THE OLD TESTAMENT STORY

"Teachers struggling to teach the strange world of the Bible to postmodern students will welcome this textbook for three reasons. First, it's easy to read. Unlike other textbooks, undergraduates will find it difficult to get lost or even sidetracked here. Second, it's wonderfully written—creative, but not idiosyncratic; eloquent, but not fanciful; comprehensive, but never tedious. Third, this book is a cut above other Old Testament introductions because Benjamin genuinely understands and respects the faith traditions of *all* his students: Muslims, Christians, Jews, and those who profess none of the above. To a world in need of sane interreligious dialogue, *The Old Testament Story* is an answer to prayer."

MICHAEL S. MOORE
Fuller Theological Seminary Southwest

"Benjamin's willingness to employ several critical techniques in one unified approach brings new insights with every chapter. His insights into the Old Testament breathe new life into the ancient text, and free it up to breathe new life into those of us who study and love it."

CLIFTON A. MANN
Rector, St. Andrew's Episcopal Church (Amarillo, Texas)

THE OLD TESTAMENT STORY

AN INTRODUCTION
WITH CD-ROM

DON C. BENJAMIN

Fortress Press
Minneapolis

THE OLD TESTAMENT STORY
An Introduction with CD-ROM

Cover design: Jessica Thoreson
Cover image: Anonymous, 20th century. Untitled [Stories from Genesis]. 1920–1930. Copyright Ricco/Maresca Gallery (New York, NY, U.S.A.) / Art Resource. Used with permission.
Maps: Lucidity Information Design, LLC
Illustrations: Katie Meier
Book design: City Desktop Productions

Material from Victor H. Matthews and Don C. Benjamin, *Old Testament Parallels: Laws and Stories from the Ancient Near East,* Rev. ed., is copyright © 1997, Paulist Press. Used with permission.

The paper used in this publication meets the minimum requirements of American National Standard for Information Sciences—Permanence of Paper for Printed Library Materials, ANSI Z329-1984.

ISBN 0-8006-3621-X

Manufactured in Canada.

08   07   06   05   04   1   2   3   4   5   6   7   8   9   10

CONTENTS

Maps   xiv
Illustrations and Figures   xviii
Abbreviations   xxiv

1 LEARNING THE BIBLE   1
   How Old Is the Bible?   2
   Is the Bible History or Story?   4
   Who Were the Hebrews?   6
   Who Wrote the Bible?   9
   In What Language Was the Bible Written?   11
   Why Are There So Many Different Bibles?   12
   Who Divided the Bible into Books, Chapters,
      and Verses?   15
   What Is the Difference between Bible Study
      and Biblical Studies?   17

2 BOOK OF GENESIS (GEN 1:1—EXOD 1:6)   21
   Creation Stories (Gen 1:1—11:26)   21
      Stories of Adam and Eve (Gen 2:4—4:2) / 21

Ancestor Stories (Gen 11:27—37:2)   40

Stories of Abraham and Sarah
(Gen 11:27—25:18) / 40
Stories of Isaac and Rebekah / 69
Stories of Jacob, Leah, and Rachel
(Gen 25:20—37:2) / 70

3 BOOKS OF EXODUS, LEVITICUS, NUMBERS
(EXOD 1:7—NUM 27:11)   73

Creation Stories (Exod 1:7—Num 27:11)   74

Death of the Firstborn of Egypt (Exod 1:7—13:16)   74

Sterility Affidavit (Exod 1:7—7:13) / 75
Cosmogony: Plagues Stories (Exod 7:14—13:10) / 89
Covenant: Passover (Exod 12:1—13:16) / 92

Creation of the Firstborn of Israel
(Exod 13:17—Num 27:11)   93

Sterility Affidavit (Exod 13:17—14:20) / 93
Cosmogony (Exod 14:21-31) / 94
Covenant (Exod 15:1—Num 27:11) / 95
Covenant between Yahweh and Israel
(Exod 19:1—24:18) / 95

The Book of Deuteronomy (Num 27:12—Deut 34:12)   122

4 BOOKS OF JOSHUA AND JUDGES
(JOSH 1:1—JUDG 21:25)   125

Covenant between Yahweh and Israel (Josh 1:1-8)   127

Story of Rahab as Host (Josh 2:1-24 + 6:22-25)   128

Inauguration of Joshua at Jericho (Josh 5:13—6:27)   133

Crisis Episode (Josh 5:13) / 137
Climax Episode (Josh 5:14) / 140
Denoument Episode (Josh 6:1-27) / 140

Othniel Delivers Israel from Aram (Judg 3:7-11)   141

Ehud Delivers Israel from Moab (Judg 3:12-30)   145

Saga of Deborah and Jael (Judg 4:1—5:31)   146

Deborah Delivers Israel from Hazor
    (Judg 4:1-16 + 5:31) / 146
Jael Delivers Israel from Harosheth-ha-goiim
    (Judg 4:17-24) / 147
Hymn (Judg 5:1-31) / 152

Jephthah Delivers Israel from Ammon (Judg 11:1-40)   152

Saga of Samson (Judg 13:1—16:31)   155

Annunciation to the Wife of Manoah
    (Judg 13:1-25) / 156
Samson Courts the Woman of Timnah
    (Judg 14:1-4+10) / 157
Samson Slays the Lion of Timnah (Judg 14:5-9) / 158
Samson Kills the Warriors of Ashkelon
    (Judg 14:11-20) / 158
Samson Burns the Crops of Timnah (Judg 15:1-8) / 159
Samson Massacres the Garrison of Lehi
    (Judg 15:9-17) / 159
Samson Raids the Spring at Hakkore
    (Judg 15:18-20) / 161
Samson Wrecks the Gates of Gaza (Judg 16:1-3) / 161
Samson Terrorizes the Wadi Sorek (Judg 16:4-22) / 162
Samson Destroys the House of Dagon
    (Judg 16:23-31) / 163

5 BOOK OF RUTH
(RUTH 1:1—4:22)   165
Parable of a Persevering Widow (Ruth 1:1-22)   165

Crisis Episode (Ruth 1:1-7) / 166
Climax Episode (Ruth 1:8-18) / 167
Denoument Episode (Ruth 1:19-22) / 168
Parable of Workers in a Wheat Field (Ruth 2:1-23)   169

Crisis Episode (Ruth 2:1-3) / 169
Climax Episode (Ruth 2:3-7) / 169
Denoument Episode (Ruth 2:8-23) / 170

Story of Ruth as a Persevering Widow (Ruth 3:1-18)   171

Crisis Episode (Ruth 3:1-9) / 171
Climax Episode (Ruth 3:9-13) / 172
Denoument Episode (Ruth 3:14-17) / 172

Story of Boaz as Legal Guardian (Ruth 4:1-22)   173

Crisis Episode (Ruth 4:1-4) / 173
Climax Episode (Ruth 4:5-12) / 174
Denoument Episode (Ruth 4:13-22) / 174

6 BOOKS OF SAMUEL AND KINGS
(1 SAM 1:1—2 KGS 25:30)   177

Stories of Samuel (1 Sam 1:1—8:3)   178

Annunciation to Hannah (1 Sam 1:1—2:11) / 178
Trial of Eli and His Sons (1 Sam 2:12—4:22) / 180
The Ark Delivers Israel from Philistia
  (1 Sam 4:1—7:1 + 2 Sam 6:2-23) / 181

Stories of David's Rise to Power
  (1 Sam 8:4—2 Sam 8:13)   184

Stories of Saul (1 Sam 8:4—15:35) / 184

Stories of David (1 Sam 16:1—2 Sam 8:13) / 192

Stories of David's Successor
  (2 Sam 9:1—20:26+1 Kgs 1:1—11:43)   204

Stories of Merib-baal
  (2 Sam 9:1-13; 16:1-4; 19:24-30) / 204
Trial of David (2 Sam 10:1—12:31) / 209
Trial of Amnon (2 Sam 13:1—14:33) / 213
Trial of Absalom (2 Sam 15:1—20:23) / 218
Trial of Adonijah (1 Kgs 1:1-53) / 221
Trial of Solomon, 1000–925 B.C.E.
  (1 Kgs 2:1—11:43) / 221

**Review of the Annals for the Monarchs of Israel
  and Judah** (1 Kgs 11:44—2 Kgs 25:30)   222

Trial of Ahab and Jezebel (1 Kgs 16:29—22:40) / 223
Trial of Ahaziah (2 Kgs 1:1—2:25) / 236
Trial of Jehoram (2 Kgs 3:1—8:24) / 240

7 BOOK OF JOB

(JOB 1:1—42:17)   247

Credential Hearings (Job 1:1—2:13)   251

Indictment Hearings (Job 3:1—42:17)   255

Indictment (Job 3:1-28) / 255
Lament (Job 3:1-26) / 256
Legal Arguments (Job 4:1—42:6) / 257

Entitlement Hearing (Job 42:7-17)   261

8 BOOK OF PSALMS

(Pss 1:1—150:6)   263

Teachings   264

Teaching on Prayer (Ps 1:1-6) / 264

Hymns   267

Hymn (Ps 8:1-9) / 267
Hymn (Ps 23:1-6) / 268
Hymn (Ps 150:1-6) / 271

Laments   272

Lament (Ps 44:1-26) / 272
Lament (Ps 3:1-8) / 273
Lament (Ps 137:1-9) / 275
A Hymn and a Lament (Ps 66:1-20) / 277
Lament (Ps 22:1-31) / 278

9 BOOK OF PROVERBS

(PROV 1:1—31:31)   287

Part One: Courtyard Teachings (Prov 1:1—9:18)   290

Teaching on Wisdom (Prov 1:1-7) / 292
Teaching on Foolishness (Prov 1:8-19) / 293
Teaching on Wise Teachers (Prov 3:13-18) / 294
Teaching on Foolish Teachers (Prov 5:1-23) / 295
Teaching of the Wise Woman (Prov 8:1-36) / 295

Part Two: Great Room Teachings
(Prov 10:1—22:16)   300

Sayings, Adages, Proverbs about Mothers of Households / 300

Part Three: Holy of Holies Teachings
(Prov 22:17—31:31)   302

Hymn (Prov 31:10-31) / 302

10 BOOK OF ECCLESIASTES
(ECCL 1:1—12:14)   305
Audit of Work (Eccl 1:2-11)   306
Audit of Wisdom (Eccl 1:12-18)   307
Audit of Possessions (Eccl 2:4-11)   308
Audit of Harmony (Eccl 3:1-15)   308
Audit of Students (Eccl 7:23-29)   309
Audit of Learning (Eccl 11:7—12:8)   310
Audit of Learning (Eccl 12:9-14)   313

11 SONG OF SOLOMON
(SONG 1:1—8:14)   315
Propositions   318

Woman's Proposition (Song 1:2-4) / 319
Man's Proposition (Song 2:8-13) / 320
Woman's Proposition (Song 2:16-17) / 320
Man's Proposition (Song 4:8-9) / 321
Man's Proposition (Song 7:1-6) / 321

Tours-Burlesque   322

Tour-Burlesque of the Woman's Body
(Song 1:5-6) / 322
Tour-Burlesque of the Woman's Body
(Song 4:1-5) / 325
Tour-Burlesque of the Man's Body
(Song 5:11-16) / 326

Erotic Fantasies   326

Erotic Fantasy (Song 1:9—2:7) / 327
Erotic Fantasy (Song 3:2-8) / 328

Teases   328

    Tease (Song 2:15) / 328
    Tease (Song 8:8-10) / 330

Boasts   330

    Boast (Song 5:9) / 330
    Boast (Song 6:8-9) / 330

12 BOOK OF ISAIAH

(ISA 1:1—66:24)   333

  Trials of Judah (Isa 1:1—39:8)   335

    Isaiah Movement, Phase One, 740–700 B.C.E. / 335
    Trial of Judah (Isa 1:2-31) / 335
    Trial of Jotham, 750–735 B.C.E. *(Isa 5:1-7) / 338*
    Inauguration of Isaiah at Jerusalem (Isa 6:1-13) / 342
    Trial of Ahaz, 735–715 B.C.E. *(Isa 7:1—12:6) / 346*
    Trials of Judah and Its Covenant Partners
      (Isa 13:1—23:18) / 355
    Creation of New Heavens and a New Earth
      (Isa 24:1—27:13) / 357

  Creation of Zion (Isa 40:1—55:13)   362

    Isaiah Movement, Phase Two, 587–537 B.C.E. / 362
    Sterility Affidavit (Isa 40:1-31) / 363
    Cosmogony (Isa 41:1—48:22) / 364

  Isaiah's Book of Psalms (Isa 56:1—66:24)   369

    Isaiah Movement, Phase Three, 537–332 B.C.E. / 369
    Hymn (Isa 60:1-22) / 370
    Hymn (Isa 65:17-25) / 371

13 BOOK OF JEREMIAH

(JER 1:1—52:32)   373

  Inauguration of Jeremiah in His Mother's Womb
    (Jer 1:4-19)   374

  Trial of Jerusalem (Jer 2:1—3:5)   376

  Trial of Judah and Jerusalem (Jer 13:1-11)   378

  Trial of Judah (Jer 13:12-14)   379

  Trial of Jerusalem (Jer 16:1-13)   379

Trial of Jerusalem and Judah (Jer 19:1-15)   380

Lament of Jeremiah (Jer 20:7-18)   381

Trial of Jerusalem (Jer 34:1—35:19)   382

14 BOOK OF EZEKIEL
(EZEK 1:1—48:35)   385

Creation of the City of Immanuel
(Ezek 1:1—48:35)   386

Sterility Affidavit (Ezek 1:4—12:28) / 386
Cosmogony (Ezek 13:1—32:32) / 391
Covenant (Ezek 33:1—48:35) / 397

15 BOOK OF DANIEL
(DAN 1:1—12:13)   405

Teaching Stories (Dan 1:1—6:29)   407

*Daniel and Three Friends Thrive on Vegetables
and Water* (Dan 1:1-21) / 409

Apocalypse Stories (Dan 7:1—12:13)   411

Ordination of a Son of Man (Dan 7:1-28) / 413
New Heavens and a New Earth in 3½ Years
(Dan 8:1-27) / 416
New Heavens and a New Earth in 7x70 Years
(Dan 9:1-27) / 418
Resurrection of the Dead (Dan 10:1—12:13) / 421

Teaching Stories (Dan 13:1—14:46)   425

A Beautiful Woman Remains Faithful
(Dan 13:1-64) / 426

16 BOOK OF HOSEA
(HOS 1:1—14:9)   429

Trial of Israel (Hos 1:2-3)   433

Trial of Israel (Hos 1:3-5)   435

Trial of Israel (Hos 2:2—3:5)   435

Trial of Israel (Hos 11:1-11)   439

17 BOOK OF AMOS

(AMOS 1:1—9:15)   435

Trials of Israel and Its Covenant Partners
(Amos 1:3—2:16)   444

Trial of Israel (Amos 7:1—9:15)   448

18 BOOK OF JONAH

(JONAH 1:1—4:11)   451

Crisis Episode (Jonah 1:1—3:9) / 451
Climax Episode (Jonah 3:10—4:8) / 457
Denoument Episode (4:9-11) / 458

19 LIVING THE BIBLE   461

What Does the Bible Teach?   461

Why Do We Say the Bible Is Inspired?   466

Works Cited   469

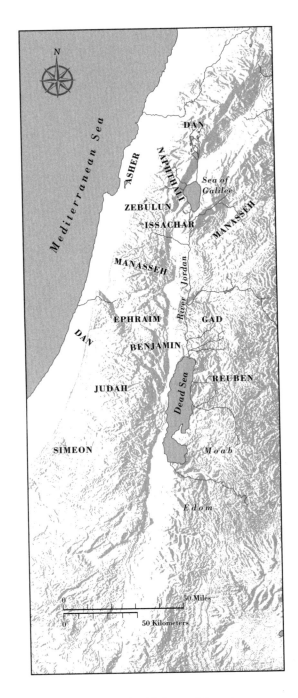

The Twelve Tribes of Israel

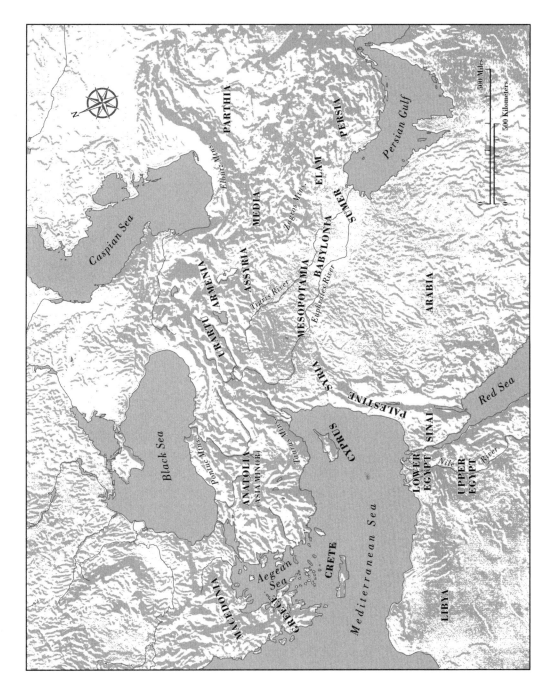

The Ancient Near East

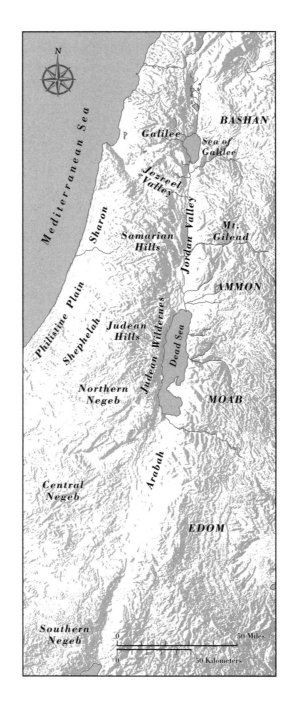

Geographic Subregions of Palestine

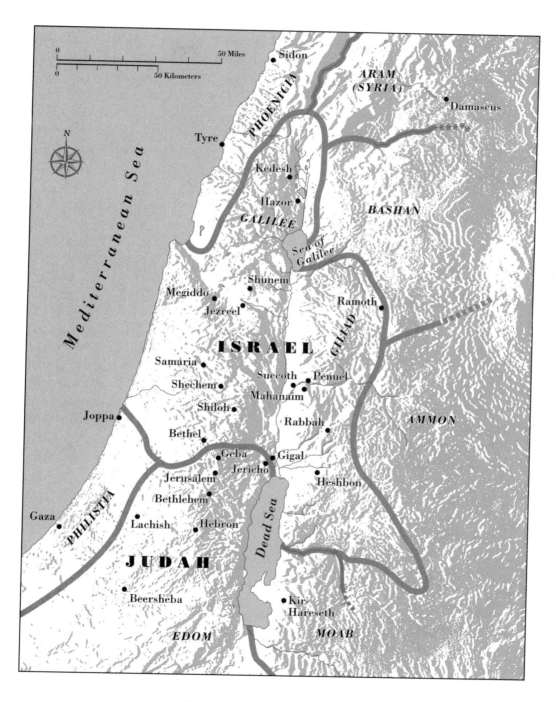

Kingdoms of Israel and Judah

ILLUSTRATIONS AND FIGURES

Illustrations

Points of Interest (Chapter 1) — xxvi

Household of Absha from Syria-Palestine Entering Egypt
(Beni Hasan 2050–1800 B.C.E.; fresco 24 m) — 5

Points of Interest (Chapter 2) — 20

Men Lead a Bull to the King of Ur
(Ur 2400 B.C.E.; mosaic) — 26

Points of Interest (Chapter 3) — 72

Man Riding an Ass
(Syria 2000 B.C.E.; bronze 13 cm) — 77

Points of Interest (Chapter 4) — 124

Lion Slays a Man
(Nimrud 900–700 B.C.E.; ivory 10 x 10 cm) — 127

Points of Interest (Chapter 5) — 164

Expectant Mother
(Akhziv 700–600 B.C.E.; ceramic 23.5 cm) — 167

Points of Interest (Chapter 6) — 176

Ships of Tyre Unload Cedar for Palace of Sargon II
(Khorsbad 721-705 B.C.E.; alabaster 2.83 m) — 179

Points of Interest (Chapter 7) — 246

Hippopotamus Grazing Riverbank
(Dra Aboul Naga 2040–1640 B.C.E.; faience 12.7 cm) — 249

Points of Interest (Chapter 8)

262

Mourners Strike Their Heads in Grief
(Tell 'Aitun 1200–1100 B.C.E.; terra cotta)

265

Points of Interest (Chapter 9)

286

Godmother with Great Hips, Full Breasts and a Pointed Crown
(Horvat Minha 6000 B.C.E.; terra cotta 11 x 65cm)

289

Points of Interest (Chapter 10)

304

Teacher like Amen-em-ope Whom Ecclesiastes Audits
(Saqqara 2575–2134 B.C.E.; limestone 53.7 cm)

307

Points of Interest (Chapter 11)

314

"Your Navel is a Rounded Bowl, Your Belly is a Heap of Wheat" (Song 7:2)
(Safadi 4300–3300 B.C.E.; ivory 10 cm)

317

Points of Interest (Chapter 12)

332

Assyrian Cherubim Guard Palace of the Great King
(Nimrud 883–859 B.C.E.; alabaster 4.4 m)

339

Points of Interest (Chapter 13)

372

Amun Calls Tutakhamun from a Lotus Womb
(Valley of the Kings 1333–1323 B.C.E.; wood)

375

Points of Interest (Chapter 14)

384

Hebrew Refugees Flee Lachish with Wagon
(Nineveh 694 B.C.E.; limestone 250 cm x 18.9 m)

387

Points of Interest (Chapter 15)

404

Splendor of Greece—an "Abomination" in Dan 11:31
(Pergamon 200 B.C.E.; marble 39.5 cm)

409

Points of Interest (Chapter 16)

428

Noble Woman like Gomer Gazes from Her Window
(Nimrud 800–750 B.C.E.; ivory 10.7 cm)

431

Points of Interest (Chapter 17)

442

Divine Gardener like Amos Dresses Tree (Amos 7:14)
(Nimrud 875–860 B.C.E.; alabaster 141 x 95 cm)

445

Points of Interest (Chapter 18)

450

Jonah 3:6-9 Reverses Humiliation of Jehu before Shalmaneser
(Nimrud 858–824 B.C.E.; alabaster 2 x 0.6 m)

453

Anonymous, 20th century. Untitled [Stories from Genesis]. 1920–1930.
Ricco/Maresca Gallery (New York, NY, U.S.A.).

460

Dome of the Rock (right) and Dome of Holy Sepulchre Church
Frame the Walled City of Jerusalem

465

Figures

1. Raw Materials for Tools and Weapons 3
2. Gezer Almanac (Matthews and Benjamin 1997: 145-46) 6
3. Hymn to Yahweh (Ps 66:1-12) 7
4. Traditions of Judaism, Christianity, and Islam 13
5. Covenant between Yahweh and Israel (Jer 31:31-33) 14
6. The Book of Genesis (Gen 1:1—Exod 1:6) 22
7. Story of the 'Adam as a Farmer (Gen 2:4-17) 25
8. Story of the 'Adam as a Herder (Gen 2:18-20) 28
9. Story of the 'Adam as a Man and a Woman (Gen 2:20-24) 29
10. Teaching on Women (Sir 25:21-26) 32
11. Story of Adam and Eve as Farmers and Child-bearers (Gen 2:25—4:2) 34
12. Story of Adam and Eve as Farmers and Child-bearers (cont.) (Gen 2:25—4:2) 36–37
13. Story of Adam and Eve as Farmers and Child-bearers (cont.) (Gen 2:25—4:2) 41
14. Abraham and Sarah Negotiate with Yahweh (Gen 11:17—12:8) 45
15. Abraham Negotiates with Lot (Gen 13:5-18) 49
16. Abraham Negotiates with Lot (cont.) (Gen 14:1-24) 53
17. Story of Hagar from Beer-lahai-roi (Gen 16:1-16) 56
18. The Code of Hammurabi (Matthews and Benjamin 1997: 104–5) 57
19. Lot and His Daughters as Hosts (Gen 19:1-11) 59
20. Creation of Moab and Ammon (Gen 19:12-38) 63
21. Story of Abraham on Mt. Moriah (Gen 21:1-14 + 22:1-19) 63–67
22. Land Grant to Slaves Set Free (Num 26:1—27:11) 74
23. Death of the Firstborn of Egypt (Exod 1:7—13:16) 76
24. Story of Two Shrewd Midwives (Exod 1:12-21) 79
25. Seven-Day Pattern in Plagues Stories (:: comparison) 91
26. Patterns in the Creation of the Firstborn of Israel (Exod 13:17—Num 27:11) 94
27. Patterns in a Covenant between Yahweh and Israel (Exod 19:1—Lev 27:34) 99
28. Annals of Mesha (Matthews and Benjamin, 1997: 157–59) 117
29. Amarna Letters (Matthews and Benjamin 1997: 138) 129
30. Jericho's Archaeological Record 135

31. Inauguration of Joshua at Jericho (Josh 5:13—6:27) 139
32. Jael Delivers Israel from Harosheth-ha-goiim (Judg 4:11 + 15-22) 148
33. Trial of Jehu (2 Kgs 9:29-33) 149
34. Jephthah Delivers Israel from Ammon (Judg 11:1-40) 155
35. Stories of Samson (Judg 14:1-10) 157
36. Stories of Jacob, Leah, and Rachel (Gen 30:31-39) 160
37. Egyptian Love Song
    (Matthews and Benjamin 1997: 300-01) 161
38. Saul Delivers Jabesh-gilead from Ammon (4QSam^a + 1 Sam 11:1-3) 187
39. Creation of the City of David (2 Sam 5:6-16) 198–99
40. Stories of David's Rise to Power (2 Sam 5:22-25) 204
41. Stories of Merib-baal (2 Sam 9:1-13) 205
42. Four Friends Thrive on Vegetables and Water (Dan 1:1-5) 206
43. Stories of Merib-baal (cont.) (2 Sam 16:1-4) 207
44. Stories of Merib-baal (cont.) (2 Sam 19:24-30) 209
45. Abimelech Delivers Israel from Thebez (Judg 9:50-57) 212
46. Tour-Burlesque of the Woman's Body (Song 7:1-5) 214
47. Teachings of Amen-em-ope (Matthews and Benjamin 1997: 278) 215
48. Hittite Cure for Impotence
    (KUB, vii, 5; KUB, vii, 8; KUB ix, 27) 216
49. Middle Assyrian Code, art. 55 (Matthews and Benjamin 1997: 122) 217
50. Stories of David's Successor (Sam 16:5-12) 219
51. City of Tyre 223
52. False Prophets 227
53. Shamans 228
54. Dancing 231
55. Stories of Abraham and Sarah (Gen 24: 61-67) 233
56. Hymn (Ps 29:1-11) 234
57. Healing 237
58. Channeling 242
59. Patterns in the Book of Job: A Pretrial Hearing (Job 1:1—42:17) 253
60. Teaching on Prayer (Ps 1:1-6) 266
61. Hymn (Ps 8:1-9) 269
62. Hymn (Ps 23:1-6) 270
63. Hymn (Ps 150:1-6) 272

64. Lament (Ps 44:10-17)   274

65. Lament (Ps 3:7)   275

66. Lament (Ps 137:1-9)   276

67. A Hymn and a Lament (Ps 66:1-20)   282–83

68. Lament (Ps 22:1-31)   284–85

69. Patterns in the Book of Proverbs   291

70. Teaching on Wisdom (Prov 1:1-7)   293

71. Teaching on Foolishness (Prov 1:8-19)   294

72. Teaching on Foolish Teachers (Prov 5:1-23)   296–97

73. Teaching of the Wise Woman at Creation (Prov 8:1-36)   299

74. Teaching on the Mother of a Household (Sir 26:1-4)   302

75. Audit of Learning (Eccl 11:7—12:8)   312–13

76. Egyptian Love Songs (Matthews and Benjamin 1997: 297–98)   318

77. Tammuz and Ishtar (Matthews and Benjamin 1997: 306–07)   324

78. Erotic Fantasy (Song 2:4-6)   327

79. Middle Assyrian Code (Matthews and Benjamin 1997: 119–20)   329

80. Patterns in the Book of Isaiah (Isa 1:1—66:24)   334

81. Trial of Judah (Isa 1:1-31)   336–37

82. Trial of Jotham, 740–726 B.C.E. (Isa 5:1-7)   340

83. Inauguration of Isaiah at Jerusalem (Isa 6:1-13)   344

84. Trial of Ahaz (Isa 7:1-25)   348–49

85. Categories of Prophetic Pantomimes   350

86. Annals for Ahaz of Judah (735–715 B.C.E.) (2 Kgs 16:1-20)   352

87. Patterns in Trials of Judah and Its Covenant Partners (Isa 13:1—23:18)   356

88. Patterns in a Creation of New Heavens and a New Earth (Isa 24:1—27:13)   359

89. Creation of New Heavens and a New Earth (Isa 25:7-8)   360

90. Decree of Cyrus (Matthews and Benjamin 1997: 193–95)   368

91. Hymn (Deut 33:26-29)   389

92. Trial of Jerusalem (Ezek 16:1-63)   394

93. Stories of Atrahasis, I:200–230 (Matthews and Benjamin 1997: 33)   399

94. Patterns in Dedication of the City of Immanuel (Ezek 40:1—48:35)   401

95. Stories of Aqhat (Matthews and Benjamin 1997: 67)   406

96. Stories of Wen-Amon (Matthews and Benjamin 1997: 325)   412

97. Hymn to Yahweh (Ps 68:1-5) 415
98. New Heavens and a New Earth in 7x70 Years (Dan 9:1-27) 419
99. Calendar in the Book of Daniel 420
100. Catechism (Dan 10:1-14) 421
101. Catechism (Dan 10:15—12:4) 423
102. Annals of Solomon (1 Kgs 11:1-3) 433
103. Trial of Israel (Hos 11:1-4) 440–41
104. Crisis Episodes (Jonah 1:1—3:9) 454–55
105. A Lament for Jonah (Jonah 2:3-9) 456
106. Denouement Episodes (Jonah 4:9-11) 459
107. The Books of the Bible 462

Abbreviations

4QSam^a	scroll of the books of 1–2 Samuel from Qumran (4Q51)
Aqhat	The Story of Aqhat (Ugaritic epic)
ARM	Archives royales de Mari (tablets from the royal archives of Mari)
Atra	Atrahasis (Babylonian epic of creation and the great flood)
b.	Babylonian Talmud tractates
CH	Code of Hammurabi (Babylonian stele with legal regulations)
DTH	Deuteronomistic History
Enuma	Enuma Elish (Babylonian epic of creation)
Gilg	Gilgamesh (Babylonian epic of king Gilgamesh)
KUB	Keilschrifturkunden aus Boghazköi (collection of Hittite documents)
Meg.	*Megillah* (The Scroll [of Esther]); a rabbinic tractate
NAB	New American Bible
NRSV	New Revised Standard Version

Old Testament Books (in canonical order)

Gen	Genesis
Exod	Exodus
Lev	Leviticus
Num	Numbers
Deut	Deuteronomy
Josh	Joshua
Judg	Judges
Ruth	Ruth
1 Sam	1 Samuel
2 Sam	2 Samuel
1 Kgs	1 Kings
2 Kgs	2 Kings
1 Chr	1 Chronicles
2 Chr	2 Chronicles
Ezra	Ezra
Neh	Nehemiah
Esth	Esther
Job	Job
Ps / Pss	Psalms
Prov	Proverbs
Eccl	Ecclesiastes
Song	Song of Songs
Isa	Isaiah
Jer	Jeremiah
Ezek	Ezekiel
Dan	Daniel
Hos	Hosea
Joel	Joel
Amos	Amos
Obad	Obadiah
Jonah	Jonah
Mic	Micah
Nah	Nahum
Hab	Habakkuk
Zeph	Zephaniah
Hag	Haggai
Zech	Zechariah
Mal	Malachi

Apocryphal Books

Bar	Baruch
Add Dan	Additions to Daniel
Pr Az	Prayer of Azariah
Bel	Bel and the Dragon
Sg Three	Song of the Three Young Men
Sus	Susanna
1 Esd	1 Esdras
2 Esd	2 Esdras
Add Esth	Additions to Esther
Ep Jer	Epistle of Jeremiah
Jdt	Judith
1 Macc	1 Maccabees
2 Macc	2 Maccabees
3 Macc	3 Maccabees
4 Macc	4 Maccabees
Pr Man	Prayer of Manasseh
Ps 151	Psalm 151
Sir	Sirach (Ecclesiasticus)
Tob	Tobit
Wis	Wisdom of Solomon

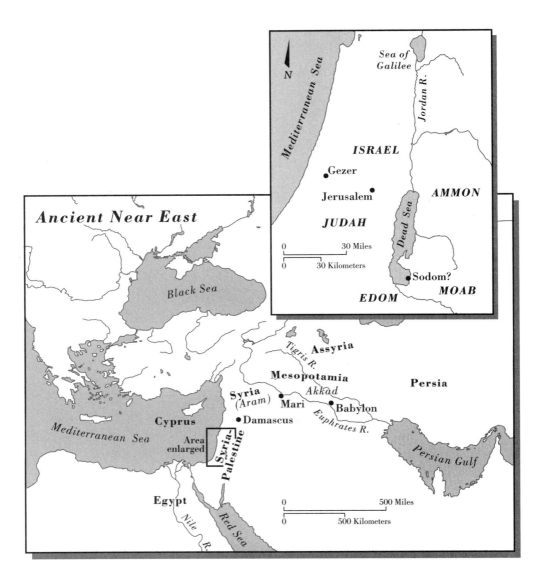

Points of Interest (Chapter 1)

1

LEARNING THE BIBLE

The Bible of ancient Israel is a masterpiece of storytelling. Many cultures governed greater empires. Many built larger temples. Many celebrated more spectacular rituals, but the Hebrews who lived in the hills along the Jordan River more than 3,000 years ago were masters at crafting words. Their words made radical changes in their own world and have had enduring influence in worlds they never knew. The Bible preserves the worldview of these amazing people. These Hebrews lived fully, acted courageously, and suffered profoundly, but what makes them important is that they handed on their riveting reflections on their lives, their actions, and their suffering.

The Old Testament Story is a guide to the world of the Hebrew states of Israel and Judah, and to the times of the Iron Age (1200–586 B.C.E.) when these Hebrews lived. But, more importantly, it is an interpreter of the enduring traditions in the Bible whose words describe how they thought about Yahweh, their divine patron, how they understood themselves, how they dealt with their neighbors, and how they treated the earth.

The Hebrews shaped their words, and not only in story. The Hebrews used laws and proverbs and trials and hymns and laments and other genres as well. Yet when this wonderful collection was organized into the Bible, it became a story of the relationship, the covenant, between this ancient people and their divine patron. Christians described the story as the "Old Testament," not because they considered it to be outdated, but because it was the original and enduring testament from which their own traditions—the New Testament—developed.

Stories and laws are traditions that always begin with experience. Something happens, and these traditions develop in order to understand what the experience means. Sound interpretations are handed on, unsound interpretations are not. The Bible represents only the traditions that convincingly explained what the experiences of the people of ancient Israel and Judah meant. Some of these traditions in the Bible, like the Stories of Adam and Eve in the book of Genesis, were common throughout the ancient Near East. Some, like the Stories of the Death of the Firstborn of Egypt, and the Stories of the Birth of the Firstborn of Israel in the book of Exodus, were unique in ancient Israel.

The medium of traditions is words. Today the words of the Bible are written. Originally, the words of the Bible were told. They were not something to read like newspapers, magazines, and journals; they were something to hear like music. These words were to be heard, not seen. In the beginning the Bible was a sound; now it is a shape. Yesterday, the Bible was language; today it is literature. Understanding how the Hebrews crafted their words is essential to understanding the stories themselves.

How Old Is the Bible?

There are two kinds of time in biblical traditions. First, there is the time in a tradition. For example, in the Stories of Abraham and Sarah in the book of Genesis, these ancestors of ancient Israel live in the Middle Bronze period (2000–1550 B.C.E.). Second, there is the time when these stories, which are preserved in the Bible today, were told. For example, these Stories of Abraham and Sarah are preserved in the Bible today as they were told during first period of the Iron Age (ca. 1000–925 B.C.E.). The stories may have developed earlier than the Iron Age, but the version of these stories in the Bible is from the Iron Age, not the Middle Bronze period or the Late Bronze period (1550–1200 B.C.E.). The time in a tradition, and the time when the tradition was told are almost never the same. Yet, it is as important to know something about the time when a particular book of the Bible was told as it is to know the time about which the book itself tells.

Jews, Catholics, Protestant Christians, Orthodox Christians, and Christians from Egypt include different books in their Bibles and arrange them differently. But neither the order of the books of the Bible nor their contents are keys to their age. Genesis, for example, is the first book in the Bible, and it tells about the beginning of the world, but Genesis is not the Bible's oldest book. The Hymn of Miriam (Exod 15:20-21), the Blessings of Land and Children by Balaam (Num 22:1—24:25), the stories How Deborah Delivers Israel from Hazor (Judg 4:1-16) and How Jael Delivers Israel from Harosheth-ha-goiim (Judg 4:17-24) are much older. Likewise, a Blessing of the Household of Jacob (Gen 49:1-27), a Blessing of the Household of Israel (Deut 33:1-29), a Lament for Saul and Jonathan (2 Sam 1:19-27), Hymns to Yahweh as a Divine Warrior (2 Sam 22:2-51; Ps 18:1-51; Ps 29:1-11; Ps 68), and a Teaching of David (2 Sam 23:1-7) are also among the oldest traditions in the Bible. The Hebrew vocabulary and grammar in these traditions, as well as how these traditions describe their social world, indicate that the versions of these traditions preserved in the Bible sound much the same as they did at the beginning of the Iron Age.

Dates for the world of the Bible are labeled either "B.C.E." or "C.E." Therefore, David and Solomon ruled Israel from about 1000 to 932 B.C.E., and the Babylonians destroyed Jerusalem in 587 B.C.E. Herod was King of Judea from 37 to 4 B.C.E., and Pontius Pilate was the Roman governor of Judea from 27 to 37 C.E. The abbreviations mean "Before the Common Era" and "Common Era." This "Common Calendar" is almost identical to the Christian Calendar introduced by Pope Gregory XIII in 1582. The Christian Calendar celebrated the birth of Jesus in 1 A.D. "A.D." is an abbreviation for the Latin phrase *anno Domini* meaning "in the year of the Lord." Dates before 1 A.D. carry the label "B.C.," an abbreviation for the English phrase "Before Christ." The numbers for the years in the Common Calendar and the Christian Calendar are the same. The abbreviations in the Common Calendar, however, avoid imposing Christian terminology on non-Christians, and they keep both abbreviations in the same language.

The Archaeological Calendar is altogether different from either the Common Calendar or the Christian Calendar. Archaeologists named periods of culture for the raw materials that humans used to make tools and weapons. The Stone Age lasted until 4300 B.C.E., during which flint was the primary raw material. The Chalcolithic Age, from the Greek words for "copper" and "flint," begins about 4300 B.C.E. The Bronze Age begins about 3300 B.C.E. and the Iron Age about 1200 B.C.E. (Fig. 1).

The Hebrews were a people of the Iron Age. Hebrew villages appeared in Syria-Palestine around 1200 B.C.E. About 1000 B.C.E., these villagers founded the states of Israel in the north and Judah in the south. The state of ancient Israel lasted until about 721 B.C.E., when it was conquered by the Assyrians from Mesopotamia. Judah lasted until about 587 B.C.E., when it was conquered by the Babylonians, who were also from Mesopotamia. The Hebrews inherit some of their traditions from the great cultures of

Stone Age: flint quartz quarried throughout Syria-Palestine

Chalcolithic Age: copper containing arsenic mined in Cyprus, Turkey, and Sinai

Bronze Age: bronze manufactured by alloying copper with 2-10 percent tin mined in Russia, Turkey, and Afghanistan

Iron Age: iron originally mined from meteorites, then in Turkey

FIGURE 1   Raw Materials for Tools and Weapons

Egypt and Mesopotamia. The literary origins of the Flood Stories in the book of Genesis or the Teachings of Amen-em-ope in the book of Proverbs may reach back into the Bronze Age. The Hebrews also tell their own stories. The literary origins of the Death of the Firstborn of Egypt in the book of Exodus may reach back into the Iron Age. The time in a tradition is always easier to identify than the time when a story was first told, or the time when the telling of the story preserved in the Bible was told.

The dates for the archaeological periods in *The Old Testament Story* follow Amihai Mazar, *Archaeology of the Land of the Bible 10,000–586* B.C.E. (1990: 30). The dates for the pharaohs of Egypt follow John Baines and Jeromir Malek, *Atlas of Ancient Egypt* (1980: 36–37). The dates for the great kings of Mesopotamia follow Michael Roaf, *Cultural Atlas of Mesopotamia and the Ancient Near East* (1991). The dates for the rulers of Israel and Judah follow John H. Hays and J. Maxwell Miller, *Israelite and Judean History* (1977: 678–83).

Is the Bible History or Story?

The Bible is more story than history. The genre of history, which developed in the Western industrial cultures of Europe and North America during the nineteenth century, compiles chronological records of military and political events to explain why these events happened. History quickly became the genre of choice for understanding and directing human experience. Because the scholars and ordinary people in the nineteenth and twentieth centuries had such a love of history, they assumed that the peoples of Mesopotamia, Egypt, ancient Israel, Greece, and Rome also loved history. So, they read the Bible, and Herodotus and Thucydides, as history. In fact, they honored the people of ancient Israel for having been the first to use history to understand God. While such enthusiasm for history is understandable, there is little evidence that before the late eighteenth century history played any role in education in any ancient culture, or that any culture claimed that history provided an interpretation of human life as a whole.

The genre of choice in antiquity was story, which was more interested in what events mean than in why events happen. The stories in the Bible are an enduring incarnation of Israel's faith and way of looking at the world. They continue to challenge audiences to look at life in new and exciting ways. They take their listeners on sensual pilgrimages, teaching them to hear, see, smell, taste, and feel the world with new recognition and increased reverence. The sheer volume of music, sculpture, architecture, painting, mosaic, metalwork, weaving, drama, and literature that the Bible continues to inspire identifies it as a penetrating and dynamic interpretation of reality. Stories make humans more human by enlarging their awareness of the world of the senses and of the world which cannot be sensed. Story soothes, inspires, motivates, refreshes, and awes. Story

Household of Absha from Syria-Palestine Entering Egypt
(Beni Hasan 2050–1800 B.C.E.; fresco 24 m)

is about life, not about time. It frames one part of life at a time, and cuts off everything else so that audiences can concentrate on the subject at hand.

Not all biblical traditions are stories. There are other patterns and shapes. Story and law are the two most common, but there are trials, pantomimes, audits, teachings, hymns, laments, and even erotica. Ancient audiences knew these patterns as well as their performers. The Bible never defines its genres, but by a careful reading of the traditions of ancient Israel, and of its neighbors in Syria-Palestine, Egypt, and Mesopotamia, it is possible to determine which parts are generic and which are not. Being able to recognize genres does not take the excitement out of listening to the Bible. Genre only orients the development of a tradition. It does not dominate it. Storytellers and lawgivers do not simply copy the genre. They select the appropriate genre and then creatively adapt it into a suitable structure for a particular audience.

Biblical traditions are the products of both an Eastern and an ancient culture. They are seldom, if ever, identical with the traditions used in Western cultures, even with those traditions used in religious worship. The way in which Jews, Christians, and Muslims today read, sing, or preach the Bible is different from the way in which the Bible was told and lived in its own world.

Lawmakers and storytellers worked their mediums with skill and craft for specific purposes. They taught people how to survive. All art was art for a purpose rather than art for its own sake. Laws and stories preserved and protected society. Once society cut the connection between art and society in the nineteenth century, the only measure of art was in the eye of the beholder. Art for its own sake does not need to reflect tradition or to serve a social purpose. Biblical traditions served very specific needs in the lives of very real people.

All cultures develop survival systems to feed, clothe, and shelter their people. They use laws and stories to institutionalize these systems. The almanac that R. A. S. Macalister recovered in 1908 during his excavation of Gezer in Israel, today shows how closely art and society are related. Sometime after 1000 B.C.E., an Israelite copied this almanac on a piece of soft rectangular limestone about four inches long and four inches wide. It matched each month of the year with a particular farm chore. It had the same number of parts as the year, and like the agricultural cycle, the calendar arranged the parts in a harvesting-planting-cultivating pattern (Fig. 2).

Worship, like farming, was an important institution in ancient societies. It was the official way to determine who did or did not belong to a village or state. Households, like citizens pledging their allegiance to their flags or congregations professing their creeds today, participated in worship to identify themselves as members-in-good-standing of their clans and, therefore, entitled to all their rights and privileges. The liturgy of ancient Israel developed two important traditions: hymn and creation story. Hymns like those in the book of Psalms have a call to worship (Ps 66:1-5) and a creation story (Ps 66:5-12). Like the social institution of worship where they developed, these genres preserve the approved traditions of their culture. Only households able to sing hymns and recite creation stories were eligible for Yahweh's blessings of food and protection (Fig. 3).

Who Were the Hebrews?

The Hebrews were one of the peoples who lived in Syria-Palestine during the Late Bronze period and the Iron Age. "Syria-Palestine" is a geographical, not a political term.

August and September to pick the olives,
October to sow the barley,

December and January to sow the wheat,
February to pull the flax,

March and April to harvest the barley,
April to harvest the wheat and to feast,

May and June to prune the vines,
July to pick the fruit of summer.

FIGURE 2   Gezer Almanac (Matthews and Benjamin 1997: 145-46)

call to worship (Ps 66:1-5)

> *Make a joyful noise to our Creator, all the earth;*
> *Sing the glory of the name;*
> *Give to our Creator glorious praise.*

> *Say to our Creator, "How awesome are your deeds!*
> *Because of your great power, your enemies cringe. . . .*

> *Let all the earth worship you;*
> *Let it sing hymns to you,*
> *Let it sing praises to your name."*

> *Come! See what our Creator has done;*
> *our Creator is awesome in deeds among humans.*

creation story (Ps 66:6-12)

> *Our Creator turned the sea into dry land;*
> *They passed through the river on foot.*

> *There we rejoiced in our Creator,*
> *Who rules by might forever,*

> *Whose eyes keep watch on the nations—*
> *Let the rebellious not exalt themselves.*

> *Give thanks to Our Creator, peoples of the earth,*
> *Let the sound of praise be heard,*

> *Our Creator has kept us among the living,*
> *Our Creator has not let our feet slip.*

> *For you, Our Creator, have trained us;*
> *You have refined us as silver is refined.*

> *You brought us into the net;*
> *You laid burdens on our backs;*
> *You let people ride over our heads;*

> *We went through fire and through water;*
> *Yet you have brought us out to a spacious place.*

FIGURE 3   Hymn to Yahweh (Ps 66:1-12)

The geography of Syria-Palestine today covers a number of states: Syria, Lebanon, Israel, Palestine, Jordan, to name a few. Likewise, "Hebrew" is a cultural or ethnic term. It does not refer to political citizenship.

In the Amarna Letters written to Amenophis III (1398–1361 B.C.E.) and Akhenaton (1352–1335 B.C.E.) by their governors in Syria-Palestine, the word 'apiru refers to people without honor, who lack recognized social status. They are ethnically diverse. They are a culture without honor. The governors use the word to describe the mercenaries hired by their fellow governors to raid their caravans, plunder their harvests and rustle their cattle as 'apiru. They also accuse fellow governors of being 'apiru for being disloyal to Pharaoh.

Some of the Hebrews in the Bible were 'apiru. Most were farmers and herders. The story Abraham Negotiates with Lot (Gen 13:5—14:24) describes Abraham as 'apiru when he delivers Sodom and Melchizedek from Elam, their enemy. When the father of the household of Gilead excommunicates Jephthah, he joins the 'apiru and supports himself raiding caravans (Judg 11:1-40). In the Covenant between Abigail and David (1 Sam 25:2-43), Nabal accuses David of being 'apiru because he extorts protection money from households for protecting their herds. Nonetheless, there is little evidence today for identifying the 'apiru in the Amarna Letters with the Hebrews in the Bible. Nonetheless, this social unrest in Syria-Palestine during the New Kingdom is comparable to the social unrest in Syria-Palestine during the early Iron Age period described in the books of Joshua and Judges.

Some stories in the Bible describe the Hebrews as conquerors, others describe them as immigrants, others as revolutionaries. But it is unlikely that the Hebrews invaded Syria-Palestine like the Sea Peoples from Cyprus, or migrated into unoccupied areas of Syria-Palestine from east of the Jordan River, or revolted against their patrons in the great cities along the coast of the Mediterranean Sea. The material remains in their villages are neither foreign to Syria-Palestine nor military. These villagers were farmers and herders from the cities of Syria-Palestine. They were not nomads from the desert, nor pirates from the sea. They came from inside, not outside, Syria-Palestine. The writing, language, material culture, and religious traditions of the Hebrews who resettled or founded the villages in the hills west of the Jordan River are the same as those of the other cultures throughout Syria-Palestine. Nonetheless, their villages were not colonies of the great cities. These villages were founded by social survivors who fled the famine, plague, and war that brought the Bronze Age to an end. These Hebrews did not wage war; they survived war. They fled the centralized, surplus economies of the great cities of Syria-Palestine and founded a decentralized subsistence economy of some three hundred villages in the hills along the Jordan River.

Royal annals were published by monarchs as yearly reports to their divine patrons of their stewardship of the land and children that these divine patrons had placed in their care. In his annals, Pharaoh Merneptah (1224–1214 B.C.E.) boasted of conquering these villages. "I have decimated the people of Israel and put their children to death," he carved into a victory stela. Around 1000 B.C.E. David united these Hebrew villages into a state called "Israel." Its citizens were called "Israelites." When civil war cut Israel into two states, the Hebrew state in the south was called "Judah." Its citizens were "the people of Judah." The Hebrew state in the north continued to be called "Israel." The terms "Israelites" and "people of Judah" define the political citizenship of the populations of two different states with the same culture.

Who Wrote the Bible?

The Hebrews told, and then wrote, the Bible. Some of these Hebrews were Israelites. Some were the people of Judah.

The Bible is the word of God, but it is not the autobiography of God. God is not the one who tells the story, but the one about whom the story is told. Likewise, the Bible begins with the Books of Moses, but they were not written by Moses. Moses is the ancestor to whom the scrolls of Genesis, Exodus, Leviticus, Numbers, and Deuteronomy are dedicated. The ancient art of storytelling was highly democratic. It was not an elite recreation. Storytelling was a common craft. Today's author, whose personal charisma wields penetrating insights into wonderfully crafted words, was unknown in the ancient Near East. Today an essay, a novel, or a poem captures the muse of a single prodigy. The Bible hands on the faith and vision of an entire people telling, singing, praying, laughing, negotiating, preaching, boasting, loving, remembering, and suffering.

Storytellers seldom signed their work, but they did leave clues to their identity in the characters that appear in their traditions. Tellers are most likely to hand on stories with protagonists who look like they look, act like they act, do what they do, and know what they know. Mothers and fathers of households were two important groups of lawmakers and storytellers in the villages of early Israel. The mothers of households made laws for and told stories to women and children inside the household. The fathers of households made laws for and told stories to men at village sanctuaries. The stories and laws of the fathers of Israel's households have had a greater influence in the formation of the Bible than the stories and laws of its mothers.

When Hebrew villages became the states of Israel and Judah, their laws and stories grew into great traditions. State storytelling took place at major sanctuaries where every household was required to send its seasonal harvests and herds to be taxed. Priests representing the state, rather than fathers representing their households, told the great stories that forged Israel's identity as the people of Yahweh. There are no existing copies of any of these traditions, but scholars reconstruct four of them from the books of Genesis, Exodus, Leviticus, Numbers, and Deuteronomy. They are called the Yahwist Tradition (J), the Elohist Tradition (E), the Deuteronomist Tradition (D), and the Priests' Tradition (P).

The Yahwist and the Elohist Traditions developed when David and Solomon ruled Israel. The Yahwist Tradition was popular in the villages of the south, where Abraham and Sarah were their ancestors and David was their chief.

David enlarged the state of Israel by conquest and by covenant, first with the Hebrew villages to the north and then non-Hebrew states like Syria, Ammon, Moab, and Edom to the east. Israel and its covenant partners were part of the geographical spheres of influence of both Egypt and Mesopotamia. Mesopotamia is the region between the Euphrates River to the west and the Tigris River to the East. Since 1958, it is the location of the republic of Iraq, whose capital is Baghdad. To the east of the Tigris River is the ancient land of Persia. Since 1979, it is the location of the Islamic republic of Iran, whose capital is Tehran. To the west of the Euphrates River is Syria-Palestine. Since 1944, it is the location of the republic of Syria, whose capital is Damascus. Today's Lebanon, Israel, and Jordan were also part of Syria-Palestine in antiquity.

Under Solomon, Israel's covenant partners became restless. The cost of belonging to Israel began to outweigh its benefits, and they declared their independence from Israel. This is the climate of emerging nationalism in which one great tradition promising military security and economic aid to those who remained loyal to the household of David and Solomon developed. Its storytellers referred to the divine patron of the Hebrews as "Yahweh." Their stories described Yahweh with very human metaphors. Yahweh made pottery, planted crops, and trudged along the paths of Syria-Palestine to find Hebrews who would help in the work of feeding and protecting the people. Scholars refer to these storytellers as "Yahwists," and to their laws and stories as the "Yahwist Tradition," which is abbreviated "J" from the German spelling of "Yahweh" as *Jahve*.

The Elohist Tradition developed in Hebrew villages in the north. This tradition celebrated Jacob, Leah, and Rachel as the ancestors of Israel, and referred to its divine patron of the Hebrews as "Elohim," a title used by cultures in Syria-Palestine to identify their "God-parent." The traditions described Elohim ruling like the monarch of a great state, surrounded by messengers or angels who came and went seeing to the care of the Hebrews. Scholars label these storytellers as "Elohists," and call their laws and stories the "Elohist Tradition," which is abbreviated "E." J and E are traditions of empire building, inspiring the Hebrews to reach out and acquire colonies in Syria-Palestine.

The Deuteronomist Tradition developed in Jerusalem during the reign of Josiah (640–609 B.C.E.). The laws and stories of the Deuteronomists, which are labeled "D," were named for their masterpiece, the book of Deuteronomy. The intention of the Deuteronomist Tradition was to avoid the complete destruction of the culture of Judah by the Babylonians. In this tradition, Yahweh calls the Hebrews not to become an empire, but to set themselves apart from other states. Isolationism replaces colonialism.

The Priests' Tradition appears after Jerusalem is destroyed. A tragic series of wars between the state of Judah and the Mesopotamian empire of Babylon ended when the armies of Nebuchadnezzar (604–562 B.C.E.) broke through the walls of Jerusalem and forced King Zedekiah's government to surrender. Nebuchadnezzar's terms were devastating. Virtually every household connected with the government of Judah was deported to Mesopotamia. Jerusalem and the temple were razed to the ground. Land and livestock were redistributed to households that the Babylonians could trust. Without a government, without a capital city, without a temple and without control of their land it seemed almost impossible that either the households deported to Mesopotamia or those who remained in Syria-Palestine could survive assimilation. The exile was the most painful, and yet the most prolific, period in the history of ancient Israel. The people of Judah not only survived, they prospered. The survival skill that the exiles used best was their ability to tell a story. Performance, however, gave way to preservation. The stories were no longer told; they were written. The writers were the priests who had been charged with caring for the traditions of ancient Israel since the days of David and Solomon. They now undertook their greatest task. It was this story told by priests, abbreviated "P," which developed in Babylon during the exile that gave the Bible much of the shape that it has today.

In What Language Was the Bible Written?

Two important language families appear in the ancient Near East. One is Indo-European and the other is Semitic. Hittite and Persian are the only Indo-European languages in the world of the Bible. They are related to the languages of India to the east, and of Britain, Germany, Italy, and the Baltic and Slavic countries to the west.

Semitic languages are divided into east Semitic languages and northwest Semitic languages. Akkadian is the only east Semitic language. It was named for Akkad in southern Mesopotamia, where the first inscriptions in this language were recovered by archaeologists. Babylonian and Assyrian are dialects of Akkadian. Babylonia was the cultural heartland of Mesopotamia where the art and traditions characteristic of all Mesopotamian cultures developed. During the Middle Bronze period (2000–1550 B.C.E.) Mari, north of Babylon on the Euphrates River near Deir-ez-Zor, Iraq today, served as a gateway for Babylonian culture to enter Syria-Palestine. Assyria (1000–614 B.C.E.) was a culture that developed the technologies of government and military science, but borrowed heavily from Babylonia for its art and tradition.

The dominant northwest Semitic language is Aramaic. It is written with an alphabet of just twenty-two letters instead of the hundreds of Akkadian symbols. Aramaic replaced Akkadian as the language of diplomacy after 1000 B.C.E. Arameans were from Aram or Damascus, but appear throughout Mesopotamia and Syria-Palestine. Hebrew is a dialect of Aramaic. Most of the Bible is written in Hebrew, although part of the book of Daniel (Dan 2:4—7:28) and a few other sections are written in Aramaic (Gen 31:47; Jer 10:11; Ezra 4:8—6:18; 7:12-26).

Why Are There So Many Different Bibles?

Eventually, the books of Genesis, Exodus, Leviticus, Numbers, and Deuteronomy became the basic teaching or core curriculum of the Bible, which Jews call the "Tanak." "Tanak" is an abbreviation for the three sections of the Hebrew Bible: the Torah, the Nebiim, and the Ketubim. The Torah continued to be applied in different times to new challenges. The Nebiim or the Books of the Prophets like Samuel-Kings and Isaiah and the Ketubim or the Books of the Writings like Proverbs and Job develop the understanding of the Torah in different ways. For example, the Prophets challenged ancient Israel to face the dangers of becoming a state with monarchs, taxes, soldiers, slaves, and cities. Likewise, the Writings challenged ancient Israel to become a special partner in the family of nations. They wanted Israel to take its place in a world where Yahweh was not only the divine patron of Israel but the creator of the universe.

As early as 721 B.C.E., when the Assyrians captured and destroyed the state of Israel and Samaria, its capital city, Israelites who survived emigrated from their homeland to Egypt and other states in the ancient Near East. This great emigration continued for the next thousand years, creating communities of Hebrews living outside Israel and Judah in the "Diaspora." The Bible continued to help these diaspora communities preserve their roots and adapt to new cultures.

Greek was the language of daily life for people throughout all the countries in the Mediterranean conquered by Alexander of Macedonia (356–323 B.C.E.). The common culture of all the Greek-speaking lands is called "Hellenism." Greek-speaking Jews in Egypt translated the Bible into Greek, and developed new traditions in Greek to help them avoid assimilation and preserve their own cultural identity. Old stories of Jews who were strangers in strange lands like Joseph in Egypt took on new meaning. New stories like Esther in Persia and Daniel in Babylon were incorporated into the Greek Bible of the Diaspora or "Septuagint." Septuagint means "seventy" in Greek. The word recalls a tradition that describes the translation of the Hebrew Bible into Greek by seventy teachers in Egypt (Fig. 4).

Books that appear in the Septuagint, but not in the Hebrew Bible, are called "apocryphal" or "deutero-canonical" books. "Apocryphal" emphasizes that these traditions clarify or reveal the obscure or hidden significance of the Hebrew Bible. "Deutero-canonical" labels these traditions as a supplementary or second collection of traditions that are normative for life and teaching in biblical communities. For the communities of Jews who became Christians, the Septuagint was the Bible, which their New Testament traditions interpreted.

By the time of Jesus, most Jews considered the Bible as a covenant or testament negotiated by Yahweh and Israel. Covenant is a genre developed by diplomats in the ancient Near East who negotiated treaties between one village or state and another to prevent or to end wars. The intention of covenant, like the function of diplomacy, was to clearly identify the responsibilities the negotiators had toward one another. The technical term in ancient Israel for fulfilling these responsibilities was *hesed,* or "love." Love here is not simply an emotional attachment; it is a binding contractual obligation. The intention of a covenant was to help two communities "to love one another" or to live in peace.

As a covenant, the Bible characterizes Yahweh as the divine patron of ancient Israel and Israel as the client people of Yahweh. "I, Yahweh, their Godparent, am with them . . . they, the house of Israel, are my people . . . you are my sheep, the sheep of my pasture, and I am your Creator" (Ezek 34:30-31). In this covenant Yahweh agreed to

---

Judaism

canon Hebrew Bible (1000–165 B.C.E.); Masorah (70 C.E.)

commentary Mishnah (200 C.E.); Talmud (600 C.E.)

translations Aramaic Targums (500 B.C.E.); Greek Apocrypha (300 B.C.E.); Syriac Peshitta (100 C.E.)

copies Hebrew Dead Sea Scrolls (150 B.C.E.–70 C.E.)

Christianity

Hebrew Bible (1000–165 B.C.E.); Greek Septuagint (300 B.C.E.); Greek New Testament (49–110 C.E.)

Islam

Hebrew Bible (1000–165 B.C.E.); Greek New Testament (49–110 C.E.); Arabic Qur'an (600 C.E.)

(all dates are approximate)

FIGURE 4 Traditions of Judaism, Christianity, and Islam

protect and to provide for Israel and Judah, and the people of Israel and Judah agreed to make no covenants with any other divine patron. Jews who became Christians believed that, as the book of Jeremiah (Jer 31:31-34) had promised, Jesus had renegotiated Israel's covenant with Yahweh (Fig. 5). Therefore, they began calling the Hebrew Bible the "Old Covenant" or "Old Testament," and their own interpretations of it the "New Covenant" or "New Testament." Christians did not consider themselves a new religion, but a renewed religion. Therefore, Moses, Micah, Jesus, and Akiva all summarize the Bible with the same words: "love the Lord, your God, with all your heart, and with all your soul, and with all your strength" (Deut 6:5; Mic 6:6; Matt 22:37-40; Mark 12:29-31; Luke 10:27; *Genesis Rabbah* 24, 7).

After 100 C.E. neither Jews nor Christians added any new traditions to the Bible. Preaching and teaching became the ongoing story in each tradition. About 200 C.E., Jewish teachers or "rabbis" collected their laws and stories into the "Mishnah." This legal code, written in Hebrew, contains regulations and beliefs foundational of rabbinic Judaism and thus of all later Jewish thought. The word *mishnah* means those traditions that are "repeated" (Hebrew: *shanah*) or "retold." The second official commentary in the Jewish community appeared about 400 C.E. in both Hebrew and Aramaic. It is called the "Talmud," which means "study" or "learning" in Hebrew. The Talmud is a commentary on the Mishnah. There are two Talmud traditions. The one, which developed in Mesopotamia, is called the "Babylonian Talmud." The other, which developed in Syria-Palestine, is called the "Palestinian Talmud." Mishnah and Talmud continue to play an important role in the teaching and way of life of Jews today.

Eventually Latin replaced Greek as the daily language throughout the Hellenistic world. By 400 C.E., Jerome, who was a Christian hermit in Bethlehem, translated the Hebrew Bible and the Greek New Testament into Latin. Jerome's translation or "Vulgate" was the prayer book and the official Bible of Western Christians until the reformation

> The days are surely coming, (WORD OF YAHWEH!), when I will make a new covenant with the Household of Israel and the Household of Judah. It will not be like the covenant that I made with their ancestors when I took them by the hand to bring them out of the land of Egypt—a covenant that they broke, though I was their husband, (WORD OF YAHWEH!). But this is the covenant that I will make with the Household of Israel after those days, (WORD OF YAHWEH!): I will put my law within them, and I will write it on their hearts: and I will be their God, and they shall be my people.

FIGURE 5   Covenant between Yahweh and Israel (Jer 31:31-33)

of Martin Luther (1483–1546) in northern Europe and for Catholics throughout the world until Vatican Council II (1962–65), when modern-language versions of the Bible came into use.

Today there are several very readable translations of the Bible from Hebrew, Greek, and Aramaic into the English spoken in the United States. Among them are the *New Revised Standard Version* (1989), *Tanakh: The Holy Scriptures* (1985), and the *New American Bible* (1970). Introductions printed with the translations describe the principles used by the scholars who did the work. The *New Revised Standard Version* reflects how most biblical scholars are reading the Bible today. HarperCollins publishes an excellent study edition, which contains the standard interpretations taught in most introductory courses at universities that are not religiously affiliated. *Tanakh: The Holy Scriptures* is a reading of the Bible in light of Jewish traditions of interpretation. Christians already familiar with the Bible will find the *Tanakh* a refreshing way to revitalize passages that have become overly familiar. The new language of the *Tanakh* is also a helpful reminder that all translations are interpretations. The *New American Bible* is a reading of the Bible by Catholic and non-Catholic scholars that is sensitive to the way in which Catholic theology understands various passages. Oxford University Press publishes the best study edition. In most cases the interpretations in the more recent introductory material are more reliable. The translations in *The Old Testament Story* are my own. They are not literal, visual, or text-oriented, but reader-oriented. Their vocabulary and idiom reflect the aspects of those traditions that I am emphasizing.

Who Divided the Bible into Books, Chapters, and Verses?

Jews divide the Bible into scrolls. Christians divide it into books. Scrolls were an earlier storage format than books. Some books and scrolls were made of animal skins called "vellum" or "parchment." Others were manufactured from plant fibers called "papyrus." Paper was not used for writing until the explorer Marco Polo (1254–1324) brought it from China to Europe. A scroll looks like a roll of paper towels about ten inches from top to bottom. A tightly rolled scroll was about two and one-half inches in diameter. Each end of the scroll was connected to a roller. Rollers were about the diameter of a broomstick, and about ten inches longer than the scrolls that were attached to them were wide. Therefore about five inches of the rollers extended beyond the top and bottom of the scroll itself to be used as handles. These rollers allowed readers to use scrolls without touching the scrolls themselves. Readers held the roller with the unread portion of the scroll in their left hand, and the roller with the read portion of the scroll in their right.

Because a scroll was turned or rolled as it was read, it was also called a "volume." The average scroll was between twenty and thirty feet long. Longer scrolls were unmanageable. They were too heavy and too awkward. The longest surviving scroll is the Harris Papyrus in the British Museum. It is about 133 feet long, but scrolls of this length were ceremonial and not intended for practical use. A large and important collection of ancient biblical manuscripts was discovered in a series of caves along the western shore of the Dead Sea in 1947. Some may have been made as early as 200 B.C.E., almost a thousand years older than any biblical manuscript available until then. The first of the Dead Sea Scrolls contained the book of Isaiah (1QIsa^a), which was made from seventeen sheepskins and is about ten inches wide and twenty-four feet long.

The beginning and the end of many of the books in the Bible today say more about the physical size of the scrolls on which they were traditionally copied than about their literary divisions. Scribes copied as much of the biblical text as would fit on a standard-size scroll, without a great deal of regard for whether or not the last lines of text on a scroll coincided with an actual literary division of the text. They copied texts onto scrolls like a computer filling a CD with data. They used all the space available on one scroll before going on to the next. Readers, not scribes, were responsible for knowing where the literary divisions of the text occurred. For example, the Torah was divided into five sections of roughly the same physical length in order to fit onto five standard-length scrolls. Today, each of these five scrolls or "Pentateuch," has its own name. The first scroll is called "The Book of Genesis" or "The First Book of Moses." The second is "The Book of Exodus" or "The Second Book of Moses." The third is "The Book of Leviticus" or "The Third Book of Moses." The fourth is "The Book of Numbers" or "The Fourth Book of Moses." The fifth is "The Book of Deuteronomy" or "The Fifth Book of Moses." The Books of Samuel-Kings and the Books of Chronicles-Ezra-Nehemiah were also physically divided so as to fit the normal capacity of a twenty to thirty foot scroll. Conversely, twelve short traditions, today called the Books of Hosea, Joel, Amos, Obadiah, Jonah, Micah, Nahum, Habakkuk, Zephaniah, Haggai, Zechariah, and Malachi, were copied together on a single scroll. Even the sixty-six chapters of the book of Isaiah, which is the longest book in the Bible today, developed from the practice of copying two or three originally separate traditions on a single twenty- to thirty-foot scroll.

Likewise, the books of Bible were not originally divided into chapters and verses as printed Bibles are today. It was Stephen Langton of Canterbury who divided a Latin translation of the Bible into chapters about 1226 C.E. Solomon ben Ishmael later divided a Hebrew scroll into chapters for the first time. As early as 200 C.E., the Talmud divided the Torah into verses, but not always at the same places. Robert Lyon, a printer, first numbered the verses of the Vulgate in 1551 C.E. Therefore, chapter and verse divisions reflect the way the Bible was interpreted at various times in its history, but they are not very reliable guides for interpreting it today.

What Is the Difference between Bible Study and Biblical Studies?

The study of the Bible is part of the study of religion. One important role of religion is to preserve the myth and ritual of a culture. Unlike the way "myth" and "ritual" are used in everyday speech, neither word, when it is used technically, carries the connotation that religion is meaningless, mechanical, or misleading. Myth describes what a culture believes. Ritual defines how the people in a culture are expected to behave. Departments of Theology in religiously affiliated colleges or universities generally study a single religion or denomination. Departments of Religious Studies investigate the religions of many different cultures. Biblical Studies is the specialty in Religious Studies dedicated to understanding and appreciating the "words" and the languages of ancient Israel and early Christianity. The History of Religion studies the leaders and movements that have contributed significantly to the development of a religion. Philosophy of Religion, which in the Christian tradition is called "systematic" or "dogmatic" theology, seeks to understand the underlying principles or metaphysics on which a religion operates. Ethics analyzes religious behavior, whether it is the liturgical behavior called "worship" or the ordinary behavior of daily life called "morality." Psychology of Religion studies the attitudes, spirituality, piety, asceticism, and prayer that religions teach.

Biblical Studies is not the same as Bible Study. Biblical Studies is a class; Bible Study is a community. Biblical Studies is an academic discipline. Bible Study is a religious devotion. A Bible Study is a small group of people with a common faith, even though they may belong to different churches. They come together on a regular basis. Between meetings members of the group read and pray the same passages of the Bible. During meetings members speak in turn about how the passage helped clarify God's will for them, and what decisions the passage was helping them make. Sometimes, to enrich their reflections, members of a Bible Study do compare different modern-language translations of the Bible and read simple commentaries. A Bible Study is a community whose members become companions supporting one another in their desire to better live out the commitments of their faith in God.

Biblical Studies developed following the Enlightenment in the eighteenth century. It was one of many new fields of inquiry stimulated by the kind of learning and research common in universities today. The Enlightenment assumed that human experience, and even human religious experience, made sense. The medieval worldview, which preceded the Enlightenment, considered human experience, and especially human religious experience, as a mystery that defied human understanding. The Enlightenment established a renewed confidence in the human mind and its ability to understand human experience. Therefore biblical scholars, like their colleagues in other areas of study, began to collect data on the Bible. They used the data to develop methods for understanding and appreciating its traditions. These methods were continually reviewed and tested, and then adapted or replaced by new methods. Slowly the world of the Bible and the religious traditions of ancient Israel began to become better understood.

Methods used in Biblical Studies are called "criticisms." Criticism, in spite of the way it is used in everyday speech, is not just saying something derogatory. Technically, criticism analyzes and evaluates art and culture. It judges both strengths and weaknesses. Art endures when it possesses the quality of being able to communicate with different people in different places at different times. The Bible is clearly art. It continues to enlighten and to inspire and to inform those who hear it today as it has done for centuries. The purpose of biblical criticism is not to destroy, or even to monitor, the special encounter that takes place between the Bible and those who hear it. The purpose of biblical criticism is to build on that encounter. Biblical criticism helps those who hear the Bible, and are enlightened, inspired, and informed by it, to hear the Bible better, to understand it better, and, hopefully, to be more inspired by it.

When people ask, "Do you take the Bible literally?" they are really asking, "Will you accept my interpretation of the Bible, or the interpretation of my teacher, or my congregation?" Biblical Studies assumes it is impossible to encounter the Bible without interpreting it. Biblical Studies teaches audiences how to develop appropriate and healthy reactions to the Bible. Encounters with the Bible, like encounters with all classic works of art, open the human mind. A closed mind is not an appropriate reaction to an encounter with the Bible. Therefore, whenever the question, "Do you take the Bible literally?" means "Have you closed your mind to every other interpretation of the Bible but mine?" the appropriate answer is "No." Encounters with the Bible can, do, and should lead to conviction and to commitment, but encounters with the Bible should never lead to arrogance, elitism, and religious persecution. Sadly, they have, and they do, but they should not.

Before 1900, most introductions to the Bible were theological or confessional. They explained the doctrines of particular religious traditions, and used the Bible to footnote these theologies. After 1900, most introductions to the Bible were historical-critical, and taught students that the Bible had a time and a place and a message of its own. *Understanding the Old Testament* by Bernhard W. Anderson was one of the best introductions. When this widely used textbook was first published there was a consensus among teachers that historical criticism was the best method to use with students in introductory classes. Today many teachers still choose a historical-critical introduction for their students, but many historical-critical introductions are still too much history and too little criticism. Anderson's opening chapter, for example, offers thirty-four pages of well-balanced and reliable history of the Middle Bronze period without critically discussing a single biblical tradition.

A new consensus is emerging among teachers, but nothing like the consensus for which Anderson published. Teachers still want their students to understand how the Bible functioned in its own world, without overemphasizing the importance of this community of origin. Nevertheless, they also want their students to recognize how each time and place where the Bible is heard continues to enrich and unfold its meaning. *The Old Testament Story* represents a new generation of introductions to the Bible that integrate what historical criticism taught with what narrative criticism, social-scientific criticism, and feminist criticism are teaching. Here there is more criticism, less history. This introduction teaches students how to listen to the words that the Bible speaks, and how to understand the people of ancient Israel who crafted these remarkable words.

Teachers today seldom arrange the syllabus for their classes chronologically and begin with the book of Exodus, as Anderson does, even though historical critics agree that it contains the oldest, and most characteristically Hebrew, traditions in the Bible. Likewise, teachers are less likely to teach the book of Deuteronomy as an introduction to the book of Jeremiah, as Anderson does, even though historical critics have demonstrated that both developed during the same period shortly before the destruction of Jerusalem in 587 B.C.E. More and more teachers today arrange their course along the lines of the canon, so the contents of *The Old Testament Story* follow the order of the English canon.

Since it is the biblical traditions themselves that draw students to study the Bible in the first place, *The Old Testament Story* studies the Bible by studying traditions from the Bible. These interpretations are not full commentaries. So, for example, there are interpretations for Stories of Abraham and Sarah, but not for the Stories of Isaac and Rebekah. There are interpretations for the book of Exodus, but not for the book of Deuteronomy. There are interpretations for the Books of Samuel-Kings, but not for the Books of Chronicles.

The Old Testament Story provides not only interpretations, but also offers an invitation to a life of learning. The Bible recognizes that what endures over time is seldom the answers, but the questions about life and death, about right and wrong, about the divine, about the human, and about the earth. The Bible is a powerful testimony to the consistency with which humans engage God, one another, and the earth. These shared questions demonstrate how human beings have faced troubles before, troubles that they have managed well or have managed badly. The Bible crosses social boundaries and challenges dominant worldviews. The Bible unveils a faith that is larger than cultures and has survived for thousands of years. The Bible is not a textbook in the theology of Judaism, Christianity, Islam, or even the American way of life, but an exquisite expression of the questions with which, eventually, every human being must struggle.

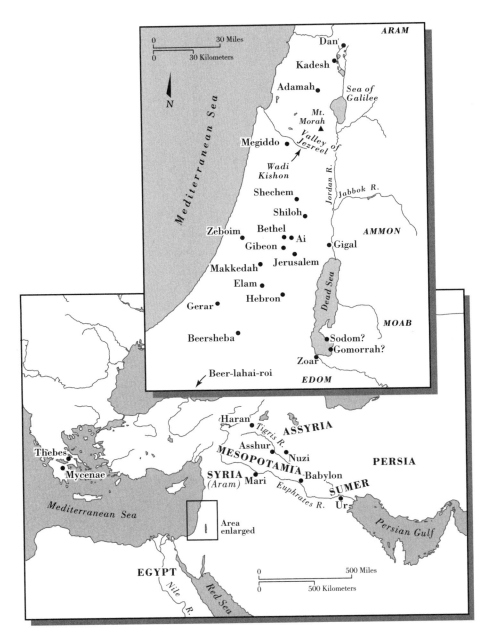

Points of Interest (Chapter 2)

2

BOOK OF GENESIS

(GEN 1:1 — EXOD 1:6)

Creation Stories
(GEN 1:1 — 11:26)

The book of Genesis (Hebrew: *Bereshit*) opens with an unforgettable set of creation stories. (Fig. 6) They are followed by two fascinating cycles of ancestor stories. One cycle tells about the household of Abraham and Sarah, and the other about the household of Jacob, Leah, and Rachel. Genesis concludes with the Teachings of Joseph. Creation stories and teaching stories hand on the traditions of the powerful. Ancestor stories hand on the traditions of the powerless. In creation stories the powerful demonstrate how a culture works. In teaching stories the powerful explain to their audiences how to work within the system that creation stories describe. In ancestor stories the powerless teach their audiences how to get the system to work for them.

Stories of Adam and Eve
(GEN 2:4 — 4:2)

In the book of Genesis the Hebrews tell their own versions of the creation stories of Babylon, in whose sphere of influence they lived after 587 B.C.E. These traditions include the stories of the Heavens and the Earth (Gen 1:1—2:4), the Stories of Adam and Eve (Gen 2:4—4:2), the Stories of Cain and Abel (Gen 4:3—5:32), and the Flood Stories (Gen 6:1—11:26). They provide little truly scientific information about the origins of the world or the origins of humanity. Planetary geology, paleontology, and archaeology are modern, not ancient interests. The Hebrews lacked both the data for and the

---

A. CREATION STORIES (Gen 1:1—11:26)

1. *Creation of the Heavens and the Earth (Gen 1:1—2:4)*

2. *Stories of Adam and Eve (Gen 2:4—4:2)*

3. *Stories of Cain and Abel (Gen 4:3—5:32)*

4. *Flood Stories (Gen 6:1—11:26)*

B. ANCESTOR STORIES (Gen 11:27—37:2a)

1. *Stories of Abraham and Sarah (Gen 11:17—25:18)*

2. *Stories of Jacob, Leah, and Rachel (Gen 25:19—37:2)*

C. TEACHINGS of Joseph (Gen 37:2—Exod 1:6)

FIGURE 6   The Book of Genesis (Gen 1:1—Exod 1:6)

interest in forging a chain between themselves and early humans. Instead they told creation stories to put human life in their time into perspective. Their creation stories are not reports on the past. They are timeless reflections on human life. They explore questions about life and death. People in every culture raise these questions to orient themselves to the greater world in which they live. Therefore, biblical storytellers set creation stories during the epoch primeval, which does not date events, it qualifies them. Setting the action of a story in the epoch primeval does not explain when something took place, but why things are the way they are in the time when the story itself is told. Only events of universal significance take place in the epoch primeval. Stories set in the epoch primeval are philosophical or theological, not geological or paleontological.

Story of the *'Adam* as a Farmer
(GEN 2:4-17)

The Stories of Adam and Eve (Gen 2:4—4:2) develop from shorter creation stories that are now artistically nested one inside the other. Each investigates different questions about human life. Together they are as important for understanding the culture of ancient Israel as are the stories of the deliverance of the Hebrews from slavery in Egypt and their settlement in Syria-Palestine in the book of Exodus.

Like all stories, creation stories have plots with three episodes: a crisis, a climax, and a denouement. The crisis episode in a creation story is a sterility affidavit, which certifies that the conditions for land and children are missing. The climax episode is a cosmogony, which describes the creator giving birth to the world. The denouement episode is a covenant, which endows humans with gifts and teaches them how to live in this new world (Fig. 7).

The Story of the *'Adam* as a Farmer (Gen 2:4-17) certifies that when Yahweh began to create, none of the conditions for agriculture existed. First, there were no grapes or olives, and there were no grains. Grain, wine, and olive oil were farm products in the world of the Bible. Second, there was no rain at the end of the long, hot summer to soften the soil enough for farmers to plow, and there was no rain near the end of the growing season to bring crops to full fruit. To prevent crop failure these twin rains must come at the right time and in the right quantity. Third, there was no farmer, and there was no farmland. Land was life. Without good farmland, no farmer could survive. Without good farmers, no farmland would exist. Fourth, there was water everywhere. Some translations describe this flood as if it were an irrigation system parallel to the imagery in the Stories of Enki from Sumer where his semen irrigates the vulva of Nintu before she gives birth to the plants and animals. The waters in the Story of the *'Adam* as a Farmer do not give life; they bring death. They are not a cloud, a mist, a spring, or a stream that irrigates crops, but rather a flood that inundates everything in its path.

Yahweh's first work in the cosmogony is the *'adam*. Some cosmogonies describe the creator fighting with chaos; some do not. Yahweh battles the waters of chaos in the Flood Stories and in the Death of the Firstborn of Egypt stories and in the Creation of the Firstborn of Israel stories. Here, however, Yahweh is not a warrior, but an artist or a potter. This image of the creator as a potter also appears in a Trial of Judah and Jerusalem in the book of Jeremiah (Jer 18:1-12), and in the Stories of Atrahasis as they were told in Babylon.

Between 10,000 and 4,000 B.C.E. Stone Age humans took two momentous steps toward civilization. They learned to farm and they learned to make pottery. These inventions created a new world. Consequently, their creation stories often describe their divine patrons as potters or farmers. The metaphor is modified so that the techniques of the divine and human potters are similar, but not identical. All potters work with two ingredients. One ingredient is firm and the other is fluid. Human potters mix clay with water. Divine potters use a variety of thinners. The divine midwife, Nintu-Mami, thins her clay with blood (Atra 1:229-234). The godmother, Aruru, uses saliva (Gilg 1:30-40). Here Yahweh wets the clay with only the condensation created by breathing on it. Many translations refer to the human element that Yahweh uses as "dust," not clay, and do not continue the image of Yahweh as a potter from the beginning of the verse: "then Yahweh, our Creator, formed the *'adam* from the dust of the ground" (Gen

sterility affidavit (Gen 2:4-6)

> *When Yahweh, Our Creator,*
>
> *Began to create the heavens and the earth,*
>> *There were no orchards,*
>
> *There were no fields of grain.*
>> *There were no planting rains,*
>
> *There were no harvesting rains.*
>> *There was no one to work the soil,*
>
> *There was no soil to work.*
>> *Only water pouring through dikes of clay,*
>
> *Only water flooding the earth.*

cosmogony (Gen 2:7-14)

> *Then Yahweh sculpted an 'adam from clay,*
>
> *Made it live by breathing moisture onto the clay.*
>> *Yahweh, Our Creator, built a plantation,*
>
> *Yahweh installed the 'adam in Eden.*
>> *There were trees delightful to see,*
>
> *Fruit good to eat*
>> *The Tree of Life was in the middle of Eden,*
>
> *And The Tree of the Knowledge of Good and Evil.*
>> *There were rivers,*
>
> *Abundant water for the garden.*
>> *The Pishon flowing through the desert of Havilah in Arabia,*
>
> *The Gihon running through the land of Cush in Ethiopia.*
>> *The Tigris rolling east of Asshur in Iraq,*
>
> *The Euphrates.*
>> *There was gold,*

(continued)

> Twenty-four carat gold.
>   There was the gemstone, bdellium,
>
> There was lapis lazuli.
>
> **covenant** (Gen 2:15-17)
>
>   Finally Yahweh, Our Creator, gave Eden to the 'adam to
>   cultivate,
>
> The 'adam was to care for the plantation of Yahweh.
>   Yahweh decreed: "You shall eat from any tree in Eden,
>
> Except the Tree of Knowledge of Good and Evil.
>   Anyone who eats from this tree shall die."

FIGURE 7   Story of the 'Adam as a Farmer (Gen 2:4-17)

2:7), to the end of the verse: "and breathed into its nostrils the breath of life" (Gen 2:7). Consequently, these translations consider the divine element to be breath, not fluid (Ps 104:27-30; Job 34:14-15). There is no parallel in Mesopotamia for breathing life into clay. In Egypt, Amon Ra is portrayed as breathing into the pharaoh's nose to authorize his coronation, but this breathing motif appears in coronation stories, not in creation stories. The defining metaphors in the stories of Adam and Eve are from Mesopotamia, not Egypt. For the Hebrews, a living creature is moist, not inflated. Blood, sperm, tears, and saliva distinguish the living from the dead, the moist from the dry. Therefore, it is more consistent with parallels from Mesopotamia to portray Yahweh as a divine potter who shapes the 'adam from clay and then gently moistens and polishes the 'adam with saliva.

To emphasize that the first creatures were extraordinary, storytellers gave them special names. The Enuma Elish Stories and the Stories of Atrahasis call the people primeval *lullu*. The Stories of Gilgamesh call their person primeval *enkidu*. Here Yahweh's first creature is not "Adam" or a "man," but an 'adam. Creation stories describe the differences between ordinary human beings and their predecessors in various ways. Ordinary human beings are fertile and mortal, but the *lullu* are fertile and immortal (Atra iii, 8:1) and the *enkidu* is infertile and mortal. The Stories of Adam and Eve assume both the 'adam (Gen 2:7) and the man and the woman (Gen 3:23) are immortal like the *lullu* and infertile like the *enkidu*. They are living, but not fully human. The 'adam is a being without gender, neither male nor female. The man and the woman have gender, but are sterile. The first truly human beings in the stories are the Adam and Eve who appear at the very end of the stories (Gen 4:1-2). Unlike the 'adam, and the man and the woman, only Adam and Eve have names. Only they have children, and only they work the land.

The world that Yahweh creates for the 'adam is called 'eden (Gen 2:8). Romanticism in the eighteenth century branded the city as an unfit environment for humans. For English poets like Blake, Wordsworth, Coleridge, Byron, Shelley, and Keats, a city could never be a paradise. Their exaltation of human life in the open continues to evoke condemnations of urban life today, and this Romantic perspective has had an enduring effect on the interpretation of the Bible. Consequently, many still describe Eden as an unspoiled wilderness. In the world of the Bible, however, there was no Romantic movement to celebrate naturalism or primitivism. Cultures in the ancient Near East considered the untamed wilderness unfit for humans, who were created to live in cities, not in the desert. The people primeval are wild and barbaric until the wise tutor them in the arts of sexual intercourse, government, trades, skills, and crafts so that they can build cities. Eden in the story of the 'adam is a landscaped garden or urban masterpiece, like the Hanging Gardens of Nebuchadnezzar in Babylon, not an undeveloped wilderness or a geological wonder. Like the chaos that it replaces, Eden is described with parallels reflecting order, balance, and abundance. It is built from pairs or twins.

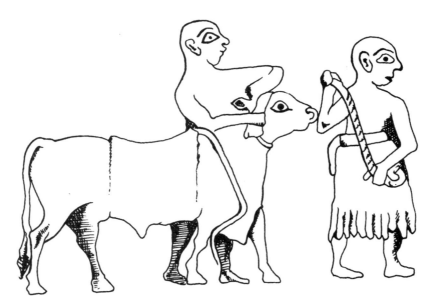

Men Lead a Bull to the King of Ur
(Ur 2400 B.C.E.; mosaic)

There are two of everything: two trees, two sets of rivers, two kinds of gold, two kinds of gems.

The covenant that closes the story gives Eden to the *'adam* and decrees that the *'adam* will survive in this new world by eating the fruit from every tree but the Tree of the Knowledge of Good and Evil. The apple tree was virtually unknown in the world of the Bible, but the quince tree with its apple-shaped and yellow fruit whose shade, beauty, fragrance, and taste was widely associated with fertility (Song 2:3-5; 7:9; 8:5; Joel 1:12; Prov 25:1). At some point the quince tree in the Song of Solomon (Song 8:5) was identified with Tree of the Knowledge of Good and Evil and, subsequently, the art and literature of western Europe began to describe it as an apple tree.

The intention of the covenant in the denouement is not to restrict or to tempt. Yahweh does not trap and test the Hebrews, but teaches them how to survive. This covenant teaches the *'adam* how to survive in Eden. The covenant stipulates: "You shall eat from any tree in Eden, except the Tree of Knowledge of Good and Evil. Anyone who eats from this tree shall die" (Gen 2:16-17). The balance between eating from some trees, and not eating from one tree creates a parallelism. This parallelism teaches that in Eden—and in all human life—every decision is really two decisions. There is a decision to do something and a decision not to do something. Every yes has a corresponding no. Anyone who ignores the no-consequences of a yes-decision will die. The covenant with which the story ends describes a consequence, not a punishment.

Story of the *'Adam* as a Herder
(GEN 2:18-20)

The sterility affidavit that opens the Story of the *'Adam* as a Herder certifies that everything around the *'adam* is twinned and thriving, but the *'adam* is alone and infertile. Gender, and therefore truly human life, is missing (Fig. 8).

The cosmogony describes Yahweh sculpting animals from clay. They are created like the *'adam* to be companions for the *'adam*.

In the covenant Yahweh endows the *'adam* with the animals. The *'adam* then takes legal possession of the gifts by naming them.

Storytellers found humor in Yahweh's failure to find a partner for the *'adam* among the animals. Like the denouement of the previous creation story, the denouement of the Story of the *'Adam* as a Herder leaves its crisis only partially resolved. There is a bond between the *'adam* and the animals, but there is no partner for the *'adam* among the animals.

---

sterility affidavit (Gen 2:18)

When Yahweh, Our Creator, said:

"It is not good, for the *'adam* to be alone."

cosmogony (Gen 2:18-19)

Then Yahweh, Our Creator, called out: "Let there be a partner for the
    'adam!"

So Yahweh, Our Creator, began to sculpt beasts and birds.

covenant (Gen 2:19-20)

Finally Yahweh, Our Creator, gave them to the *'adam,*

Let the *'adam* name them.
Whatever the *'adam* called each,

Became its name.
The *'adam* named all the cattle,

Every bird of the sky, every beast.

FIGURE 8   Story of the *'Adam* as a Herder (Gen 2:18-20)

Story of the *'Adam* as a Man and a Woman
(GEN 2:20-24)

The sterility affidavit in the Story of the *'Adam* as a Man and a Woman certifies that
there is still no "helper," no "partner," no "helpmeet" for the *'adam* (Fig. 9). "Helper" is not
a patronizing term in the Bible; it is one of Yahweh's titles (Deut 33:1-7; Ps 33:20-22;
121:1-2). For example, Moses prays: "The divine patron of my father, who delivered me
from the sword of Pharaoh, was My Help" (Exod 18:4).

    To begin the cosmogony Yahweh puts the *'adam* to sleep (Gen 2:21-22). Humans
may not watch Yahweh at work and live (Exod 33:20). This sleep is not rest, but a unique
coma which allows Yahweh to work unobserved and protects the *'adam* from harm (Gen
15:12; Job 4:13; 33:15). Although Yahweh fashions both the *'adam* and the animals from
clay, the raw material for the woman is a rib. The technique is not sexist indicating she
is inferior. The *'adam* and the animals are new creations. The man and the woman are
re-creations. Yahweh redesigns the *'adam* into a man and a woman. In Mesopotamia,
creation stories regularly play on the words "rib" and "living" because both are spelled

ti in the Sumerian language. The God-mother is *Nin-ti*, whose name means both "life-giver" and "rib-lady." The same wordplay appears in the story of Adam and Eve as Farmers and Child-bearers, where Eve is both the woman created from a rib and the woman who creates all the living (Gen 3:20). The puns develop from a similarity in the sounds of the two words, but not necessarily from any parallelism in meaning.

The story comes to a close with a marriage covenant (Gen 2:22-24). The word for marriage does not appear in the story itself, but Yahweh walks in procession with the

---

sterility affidavit (Gen 2:20)
But when there was not one,
not a single partner for the *'adam*.

cosmogony (Gen 2:21-22)
Then Yahweh, Our Creator, cast a spell on the *'adam*,
Put the *'ish* to sleep.

Yahweh, Our Creator, took a rib,
Moistened it with flesh.

Yahweh, Our Creator, took a rib from *'ish*,
And created *'ishah*.

covenant (Gen 2:22-24)
Finally Yahweh, Our Creator, brought *'ishah* to *'ish*,
"This one, at last, is bone of my bones,
flesh of my flesh.

This one shall be called "*ishah*,'
'ishah from the *'ish*."

And Yahweh, Our Creator, decreed:
"Man must leave father and mother, must join woman,
The two must become one."

FIGURE 9   Story of the *'Adam* as a Man and a Woman (Gen 2:20-24)

woman to the man like the father of a household bringing his daughter to her groom (Gen 29:23). Furthermore, the covenants in creation stories regularly inaugurate social institutions like marriage.

To celebrate the woman's creation, the man sings a hymn. He is not naming or taking possession of the woman here, the way he names and takes possession of the animals and birds in the Story of the 'Adam as a Herder. There his language is legal; here the language is liturgical. Like hymns in the book of Psalms, the man's words here praise Yahweh for a work of creation.

Before the Story of the 'Adam as a Man and a Woman became an episode in the Stories of Adam and Eve, their characters would have been fully human and capable of reproduction. For many the work that Yahweh begins in the Story of the 'Adam as a Herder (Gen 2:4) is completed at this point in the Story of the 'Adam as a Man and a Woman (Gen 2:25), rather than when Eve gives birth to Cain and Abel (Gen 4:2). In the Bible today, however, the development from gendered to fertile now takes place in the Story of Adam and Eve as Farmers and Child-bearers.

Story of Adam and Eve as Farmers and Child-bearers
(GEN 2:25—4:2)

The Story of Adam and Eve as Farmers and Child-bearers opens with a sophisticated pun that is almost erased when it is translated as: "and the man and his wife were both naked, and were not ashamed" (Gen 2:25) and "the snake was more crafty than any other wild animal" (Gen 3:1). In Hebrew the verses are joined by a play on the words "naked" (Gen 2:25) and "cunning" (Gen 3:1). "The man and the woman have no clothes" (Hebrew: 'arummim) and the snake has "no rivals" (Hebrew: 'arum). Both words contain the same three Hebrew letters: 'ayin, resh, and mem. By describing the man and the woman as naked, storytellers indicate that they are not yet ordinary human beings. They are still people primeval, more divine than human (Gilg 2:28). The snake in this story is also hardly an ordinary reptile. It talks. The talking snake (Gen 3:1) and the teaching tree (Gen 3:6-7) are examples of fable that gives plants and animals anthropomorphic or human characteristics. Even though the extraordinary title "more subtle than any other wild animal that Yahweh, our Creator, had made" (Gen 3:1) identifies the snake as a creature, it still plays the role of a member of the divine assembly, just as the Satan does in the book of Job (Job 1:1—2:13).

The divine assembly was analogous to the village or city assembly in the world of the Bible. The fathers of the households made up the village or city assembly. The divine assembly was made up of Yahweh and advisers like the Heavens and the Earth, the Sun and the Moon. Both judicial bodies met at a threshold to resolve a crisis that put land and children at risk. The village assembly met at the threshing floor where the grain harvest was processed. The city assembly met at the gates. The divine assembly convened at the beginning of each new year at a sanctuary. Sometimes a member of the divine assembly, like the snake in the Stories of Adam and Eve or the Satan in the book of Job, opened the hearing. Sometimes, prophets filed a lawsuit against monarchs who did not fulfill their covenant obligations to Yahweh. Here the snake wants to know whether the woman can conceive a child, and the man can grow a harvest.

Sometime after 300 B.C.E., both biblical and nonbiblical traditions began identifying the snake as the devil, and the woman as seductive (Wis 2:24; Rev 12:9; 20:2). The best-known Christian interpretation of these stories considers them to be stories about sin or original sin, which tell how God created a perfect world for humans in the Stories of the Heavens and the Earth and in the first three Stories of Adam and Eve (Gen 2:4-24). Nonetheless, in the Story of Adam and Eve as Farmers and Child-bearers, they sinned (Genesis 3), setting in motion a chain reaction of sins in the Stories of Cain and Abel (Genesis 4–5), which eventually destroyed God's once-perfect world in the Flood Stories (Genesis 6–11). Subsequently, every human born into this now imperfect world was born sinful or alienated from God, even without having personally sinned. To re-create a perfect world, God introduced religion in the Stories of Abraham and Sarah (Gen 11:27—25:18). Now, humans could overcome their alienation from God by entering this religion and rejecting the radical sinfulness of the world around them.

Neither the Hebrew Bible nor the Gospels refer to original sin. Furthermore, the first reference to the woman as evil does not appear until after 180 B.C.E. in the book of Sirach (Sir 25:21-26) from the Septuagint used by Greek-speaking Jews in Egypt (Fig. 10). It was never part of the Hebrew Bible used by Jews in Syria-Palestine. The *Life of Adam and Eve* and the *Apocalypse of Moses*, which were popular nonbiblical books in the Jewish community around 100 B.C.E., share Sirach's portrayal. By 100 C.E., the New Testament had canonized the image of Eve as the mother of sin and death, and after 382 C.E. Jerome's Latin translation of the Bible distributed it throughout the Christian world.

The original-sin reading of the Stories of Adam and Eve developed from a commentary by Augustine on the letter to the Corinthians (1 Cor 15:20-28) and the Letter to the Romans (Rom 5:12-23). Augustine (354–430) was a bishop near the ancient city of Carthage in Tunisia, North Africa. He became an influential teacher in the early Christian church. The Council of Trent (1542–63) in Italy adopted his commentary as the official teaching of the church.

Prior to Augustine, readings of the Stories of Adam and Eve indicated that human beings were free to choose good or evil. Augustine stressed that human beings were slaves to sin. For Augustine the emancipation of human beings from sin required not only faith and baptism, but a commitment to a life of celibacy and self-sacrifice. Augustine's teaching is quite negative, but its corollaries are quite positive, which may account for its enduring popularity. Everyone is free to accept or reject God, who does not impose

> *Do not be ensnared by a woman's beauty,*
>   *Do not desire a woman's possessions.*
>
> *There is quarreling, disobedience, and a loss of face,*
>   *When a wife supports her husband.*
>
> *A dejected mind, a gloomy face,*
>   *A broken heart are caused by a bad wife.*
>
> *Powerless hands and weak knees are the result of a wife,*
>   *Who does not make her husband happy.*
>
> *From a woman, sin had its beginning,*
>   *Because of a woman, we all die.*
>
> *Allow water no outlet,*
>   *Give a bad wife no voice.*
>
> *If your wife does not obey,*
>   *Divorce her.*

FIGURE 10   Teaching on Women (Sir 25:21-26)

grace or salvation on anyone. Augustine's interpretation was more than theological reflection; it was a constitution for the political order of his day. Government, for Augustine, was an indispensable defense against the forces that sin unleashed in human nature. Augustine drafted the concordat that united the church and the Roman Empire and has served as the basis for all subsequent societies with an established religion.

Although biblical scholars generally concurred with Augustine's commentary, some noted it was anomalous. For many the story of Adam and Eve as Farmers and Child-bearers still introduces discordant elements into the worldview of the Bible. A wily snake entices, the woman disobeys, and the man passively follows suit. Eve is a criminal. She is created after Adam, from Adam, as Adam's helper and named by Adam. She is seduced by the snake and then seduces Adam. The sad legacy of this long tradition of interpretation is the gruesome theological anthropology that views women as condemned by God to agonizing deliveries of their children as a sentence for seducing men to whom they are intellectually and morally inferior.

A reassessment of Augustine's reading is taking place in more than one area of study today. There are scholars of classical antiquity researching Graeco-Roman attitudes toward sexuality, moral freedom, and human value in Augustine's world. There are feminist scholars working to reduce the impact of sexism on the interpretation of women's roles in the Bible. Compelling arguments for revising Augustine are also emerging from the world of the Bible itself, where snakes and women appear more often as teachers than as tempters.

Snake characters are not just adversaries, they are also helpers. Both are wise. As adversaries snakes take away life; as helpers they renew it. Adversary snakes trick protagonists into trading away their youth. Helpers teach them the secret of eternal youth. In the Stories of Adapa from Mesopotamia, Gishzida, the snake who guards the gate to the divine plane, is a helper. It tells Adapa the priest to eat and drink the Bread and Water of Life in order to become immortal. In the Stories of Gilgamesh from Mesopotamia, the snake that tricks Gilgamesh out of the plant that would make him immortal is an adversary.

The snake in the Story of Adam and Eve as Farmers and Child-bearers is more a helper than an adversary (Fig. 11). It is more informed and questioning than malicious. It is subtle or cunning like a sage pondering the age-old questions of life and death. The snake knows the decree of Yahweh. It walks in the garden just as Yahweh walks in the garden. Neither the man nor the woman fear the snake when they meet, but talk quite openly.

The snake and the woman speak of delicate subjects, using socially acceptable metaphors. "Eating" and "knowing" are euphemisms for "having sexual intercourse" and "conceiving a child." In Semitic languages vocabulary for sexual intercourse, learning, eating, farming, fighting, and sacrificing overlap (Gilg i 4:16; Song of Solomon). Therefore, when the snake asks the woman: "Did Yahweh, our Creator, say, "You shall not eat from any tree in the garden?" it means: "Are you fertile?" When it says: "when you eat of it your eyes will be opened . . . knowing good and evil," it means: "You will become fertile." Just as the word "life" is ambivalent in the discussion between the woman and the snake, so is the word "death." The woman will not be summarily executed for eating of the fruit of the tree. Instead the woman will labor and, eventually, die in exchange for the ability to bear children. The snake and the woman discuss whether humans should be mortal or immortal, fertile or infertile. The snake does not offer immortality to the man and the woman. They are already immortal when the story begins. The snake does not steal immortality from them. It simply convinces them to exchange their immortality for fertility by pointing out that the wise know that human life, which is good, requires suffering, which is bad. The snake teaches the man and the woman that they must labor to have children and a harvest.

The man and the woman in this story share in Yahweh's work of making them fully human. There is tension between Yahweh and the people primeval. The tension leads to changes, but it is too simple to reduce that tension to raw human disobedience. Truly human life results not simply from a grand divine plan, but from the interaction, the cooperation, the tension between Yahweh the Godparent and the first creatures. People

sterility affidavit (Gen 2:25—3:5)

When the man and the woman had no clothes and no shame,

When the snake had no rivals among the creatures of Yahweh,
      Our Creator.

The snake asked:
      "Did Yahweh, Our Creator, say: "You shall not eat from any
      tree in the garden?"

"We may eat fruit from Eden's trees,"
      The woman answered.

"But anyone who touches the Tree shall die,"
      The woman explained.

"No one shall die!"
      The snake argued.

"What Yahweh, Our Creator, knows is:
      Anyone eating shall have her eyes opened.

"What Yahweh, Our Creator, knows,
      She shall know.

"What is good,
      What is bad!"

cosmogony (Gen 3:6)

Then woman saw that the Tree was good for food,
      Pleasing to the eyes, desirable for gaining wisdom.

So, she picked its fruit,
      She ate its fruit.

She gave its fruit to the man, her partner,
      The man ate its fruit. . . .

FIGURE 11   Story of Adam and Eve as Farmers and Child-bearers (Gen 2:25—4:2)

primeval become human not because of their disobedience, but because of their intimacy with and imitation of their creator. The tensions lead to the creation of a world in which Adam and Eve can have children, who can herd and farm the land.

The snake chooses to speak with the woman not because she is gullible, but because women play a more important role than men in human reproduction, which is the subject of the conversation. Storytellers also take advantage of at least two other motifs by having the snake and the woman speak with one another. With only a slight change in pronunciation, the same word can mean either "a female snake" or "Eve." The pun emphasizes the reciprocity between the snake who understands fertility and the woman who must decide whether or not to become fertile. The selection of the woman to teach the man how to have intercourse in the Story of Adam and Eve as Farmers and Child-bearers is parallel to the commissioning of the Wise Woman by the divine assembly in the Stories of Gilgamesh to teach the *enkidu* how to have intercourse.

In contrast to the remarkably universal postbiblical interpretation of Eve as evil, biblical storytellers portrayed Eve as intelligent, moral, and selfless. Eve shows her intelligence in the accuracy with which she quotes Yahweh's decree. She shows her moral integrity in the strictness with which she interprets the decree, by extending it from a prohibition against eating the fruit of the tree to touching it. She shows her selflessness in making the choice to bear children, even though it demands labor. On the basis of her discussion with the snake about the quality of their life primeval, she decides to lay down her life in order to create life. The woman is willing to create and to die, and so, by implication, is the man. The woman goes to the man, not to seduce him, but because she has discovered his role in the technique of sexual intercourse by which she can conceive a child.

The covenant with which the Story of Adam and Eve as Farmers and Child-bearers concludes is commonly read as a criminal sentence (Gen 3:13-19). Consequently, humans today often consider the labor of having a child or working a field to be a divine punishment for sin. There is certainly legal language in the tradition, but there is no need to impose a criminal character on the story as a whole. The syntax and legal anthropology do not definitively identify the words in the covenant as a prescriptive and promulgated law, or an adjudicatory judgment and court verdict. None of the technical terms for crime or sin are applied to actions of the snake, the woman, or the man, and only the snake and the soil are cursed. The man and the woman are not cursed. Finally, a divine judge like Yahweh here is more of a creator of a new world than a magistrate who rewards and punishes (Fig. 12).

The intention of the story is not to punish, but to persuade listeners that the blessings of fertility are worth the labor. By farming and childbearing the man and the woman, and subsequently all humans, imitate Yahweh, even though human creativity demands labor and divine creativity does not. Labor marks humans as different from Yahweh, not disobedient to Yahweh. For humans, the ecstasy of giving life to another human being in birth or to the earth in farming demands the agony of labor. Yahweh here is more a midwife than a judge. Midwives do not impose labor pain upon mothers as a sentence for conceiving a child. They interpret labor pain and all the consequences of parenthood.

By teaching the man and the woman how to become human, the snake establishes an ongoing relationship with the man and the woman. Snakes became reminders of the labor that human creativity demands. The story explains why snakes crawl and why they strike at humans. These explanations teach simple lessons. Crawling reminds snakes that they must continue to tutor humans in the cost of fertility, and snake bites remind humans that they must labor to have a child and bring in a harvest. Like all learning,

---

first covenant (Gen 3:7+3:22—4:2)

> *The eyes of both were opened,*
> *They realized they had no clothes.*
>
> *They wove fig leaves together,*
> *They made clothes for themselves.*

second covenant (Gen 3:8-21)

> *Finally Yahweh, Our Creator, moved into Eden as gently*
> *as a breeze.*
> *The Man and the Woman hid in the trees.*
>
> *"Man! Woman! Where are you?"*
> *Yahweh, Our Creator, called out.*
>
> *"I heard you in Eden and I was afraid.*
> *I was naked, so I hid."*
>
> *"How did you know you are naked?"*
> *Yahweh, Our Creator, asked.*
>
> *"You have eaten from the forbidden tree!"*
> *Yahweh, Our Creator, charged.*
>
> *"The Woman,*
> *The partner you gave me—*
>
> *"Gave me the fruit*
> *and I ate!" the Man answered in his defense.*
>
> *"Why did you do such a thing?"*
> *Yahweh, Our Creator, continued.*

(continued)

"The Snake tricked me into eating the fruit."
The Woman answered in her defense.

So Yahweh, Our Creator, decreed: **Snake!** *Because*
you have done this,
You shall have no companions—cattle or beasts.

You shall crawl on your belly,
You shall eat dirt all the days of your life.

You and the Woman will be enemies,
Your children will kill her children.

Her child will stomp on your head,
Your child will strike at his heel.

Your instinct will be to strike at humans,
Even though they will master you (Gen 3:16b).

Woman! *(Gen 3:16a): Your labor in childbirth will be*
excruciating,
You shall birth your children in pain.

Man! *Because you obeyed the Woman,*
Because you ate the forbidden fruit

You will curse the soil,
You will labor to eat all the days of your life.

The soil shall only produce thorns and thistles,
You shall be forced to eat wild plants.

You shall earn your bread by the sweat of your brow,
You shall return to the soil from which you come.

You are soil,
You shall return to the soil.

The Man named the Woman "Eve,"
He called her "Mother of All the Living."

Yahweh gave the Man and the Woman leather,
Our Creator clothed them in rawhide. . . .

FIGURE 12 Story of Adam and Eve as Farmers and Child-bearers (cont.)
(Gen 2:25—4:2)

crawling and snake bites are painful, but something can be learned from the pain. Such etiologies by no means struggle with the profound questions that are the main subject of creation stories. Nonetheless, they teach how to turn human curiosity into a learning experience. Therefore, Yahweh reminds the snake that the task of teaching the people primeval how to become fertile and mortal is far from easy and far from over.

The woman's choice to create has consequences for her relationship to her children. She will be able to give birth, but not without labor. If the woman actually made a choice, why does she seemingly deny it (Gen 3:13)? Refusing to take responsibility for the choice may be a demur. She has acted courageously, but it would be inappropriate for her to brag about what she has done. So, she simply says it was nothing. The woman's response to Yahweh may also reflect a basic human question about life: "Did humans freely choose to become fertile and mortal or were they tricked?" The woman's response raises the question to which these stories provide an answer. They want their audiences to regard fertility as a freely chosen blessing and to embrace the asceticism of laying down their lives by childbearing and farming.

Another objection to the characterization of Eve as having made a heroic choice is the long-standing tradition of interpretation that emphasizes the negative consequences which her actions have on her relationship to her man (Gen 3:14-16). As it now stands, the woman seems sentenced to be subordinate to the man. But originally this consequence may have applied to the snake, not to the woman. A parallel from the Stories of Cain and Abel (Gen 4:7) may provide a clue both to the original meaning and to the position of the words: "and he shall rule over you" (Gen 3:16).

Crawling snakes are not tortured or humiliated; they are on the hunt. Snakes crawl in the dust like warriors to ambush humans who are creatures of dust. Both the *robets*-snake in the Stories of Cain and Abel (Gen 4:7) and the *nahash*-snake in the Stories of Adam and Eve (Gen 3:14) lurk at doorways to strike out at those who enter and leave. The nouns are synonymous and their verbs are identical (Hebrew: *teshuqat*). Rather than consider one verb to refer to the woman's urge to have sexual intercourse with her husband, and the other to refer to the instinct of the *robets*-snake to strike at anyone who threatens it, it would be better to read both verbs as referring to a snake's instinct to strike. Just as one snake stalks Cain, the other stalks Eve's children. Snakes are sentenced to continue these engagements, even though humans continue to crush their heads with their heels. Therefore, instead of instructing the woman that "your desire will be for your husband, and he will rule over you," Yahweh instructs the *nahash*-snake: "your instinct will be to strike at humans, even though they will master you" (Gen 3:16b). Yahweh's only instruction to the woman is: "I will greatly increase your pangs in childbearing; in pain you shall bring forth children" (Gen 3:16a). There is still no evidence in the tradition of the text that shows when this part of the verse was detached from Yahweh's instruction of the snake and attached to the instruction of the woman. Yet, as more and more negative characterizations of the woman in this story became standard, it is easy enough to understand why the transposition may have taken place.

The man's choice to create has consequences for his relationship to the land. He will be able to bring in a harvest, but not without labor. The Stories of Adam and Eve begin with a sterility affidavit that clearly observes that the essentials for agriculture are missing, but the Story of Adam and Eve as Farmers and Child-bearers tells only her story. Yet, storytellers assume that the man goes through a similar process of discovery to become fertile. His story now appears in the Stories of Cain and Abel.

Many interpreters end the Stories of Adam and Eve with the words: "after he drove the man out he placed on the east side of Eden cherubim and a flaming sword flashing back and forth to guard the way to the tree of life" (Gen 3:24). Standard creation stories, however, never end one world without inaugurating another. Therefore, it is more likely that this story ends, not with the closing of the old world of Eden, but with the opening of a new world of the East. The work that Yahweh began in the Story of the 'Adam as a Farmer is completed only when Eve gives birth to Cain and Abel (Gen 4:2). In the Story of the 'Adam as a Farmer, only Yahweh farms; the 'adam simply tends (Gen 2:15), whereas in the Story of Adam and Eve as Farmers and Child-bearers, the man actually farms (Gen 3:23).

In its conclusion, the Story of Adam and Eve as Farmers and Child-bearers celebrates Eve in the much the same way that the Stories of Atrahasis celebrate Nintu-Mami (Fig. 13). Both women carry the title "Mother of All" (Atra 1:245-246; Gen 3:20). Nintu-Mami gives birth to seven sets of twins. Eve gives birth to two sons. Nintu-Mami celebrates her delivery by singing: "You commanded me a task, I have completed it" (Atra 1:237-238). Eve sings to celebrate her sons: "With the help of Yahweh, as my midwife, I have given birth!" (Gen 4:1). She names her dominant son "Cain," because he is "Strong as Iron." She names her recessive son "Abel," because he is "Fragile as a Breath of Air" (Eccl 1:14). In many ways, Eve's hymn summarizes what the Stories of Adam and Eve teach. She is as delighted that she has learned how to use her power to create as the man was delighted in Yahweh's creation of her (Gen 2:23). She sees the successful birth of a child as a divine work.

The Stories of Adam and Eve are part of an ancient quest to understand human life. As others have done, and will continue to do, these wonderful stories ask: "Does immortality or creativity better define human life?" The search of the Stories of Adam and Eve for an answer is positive and inspiring, not cynical or complaining. These stories ponder both the life of Yahweh and the life of the people primeval to better understand human life. Yahweh is immortal and fertile. Yahweh lives forever and Yahweh creates. The people primeval are immortal, but infertile. The 'adam, the man, and the woman live forever, but cannot create. Ordinary humans like Adam and Eve are mortal, but can create. The tellers of the Stories of Adam and Eve were not utopian dreamers. Their investigation of the assets and liabilities of both immortality and fertility is brutally realistic. The immortal life of the people primeval was certainly enjoyable, but not completely satisfying. Human creativity is godlike, but painful. Childbirth is agonizing and farming exhausting. Nonetheless, the stories conclude that humans are most like God when they create, not when they live forever.

Ancestor Stories
(GEN 11:27—37:2)

Stories of Abraham and Sarah
(GEN 11:27—25:18)

Three stories celebrating Abraham and Sarah introduce two great cycles in the book of Genesis. The first cycle tells the Stories of Abraham and Sarah (Gen 11:27—25:18); the second tells the Stories of Jacob, Leah, and Rachel (Gen 25:19—37:2). They are ancestor stories told by clans to celebrate those who taught their households how to survive. These stories describe Abraham and Sarah as people of the Middle Bronze period. During this remarkable time, refugees from the Early Bronze period returned from the hills and deserts to rebuild old cities and found new ones. Their cities were magnificent. Throughout the entire Bronze Age, there were none larger, none more heavily fortified. Walls twenty-five feet thick and a mile long were built with stones weighing over two thousand pounds. City people in the Middle Bronze were merchants. Villagers were herders and farmers. Some were rich and some were poor. The wealthy were served by warriors, bureaucrats, artists, tradespeople, and slaves. They were masters of the planning, organization, production, distribution, and enforcement that the construction and operation of great cities demands. They invented the alphabet. Hundreds of word-pictures in Mesopotamian cuneiform and Egyptian hieroglyphics were reduced to thirty hieroglyphics in Ugaritic and twenty-two letters in Hebrew. Ordinary people, not just an elite corps of scribes, could now read and write. They manufactured bronze tools and weapons with tin imported from Afghanistan. They crafted jewelry with alabaster and faience from Egypt. They turned exquisite pottery on new high-speed wheels. They carved fine wooden furniture inlaid with ivory from Syria. They exported grain, olive oil, wine, cattle, timber, and slaves. During the Middle Bronze period colonists and warriors from Syria-Palestine, whom native Egyptians despised as "Hyksos" or "northerners," occupied the delta where the Nile River flows into the Mediterranean Sea. From there the Hyksos ruled Egypt (1630–1539 B.C.E.) three hundred miles south to Thebes, which is today's Luxor. Middle Bronze culture thrived until 1540 B.C.E. when Kamose declared Egypt's independence from the Hyksos. For the next 150 years,

first covenant (cont.)

> Finally, Yahweh, Our Creator, decreed:
>   "If the 'adam now looks like us,
>   knows what is good and what is evil,
>
> Then the 'adam must not be allowed to pick
>   from the Tree of Life,
>   The 'adam must not eat it and live forever."
>
> Then Yahweh, Our Creator, sent the 'adam out of Eden,
>   to farm the soil of which the 'adam was made.
>
> Yahweh, Our Creator, sent the 'adam forth,
>   Yahweh, Our Creator, dispatched the 'adam from Eden.
>
> Yahweh, Our Creator, stationed Cherubim
>   and the Flaming Sword,
>   To guard the gate to the Tree of Life.
>
> Adam had intercourse with Eve.
>   She conceived.
>
> Eve gave birth to Cain, singing:
>   "With Yahweh, Our Creator, as my midwife,
>   I have given birth!"
>
> Then she gave birth to his brother, Abel, singing:
>   "Abel will be the first herder, and Cain the first farmer."

FIGURE 13 Story of Adam and Eve as Farmers and Child-bearers (cont.)
(Gen 2:25—4:2)

pharaohs systematically razed their cities and exterminated their culture from Avaris in the delta of Egypt north to Megiddo in the valley of Jezreel in Syria-Palestine.

The Hebrews who told the Stories of Abraham and Sarah lived in Syria-Palestine during the Iron Age. When their villages first began to appear in the hills north of Jerusalem, the Middle Bronze period was only a memory, but it was a wonderful memory. They were a simple people, but they re-created the splendor of those grand Middle Bronze cities in the stories that they told about their ancestors. Until the twentieth century, when archaeologists began to uncover the cities of this period once again, these stories were virtually our the only window on that time.

Like all stories, ancestor stories have plots with three episodes: a crisis, a climax, and a denouement. The crisis disturbs the peace by placing the land and children of a household at risk. The climax places the protagonists at a threshold where they must choose between life and death for their household. The denouement restores peace to the household so that it is, once again, fertile and capable of bearing children and bringing in a harvest. The plots in ancestor stories are simple and one-dimensional. Only one story is told at a time.

Description in ancestor stories is also one-dimensional. Everything is handled as simply as possible. Things of the same kind are described as nearly alike as possible. Ancestor stories also delight in repetition. Three is a standard number of times to repeat an episode or motif. These stories also make generous use of the literary technique of irony. Hence, the youngest, rather than the oldest, often becomes the "beloved son."

Ancestor stories have only three main characters, and only two appear together at a time. To include more than three characters, tellers use twins, who share one part. The stories also cast their characters in contrasting, dialectic, or polarized roles. There is always a protagonist who is the hero and an antagonist who is the villain. One character is good; the other is bad. Only the quality that directly affects the story is mentioned, and no hint is given that these characters have any life outside the story.

Characterization in ancestor stories is very distinct from characterization in creation stories. Characters in ancestor stories are human beings. Characters in creation stories are not. Few scholars label the Stories of Abraham and Sarah as creation stories, but many identify Yahweh, a divine character, as the protagonist who is negotiating a covenant with Abraham and Sarah, who stand in the way of Yahweh's kindness. The resulting theology of Yahweh as a divine patron who patiently loves a sinful people is cherished by many Jews, Christians, and Muslims today. Ancestor stories, however, celebrate human ancestors like Abraham and Sarah, not divine patrons like Yahweh. Therefore, it is better to understand Abraham and Sarah as protagonists negotiating a covenant with Yahweh.

The stories characterize Abraham and Sarah Israel as seminomadic herders who negotiate covenants with villages to manage their livestock. Nomadic herders do no farming at all. They have no permanent relationship with any villages. They are economically self-sufficient. Today, truly nomadic herders live in Russia, Mongolia, Afghanistan, Turkestan, Uzbekistan, Kazakhstan, Saudi Arabia, and the Sahara. Seminomadic herders settle down and become villagers when economic factors demand it. They migrate from regions that could only support herding to regions that could support both herding and farming. The same economic factors that force nomadic herders to become seminomadic can also force them to become nomadic once again.

Ancestors are not simply biological forebears, but those who taught their households how to survive. Ancestor stories do not establish a universal system of values, but inspire audiences to imitate the survival skills of their protagonists. Some of these skills, like hospitality to strangers, are more important in the world of the Bible than others.

Ancestor stories celebrate only one particular characteristic of an ancestor. They never portray their main characters as perfect. The limitations of ancestors are always obvious. They are flawed, which gives them a very human, very imitable quality. Storytellers want their audiences to relate to their ancestors as companions and models.

Technically, "ancestor story" is a synonym for "legend" or "tale," but these words have too many negative connotations in ordinary conversation today. Legends and tales are entertaining. Ancestor stories are about survival. Ancestor stories want their audiences to imitate the virtue that the ancestors demonstrate in life-threatening situations. Ancestor stories teach households to survive by imitating the crisis virtue of their protagonists. Theoretically, ancestor stories can describe any virtue that the protagonist employs to overcome chaos and restore order. The most celebrated virtue is hospitality to strangers. Convinced that a household exists because its divine patron hospitably grants it both land and children, ancestor stories celebrate the cordial and generous reception ancestors extend to strangers.

The versions of the Stories of Abraham and Sarah and the Stories of Jacob, Leah, and Rachel preserved in the book of Genesis also played an important role in creating the states of Israel and Judah and authorizing the rulers who governed them between 1000 and 587 B.C.E. No precise dates from the Iron Age, and no exact references to any events from the Iron Age, are explicitly mentioned in these stories, but storytellers from the Iron Age describe Bronze Age events against the background of their own day. Bronze Age Abraham, Sarah, Jacob, Leah, and Rachel visit all the sanctuaries that are important during the Iron Age. When Abraham fights his Bronze Age enemies he uses David's Iron Age tactics. Likewise, the names "Canaan" and "Yahweh" are anachronisms that are chronologically out of place in the stories. The divine patron of Israel was only called "Yahweh" and the land into which Abraham and Sarah migrated was only called "Canaan" during the Iron Age. Abraham and Sarah live in the Middle Bronze period, but talk like people in the Iron Age. Therefore, in the Bible today we are hearing a version of the Stories of Abraham and Sarah that was popular in the Iron Age.

Unlike the Bronze Age when there were great empires, the Iron Age was a time of small states. The last great Bronze Age empires were Mycenae in Greece, Hatti in Turkey, and Egypt in Africa. They destroyed one another competing for economic control of the eastern Mediterranean. One of the last great military battles in the Bronze Age took place in about 1280 B.C.E. at Kadesh in Syria. Here, on the Orontes River, Hattusilis III ambushed Ramses II of Egypt. The battle was inconclusive, but its treaty was a diplomatic masterpiece that prevented war for the next fifty years. The years following the battle of Kadesh created a political vacuum in Syria-Palestine. Small states like Israel developed west of the Jordan River, and Ammon, Moab, and Edom developed to the east of it. About 1000 B.C.E., David federated the Hebrew villages into one state called "Israel," centered in Jerusalem.

Abraham and Sarah Negotiate with Yahweh
(GEN 11:27—12:8)

Abraham and Sarah Negotiate with Yahweh is a story that celebrates their ability to negotiate a covenant with their divine patron. Abraham and Sarah Negotiate with Pharaoh is a story that celebrates their ability to negotiate a covenant with their enemy. Abraham Negotiates with Lot is a story that celebrates their ability to negotiate a covenant with their neighbors. Whether their negotiating partners were human or divine, friend or foe, Abraham and Sarah were masters of the art of covenant making. Later stories would celebrate ancestors who purchase land (Gen 23:1-20) or ancestors who conquer it, but here the land belongs to those who can negotiate for it.

The story opens with a genealogy (Gen 11:27-32). Technically, a genealogy is not a story at all, but a law that authorizes fathers of households to exercise authority in their villages. This genealogy authorizes Abraham and Sarah to head the household of Terah by relating them as villagers from the villages of Syria-Palestine to the great city of Ur in Mesopotamia (Fig. 14).

The Ubaid people founded Ur in 4000 B.C.E. The city lasted until 300 B.C.E. By 2800 B.C.E., it had developed a unique culture magnificently displayed in the tombs of its rulers, buried amid numerous objects fashioned in gold and precious stones. The code of Ur-Nammu (2050–1950 B.C.E.), which is the oldest legal tradition recovered from the world of the Bible, is also developed at Ur. In this wonderful city, Terah is father of a household with three sons.

Audiences expect a father with three sons to prosper. Terah himself succeeds, but he cannot pass on his success. His genealogy subtly reflects one disaster after another. Terah loses his first son, Haran, to death. Terah successfully arranges a marriage for Haran, but after having only one son—Lot, and two daughters—Milcah and Iscah, he dies. Fathers expect to see their sons come from the womb, but not to lay them in the tomb. It is the duty of sons to bury their fathers, not of fathers to bury their sons.

Terah loses his second son, Nahor, to debt. As the legal guardian for the household of Haran, Nahor must marry Milcah, and adopt Lot and Iscah. They remain unmarried and at risk. Nothing in the genealogy indicates that Nahor's efforts to restore the household of Haran are successful.

Terah loses his third son, Abraham, to infertility. Abraham and Sarah are unable to have children. Consequently, Terah leaves Ur and follows the River Euphrates north. In the end Terah loses even his own life. His exodus ends in death, not deliverance.

Nevertheless, the death of Terah is a call for Abraham and Sarah, who turn from Sin, divine patron of the moon, who had watched over their household in Ur, and negotiate a covenant with Yahweh, who will bless them with land and children in Syria-Palestine. The household of Terah and the old world of Ur and Haran die. The household of Abraham and Sarah cross the Euphrates River, leave the old world of Mesopotamia,

title (Gen 11:27a)

This is the story of Terah and his three sons: Abraham, Nahor, and Haran.

crisis (Gen 11:27b-32)

Terah's son, Haran, had only one son, Lot, and two daughters, Milcah and Iscah. Terah watched Haran die and buried him in Ur, where he was born. Terah's son, Abraham, married Sarah. His son, Nahor, married Milcah. Sarah, however, was infertile and had no children. So, Terah took Abraham, Lot, and Sarah and departed Ur for Canaan. They only got as far as Haran, where Terah died at the age of 250.

climax (Gen 12:1-6)

Then Yahweh spoke:

"Depart from the old land of your people,
 Depart from the household of your father,
 Depart for a new land where I will look after you.

"I will make you a great nation,
 I will bless you.

"I will make your name great,
 I will make you a blessing.

"I will bless those who bless you,
 I will curse those who curse you.

All the earth shall find blessing in you."

Abraham answered Yahweh and departed with Lot for Canaan. When Abraham departed from Haran, he was seventy-five years old. He took Sarah and Lot, whom he had brought from Ur, with every last possession and slave they owned. Abraham traveled through the Land of Canaan as far as the sacred tree of Moreh in the sanctuary of Shechem.

denouement (Gen 12:7-8)

Here Yahweh looked after Abraham and promised: "I will turn this land over to the household of Abraham." Abraham marked the site by erecting an altar for Yahweh, who looked after him. From there Abraham moved on to the hill country east of Beth-El, pitching his tent with Beth-El to the west and Ai to the east. He marked the site by erecting another altar dedicated to Yahweh.

FIGURE 14   Abraham and Sarah Negotiate with Yahweh (Gen 11:17—12:8)

and enter the new world of Syria-Palestine. This motif of going into the water as slaves and coming out of the water as free people appears also in the Stories of Moses leading the Hebrews across the Red Sea and in the Stories of Joshua leading the Hebrews across the Jordan River.

The Stories of Abraham and Sarah refer to Syria-Palestine as "Canaan." "Canaan" is a generic word for the purple dye manufactured along the Mediterranean coast of Syria-Palestine in Lebanon today. The murex shell was the natural source of the coloring. Because cloth dyed purple was popular throughout the panhandle of Syria-Palestine, the region itself was called "Canaan." Originally, only the merchants who sold the cloth were called "Canaanites," but eventually, all who lived in the marketing area were also called "Canaanites."

Abraham and Sarah visit Shechem, Bethel, and Ai, which, like Shiloh, Gibeon, Beersheba, Gilgal, Dan, and Jerusalem, were sacred centers in Syria-Palestine. Their pilgrimage establishes their credentials as ancestors who can tap the resources of these sacred centers and bring the land to life. Ancient peoples had little idea that the earth was round, but they did think of their own lands as emanating from a center, like water rings from a stone tossed into a pond. For them, life radiated from a sacred center, which was its navel. Sacred centers were reservoirs from which life flowed to the villages around them. Here an umbilical cord joined their land to its Godmother. The richest parts of the land were those closest to its omphalos. The tradition of the omphalos hands on a wonderfully maternal metaphor. Divine patrons maintain their lands and people just as an expectant mother silently feeds the fetus she carries in her womb.

Sacred centers are marked with a tree, a mountain, a river source, a city, or a statue. These works of nature or of art at sanctuaries are microcosms or models that reflect the worldview of their cultures. Without a word of explanation, pilgrims can stand in a sanctuary and understand how their cultures look at life. The sanctuaries that Abraham and Sarah visit are marked with trees of life or "terebinths," the great turpentine-producing sumac trees in Syria-Palestine. Abraham and Sarah walk off and mark the boundaries of their land grant with altars. These cairns of fieldstones identify them as clients of Yahweh. The altars at Bethel (Gen 12:7), Ai (Gen 12:8), and Hebron (Gen 13:18) form the triangle of Abraham and Sarah's first estate. At each marker Yahweh stands guard to protect the land. A covenant between Yahweh and Israel in the book of Deuteronomy (Deut 27:1-26) envisions a fairly elaborate process of documenting a land grant on a series of such stone markers. Similarly, Job charges Yahweh with failing to prosecute those who remove landmarks (Job 24:2). The Middle Assyrian Code from Ashur in Iraq legislates the use of these *tahumu rabu* boundary markers. They divide the fields and pastures of households bound together by covenant. Some markers may have been little more than a furrow cut with a plow, a ditch, a stream, or perhaps a low wall marked off at intervals with stones protected by divine sanctions. The *kudurrum* markers in Akkadian law have curses inscribed on them.

The clan of Abraham and Sarah told these stories to celebrate their ancestors for teaching them how to make peace and to keep the peace by negotiating covenants. They handed on these stories to remind each generation that title to their land was dependent on their ability to make good covenants. The Hebrews were not wealthy, and the Hebrews were not warriors; they were people of the covenant.

Abraham and Sarah Negotiate with Pharaoh
(GEN 12:9—13:1)

Like Abraham and Sara Negotiate with Yahweh, Abraham and Sarah Negotiate with Pharaoh is an ancestor story that celebrates their ability to cut a covenant. The antagonists in the story are famine and Pharaoh.

The crisis in the story is a crop failure in Syria-Palestine that forces Abraham and Sarah to migrate to Egypt. They must first negotiate with the soldiers at the border to let them cross. Abraham uses words to negotiate; Sarah uses only her appearance. She is good-looking; he is fast-talking. The powerless in many folk traditions use these same traits to trick the powerful into endowing them with land and children.

Abraham allows the Egyptians to think that Sarah is his sister, not his wife, and therefore marriageable. Nevertheless, the Egyptians are impotent voyeurs. Seven times they "look at" Sarah and find her "good-looking," but they can do nothing. They are physically unable to have intercourse with her.

In the negotiations at the border, Abraham and Sarah are shrewd, not liars. Lying, even to your enemies, is seldom a virtue in any culture. They do not lie. They persuade the Egyptians to draw their own conclusions. The Egyptians' lust for Sarah drives them to use their power in a way that will benefit Abraham and Sarah, who say or do nothing to keep them from doing so. As a result, Sarah's marriage to Pharaoh seals the covenant that allows their household to enter Egypt with their livestock.

Seminomadic herders like Abraham and Sarah were an integral part of village life throughout the world of the Bible. Villages were economically dimorphic. Farmers exploited natural resources in one way, and herders in another. Herders could not survive without farmers, and farmers could not survive without herders. They were mutually dependent or symbiotic. Herders did not only graze near their own villages, but in pastures some distance away as well. These herders had to be shrewd to successfully negotiate with strangers for access to the limited pastures and water. Herders compensated for their lack of power by an ability to manipulate the power of others. They were not outlaws, but they knew how to work the system to their own advantage. Egypt's farmers and herders considered herders from Syria-Palestine to be spies or tricksters, who preyed on their land and water. To change these strangers from enemies to friends, they cut covenants with them. In return, these strangers would herd Egypt's livestock, and as the herds of these strangers grazed stubble of Egypt's harvest, they fertilized the fields with the dung they dropped.

The story also does not portray Sarah as sexually abused, but as resourceful in setting her household free. The soldiers want to rape her but cannot. In the climax of the story Pharaoh discovers Abraham and Sarah have tricked him. Pharaoh takes her as his wife with the intention of having sexual intercourse with her; he also cannot. Impotence plagues his efforts.

The story delights in the irony of Pharaoh who thought he was the dominate partner in the covenant. In the denouement of the story, Abraham and Sarah profit most from the covenant when Pharaoh offers them a generous settlement to leave Egypt in order to cure his impotence. Everything is completely reversed. Normally, clients like Abraham and Sarah buy their freedom from patrons like Pharaoh after six years (Exod 21:1-5). Here Pharaoh buys his freedom from Abraham and Sarah.

The story celebrates Abraham and Sarah as ancestors who use their ability to negotiate well even with the pharaoh of Egypt. Their household has neither the land nor the children to compete with Pharaoh, but Abraham compensates by being shrewd, Sarah by being attractive. Tellers never consider whether Abraham is also a liar and Sarah the victim of a chauvinist husband and an employer who harasses her sexually. Their story celebrates these ancestors for a single virtue and takes for granted that even Israel's ancestors were not perfect.

Abraham Negotiates with Lot
(GEN 13:5—14:24)

Abraham Negotiates with Lot is a story that celebrates not only Abraham's ability to make a covenant, but his ability to keep a covenant regardless of the cost. The story opens with Abraham and Lot negotiating a covenant to end the war between their herders for water and pasture (Fig. 15).

Some traditions of interpretation argue that Lot is greedy. He picks the best part of the land, even though his choice turns out to be disastrous, and his very life depends on the selflessness and loyalty of the uncle he has alienated. Lot's character has also been seen as quarreling (Gen 13:7), selfish (Gen 13:10-11), and easily duped (Gen 14:12). He has been described as indecisive (Gen 19:15-16), cowardly (Gen 19:30), married to an addle-minded woman (Gen 19:26), and content to leave the future of his household to his daughters (Gen 19:30-38).

Abraham and Lot, however, are better understood as covenant partners. Abraham is not Lot's patron. The episodes describing Abraham's delivering Sodom from Elam (Gen 14:1-24) are the fulfillment of their covenant. Lot does not separate from the household of Abraham and Sarah, but negotiates a covenant to remain related to it. It is this

story of the conflict (Gen 13:5-7)

The Household of Lot and the Household of Abraham lived together in the same village. But there were too many flocks, herds, and tents. One land could not support two households. With the Canaanites and the Perizzites in the land, skirmishes developed between the herders of Lot and the herders of Abraham. So Abraham negotiated this covenant with Lot.

stipulations terms (Gen 13:8-13)

"Let there be peace between you and me. Let us be brothers."

"Go anywhere! Is not the whole land at your disposal? Please separate from me. If you prefer the north, I will go to the south; if you prefer the south, I will go to the north." Lot looked about and saw how well watered the whole Jordan Valley was as far as Zoar, like the Garden of Yahweh or like Egypt. This was before Yahweh had destroyed Sodom and Gomorrah. Lot, therefore, chose the Jordan Valley and set out eastward. Thus they separated from each other. The Household of Abraham stayed in the Land of Canaan, while the Household of Lot settled among the Cities of the Plain, pitching his tents near Sodom. Now the inhabitants of Sodom were shameful. They committed sins against Yahweh.

litany of curses and blessings (Gen 13:14-17)

After Lot had left, Yahweh said to Abraham: "Look about you. From where you are standing, look to the north, the south, the east, and the west. I will give to you and to your household all the land which you see forever. I will make your household like the dust of the earth. If anyone could count the dust of the earth, your household too might be counted. Walk off from here the length and width of the land which I will give you."

promulgation (Gen 13:18)

Abraham struck his tents and pitched them near the sacred tree of Mamre at Hebron. There he built an altar dedicated to Yahweh.

FIGURE 15   Abraham Negotiates with Lot (Gen 13:5-18)

covenant that allows his household to survive. Lot is not selfish; he is farsighted. The story does not celebrate Abraham as a generous patron who delivers a foolish client, but as a covenant partner who fulfills his legal obligations.

Covenants in ancient Israel parallel treaties in the Hittite empire. About 1600 B.C.E., the Hittite empire appeared in central Turkey. Standard Hittite treaties contained at least six components. They open by (1) giving the credentials of the signatories to the treaty and (2) issuing a new and official story of their relationship with one another. Then they (3) lay out the terms in careful legal language. These are followed by (4) a list of witnesses to the treaty, (5) a litany of curses for treaty violations and blessings for treaty compliance, and finally (6) provisions for recording and promulgating the treaty. The treaty of Ramses II and Hattusilis III following the battle of Kadesh in 1280 B.C.E. is a textbook for conventional treaty style and language. Archaeologists recovered both Egyptian and Hittite copies of this treaty. In the Egyptian edition, Ramses flamboyantly elaborates his role in negotiating the treaty. The Hittite edition is more sober. Although only the history of the conflict, the terms, and the litany are clearly present in Abraham Negotiates with Lot, it faithfully mirrors the characteristic language and content of the genre.

The covenant between Abraham and Lot presents the official background to the conflict between their households: "there were too many flocks, herds, and tents for one land to support and for both households to camp together. War broke out between the herders of Lot and the herders of Abraham" (Gen 13:5-7).

The treaty between Ramses and Hattusilis not only declares that Egypt and Hatti are officially at peace with one another, but also that they are "brothers" or covenant partners: "Hattusilis agrees to this treaty with Ramses, creating peace and an eternal alliance between us. We are brothers and are at peace with each other forever." Likewise, the ancestor story proclaims: "then Abraham said to Lot, 'Let there be no strife between you and me, and between your herders and my herders'" (Gen 13:8). Although only Abraham's declaration now appears, it should be assumed that Lot made a similar declaration. The covenant between Abraham and Lot also declares that the ancestors of both households are brothers.

The terms of the treaty between Ramses and Hattusilis include a mutual non-aggression pact: "in the future, the great king of Hatti shall neither invade, nor raid Egypt, and Ramses shall neither invade, nor raid Hatti." Abraham and Lot negotiate similar terms: "is not the whole land before you? Separate yourself from me. If you take the left hand, then I will go to the right; or if you take the right hand, then I will go to the left."

Finally, Ramses and Hattusilis conclude their treaty by blessing compliance with land and population: "blessed by the divine assembly of Hatti and Egypt with prosperity and long life be the homes and lands and slaves of those Egyptians and Hittites who observe and carry out faithfully the treaty between Hatti and Egypt inscribed on this silver tablet." The covenant between Abraham and Lot also concludes with blessings.

Hittite treaties regularly established a defensive alliance between the signatories: "if a foreign army invades the lands of Ramses, and he sends a message to the great king of Hatti, saying: 'Come and help me against this enemy,' the great king of Hatti shall come and fight against the enemy of Egypt, his ally. . . . If a foreign army attacks the great king of Hatti, Ramses shall come and fight against the enemy of Hatti, his ally. . . . Ramses shall send infantry and chariots. . . . Once order has been restored in Hatti, they shall return to Egypt." In this ancestor story, there is no mention of this stipulation in the covenant between Abraham and Lot, but the story that follows assumes such an agreement was, in fact, in place.

An elaborate title introduces the story of how Abraham Delivers Lot from Elam (Gen 14:1-3).

Technically, the crisis does not begin until Elam's clients default on their covenant obligations, leading Elam to take reprisals against them (Gen 14:4-7). Sodom also declares its independence by refusing to send its annual taxes to Elam. Under the terms of its covenant with Elam, Sodom was committed to align itself with Elam's foreign policy and offer logistical and military assistance to Elam's army. The most common declaration of independence is defaulting on these obligations to draft soldiers to serve in the patron's army and to pay taxes on all crops, herds, raw materials, and manufactured goods. Every war of independence was a taxpayers' revolt. There was no need to launch a military attack; the first blow was always economic (Fig. 16).

To collect its taxes, Elam declares war on Sodom. Only two of the personal names of the four rulers loyal to Chedorlaomer have been identified. Ellasar is generally understood to be Assyria. Arioch or Arriwuku was a ruler of Mari, which is on the Euphrates River between Syria and Iraq. Tidal or Tudhalias was a ruler of Hatti, the land of the Hittites. Shinar is another name for Babylon (Gen 11:2).

Sodom and the other cities of the plain prepare to defend themselves against Elam (Gen 14:8-12). The armies of Elam rout, but do not annihilate, Sodom and Gomorrah's army. The rulers of the cities of the plain and some of the soldiers escape (Gen 14:10). These rulers do not accidentally fall, nor do they throw themselves into the tar pits to commit suicide. They crouch down and hide in the tar pits from Elam's soldiers who rush by them in hot pursuit. When Joshua routs the Amorites at Gibeon, their rulers use the same strategy to hide from him in a cave at Makkedah (Josh 10:16). The language of the story is wonderfully subtle. The Hebrew word not only describes the physical position of the rulers as they "crouch down" to create a low profile in order to avoid detection by their pursuers, but also carries the connotation that the rulers are once again "prostrate" as clients before Chedorlaomer. The armies of Elam do not plunder Sodom wantonly, which would destroy a rich source of income for Elam. Instead, they simply collect their back taxes or exact reparations from Sodom by confiscating the city's grain and livestock. In addition Chedorlaomer takes the household of Lot for ransom.

The household of Lot sends a message to Abraham saying: "Come and help me" (Gen 14:13-16). The person who comes to Abraham is not a fugitive, nor even simply a survivor of the battle for Sodom, but a runner on a diplomatic mission. Messengers were an important means of communication between the great cities. Rulers carefully maintained corps of messengers to keep themselves informed of events throughout their territory. Abraham responds by declaring war on Elam.

title (Gen 14:1-3)

This is the story of the war between Elam and the Cities of the Plain. With Elam were Amraphel, ruler of Babylon, Arriwuku, ruler of Mari, Chedorlaomer, ruler of Elam, and Tudhalias, ruler of Hatti. With the Cities of the Plain were Bera, ruler of Sodom, Birsha, ruler of Gomorrah, Shinab, ruler of Admah, Shemeber, ruler of Zeboiim, and the ruler of Bela-Zoar.

crisis episode (Gen 14:4-12)

For twelve years the Cities of the Plain were clients to Chedorlaomer, but in the thirteenth year, they declared their independence of him. In the fourteenth year, Chedorlaomer and the rulers who remained loyal to him attacked and put down the revolt of the Rephaim at Ashteroth-karnaim, of the Zuzim at Ham, of the Emim at Shaveh-kiriathaim, and of the Horites in the hills of Seir, routing them as far as El-paran on the desert border. Then they turned and attacked the sanctuary of En-mishpat and put down revolt through the land of the Amalekites and of the Amorites living around Hazazon-tamar.

Therefore, the rulers of Sodom, Gomorrah, Admah, Zeboiim, and Bela-Zoar deployed their armies in the Valley of Siddim and prepared to defend themselves against Chedorlaomer of Elam, Tudhalias of Hatti, Amraphel of Babylon, and Arriwuku of Mari. Four rulers against five. There were tar pits everywhere in the Valley of Siddim. So, after the rulers of Sodom and Gomorrah were routed and, they crouched down in those tar pits hid themselves there, while their soldiers fled to the hills. The armies of Elam plundered all the livestock and granaries of Sodom and Gomorrah before withdrawing. They also took the Household of Lot, Abraham's covenant partner, who was living in Sodom, and his livestock.

climax (Gen 14:13-16)

A messenger reported everything to the Hebrew chief, Abraham. He was camped under the sacred tree of the Amorite chief, Mamre, who was a covenant partner with Eschol and Aner, who were Abraham's covenant partners. When Abraham learned that the household of Lot was being held hostage, he armed his most trusted slaves, three hundred eighteen in all, and set out for Dan. Abraham and his warriors cleverly deployed against the armies of Elam at night, and then attacked and routed them as far as Hobah, north of Damascus.

denouement episode (Gen 14:17-24)

When Abraham returned from his victory over Chedorlaomer and the rulers who remained loyal to him, the ruler of Sodom went out to greet him in the Valley of

(*continued*)

Shaveh, which was royal land. Melchizedek, ruler of Salem, brought out bread and wine, and, being a priest of El most high, he blessed Abraham with these words:

> "Blessed be Abraham by El most high, who created
> the heavens and the earth.
>
> Blessed be Abraham by El most high, who turned
> the enemy over to you."
>
> Then, Abraham gave him a tenth of everything.
>
> The ruler of Sodom said to Abraham: "Give me
> the hostages, but keep the rest of the plunder."
>
> But Abraham replied:
>
> "I have raised my hand before Yahweh,
> before Yahweh, Our Creator, who is the most high,
> before Yahweh, Our Creator, who created
> the heavens and the earth.

"I will not accept even a length of cloth or a single tract of land from you, so you cannot brag: 'I am the one who blessed Abraham.' Forget me. Just repay my warriors for what they have eaten, and give them and my covenant partners who fought with me, Aner, Eshcol and Mamre, their shares of the plunder."

FIGURE 16 Abraham Negotiates with Lot (cont.) (Gen 14:1-24)

Abraham does not attack Elam at night (Gen 14:15). He deploys at night to attack at dawn. Gideon attacks the Midianites at night (Judg 7:19), but his story is careful to explain that Gideon's warriors use torches in the darkness. By waiting until night to deploy, Abraham prevents Elam from knowing what kind of attack is pending and thus from making preparations to defend itself. This is the same strategy that David uses against the Amalekites (1 Sam 30:17). The timing of the attacks is not the only parallel between this story and the story of how David delivers Ziklag from Amalek (1 Sam 30:1-31). In fact, there are enough parallels to argue that both stories were popular between 1000 and 932 B.C.E., when David and Solomon were the rulers of Israel. Repeated performances by the same tellers, as well as the popular identification of David with Abraham, led to the similarities. In both, a city is raided and hostages are seized, a messenger provides information on the attack, the rout of the raiders is decisive, and the protagonist keeps none of the plunder, but instead divides it among his soldiers and the cities that were raided.

After a decisive defeat of Elam, Melchizedek brings out bread and wine to declare that the war has ended. Only when there is peace can farmers properly tend vines and work fields so that they can produce bread and wine. The rations of war are unleavened bread and water.

Melchizedek then certifies that Abraham has fulfilled his covenant obligations, and is eligible to keep his plunder. Abraham, however, magnanimously distributes the spoils to Melchizedek, to his warriors, and to Sodom because to accept goods or land from Sodom would create a conflict of interest and make his household a client of Sodom. Yahweh alone blesses the household of Abraham and Sarah with goods and land. The ruler of Sodom does not bless their household. Therefore, Abraham will not accept a "thread"—rather, movable and manufactured goods such as cloth, or a "sandal thong"— immovable property or land. Landowners walked off the dimensions of their land in sandals, which became their legal title.

The story concludes by celebrating not only the faithfulness of Abraham to his covenant partners, but also his generosity in victory and his unconditional confidence that Yahweh would feed and protect his household. Each virtue was highly prized in ancient Israel. Each virtue was handed on from generation to generation in these stories so that every generation would know that it was not power, nor wealth, but faithfulness and generosity and confidence in Yahweh that made this people to be Israel.

Story of Hagar from Beer-lahai-roi
(Gen 16:1-16)

The Story of Hagar from Beer-lahai-roi, the Story of Hagar from Beersheba (Gen 21:1-21), and the Story of Abraham on Mt. Moriah (Gen 21:33—22:19) are not chronological sequels, they are parallels. The same basic story is repeated three times (Fig. 17).

All three stories are ancestor stories. In the two Stories of Hagar, Abraham and Sarah are the antagonists. Neither reaches a goal or undergoes a change in the story. Abraham is indecisive throughout and his actions only ratify the actions of Sarah. Abraham is Sarah's helper.

Hagar is the protagonist. She sets out at the beginning of the story to obtain land and children and, at the end of the story, she accomplishes her goal. She is relentless in her desire to set her household free from slavery in the household of Sarah and Abraham.

Sometimes the names of protagonists become summaries of the stories themselves. "Adam" is "the man who learns to farm" (Gen 2:5), "Eve" is "the woman who learns to bear a child" (Gen 3:20), and "Isaac" is "the child who makes his parents laugh" (Gen 21:9). "Hagar" is "the homeless woman who becomes the mother of a household."

The story does not say whether Sarah is physically unable to have a child, or whether she has made a vow not to bear children. At Sumer, women who were *naditu* priests made a vow not to have children so that the inheritance of the households of their fathers could remain intact. The Code of Hammurabi permits *naditu* priests to marry, but they must first negotiate a covenant with a surrogate to bear children for their husbands (CH arts. 144-146). Only the mothers of households, not the fathers, could negotiate covenants for a surrogate. Like men who were the legal guardians of a household, women who were surrogates for households had to already be members of the household (Deut 25:10-25). The children of surrogates inherit only from the fathers of their households, not from the mothers of their households. Mothers of households are not shamed by designating surrogates; instead, this legal remedy protects their honor.

Hagar agrees to bear Sarah a child. She abrogates their covenant when her unborn child kicks in her womb. The movements of an unborn were significant (Gen 25:22-23). Hagar considers the child's kick to be a declaration of independence.

Hagar's response to the child's movement is generally translated: "she looked with contempt upon her mistress" (Gen 16:4), but Hagar's words may have originally been a hymn, not an insult. When she feels the child kick, Hagar sings: "I am going to give birth to a wild ass of a man." Mothers regularly celebrate the birth of their children with a hymn like those now preserved in the words of the messenger of Yahweh to Hagar who sings: "he shall be a wild ass of a man, with his hand against everyone, and everyone's hand against him; and he shall live at odds with all his kin" (Gen 16:12). The Hebrew word commonly translated "to look on with contempt" also has the meaning "to jettison" or "to unload." In the book of Jonah the sailors jettison the cargo of the ship into the sea, to lighten it for them (Jonah 1:5). In the books of Samuel-Kings, the people say to Rehoboam, "Lighten the yoke that your father, Solomon, put on us" (1 Kgs 12:10). Since the messenger describes Ishmael as a wild ass, it would be consistent for Hagar to describe his birth as if she were "throwing" or "dropping" a foal. Her words celebrate the strength and vigor that he began to exhibit even in the womb.

Likewise, the Hebrew word commonly translated as "mistress," and used in reference to Sarah (Gen 16:4), can also mean a "champion" or "stallion." Goliath is a champion of the Philistines (1 Sam 17:51). Yahweh does not "delight in the stallion" (Ps 147:10). At this point in the story, Hagar anticipates giving birth to a champion or a stallion. Hagar compares the kick of her unborn child to the kick of the wild ass common in Syria-Palestine, which was notoriously difficult to break and ride. Hagar's attention is not on Sarah, but on the son she expects. It is Sarah who first taunts Hagar and twists the words of Hagar's hymn when she reports to Abraham. Hagar sings: "I am going to deliver a real fighter" (Gen 16:4), but Sarah taunts: "this pregnant slave is picking a real fight with me" (Gen 16:5).

Sarah's indictment is not without precedent. Law allowed Sarah to punish or demote a surrogate, but not sell her (Exod 21:1-6; CH art. 147). Both the Code of Ur-Nammu

crisis (Gen 16:1-6)

Sarah, wife of Abraham, could not bear him a child. So, she made a covenant with her slave, Hagar the Egyptian. Sarah said to Abraham: "Yahweh has forbidden me to bear a child. Have intercourse with my slave, and she will bear my child." After ten years in Canaan, Abraham fulfilled Sarah's covenant with Hagar to be her child-bearer. He had intercourse with Hagar, who conceived a child.

Hagar celebrated her pregnancy, singing, "I am going to deliver a real fighter." Consequently, Sarah said to Abraham: "You have caused me to lose face, after I saved your face by providing you a child-bearer. This pregnant slave is picking a real fight with me." Abraham told Sarah: "She is your slave, therefore you must deal with her." Sarah swore: "May Yahweh decide between you and me," and she punished Hagar.

climax (Gen 16:6-8)

Then, Sarah submitted Hagar to a grueling ordeal in the desert, where Hagar sought sanctuary with Yahweh at a spring on the road to Shur. Here a messenger of Yahweh cross-examined Hagar: "Hagar, slave of Sarah, where have you come from, and where are you going?" Hagar answered in her defense, "I want to free my household from the Household of Sarah."

denouement (Gen 16:8-16)

Then the messenger of Yahweh decreed: "Go back to Sarah, your patron, and carry out the labor of childbirth for her. I will make your children so numerous, they will be too many to count. You have conceived and will bear a son and will name him 'Ishmael.' For Yahweh has heard your prayer. This child will be afraid of no one, but everyone will be afraid of him. He will be a real fighter, even when he has to stand alone."

Hagar named the spring "Where I looked for Yahweh," singing: "At Beer-lahai-roi, Yahweh will look after you, and you can look from Kadesh to Bered." She gave birth to a son. Abraham named the son, whom Hagar bore him when he was eighty-six years old, "Ishmael."

FIGURE 17   Story of Hagar from Beer-lahai-roi (Gen 16:1-16)

and the Code of Hammurabi establish procedures for dealing with slaves who challenge their owners. Mothers of households have the authority to punish any woman who fails to honor them. The Code of Ur-Nammu, for example, allows mothers of households to rub salt into the gums of surrogates who break their covenants. Therefore, Abraham tells Sarah: "Your slave is your property; do whatever you please with her" (Gen 16:6).

If the woman was a surrogate who had actually borne a child for the father of the household, however, "she could not be sold out of the house and, after her master's death she could, together with her children, gain freedom; if recognized by the father, her children had even the right of inheritance" (CH art. 170-171). Because Hagar has already conceived a child when she breaks her covenant with Sarah, she can only be punished. She cannot be sold out of the household. Therefore, Hagar is not running away or being expelled from the household of Abraham and Sarah. Sarah is law-abiding, not law-breaking. She does not violate Hagar's legal rights to remain in the household once she has conceived or given birth to a child. Instead, Sarah submits Hagar to an ordeal, and allows Yahweh to decide whether Hagar's child would legally belong to Hagar or to Sarah.

In traditional cultures, the ordeal was a judicial institution that resolved conflicts between households which could not be resolved by the elders in a village assembly. It was an extraordinary means to reestablish harmony within the village. Crimes that carried the death penalty, such as adultery and jealousy, required the indictment to be supported by the testimony of two eyewitnesses. Without eyewitnesses, plaintiffs had no recourse. Harmony in the village was essential for its economy to prosper. Ordeals break stalemates and allow the village to make a decision between the households.

Defendants in ordeals were exposed to strenuous, life-threatening experiences. If they survived, then the divine assembly had cleared them of the charges made against them, and the honor of their households was reaffirmed. If they did not, then their households were shamed. Ordeals were legally constructed days of judgment (Deut 32:34-36, Ps 18:7; 32:6; Job 21:30). In one ordeal, defendants were thrown into the river as they cried out for deliverance (CH arts. 129, 132; Fig. 18). If they survived they were innocent. If they drowned they were guilty and their property was confiscated (Job 21:17). In the books of Samuel-Kings, Elijah submits the prophets of Ba'al to an ordeal by water in the Wadi Kishon: "Elijah said to them, 'Seize the prophets of Ba'al. Do not let one of them escape.' Then the people seized them, and Elijah had them thrown into the Wadi Kishon" (1 Kgs 18:40).

Sarah submits Hagar to an ordeal in the desert, rather than in a river. The desert here is not a place of punishment, but a place of judgment. Hagar appeals to Yahweh for a judgment against Sarah by taking Ishmael into the desert in the book of Genesis just as Moses appeals to Yahweh for a

Art. 129 If the wife of a citizen commits adultery, then she and her partner are to be tied up and tried by ordeal in a river. If, however, the woman's husband pardons her, then the monarch can pardon her partner.

Art. 132 If a citizen charges a woman with adultery, but has no evidence, then she is to be tried by ordeal in the river to restore the honor of her husband. If she survives, then she must pay a fine.

FIGURE 18   The Code of Hammurabi (Matthews and Benjamin 1997: 104–5)

judgment against Pharaoh by taking the Hebrews into the desert in the book of Exodus. Hagar places Ishmael under a sacred tree, and cries out to Yahweh for justice (Ps 18:7; 69:15-16; Jonah 2:3). Yahweh then subpoenas Hagar with the same formula used to subpoena Adam and Eve (Gen 3:9). The legal language continues as Hagar serves as her own defense attorney: "I want to free my household from the household of Sarah" (Gen 16:8).

The verdict of the ordeal is a covenant between Yahweh and Hagar. Although the covenant blesses Hagar with both land and children, it also imposes the stipulation: "go back to Sarah your patron and carry out the labor of childbirth for her" (Gen 16:9). Yahweh is not authorizing the physical abuse of Hagar, but rather informing Hagar that her decision to become the mother of a household will demand labor. Hagar, like Eve, cannot bear her child without labor. Yahweh's words to Hagar are virtually identical to Yahweh's words to Abraham (Gen 12:2-3). Yahweh endows Hagar with children and land, and tutors her in the requirements of her newly acquired fertility. She will have a son and take possession of the oasis of Beer-lahai-roi. She will no longer be a slave, but the mother of a household. Nonetheless, that fertility requires labor. The ecstasy of giving life to another human being in birth, or to the harvest in farming, demands the agony of labor. As in the Stories of Adam and Eve, Yahweh here in the Stories of Hagar is more a midwife than a judge. Midwives do not impose labor pain upon a mother as a sentence for conceiving a child, they interpret it. Hagar must bear children, manage resources, educate women and children, and mediate disputes. She must labor to become mother of a household.

Stories of Lot and His Daughters
(GEN 19:1-38)

In the world of the Bible, fathers of households use the diplomacy of hospitality to determine whether strangers are friends or enemies. Strangers who pass the test become covenant partners. Strangers who fail are exiled. The Bible celebrates both Abraham and Sarah (Gen 18:1-15) and Lot and his daughters (Gen 19:1-11) for their hospitality to strangers (Fig. 19).

The "men" (Gen 18:16) or "angels" (Gen 19:1) who are guests of Lot and his daughters are messengers. Messengers created a communications network that allowed rulers to govern great states from a single city. In Mesopotamia, *mar sipri* messengers were responsible for communications and negotiations between one ruler and another. Several kinds of messengers appear in the Royal Archives of Mari (ARM). *Suharu* messengers carried letters from one ruler to another (ARM XII 131; II 21:15–22), usually announcing the arrival of an important official or an army. *Sa sikkim* messengers carried letters of introduction authorizing them to negotiate covenants.

crisis (Gen 19:1-3)

Two strangers reached Sodom in the evening, where Lot was sitting at the gate. He got up to greet them, and bowing with his face to the ground, he said, "Please, honor my household as its guests. Stay the night and bathe your feet. You can get up early to continue your journey." They replied, "No, we shall spend the night here at the gate." When Lot repeated his invitation, however, they went to his house. He prepared a meal for them, baking bread without leaven, and they ate.

climax (Gen 19:4-9)

Before they went to bed, every elder and warrior in Sodom assembled in front of the house. They shouted to Lot: "Where are the strangers who came to your house tonight? Bring them out so that we may show them that they are powerless here." Lot stepped out of the door. When he had shut the door behind him, he tried to reason with them: "Neighbors, you don't know what you are doing. I have two unmarried daughters. I would rather bring them out to you, and have you rape them, than have you lay a hand on these strangers who are my guests." The citizens of Sodom replied, "Get out of the way, you old fool. You are a stranger here yourself. You have no authority to host strangers. We will rape you as well as them." Then they knocked Lot against the door and began to break it down.

denouement (Gen 19:10-11)

At that moment, the guests stretched out their hands, pulled Lot inside, and closed the door. They paralyzed everyone rushing the house with a glance. No one could reach the door.

FIGURE 19   Lot and His Daughters as Hosts (Gen 19:1-11)

Messengers and other people on foot were often considered to be spies (Gen 42:16; Judg 4:7). Although hosts lavished messengers with food, clothing, and slaves, they also assigned them bodyguards to protect them from harm while they were in their land and to prevent them from spying.

The messengers in the household of Lot and his daughters are divine. Hospitality stories often cast Yahweh as a traveler on foot inspecting how households treat strangers (Gen 19:1; 21:17; Josh 6:17+25; Job 1:7; Isa 1:1-31; Zech 1:10; Dan 7:9-27). Hosts never immediately recognize their guests as divine because they are disguised. The Story of Abraham and Sarah introduces the strangers as Yahweh, but Abraham sees only three messengers (Gen 18:1-2). The disguise prevents hosts from showing partiality. Until they strike the city assembly of Sodom with blindness (Gen 19:11), the true identity of the messengers remains hidden. Since only Yahweh can blind (Gen 19:11; 2 Kgs 6:18) or paralyze ene-mies with a glance (Exod 14:24), their strategy for protecting Lot and his daughters at the door of their household clearly identifies them as members of the divine assembly.

Lot begins his test of the strangers by inviting them to his house. They decline. The invitation is repeated and they accept. By declining the first invitation and then accept-ing the second, the strangers pass this first test. To accept a first offer of hospitality would make strangers appear imposing. To decline a second offer would make them appear ungrateful. Lot and his daughters celebrate the completion of this first test by washing the feet of the messengers and graduating them from strangers to guests. As guests they will remain under the protection of Lot and his daughters for three days.

The second test begins when Lot and his daughters serve them a meal. Eating involves all five senses. Like sexual intercourse, farming, fighting, offering sacrifice, and learning, eating demands undivided attention. The way in which the guests eat will demonstrate whether they will bless or curse Sodom.

The assembly of Sodom interrupts the second test. Assemblies normally convene at thresholds like the gates of a city or the threshing floor of a village. Here it con-venes at the threshold of the house of Lot and his daughters. The phrase "both young and old" does not indicate that even very young and very old men in Sodom were homo-sexuals. The story is not describing a sex riot, but a legal assembly. In the world of the Bible, men are either warriors or elders. The terms do not refer to age, but to politi-cal status. The assembly of Sodom is composed of both warriors and elders. Not one member of the assembly was absent, and they unanimously agree that the strangers are enemies of Sodom.

Rape, here, is not only an act of passion (1 Sam 24:1-17; 2 Sam 9:8). Rape will label the messengers as powerless to harm Sodom. The story does not indict the elders and warriors of Sodom for sexual misconduct, but for social injustice. The sentence imposed on the messengers by the assembly of Sodom is virtually identical to the sen-tence imposed on the Levite and his concubine (Judg 19:1—21:25). In one tradition, however, the rape is homosexual; in the other it is heterosexual. The Middle Assyrian Code legislates that if the father of the household is convicted of adultery with the wife of his neighbor, the members of the village assembly shall rape him, and then castrate him. In the Stories of Osiris and Seth, Horus rapes Seth for challenging his right to rule Egypt. Shechem rapes Dinah in a takeover bid to control the assets of the house-hold of Jacob (Gen 34:1-31). Amnon rapes Tamar in a bid to take over the household of David (2 Sam 13:1-22). Absalom rapes ten concubines (2 Sam 15:16-17+16:20-22) in a bid for economic control of the ten most important covenants negotiated by the household of David which these women represent.

The Stories of Lot and His Daughters are often cited as biblical precedents for con-demning same-sex relations between adults. These stories, however, condemned the inhospitable, not the homosexual. Rape, whether it was homosexual or heterosexual, flagrantly demonstrated a lack of hospitality. The outcry against Sodom in the story of Abraham and Sarah as hosts (Gen 18:20) charges the city with social injustice, not sexual misconduct. Outcries to Yahweh in the Bible never involve homosexuality. The outcry in the book of Exodus (Exod 2:23) is against slavery. In the book of Judges (Judg 10:10), it is against idolatry. In the book of Jonah (Jonah 1:14), it is against murder. Furthermore, no other traditions in the Bible understand the actions of the assembly of Sodom to be evidence that homosexuality was common in the city.

The assembly attempts to execute the sentence of rape on the strangers at the threshold of the household of Lot, but he appeals their decision. "Neighbors, you don't know what you are doing. I have two unmarried daughters. I would rather bring them out to you, and have you rape them, than have you lay a hand on these strangers who are my guests" (Gen 19:7-8). Lot is willing to sacrifice his daughters, not to protect himself, but precisely because they are more valuable than himself. The daughters of a household are its economic portfolio. Without daughters, Lot will have no heir, and the household will be destroyed. Sentencing a woman to death by rape is to sentence her to die by the act through which she should live. It converts intercourse from an act of life to an act of death. Sentencing a woman to death by rape also sentences the father of her household or her husband to death (Gen 3:10-16). The death sentence is immediate for the women, but drawn out for their men. Without his daughters, Lot will be without an heir, and therefore without anyone to care for him and his household. A father of a household who does not fulfill his responsibility as a host sentences himself to live out his life without heirs. Lot is willing to accept the death of his daughters by rape, and his own death by exile, to defend the lives of his guests.

The first story of Lot and His Daughters ends when the messengers save their lives. Lot saves the lives of the messengers at the gate when the story begins (Gen 19:1-3). They return the favor when the story ends (Gen 19:11). Hospitality is the act of keeping the stranger alive. Hosts feed and protect their guests, and in return guests feed and protect their hosts. Guests often acknowledge the status of their hosts as life givers by bringing them a living, or life-giving, gift. The three strangers who visit Abraham and Sarah promise them a child (Gen 18:9-15). Today, guests often bring hosts something living like a plant, or something life-giving like wine or a special food like chocolate.

Hospitality was the key to life. Only the hospitable survived. The tellers of the Stories of Lot and His Daughters wanted to emphasize not only that their hospitality won them the gift of life in the old world to which Sodom belonged, but that in the new world the divine assembly created after Sodom was gone. Therefore, the first story of Lot and His Daughters, which is an ancestor story, is followed by a second, which is a creation story (Fig. 20).

sterility affidavit (Gen 19:12-29)

The messengers said to Lot: "Who else belongs to your household? Take every man and woman in your household out of the city. We are about to destroy this place, for the outcry reaching Yahweh against those in the city is so great."

Then Lot assembled his household. "We need to evacuate this place," he told them. "Yahweh is about to destroy the city." The men of his household laughed.

As dawn was breaking, the messengers said to Lot: "You need to get out of here. At least, evacuate your household or you will all be killed when we destroy the city."

When Lot continued to delay, the messengers led him, his wife, and his two daughters by force out of the city. The strangers ordered them: "Run for your lives. Don't look back or stop anywhere on the plain. Go into the hills or you will all die."

"Oh, no, honored guests," Lot replied. "You have already saved my life once. I cannot run off to the hills to keep this disaster from overtaking me, and so I shall die. There is a village ahead. If I am not being too picky, let us take refuge there. Now that's not being too picky, is it?"

"All right," the strangers replied, "Yahweh grants this petition and exempts this one little village from destruction. Hurry, escape there. Yahweh will not do anything until you arrive." That is why the village is called "Picayune."

The sun was just rising when Lot arrived in Picayune. Yahweh rained sulfur upon Sodom and Gomorrah until all their people and land were destroyed. Lot's wife turned back and was turned into a pillar of salt.

Early the next morning, Abraham went to the place where he had stood in Yahweh's presence. As he looked down toward Sodom, Gomorrah, and all the cities of the plain, he saw dense smoke over the land rising like fumes from a furnace.

Title colophon

This is the story of how Yahweh destroyed the Cities of the Plain, and remembered the Covenant with Abraham and Sarah by protecting the household of Lot.

cosmogony (Gen 19:31-36)

Lot was afraid to stay in Picayune, so he and his two daughters went up and settled in the hills, where they lived in a cave. The first night, the older daughter said to the younger: "Our father is old, and there is not a man on earth to father children for this household. Let us offer wine to our father, and have intercourse with him, that we may have children." They offered their father wine, and the older one went in and had intercourse with him, even though Lot did not remember anything. *(continued)*

The second night, the older one said to the younger: "Last night I had intercourse with my father. Let us offer him wine again tonight, and then you go in and have intercourse with him, that we may both have children." So that night, too, they offered their father wine, and then the younger one went in and had intercourse with him, even though he did not remember anything.

covenant (Gen 19:37-38)

Both of Lot's daughters became pregnant. The older one gave birth to a son whom she named Moab, singing: "This child is a gift from my father." He is the ancestor of the Moabites of today.

The younger one, too, gave birth to a son, and she named him Ammon, singing: "This child is the heir of my household." He is the ancestor of the Ammonites of today.

FIGURE 20   Creation of Moab and Ammon (Gen 19:12-38)

Natural disasters always threaten human security. Tornadoes, hurricanes, floods, monsoons, earthquakes, volcanic eruptions leave permanent marks on human memory long after the generation that suffered them has died. The Flood Stories in the book of Genesis (Gen 6:1—11:26) are creation stories that developed in clans regularly threatened by flooding. Hence they describe chaos as water. For the clans who lived along the Dead Sea on the fault line created by the African and Asian tectonic plates, earthquakes and volcanic activity were the most common natural disasters. In their creation stories, chaos is not water, but earthquake and volcanic activity (Gen 19:23-25). The Stories of Lot and His Daughters teach their audiences that the same Yahweh who sends volcanic eruptions to destroy Sodom also leads Lot and his daughters to safety (Gen 19:16). Yahweh never destroys without creating. The same Yahweh who destroys the Egyptians, delivers the Hebrews. Good and evil are always partners in human experience. There are always survivors. Destruction is never total.

Lot had the good sense to negotiate a covenant with Abraham. The household of David, which regarded Abraham as its ancestor, told the Story of the Creation of Ammon and Moab, which regarded Lot as their ancestor, to convince them to be faithful to their covenants with Israel as the household of Lot had done before them.

Like the ancestor Story of Lot and His Daughters as Hosts (Gen 19:1-11), the Creation of Moab and Ammon (Gen 19:12-38) begins with an invitation offered and declined. Here the protagonists invite Lot's household to leave the city. Lot meets with his sons-in-law, who laugh and refuse to leave the city.

Laughter here declines or demurs an invitation (Gen 17:17; 18:12; 19:14; Job 5:22; 39:22; 41:29). Just as the messengers in the ancestor story declined Lot's invitation, so

Lot's sons-in-law decline the invitation of the messengers to evacuate Sodom. Just as Lot reiterates his invitation in the ancestor story, the messengers repeat their invitation in the creation story, but only Lot, his wife, and his two daughters accept.

The deliverance of Lot's daughters is a reward for their hospitality. They are not silent victims of their sexist father and his neighbors. If they had not been willing to lay down their lives for their guests, there would be no reason for the guests to return the favor to them by delivering them from Sodom. Because the daughters of Lot are hospitable, their husbands are also eligible for deliverance, just as because Lot was hospitable, so the wife of Lot is eligible for deliverance.

The episode at the village of Zoar is an etiology (Gen 19:18-22) that identifies the salt miners and asphalt workers from Zoar as the tellers of the Stories of Lot and His Daughters. This small village on the frontiers of Ammon and Moab nonetheless marks out for itself a major role in the stories of these great peoples. It is ironic that the village of Zoar survives the cataclysm, while the grand cities of Sodom, Gomorrah, Adamah, and Zeboiim do not. The villagers credit their survival to the hospitality that they extended to Lot and his daughters. Like colonial inns and homes on the Atlantic coast of the United States who proudly remember that "George Washington Slept Here," the village of Zoar recalled its hospitality to Lot, which allowed it to survive.

Zoar's signature plays on its name, which people from Louisiana would call "picayune." When Sodom and the other cities of the plain were booming, they considered Zoar to be "of little or no importance." Lot tells the messengers: "'Look, there is a village where we will be safe. If I'm not being too picky, let me flee there for sanctuary. Now that's not being too picky, is it? . . . That is why the village is called 'Picayune.'"

Salt and asphalt production are the primary industries by which the peoples of the Dead Sea valley traditionally have made their living. Today, potash is taken from the Dead Sea for fertilizers and explosives. In the world of the Bible, these salt blocks were used to start fires. Asphalt was used as an adhesive to haft stone blades to wooden handles, and as caulking for boats with wooden hulls. Since both salt and asphalt were such important economic commodities, they appear in this creation story as divine endowments. Salt miners may well have considered Lot's wife to be their special patron, so she appears here, not so much as a warning against curiosity, but as the woman who could not leave the villages in the Dead Sea valley without some way to make a living after the old world of Sodom and Gomorrah was gone.

The divine assembly not only endows this new world with natural resources like salt and asphalt, but with a new people as well. The daughters of Lot discover how to reproduce. In the Stories of Adam and Eve, the aphrodisiac that leads to sexual intercourse is the fruit from the tree. In the Flood Stories and here in the Creation of Moab and Ammon, it is wine. The drunkenness in these stories is not a social disease or physical dependency, but induces the trance or ecstasy that allows those who are about to participate in a divine work to leave the human plane and enter the divine plane.

The Stories of Adam and Eve, the Flood Stories, and the Creation of Moab and Ammon each describe this inaugural act of sexual reproduction differently. In the Stories of Adam and Eve, the act is heterosexual (Gen 4:1). In the Flood Stories this inaugural act of sexual reproduction seems homosexual (Gen 9:20-23). Here in the Creation of Moab and Ammon it is incestuous (Gen 19:30-38). The intention of these creation stories is not to endorse heterosexuality, nor to condemn homosexuality and incest, but to identify the inaugural act of sexual reproduction as unique.

Story of Abraham on Mt. Moriah
(GEN 21:33—22:19)

Ancestor stories are often framed by formulas declaring there is peace in the land. The Story of Abraham on Mt. Moriah begins when Abraham plants a sacred tree and lives at peace in Beersheba (Gen 23:33), and ends when Abraham returns to Beersheba (Gen 22:19). Like building an altar, planting a tree establishes a sanctuary and takes possession of the land. A sanctuary is a sacred center where life comes into the human plane from the divine. The tree is a birth canal that unites the human plane with the divine plane. The same connotations appear in the children's story "Jack and the Bean Stalk," where the bean stalk allows Jack to leave the earth and enter a special and mysteriously different world (Fig. 21).

Abraham is the protagonist. He has two sons. Isaac is the "beloved" and the "boy." The titles legally designate him as the heir apparent, not just as Abraham's favorite. Ishmael is "a wild ass of a man" (Gen 16:12). When Abraham orders his slaves "stay here with the ass; the boy and I will go over there" (Gen 22:5), he is referring to the two sons between whom Yahweh must decide, and not to the ass that he saddled when the story opened (Gen 22:3). The slaves are to guard Ishmael, "the ass," while Abraham takes Isaac, "the boy," forward for the ordeal.

The symmetry between the Stories of Hagar and the Story of Abraham on Mt. Moriah is critical for understanding important aspects of this story. Key words (Gen 21:14—22:3) and key themes shared by these stories suggest that they were originally closer parallels than they appear to be in the Bible today. In one tradition, the ordeal that Sarah demands (Gen 21:9-11) would have been conducted by Hagar (Gen 21:12-16), in the other by Abraham (Gen 22:1-10).

The identity of the candidate for the ordeal in the Stories of Hagar was not as significant in the world of the Bible as it has become in the world of ongoing tensions between Muslims and Jews today. The unresolved question in all three stories is: "Who

crisis (Gen 21:1-10)

Yahweh kept the stipulations of the Covenant with Sarah, who conceived and bore Abraham a son in his old age. Abraham named the son to whom Sarah gave birth "Isaac" (Hebrew: *tsahaq*), and circumcised him when he was eight days old, as Yahweh had stipulated. Abraham was a hundred years old when his son Isaac was born and when Sarah sang:

> *"Yahweh has made me laugh (Hebrew:* **tsahaq***);*
>
> *Everyone who hears will laugh with me. . . .*
>
> *Who would have said Sarah will nurse a child?*
>
> *Yet I have borne Abraham a son in his old age."*

The child grew. On the day he was weaned Abraham celebrated a great feast. Then Sarah saw the son to whom Hagar the Egyptian had given birth with Abraham sexually abusing (Hebrew: *metsaheq*) son Isaac (Gen 26:8; 39:14-17; Judg 16:25).

climax (Gen 21:11-18)

So she said to Abraham, "Expel this slave with her son, for the son of this slave shall not inherit along with my son Isaac." Sarah's indictment of Ishmael troubled Abraham. But Yahweh said to Abraham: "Do not worry about this young man Ishmael and the slave Hagar. Do whatever Sarah asks you to do, because it is Isaac's children who will remember (Hebrew: *qara'*) you. As for the son of the slave, I will make a great people of him as well, because he is your son." So Abraham rose early in the morning. . . .

climax (Gen 22:1-10)

Abraham planted a sacred tree at Beersheba, which he dedicated to Yahweh, Our Creator Everlasting (Hebrew: *el 'olam*). Abraham remained a stranger in the Land of the Philistines for a long time. Some time later, Yahweh appeared (Hebrew: *nissah*) to Abraham and said: "Abraham." "Here I am," Abraham responded. Then, Yahweh gave Abraham this command: "Take your son, your heir, Isaac, and depart for the Land of Moriah, where you will offer sacrifice on the hill which I will reveal to you." So Abraham rose early in the morning. . . .

. . . saddled an ass, took his son, Isaac, two slaves, and the wood that he had cut for the sacrifice. Then he departed for the sanctuary that Our Creator would reveal to him.

On the third day, Abraham saw the sanctuary in the distance. Then Abraham ordered his slaves: "Stay here and take care of Ishmael (Hebrew: *hamor*). This young

(continued)

man and I will go on ahead. After we offer the sacrifice, we will return." Abraham let Isaac carry the wood for the sacrifice. Abraham himself carried the flint and steel to light the fire. As the two of them were walking along together, Isaac called out to his father, Abraham: "My father." "Here I am, my son," Abraham replied. "Look. There is fire and wood, but there is no sheep for the sacrifice." "My son, Our Creator, will see to it that there is a sheep for the sacrifice." The two of them continued walking along together. When they came to the sanctuary that Yahweh had chosen, Abraham built an altar, and laid firewood on it. Then he raised the steel knife in his hand to sacrifice his son.

denouement (Gen 22:11-14)

But the messenger of Yahweh called out from the heavens, "Abraham, Abraham!" He said, "Here I am." "Do not sacrifice this young man. Do not harm him. Yahweh, the divine patron of your household, knows that you have placed your heir in his hands." Abraham looked around and saw a ram caught by its horns in the maquis brush. So he went and took the ram and sacrificed it in place of his son. Abraham named the sanctuary "Where I looked for our Creator," where people now sing: "On this mountain Our Creator will look after you."

denouement (Gen 22:15-19)

Again the messenger of Yahweh called to Abraham from the heavens. This is the word of Yahweh: "Because you would not withhold even your heir from me, I will bless you abundantly and make your children as countless as the stars of the sky and the sand on the shore. I will give your children the cities of their enemies. I will bless all the nations of the earth with your children because you obeyed my command." Abraham returned to his slaves, and they set out together for Beersheba, where Abraham made his home.

FIGURE 21   Story of Abraham on Mt. Moriah (Gen 21:1-14 + 22:1-19)

is to be the heir to the household of Abraham? Is it Ishmael, or is it Isaac?" Submitting Isaac to an ordeal, as tellers do in the Story of Abraham on Mt. Moriah, or submitting Ishmael as they do in the Stories of Hagar from Beer-lahai-roi and from Beersheba, equally resolves the issue. In all three stories Yahweh accepts both Ishmael and Isaac as heirs with virtually equal rights and privileges. Both will have land and children. Ishmael will inherit the land of Abraham and Hagar which can be seen from Beer-lahai-roi. Isaac will inherit the land of Abraham and Sarah which can be seen from Moriah. Ishmael will endow his descendants with the bow so that they can survive in the desert.

Isaac will endow his descendants with stories so that they can survive assimilation any-where on the face of the earth (Gen 21:12).

Hagar, Sarah, and Abraham struggle to resolve an external legal claim, not to resolve an interior crisis of faith. The ordeal clarifies Yahweh's covenant with them. In contrast to western European literature today, biblical traditions have little interest in the inter-nal emotions of characters. Only external actions move the plot. Sometimes traditions of biblical interpretation reflect more about the culture of the interpreters than about the culture of ancient Israel, and some interpretations of the Story of Abraham on Mt. Moriah are good examples. Many Jews, Christians, and Muslims read the story as a les-son in contemporary human relationships with God and with one another, especially when those relationships are difficult and painful. These readings focus on God–human and parent–child relationships, and portray Abraham as torn between being the loving par-ent, who carries the fire and the knife so that Isaac would not get hurt, and being a reli-gious fanatic who sacrifices his own son to please God. They portray Isaac as a completely trusting and completely innocent victim manipulated by both parental love and parental violence. Sarah is portrayed as a wife and mother resigned to the loss of both her hus-band and her son to their divine patron. Interpretations that focus on the thoughts or feelings of Sarah, Abraham, or Isaac treat the Bible as if it were western European lit-erature. Biblical characters are developed by what they say and what they do, not by what they think and what they feel. For example, "the fire and the knife" is an idiom like "flint and steel," which identifies the tools that Abraham will use to light the fire. He is not carrying burning coals. The knife was used against the flint to raise a spark, as well as to butcher the offering (Gen 22:10). Abraham carries these tools, not because he does not want Isaac to hurt himself, but because he is the father of the household. These are the instruments of his office, and with which he will offer the sacrifice.

Yahweh is not testing Abraham to see if he is obedient. The Hebrews seldom, if ever, portrayed Yahweh as testing human beings, even in the book of Job. When the word "test" does appear it carries the connotations of "coaching" or "training." Yahweh trains the Hebrews so that they can meet and survive the challenges they will face. Yah-weh trains the Hebrews to protect them from harm, not to torment them to see how they will react. This story does not celebrate Abraham and Sarah for blind obedience to a divine patron who toys with their feelings by giving them a child and then pretends to take that child away. The story more likely remembers them as ancestors who strug-gled for land and children of their own in a world where slavery seemed inevitable. In the story, Yahweh is not their enemy, but their covenant partner who helps them resolve the conflict as to who should be their heir.

Likewise, the Story of Abraham on Mt. Moriah is not a story about human sacri-fice. It is a story about who will be the heir of Abraham. Human sacrifice demonstrated the complete dependence of a household upon its divine patron. Human sacrifice was offered when the father of a household set off to war or founded a city. Ahaz sacrifices his son as he prepares to declare war on Israel and Aram. Hiel sacrifices both his oldest and youngest sons during the reconstruction of Jericho (1 Kgs 16:35). In this story Abraham is neither setting off to war nor founding a city. Furthermore, he tells Ishmael and his slaves that both he and Isaac will return to the camp (Gen 22:5).

There are two denouement episodes in the Story of Abraham on Mt. Moriah (Gen 22:12-14 and 22:15-19). Each is introduced with the words "the messenger of Yahweh called to Abraham . . . from heaven." In one denouement, Yahweh delivers Isaac, and in the other Yahweh blesses him.

From Mt. Moriah Yahweh lets Abraham and Isaac look over the land where Yahweh will look after them. Therefore, Abraham names the sanctuary "Where I looked for Yahweh." It will be the sanctuary where the household of Abraham and Sarah will sing: "On this mountain, Yahweh will look after you" (Gen 22:14). All the land that Abraham and Isaac can see from the sanctuary on Mt. Moriah will belong to the household of Abraham and Sarah. As their heir, Isaac will inherit it all. Ishmael, as the heir of Abraham and Hagar, will inherit all the land that can been seen from the sanctuary at Beer-lahai-roi. The story designates Isaac as heir to the household of Abraham and Sarah, just as the Stories of Hagar designate Ishmael heir to the household of Abraham and Hagar. These ancestor stories celebrate Abraham, Sarah, and Hagar for their faith and perseverance in moving their households from slavery to freedom—from being slaves without land and children, to being free or Hebrew, blessed by Yahweh with the children of Ishmael and Isaac and the lands of Beersheba and Moriah.

Stories of Isaac and Rebekah

The Stories of Isaac and Rebekah are not a fully developed cycle. Isaac and Rebekah appear only as names (Exod 2:24; 3:6; Jer 33:25; Amos 7:7-9; 1 Chr 1:34; Sir 44:16-23). They never speak for themselves, but only through the Stories of Abraham and Sarah and the Stories of Jacob, Leah, and Rachel, where they appear without definition or development. Not even how the Hebrews came to call their divine patron the "Fear of Isaac" (Gen 31:42, 53) is explained.

Only the Annunciation to Rebekah (Gen 25:19-26) and the Blessing of Jacob and Esau (Gen 27:1-45) are without parallels in the Stories of Abraham and Sarah and the Stories of Jacob, Leah, and Rachel. In no story is Isaac himself an unparalleled protagonist. In the Annunciation to Sarah (Gen 18:1-15; 21:1-8), Sarah is the protagonist. In the Story of Abraham on Mt. Moriah (Gen 22:1-19) and the Story of Isaac's Marriage (Gen 24:1-67), Abraham is the protagonist. Even the Obituary of

Isaac (Gen 35:28-29) is part of the genealogy of Jacob (Gen 35:22-29). Traditions in which Isaac is technically the protagonist are all parallels of stories about other ancestors. The story of how Isaac and Rebekah Negotiate with Abimelech (Gen 26:1-11) retells Abraham and Sarah Negotiate with Pharaoh (Gen 11:9—13:1) and Abraham and Sarah Negotiate with Abimelech (Gen 20:1-8). Likewise, the story of how Isaac Negotiates with the Herders of Gerar (Gen 26:12-33) retells Abraham Negotiates with Abimelech (Gen 21:22-24).

Stories of Jacob, Leah, and Rachel
(GEN 25:20 — 37:2)

The Stories of Jacob, Leah, and Rachel are a window through which to view the Hebrews' struggle for survival in the hostile world of the Iron Age. They remembered these ancestors the way they understood themselves: as survivors who compensated for lack of power by an ability to manipulate the power of others.

Jacob or Israel was a favorite ancestor of a Middle– or Late Bronze–period people who appear both in the Bible and in traditions from Mesopotamia and Egypt. They lived north of Jerusalem and on both sides of the Jordan River. Jacob's rivals all lived along the frontiers of this area. Esau lived in Edom along the south. Laban lived in Aram along the north and Shechem along the west. Jacob's encounters with his divine patron take place at Jabbok and Bethel, important sanctuaries in the area (Gen 28:10-22).

Bethel marks the intersection of two great ancient highways fifteen miles north of Jerusalem. Founded after 2000 B.C.E., Bethel was a border city separating Israel from Judah. Its sister city, Dan, separated Israel from Syria. For the Israelites, Dan and Bethel were holy cities dedicated to Yahweh. For the people of Judah, however, Dan and Bethel were cities whose worship was sacrilegious, because the Israelites erected golden calves as pedestals for Yahweh in their sanctuaries. The only fitting pedestal for Yahweh, according to the people of Judah, was Ark of the Covenant, as "Luz," Bethel, like its sister city Dan, is a border city, a holy city, a sacrilegious city. Bethel belongs to the heartland of ancient Israel where some of the Bible's most-told traditions developed. Near Bethel are Jericho and Ai, where villagers celebrated Yahweh's gift of new land to them by telling stories like those in the book of Joshua (Josh 2–8). Bethel was also part of the territory where the ark of the covenant stories (1 Samuel 4–6; 2 Samuel 6) and the Stories of Samuel were told.

Hebrews laid claim to Bethel with the story of how Abraham Negotiates with Yahweh (Gen 11:27—13:18) and the Inauguration of Jacob at Bethel (Gen 28:10-22). These ancestors celebrate their commitment to their divine patron by erecting a great stone there. In his inauguration, Jacob does not actually see a ladder, but Esagila, a ziggurat or great stepped-platform which the members of the divine assembly use to enter and leave Babylon. The Flood Stories (Gen 11:1-9) satirize the same ziggurat as the "Tower of Babel." The stories confer the status of the "Gate (*Bab-*) of our Divine Patron (*-Elyon*)" in Mesopotamia on the "House (*Beth-*) of our Divine Patron (*-El*)" in Syria-Palestine.

The villages where the Stories of Jacob, Leah, and Rachel were told were always threatened by rivalry from within and invasion from without. Similarly, Jacob is always embroiled in conflict. He struggles with Esau, his brother, and with Laban, his uncle; with Levi and Simeon, his sons; and even with Yahweh, his divine patron. Storytellers did not wish to remember the household of Jacob, Leah, and Rachel as troublemakers, but as survivors. Their position was never secure and had to be continually defended.

The Hebrews were a people on the margins of their world. Like all marginal peoples, the Hebrews admired the clever who improved themselves at the expense of the establishment. Cleverness was the wisdom of the poor. Therefore, Jacob tricks Esau into selling him his birthright (Gen 25:19-34), Isaac into designating him as his heir (Gen 27:1-45), Laban into selling him his sheep (Gen 30:25-43) and his land (Gen 31:1—32:3), and even Yahweh into letting him cross the Jabbok into the promised land (Gen 32:23-33). The household of Jacob, Leah, and Rachel knew how to work the system to their own advantage. Cuneiform tablets from Nuzi, an important Mesopotamian city around 1500 B.C.E., now document the household of Jacob's legal sophistication by showing that birthrights could be bought and sold; that oral wills, even when conferred on the wrong beneficiary, were irrevocable; that fathers of households without natural heirs like Laban could adopt an heir like Jacob (Gen 29:1-30); and that the titles to property belonged to whomever could produce the *teraphim* statues of a household's divine patrons (Gen 31:19-35).

Jacob, Leah, and Rachel could not only manipulate the powerful, but use nature to their advantage as well. Leah uses mandrake plants to conceive a child (Gen 30:14-21). Mandrakes are only one plant that the clever in traditional societies use to help the childless conceive. Likewise, Jacob builds a breeding corral from multicolored poles so that his sheep will conceive multicolored lambs. Traditional societies have a wonderful inventory of techniques like this for priming nature to imitate human behavior.

Nonetheless, the Stories of Jacob, Leah, and Rachel are quite balanced in their assessment of cleverness, which is, at best, only a temporary challenge to the establishment. The clever are fugitives at risk. Consequently, the household of Jacob is always on the run, a wandering Aramean (Deut 26:5-10). Esau (Gen 27:30-45), Isaac (Gen 27:46—28:9), and Laban (Gen 31:1-24) all exile the household of Jacob when they discover their losses. The household of Jacob that outwits Isaac is eventually outwitted by Simon and Levi (Gen 34:1-31). Their stories do not celebrate cleverness to teach that cheating and stealing is all right for ancestors, but not for ordinary people. Biblical cleverness celebrates the tenacity with which the poor survive and honors the divine patron of Jacob, Leah, and Rachel for helping the poor, rather than supporting the powerful (Gen 49:24; Isa 1:24; 49:26; 60:16; Ps 132:3-5).

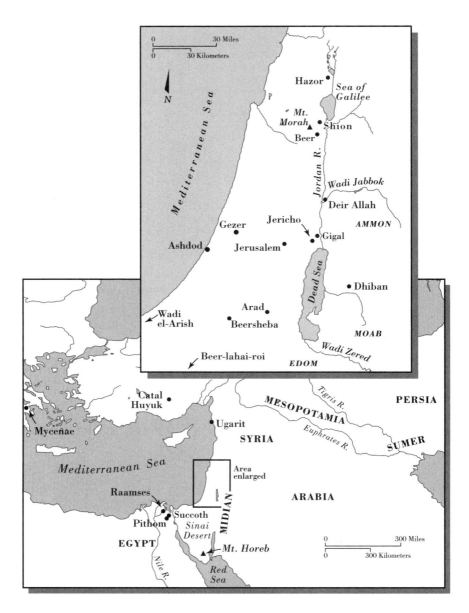

Points of Interest (Chapter 3)

3

BOOKS OF
EXODUS, LEVITICUS,
NUMBERS

(EXOD 1:7—NUM 27:11)

In 1958, when film director Cecil B. DeMille (1881–1959) cast actor Charlton Heston as Moses in *The Ten Commandments*, he created a set of images for the theater-going public more enduring for many than those of the Bible itself. Nevertheless, DeMille's epic film reminded twentieth-century audiences that the book of Exodus (Hebrew: *Shemot*) tells more than the story of a single people, but portrays the timeless confrontation of life and death celebrated in the creation stories of all cultures. Here Amon Ra and Yahweh struggle for control of the Hebrews who work the land and bear the children. The book of Exodus tells the story of how Yahweh delivers the Hebrews from slavery, and tells the Hebrews how to live lives of gratitude for the freedom that land and children bring. "I am Yahweh, your divine patron, who brought you out of the land of Egypt, out of the house of slaves" (Exod 20:2) is the creed of ancient Israel.

The physical beginning and end of the book of Exodus (Exod 1:1—40:38) does not correspond with the literary beginning and end of the book, nor do changes in the geography of the action correspond with its most important literary divisions. There is a tradition of interpretation that divides the story at itinerary formulas like "the Israelites journeyed from Ramses to Succoth" (Exod 13:11), which separate the actions that take place in Egypt (Exod 1:7—13:16) from those that take place in the desert (Exod 13:17—18:27) and at the sacred mountain (Exod 19:1—40:38). Geography alone, however, seldom adequately determines the structure of biblical traditions. Artistically, the book of Exodus begins with a story of slaves who prosper (Exod 1:7-12) in the book of Exodus and ends with a land grant to slaves set free in the book of Numbers (Num 26:1—27:11). In the beginning, the Hebrews are slaves without land or children of their own in the old world of Egypt. At the end there are over six hundred free households, with land guaranteed to each in perpetuity. Not even the lack of a male heir is grounds for taking the land away from a household in this new world of Israel (27:1-11; Fig. 22).

Creation Stories
(EXOD 1:7—NUM 27:11)

The book of Exodus is best understood as a creation story. The language and structure characteristic of ancient Near Eastern creation stories is not limited to the hymn of Moses and Miriam (Exodus 15), but can be found throughout the Death of the First-born of Egypt (Exod 1:7—13:16) and the Creation of the Firstborn of Israel (Exod 13:17—Num 27:11). These creation stories of ancient Israel follow the same basic pattern as the Enuma Elish Stories about Marduk who delivers Babylon from Tiamat and Kingu, and the Stories of Ea and Enki who deliver the household of Gilgamesh from Enlil, and the Stories of Ba'al and Anat who deliver Ugarit from Yam and Nahar.

Death of the Firstborn of Egypt
(EXOD 1:7—13:16)

Yahweh, Moses, and Aaron are the protagonists in the Death of the Firstborn of Egypt. Amon Ra, Pharaoh, and the priests of Egypt are the antagonists. The crisis of the story is a long and involved apocalypse that decommissions the old world of Egypt by unmasking Pharaoh and revealing Egypt as a land of the dead.

> Yahweh said to Moses and to Eleazar, son of Aaron the priest, "Take a census of the Israelites, from twenty years old and upward, by households, everyone in Israel able to go to war" (Num 26:1). There were 601,730 warriors. . . . Then Yahweh said to Moses: "Divide the land among these warriors" (Num 26:51-53).
>
> Then the daughters of Zelophehad came forward. . . . They stood before Moses, Eleazar the priest, and all the elders and warriors at the entrance of the tent of meeting, and they said, "Why should the name of our father be taken away because he had no son? Give to us a possession among our father's brothers" (Num 27:1+4). Then Yahweh told Moses: "If the father of a household dies, and has no son, then you shall pass his inheritance on to his daughter. If he has no daughter, then. . . ." (Num 27:6+8-9).

FIGURE 22   Land Grant to Slaves Set Free (Num 26:1—27:11)

The crisis opens with a series of ancestor stories: Slaves Who Prosper, Two Shrewd Midwives, the Birth of Moses, and Moses in the Desert. In each story Pharaoh is disturbed by a population that is not just too large, but is "out of place." Therefore, Pharaoh conspires to destroy his Hebrew slaves. This displacement motif appears in other creation stories like the Flood Stories (Gen 6:1-4) and the Stories of Atrahasis in Mesopotamia, where the good idea of creating humans as slaves to maintain the cosmos sours when they become "many" (Exod 5:5), or "restless and noisy" (Atra 1:305), threatening revolt (Fig. 23).

Sterility Affidavit
(Exod 1:7—7:13)

Slaves Who Prosper
(Exod 1:7-12)

Tellers often framed a story by repeating the words with which the story began at the end of the story. The technique is called a frame or "chiasm" after the Greek letter *chi* which is printed X. The top shape of the letter is mirrored by its base shape just as the opening of a story is repeated at its closing. The Slaves Who Prosper (Exod 1:7-12) begins with the words: "the Israelites were fruitful and prolific; they multiplied and grew exceedingly" (Exod 1:7), and ends with almost the same words: "the more they were oppressed, the more they multiplied and spread" (Exod 1:12). When it begins, the slaves are fruitful and prolific, and when it ends they multiply and spread. Using words like "fruitful and prolific" in pairs is a technique called "hendiadys," which is a form of repetition or parallelism. The two words in these pairings do not express two different characteristics, but the same characteristic in two different ways. These words affirm that the conditions necessary for life are present. Peace is normal, while crisis, threatening the ability of a household to rear its children and farm its land, is not.

The protagonists in the story are slaves. Even though these slaves make the land of Egypt produce and even though they themselves reproduce, the land they work is the land of Pharaoh and the children they bear are the slaves of Pharaoh. Therefore, they have no land and they have no children. They are not fully human, not fully alive. Here, and in the two stories that follow, the protagonists are slave mothers who bear the children who threaten the pharaoh. This gender-specific task takes on political significance in the struggle for freedom. Birth is an implicitly female expression of divine power; therefore these women are not only protagonists, but also stand in for Yahweh, who does not appear in the story at all. Storytellers often disguise themselves as protagonists in their stories, so this story may have first been told by slave mothers.

I. *Crisis episodes* (Exod 1:7—12:28)

  A. Slaves Who Prosper (Exod 1:7-12a)

  B. Two Shrewd Midwives (Exod 1:12b-21)

  C. Jochebed Gives Birth to Moses (Exod 1:22—2:10), an apology for a collaborator

  D. Moses in the Desert (Exod 2:11-22), an apology for a fugitive

  E. Inauguration of Moses on Mt. Horeb (Exod 3:1—4:23)

  F. Labor of Moses and Zipporah against Yahweh (Exod 4:24-26)

  G. Labor of Moses against Pharaoh (Exod 4:27—6:1)

  H. Inauguration of Moses in Egypt (Exod 6:2—7:13)

II. *Cosmogony:* **Plagues Stories** (Exod 7:14—11:10)

III. *Covenant:* **Passover** (Exod 12:1—13:16)

FIGURE 23   Death of the Firstborn of Egypt (Exod 1:7—13:16)

Throughout the Death of the Firstborn of Egypt, the character of Yahweh is modeled, to some extent, on the character of Enki in the Stories of Atrahasis or on the character of Ea in the Stories of Gilgamesh. Like Ea and Enki, Yahweh is a friend to humans. Like Ea and Enki, Yahweh prevents the divine assembly from completely destroying humans with a flood, and like Ea and Enki, Yahweh requires the people to leave the land of their divine enemy.

Similarly, the character of Pharaoh is modeled on Enlil in the Stories of Atrahasis and in the Stories of Gilgamesh. Enlil and Pharaoh are both members of the divine assembly. They are both disturbed by their slaves, and both try a number of strategies to control them. Enlil tries plague, drought, and floods. The pharaoh tries slave labor, aborting male newborns, and exposing male infants on the banks of the Nile.

The Slaves Who Prosper, the Two Shrewd Midwives, and the Birth of Moses all show that the pharaoh's power to command has less and less effect in Egypt. Slave drivers do not obey his command to cripple the Hebrews with hard work. Midwives do not obey his command to abort the newborn. The wife of the Levite circumvents his command to expose her son on the banks of the Nile. This great and arrogant male,

Man Riding an Ass
(Syria 2000 B.C.E.; bronze 13 cm)

father of the land and father of the people in Egypt, is impotent. Here the land and its people belong to Yahweh, and not to Pharaoh. Ancestor stories are the legacy of the powerless, who use them to compensate for their lack of power. The New Kingdom

(1550–1070 B.C.E.) was ancient Egypt's high point. Nonetheless, Hebrew slaves caricature the pharaoh of the great New Kingdom in their ancestor stories.

The slave women in this story turn persecution into progress. Pharaoh does not control the population of his slaves. It hardens their resolve to survive by bearing children. Pharaoh defeats men in battle, but is conquered by women in labor. This reversal encourages the descendants of these slave women to use persecution to thrive. The Slaves Who Prosper also introduces a fertility motif. Throughout the book of Exodus, fertility is a blessing for the Hebrews, but a curse for their enemies like Egypt and Moab (Num 22:2—24:25).

Ancestor stories narrate only the essentials. The Slaves Who Prosper gives no details on the confrontation between the pharaoh and the slaves. It explains neither the threat of war nor the basis for the pharaoh's fear of treason among the slaves. The Egyptians treated all strangers like the Hyksos who swept out of Syria-Palestine and conquered Egypt in 1720 B.C.E. The nickname "Hyksos" carried the same connotations as "damn Yankees" during the reconstruction after the war between the states in the American South. The personal names of these Hyksos indicate they were culturally diverse, but were primarily Semitic people. After they conquered Egypt the Hyksos Pharaohs opened its borders and government to Semites like Joseph. In 1552 B.C.E. Kamose and Ahmose (1539–1514 B.C.E.), who were native-born Egyptians from the south, liberated Egypt. After this revolution, the social standing of all Semites rapidly deteriorated. More than one hundred years after the fall of the Hyksos, Pharaoh Hatshepsut (1478–1458 B.C.E.) can still vividly describe their oppression of Egypt, as can Manetho more than one thousand years later. The Slaves Who Prosper reflects Egypt's fear of strangers.

State slavery is not the draconian scheme of this one pharaoh. Monarchs throughout the world of the Bible had the authority to use villagers for public works. "Pharaoh" means the "builder of great houses." Pharaohs were obsessed with building. Obelisks, colossal statues, palaces, temples, and cities covered the land. The scale of their projects is staggering. One colossal statue of Ramses II (1279–1213 B.C.E.) is twenty-four feet seven inches high and weighs forty-seven tons. Quarries rang with the sound of picks and hammers hewing out blocks of granite, limestone, sandstone, and quartzite. Copper chisels, wooden mallets, and heavy hematite ball-hammers were used to pound out narrow trenches around all four sides of the stone and to drive wooden wedges beneath it. When wet, the wedges expanded and helped to crack the block from the stone below. Stones were measured with cubit sticks, squares, and plumb lines and finished with chisels, adzes, mallets, and sanding stones. Barges floated the blocks to building sites.

Two Shrewd Midwives
(EXOD 1:12-21)

A story of Two Shrewd Midwives (Exod 1:12-21) opens with the words: "the number of slaves continued to increase," and closes with words: "the number of slaves whose midwives were faithful to Yahweh continued to increase." Two crises threaten the Hebrews. One is the impossible task of making bricks and of farming at the same time. The other is the abortion of their male newborns. Like the Slaves Who Prosper and the Birth of Moses, this story teaches that the more the Egyptians oppress the Hebrews, the more they thrive, and it celebrates the contribution of midwives and mothers to the liberation of the Hebrews from slavery (Fig. 24).

The logical thing for Pharaoh to do was to kill the females who bear children. Killing males deprived him of his workforce. Ironically, Pharaoh spares females, who, with stories like the Two Shrewd Midwives and the Birth of Moses, teach slaves how to outsmart him.

The story also mocks Pharaoh as a fool gullible enough to believe the midwives' shrewdly worded report that "Hebrew women are different from Egyptian women. They are strong enough to birth their children before we arrive" (Exod 1:19). The audience knows, even if Pharaoh does not, that unaided childbirth is not a normal practice in any culture, no matter how strong its women may be. For the powerless, shrewdness is

The number of slaves continued to increase. The Egyptians, believing the Hebrews were a threat, began enslaving them to work on state construction projects and state farms. In fact, whenever the Egyptians needed slaves, they used the Hebrews. Finally, Pharaoh ordered Shiphrah and Puah, the Hebrew midwives: "Whenever you deliver Hebrew mothers, keep your eye on the birthing stool, and if the newborn is male, abort it; but if it is female, deliver it alive!"

The midwives, however, were people of Yahweh, so they disregarded Pharaoh's orders and delivered males alive.

Consequently, Pharaoh indicted the midwives for malpractice: "Why are you delivering males alive?"

In their defense, the midwives argued: "Hebrew women are different from Egyptian women. They are strong enough to birth their children before we arrive."

Therefore, Yahweh blessed the midwives. As a result, the number of slaves whose midwives were faithful to Yahweh continued to increase.

FIGURE 24   Story of Two Shrewd Midwives (Exod 1:12-21)

a survival skill. It is not a gender-specific virtue. The Bible celebrates the shrewdness of men like Abraham (Gen 12:9—13:1; 20:1-17) and Isaac (Gen 26:1-11) and women like these midwives. These women are strong in word, and the mothers are strong in deed. Slave midwives can outtalk Pharaoh, and slave mothers can outdeliver Egyptian mothers. Like the mothers in the previous story who do the divine work of bearing children, midwives also do the work of Yahweh.

Yahweh was sometimes described with metaphors that were male, and sometimes with metaphors that were female. The Bible portrays Yahweh as a mother or a midwife or a wet nurse. As mother, Yahweh labors to give birth to rain and sleet (Job 38:28-29), carries humanity in the womb (Deut 32:18; Num 11:12-13), labors to give birth to humanity (Deut 32:18; Isa 42:14), teaches humanity to walk (Hos 11:3-4), wipes humanity's tears when it cries (Isa 66:13-14). As midwife, Yahweh delivers the sea (Job 38:8), delivers Zion's child (Isa 66:9), bathes humanity (Ezek 36:25), clothes the sea (Job 38:8-9), clothes humanity (Gen 3:21; Job 10:10-12), places humanity in its mother's arms (Ps 22:9-10). As wet nurse, Yahweh rocks humanity (Hos 11:3-4; Isa 46:3-4), nurses humanity (Isa 49:15; Ps 34:9; Hos 11:4; 2 Esd 1:28-29), weans humanity from breast milk to solid food (Ps 131:1-2; Wis 16:20-21). These powerful female images for Yahweh are a profound part of the biblical heritage.

Midwives provided clinical services to women before conception, during pregnancy, during labor, and after delivery. Before conception midwives taught mothers-to-be how to care for themselves during menstruation and how to identify periods of fertility. During pregnancy they advised expectant mothers on proper nutrition and helped them deal with midterm traumas.

Paleolithic (25,000–10,000 B.C.E.) rock drawings from Europe and a Neolithic (8000–3800 B.C.E.) clay figurine from Çatal Hüyük, Turkey, which was a sister city to Jericho, show large-hipped women birthing children in squatting positions. Prehistoric mothers delivered children kneeling, squatting, sitting, or standing. They used stones as birthing stools to support their buttocks. When pregnancy comes to term in the Stories of Atrahasis, Nintu-Mami puts on her cap and apron and sets up a brick for a birthing stool (Atra 1:282). Moses puts Israel on trial with the words: "he abandoned Yahweh who made him, and scoffed at the rock of his salvation" (Deut 32:15). The metaphor may compare Yahweh with nature. Yahweh is the hills (Num 23:9) or a mountain. "Mountain" is also a title for Ba'al, the divine patron of Ugarit. The metaphor may compare Yahweh with architecture. Yahweh is the foundation for a building, a city or a fortress (Ps 144:1-10; 1 Sam 2:1-10). The metaphor may compare Yahweh with the rock that midwives use to support a mother in labor. So when Pharaoh orders the midwives to "keep your eye on the rock," he wants them to watch the birthing stool.

Because midwives performed such significant clinical and legal responsibilities, they were highly regarded not only by the parents they helped conceive, birth, and rear children, but by the whole village, which learned from observing how these women worked to better understand how Yahweh creates. Israel's gratitude to these women remains enshrined in the powerful midwife-metaphors that the Bible uses to describe the creation of the cosmos, the beginning of each new day, and the labor of the eschaton. Similarly, the creation of people primeval, the formation of states, the education of the young, the burial of the dead, the resurrection of the dead, child sacrifice, and the desecration of the dead are all modeled on the services of midwives. The Two Shrewd Midwives is part of this noble tradition.

The Birth of Moses
(EXOD 1:22—2:10)

The Stories of Moses (Exod 1:7—7:13) portray Moses rehearsing the major events through which he will subsequently lead the Hebrews. Moses goes into the Nile and is lifted up out of the Nile just as the Hebrews will go into the Red Sea and be lifted up out of it. He strikes down one Egyptian who was beating a Hebrew, just as Yahweh will strike down all the firstborn in Egypt. He goes into the desert and encounters Yahweh, just as the Hebrews will go into the desert and encounter Yahweh.

The Birth of Moses (Exod 1:22—2:10) opens with Pharaoh's decree to expose the Hebrews' newborn sons on the banks of the Nile and closes with the newborn Moses being drawn from the water. In the beginning of the story, the water is a tomb; at the end of the story, the water is a womb. With the help of women like the Levite's wife and Pharaoh's daughter, Yahweh plays the role of Ea Enki, the divine patron of fresh water in the Stories of Atrahasis. Enlil orders Ea Enki to drown all the humans, but Ea Enki teaches Atrahasis how to build a boat so that he and his household can survive.

The daughter of Pharaoh takes pity on the child she finds in the basket. She "spares" the newborn (1 Sam 15:3; 2 Sam 12:4+6; Isa 30:14; Lam 2:2; Jer 50:14; Job 20:13). She acts like Yahweh. She is compassionate (Hebrew: *hesed*). Justice treats others as they deserve. Compassion treats others as they do not deserve.

In birth stories the qualities for which heroes were known in their adult lives are often predicted in the extraordinary events that surrounded their births. The Birth of Moses shows that he was a miracle child destined by Yahweh from the very beginning of his life to fulfill a special role in Israel. Since, as an adult, Moses was the ancestor who led the Hebrews through the water, this story honors him for going into the water even as an infant. The waters of the Nile and the Red Sea are both primeval waters of chaos like Tiamat or Apsu in the Enuma Elish stories. Both Moses and the Hebrews are drawn out of these primeval waters.

The stories also defend Moses against criticism leveled against him in his own day and by Hebrews in later periods. The Birth of Moses explains that he escapes death not because he was a collaborator, but because his mother showed the same courage as the two shrewd midwives. The mother of Moses obeys the letter of the law and exposes her child on the banks of the Nile, while she carefully plans to prevent his death. The connotations of the verbs are carefully chosen. She does not abandon the child, she places him in a basket at a strategic location on the banks of the Nile. She fulfills the decree, while circumventing it.

The Birth of Moses is an apology. An apology is a variety of ancestor story that defends its protagonist against assumed, but unmentioned, criticism. The Birth of Moses assumes critics are attacking the household of Moses for being Egyptian sympathizers (Num 12:1-16; 14:1-12; 16:1-50), and therefore unfit to exercise authority in Israel. The objection is voiced by the slave who says to Moses: "Who made you ruler and judge over us?" (Exod 2:14). The household of Moses is accused of being soft on Egyptian imperialism because Moses was not a native, because Moses had an Egyptian name, and because Moses was reared in the household of Pharaoh. Like the names "Ah-moses" and "Ra-moses," the name "Moses" means a "child," "son," or "heir." "Ra-moses" is the son of Ra, but "Moses" is simply the "son," without a divine patron.

Sole survivors of tragedies often suffer a sense of guilt that they survived because of cowardice or collaboration with the enemy. Cultures compensate for this guilt by the use of birth stories in which a sole survivor is celebrated as someone who has died and been brought back to life for the sole purpose of doing a special task. So the story of the Birth of Moses admits that he did survive the massacre of the Hebrew children so that he could free the Hebrews from slavery; that he was reared in an Egyptian household to prepare him to negotiate with Pharaoh; and that he had a name that sounded patriotic to the Egyptians, and revolutionary to the Hebrews.

Moses in the Desert
(EXOD 2:11-22)

Like the Birth of Moses, the story of Moses in the Desert (Exod 2:11-22) is an ancestor story and an apology. It defends Moses and his household against criticism that they are all murderers and fugitives, who live like pharaohs while other Hebrews suffer as slaves. The story admits that Moses does kill an Egyptian, but only as a freedom fighter striking the first blow against the Egyptians. Yahweh will endorse Moses by killing "all the firstborn in the land of Egypt, from the firstborn of Pharaoh who sat on his throne to the firstborn of the prisoner in the dungeon, and the firstborn of the cattle" (Exod 12:29). What Henry Wadsworth Longfellow (1807–82), an American poet, did to reinterpret the shots fired by the colonial Minutemen on Concord bridge against British soldiers at the beginning of the War of Independence, this story does for Moses' killing of the Egyptian. It was the "shot heard 'round the world." The story also argues that Moses is not a fugitive from justice, but preparing for his mission as the deliverer of Israel. Moses is not hiding in Midian, but enduring "as a stranger in a strange land" (Exod 2:22), which is precisely the kind of suffering that the Hebrews experience as slaves in Egypt. The story describes his experience in Midian as a novitiate preparing Moses for the role he is to play. The desert tempers his anger, deepens his commitment, and purifies his will to set the Hebrews free.

The story argues that Moses was in Midian not as in flight to avoid prosecution, but to appeal for a change of venue for his trial (Deut 4:41-43; 19:1-13). He left Egypt and settled at The Well—Beer, Beer-Sheba, or Beer-lahai-roi. The people of a village come together wherever they draw water. Because young women draw water for their households, young men often go to the well to look at the young women eligible for marriage. Moses' courage, above and beyond the call of duty, in defending the daughters of Reuel demonstrates to the elders that he acted with similar virtue in defending the slave. The verdict of the assembly is ratified by the marriage of Moses and Zipporah. Zipporah is not only a wife, but also a witness that Moses is not guilty. The daughters of Reuel restore honor to the household of Moses.

The Levites who belong to the household of Moses may have been the clan that developed and told the Stories of Moses. They may have used these stories to describe how they understood their own leadership in Israel. Like Moses, who freed the slaves and created Israel, the Levites considered themselves the guardians of freedom and the custodians of the covenant in early Israel.

Inauguration of Moses at Mt. Horeb
(EXOD 2:23—4:23)

The Story of Slaves Who Prosper, the Story of Two Shrewd Midwives, the Story of the Birth of Moses, and the Story of Moses in the Desert each demonstrate that the decline and fall of Egypt has begun. The old world is ending, and a deliverer is chosen to look for survivors. The Enuma Elish Stories in Mesopotamia describe a similar sequence of events. There is a declaration of independence (Enuma 1:21-28), a meeting of the divine assembly (Enuma 1:29-54), and the inauguration of a deliverer (Enuma 1:55-76). The protagonist in the Inauguration of Moses is Yahweh, who recruits Moses to deliver the Hebrews and pioneer a new world (Exod 2:23—4:31). Moses is the antagonist whom Yahweh must convince to become a prophet.

Inauguration stories open with theophanies. Theophanies allow candidates to encounter Yahweh. Images of Yahweh were forbidden in ancient Israel (Deut 5:8-10). Theophanies reveal the presence of Yahweh without technically violating the prohibition. Candidates sense more than they actually see. When they do see something it is either the fire or lightning that is Yahweh's weapon, or the cloud of dust churned up by his war chariot, or an angel or messenger (Exod 3:2; Judg 13:6). Here a messenger appears to Moses (Exod 3:2) before Yahweh speaks (Exod 3:6).

Candidates respond to theophanies by investigating them. The burning bush attracts the attention of Moses, who then turns aside to look at the great sight (Exod 3:3). This first episode in the inauguration records Yahweh's successful contact with the candidate. The relationship between Yahweh and the candidate is like a game of tag. Yahweh is "it," and the candidate does not want to be caught. Yahweh ambushes the candidate with a lure such as the burning bush, which seems harmless enough and attracts the curiosity of the candidate. Once the candidate gets close enough, Yahweh tags him with the greeting. Yahweh usually addresses the candidate formally by calling his name twice. As Moses approaches the burning bush, Yahweh greets him with "Moses! Moses!"

Once he hears his name, Moses realizes he is in the presence of Yahweh, and responds to the greeting with the formula: "Here I am" (Exod 3:4). Like soldiers or students answering to their names in a roll call, candidates answer: "Present!" Their words are sometimes accompanied by a gesture of humiliation. Those who see Yahweh must remain forever in the presence of Yahweh by dying. Death here is not a punishment, but a passage from the human plane to the divine plane. Humans pass from one plane to the other only in birth and death. Through the womb from which they are born, and the tomb where they are buried, humans leave and return to the divine plane. The position in which both the fetus and the cadaver begin their journeys is fetal. In its mother's womb, a fetus tucks its knees against its chest, and in the graves of many Neolithic period cultures the bodies of the dead are arranged in the same position. Therefore, candidates often prostrate themselves on the earth with their chests tight against their knees, ready to leave the human plane for the divine. The fetal position is an ancient human gesture of humiliation or *kenosis*, and it is a prayer posture for Muslims today. The term *kenosis* is Greek for "emptying." Whether coming into the world or going out of the world, the proper posture for the journey is the fetal position. The *kenosis* demonstrates candidates' complete lack of ambition, and argues that the exercise of power by prophets in their communities is not the result of a selfish quest for power, but a response to a call from Yahweh.

With the formula "Fear not!" Yahweh postpones candidates' deaths, so that they can carry out a divine mission. When candidates prostrate, their human lives come to an end. When they stand and return to the human community to carry out a divine mission, they do so not simply as members of that community, but as prophets sent by the divine assembly. The inauguration of a prophet is a rite of passage. Sometimes, instead of using the fear-not formula, Yahweh simply teaches candidates how to act in the presence of the divine assembly. Here Yahweh instructs Moses to remove his sandals (Exod 3:5). Members of the divine assembly were holy. Holiness in the world of the Bible is like radioactivity. Both physically alter humans unless they take proper precautions, therefore, the community quarantines, ostracizes, or executes those whom, like Moses, the presence of Yahweh transforms. If candidates follow the protocol in which Yahweh instructs them, then they can return safely to the human community without threatening it with holiness.

When fathers of households entered a sanctuary, they covered their genitals (Exod 28:42) and they removed their sandals (Exod 3:5). Sandals were not only footwear, but also the uniform of landowners (1 Kgs 21:16-17). Buyers walked off their land in sandals, which then became the movable title to that land. Sandals were a symbol of power over land. Genitals were a symbol of power over children. No symbols of reproduction or land ownership were displayed before Yahweh, who alone blessed the Hebrews with land and children. Human parenthood and land ownership were only by proxy. Wearing sandals onto the holy ground of a sanctuary would be tantamount to challenging Yahweh.

Having greeted and briefed candidates, Yahweh then commissions them to carry out a divine mission. A command (Exod 3:8-10), decalogue (Deut 5:6-21), or covenant is the standard commission. Candidates respond to the commission by demurring. It would be arrogant for candidates to accept their commissions without first declining on the basis that they are not worthy to fulfill a divine task.

Yahweh responds to candidates' demurrals with a talisman. Talismans are offensive weapons. Amulets are defensive weapons that protect candidates from their enemies. This talisman serves as a passport certifying the validity of their mission, and as a weapon against their enemies. The talisman that Yahweh gives Moses is the promise: "I will be with you" (Exod 3:12). The mission is a divine mission, and it will be accomplished not by means of the talents and skills of Moses, but only by Yahweh.

Almost ignoring the talisman offered, Moses asks for a name. Yahweh refuses (Exod 3:13-14). Although the response "I am, who am" has been an incentive for generations of reflections, it was not originally meant to be a key to the nature of God as the source of being or the cause of all being. The response tells Moses nothing. "I am, who am" is a nonsense riddle like "name-smame." Outside the Bible, the name "Yahweh" appears on ostraca from Arad after 700–600 B.C.E. The place-name "Bet Yahweh" appears in Egyptian lists dated to Amenophis III (1417–1379 B.C.E.) and Ramses II (1304–1237 B.C.E.). Archaeologists have identified Bet Yahweh with Qurayyah, a site in Late Bronze period Midian, today found forty-five miles northwest of Tabuk, Saudi Arabia; fifteen miles westsouthwest of Bir Ibn Hirmas; and forty miles from Mudawwara, Jordan. A name is power. Those who give names or call names have power over those who answer to their names. Owners name their animals. Parents name their children. Many husbands still name their wives. Moses' request is inappropriate because if he knows the divine name, then he can call or control Yahweh. Thus, Yahweh's response simply continues Moses' protocol lesson. No human, not even a prophet, should ask for power over Yahweh.

Labor of Moses and Zipporah against Yahweh
(EXOD 4:24-26)

The Labor of Moses and Zipporah against Yahweh at the Wadi el-'Arish, which marked the frontier between Syria-Palestine and Egypt (Exod 4:24-26), is parallel to the Labor of Jacob against Yahweh at the Wadi Jabbok, which marked the frontier of Sihon (Gen 32:23-33). In both stories ancestors cross a threshold en route back to their people.

Yahweh is the guardian of the land that the ancestors seek to enter. The role of the guardian is not to kill the ancestors, but rather to test and prepare them for the challenges that lie ahead. The guardian is a coach, a trainer, or a teacher, not an enemy. Ancestors must demonstrate that they are worthy of the missions they have accepted. In the Labor of Moses and Zipporah, Yahweh meets the ancestors at the frontier of Egypt to prepare them for their labor against Pharaoh.

Pilgrims to the temple in Jerusalem also labored against Yahweh. As they climbed Mt. Moriah toward the sanctuary, priests would challenge them with questions (Psalms 15, 24). This labor was an examination of conscience that prepared pilgrims to enter the presence of Yahweh.

Labors also appear in children's stories like "Three Billy Goats Gruff." The guardian of the threshold, which is a bridge, is a troll. The smallest goat crosses the threshold by manipulating the troll's greed. "Why would you want to eat a goat as small as I am?" it asks. The same strategy wins passage for the medium-sized goat. When the largest goat arrives at the bridge, it is physically large enough to butt the troll off the bridge and into the canyon below.

To cross the threshold successfully, the ancestor must fool the guardian. It is Zipporah who fools Yahweh. To fool Yahweh into thinking that Moses is dead, Zipporah circumcises their son and smears Moses with the son's blood. Playing dead is sometimes an effective technique against a stronger enemy. Zipporah helps Moses feign death, and therefore they survive.

Like most of the Stories of Moses, the Labor of Moses and Zipporah against Yahweh is a rehearsal for one of the great works that Moses will do in delivering the people. She rehearses the same strategy that Moses will teach the Hebrews to use during the Death of the Firstborn. When Yahweh attacks the firstborn of Egypt, the Hebrews fool Yahweh into passing over them and their firstborn by slaughtering a lamb and smearing its blood on the doors (Exod 12:21-23). When firefighters today evacuate a burning building, they use a piece of chalk to mark the door of each room they have cleared with a "X." It tells other firefighters that the room is secure, and not to risk their lives searching it again. In antiquity, soldiers securing a village or city used the blood of their victims inside each house they searched to mark its door. The blood told other soldiers that the house was secure and to pass it by.

The household of Moses and Zipporah uses circumcision as enduring proof of their labor against Yahweh. Circumcision is one of several ways in which cultures alter or mutilate the human body. Besides cutting skin off the tip of the penis, humans also shave the hair from their bodies, pierce their earlobes, tattoo their skin, bind their feet, and stretch their necks and lips. These alterations are seen as necessary physical improvements that allow a child to become an adult. The changes are also regarded as sexually alluring or attractive. Likewise, ancestors carry permanent physical souvenirs of their labors. The child of Moses and Zipporah is marked by circumcision. Jacob is marked with a broken hip. The marks are not simply wounds of war, but, like the tattoo with which Yahweh marks Cain, they alert people to the character of those who bear them as survivors or "bridegrooms of blood" (Exod 4:26). The scars also raise the question, "How did that happen?" which allows the scarred to tell the story of the divine mission of their households.

Circumcision was standard in the Semitic cultures of the eastern Mediterranean, but not the Greek and Roman cultures of the west. Semitic and African cultures circumcise males to initiate into adulthood from puberty. Circumcision indicates that a boy has become a man and is now sexually active. The Hebrews circumcised infants as an indication that they were blessed by Yahweh with fertility from birth, not just from puberty. Western Mediterranean or Hellenistic cultures like the Greeks, Romans, and Philistines considered circumcision to be obscene. Eastern Mediterranean cultures like the Hebrews considered the "uncircumcised" to be women or children. Western Mediterranean cultures considered the human body to be an exquisite creation, which was to be diligently developed in the bath and gymnasium. It was a sacrilege to mutilate the human body. Hellenistic rulers of Syria-Palestine mounted a futile campaign after 200 B.C.E. to prevent the Jews from circumcising themselves.

Moses and Aaron Negotiate with Pharaoh
(EXOD 4:27—6:1)

Negotiations between Moses, Aaron, and Pharaoh open when Yahweh orders Pharaoh to let his Hebrews go. The challenge pits the authority of Yahweh against the authority of Pharaoh. Pharaoh has Yahweh's firstborn at work building sanctuaries at Pithom and Ramses. Moses orders Pharaoh to put them to work in the desert building a sanctuary for Yahweh.

Before the Plagues Stories were integrated into the stories of the Death of the First-born of Egypt, there may have been only the story of Moses and Aaron Negotiate with Pharaoh (Exod 4:27—5:5) and the story of the Egyptian Overseers Negotiate with Pharaoh (Exod 5:6—6:1). When neither negotiation was successful in emancipating the Hebrews, Yahweh put the firstborn of every household in Egypt to death (Exod 12:29-30). There were no plagues stories. Moses and Aaron Negotiate with Pharaoh and the Egyptian Overseers Negotiate with Pharaoh are now episodes in the crisis of the stories of the Death of the Firstborn of Egypt. The Plagues Stories are its climax.

Labor of Moses and Aaron against the Priests
(EXOD 6:2—7:13)

The Labor of Moses and Aaron against the Priests opens with an Inauguration of Moses parallel to the Inauguration of Moses on Mt. Horeb. Unlike the Inauguration of Moses on Mt. Horeb, however, this inauguration has only a commission episode. There is no lure, no greeting, and no demur. Yahweh commissions Moses to remind the Hebrews that Pharaoh is not their divine patron, and to indict Pharaoh for kidnapping the Hebrews and forcing them to work in Egypt. The second commission is repeated.

Moses protests Yahweh's commission: "I am a poor speaker; why would Pharaoh listen to me?" (Exod 6:10+30). Moses does not have a speech impediment. His demurral means that he is unworthy to speak a divine word. The word of the divine assembly was a decree that set into motion the end of one world and the creation of another. Any inappropriate use of such a divine word produced disastrous results.

Traditional cultures consider the use of unlimited power a measure of the honor or shame of a household. In some cultures candidates are given three wishes to test their virtue. Honorable households use their wishes or divine words to do good, shameful households to do evil. Three general types of fools appear in these stories. In anger a husband makes two foolish wishes, and then must make a wise wish to return the life of his household to normal. The demurral of Moses acknowledges how difficult it is for any human being to wield divine power, for a human being to speak a divine word. Yahweh counters by assigning Aaron to care for the word. Since the use of the divine word would now require that both Moses and Aaron agree on its use, chance of misuse is reduced.

In addition to Aaron as a helper, Yahweh gives Moses another talisman. Both Yahweh and Pharaoh arm their heroes with staffs, arrows, or lightning bolts, which are phallic symbols of male power (Gen 19:11). Yahweh arms Moses with a snake staff (Exod 4:1-5), with healing (Exod 4:6-9), and with a word to be carried by Aaron (Exod 4:10-17). Moses' snake staff is a counterpart to the *uraeus*-snake that pharaohs wear around their heads like a crown.

The Inauguration of Moses is followed by a miracle story (Exod 7:8-13). A parallel miracle story appears in the books of Samuel-Kings (1 Kgs 12:33—13:10). A miracle story is a duel between a prophet and a king that challenges the ability of rulers to protect and provide for the people and the land. Both stories open with some "pregame" coverage in the crisis episode. Here storytellers describe Yahweh as a coach reviewing strategy with his team. A "play-by-play commentary" makes up the climax episode in which there are two rounds. Moses and Aaron lead off both rounds. The first round is a tie. Yahweh's team changes its staff into a snake and Pharaoh's team changes its staff into a snake. Pharaoh's team forfeits the second round. Yahweh's team uses its snake to swallow the snake of Pharaoh's team. Snake handlers in Egypt paralyze a particular species of cobra by applying pressure just below the head. The cobra becomes rigid as a stick, but when it is thrown on the ground it recovers and is ready to strike. The denouement episode of a miracle story scores the contestants in the duel between Moses, Aaron, and Pharaoh; the results are contested and Pharaoh refuses to free his slaves.

The combination of word and work, which Moses and Aaron use against the priests of Egypt, is also characteristic of how prophets confront monarchs in Israel. Prophetic works like those of Moses and Aaron have been described as both miracle and magic. Miracle and magic are both uses of divine power. One term does not describe one kind of power, and the other another kind of power. Describing a prophet's use of power as miracle or magic identifies the tellers of a story, not the power which a protagonist wields. Prophets are miracle workers for the powerless whom they deliver from slavery, but they are magicians for the powerful whom they indict for enslaving their people. To the Hebrews, Moses and Aaron are miracle workers, while to Pharaoh they are magicians. Technically, prophetic works are better described as pantomimes that set in motion the decommissioning of old worlds and the creation of new worlds.

Cosmogony: Plagues Stories
(EXOD 7:14—13:10)

The Plagues Stories demonstrate the sterility of the old world that the pharaohs built. They are a parody or satire that ridicules Egypt and its traditions by treating them flippantly and by telling the creation stories of Egypt in an inappropriate and trivial manner. They contrast the Egypt of the pharaohs with the world of Yahweh. In the Stories of the Heavens and the Earth (Gen 1:1—2:3) the world of Yahweh is orderly and its creatures are noble. The firstborn of this world plant the land and populate it with children. In the Plagues Stories the world of the pharaohs is disorderly and polluted with ignoble creatures. In the Stories of the Heavens and the Earth Yahweh hangs a light and then creates a world. In the Plagues Stories Yahweh decommissions the world of Egypt and then turns out the light. Pharaoh's firstborn are stillborn.

In the Egypt that the pharaohs create, fertility is a curse. In the Israel that Yahweh creates, fertility is a blessing. The plagues do not destroy Egypt, but simply dramatize that its fertility is superficial. They demonstrate that the fertility of Egypt only plagues the cosmos with creatures that are out of place. They portray Egypt as destroying life rather than supporting it. Egypt is a house of slaves and a land of death. The Nile River brings not only the life-giving organisms and minerals to the plants and animals of Egypt, but deadly red clay from landslides upriver as well. Swamp frogs not only control the populations of insects like gnats and flies, but attract these germ-bearers to animals and humans as well. Livestock not only enriches the diet of humans and lightens their work, but infects them with hoof-and-mouth disease. Rain not only causes the crops to grow, but the locusts to migrate. The same principle of fertility that creates the world of the pharaohs also destroys it.

To understand the Plagues Stories it is necessary to understand something of both the technology and the traditions of Egypt. The creatures in the plagues are caricatures of the great households of Egypt and their totems. Totems are the animal ancestors who give birth to humans and then protect and befriend them. The Nile is the totem of the household of Hapy. The sun is the totem of the household of Ra. The bull is the totem of the household of Apis. Plagues shame these great households. The Nile and its canals, which were the pride of Egypt, are satirized as a sewer that pollutes the fields and infects the villages. The cattle bred by temple ranchers and the great Apis bull are scorned as carriers of the hoof-and-mouth disease that decimates Egypt's population.

One pattern proposed for the Plagues Stories divides them into ten episodes with one plague in each episode. There are plagues (1) of water pollution, (2) of frogs, (3) of mosquitoes, (4) of flies, (5) of hoof-and-mouth disease, (6) of boils, (7) of hail, (8) of locusts, (9) of darkness, and finally, (10) of sudden infant death. This popular pattern of ten is understood as having developed from earlier stories with patterns of eight, seven, three, one, or no plagues at all.

Other patterns proposed for the Plagues Stories divide them into three episodes on the basis of the weapons that Moses and Aaron use against Egypt. The Enuma Elish Stories from Mesopotamia arm Marduk from a vast arsenal. He wields snakes (Enuma 1:134), spells (Enuma 1:161), scepters (Enuma 4:29), arrows (Enuma 4:35-40), or winds (Enuma 4:47-49). Moses and Aaron wield divine power simply by stretching out their hands (Exod 9:15, 22, 29, 33; 10:21-22) or use a staff called the "finger of God" (Exod 7:15-20; 8:1-15; 10:12-13). Sometimes, Moses and Aaron throw soot into the air to bring on the plague of darkness (Exod 9:8).

The pattern used here for the Plagues Stories is based on the pattern in the Stories of the Heavens and the Earth (Fig. 25). The intention of both creation stories is to demonstrate that Yahweh alone destroys chaos and creates cosmos. Creation-story language appears throughout the Plagues Stories. The divine title "Yahweh, our Creator"

Day one: Nile and Canals (Exod 7:14-24 :: Water Below and Water Above (Gen 1:6-8)

Day two: Frogs and Mosquitoes (Exod 7:25—8:3) :: Fish and Birds (Gen 1:20-23)

Day three: Cattle and Humans (Exod 9:1-12 :: Cattle and Humans (Gen 1:24-31)

Day four: Grain and Dates (Exod 9:13—10:20) :: Earth and Sea (Gen 1:9-13)

Day five: Darkness and Light (Exod 10:21-29) :: Light and Darkness (Gen 1:3-5)

Day six: Firstborn and Heirs (Exod 11:1-10+12:29-32) :: Male and Female (Gen 1:26-31)

Day seven: Passover (Exod 12:1—13:16) :: Sabbath (Gen 2:1-4)

FIGURE 25   Seven-Day Pattern in Plagues Stories
(:: comparison)

(Exod 9:30) rarely occurs in the Bible, except in the Stories of the Heavens and the Earth and here. Furthermore, the events of each day are labeled as works of creation—"signs" (Exod 4:21; 7:3, 21) and "wonders" (Exod 4:21).

The centerpiece of the Stories of the Heavens and the Earth is a cosmogony (Gen 1:3-31) of six days on which noble twins like light and darkness (Gen 1:3-5) are born. On the seventh day, Yahweh endows this new world with the gift of Sabbath. Similarly, the centerpiece of the Plagues Stories is also a cosmogony of six days on which ignoble twins like the Nile and its canals (Exod 7:14-24 :: Gen 1:6-8) are born. On the seventh day, Yahweh endows this new world with the gift of Passover. Virtually the same twins are paired in both stories, but their birth order is different. The Nile and its canals (Exod 7:14-24) are followed by frogs and mosquitoes (Exod 7:25—8:28), cattle and humans (Exod 9:1-12), fields of grain and date palms (Exod 9:13—10:20), darkness and light (Exod 10:21-28), and then the firstborn and heirs (Exod 11:1-10). Just as the Stories of the Heavens and the Earth lead up to the seventh day with two three-day episodes, the Plagues Stories lead up to the final plague with two three-plague episodes.

On the six days, the old world of Egypt is decommissioned, and on the seventh day Passover is celebrated. The gnats (Exod 8:16-19) and the flies (Exod 8:20-32) are a pair. The plague upon cattle (Exod 9:1-7) and the boils (Exod 9:8-12) are a pair. The locusts (Exod 10:1-20) and the darkness (Exod 10:21-29) are a pair. The Nile and the canals (Exod 7:14-24) are parallel to the waters under and above (Gen 1:6-8). The frogs and mosquitoes (Exod 7:25—8:28) are parallel to the water creatures and birds (Gen 1:20-33). The cattle and humans in the book of Exodus (Exod 9:1-12) are parallel to the cattle and humans in the book of Genesis (Gen 1:24-31). The fields of grain and date palms (Exod 9:13—10:20) are parallel to the earth and sea (Gen 1:9-13). The darkness and light in the book of Exodus (Exod 10:21-28) are parallel to the light and darkness in the book of Genesis (Gen 1:3-5) and the firstborn and heirs (Exod 11:1-10) are parallel to the man and the woman (Gen 1:26-31).

The frogs-mosquitoes (Exod 7:25—8:28), darkness-light (Exod 10:21-28), and firstborn-heirs (Exod 11:1-10) twins remain the same whether the climax episode in the stories of the Death of the Firstborn of Egypt (Exod 7:14—10:29) is a story about ten plagues or seven days. The rest of the twins, however, are replaced by their victims in the Plagues Stories in the Bible today. For example, the Nile and its canals replace blood (Exod 7:14-24).

Cattle appear twice in the Plagues Stories (Exod 9:1-7, 13-34). The twins in one episode are cattle and humans, in the other they are fields of grain and date palms, which preserves both the seven-day pattern and the parallel to two sets of twins in the Stories of the Heavens and the Earth.

The greater and lesser lights in the Stories of the Heavens and the Earth (Gen 1:14-19) are missing in the Plagues Stories. The sun and the moon were such popular members of the divine assembly that the Stories of the Heavens and the Earth includes them, but does not refer to them by their liturgical titles: "The Sun" and "The Moon." The same reticence may have led the Plagues Stories to omit them altogether and replace them with Passover, which is a moon feast.

Technically, the entry for the firstborn and heirs (Exod 11:1-10) is a death certificate or a death sentence. The firstborn and heirs are stillborn. Although the certificate refers only to "firstborn," the parallel: "firstborn" (Exod 4:22-23) and "son" appears elsewhere in the Plagues Stories. "Firstborn" is regularly used by itself without "son." There are only six exceptions (Gen 27:32; Exod 4:22-23; Deut 2:15; 1 Sam 8:2; 1 Chr 8:30; 9:36). Nonetheless, the parallelism is at least implied here and would strengthen the connection between the Birth of Moses where Pharaoh drowns the firstborn and heirs of Yahweh in the Nile and here where Yahweh executes the firstborn and heirs of Egypt.

Covenant: Passover
(EXOD 12:1—13:16)

The denouement of the Death of the Firstborn of Egypt (Exod 12:1—13:16) is short, because it is elaborated by the Creation of the Firstborn of Israel. In the denouement,

Yahweh lays claim to the Hebrews who are to acknowledge Yahweh, and not Pharaoh, as their divine patron. Therefore, in the covenant with which the Death of the Firstborn ends, Pharaoh transfers the Hebrews from his jurisdiction to Yahweh's jurisdiction.

Immediately, Yahweh begins to shape the new world inaugurated when Moses was sent to lead the Hebrews out of the chaos of Egypt. As a down payment on the fertility of this new world, Yahweh sends them out of Egypt with food in their stomachs, clothes on their backs, and rings on their fingers. Yahweh also endows the Hebrews with the skill to make bread (Exod 12:33-34). Yahweh similarly endows Adam and Eve, and Abraham and Sarah (Gen 12:9—13:4) before their exodus. Just as the Stories of the Heavens and the Earth end with the endowment of Sabbath, the Death of the Firstborn of Egypt ends with the endowment of Passover. Sabbath and Passover both teach the Hebrews how to acknowledge Yahweh as their divine patron.

Passover and the Feast of Unleavened Bread were originally celebrated separately. At Passover, shepherds butchered and ate the first lambs born during the grazing season. At the Feast of Unleavened Bread, farmers baked the first grain from the harvest. Eating the firstfruits of the herd and field acknowledged that these were divine gifts, and not human wages. It also demonstrated the confidence of the farmers and herders that Yahweh would continue to bless them with herds and harvests, so the households did not have to hoard the firstfruits as a hedge against famine.

Creation of the Firstborn of Israel
(Exod 13:17—Num 27:11)

The Death of the Firstborn of Egypt and the Creation of the Firstborn of Israel are companion stories. The first uses the Plagues Stories to elaborate Yahweh's work in the decommissioning of the old world of Egypt. The second uses a Covenant between Yahweh and Israel to elaborate Yahweh's work in commissioning the new world of Israel.

Sterility Affidavit
(Exod 13:17—14:20)

The Creation of the Firstborn of Israel begins when Pharaoh sets out in hot pursuit of the fleeing Hebrews (Exod 13:17—14:18). As they do at the beginning of the Death of the Firstborn of Egypt, the Hebrews cry out to Yahweh, who inaugurates Moses to deliver them (Fig. 26).

I. *Sterility Affidavit* (Exod 13:17—14:20)

II. *Cosmogony* (Exod 14:21-31)

    A. Hebrews Escape through the Red Sea (Exod 14:21-25)

    B. Egyptians Drown in the Red Sea (Exod 14:26-31)

III. *Covenant* (Exod 15:1—Num 27:11)

    A. endowment: music (Exod 15:1-21)

    B. endowment: living water (Exod 15:22-27+17:1-7)

    C. endowment: manna (Exod 16:1-35)

    D. endowment: no foreign aggression (Exod 17:8-15)

    E. endowment: no domestic turmoil (Exod 18:1—Num 27:11)

       1. Law (Exod 18:1-27)

       2. Covenant between Yahweh and Israel (Exod 19:1—Lev 27:34)

          a. Credentials (Exod 19:1—20:2)

          b. Story (Exod 20:2b)

          c. Stipulations (Exod 20:3—23:19)

             (1) Decalogue (Exod 20:3-17)

             (2) Covenant Code (Exod 20:24—23:33)

          d. List of Witnesses (Exod 24:1-8)

          e. Promulgation and Documentation (Exod 24:9—Lev 27:34)

          f. Litany of Blessings and Curses (Num 1:1—27:11)

FIGURE 26   Patterns in the Creation of the Firstborn of Israel
(Exod 13:17—Num 27:11)

Cosmogony

(EXOD 14:21-31)

The Creation of the Firstborn of Israel comes to a climax in a great battle in which Pharaoh and the sea are defeated by Yahweh and the east wind (Exod 14:19-31). There are actually two different accounts of the battle. In one account, Yahweh uses the east wind to cut the Red Sea in two, creating a highway of dry land through it on which the Hebrews escape (Exod 14:21-25). Frightened by this great work, Pharaoh orders the chariots of Egypt to withdraw: "Let us flee from the Israelites, for Yahweh is fighting for them against Egypt" (Exod 14:25). In the other, Yahweh hides the Hebrews with a cloud on the shore of the Red Sea (Exod 14:19-20). Pharaoh assumes that they have crossed the sea, and orders his chariots into barges to pursue them. As the Hebrews watch, Yahweh uses the east wind to capsize the barges and drown Pharaoh in the Red Sea (Exod 14:26-31).

The weapons that Moses uses against the Red Sea are similar to the weapons that Marduk uses against Tiamat in the Enuma Elish Stories. Marduk waits until the water monster of chaos opens its mouth to roar and then inflates it with his wind weapon. When Tiamat is completely distended, Marduk punctures the monster with an arrow, and the pressure tears it to pieces. Moses uses both his staff, which is a spear or arrow (Exod 14:10), and the wind (Exod 15:8) to cut the Red Sea in two and deliver the Hebrews. This classic strategy for destroying a water monster also appears in Steven Spielberg's 1975 movie *Jaws*. When the great shark rams the boat of its hunters, they shove an oxygen tank into the shark's mouth and then detonate the tank with rifle shot. The explosion blows the great shark to pieces.

Covenant
(EXOD 15:1 — NUM 27:11)

The denouement of the Creation of the Firstborn of Israel constructs a new world that is full of singing (Exod 15:1-19) and tambourine playing (Exod 15:20-21), not mourning (Exod 12:30). In this new world, the Hebrews drink living spring water (Exod 15:22-27+17:1-7), not stagnant water from the canals of Egypt. They eat the manna that Yahweh effortlessly prepares (Exod 15:28—16:36), and not bread worked laboriously from the soil of Egypt.

The firstborn of Israel will not be destroyed by enemies who attack them (Exod 17:8-15), because Yahweh will lift up heroes like Moses and Aaron to deliver them. The firstborn of Israel will not be destroyed by domestic turmoil, because Moses appoints elders (Exod 18:1-27) to resolve disputes between households (Exod 19:1—24:17). In this new world Yahweh dwells alongside the Hebrews in a splendid sanctuary (Exod 25:1—Num 27:11).

Covenant between Yahweh and Israel
(EXOD 19:1 — 24:18)

Ur-nammu (2050–1950 B.C.E.) authorized the publication of a law code that is still the oldest recovered by archaeologists. The code and the cuneiform language in which it was written were the most important subjects studied by candidates for state jobs in

Sumer. They wrote out, again and again, the technical terms and phrases from the code, which would appear in their examinations. The code reflects a tradition of jurisprudence or court practice whose standards were followed by many Bronze Age cultures. The Code of Hammurabi (1792–1750 B.C.E.), the Hittite Code (1450–1200 B.C.E.), and the Middle Assyrian Code (1115–1027 B.C.E.) all reflect the principles and practice in the Code of Ur-nammu. The continuity in this legal tradition is explicitly acknowledged in the Hittite code, which inserts "formerly" at the beginning of each precedent from the code of Ur-nammu before introducing its revision with the words "but now."

Covenant stipulations were set down in a pattern called "case law." Standard case laws have two parts. There is a dependent clause and a main clause. The dependent clause is introduced by the conjunction "if" or "when" and describes a situation. The Code of Hammurabi stipulates: "If one citizen charges another with murder, without the evidence to prove it" (CH art. 1). Likewise, the book of Exodus stipulates: "When you purchase a Hebrew slave" (Exod 21:1). Both are dependent clauses. The main clause is introduced by the adverb "then" and imposes a sentence or mandates a procedure to resolve the grievance. Again, the Code of Hammurabi stipulates: "then the plaintiff is to be sentenced to death" (CH art. 1). The book of Exodus stipulates: "he is to serve you for no more than six years, but in the seventh year he shall be given his freedom without cost" (Exod 21:1). Both are main clauses.

The stipulations in the Code of Ur-nammu reflect uniform principles of justice. They also divide society into distinct social-economic groups such as citizens, priests, widows, orphans, and slaves. The law deals comparably with the members of each group. Likewise, the Code of Ur-nammu develops standards for each social institution such as the standardization of weights and measures for merchants.

Sentencing in the Code of Ur-nammu preferred restitution paid to the victim in preference to punishment inflicted on the criminal. The Hittite Code further refines this aspect of the tradition by commuting death sentences to corporal punishment, and sentences of corporal punishment to fines. The covenant between Yahweh and Israel also uses the principle of talion or retaliation, which tailors the punishment to the crime. "Talion" is from a Latin word *talis* meaning "just as." Hence the sentence should be "just as" or "fit" the crime.

The Hittites, who lived in what is today central Turkey during the Late Bronze period, developed the covenant pattern of negotiating. The intention of a covenant is to identify clearly the responsibilities that the negotiators have toward one another so that they can live in peace. Other cultures, like Egypt and early Israel, adapted the genre to their own needs. There are examples of covenants in the stories of Abraham and Sarah in the book of Genesis, but the most outstanding example in the Bible is the covenant between Yahweh and Israel in the book of Exodus (Exod 19:1—24:18).

Standard Hittite treaties have at least six components. The credentials of each partner to the covenant are listed, and a new and official story of the peoples affected by
the covenant is told. The covenant then lays out the stipulations governing this new
relationship. It closes with a list of witnesses, a litany of curses for covenant violations,
and blessings for covenant compliance. Finally, there are provisions to record and promulgate the covenant.

There are two types of covenants, parity covenants and vassal or suzerainty
covenants. In parity covenants the partners are peers. In vassal covenants one partner
is superior to the others. Superior partners or patrons are addressed as "suzerains," "sov-
ereigns," or "lords." Inferior partners or clients are addressed as "colonies," "servants,"
"slaves," or "vassals."

Credentials
(Exod 19:3—20:2)

The simplest form of credential for Yahweh is: "I am Yahweh, your divine patron" (Exod
20:2). In the covenant between Yahweh and Israel (Exod 19:3—20:2), Yahweh begins:
"I am the Old One on the Mountain" (Exod 19:3-8). "I am the Sky Father" (Exod 19:9-
15). "I am the Thunder Roller and the Lightning Chucker" (Exod 19:16-17). "I am the
Volcano Stoker" (Exod 19:18-25). "I am Yahweh, your Creator " (Exod 20:1-2; Fig. 27).

"The Old One" best preserves Yahweh's title as creator. Virtually the same title
appears in some Native American traditions. This motif of the creator as "old" appears
in English as "my old man" or "my old lady." These titles are not originally derogatory,
but identify the speaker's parent or creator.

The cloud descending on the mountain identifies Yahweh as the Sky Father. The
Sky Father is one of the two original world parents in the creation stories of the Zuni,
Pima, Mohave, and Yuma peoples. Their stories address the earth as "Mother" and the
sky as "Father." In the beginning, earth and sky were joined together. Slowly sky was
pushed up to make room for humans to live on the earth. Similarly, Moses encounters
Yahweh at a cosmic hinge where the world of the Earth Mountain Mother and Sky Father
are joined.

Yahweh is also introduced to Israel with the title "your El," which abbreviates "I am
the creator or divine patron of your ancestors, the divine patron of Abraham, the divine
patron of Isaac, and the divine patron of Jacob" (Exod 3:6).

I. Credentials (Exod 19:1—20:2)

   A. Old One on the Mountain (Exod 19:3-8)

   B. Sky Parent (Exod 19:9-15)

   C. Thunder Roller, Lightning Chucker (Exod 19:16-17)

   D. Volcano Stoker (Exod 19:18-25)

   E. Yahweh (Exod 20:1-2)

II. Story (Exod 20:2b)

III. Stipulations (Exod 20:3—23:19)

   A. Decalogue (Exod 20:3-17)
     1. stipulation (Exod 20:3)
     2. stipulation (Exod 20:4-6)
     3. stipulation (Exod 20:7)
     4. stipulation (Exod 20:8-11)
     5. stipulation (Exod 20:12)
     6. stipulation (Exod 20:13)
     7. stipulation (Exod 20:14)
     8. stipulation (Exod 20:15)
     9. stipulation (Exod 20:16)
    10. stipulation (Exod 20:17)

   B. Covenant Code (Exod 20:18—23:33)

IV. List of Witnesses (Exod 24:1-8)

V. Promulgation and Documentation (Exod 24:9—Lev. 27:34)

   A. ratification of covenant (Exod 24:9-18)

   B. erection of a sanctuary (Exod 25:1—40:38)

   C. schedule for sacrifices (Lev 1:1—7:37)

   D. personnel (Lev 8:1—21:24)
     1. ordination of priests (Lev 8:1—10:20)
     2. honor and shame stipulations (Lev 11:1—16:34)

(continued)

3. holiness code (Lev 17:1—26:46)
4. schedule for offerings (Lev 27:1-34)

VI. Litany of Blessings and Curses (Num 1:1—27:11)

  A. Blessing (Children) (Num 1:1—22:1)
    1. Military Census (Num 1:19-46)
    2. Teaching on Jealousy and Adultery (Num 5:11-21)
    3. Obituary for Aaron

  B. Blessing (Land) (Num 21:1—27:11)
    1. Stories of Balaam (Num 21:1—24:25)
    2. Trial of Zimri (Num 25:1-18)
    3. Land Grant to Slaves Set Free (Num 26:1—27:11)

FIGURE 27   Patterns in a Covenant between Yahweh and Israel
(Exod 19:1—Lev 27:34)

Story
(EXOD 20:2)

In vassal covenants, the story describes what patrons have done for their clients and how they have blessed them. The story in the Covenant between Yahweh and Israel is simply the exodus formula: "who brought you out of the land of Egypt, out of the house of slaves" (Exod 20:2). This formula abbreviates the story of the Death of the Firstborn of Egypt. Yahweh's fundamental blessing of the Hebrews is having delivered them from slavery. The covenant reestablishes the proper relationship between Yahweh and Israel, which had been broken when the Hebrews became slaves of Pharaoh, who has done nothing for them.

Stipulations
(EXOD 20:3—23:19)

After describing what patrons have done for their clients, covenants stipulate what clients will do for their patrons. By obeying the stipulations clients show gratitude to their patrons for the blessings that they receive.

When the stipulations are many and complex, as they are in the covenant between Yahweh and Israel, a decalogue often introduces and summarizes the list (Exod 20:3-17). Decalogues are manuals or handbooks with ten or twelve stipulations. Each stipulation is either a command or a prohibition.

The first stipulation in the decalogue that introduces the covenant between Yahweh and Israel is a prohibition: "you shall have no other divine patrons before me" (Exod 20:3). This prohibition summarizes the argument made by the Death of the Firstborn of Egypt. Yahweh, and not Pharaoh, is the divine patron of the Hebrews. Monotheism as it is taught by Jews, Christians, and Muslims today argues that only one God exists. This prohibition affirms that the Hebrews have only one God.

Some rabbinic traditions of interpretation divided the stipulations in the covenant into two sets. The five that mentioned the name of Yahweh addressed the relationship between humans and God. The other five addressed the relationship of human beings with one another. Similarly, some Christian traditions also divide the stipulations into two sets, but consider three or four stipulations to deal with the relationship of humans to God and six or seven to the relationship of human beings with one another.

Not all Christians number the stipulations in the decalogue in the same way. Like Augustine (354–430), an influential African bishop and teacher, some combine the prohibition: "You shall have no other gods but me" (Exod 20:3) with the prohibition: "You shall not make statues in the form of anything that is in heaven above, or that is on the earth beneath, or that is in the water under the earth" (Exod 20:4-6) to create their first commandment. For others their first commandment is: "you shall have no other divine patrons but me" (Exod 20:3). Their second commandment begins, "you shall not make statues in the form of anything" (Exod 20:4-6). All Christians have only ten commandments. Again following Augustine, some separate the prohibition: "you shall not covet your neighbor's house" (Exod 20:17) from the prohibition: "you shall not covet your neighbor's wife" (Exod 20:17) to create their ninth and tenth commandments. One way of counting the commandments reflects the tradition in the book of Exodus, while the other reflects the tradition in the book of Deuteronomy (Deut 5:21).

The second stipulation in the decalogue is the prohibition: "you shall not make statues in the form of anything that is in heaven above, or that is on the earth beneath, or that is in the water under the earth. You shall not bow down to them or worship them; for I, Yahweh, your divine patron, am jealous, punishing descendants for the iniquity of their ancestors, to the third and the fourth generation of those who reject me, but showing steadfast love to the thousandth generation of those who love me and keep my commandments" (Exod 20:4-6). This prohibition outlaws statues of Yahweh. Statues were an essential piece of liturgical furniture throughout the world of the Bible. The cultures of Egypt, Syria-Palestine, and Mesopotamia all used statues. The Hebrews did not. Virtually no culture, ancient or existing, considers its statues to be divine. These images are theophanies or sacraments of the divine patrons of the peoples who are their clients. In antiquity, people express their devotion for their divine patrons by caring for their statues. They wake them, bathe them, dress them, feed them, take them out of their sanctuaries to visit their land and their people.

Some cultures, like ancient Israel, are iconoclastic and consider statues to be inappropriate. The Hebrews outlawed statues because they considered them to be a human attempt to control the divine. Anything that could be drawn or sculpted could be controlled. Yahweh feeds and protects the Hebrews. The Hebrews do not feed and protect Yahweh. The Hebrews prohibited statues of Yahweh to emphasize that they had absolutely no control over their divine patron. For the Hebrews, Yahweh was absolutely free of human control. They did not force Yahweh to deliver them from slavery. They did not force Yahweh to bless them with land and children. To emphasize that their land and children were gratuitous acts of kindness, they remembered Yahweh with stories, not with statues. Yahweh appeared among the Hebrews in the telling, not in sculpting.

The third stipulation in the decalogue is the prohibition: "you shall not perjure the name of Yahweh, your divine patron, for Yahweh will not acquit anyone who misuses the name" (Exod 20:7). The prohibition forbids the misrepresentation of the economic resources of a household, not vulgarity. In English, vulgarity is rude, and a dangerous form of verbal violence. The languages of the densely populated lands of China and Japan long ago deleted vulgarity in order to reduce the physical violence that verbal violence often initiates. Hebrew was the language of a sparsely populated land. It never addressed the use of vulgarity. The Hebrews were an oral culture whose word was law. When cultures negotiated covenants they called on each of the members of their divine assemblies to serve as witnesses that they were ready, willing, and able to fulfill the stipulations. Calling upon Yahweh to witness a covenant that a household was unable or unwilling to keep perjured the name of Yahweh. The Hebrews did not lie to one another because Yahweh did not lie to them.

The fourth stipulation in the decalogue is a commandment: "remember the Sabbath day, and keep it holy. Six days you shall labor and do all your work. But the seventh day is a Sabbath to Yahweh, your divine patron. You shall not do any work—you, your son or your daughter, your male or female slave, your livestock, or the strangers living in your villages. For in six days Yahweh made heaven and earth, the sea, and all that is in them, but rested the seventh day; therefore Yahweh blessed the Sabbath day and set it apart" (Exod 20:8-11). Technically there are only two commandments in the decalogue: "remember the Sabbath" (Exod 20:8-11) and "honor your father and mother" (Exod 20:12). Commands are stipulations to do something. Prohibitions are stipulations not to do something. Commands are not a morally superior legal genre to prohibitions. The two genres are parallel. The Sabbath is a day to remember. In their own villages and states, the Hebrews observed Sabbath as a day on which to tell the Stories of the

Heavens and the Earth in the book of Genesis, and the stories of the Death of the First-born of Egypt and the Creation of the Firstborn of Israel in the book of Exodus. As strangers in strange lands (721–332 B.C.E.), Jews observed Sabbath as a day on which to be still and to contemplate the quiet working of a world maintained by Yahweh alone. The action of telling the stories of the works that Yahweh has done, and the contemplation of resting to appreciate the work that Yahweh is doing are comparable. Using the Sabbath as a day of rest involves the same social dynamics as a union strike today. In a strike, work ceases in order to draw attention to all the ways in which workers contribute to public life. On the Sabbath as a day of rest, work ceases in order to draw attention to all the ways in which it is the work of Yahweh and not human work that makes life possible. It is an antistructural ritual that invites humans to do nothing, not to do something.

The fifth stipulation in the decalogue is the command: "honor your father and your mother, so that your days may be long in the land that Yahweh, your divine patron, is giving you" (Exod 20:12). The stipulation assigns fathers of households in ancient Israel the responsibility of feeding and protecting the parents who had fed and protected the household before them. This was the only retirement plan. These parents were powerless. If the father of their household did not feed and protect them, they died of starvation.

The sixth and seventh stipulations in the decalogue are the prohibitions: "you shall not murder" (Exod 20:13) and "you shall not commit adultery" (Exod 20:14). They outlawed competition between the father of one Hebrew household and the father of another for land and children. The sixth stipulation did not prohibit war or capital punishment, but the killing of one Hebrew by another in order to enslave the members of his household. The members of every Hebrew household were the children promised to Abraham and Sarah by Yahweh. They were the children of Yahweh. Yahweh gave these lives, and only Yahweh could take them away. To murder another Hebrew was to act like Yahweh. It was a sacrilege. Similarly, for the father of one Hebrew household to have intercourse with a wife of the father of another Hebrew household was adultery. Adultery was not just a sexual assault on a married woman, but an act of economic aggression by one household against another for its land, represented by the mother of the household. In the world of the Bible, marriages ratified covenants between two households for the right to bear children and to plant or graze the land. When the father of one household had sexual intercourse with a wife of another, he challenged the right of his neighbor's household to its land and children. Again, Yahweh had promised Abraham and Sarah that their descendants would enjoy an uncontested right to their land. Fathers of households who committed adultery made Yahweh look like a liar.

The eighth stipulation of the decalogue is the prohibition: "you shall not steal" (Exod 20:15). This stipulation outlawed the kidnapping of the members of one Hebrew household by another in order to sell them as slaves (Exod 21:16; Deut 24:7). The prohibition summarizes the two stipulations that precede it. Yahweh had emancipated the Hebrews from slavery and given them land and children. Without land and children, a household was once again reduced to slavery, and returned to the days without Yahweh.

The ninth stipulation in the decalogue is the prohibition: "you shall not bear false witness against your neighbor" (Exod 20:16). It outlaws perjury or lying to the village assembly of the elders responsible for resolving conflicts of interest between one household and another. Physical evidence plays a significant role in trials today, but, in the world of the Bible, trials depended almost entirely on only oral testimony. A household charged with a capital crime could be convicted on the oral testimony of just two witnesses. Perjury destroyed the ability of villages to resolve problems nonviolently, and plunged Israel into anarchy.

The prohibition: "you shall not covet your neighbor's house; you shall not covet your neighbor's wife, or male or female slave, or ox, or ass, or anything that belongs to your neighbor" (Exod 20:17) stipulates that the father of one Hebrew household shall not find ways to benefit unjustly from the goods of another. "To covet" does not mean simply to daydream about having someone or something which belongs to someone else, but actually to take steps to profit from it. Again, Yahweh guarantees the economic integrity of every household in Israel. When the father of one household profits unjustly from the father of another, the thief is stealing from Yahweh.

The decalogue reveals the picture that the Hebrews drew of Yahweh to determine the way they were expected to treat one another. As the stipulation to observe the Sabbath shows, they were convinced that exploitation was the result of narrow-mindedness, and selfishness was the consequence of a bad memory of their own bad times. Sabbath was not simply the right of the Hebrews themselves, but of their slaves, and of their livestock, and of their strangers as well. The Hebrews thought of Yahweh traveling from one end of Israel to the other, inspecting and improving one aspect or the other of the land and its people. Yahweh went about these chores not as a monarch or a warrior, but as a widow, an orphan, a stranger. Yahweh's pride of ownership showed in the willingness to do anything that needed to be done. For the Hebrews, Yahweh was not an absentee owner, but a manager always on the premises. As long as Yahweh wanders dressed as a stranger, a widow, an orphan, no one can molest, oppress, wrong, or extort them. To take advantage of the poor would be to take advantage of Yahweh. It was the unassuming presence of this all-powerful divine patron that inspired the Hebrews to envision a more gentle world in which even the weak could survive.

The Hebrews realized that greed and violence were more possible when their households were halfhearted. A household that loves with a whole heart, and a whole soul, and a whole mind cannot fail to love its neighbor as itself. Hatred, oppression, extortion are the works of the halfhearted, who can only see their own needs. Only they can throw a cloak taken as collateral into a heap against the wall of their house without ever wondering what it is like to spend a winter night curled up naked in an open field. For the Hebrews, nature and society both revolt against the exploiters, who burn the earth with famines and batter it with wars. Gentleness is the mark of the wholehearted. Israel is not to be competitive, but to be a community where even the powerless rest.

Likewise for the Hebrews, gentleness is the result of a good memory for the bad times. Only households with bad memories can forget what it was like to be strangers with no place to go, no job to work, no words to speak. "You shall not molest or oppress an alien, for you were once aliens yourselves in the land of Egypt" (Exod 22:21). Only households who believe in a Yahweh who is poor can remember their own sufferings well enough to live wholehearted lives that are gentle and compassionate. Only then can they risk their whole hearts and souls and minds by forgoing greed and competition, living simply so that others may simply live.

Following the decalogue is a covenant code describing a characteristically Israelite way of life. Throughout this code, two basic principles serve as a focus for all these stipulations. The first is that Yahweh alone provides Israel with land and children, and the second is that Yahweh alone protects Israel from its enemies. In some way, the stipulations in the covenant code reflect a concern to emphasize these two prerogatives of Yahweh and to prevent the Hebrews from challenging them. Common themes and key words gather the stipulations in the code into clusters.

The code opens with a cluster of stipulations dealing with worship. Moses is to preside over the ratification of the covenant (Exod 20:18-21). The use of precious metals like gold and silver as well as sacred sculpture are prohibited (Exod 20:22-23). Since technically there was no theophany or vision of Yahweh on Sinai, there was to be no image of Yahweh in Israel. Altars in Israel are to be built of earth (Exod 20:24). Stone altars are permitted as long as the stone is uncut (Exod 20:25). Yahweh is the sculptor of uncut stone, humans the sculptors of dressed stone. The altars of Israel are to focus on the work of Yahweh, not human work. Altars may not be mounted on a raised platform (Exod 20:26). The raised platform would not only allow the congregation a better view of the liturgy, but also of the genitals of the priests around the altar as well. The stipulation is not concerned with scandalizing the congregation, but rather violating the protocol for a sanctuary of Yahweh. Yahweh was the creator of land and children. The Hebrews must be careful to acknowledge these prerogatives by never appearing before Yahweh with their feet covered or their genitals uncovered (Deut 28:57; 1 Kgs 15:23; 2 Chr 16:12; Isa 6:2; 7:20, Ruth 3:4-7). Only landowners wore sandals, and the fathers of households uncovered their genitals only when preparing to sire a child.

There is also a cluster of stipulations dealing with slavery (Exod 21:1). Slavery in the ancient Near East is not the crime of human bondage that appeared in such cruel forms in the colonization of the Americas, when Native Americans and then Africans were trapped, sold, and worked like animals. Slavery was a form of financing used to borrow money and to pay debts to both households and to the state. Therefore, like laws regulating financing today, these laws regulated debt slavery. There are time limitations for debt slaves (Exod 21:2), and stipulations governing the disposition of the property of male slaves upon final payment of their debts (Exod 21:3-4). There is a procedure for permanently changing the status of a household from free to slave (Exod 21:5-6). The conversion protected the household from taxes and creditors, much like declaring bankruptcy today. The disposition of a slave designated to become the mother or the daughter of the household as part of a covenant that has been abrogated is also carefully regulated (Exod 21:7-11). The father of the household may not sell her as a slave to any other household. He may negotiate a new covenant with her household or he may return her to her household as long as he has not had sexual intercourse with her. He may also allow his son to marry her; he may keep her as a secondary wife as long as he provides her with food, clothing, and has sexual intercourse with her; or he may allow her to leave as a free woman.

Another cluster deals with assault. Premeditated murder is prohibited (Exod 21:12). Sanctuary for defendants in cases of manslaughter is permitted, but prohibited for defendants in cases of murder. Battery of a father or mother of the household is punished by death (Exod 21:15), as is kidnapping and selling or attempting to sell the free into slavery (Exod 21:16). Cursing, which is failing to financially support the father or mother of the household, is also a capital crime (Exod 21:17).

Restitution for the period of lost workdays is to be paid by a household when one of its members is involved in a quarrel with a member of another household (Exod 21:18-19).

Flogging is the punishment for the father of a household who beats his slave to death (Exod 21:20), but he is acquitted if the slave dies two or three days after his beating on the grounds that the household owns the slave and thus can dispose of him as it wishes (Exod 21:21). Fathers of households who beat their slaves so badly that they knock out one of their teeth must emancipate them (Exod 21:17).

A fine is imposed upon a household if one of its members is involved in a fight during which a pregnant woman is injured and subsequently miscarries (Exod 21:22-24). The amount of the fine is to be set by the woman's husband and approved by the village assembly.

List of Witnesses
(EXOD 24:1-8)

Every covenant must be ratified by a list of witnesses. Ordinarily, covenants in the ancient Near East were valid only when witnessed by the divine assemblies of each covenant partner. In the covenant between Yahweh and Israel, however, the list of witnesses names only human witnesses: Nadab, Abihu, and the seventy elders who go with Moses.

Promulgation and Documentation
(EXOD 24:9—LEV 27:34)

The Covenant between Yahweh and Israel is documented on "tablets of stone" (Exod 24:12). Great stone monoliths were often erected at sanctuaries where the ratification of a covenant took place. Sometimes these stones were large undressed shafts of natural rock; sometimes they were dressed and inscribed. A stand of colossal limestone *matseboth* were excavated at Gezer in Israel today by William G. Dever and an assemblage of smaller basalt stelae were recovered by Yigael Yadin at Hazor. The tablets of stone here in the covenant between Yahweh and Israel were more likely basalt stelae similar to those from Hazor. The stones that Joshua erects at Gilgal were more likely limestone *matseboth* like those from Gezer (Josh 4:1—5:1).

Once the covenant is documented in stone, Yahweh serves as the divine architect for the construction of a sanctuary where it will be regularly promulgated. In the book of Exodus (Exodus 25–31 + 35–40), the sanctuary is a Great Tent in the Sinai. In the book of Ezekiel, the sanctuary is a great stone temple at Jerusalem (Ezek 40:1—48:35). In traditional societies like ancient Israel, trades are all learned from a divine patron. To complete the construction of the Great Tent sanctuary, Yahweh endows carpenters, tailors, and metalworkers with their crafts.

The great tent in the Sinai and the temple in Jerusalem were houses of Yahweh, not meeting halls for the Hebrews. These sanctuaries were the places where Yahweh stayed during feasts when the households of Israel assembled to acknowledge Yahweh as their divine patron by offering sacrifice. Yahweh teaches the Hebrews not only how to construct the great tent, but also how to select crops and livestock and how to prepare or sacrifice them. The Hebrews used sacrifices to redistribute goods more equitably throughout Israel, and, in some way, every sacrifice acknowledged that the land and children of the Hebrews were gifts of Yahweh, and not possessions that they as humans had earned. Therefore, they brought children to the sanctuary so that Yahweh, like a human grandparent, could see them. Certain children remained at the house of

Yahweh as priests to remind the Hebrews that all their children were the children of Yahweh. Likewise, at the end of every growing and herding season, the households of Israel brought their harvest and their herds for Yahweh to see and to eat. As this produce of the land was cooked and eaten, the stories of the Death of the Firstborn of Egypt and the Creation of the Firstborn of Israel were told, and the covenant between Yahweh and Israel was promulgated once again.

Teachings on Cattle, Sheep, Goats, and Poultry (LEV 1:1-17)

The book of Leviticus (Lev 1:1—27:34) serves as a calendar in the Covenant between Yahweh and Israel that closes the Creation of the Firstborn of Israel. It tells the Hebrews when and how to offer sacrifices. Leviticus also provides job descriptions for the priests who will supervise the collection of these sacrifices (Lev 8:1—10:20), as well as regulations for the households of Israel to remain in good standing (Lev 11:1—26:46).

Legal instruction or teaching is the most common genre in the book of Leviticus. These teachings combine a citation of the law with a commentary. The type of law most often cited is case law whose dependent clause describes the actions of a household, and whose main clause describes the reactions of its village. "Whoever curses his father or mother" describes an action; "shall be put to death" a reaction (Exod 21:17). The other kind of law is apodictic law which simply states: "you shall not kill" (Exod 20:13) and "remember to keep holy the Sabbath day" (Exod 20:8).

A Teaching on Cattle, Sheep, Goats, and Poultry gives step-by-step instructions for selecting and cooking these animals (Lev 1:1-17). Cattle, sheep, and goats were the standard herd animals. They were also the currency in which farmers and herders paid their taxes at local sanctuaries. Taxes in ancient Israel were modest in contrast to the taxes imposed by the Egyptian governors, who collected up to ninety-five percent of everything households herded and farmed.

The teaching contains three recipes (Lev 1:3-17). Each recipe begins: "If the holocaust. . . . is from," and ends: "a sweet smelling oblation." Recipes combine a list of ingredients (Lev 1:3) and a series of directions (Lev 1:3-9). The first recipe is for a bull. The bull here must be a "male without blemish"; it must be whole or healthy. It is impossible to cook a nourishing meal with rancid food, and it is illegal to pay taxes with sick animals.

There are two sets of directions: one for laypeople and one for priests. The directions for laypeople describe a para-liturgy in a village, the directions for priests describe a liturgy at a sanctuary. Liturgy is official worship; para-liturgy is unofficial worship. Holidays in many cultures involve not only sanctuary liturgy celebrated by men, but also elaborate household meals or kitchen liturgies celebrated by women. The steps of the kitchen liturgies parallel the steps of the sanctuary liturgies. This teaching instructs the father of a household to conduct a liturgy in his village that parallels the liturgy conducted by the priests at the sanctuary.

A priest is a butcher and a cook who prepares meals for Yahweh. The teaching authorizes fathers of the households of Israel to butcher and cook meat for Yahweh without the presence of a priest. The father of the household leads the animal in procession to the sanctuary (Lev 1:3), lays his hands on its head to legally identify the household with the animal (Lev 1:4), and then slaughters the animal (Lev 1:5). He skins the animal, butchers it (Lev 1:6), and washes the organ meats (Lev 1:9).

The teaching guides the fathers of households through these important procedures to acknowledge that cattle, sheep, goats, and poultry belong to Yahweh, and not to the households of ancient Israel. None can be slaughtered or harvested without permission. Trespassing or poaching on the livestock of Yahweh is severely punished. Even with permission these animals must be slaughtered with great care.

Teachings on Clean and Unclean (LEV 11:1—16:34)

The word "clean" in the books of Exodus, Leviticus, and Numbers, and "wise" in the books of Proverbs, Ecclesiastes, and Job, are parallel labels that describe acceptable or honorable physical conditions and human behavior. The words "unclean" and "foolish" describe unacceptable or shameful conditions or behavior. In the Bible "clean" and "unclean" have little to do with hygiene. These labels define the status of a household in the village. The labels are analogous to credit ratings today and distinguished households in good social and economic standing from those that were not. They do not indicate so much what a household was actually doing or not doing, but rather how their villages reacted to their behavior.

Labels teach each generation a specific way of looking at life. Some formal education did take place in schools whose teachers explained to students why certain ways of doing things were clean, and others were unclean, but most education was informal. Labeling was the principal means of informal education. Villagers applied labels with words, gestures, facial expressions, or tone of voice.

Clean behavior entitled a household to life. The clean ate moderately, did not get drunk, worked hard, made good friends, sought advice before acting, held their temper, paid their taxes, and imposed fair legal judgments. The clean were careful in dealing with one another during menstruation, sexual intercourse, childbirth, and death. The clean were equally conscientious about what food they ate, what clothes they wore, what animals they herded, and what crops they planted in their fields. Clean households could care for their own members and were prepared to help their neighbors. "Clean" was the label for a household in good standing, licensed to make a living in the village, and entitled to its support. Only the clean were entitled to buy, sell, trade, marry, arrange marriages, serve in assemblies, and send warriors to the tribe. Only the clean were entitled to make wills, appoint heirs, and serve as legal guardians to care for households endangered by drought, war, and epidemic. The clean were in place and functioning well.

Unclean behavior sentenced a household to death by placing its land and children at risk. The unclean ate too much, drank too much, were lazy, quarrelsome, selfish, and thought nothing about lying to the village assembly. They were thoughtless in their sexual relationships, and disrespectful of the newborn and the dead. The herds of the unclean were mangy, and their farms run-down. Unclean households did not fulfill their responsibilities to their own members or their neighbors. "Unclean" is the label for households on probation. The unclean were out of place and not functioning properly. Consequently, both their contributions to the village and their eligibility for its support were suspended. The unclean label downgraded the status of a household, until it demonstrated that it was once again contributing to the village. The code of honor and shame in ancient Israel changed significantly at least twice: after the end of the war between Babylon and Judah in 587 B.C.E., and after Alexander brought Hellenistic culture to the eastern Mediterranean in 332 B.C.E.

Teachings on Leprosy (LEV 13:9-23; 14:54-57)

In 1869, Gerhard Henrik Armauer Hansen of Norway identified the bacteria that cause leprosy. Consequently, medicine began referring to the condition as "Hansen's disease" instead of "leprosy." Western European societies stopped sentencing lepers to remote colonies like Molokai, Hawaii, and the persecution of lepers came to a close.

There is no hard evidence for Hansen's disease in the world of the Bible until after 332 B.C.E., when Alexander's soldiers returned from India. None of the symptoms in the book of Leviticus (Lev 13:9-23; 14:54-57) are exclusively associated with Hansen's disease, and descriptions in Hippocrates and Polybius are equally inconclusive. In the Bible, "leprosy" refers to a variety of skin disorders such as psoriasis, eczema, seborrhea, or ringworm. To some extent, this teaching views these conditions as diseases, but primarily it treats them as social disorders.

The bodies of the men and women of a household were considered to be microcosms or households in miniature. The penis, anus, vagina, nipples, mouth, eyes, ears, and nose were the borders where these microcosms opened to the outside world. Emissions from these portals defined the status of the household itself. Emissions associated with women, with death, or which are uncontrollable indicate a household is at risk or unclean. Emissions associated with men, with life, or which are controllable indicate a household is in good standing or clean.

Lepers break out. Rashes, flakes, scales, and boils on human skin, as well as molds on the walls of houses and on clothes were symptoms of chaos. The human body or the house was in revolt. Reactions to these conditions reflect the Hebrews' sense of social organization more than their medical knowledge. Any disorder on these frontiers is like a hole in the dike, which would quickly expand. Lepers were the incarnation of households in revolt against the codes of honor necessary for life in the village to continue. Households that conformed to those codes, as well as those who deviated from them, must be clearly labeled. Otherwise, social organization would disappear, everyone would be out of place, and life would become impossible.

The procedure for diagnosing and treating leprosy was neither hasty nor cruel. When symptoms appeared, priests examined patients for changes in skin and hair color. After a seven-day waiting period patients were reexamined (Lev 13:12-17). One cure for leprosy was humility. Confirmed lepers were treated with a protocol of ritual degradation. They were allowed to die and to be reborn. They dressed like corpses, shrouded their faces, did not cut their hair, and wailed like mourners (Lev 13:45; Num 5:18; Mic 3:7; Isa 52:11). When the symptoms of leprosy subsided, and when they were ready to care for, rather than abuse, neighboring households, priests readmitted lepers to their places in the village.

Teaching on the Household of the Father (LEV 18:1-30)

Societies have different base communities. Base communities are the smallest self-supporting units in society. In Western European cultures like the United States and Canada, an unmarried adult between eighteen and sixty-five years of age is a base community, whereas in the world of the Bible, such unmarried adults could not survive. Israel's base community of four generations is reflected in a Teaching on the Household of the Father (Lev 18:1-30). This teaching was important enough to be preserved as a covenant, with a credential (Lev 18:2) and stipulations introduced by a decalogue (Lev 18:6-23). There is also a litany of blessings and curses (Lev 18:24-30), but no list of witnesses or a liturgy describing its documentation and promulgation.

The teaching sets women from each generation off-limits to men within their households. Childbearing women were the portfolio for a household. The teaching envisions a household where the father has more than one wife and where these wives are not the only childbearing women. It explicitly protects mothers, sisters, and granddaughters and, by implication, it also protects daughters by setting them off-limits. The prohibition of sexual intercourse with a daughter should appear after the prohibition: "you shall not uncover the nakedness of your sister" (Lev 18:9), but it was lost. The repetitive style made it easy for scribes to skip from the prohibition of intercourse with a sister to the prohibition of intercourse with a granddaughter. The lost prohibition protecting the daughter and the prohibition protecting the granddaughter both started with exactly the same words: "you shall not uncover the nakedness of your (grand-)daughter." A scribe's eye skipped from the beginning of the first prohibition to the end of the second, thus omitting the prohibition protecting the daughter.

The words: "you shall not uncover the nakedness of" technically means: "you shall not have intercourse with" or "you shall not marry." The prohibition: "you shall not uncover the nakedness of your father" (Lev 18:7) does not protect the father of the household from homosexuality. It protects the mother of the household. She is "the nakedness of the father." No other men are mentioned in the decalogue, which otherwise deals exclusively with protected women. Furthermore, the expression "nakedness of" which occurs twice in this prohibition as "nakedness of your father" and "nakedness of your mother" occurs only once in each of the other prohibitions referring to more than one protected person. Finally, neither the motivation: "she is your mother" nor the repetition: "you shall not uncover her nakedness" mentions the father.

Covenants sealed by marriage were an important investment that allowed households to survive and prosper. The most valuable women for such covenant marriages are those mentioned in the teaching. These women served two roles: they were hostages and advocates. As hostages they guaranteed that the household of the vendor or father would fulfill the terms of the covenant. As advocates they worked to assure that the household of the consumer or their husband continued to have a need for the products or services on which the household of their father depended for a living.

The teaching is prohibiting not only incest, but also highly competitive economic policies. Although the villages of early Israel had subsistence economies and were not particularly competitive, the states of Israel and Judah were intensely competitive surplus societies. State households pursued aggressive economic policies in which they frequently negotiated highly competitive covenants with one another. Such challenges were made when the head of one household had intercourse with the women of another household, but not just with any women, but those whose marriages represented the significant covenants of the household. The teaching serves as a legal digest or companion for fathers of households, who could use it to handle any challenge that confronted them with this simple set of ten or twelve commandments and prohibitions. It spells out the laws dealing with conflicts of interest regarding potentially confusing sexual relationships, and tries to control the damage that unbridled competition could do to a household by limiting the covenants that it could make.

The teaching begins with a stipulation affirming the general principle: "none of you shall approach anyone near of kin to uncover nakedness" (Lev 18:6). The centerpiece of the teaching is a pattern, which is a set of ten or twelve stipulations (Exod 20:3-17; Lev 18:6-17). Each stipulation cites a command or a prohibition. Commentaries refine the stipulation. The commentary "whether she is your father's or your mother's daughter" (Lev 18:9) defines "sister" in the stipulation "you shall not uncover the nakedness of your sister" as both a congenital and a legal relative. Likewise, "whether born at home or born abroad" (Lev 18:9) identifies sister as both an absent as well as a resident relative. "She is your mother" (Lev 19:7) specifies the charge to be brought against the defendant. Similar declarations appear in store windows today. "Shoplifting is a crime (misdemeanor)!" is a declaration advising customers that the store prosecutes shoplifters.

The intention of the teaching is to remove any obstacles that households have to obeying a law. These teachings are persuasive genres. "My ordinances you shall observe and my statutes you shall keep, following them: I am Yahweh, your divine patron. You shall keep my statutes and my ordinances; by doing so one shall live: I am your divine patron" (Lev 18:4-5) is a common motivation. The household that carries out the stipulations will live. Yahweh is the only life-giver. The presence of Yahweh is a blessing that brings the fertility that allows everything to live. The absence of Yahweh is a curse that allows everything to die. This motivation (Lev 18:2-3, 5-6, 30) uses Yahweh's title like the refrain to affirm, again and again, that Yahweh is the lawgiver (Lev 18:2), the life-giver (Lev 18:5), the protector and provider of Israel (Lev 18:6), and the one whose absence from Israel leaves it open to being "vomited out" and "cut off" from the land (Lev 18:30).

The decalogue ends with the prohibition: "you shall not uncover the nakedness of a woman and her daughter, and you shall not take her son's daughter or her daughter's daughter" (Lev 18:17). The prohibition: "you shall not take a woman as a rival to her sister" (Lev 18:18) repeats the prohibition of having intercourse with a sister-in-law in the decalogue (Lev 18:16), but is a completely different kind of prohibition. Each stipulation in the decalogue uses the form "you shall not uncover the nakedness of...," but this prohibition does not. It originally introduced the short law code that followed the decalogue, and became part of this decalogue to fill out the number twelve after the prohibition protecting the daughter was accidentally lost. Instead of reinserting the prohibition protecting the daughter, later copyists simply moved the second prohibition protecting sisters-in-law to the end of the decalogue.

Litany of Blessings and Curses
(NUM 1:1—27:11)

The book of Numbers is a litany of blessings and curses for the Covenant between Yahweh and Israel. The generation that never entered the land is cursed; the generation that did enter the land is blessed.

Blessing of Children: Military Census (NUM 1:19-47)

There are two long census lists or "numbers" in the tradition (Num 1:1—25:18; 26:1—27:11). Each consists of shorter lists like a census of the twelve tribes in the Sinai desert

(Num 1:19-46). Most translations calculate that a single tribe like Reuben could muster 46,500 warriors (Num 1:21) and that the twelve tribes could field 603,550 warriors (Num 1:46). The Sinai lacks adequate natural resources to feed so many for forty years. Similarly, the daunting logistics necessary to maneuver over half a million warriors and their households make it unlikely that the standard translations are accurate. It is better to read the word traditionally translated as "thousand" as "military detachment." Therefore, Reuben musters forty-six detachments, not forty-six thousand warriors. Only the words following "detachment" identify the total number of warriors that a tribe was prepared to send into battle. Therefore, Reuben drafts five hundred, not 46,500 warriors: "the tribe of Reuben mustered forty-six detachments totaling five hundred warriors" (Num 1:21). This formula of interpretation, however, is not universally applicable. For example, the twelve tribes could not field 603 detachments with only a total of 550 warriors (Num 1:26).

In the Covenant between Yahweh and Israel, Yahweh agrees to feed and protect the Hebrews, and the Hebrews agree to let Yahweh be their sole provider and protector. The census lists reflect a policy that the Hebrews are to draft warriors only in times of crisis, not maintain a standing army of soldiers like the Egyptians and the Philistines. Yahweh, not professional soldiers, protects the Hebrews. Hebrew warriors are herders and farmers responding to a temporary crisis, not soldiers in a standing army. Furthermore, they never go into battle outnumbering their enemies. They always fight only in support of Yahweh and the divine warriors who lead the attack. The Hebrews developed this military policy to remind themselves that Yahweh alone is the guardian of Israel.

Blessing of Children: Teachings on Adultery and Jealousy (NUM 5:12-31)

Teachings on Adultery and Jealousy are part of a litany that blesses with children those who fulfill the stipulation, "you shall not commit adultery" (Exod 20:14), and punishes with infertility those who do not. In the tradition on adultery the defendant is a woman; in the tradition on jealousy the defendant is a man. The woman is charged with adultery for which there are no witnesses (Num 5:12-13). The man is charged with jealousy for which there are also no witnesses (Num 5:14). Nonetheless, the teachings require that the wife represent the household in both. Jealousy or adultery both jeopardize the ability of the woman to conceive a child. The breakdown affects her sphere of influence. Furthermore, the world of the Bible considered semen as the evidence of intercourse, and it remained in the woman, not in the man.

Crimes that carried the death penalty required that the plaintiff's charge be supported by the testimony of two eyewitnesses. Without two eyewitnesses, the assembly could not use the standard legal remedies to restore the honor of the household. To resolve such a deadlock, traditional cultures use an ordeal. Ordeals allow a decision to be made. In an ordeal, defendants are exposed to strenuous, life-threatening experiences. If they survive, then the divine assembly has cleared them of the charges made against them, and the honor of their households is reaffirmed. If they do not, then their households are shamed.

Decisions must be made for human life to continue. To facilitate making difficult decisions, cultures develop tie-breaking rituals. The results are never absolute. There are always unknowns. When research fails to identify a preference, cultures resort to ordeal. Remnants of ordeals remain in industrial cultures today. Occasionally, lovers still pull petals off a daisy to determine if their love is unrequited. Children still alternate their hands along the handle of a baseball bat to determine which team should bat first, and officials still flip a coin to determine who kicks and who receives at the start of a football game.

The seven rubrics for an ordeal that uses a mixture of clay, water, and ink are nested inside the seven rubrics for an ordeal that uses a bowl of grain. The rubric directing a priest to administer an oath to the woman is part of both ordeals (Num 5:19-21). Rubrics are directions. "Rubric" means "red," from the custom of writing the actions to be performed by priests with red ink and the words to be said with black ink.

The ordeal that uses a bowl of grain places the husband on trial for jealousy. The ordeal begins when the husband (1) brings both the woman (Num 5:15) and (2) a bowl of grain to the sanctuary (Num 5:15). A priest (3) officially arraigns the woman (Num 5:18), (4) removes her veil (Num 5:18), (5) places the bowl of grain in her hands (Num 5:18), and (6) administers an oath to determine whether the woman is faithful or unfaithful to her husband. The woman swears that if she has only had intercourse with her husband, then she will be able conceive a child with him (Num 5:26), but if she has had intercourse with anyone else, she will never again be able to conceive a child with her husband (Num 5:19-21). If the husband and wife conceive a child after they resume sexual relations, the husband is guilty of jealousy. If they are unable to conceive a child, he is innocent. (7) A handful of grain from her bowl is then scattered or sown on the sterile dirt floor of the sanctuary (Num 5:26). The grain represents the semen of the woman's husband. The action confirms the words of her oath. If she has scattered the seed of her husband by adultery, then their seed will be infertile.

The number seven characterizes ordeals as procedures that restore fertility to a household threatened by infidelity or jealousy. At least two observations contributed to the association of the number seven with fertility. First, only the sun, the moon, and five planets are visible with the unaided eye. Second, the moon completes its cycle of twenty-eight days in four seven-day weeks. The Hebrews concluded that it took Yahweh seven days to create the world and seven days to re-create it. It took seven days to go from chaos to cosmos, from death to life. Therefore, it takes seven days to tell the Stories of the Heavens and the Earth. The seventh day is the day on which the world comes to life. Fertility is the sign of Yahweh's presence. Sterility is the curse of Yahweh's absence. The curse in these ordeals asks Yahweh to leave a household guilty of jealousy or adultery.

The ordeal that uses clay, water, and ink places the woman on trial for adultery. A priest (1) brings the woman into the sanctuary (Num 5:16), (2) thins clay from the floor of the sanctuary with water in a bowl (Num 5:17), and (3) administers an oath to determine whether the woman is faithful or unfaithful to her husband. The priest announces that if the woman has had intercourse with anyone other than her husband, her uterus will become infected and prolapse when she drinks the mixture, but if she has only had intercourse with her husband, then nothing will happen (Num 5:19–21). The same symptoms appear among the women of Ashdod in the books of Samuel-Kings (1 Sam 4:1—7:2) after their husbands bring home the ark of the covenant as a war trophy. The woman (4) accepts the conditions (Num 5:22), the priest (5) writes the words of the oath on a broken piece of pottery (Num 5:23), (6) washes the ink off into the mixture of clay and water (Num 5:23), and (7) the woman drinks it (Num 5: 24). If her uterus becomes infected and prolapses, she is guilty of adultery. If she drinks the potion without a reaction, she is innocent of adultery.

The economy of ancient Israel depended on a high level of cooperation regulated by covenants and notarized by marriages. Infidelity and jealousy paralyzed the economy. The teachings on jealousy and adultery teach the Hebrews how to use ordeals to end the deadlock of infidelity and jealousy, to restore harmony, and to get the village back to work.

Blessing of Land: Balaam Delivers Israel from Moab (NUM 22:1—24:25)

The census lists with which the book of Numbers opens describe how Yahweh blesses the Hebrews with children. Balaam Delivers Israel from Moab (Num 22:1—24:25), together with the Trial of Zimri (Num 25:1-18) and a Land Grant to Slaves Set Free (Num 26:1—27:11), describe how Yahweh blesses the Hebrews with land.

The Balaam character is always a famous prophet. Balaam is a master of divination and imitative ritual. Although he is most at home in East Jordan, traditions also place him alongside Noah, Daniel, and Job as a hero. In 1967 Hendricus Jacobus Franken directed the team that recovered a delightful nonbiblical tradition about Balaam. It was written in a dialect of Aramaic in red and black ink either on the plaster finish of a stele or on the walls of a sanctuary at Deir 'Alla in Jordan today. No doubt, these monuments were dedicated to the members of the divine assembly named in the inscription, and intended to protect the villages around the sanctuary from the disasters that it describes. The artifacts found with the plaster and the style of writing date the construction of the sanctuary to 700 B.C.E.

Balaam Delivers Israel from Moab is a hero story like those in the Saga of Samson. Samson and Balaam are both chiefs without honor. Stories about chiefs without honor demonstrate that Yahweh, the silent protagonist in every hero story, can use even fools to free the Hebrews from their enemies. Balaam is not only a fool like Samson, but he is also a stranger. Samson, although married to a Philistine, is at least technically a Hebrew; Balaam is not. Yahweh can lift up not only a fool, but also a stranger to deliver Israel from its enemies This hero story demonstrates the hopelessness of opposing the people of Yahweh who march through the desert like an army (Num 1:19-46). Yahweh is the unchallenged ruler of the cosmos, and therefore the people of Yahweh are invincible. The army that Yahweh fields in the opening chapters of the book of Numbers cannot be destroyed by mutiny from within (Num 11:1-35; 12:1—14:45; 16:1—17:15; 20:1-13) nor attack from without (Num 21:1—22:1; 22:2—24:25). The Hebrews are vulnerable only to Yahweh (Num 25:1-18).

Two episodes in the crisis of Balaam Delivers Israel from Moab describe how Moab threatens the Hebrews. Three episodes intensify the threat in the climax of the story. Finally, four episodes describe how Balaam resolves the crisis in the denouement.

Moab is a plateau of land that rises three thousand feet above sea level on the eastern shore of the Dead Sea. Today, Moab would stretch across central Jordan between the city of Amman in the north to the Wadi Hesa or Wadi Zered in the south. Prevailing winds blowing off the Mediterranean Sea into the desert of Saudi Arabia brought enough rain to Moab so that its farmers could grow wheat and barley, and its herders could graze sheep and goats. Pioneers settled Moab as early as the Neolithic period. During the Early Bronze period Moab was a major civilization center. During the Middle Bronze period and the Late Bronze period, however, there is little archaeological evidence for any stable cultures in Moab, even though Ramses II (1279–1213 B.C.E.) mentions Moab in his description of Syria-Palestine on the walls of the temple complex at Luxor. The Late Bronze period was dominated by great empires like Egypt, Hatti, and Mycenae. Only when competition and war eroded their control of the eastern Mediterranean after 1200 B.C.E. did small independent states like Israel, Edom, Moab, and Ammon begin to appear. They were states, not empires. Edom, Moab, and Ammon developed into states east of the Jordan River at approximately the same time as David developed the villages of Israel to the west.

Balaam Delivers Israel from Moab is set in the time of Moses and Ramses II (1279–1213 B.C.E.). The story of how Balaam Delivers Israel from Moab is only one of the biblical and extrabiblical traditions reflecting the ongoing relationship between Edom, Moab, Ammon, and Israel. Mesha (840–820 B.C.E.), a ruler of Moab, ordered his annals carved on a curve-topped, rectangular block of basalt three feet high and two feet wide (Fig. 28). The thirty lines are written in the Moabite language using the Hebrew alphabet. The stele was located in Dhiban, Jordan, in 1868 by F. A. Klein, a

I am Mesha, King of Moab. My father reigned over Moab for 30 years and I now reign after my father. Omri, the King of Israel, controlled Moab for many years because Chemosh, our divine patron, was angry at his people. When Omri's son succeeded him, he bragged that "I too will humble Moab." In my time, however, I have triumphed over Omri's son, causing Israel to be forced out of our land forever. Omri and his son Ahab occupied our land for 40 years, but Chemosh dwells supreme there in my time. I built the city of Baal-Meon and its reservoir, and I built the city of Qaryaten.

Now long ago the tribe of Gad had claimed Ataroth, which borders Moab, for Israel. But I fought against them and captured Ataroth. I sacrificed all of the people of Ataroth to Chemosh. I brought the lion of David from the sanctuary of Ataroth and mounted it before Chemosh in the sanctuary of Kerioth. And I settled the tribes of Sharon and Maharith in the land that I had taken from Israel to claim it for Moab.

Then Chemosh said to me, "Go, take Nebo from Israel." So I went by night and fought against Nebo from daybreak until noon. I won a great victory and I sacrificed the 7,000 men, women, and children of Nebo to Ashtar and Chemosh as I had vowed I would do.

The King of Israel fortified Jahaz as a battle camp from which he invaded Moab. But Chemosh, my divine patron, drove him out before me (Josh 10:42). I settled 200 households of valiant warriors in Jahaz in order to claim it for the district of Dibon in Moab.

It was I who built Qarhoh, its gates and its towers, the palace and the reservoirs of water within the town. I also ordered the people, "Let each of you make a cistern for himself in his house." I had Israelite prisoners of war cut the beams for the royal buildings in Qarhoh. I built Aroer, and the highway in the Arnon valley. I also rebuilt the destroyed cities of Beth-bamoth and Bezer using 50 households loyal to me in Dibon.

I reigned in peace over the 100 villages that I had added to the land, and Chemosh dwelt there in my time.

FIGURE 28   Annals of Mesha (Matthews and Benjamin, 1997: 157–159)

German missionary. Subsequently, Charles Clermont-Ganneau (1846–1923), a French scholar, had a paper squeeze made of the inscription. Reacting to the attention these Europeans were giving their artifact, local people heated the stele in a fire and then smashed it into pieces with cold water to see if it was filled with treasure. Thirty percent of the stele was permanently destroyed. In 1870 the remains were restored by the Louvre Museum, Paris. Parallels to the Annals of Mesha appear in the books of Joshua-Judges (Josh 6:17-21) and the books of Samuel-Kings (1 Kgs 16:23-24; 2 Kgs 3:4).

Satire characterizes Balaam Delivers Israel from Moab, which begins not when the Hebrews send out a call to arms against Moab, but when Balak, the ruler of Moab, sends out a call to arms against the Hebrews who are all over Moab. For the Hebrews their exploding population is a blessing, but for their enemies it is a curse (Exod 1:7-12; Num 22:3). The warriors of Moab muster, and wait for Balaam, a prophet, to declare war.

After Balaam tells the messengers to spend the night, two separate stories, one from the Yahwist tradition (Num 22:2-19 + 22:22-35 + 22:36-40 + 23:28-24:9 + 24:10-19), the other from the Elohist tradition (Num 22:2-19 + 22:20-21 + 22:36-40 + 22:41—23:10 + 23:11-24), describe what happened "the next morning." Each ends with a similar command: "go with them, but do only what I tell you." The Story of Balaam and a King (Num 22:13-20) portrays Balaam as a fool who cannot understand his divine patron. The story of Balaam and an Ass (Num 22:21-35) portrays him as a fool who cannot even understand an animal he has owned for years. In one story Balaam is greedy; in the other he is disobedient.

In the Story of Balaam and a King, Balak thinks that the prophet is making his messengers wait until they offer him more money. The contrast between monarchs who are impatient and prophets who are patient contrasts humans, who are impatient, with Yahweh, who is patient especially in matters of judgment (1 Sam 13:4-8; Num 22:36-40). "Yahweh is slow to anger and rich in kindness, forgiving wickedness and crime" (Num 14:18). Humans are impetuous. It is their unwillingness to wait that leads to so much suffering. The test of faith is the ability to wait for Yahweh. Humans are considered impulsive. They want the cosmos to function on their schedule. It does not. Only Yahweh sets the schedule, and only Yahweh knows when the promises made by covenant with the Hebrews will be fulfilled. The belief that humans are busy, while their divine patrons are quiet, is widespread in world religions. As a result, believers in most faith traditions prepare to pray by quieting themselves, by slowing down, by centering. Even though the story opens with Balak sending Balaam a divination fee, Balaam does not summon his divine patron with divination. Balaam's divine patron comes to him in a dream.

For the divine patron of ancient Israel to come to a non-Hebrew prophet is unusual, but not unique in the Bible. For example, the book of Isaiah describes Yahweh anointing Cyrus, a non-Israelite monarch (539–530 B.C.E.), as a messiah (Isa 45:1-3).

The Story of Balaam and an Ass satirizes Balaam as a seer of the divine assembly who cannot see as well as an ass. Originally, the story was a parable that asked its audience: "Who would you rather have as an adviser? A prophet or an ass?" The tellers of the story thought prophets were fools, whose divination, magic, and visions were only so much theater, successful for getting goods and services away from their clients, but useless for understanding the ways of the divine assembly. The story has little respect for divination, magic, and visions. The key to wisdom was the ability to observe what was going on around them in the human world and in the world of nature. Even a slave knows that when a saddle-broken ass balks repeatedly something unusual is going on, but the great seer does not. Only after Yahweh approaches Balaam the third time does Balaam even do as well as the ass does. Finally, Balaam sees and responds appropriately. What the ass senses immediately, the prophet only begins to appreciate after preparation. The prophet does not understand Yahweh (Num 22:9-21), and does not even understand the world (Num 22:22-35). If prophets would just repeat the words of Yahweh like puppets, they would be of some value, but they do not (Num 22:20, 35).

There are motifs common to the Story of Balaam and an Ass, the Stories of Balaam from Deir 'Alla, and the Stories of the Farmer and the Courts from Egypt. In both the Stories of Balaam from Deir 'Alla and the Story of Balaam and an Ass, the protagonists are named Balaam. Both are seers or prophets who communicate with the divine assembly. Balaam communicates with the divine assembly using dreams or night visions, a form of prophetic trance. Both are messengers of the divine assembly who bring an unwelcome message. The tellers of both consider it possible for a human to warn others about impending misfortune. The stories use the world-turned-upside-down motif: Israel the weak will defeat Moab the strong. In both stories animals behave just the opposite of the way they behave in the presence of humans, when they are in the presence of the divine assembly.

In the Stories of the Farmer and the Courts and the Story of Balaam and an Ass, tellers use fable to include an ass as a character with a human role. In both stories, the ass recognizes danger on the path ahead, while the human character does not. Both use the motif of the troublesome ass that is punished unjustly, and the blocked-path motif or the narrow-path motif. In both stories, the protagonist adheres to a moral principle despite the fact that it is unpopular and that he is pressured to do what is convenient; in both, the divine assembly are the final judges of the just. Human courts cannot protect the poor from the rich. Both also use the motif of final justice, that for those who persevere, justice is ultimately obtainable. Balak appeals his case three times, just as the farmer appeals his case repeatedly before Rensi, the governor. Both are persevering.

The title of the divine character in the Story of Balaam and an Ass is "Yahweh," Israel's special, but not necessarily unique, title for its divine patron. Yahweh repeatedly attempts to communicate with Balaam, who repeatedly fails to discern the significance of the events that Yahweh uses. Again there is nothing unorthodox about the characterization. When the Story of Balaam and a King and the Story of Balaam and an Ass are combined, Balaam's divine patron appears to be erratic and inconsistent. It seems that Balaam's divine patron refuses him permission to work for Balak (Num 22:9-14), then grants Balaam permission to work for Balak (Num 22:15-20), then gets angry with Balaam for working for Balak (Num 22:21-34), then for a second time grants Balaam permission to work for Balak (Num 22:35).

Balaam's divine patron is neither testing him nor playing jokes on him. Likewise, Balaam does not misunderstand his divine patron. The story is not developing the character of Balaam's divine patron, but rather the character of Balaam. Balaam is the protagonist. Other characters are either ignored or only roughed in with broad strokes. The story stresses only a single aspect of Balaam's character: he is a fool about important matters. He cannot decide whether or not to work with Balak. Balaam is also a fool about ordinary matters. He cannot understand why the ass will not stay on the road. The intention of this story is to argue that Balaam is the last person you want to look to for help. The traditions are not concerned about the character of Balaam's divine patron or of Yahweh. The spotlight is on Balaam and only on Balaam, who is a fool.

Once Balaam arrives, Balak begins to offer sacrifices (Num 22:40; 23:2-6; 23:14-17; 23:29-30). Having both the monarch and the prophet present for this audit of the supplies that have been stockpiled for the campaign guarantees the accuracy of the inventory. If both the monarch and the prophet agree that households have provided enough supplies for the army, then war may be declared. If not, then the warriors must be dismissed.

At the end of this seven-day period (1 Sam 13:9), or perhaps on each of the seven days during the period (Num 23:1), sacrifices were offered. Balak offers seven bulls and seven rams on seven altars (Num 23:1). Battlefield sacrifices are emergency taxes imposed on households to provision the warriors who will defend their villages. When Jesse sends David from Bethlehem to Socoh with grain, bread, and cheese, he is not just a loving parent mailing a care package to his sons in the army (1 Sam 17:17-18). Jesse is paying his taxes to feed Saul's army. Likewise, Ziba is also paying taxes for the household of Saul when he delivers saddle-broken asses to be used as mounts, as well as bread, raisins, dried fruit, and wine to David's soldiers on the Mount of Olives (2 Sam 16:1-2).

Although the elders send out the call to arms, prophets determine whether or not Yahweh has delivered the enemy into the hands of the warriors and their chief. Prophets create an important balance to the power of monarchs in Israel. The interaction of these two officials prevents the abuse of power and the development of a dictatorship. It also creates and sustains internal tension. The prophet officially announces the decision of Yahweh to declare war with the deliverance formula. "Do you see all this huge army? When I deliver it up to you today, you will know that I am Yahweh" (1 Kgs 20:13) and "Because Aram has said that Yahweh rules the mountains, and not the plains, I will deliver up to you this large army, that you may know I am Yahweh" (1 Kgs 20:28) are both examples of the formula. If the divine assembly decides not to declare war, the prophet sends the warriors who have mustered home. "So Micaiah said: 'I see all Israel scattered on the mountains, like sheep without a shepherd, and Yahweh saying: These have no master. Let each of them go back home in peace'" (1 Kgs 22:17) is a good example of the kind of language that the prophet uses to discharge the warriors.

Once war has been declared, the prophet commissions a chief to lead the army into battle. Samuel's remarks, which now censure Saul for breaching protocol, may reflect the kind of language used in the commissioning of a chief: "Yahweh has sought out a man after his own heart; and Yahweh has appointed him to be prince over his people" (1 Sam 13:14). The prophet not only commissions Ahab as king of Israel, but appoints his officers as well. "Ahab asked, 'Through whom will this huge army be delivered up?' He answered: 'Through the retainers of the governors of the provinces.' Then Ahab asked: 'Who is to attack?' He replied: 'You are'" (1 Kgs 20:14). Certainly, the Story of Balaam and a King and the Story of Balaam and an Ass begin to reveal the playfulness with which tellers are developing this declaration of war. However, the episodes in which the prophet is supposed to announce the handing over of the enemy turn everything upside down. As audiences expect, the prophet and the monarch agree that war is imminent, but instead of announcing that Israel will be handed over to Moab, Balaam announces that Moab will be handed over to Israel.

The traditions portray Balak as frantically repeating the discernment four times. Each time the prophet determines that war is imminent, but that Moab will be destroyed. Although these stories of Balaam are certainly the best-known and best-developed prophet and monarch satires, there are precedents from both the Bible and other traditions in the ancient Near East as well.

The traditions from Deir 'Alla tell that Balaam, the son of Beor, has a dream that his city is about to be destroyed by the divine assembly. The divine assembly will turn everything in the village upside down. Tame animals will become wild. Wild animals will become tame. Poor women will use myrrh as though they were rich. The morning after his dream, Balaam is so depressed he cannot eat, drink, or speak. Nevertheless, his neighbors convince him to reveal his dream. The people take Balaam's dream as a warning and avert the destruction of their city. Nonetheless, the divine assembly condemns Balaam to death for revealing their plan.

The world-turned-upside-down motif appears in both the Stories of Balaam from Deir 'Alla and the book of Lamentations. Likewise, the motif in which a divine patron warns a human protégé of an impending disaster also appears in the Stories of Atrahasis and the Stories of Gilgamesh from Mesopotamia, as well as in the Flood Stories. The Balaam in the Bible and the Balaam from the traditions at Deir 'Allah are parallel characters. In the Bible, Balaam is more often portrayed as evil rather than good. Here Balaam appears as the prophet who would sell his skill for a price (Deut 23:4, 5; Josh 13:22; 24:9, 10; Neh 13:2; Mic 6:5).

Balaam Delivers Israel from Moab argues that the great Balaam really only does what Yahweh tells him to do. Balaam is famous throughout the world of the Bible as someone who has power with the divine assembly. Whoever Balaam blesses is blessed; whoever Balaam curses is cursed. The story of how Balaam delivers Israel from Moab domesticates this powerful figure and portrays him as subject to Yahweh. Balaam in the book of Numbers, like the great fish in the book of Jonah, is Yahweh's obedient servant.

The Book of Deuteronomy
(NUM 27:12 — DEUT 34:12)

The book of Exodus hands on the theology of ancient Israel. These constitutional traditions defined the way Hebrews understood Yahweh. Yahweh became the divine patron of Israel by delivering the Hebrews from slavery in Egypt. The exodus definitively identified Yahweh as Israel's patron and defined Israel as Yahweh's people. This confession of faith is reiterated throughout the Bible. Israel's hero stories and royal annals in the books of Joshua and Judges, of Samuel-Kings, and of Chronicles-Nehemiah celebrate the exploits of Israel's rulers as repetitions of Yahweh's great acts that led Israel out of slavery in Egypt. The verdicts of Israel's prophets in the books of Hosea, of Amos, of Micah, of Jeremiah, and of Ezekiel indict Israel for failing to acknowledge the basic relationship that should exist between slaves set free and their divine deliverer. Creation stories in the book of Psalms and in the book of Daniel portray Yahweh creating and renewing the cosmos with the same language and imagery employed in the book of Exodus.

The book of Exodus defined morality in ancient Israel by teaching how Hebrews were expected to treat one another and strangers. Again and again, teachings in the books of Exodus and of Deuteronomy motivate audiences to follow laws of all kinds, "because you were once slaves in Egypt."

The book of Exodus defined liturgy in ancient Israel by establishing its calendar. The exodus was Israel's independence day. For the books of Judges and of Samuel-Kings, the exodus marks the beginning of Israel. The book of Jeremiah similarly uses the exodus as the first date on its calendar. In the Bible the formula "since the exodus" functions in much the same way as the formula "since the founding of the land" functions in the texts of Egypt.

The book of Exodus is not only a testimony to Israel's memory of divine power in the plagues or at the Mountain of El, or Israel's moral sensitivity in the decalogue, or Israel's legal expertise in the code of the covenant, but also a testimony to Israel's ability to tell a story. The stories are not simply flights of fancy intended to distract children so that they can fall asleep, or to entertain adults during long hours of leisure or boredom. Every time it is told, the book of Exodus sets in motion the liberation that it describes. It is a creation story told to enslaved audiences in order to set them free. Every telling is an experience of the things that Yahweh can do, even against overwhelming odds. Western European cultures believe that progress is the result of scientific research. Traditional cultures like ancient Israel believe that change takes place with the telling of a story. The moments that change our lives forever are those when someone tells us a story. The Hebrews tell us the stories to help us understand that the exodus did not just happen once, but that ordinary people just like us are set free all the time. What makes the moment significant is that we believe them, and are never the same again.

The most significant retelling of the book of Exodus is preserved today in the book of Deuteronomy (Hebrew: *Devarim*). Its literary beginning describes Moses preparing to die by designating Joshua to be his heir (Num 27:12); the literary ending is his obituary (Deut 34:1-12). To prepare Joshua to lead Israel Moses retells the Stories of the Death of the Firstborn of Egypt and the Creation of the Firstborn of Israel. It is his last will and testament.

The book of Exodus is inclusive. It invites all the peoples of Syria-Palestine into the household of Abraham and Sarah. The book of Deuteronomy is exclusive. The only good Canaanite is a dead Canaanite, even though the "Canaanites" in the book of Deuteronomy are not the indigenous peoples of Syria-Palestine, but Hebrews who celebrate their Passover from slavery to freedom at the ancient sanctuaries of Carmel, Shiloh, Beersheba, or Gilgal instead of in the royal temple in Jerusalem.

In the book of Exodus, the Covenant between Yahweh and Israel is unconditional. In the book of Deuteronomy it is conditional. Yahweh will endow the Hebrews with land and children only so long as they worship Yahweh alone, and only so long as they worship Yahweh in the temple in Jerusalem. The clear sense of confidence in the book of Exodus is tinged with paranoia in the book of Deuteronomy, which argues that, in the beginning, every stranger in the land had been put to death, then here at the end, that no enemy could conquer its cities and enslave its people.

The traditions preserved in the book of Exodus today began developing in early Israel (1200–1000 B.C.E.). They proclaim a hope-filled worldview envisioning Hebrews throughout Syria-Palestine living free of monarchs who collect taxes to build cities and to pay soldiers to wage war and bring home prisoners to work as slaves. As the destruction of the states of Israel (721 B.C.E.) and Judah (587 B.C.E.) became imminent, the Hebrews struggled to put the impending tragedy of losing their divine gifts of land and children to the Assyrians and to the Babylonians into perspective. The same traditions that celebrated the foundation of ancient Israel after 1200 B.C.E. would mark its Passover to a culture without a country. Once again these ancient stories would help the people of Yahweh find their way.

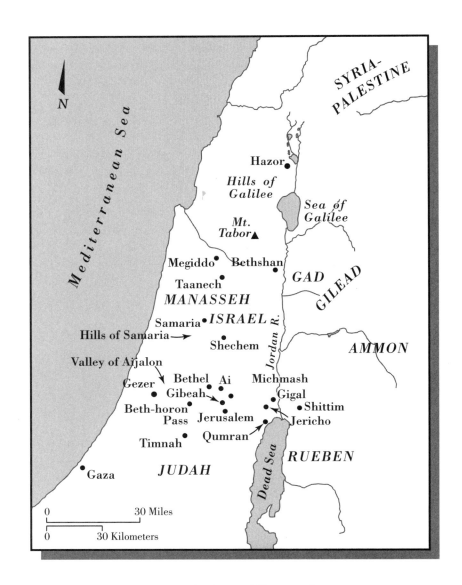

Points of Interest (Chapter 4)

4

Books of Joshua
and Judges

(Josh 1:1 — Judg 21:25)

For many, the books of Joshua (Hebrew: *Yehoshu'a*) and Judges (Hebrew: *Shofetim*) tell how miraculous military victories confirmed the Hebrews' faith in Yahweh. Nonetheless, archaeology cannot confirm that there were Hebrews in Syria-Palestine when the walls of Jericho came tumbling down. Furthermore, the genocides that took place during the Crusades, during the conquest of the Americas, and during World War II have made Jews, Christians, and Muslims painfully aware how easily any reading of the Bible that understands God to be authorizing the faithful to kill their enemies can be misused.

The events of Joshua and Judges are set in the Iron Age (1200–1000 B.C.E.) after the empires of Egypt, Hatti, and Mycenae collapsed. This political vacuum made it possible for smaller regional cultures like ancient Israel to begin their struggles for independence. The time when these events take place, however, is not the same as the time when these stories were told. The events took place between 1200 and 1000 B.C.E., but the versions of these stories in the Bible today developed after 721 B.C.E., when the Assyrians destroyed the Hebrew state of Israel and its capital city of Samaria. During this period, Josiah, a young ruler of the Hebrew state of Judah, which had miraculously survived the Assyrian invasion of Syria-Palestine, was crowned king of Judah at the age of eight, after his father's assassination. His reign lasted thirty-one years (640–609 B.C.E.). His name used the same three Hebrews letters as the name "Joshua," and he considered himself to be Joshua reborn. Josiah was a warrior-king whose soldiers campaigned from Jerusalem and Jericho in the east into the former territories of Judah in the west. Consequently, the Bible portrays Joshua conquering the same land (2 Kgs 23:19; 2 Chr 34:6).

The Assyrian empire, which had previously dominated Syria-Palestine, was in decline, making the changes that characterized Josiah's reign possible. Josiah carried out domestic reforms as well. Following the discovery of a scroll containing traditions preserved in the book of Deuteronomy, Josiah rededicated the royal temple as the state sanctuary. He began celebrating Passover as a state holiday, and decommissioned all the other regional sanctuaries of Yahweh throughout Judah. The traditions in the books of Joshua-Judges developed in this climate of nationalism, when any household that challenged Josiah's reforms was labeled a traitor, a "Canaanite," or a "prostitute" by Josiah's royal prophets. Josiah polarized Judah. Fatalism spread. There was little tolerance for diversity. Josiah's fervor led him to a martyr's death at Megiddo while trying to block Pharaoh Neco II (610–595 B.C.E.) from reinforcing the Assyrians who were retreating from the Babylonians (2 Kgs 22:1—23:30).

Judah's self-searching continued after the death of Josiah and the destruction of Jerusalem by the Babylonians in 587 B.C.E. Some of the people of Judah who were deported by the Babylonians began to reread the books of Deuteronomy, Joshua, Judges, and Samuel-Kings from a point of view that scholars today call the "Deuteronomist's History." This reading charged that it was not Yahweh who had failed to protect the land from its enemies, but the people of Yahweh who had failed to obey the Covenant between Yahweh and Israel. If the people had kept the covenant, the land would have remained in the hands of the Hebrews. If, from the days of Joshua onward, the Hebrews had put to death all those who did not worship Yahweh in Jerusalem, the land would have survived. Only when one people worshiped one God in one place would the land and children that Yahweh promised Abraham and Sarah be safe from their enemies. Until the time of Josiah, no such tradition of conformity had existed in ancient Israel. The Hebrews had worshiped Yahweh throughout the land at sanctuaries from Dan to Beersheba. Yet the exclusiveness of the Deuteronomist's History characterizes the books of Joshua and Judges today.

The traditions in the books of Joshua and Judges are companions to those in the books of Exodus, Leviticus, and Numbers (Exod 1:7—Num 27:11) and in the book of Deuteronomy (Num 27:12—Deut 34:12). The setting where these traditions developed, however, may be more liturgical than military. These traditions may say more about worship than about war. They may not celebrate wars of liberation from Egypt and wars of the conquest of Syria-Palestine. They may be traditions that celebrate Yahweh as the divine patron of the Hebrews, whom the book of Exodus remembers for blessing the Hebrews with children, and whom the books of Deuteronomy, Joshua, and Judges remember for blessing them with land.

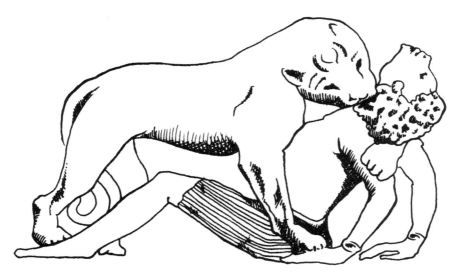

Lion Slays a Man
(Nimrud 900–700 B.C.E.; ivory 10 x 10 cm)

Covenant between Yahweh and Israel
(Josh 1:1-18)

The book of Joshua opens with a covenant entitling the Hebrews in Gilead to cross the Jordan River and settle in the land west of the river (Josh 1:1-18). Gilead is the Bible belt of early Israel. Hard-liners like Elijah came from this heartland (1 Kgs 17:1). This covenant between Yahweh and Israel is parallel to a covenant between Yahweh and Abraham (Gen 11:27—12:8). The people that Yahweh creates in the books of Genesis and Exodus are endowed with land in the books of Deuteronomy, Joshua, and Judges.

Joshua immediately executes his commission by granting land to the tribes of Reuben, Gad, and Manasseh (Josh 1:10-18). This simple transfer of title with which the book of Joshua opens is elaborately detailed in the land grants with which it closes (Josh 12:1—19:51). Ancestor stories and hero stories survey the land (Josh 2:1—12:24). Genealogies identify the tracts assigned to each household (Josh 13:1—21:45).

The Hebrews take possession of the land for which they had not labored, and villages that they had not built, and settle in them. They eat the fruits of their vineyards and olive groves that they did not plant (Josh 22:1—24:33). This land is not the prize of conquest; it is the gift of Yahweh.

The third-day motif in the covenant further emphasizes that the Hebrews' settlement in the land west of the river is the work of Yahweh, and not their work. The third day is the day of Yahweh (Gen 40:13-20; 42:17-18; Exod 19:10-16; 2 Kgs 18:9-10). It is the day on which Yahweh draws life from death, cosmos from chaos, freedom from slavery.

Story of Rahab as Host
(Josh 2:1-24 + 6:22-25)

A Story of Rahab as Host begins when Joshua dispatches two warriors from Shittim on a reconnaissance mission. The destination of the warriors is not Jericho, but simply "the land" (Josh 2:24). They go directly to the house of a woman named Rahab. She greets these strangers with hospitality, in contrast to the ruler of the city, who will threaten them with violence. Almost immediately the ruler of the land sends soldiers to question Rahab about collaborating with Joshua's warriors. The story ends when she rescues the two warriors with cleverness and courage.

The characters in the story play roles in a society shaped by the tributary economics of Egypt at the end of the Late Bronze period (1400–1200 B.C.E.). Egypt stationed governors and military detachments, like the soldiers who interrogate Rahab, in Syria-Palestine to represent its interests. These governors leased the land to rulers, like the monarch in the story, to harvest raw materials like flax and to produce manufactured goods like rope for Egypt. Surrounding trade centers, like the city in the story, were villages of farmers and herders, like the household of Rahab. Governors set quotas of goods and services for each village. Representatives of these villages, like Rahab, lived in cities to protect their goods in transit.

The political reforms of Pharaoh Akhenaten (1364–1347 B.C.E.) plunged Egypt into economic turmoil. Egypt recalled its governors and soldiers from Syria-Palestine. Those Egyptian officials who remained were powerless to harvest and process raw materials. Households began to abandon their villages and pioneer new ones in the hills above the Jordan River. Some, like Joshua and his warriors, became raiders who attacked caravans moving to and from trade centers. Officials filled diplomatic pouches to Akhenaten's government at Amarna with urgent appeals for help. These letters describe conditions similar to those in the books of Joshua and Judges (Fig. 29).

References to flax and rope in the story may suggest that the household of Rahab made rope from flax for Egypt. Wild flax is a delicate plant with beautiful blue flowers and is native to Syria-Palestine. As early as 5000 B.C.E., farmers began domesticating the first of some two hundred species eventually used throughout the world of the Bible for linseed oil, fodder, cloth, and rope. The Gezer Almanac (see Fig. 2) assigns a month for harvesting flax. Farmers pulled the stalks when the seeds were ripe and dried them. Refiners pressed the seeds to extract linseed oil. The dregs became animal fodder. After soaking the stalks to ret, or loosen, the outer fibers, they spread them on rooftops to dry. Weavers hackled, or combed, the fibers from the inner core and spun them into thread. The short, tangled fibers left over from the combing were tow (Judg 16:9), which made a coarse yarn. Flax and wool were the standard fibers used to weave clothing until the development of cotton.

"Rahab" is a nickname that praises Yahweh for enlarging a household (1 Chr 23:17; 24:21). Nevertheless, the opening episode introduces Rahab as a prostitute. Joshua's warriors may have gone to her house to have sex, but the relationship between the warriors and the woman may be much more sophisticated. The story contrasts Rahab's shameful title and honorable actions with the honorable title and shameful actions of Joshua. It uses a label like "prostitute" for Rahab in its crisis in order to refute it in the denouement. With the exception of this label of shame, the story treats Rahab with honor throughout. Even though Rahab subverts the male establishments of both Joshua and the ruler of the land, her behavior is neither prohibited nor scandalous, like the behavior of Ruth (Ruth 3:1-18), of Tamar (Gen 38:1-30), or of Bathsheba (1 Kgs 1:5-53). The story contains no demurs insisting that Rahab is not a suitable candidate for her mission. In the books of Samuel-Kings, Jesse apologizes: "here remains yet the youngest, but behold he is keeping the sheep" (1 Sam 16:11). In the book of Jeremiah, the prophet demurs: "Yahweh, our Creator, I do not know how to speak" (Jer 1:6). Not one character in this Story of Rahab, however, apologizes that she is only a prostitute.

Letter 244:1-30

Pharaoh, ruler of the heavens and earth
From: Biridiya, governor of Megiddo

I am your slave, and I renew my covenant with you as my pharaoh by bowing before you seven times seven times.

Pharaoh should know that, since he recalled his archers to Egypt, Labayu, the governor of Shechem, has not stopped raiding the land of Megiddo. The people of Megiddo cannot leave the city to shear your sheep for fear of Labayu's soldiers.

Because you have not replaced the archers, Labayu is now strong enough to attack the city of Megiddo itself. If Pharaoh does not reinforce the city, Labayu will capture it.

The people of Megiddo are already suffering from hunger and disease. I beg Pharaoh to send 150 soldiers to protect Megiddo from Labayu or he will certainly capture the city.

FIGURE 29   Amarna Letters (Matthews and Benjamin 1997: 138)

Later biblical and rabbinical traditions also treat Rahab with honor. The books of Ezra-Nehemiah-Chronicles (1 Chr 2:10) honor Rahab as the mother of Boaz. Respect for Rahab continues in the earliest translations and commentaries. Early Jewish translations of the Bible into the Aramaic language, which are called "Targumim," translate the Hebrew word for "prostitute" into Aramaic as "innkeeper." Rabbis like Rashi argue that Rahab is a "grocer." The Letter to the Hebrews honors her as a woman of faith (Heb. 11:31). The rabbis celebrate Rahab as one of the four most beautiful women in the world. The Talmud has Joshua marry Rahab, so that, ironically, he masters Syria-Palestine only to be mastered by Syria-Palestine's most engaging woman. At least eight of their descendants were prophets of the stature of Ezekiel, Jeremiah, and Huldah (*b. Meg.* 15a).

The time when the Story of Rahab as Host was told may offer one explanation for the contrast between her title and her actions. Like many of these traditions about Joshua, who lived at the end of the Late Bronze period, this story developed during the reign of Josiah. Josiah called all the people of Judah to the temple to renew the covenant (2 Kgs 23:21--23; 2 Chr 35:1-19); consequently, the book of Joshua portrays Joshua calling the Hebrews to the sanctuary at Shechem to renew their covenant with Yahweh (Josh 24:1-28). The household of Rahab considered the temple in Jerusalem as little more than a royal chapel, so may have continued to worship Yahweh at the Gilgal sanctuary of Jericho. Josiah and the household of David could go up to the temple to tell the stories of the great works that Yahweh did in Jerusalem, but the household of Rahab would go to Gilgal to tell the stories of the great works that Yahweh did at Jericho. Consequently, Josiah's prophets labeled Rahab a prostitute, not because of the work she did in the Late Bronze period, but because of the political position that her household took in the Iron Age (2 Kgs 9:22; Isa 23:16-17; Nah 3:4). She is a prostitute because her household was in political exile in the days of Josiah. A similar use of the terms appears in a Trial of Samaria in the book of Micah (Mic 1:2-7), which does not indict Samaria for failing to prosecute women and men who engage in sexual intercourse for a living. The trial indicts the state for negotiating covenants for trade and military assistance that provided luxury for a few and poverty for many. Micah parodies the titles of the women, whose marriages ratified these state covenants, by labeling them "prostitutes," and the goods and services that Samaria enjoyed from the covenants as "the wages of prostitutes." Therefore, it was not the household of Joshua in early Israel that labeled Rahab a prostitute, but the household of Josiah during the final days of the monarchy in Judah.

In contrast to the other traditions in the book of Joshua, Rahab, and not Joshua and his warriors, is the protagonist in the story. Even more unusual, in contrast to Rahab who is wise, the story casts Joshua and his warriors as fools. The tradition celebrates Rahab as more faithful to Yahweh than Joshua and his warriors, and as a better warrior. She also outwits the ruler of the land and his soldiers.

Joshua has seen all the powerful events that Yahweh has brought about at the Red Sea and east of the Jordan Valley. Rahab has only heard about these great works. Yet Joshua is doubting, while Rahab is believing. Joshua sees, and does not believe. Rahab only hears, but believes. When Yahweh commissions Joshua to take the land, the appropriate response is for him to go and take the land. Instead Joshua sends out a reconnaissance mission. Today military science requires reconnaissance, but *herem* war in the world of the Bible forbids it. Reconnaissance missions determine the strength of the enemy, which in *herem* war is irrelevant. Warriors are expected to go into *herem* war at a disadvantage in order to highlight the victory as divine rather than human. To prepare for *herem* war, a chief like Joshua may use prophets (1 Kgs 22:5), divination (2 Kgs 13:15), necromancy (1 Sam 28:6), and the ephod with its urim and thummim (1 Sam 30:7-8; 1 Sam 28:6), but not reconnaissance. Reconnaissance characterizes warriors as petty (Num 13:1—14:15), cowardly (Deut 1:19-46), greedy (Judg 1:22-26), and heretical (Judg 18:1-31). Going into battle against a superior opponent is an act of faith that highlights the victory as Yahweh's, not Israel's. Jerubbaal (Gideon) twice reduces the size of the tribe mustered to defend Israel against the Midianites (Judg 7:1-8:28). Likewise, Deuteronomy (Deut 13:13-19) assumes that the size of a city convicted of treason is of no consequence to the punitive expedition ordered against it.

Rahab has all of the military skills that Joshua lacks. Joshua personally selects the messengers to gather intelligence for him, yet they are so incompetent that the soldiers of the land detect them immediately. Rahab is a master of combat tactics. She is an expert in designing safe houses. She knows how to use camouflage and to distribute misinformation. She knows all the commando tactics necessary to scale down the walls of a city, and just how to avoid the soldiers who patrol the border along the Jordan River.

Rahab is also more faithful to Yahweh than Joshua is. She has no doubts that Yahweh will conquer the land. Therefore, she asks his warriors to spare her household when Yahweh sweeps through the city as Yahweh swept through Egypt slaying their firstborn (Exod 12:23). Like the Hebrews who celebrated their first Passover from slavery in Egypt by marking their doors with lamb's blood, Rahab celebrates the Passover of her household by marking her window with a blood-red rope (Josh 2:18; 6:25). Finally, Rahab is more powerful than the ruler of the land, who considers her both ambitious and capable of overthrowing him. He had her under surveillance. His soldiers also respect Rahab, and obey her orders to search for the messengers outside the walls.

The crisis episode (Josh 2:1) condenses the actions that appear in most hospitality stories (Gen 18:1-15; 19:1-22; Judg 19:1-30; 2 Sam 17:15-22). The commission that Joshua gives to the messengers now almost completely eclipses Rahab's actions. Since Joshua is not the protagonist, it would be better to read the commission simply as a clause that modifies the strangers to whom Rahab offers hospitality: "two warriors, whom Joshua ben Nun dispatched from a sacred grove of eucalyptus trees with the orders: 'Go and scout the land,' approached the gates of the land at sundown disguised as messengers. Rahab the prostitute saw them coming, and went to meet them. She bowed to the ground and said, 'Please, gentlemen, come to my house. Wash your feet and spend the night. Then you may rise early and go on your way" (Josh 2:1).

The climax (Josh 2:2-7) reports the shrewdness with which Rahab defends the warriors. The Bible regularly celebrates the shrewdness with which Israel's ancestors outwit foreign rulers. Abraham shrewdly outwits Pharaoh (Gen 12:9—13:1) and the ruler of Gerar (Gen 20:1-18). Isaac outwits a Philistine ruler (Gen 26:1-11). This story casts Rahab as being as shrewd as Abraham or Isaac.

There are two episodes in the denouement (Josh 2:8-24). One recounts the Covenant between Yahweh and Rahab (Josh 2:8-14), the other her celebration of Passover (Josh 2:15-24). The first episode reports Rahab's profession of faith (Deut 25:5-9). She ratifies two basic articles of Israel's creed: it is Yahweh who gives Israel land (Josh 2:8-9) and it is Yahweh who sets Israel free (Josh 2:10). Her vocabulary is almost all taken from Deuteronomy, which was the basis of Josiah's reform (Deut 6:21-23; 26:5-10). She also promises to help Joshua capture the land (Josh 2:12-13). Joshua's warriors react by granting Rahab and her household amnesty (Josh 2:14).

In the second episode of the denouement Rahab exercises her obligations as a covenant partner of Yahweh by helping Joshua's warriors escape (Josh 2:15-16). They reaffirm their promise of amnesty for her household (Josh 2:17-24). This episode uses prolepsis, which arranges events according to importance, not chronology. Rahab lets the warriors down by a rope (Josh 2:15) before negotiating a covenant with them (Josh 2:16-18). Chronologically, she would have negotiated with Joshua's warriors before lowering them over the city wall.

The point of the story is to remind its audience that Rahab is not a renegade; she is the mother of a household. The household of Rahab snapped up Josiah's label of "prostitute" and used this story to refute it (2 Kgs 23:7). How can an ancestor like Sarah (Gen 12:9—13:1), Tamar (Gen 38:1-30), Shiphrah and Puah (Exod 1:12-21), the daughter of Levi (Exod 2:1-10), and Miriam (Exod 15:20-21) be a prostitute? How can a chief like Deborah (Judg 4:1—5:31), who delivers her household from its enemies, be a prostitute?

The story warns the household of Josiah to remember that the hospitality that earned the household of Rahab honor in early Israel should not be taken away by someone whose own ancestors were its beneficiaries. The household of Rahab retains the label in introducing its ancestor Rahab, to question how a household that did not betray Joshua could betray Josiah. Without the hospitality, the military skill, and the unconditional faith of Rahab, the warriors of Joshua would have died in the gates of the land. The household of Rahab, in fact, is not a prostitute, but a covenant partner. Her household is hospitable, not hostile, to both Joshua and Josiah. To protect the warriors of Joshua, Rahab defies the orders of the ruler of the land, tricks his soldiers, and then uses one of her household's own flax ropes to help the warriors escape.

The Story of Rahab as Host was told to defend her household against a new Joshua, named "Josiah," who tried to excommunicate it for continuing to worship Yahweh outside Jerusalem. The cruel irony that the household of Rahab had welcomed as strangers those whose descendants were trying to exterminate it may have led the household to question the value of hospitality as a means of survival. The story reminded the household that the same Yahweh who delivered it once from Joshua, will would deliver it again from Josiah. By contrasting Rahab's gracious hospitality, outstanding military skill, and profound faith in Yahweh with Joshua's questioning faith and bungling strategy, the storytellers certified that her household should not be exterminated, but continue to enjoy all the rights and privileges of a covenant partner in early Israel.

The Story of Rahab as Host introduces the books of Joshua and Judges to emphasize that the Hebrews conquer the land by accepting hospitality from Rahab. She hears what Yahweh has done for the Hebrews, and negotiates a covenant of her own with Yahweh for land and children. The Hebrews join the inhabitants of the land in overthrowing the monarchs who oppress them. The story creates a stark contrast between the violence of a Joshua and the other chiefs, who exterminate strangers, and the hospitality of a Rahab and her household, who welcome them. The land belongs, not to the powerful like Joshua and his warriors who conquer its inhabitants, but to the powerless like Rahab and her household who welcome strangers with hospitality.

Inauguration of Joshua at Jericho
(JOSH 5:13—6:27)

The Bible sets the inauguration of Joshua (Josh 5:13–6:27) at Jericho. Jericho is an oasis in the Jordan River Valley some 840 feet below sea level and twenty miles north of the Dead Sea. In contrast with the Hills of Galilee, which average forty inches of rainfall a year, and with the Hills of Samaria, which average about thirty inches of rainfall a year, and with Jerusalem, which averages twenty-four inches, and with Beth-shan, which averages thirteen inches, Jericho receives only six inches of rainfall a year.

Jericho was founded on a site where two fault lines cut deep into the hill country, creating two east–west highways running between the Mediterranean Sea and the Jordan Valley. One route, called the Beth-horon Pass, ran through the Valley of Aijalon near Jerusalem; the other ran near Gibeah and Michmash. What draws the telling of the inauguration of Joshua to Jericho is not only its strategic location, but also its standing as a threshold separating chaos from cosmos. Jericho was the place where the world began, where cosmos was created. Therefore Jericho was the site where Joshua was inaugurated to teach the people of Yahweh to live in the land of Yahweh without cities like Jericho. Cities were the legacy of the pharaohs and the work of slaves. A thousand years after the days of Joshua, the people of Qumran still renewed their covenant with Yahweh by crossing the Jordan River and processing around its Jericho's ruins.

Generation after generation left marks at Jericho. Mesolithic pioneers occupied the site in 8000 B.C.E. during the Natufian era. Neolithic engineers fortified Jericho with a massive wall, tower, and dry moat between 8500 and 4300 B.C.E. Early Bronze settlers occupied the site from 2900 to 2300 B.C.E. Hyksos warriors established a battle camp at Jericho fortified with a sloping glacis and mud-brick wall in 1750–1560 B.C.E. Hezekiah (726–697 B.C.E.) and Simon (142–134 B.C.E.) were the last kings of Judah to rebuild it (Judg 3:13; 2 Sam 10:5; 1 Chr 19:5). Despite Jericho's long history, however, the site was uninhabited as often as inhabited. Jericho was a ghost town from 4000 to 2900 B.C.E., from 2300 to 1750 B.C.E., from 1560 to 716 B.C.E., and from 587 to 142 B.C.E. The existing ruins at Jericho and Ai, Jericho's sister city, date from the Early Bronze period (3300–2000 B.C.E.) or the Middle Bronze period (2000–1550 B.C.E.). As yet, there is no archaeological evidence for a city or a destruction layer at either site after 1200 B.C.E. (Fig. 30).

Kathleen Kenyon (1906–78) of the British School of Archaeology in Jerusalem was the most accomplished archaeologist to excavate Jericho (1952–58). For her, Jericho was a strongly fortified Hyksos city during the Middle Bronze period. Like the Hebrews, the Hyksos were a Semitic people. They ruled an empire that stretched from Avaris near Cairo today to the Carmel Mountains near Haifa. Their city at Jericho was destroyed more than 250 years before Joshua, and remained abandoned until 716 B.C.E., when Hezekiah rebuilt it. More than one explanation has been offered to reconcile the destruction of Jericho described in the book of Joshua with the lack of solid archaeological evidence that a city existed at the site in the days of Joshua.

Perhaps the traditions describing the conquest of Jericho and Ai (Joshua 1–9) are not battle reports, but explanations of the ruins that the Hebrews found at Jericho and at Ai. Since this proposal was first suggested, anthropologists have shown that storytellers do use striking natural phenomena and human ruins familiar to their audiences to punctuate stories, but they do not tell stories just to explain natural phenomena and human ruins.

Perhaps Jericho's Late Bronze–period city may still lie beneath a section of the tell that has not yet been excavated. No excavations have been conducted at Jericho since those directed by Kathleen Kenyon, who excavated only a small portion of the site.

Perhaps the city that Joshua conquered may have been completely eroded by Syria-Palestine's winter rains. There was a real city at the site when the Hebrew villages appeared in the area, but all trace of that city has vanished.

Perhaps the people whom Joshua conquered in the Late Bronze period were living behind Middle Bronze–period walls. They did not build their own walls in the Late Bronze period, but simply recycled those from an earlier period.

Charles Warren (1867–68) dug three thirty-foot shafts into the tell and determined that the 70-foot high, 10-acre mound (1200 N-S x 600 E-W feet) was artificial, not natural.

Ernst Sellin and Carl Watzinger (1907–09, 1911) mapped the Middle Bronze period (1600 B.C.E.) retaining wall, 15 feet high, at the base of the tell.

Using a pottery chronology now considered faulty, **John Gartstang** (1930–36) dated mud-brick wall and city at stratum iv to the Late Bronze period and their destruction to Joshua (1400–1380 B.C.E.).

Kathleen Kenyon (1952–58), whose reports were finally published in 1981–83, dug three trenches on N, W, and S sides of the tell, dated the tower (25 feet diam., 25 feet high) to Neolithic period (7000 B.C.E.), mud-brick wall (6.5 feet wide, 12 feet high) and 40-degree glacis to the Early Bronze period, but mud-brick wall and city at stratum iv to the Middle Bronze period (1350 B.C.E.) because there was no Mycenaean pottery associated with either.

Bryant G. Wood ("Did the Israelites Conquer Jericho? A New Look at the Archaeological Evidence," *BARev* 16 [March/Apr: 1990]: 44–57) did not excavate Jericho, but restudied Kenyon's records, and argues that:

1) 20 strata, 3 major destructions, 12 minor destructions cannot be assigned to only 100 years (1650–1550 B.C.E.);
2) there is Late Bronze–period local pottery in Garstang's and Kenyon's finds;
3) Jericho is not on a trade route, hence would not import Late Bronze–period Mycenaean pottery like Megiddo and Gezer;
4) Kenyon excavated an ordinary neighborhood where imported Mycenaean pottery would not occur;
5) Kenyon excavated only two 26-foot x 26-foot squares, which provides too little data to be conclusive;
6) Hyksos retreating from Egypt would not have destroyed Jericho, which was their own city;
7) Egyptians did not pursue Hyksos north of Sharuhen in the Negeb;
8) Egyptians always attacked before harvest, and six bushels of wheat recovered indicate city fell after harvest;
9) continuous scarab record in tombs from the Middle Bronze period through the Late Bronze period (1800–1400 B.C.E.) indicates a Late Bronze–period city did exist

and concludes that:

1) a landslide caused by a Late Bronze–period (1400 B.C.E.!) earthquake blocked Jordan;
2) an earthquake collapsed the Late Bronze–period mud-brick wall, which tumbled across retaining wall;
3) the Hebrews used rubble as a ladder to enter the city;
4) spontaneous fires caused by collapsing buildings destroyed the city.

FIGURE 30   Jericho's Archaeological Record

Perhaps the "Jericho" in these traditions may originally have been "Bethel," which, like Ai, was also a sister city of Jericho. There is clear evidence for Bethel's destruction in the Late Bronze period, and storytellers may eventually have transferred the battle of Bethel to the more famous Jericho.

Perhaps Kenyon simply overlooked evidence for a city at Jericho during the Late Bronze period. There may be locally made Late Bronze pottery among Kenyon's finds, even though there is no Late Bronze–period pottery imported from Mycenae. There may also be scarab seals from the Late Bronze period among the grave goods that Kenyon recovered. Burned grain recovered from the excavation may show that Jericho fell quickly and not after a prolonged siege. An earthquake may have created a landslide that held back the waters of the Jordan and tumbled the city's main mud-brick wall, providing a ramp down from the top of the tell across its glacis and retaining wall. The Hebrews may have climbed up this ramp into the city set ablaze when roofs collapsed into cooking fires.

The interpretation here, however, assumes that it was the ruins of Jericho, and not a living city, that inspired the Inauguration of Joshua at Jericho. The ruins of its lofty tower and massive walls were monuments to the affluence and organization of the peoples who once lived at Jericho. Like others who came on these ruins, the Hebrews were awestruck. The ruins made the Hebrews wonder why Yahweh allowed this great city to be destroyed, and whether or not they should rebuild it.

The Hebrews had good reasons to rebuild Jericho. Rebuilding the city would be an act of stewardship. They would be repairing the land that Yahweh had willed to them. Normally, heirs were expected to take immediate possession of their testator's estates in order to begin payment of the agreed annuity or sacrifices. Rebuilding Jericho would also allow the Hebrews to enjoy its affluence. Jericho was an economic gold mine. Obviously, the founders of Jericho knew how to make a good living in this land, and the Hebrews wanted to imitate them. The Hebrews hoped Jericho could make Israel as rich as their predecessors on the site.

The Inauguration of Joshua at Jericho reflects the idealism of early Israel. The Hebrews who built their villages in the hills above Jericho were survivors of the great slave empires of Egypt, Hatti, and Mycenae. Cities were the hallmark of these empires. While most cultures in the world of the Bible looked on cities as great accomplishments, the clan of Joshua considered cities to be monuments to slavery. Hence, the Hebrews created a village culture, not a city culture. To prevent slavery, early Israel prohibited not only cities, but monarchs, taxes, and soldiers as well. Life in early Israel would be simple, but it would be free.

Interdicts similar to the one placed on Jericho in the Inauguration of Joshua at Jericho also appear in a tradition about Babel (Gen 11:1-90) and a tradition in the book of Deuteronomy (Deut 6:10-19). To rebuild Jericho would return the Hebrews to the slavery from which Yahweh had delivered them. Cities and slavery were the antithesis of being Hebrew. The Inauguration of Joshua warns the Hebrews not to rebuild Jericho, but to leave the city in ruins, and off-limits, as a reminder that only in a land without cities can they remain free.

Crisis Episode
(JOSH 5:13)

The Inauguration of Joshua at Jericho (Josh 5:13—6:27) follows the same pattern as the Inauguration of Marduk in the Enuma Elish Stories from Mesopotamia (Fig. 31). Just as the divine assembly of Babylon inaugurates Marduk to confront Tiamat, Yahweh inaugurates Joshua to confront Jericho. Inauguration stories identify candidates to the community and authorize their use of power. These stories defend leaders against charges of ambition by portraying them as simply following the commission of their divine patrons. Inaugurations regularly open with candidates pursuing ordinary tasks.

When the book of Joshua opens, the Hebrews are east of the Jordan River. Some are content, even proud, to remain there. They have no desire to cross the frontier into the unexplored land to the west. Yahweh interrupts this peaceful existence and inaugurates Joshua to lead the Hebrews into a new world. When the inauguration opens, Joshua is on guard duty at the perimeter of the Hebrew camp. Yahweh approaches the camp as a warrior responding to a call to arms (1 Sam 13:2; 22:7; 24:3; 2 Sam 6:1). The intention of the theophany is to attract the attention of a candidate and to lure the candidate into the presence of Yahweh. The armed warrior attracts the attention of Joshua, just as the burning bush attracts the attention of Moses at Mt. Horeb (Exod 3:3). Joshua challenges the warrior to identify himself: "Are you for us, or for our enemies?" (Josh 5:13) The warrior answers, "Neither!" (Josh 5:14), which is a characteristic refusal of Yahweh to identify himself on demand. Only Yahweh asks questions. "At ease!" would be a better translation of Yahweh's refusal to give the password.

The prohibition of images of Yahweh (Deut 5:8-10) in an iconoclastic culture like ancient Israel imposes restraints on any theophany in the Bible, which technically can never be an image of Yahweh. Therefore, inaugurations regularly introduce Yahweh vaguely as a "messenger" (Exod 3:2) or a "man from the household of our Creator" (Judg 13:6). In the Inauguration of Abraham at Mt. Moriah (Gen 21:33—22:19), a messenger speaks to Abraham twice (Gen 22:10+15), before Yahweh speaks to him (Gen 22:16). In the Inauguration of Moses at Mt. Horeb (Exod 2:23—4:23), a messenger appears (Exod 3:2), before Yahweh speaks (Exod 3:6). Although the Annunciation to the Wife of Manoah (Judg 13:1-25) never formally introduces Manoah and his wife to the "man from our Creator," only Yahweh hears prayers (Judg 13:9), eats sacrifices (Judg 13:15-16), and refuses to give the candidate a name (Judg 13:17-18). The motif of Yahweh as a warrior with the a fiery sword

inauguration story crisis (Josh 5:13)

When Joshua appeared at Jericho, a warrior suddenly approached him with his sword drawn. Joshua challenged the stranger: "Friend or foe?"

inauguration story climax (Josh 5:14)

The warrior answered: "At ease! I am Yahweh, commander of the divine warriors. I am with you." Joshua fell to his knees, touching his forehead to the ground. "Your word is my command!" Yahweh Sabaoth ordered Joshua: "Take off your sandals. You are standing on holy ground." So Joshua removed his sandals.

inauguration story denouement: a creation story (Josh 6:1-27)

Jericho was unable to muster soldiers or assemble elders before the Israelites. Then Yahweh said to Joshua, "I have delivered Jericho with its ruler and all its warriors to you. Your warriors should circle the city in procession once a day for six consecutive days. Seven priests should walk in procession with their trumpets in front of the ark of Yahweh. On the seventh day, walk in processions around the city seven times. Order the priests to blow their trumpets and the warriors to shout their battle cry: 'Yahweh is Lord!' In response, the walls of the city will prostrate before the procession of warriors walking one behind the other."

So Joshua, the son of Nun, ordered the priests to shoulder the ark, and assigned seven priests with trumpets to lead it out of the camp. He ordered the warriors to circle the city in procession in front of the ark, and they carried out Joshua's orders. Seven priests blowing their trumpets led the ark of Yahweh out of the camp with warriors walking both in front of the ark and behind it. Although the priests blew their trumpets continuously, Joshua had ordered the warriors not to shout their battle cry until he gave the word. On **the first day**, the ark circled the city only once before returning to camp for the night. At dawn, Joshua ordered the priests to shoulder the ark, and assigned seven priests blowing their trumpets continuously to lead it out of the camp with warriors walking both in front of the ark and behind it. On **the second day**, they circled the city only once before returning to camp for the night. On **six consecutive days**, they repeated the ritual.

At dawn on **the seventh day**, they walked in procession around the city, in the same order, a total of seven times. It was only on the seventh day that they circled the city seven times. On the seventh time, when the priests had blown their trumpets, Joshua gave the word to the warriors: "Shout: 'Yahweh has delivered the city into our hands!' Sacrifice the city and everything in it to Yahweh. Spare only the household of Rahab the prostitute because she spared our warriors. Bring nothing from the sacrifice back to the camp. Plunder taken from a sacrifice contaminates everything it touches. Deposit the silver, gold, and bronze and iron from the sacrifice directly into the treasury of Yahweh." The warriors shouted their battle

(continued)

cry as soon as the priests blew their trumpets. In response, the walls of the city prostrated before the procession of warriors walking one behind the other. They sacrificed the entire city to Yahweh, men and women, young and old, oxen, sheep, and asses. Joshua ordered the warriors who had scouted the land: "Deliver the household of Rahab the prostitute as you swore to her you would do!" The warriors who had scouted the land delivered Rahab, her father, mother, brothers, and their slaves, and brought them to the perimeter of the camp. They offered the city as a sacrifice and deposited all the silver, gold, bronze, and iron directly into the treasury of Yahweh. Nonetheless, they spared the household of Rahab the prostitute, who are still Israelites to this day, because she spared the warriors Joshua sent to scout Jericho. Joshua placed the city under interdict: "Cursed be the ruler who rebuilds this city, Jericho. At the cost of his firstborn shall he lay its foundation, and at the cost of his youngest son shall he set up its gates." Yahweh was with Joshua, he was honored throughout the land.

FIGURE 31   Inauguration of Joshua at Jericho (Josh 5:13—6:27)

at the boundary between the old world and the new world also appears in the Story of Adam and Eve as Farmers and Child-bearers, where Yahweh stations "the cherubim, and a sword flaming and turning to guard the way to the Tree of Life" (Gen 3:24). Yahweh also appears as a warrior in the books of Samuel-Kings (2 Sam 24:16-17; 2 Kgs 19:35; 1 Chr 21:16) and in a Trial of David (2 Sam 24:16-17). The warrior who confronts David is armed only with a raised hand, but as in the Inauguration of Joshua at Jericho, the target of this warrior's commission is a city. Yahweh talks with David about the city of Jerusalem, and with Joshua about the city of Jericho.

What takes place at this threshold will determine the future of Israel. Jericho is a sacred center and Yahweh guards its threshold with a fiery sword. Joshua must use competence and courage to deal with the guardian. Once across the threshold, the candidate is endowed with the wisdom of the sacred center by this guardian. To seize this wisdom, the candidate must challenge the guardian. Only by crossing the established boundaries, only by provoking the guardian's destructive power, can the candidate obtain the guardian's constructive power, which will allow the Hebrews to pass over into a new world. To cross the threshold, candidates must develop the discipline to deny the senses that limit them to the known world, and acquire a sense of the unknown new world. Armed with the confidence of this new sense, candidates confront the guardian without fear and lead their households forward. The Labor of Moses and Zipporah against Yahweh (Exod 4:24-26) and the Labor of Jacob against Yahweh (Gen 32:23-33) are parallel stories told about ancestors crossing a frontier to undertake a divine mission.

Climax Episode
(JOSH 5:14)

In the standard inauguration stories, Yahweh greets candidates formally by calling their name twice: "Moses! Moses!" (Exod 3:4). Once addressed, candidates realize they are in the presence of Yahweh. Instead of calling Joshua by name, however, Yahweh addresses him Joshua as his commander in chief: "At ease, I am Yahweh, commander of the divine warriors" (Josh 5:14).

Joshua, like candidates in other inauguration stories, prostrates himself. His posture is a demurral that demonstrates his lack of ambition and argues that he will take possession of Jericho only in obedience and not in a selfish quest for power. With both physical and verbal demurrals candidates promise to serve the community, not dominate it. Candidates in inauguration traditions are reluctant messengers.

Yahweh often responds to the demurrals of candidates with the promise: "I am with you." This promise appears at both the beginning of the Inauguration of Joshua at Jericho when the warrior says to Joshua: "as commander of the army of Yahweh I have now come" (Josh 5:14), and at the end when the story confirms that "Yahweh was with Joshua" (Josh 6:27).

Yahweh often stays the transfer of a candidate from the human plane to the divine plane with the words "Fear not!" The delay allows candidates to carry out a divine mission. Here Yahweh delays Joshua's transfer by teaching him the protocol for an audience with his divine patron. He tells Joshua to remove his sandals, which will prevent the holiness of Yahweh from transfiguring him into a risk for the Hebrews when he returns to the camp.

Denouement Episode
(JOSH 6:1-27)

Joshua is now prepared to receive his divine commission. Standard commissions use a command (Exod 3:8-10), a decalogue (Deut 5:6-21), or a covenant. This commission, however, is a creation story like the Enuma Elish stories that developed in Mesopotamia, and the Stories of the Heavens and the Earth in the book of Genesis (Gen 1:1--2:4). "When on high" are the opening words of the Enuma Elish stories (Enuma I:1), and a good example of the standard opening words for creation stories. Likewise, "When Joshua appeared before Jericho" better translates the opening words of this inauguration. When the messenger of Yahweh appears, a radical change is imminent (Gen 39:5; Exod 12:13; 1 Sam 5:9; 7:13; 12:15).

Sterility affidavits are the standard crisis episodes in creation stories. They certify that when the creator begins to create, there is nothing but chaos.

The sterility affidavit of the creation story: "all who went out of the gate of his city" (Gen 34:24) and "all who went in at the gate of his city" (Gen 23:8-10) identify the two most important groups of men. As early as the culture of Sumer, cities were governed by warriors and elders. In the Stories of Gilgamesh, both the elders and the warriors commission him to declare war on Kish. Here in the Inauguration of Joshua, there are no warriors to protect Jericho from its enemies, and there are no elders to resolve disputes among its households. The city is as lifeless as the chaos before which Yahweh stands in the Stories of the Heavens and the Earth.

The climax episode in the creation story is a cosmogony. Yahweh directs Joshua to celebrate the end of the old world of Jericho and the beginning of the new world of Israel. This liturgy contains a series of rubrics describing what is to be done and what is to be said. For six days, the Hebrews are to walk in procession around Jericho once a day. On the seventh day, they are to process around the city seven times. These seven days of processions parallel the seven days of creation in the Stories of the Heavens and the Earth. This liturgy, however, does not draw cosmos from chaos, but returns cosmos to chaos. It is a reversed ritual that inverts the creative process.

Although some words in the liturgy do carry military connotations, they also carry liturgical connotations. For example, the same Hebrew word can mean "the army" or "the people of Yahweh" (Josh 6:8). Likewise, to carry the ark of the covenant was as much an act of war as an act of worship. In battle, the ark was a rallying point for warriors separated from their detachments. In worship, the ark was the pedestal of Yahweh toward which the congregation directed its attention.

The walls of Jericho are the divine patron of the city. They prostrate themselves, which signals that the old world of Jericho has come to an end, and acknowledges that Yahweh is the new divine patron of this land (Josh 6:20). The walls are to remain prostrate and the city is placed under interdict to remind the Hebrews that the old world of monarchs and taxes and soldiers and cities and slaves has ended. The Hebrews draw a circle as they dance with the ark around the ruin, creating a forbidden zone where only Yahweh may enter.

Othniel Delivers Israel from Aram
(JUDG 3:7-11)

The book of Judges (Judg 1:1—21:25) contains a wonderful cycle of hero stories. Like all stories, hero stories have crisis, climax, and denouement episodes. Unlike most stories, which develop action with description and dialogue, hero stories use formulas. Each episode reports the action of Yahweh, who is the protagonist, and the reaction of the Hebrews, who are the antagonist. Yahweh frees the Hebrews by feeding them and protecting them from their enemies, so that they can work their own land and rear their own children. The Hebrews block Yahweh by negotiating covenants with strangers who enslave them by offering to feed and protect them in return for their land and children.

The clan of Caleb celebrated its hero Othniel (Judg 3:7-11). The clan of Shechem celebrated Gideon (Judges 9). The clan of Dan celebrated Samson (Judges 13–16). On anniversaries and holidays there would be stories to keep the memories of these heroes alive.

Hero stories were told by oppressed Hebrew clans to vent their frustration against their enemies. As each clan became part of the state of Israel, however, it brought not only its economic and political resources into the state, but its cultural heritage as well. Those who were once heroes of only a single clan became the heroes of all Israel. The book of Judges also celebrates their exploits as reflections of the great act of liberation of the Hebrew slaves from Egypt. These hero stories are full of language and motifs that recall the Death of the Firstborn of Egypt and the Birth of the Firstborn of Israel in the book of Exodus.

Hero stories follow a standard pattern, reflected in the story Othniel Delivers Israel from Aram (Judg 3:7-11). The protagonist in hero stories is always Yahweh. Human heroes like Othniel are not proagonists, but Yahweh's helpers, referred to in English translations as "judges."

In English, judges are officers of the court, who hear complaints and hand down verdicts. Judges in early Israel are chiefs or heroes who deliver the Hebrews from their enemies. Only when Yahweh decrees that their enemies have been "given into their hands" is it possible for the Hebrews to drive them out of the land. In this sense, the chief is a judge or officer of the court who carries out sentences imposed by Yahweh and the divine assembly.

The crisis episode in hero stories assumes, but does not report, Yahweh's action of endowing the Hebrews with land and children (Judg 3:7). Because land and children are Yahweh's gifts, Yahweh alone is entitled to protect and provide for them. If the Hebrews try to protect themselves or to provide for their land and children, they will forfeit them altogether. Hero stories interpret the loss of these divine endowments as a sentence for "doing evil," "forgetting Yahweh," or "serving Baal and Asherah."

Language in formulas is tightly packed. These formulas are not specified, so the indictments remain generic. They abbreviate a story that is assumed but seldom retold. The formula: "serving Baal and Asherah" is better understood as "serving Yahweh as Yahweh Baal or Yahweh Asherah." The formulas emphasize more how Yahweh is to be worshiped than the worshiping of the divine patrons of others. Most cultures celebrated

Baal and Asherah as a divine couple. Israel generally celebrates Yahweh as both Baal and Asherah. To honor Yahweh as Asherah celebrates Yahweh as the Godmother who feeds Israel. To honor Yahweh as Baal celebrates Yahweh as the Godfather who protects it. One creates; the other saves. Both traditions authentically reflect the Hebrews' understanding of their divine patron. Yahweh is both the Godmother who gives life and the Godfather who protects it. Yahweh is integral, not sexual. For the Hebrews, only humans were gender specific; Yahweh was not.

Most cultures practiced ritual intercourse to manage the sexual relationship between Asherah and Baal that determined the quality of the farming and herding seasons of the cultures. A healthy sexual relationship between them produced a fertile land and a fertile people. If their sexual relationship was unhealthy, there was death and famine. Therefore, male rulers and female priests had intercourse with one another or with the totem animals of Baal and Asherah at the beginning of the farming and herding seasons to remind Baal and Asherah to wet the land with just the right amount of sperm, or rain.

The Hebrews did not prohibit the worship of Yahweh with ritual intercourse simply because they were excessively modest about sexuality. Prudishness about human sexuality developed in sixteenth-century England and America, not in ancient Israel. The Hebrews objected to ritual intercourse because it overemphasized the role of human beings in economic life. The Hebrews were to enjoy life, not create it (Deut 6:10-19). Yahweh freely and generously endowed Israel with life, and did not need to be reminded with ritual intercourse to feed and to protect the land and its people. The Hebrews prohibited any institution that questioned the gratuitous quality of Yahweh's actions to feed and protect the land and its people.

When the Hebrews forgot who set their households free and gave them land, or when they did evil by negotiating covenants with states to protect their land, or when they served Baal and Asherah by participating in the ritual intercourse of their state partners to guarantee successful growing and herding seasons, the anger of Yahweh was kindled against them (Judg 3:8-9). Literally, Yahweh snorts like a bull (Jer 6:29; Song 1:6; Job 39:20) through his nostrils (Gen 24:47; Job 36:13).

The anger formula is an example of a bull image of Yahweh, which, although officially forbidden, is common in the Bible (Num 19:1-10; Exod 32:1—33:11). Throughout prehistoric times, huge cattle roamed wild along the shores of the Mediterranean. Early humans revered these great animals as symbols of divine fertility. The bull was a symbol both of life and of the ability of the creator to give life. A bull that is snorting mad is sterile. When Yahweh becomes angry, the land dies. Anger is the antithesis of love in world of the Bible. The angry destroy life; the loving create it.

Unlike the formulas used in the crisis of hero stories, which are seldom expanded, the anger formula in climax episodes is often elaborated by a story, that describes in detail the enslavement of the Hebrews. Hero stories consider slavery therapeutic or educational.

Slavery teaches the Hebrews to recognize that Yahweh feeds and protects them. The Hebrews do not feed and protect themselves. Slavery tutors them to profess their faith in Yahweh by crying out. When the Hebrews cry out to Yahweh, they say "uncle." Both the Hebrew word "to cry out" and the English word "uncle" sound like what they signify, which is the sound of someone choking. The cry is a formal plea for Yahweh to set them free.

Yahweh raises up heroes designated when the spirit of Yahweh touches or comes upon them. This touched formula identifies exceptional members of societies (Judg 3:9-11). When Yahweh touches someone, it leaves a physical mark. Today, children with dimples are sometimes told that God pressed a finger into their cheeks when they were finished to show delight in the way they turned out. The Pillsbury Baking Company captures this motif in their doughboy commercials where a soft, rounded figure made of dough giggles while a giant finger presses gently into its side. Children with freckles are sometimes told they have been kissed by fairies. In traditional societies like ancient Israel, the left-handed, the tall, and the redheads were all people marked by the spirit of Yahweh for some special task. The Hebrews considered exceptional people tooled for the divine task of setting slaves free.

Once the Hebrews are free again, the land is at rest. The rest formula is a cease-fire that guarantees the villages of Israel will not be overrun, and that their people will be free to rear their children, farm their fields, and graze their herds.

Most hero stories conclude with the obituary of the hero. The obituary is a death certificate that testifies that the hero is human, not divine. The hero is Yahweh's helper. Only Yahweh lives forever, and thus only Yahweh delivers Israel.

Clans told hero stories to inspire gratitude to Yahweh in their households for having set them free from their enemies. The intention of hero stories is to unite the households of a tribe in gratitude for the power of Yahweh to deliver them. Before Babylon defeated Judah and destroyed Jerusalem, hero stories celebrated war as just and noble. Most veterans enjoyed war as a challenge and a test, and thought about war with attitudes of both terror and excitement. War is celebrated even when the cost in human life is high. On July 1, 1916, during World War I, the British army lost 19,000 killed, 35,000 wounded, 2,000 missing, and 6,000 prisoners on a front less than twenty miles long on the Somme River. There was shock, but no political or public outcry. The only generals who faced a court-martial were a few who were not aggressive enough. The wars in Vietnam (1945–75), however, changed the assessment of war in the United States. In much the same way, the wars with Babylon changed the assessment of war for those who told the hero stories in the book of Judges, which now stress the need for a total trust in Yahweh to raise up heroes for the protection of the land and its people, and indict the household of David for its militaristic policies, which ultimately destroyed the land and its people.

Ehud Delivers Israel from Moab
(Judg 3:12-30)

In the story of Ehud Delivers Israel from Moab (Judg 3:12-30), the spirit of Yahweh marks him as left-handed. Right-handed warriors found it difficult to defend themselves against left-handed warriors, just as right-handed baseball players today find it difficult to defend themselves against left-handed players. To be left-handed was a divine gift.

The Hebrews declare their independence from Moab by designating Ehud to be their chief. The Covenant between Moab and Israel was renewed each time the king of Moab collected taxes on the herds and harvest of the Hebrews. The Hebrews designate Ehud to deliver their taxes, renew their covenant with Moab at the sanctuary of Gilgal near Jericho, and then assassinate King Eglon of Moab. The strategy will outwit their enemies, who are portrayed throughout the story as fools.

Ehud prepares for his mission by making a high-tech dagger. Heroes generally use unorthodox weapons. Like the novel and film character James Bond, agent 007 of the British Secret Service, they use special weapons. Shamgar uses an ox-goad (Judg 43:31). Samson uses the jawbone of an ass (Judg 15:15), Jael uses a mallet and peg (Judg 4:21), David uses a throwing stick, and Ehud uses a two-edged sword (Judg 3:16). Yahweh does not lift up professional soldiers to lead the Hebrews from slavery to freedom. These heroes are ordinary men and women who use the tools of their trade to deliver the Hebrews from their enemies. Ehud's dagger is a customized weapon, eighteen inches long and sharpened on both sides of the blade. It is not the standard weapon of a Hebrew warrior, who would have used a sickle sword.

Gilgal is a sanctuary dedicated to Yahweh, the divine patron of the Hebrews, not to Chemosh, the divine patron of the Moabites. At Gilgal, Yahweh speaks only with Hebrews like Ehud, and not with Moabites like Eglon. Therefore, Eglon is anxious to hear what Yahweh has told Ehud to tell him, expecting, of course, that it will confirm his power. In fact, Yahweh's words for Eglon are the same as Yahweh's words for Pharaoh: "Let my people go!" Ehud leans forward to whisper the declaration into Eglon's ear, and strikes the Hebrews' first blow for independence.

Eglon's death is shameful. The language that describes his death is the same language used to describe someone having a bowel movement. "Sitting alone in his cool roof chamber" (Judg 3:20) is a euphemism, which one of Moab's guards explains: "He is only relieving himself in the closet of the cool chamber" (Judg 3:24).

Saga of Deborah and Jael
(Judg 4:1—5:31)

Deborah Delivers Israel from Hazor
(Judg 4:1-16 + 5:31)

The stories of Deborah and Jael (Judg 4:1—5:31), the stories of Gideon and Jerubbaal (Judg 6:1—8:35) and the Stories of Samson (Judg 13:1—16:31) are sagas, which combine hero stories about the birth, marriage, exploits, and deaths of similar protagonists. Sagas also develop in medieval Iceland and Scandinavia. In the "Saga of Olaf," American poet Henry Wadsworth Longfellow imitated medieval sagas like the *Heimskringla*, a collection of stories about the early rulers of Norway. Sagas like those of Deborah and Gideon contain stories only about the mission and about the death of the hero.

The Saga of Deborah and Jael combines a story of how Deborah Delivers Israel from Hazor (Judg 4:1-16 + 5:31), the story of how Jael Delivers Israel from Harosheth-ha-goiim (Judg 4:17-24), and a Hymn to Yahweh (Judg 5:1-31).

Just as the powerless in developing nations today associate the powerful in industrial societies with business suits, briefcases, and eyeglasses, the village cultures like Israel associated the powerful city cultures like Hazor with chariots. The Hyksos introduced chariots in Syria-Palestine during the Middle Bronze period. Although a federation of more than one ethnic group, the Hyksos are primarily a Semitic people. As many as four animals drew a war chariot, which had either two or four wheels. The crew of a chariot included a driver and a warrior and sometimes a shield-bearer. The Hyksos developed an entire social system around the chariot. Only Hyksos chariot warriors like the people of Hazor were eligible to become landowners for whom local villagers like the Hebrews farmed and grazed animals.

When an enemy like Hazor threatened the land or children of a Hebrew village, its elders issued a call to arms to the other villages in their tribe to draft detachments of warriors to defend their village from its enemies (Judg 5:2-12; 19:29-30; 1 Sam 11:1-8). The tribe was an insurance policy against both war and famine, and a key to Israel's ability to recover from economic crisis. Warriors mustered at a sanctuary like the "Palm of Deborah between Ramah and Bethel" (Judg 4:5).

The story introduces Deborah as "wife of Lappidoth" (Judg 4:4). Beyond this title, however, Lappidoth appears nowhere else in the Bible. It would be more characteristic of the hero story if "the wife of Lappidoth" were translated as "woman of fire." Saul is tall, David is ruddy, Ehud is left-handed, Samson is muscular, and Deborah is a "torch." She has red hair.

After the warriors of the tribe of Ephraim muster, they designate Barak to be their chief. Then they wait for Deborah the prophet to confirm their war for independence. Deborah announces to Barak that Yahweh has given Hazor into the hands of the Hebrews.

Just as the book of Exodus celebrates Yahweh's deliverance of the Hebrews by sending Moses to destroy the chariots of Egypt with the waters of the Red Sea, the book of Judges celebrates Yahweh's deliverance of the Hebrews by sending Deborah to destroy the chariots of Jabin and Sisera with the waters of the Wadi Kishon (Judg 5:21).

Jael Delivers Israel from Harosheth-ha-goiim
(JUDG 4:17-24)

In the story of how Jael Delivers Israel from Harosheth-ha-goiim (Judg 4:17-24), Jael is not a host who betrays her guest, but a hero who defends her household against its enemy (Fig. 32). Heber the Kenite sets up camp with Jael and the rest of his household beneath the Oak of Zaanannim near Kedesh (Judg 4:11). His name is derived from the same root as "Hebrew" and means "itinerant." A "kenite" is a "smith." Like tinkers in the American West, many smiths in early Israel traveled from place to place to quarry ore, and to repair tools and weapons like the chariots of Hazor. Both the name "Kedesh" and the presence of a sacred oak identify the site as a sanctuary. A sanctuary was neutral ground, where the household of Heber would be out of harm's way during the impending battle.

Sisera is the commander of the chariots at Hazor. Barak is the chief designated by the Hebrews warriors from Naphtali and Zebulun. The story keeps its audiences in suspense. Yahweh will sell Sisera into the hand of a woman (Judg 4:9), but will it be Deborah or Jael?

After the warriors of Hazor have been routed, Sisera also seeks asylum at the sanctuary. It is the sanctuary, not the camp of Heber, that offers Sisera protection. When he finds the household of Heber already at the sanctuary, Sisera tries to take over the household of Heber to restore the fortune that he has lost in battle. To take over the household of Heber, Sisera must rape Jael, the mother of the household. David uses the same strategy when he rapes Bathsheba to take over the household of Uriah (2 Sam 11:1-17). Amnon rapes Tamar to take over to the household of Absalom (2 Sam 13:1-22), and Absalom rapes ten wives of David to take over the royal household (2 Sam 16:15-22).

Every action and reaction in the story pivots on Sisera's plan to rape Jael. If Sisera were merely seeking hospitality, he would have approached the tent of Heber, not the tent of Jael. The mother of a household may share the tent of the father of the household, but fathers with more than one wife provided each wife with her own tent. Jael has a tent to herself.

Heber was a Kenite smith from the household of Hobab, the father-in-law of Moses. His household built and repaired the iron fittings on the chariots of Hazor and Harosheth-ha-goiim. When fighting broke out between them and Israel Heber remained neutral, and took refuge under the sacred tree in the sanctuary of Zaanannim.

When Sisera was told that Barak, son of Abinoam, was mustering the warriors of Israel on Mt. Tabor, he moved his nine companies of iron-fitted chariots off the heights of Harosheth-ha-goiim into the Wadi Kishon.

Then Deborah said to Barak, "Attack! This is the day of Yahweh. Yahweh has given Sisera into your hands. Yahweh will lead you into battle."

So Barak attacked from Mt. Tabor with warriors from ten villages. The glance of Yahweh paralyzed the chariots of Sisera, and Barak routed the chariots of Harosheth-ha-goiim. Every last soldier fell by the sword. No one was left. Sisera, meanwhile, dismounted his chariot and fled on foot to the sacred tree in the sanctuary of Zaanannim. Secretly, he approached the tent of Jael, wife of Heber, who had a covenant with Jabin, monarch of Hazor.

Jael came out of her tent and challenged Sisera: "Sir, this is your last chance. Put your plans to seize this household aside. If you leave me alone, no harm will come to you." Sisera, however, pushed Jael aside and barged into the tent.

Jael closed the rug flap of the tent behind him. Then Sisera ordered Jael: "Bring me water to drink. I am thirsty." So Jael opened a skin of goat's milk and gave him a drink. Then she covered him with a sleeping rug.

As he was falling to sleep, Sisera ordered Jael: "Stand at the entrance to the tent, and if anybody comes and asks you, 'Is there a man in here?' say, 'No.'" Jael, however, took a tent peg and her mallet. Secretly, she approached him, sound asleep from fatigue, and drove the peg through his temple into the ground and he died

Meanwhile, Barak arrived in pursuit of Sisera. Jael came out of her tent and announced: "Come, and I will show you 'the man' whom you are seeking." So Barak entered her tent, and there was Sisera lying dead with a tent peg through his head.

FIGURE 32   Jael Delivers Israel from Harosheth-ha-goiim (Judg 4:11 + 15-22)

Sisera does not approach Jael the way Abraham's slave approaches Rebekah (Gen 24:17). The slave approaches a woman at a well, not at her tent. He asks for permission to use the well, not for hospitality. Sisera approaches Jael's tent unnoticed (Judg 4:17). The expression usually translated "on foot" can also mean "secretly," as it does here and in the Story of Rahab as a Host where the Hebrew warriors approach Jericho "in disguise" (Josh 2:1). Whether Heber was present or not, warriors would have been in camp to protect the women (Gen 34:5). Unlike Dinah, who "went out to visit the women of the land" (Gen 34:1-2) where the men of her household could not protect her, Jael does not leave the protection of the camp (Judg 4:17). Jael confronts an intruder who has eluded her bodyguards and is trespassing. Jael's actions here are similar to those of Jezebel, who confronts Jehu after he eludes the guards and trespasses into the palace (2 Kgs 9:31; Fig. 33).

Jael's opening words to Sisera, "Turn aside. Do not be afraid" (Judg 4:18), are not an invitation. She does not want Sisera to come into her tent the way Boaz wants his neighbors to sit with him in the gate (Ruth 4:1), and she does not invite Sisera to be her guest the way Lot invites the two strangers to spend the night with his household (Gen 19:2). Jael is not the head of the household. She has no authority to offer Sisera hospitality. By themselves, the words "turn aside" can offer hospitality, but together with the words "do not be afraid" (Judg 4:18) they cannot. The words "do not be afraid" are addressed to candidates like Abraham (Gen 15:1) and Gideon (Judg 6:23) setting out on missions. Jael's words challenge Sisera to abandon his mission to take over the household of Heber (Ezek 33:11).

Jael's words also do not indicate that she is physically attracted to Sisera. Traditional societies develop only the external actions of their characters, not their internal emotions. The Bible would not evaluate the character of Jael or of Sisera on the basis of how they felt about losing a battle, about seeing a handsome warrior, or about killing an enemy threatening their household.

Jael's words do not negotiate a covenant with Sisera to overthrow Heber. Nothing suggests that Jael is acting against the father of her household. She is not like Abigail, who negotiates a covenant with David to overthrow Nabal (1 Sam 25:2-43).

When Jezebel received the report that Jehu was marching on Jezreel, she put on her royal makeup and wig, and took her place in the royal window. She indicted Jehu the moment he walked through the gate of the palace: "Have you come to surrender, you 'Zimri,' for the assassination of your king?"

The "Zimri" scoffed at his queen in the window and said, "Who is on my side? Who?"

Two or three royal bodyguards stepped forward. The "Zimri" ordered them: "Throw her down."

So they threw her down from the balcony, and her blood spattered on the wall of the palace and on the horses of the "Zimri's" chariot, which trampled her to death.

FIGURE 33   Trial of Jehu (2 Kgs 9:29-33)

Jael is not lying to Sisera. Nothing suggests that Jael and Heber are double agents working for their own advantage with both Israel and Hazor. Lies need credibility, but there is no reason for Sisera or the audience to believe her.

Jael's words are not ironic. Irony needs subtlety. Her words are absolutely clear. In contrast, Sisera's words to Jael (Judg 4:19-20) and the words between Sisera's mother and the women of her household (Judg 5:29-30) are brimming with the subtle misunderstanding irony requires.

Sisera has no right to hospitality in the tent of Jael. As long as Jabin ruled Hazor, Heber and Jael were obligated to take care of the chariots of Sisera and to provide hospitality for any member of the household of Jabin. If Jabin were still king of Hazor, Jael would have an obligation to protect Sisera from his enemies. Deborah, however, has overthrown Jabin, making the household of Heber covenant partners with the household of Deborah. Sisera is neither a monarch with whom Jael has a covenant nor a stranger seeking hospitality. Sisera is her enemy. He has lost his former status and is reduced to the role of a runaway slave.

Jael's words are a protest against Sisera, who is planning to take over the household of Heber. They are a final warning advising Sisera to abandon his mission or face the consequences. Jael's warning plays on the word "turn." She gives Sisera one last chance "to turn away from" his plan (2 Kgs 17:18; Judg 9:29; 1 Kgs 16:13). Sisera ignores her protest and "turns Jael out of his way." Jael says, "Turn aside from your plan," but Sisera "turns her aside" and invades her tent. Jael's words serve the same purpose as the words of Tamar to Amnon (2 Sam 13:12-13). Jael warns Sisera to leave her alone (Exod 8:27; Lam 4:15), to give up his plan to attack her (2 Kgs 10:29; Prov 13:14; Isa 11:13), and to disappear before he is discovered by the men of her household (1 Kgs 15:14).

Like Deborah, Jael is a liminal woman, who acts heroically when men fail to fulfill their responsibilities. When Barak fails to defend Israel against Hazor, Deborah acts. When Heber fails to defend his household, Jael acts. Both women go above and beyond the call of duty as mothers of their households. Both risk their own lives to save their households. Sisera ignores Jael's protest and turns her out of his way.

Once Jael's opening words to Sisera are read as a protest, rather than as an invitation, the significance of her actions that follow becomes clearer. Jael never regards Sisera as her guest. She declares war on him as her enemy. Sisera never regards Jael as his host. He plans to take over the household of Heber.

If Sisera were Jael's guest, she would have washed his feet (Gen 18:4; 19:2; 24:32; Judg 19:21). Jael does not omit washing Sisera's feet because such a leisurely and relaxing task is inappropriate in the middle of Barak's hot pursuit of Sisera. The omission indicates that Sisera has not been granted the status of guest.

Most translations say Jael "covered him with a rug" (Judg 4:18). At this point in the story, however, after Sisera barges past her, Jael steps into the tent behind him. She coolly and decisively draws the rug hanging as a curtain across the opening of the tent, and prepares to confront her enemy alone.

Sisera misunderstands Jael's courage. At precisely the moment that he has fallen into the power of a woman (Judg 4:9), he assumes that she is now in his power. Unaware that he is in danger, Sisera orders Jael to wait on him like a slave by bringing him a drink. If Sisera were Jael's guest, he would not ask her for anything. She "opens a skin of milk and gives him a drink" (Judg 4:19). Abraham offers his guests "a morsel of bread" (Gen 18:4-5), and then upgrades it to pastry, a calf, curds, and milk, but Jael is not a host providing the best for her guest. When Jael gives Sisera milk to drink, she is a hunter stalking prey. Jael manipulates Sisera, not by treating him like a child, but by distracting him as if he were her lover. Goat's milk is a wedding drink with which a man and woman toast their marriage. Milk is also contains lactic acid, which soothes away the anxieties that prevent sleep. Sisera drinks the milk to prepare for sex. Jael serves the milk to prepare him for the sleep of death (Judg 16:14-19; CTA 19.213-224).

After Jael serves Sisera a drink, she covers him with a rug (Judg 4:19). This rug is the shroud in which his body will be carried home to his mother. (Judg 5:30). Jael stalks Sisera the way Judith stalks Holofernes in the book of Judith (Jdt 12:10—13:10), and Pughat stalks Yatpan in the Story of Aqhat from Ugarit (CTA 19.205-221). Sisera, Holofernes, and Yatpan all foolishly taunt the women they plan to rape with the foreplay of eating and drinking, while all the women wisely first put them to sleep, and then to death. Jael, Judith, and Pughat hunt and kill their enemies to set their households free.

Sisera also orders Jael to guard the door to the tent. He continues to command Jael as if she were a soldier in his now vanished army. "If anyone comes and asks you, 'Is there a man in this woman's tent?' say, 'No!'" Hosts like Lot, Rahab, or the slave at En-rogel (2 Sam 17:17-21) do guard the door to protect their guests, but guests can never order a host to stand guard. Sisera's order dramatizes his powerlessness as he cries out like a child afraid of the dark. The story uses a word that means both "anyone" and "a man" to force this once-great warrior to unwittingly admit that he is no longer a man. Sisera orders Jael to lie, but she can use his exact words and tell the truth.

Jael fetches the hammer and peg that she uses to pitch her tent. Her weapons are unorthodox, but they are familiar. The same skills and strength that Jael uses to erect her tent, she uses to defend it. She drives the peg through Sisera's skull with the same speed with which she normally sinks it into the ground. The man who penetrated the door of her tent is penetrated by the woman he threatened.

From the moment he passes through the door of her tent, Sisera is guilty of rape. The door of a house or a tent is a metaphor in love songs from both Egypt (Papyrus Harris 500) and the Song of Solomon (Song 5:4) for the woman herself. Although Sisera enters her tent, he never has sexual intercourse with Jael. He is impotent, and "falls between her legs" (Judg 5:27), as much a failure against Jael as he had been against Deborah (Judg 4:15). On neither field does he mount a successful assault. He tries to bring shame upon Barak and Heber, and instead suffers the shame of death at a woman's hand (Judg 9:53).

Like Deborah, who leads Barak to Sisera on the battlefield (Judg 4:14-16), Jael now leads Barak to Sisera on the floor of her tent. This final episode (Judg 4:22), with the opening episode (Judg 4:18), creates a frame around the stories.

Hymn
(JUDG 5:1-31)

When Hebrew warriors returned to their villages after battle, women sang hymns to celebrate Yahweh's victories over their enemies. Miriam sings after Yahweh delivers the Hebrews from the Egyptians at the Red Sea (Exod 15:20-21). Jephthah's daughter sings after Yahweh delivers the Hebrews from the Ammonites (Judg 11:34). Here Deborah sings to celebrate Yahweh's deliverance of the Hebrews from the rulers of Syria-Palestine at Taanach (Judg 5:19).

The hymn celebrates both Deborah and Jael as mothers in Israel, who delivered their households from the enemy. Mothers in Israel were selfless, not only in birthing and rearing their children, but in protecting them. In contrast, the mother of Sisera pines selfishly for a child to feed and protect her (Judg 5:28-30).

The irony with which the mother of Sisera speaks is exquisite. She rationalizes Sisera's delay by assuming her warrior son is busy handling the two women he has taken prisoner. In fact, it is Sisera who has fallen into the hands of two women. Sisera's mother imagines her loving son arriving with a bolt of fabric dyed in royal purple for her. In fact, her son will soon arrive shrouded in the carpet he has dyed with his blood.

In the hymn, Deborah and Jael are "blessed among women" (Judg 5:24). The title is superlative and confers on the two women honor equal to that of Othniel, Ehud, Gideon, Jephthah, Samson, Saul, Jonathan, and David. Deborah and Jael were "friends of Yahweh" (Judg 5:31) who set their households free.

Jephthah Delivers Israel from Ammon
(JUDG 11:1-40)

In the story of how Jephthah Delivers Israel from Ammon, a father offers his daughter as a human sacrifice in thanksgiving to Yahweh for delivering his household from its enemies (Fig. 34). Today Jephthah's actions would be child abuse and murder.

Like Jacob, Jephthah becomes the father of his household, not by birth, but by achievement. His birth mother is not the mother of the household, but a secondary wife, although her title is generally translated into English as "harlot," "concubine," or "prostitute." Jephthah's father did not designate Jephthah to be his heir, but chose a son from the mother of the household. The heir and his brothers exile Jephthah to protect their status in the household, just as the sons of Jacob exile Joseph. Gilead exercises his authority to appoint an heir, and his heir exercises his authority as the new father of the household to adopt and to exile members by forcing Jephthah to become a man without a household. The same belligerence that made Jephthah a threat to this new father of the household, however, becomes an asset to other exiles who join Jephthah and support their households by raiding caravans.

When the people of Ammon invade the land of Gilead, however, the same sons who drove Jephthah into exile send him a call to arms and designate him as the chief who will deliver them from their enemies. He reminds them: "Did you not shame me, and excommunicate me from the household of my father?" (Judg 11:7). Then he negotiates with them for his reinstatement. He will serve as their chief on condition that, if he defeats the Ammonites, they will designate him as the father of their of household. The covenant they negotiate with Jephthah is comparable to the covenant made between the divine assembly and Marduk in the Enuma Elish Stories. Marduk demands: "If I agree to serve as your deliverer, if I am sucessful in defeating Tiamat, if I save your lives, you must proclaim me the ruler of the divine assembly. My word, not yours, must determine all things. What I create must not change; what I command must not be revoked or altered" (Enuma IV:3-41).

As a chief, Jephthah vows not only a portion of the plunder that his warriors will take from the Ammonites, but also "whoever comes forth from the doors of my house to meet me, when I return victorious from the Ammonites" (Judg 11:30-31). His vow is part of the ritual of herem war. Like David, who shared his plunder with those who remained with the pack animals, Jephthah shares the price of war with those who remained in the village (1 Sam 30:21-25).

The first person to greet Jephthah after the battle is his daughter. She comes out of the village playing a tambourine and dancing (Exod 15:20; 1 Sam 18:6). She is Jephthah's "only child" (Judg 11:34). This is the child that Jephthah designated to be his heir.

When Jephthah realizes the implications of his vow, he has second thoughts, but his daughter is resolute. She knows that the honor of the household must be maintained. She insists that her father fulfill his vow. The daughter of Jephthah, like the daughters of Lot, is not a tragic or pathetic figure. She is heroic. Unlike the daughters of Lot, she is not silent. Her words reinforce her actions, and she makes the decision to lay down her life for her household.

Every year, Hebrew women remember the daughter of Jephthah. They lament not only her premature death, but also her inability to fulfill her role as a mother.

At the beginning of the story, Jephthah has a child, but no land. At the end of the story, he has land, but no child. He regains his position within the household of Gilead, but he is unable to pass on his inheritance. The story remembers Jephthah as a father who paid a terrible price for trying to defend his village, and to provide an heir for his household on his own. Like all hero stories, Jephthah Delivers Israel from Ammon reminds the Hebrews that only Yahweh can bless a household with land and children. Without Yahweh, fathers of households are powerless.

crisis (Judg 11:1-3)

There was a chief from the household of Gilead named "Jephthah," who was the son of Gilead and a secondary wife. Besides Jephthah, Gilead had sons with his primary wife. When the sons of Gilead with his primary wife became elders, they excommunicated Jephthah. "Because you are the son of stranger, you shall inherit nothing."

Jephthah went into exile in the land of Tob, about twelve miles north of Ramoth-gilead near the border of Jordan and Syria today. Other exiles joined him and they supported their households by raiding.

climax (Judg 11:4-33)

Some time later, when Ammon began to attack Israel, the elders of Gilead sent messengers to Jephthah in the land of Tob. "Come," they said to Jephthah, "be our chief that we may defend ourselves against Ammon."

"Are you not the elders who excommunicated me from the household of my father?" Jephthah replied. "Why do you come to me now, when you are in distress?"

The elders of Gilead replied to Jephthah, "In spite of our actions then, we are now asking you to return as the chief of Gilead and defend us against Ammon."

Jephthah told the messengers to reply to the elders of Gilead: "If you allow me to return and Yahweh delivers Ammon up to me, then you must recognize me as the father of the household of Gilead."

The elders of Gilead replied: "We will do as you say. Yahweh is our witness."

So Jephthah returned to Gilead with the messengers, and the warriors of Gilead inaugurated him as their chief before Yahweh at the sanctuary of Mizpah.

Then Jephthah sent messengers to the ruler of Ammon with the message: "What have you against me that you attack me in my land?" (Judg 11:12).

(continued)

The spirit of Yahweh came upon Jephthah (Judg. 11:29). He reconquered Gilead and Manasseh, and Mizpah-Gilead as well, and from there he went on to attack Rabbath-Ammon.

Before the battle, Jephthah made a vow to Yahweh: "If you deliver Ammon up to me, I will sacrifice to you the first to come out of the doors of my house to meet me when I return in triumph."

Then Jephthah attacked Rabbath-Ammon and Yahweh delivered Ammon up to him. His victory was complete. He destroyed twenty villages between Aroer and Minnith and Abel-keramim, and sold the Ammonites as slaves in Israel.

denouement (Judg 11:34-40)

When Jephthah returned to Mizpah, his daughter was the first person to come out of his house, praising Yahweh with her tambourines and dancing. She was his heir. Jephthah had no other sons or daughters. When Jephthah saw her, he tore his clothes in mourning, and cried out: "Oh my daughter, the words of your song are a death sentence for our household. For I have made a vow to Yahweh and I must fulfill it."

"Father," she replied, "you have made a vow to Yahweh. Do with me as you have vowed, because Yahweh has delivered your enemies up to you. But grant me this favor. For two months, let me and the other marriageable women in the household go off to the mountains to mourn our infertility."

"Go," he replied, and sent her away for two months.

She departed with the other marriageable women and they mourned their infertility on the mountains. After two months she returned to her father without ever having had sexual intercourse, and her father sacrificed her to Yahweh as he had vowed. It then became an annual custom for the women of Israel to mourn the daughter of Jephthah from Gilead for four days.

FIGURE 34   Jephthah Delivers Israel from Ammon (Judg 11:1-40)

Saga of Samson
(JUDG 13:1 — 16:31)

Ugarit was a state strategically located on the trade lanes between Egypt to the south, islands like Crete to the west, and Mesopotamia to the east. Ugarit prospered during the Late Bronze period. Among the traditions of this wonderful culture, excavated by the French team of Claude A. Schaeffer during twenty-two seasons between 1929 and 1960, are the Stories of Aqhat. The Stories of Aqhat were popular throughout the world of the Bible. The Saga of Samson parallels the Stories of Aqhat. The Hebrews may have first heard them in Philistine ports like Gaza and Ashkelon, where Ugarit's merchant ships called, or border towns like Timnah.

The crisis episode in the Saga of Samson is simply two formulas: "The Israelites again offended Yahweh, who therefore delivered them into the power of the Philistines for forty years" (Judg 13:1). The climax episodes are developed by a series of seven hero stories. The first is simply the formula: "the spirit of Yahweh first stirred him in Mahaneh-dan" (Judg 13:25), which is attached to the Annunciation to the Wife of Manoah.

Annunciation to the Wife of Manoah
(JUDG 13:1-25)

In an Annunciation to the Wife of Manoah, Samson's parents-to-be, like Danil and Danatiya in the Stories of Aqhat, have no children. Yahweh, like Baal in the Stories of Aqhat, intervenes and Manoah and his wife have a son. This barren-wife motif also appears in the Stories of Abraham and Sarah (Gen 15:1-4; 16:1-15; 18:9-15; 25:21; 30:1-24), the Stories of Samuel, and the Stories of Elijah and Elisha (1 Sam 1:2-17; 2 Kgs 4:8-17).

Samson and Aqhat both grow up to become fearless hunters. Undaunted by animals, they are defeated by women. Delilah, a Philistine woman, outwits Samson, just as Anat, the divine patron of love and war, outwits Aqhat. The deaths of both Aqhat and Samson are avenged by their divine patrons.

The wife of Manoah is wise. Because the message involves childbirth, and because women have a greater role in childbirth than men, the messenger deals with the wife of Manoah, rather than with Manoah. The same motif appears in the Stories of Adam and Eve. The snake talks with the woman, not because women are prey to temptation, but because the consequences of fertility have more to do with them than with their partners. The wife of Manoah respects the messenger, pays close attention to the directions, and conscientiously tells Manoah what the messenger told her to do for their son.

In contrast, Manoah is a fool who not only knows little or nothing about childbearing, but also does not listen to his wife, who does. Manoah also violates the protocol of a host by asking the messenger for his name. The foolishness of fathers in annunciation stories does not just make fun of them, but emphasizes the powerlessness of human beings to save themselves. Annunciation stories celebrate the power of Yahweh to give birth to children even from infertile couples. The infertility of the mothers of great men celebrates their births as the work of Yahweh, rather than as human work. Infertile women are liminal women, who, like Israel itself, are without status, but infertile women, like Israel itself, are chosen by Yahweh to free the slaves.

Samson Courts the Woman of Timnah
(JUDG 14:1-4 + 10)

Samson is named for Shamash, the divine patron of the sun. He is a sun child. Traditions celebrate the sun as a voyeur who spends his day gazing down on all the women on earth. The Saga of Samson characterizes him as a womanizer, who seduces the woman of Timnah and the woman of Gaza, and is seduced by Delilah. The wife of Manoah is a Hebrew. She is the mother of a household in Israel. The other three women in the Saga of Samson are Philistines. They are strangers. The wife of Manoah is the insider whom Yahweh protects. The woman of Timnah, the woman of Gaza, and Delilah are the outsiders from whom Yahweh protects the Hebrews (Fig. 35).

Samson Courts the Woman of Timnah
(Judg 14:1-4 + 10)

Once Samson went down to Timnah, and had intercourse with a Philistine woman. When he came back to his own village, he told his father and mother: "I had intercourse with a Philistine woman at Timnah with whom I want you to arrange a wedding for me." His father and mother refused. "Are there no Hebrew women for you to marry? Why do you want to marry the daughter of an uncircumcised Philistine?" Samson, however, insisted. "Arrange a wedding for me with the woman I want." His father and mother did not know that Yahweh was going to use Samson to shame the Philistines, who ruled the villages of Israel.

Samson Slays the Lion of Timnah
(Judg 14:5-9)

Samson went down to Timnah. . . . When he came to the vineyards of Timnah, a female lion suddenly attacked him. The spirit of Yahweh possessed Samson, and he tore the lion apart bare handed as easily as if she were a newborn goat. He did not tell his father or his mother what he had done. Then Samson proposed to the Philistine woman he wanted to marry. When Samson returned to marry her, he left the road to look at the carcass of the lion. A swarm of bees had built a hive in her carcass, and filled it with honey. Samson scooped out the honeycomb with his bare hands, and ate the honey as he walked on down the road. When he met his father and mother, he gave them some honey, and they ate it. Samson did not tell them that he had collected the honey from the carcass of the lion. While his father negotiated with the woman, Samson began the traditional celebration with the other young men in the village.

FIGURE 35   Stories of Samson (Judg 14:1-10)

The sight of the woman of Timnah and the woman of Gaza sexually arouses Samson, who is a fool for seeking to have intercourse with strange women. He crosses back and forth over the frontier separating Hebrew and Philistine villages. He marries outside his tribe.

Samson Slays the Lion of Timnah
(JUDG 14:5-9)

The story of how Samson Slays the Lion of Timnah is framed by the sentences: "Samson went down" (Judg 14:5) and "his father went down" (Judg 14:10). Samson is the protagonist in both stories, and the woman or lion of Timnah is the antagonist.

Samson's weapons in these stories are his bare hands. The Hebrews considered Philistine weapons to be state of the art. The Philistines had the best available arsenal of military hardware, yet the best iron weapons that the Philistines could forge were no match for the hands of Samson, or the jawbone of an ass, when these unorthodox weapons are wielded by heroes lifted up by Yahweh to deliver the Hebrews from slavery.

Double entendre is used throughout the Stories of Samson. Words frequently have more than one meaning. One meaning is always sexual, the other meaning is not. The woman of Timnah is a female lion. She roars or taunts Samson, who, nonetheless, overpowers her. Eating the honey from the body of the lion is a double entendre for Samson's enjoyment of his sexual conquest.

Samson Kills the Warriors of Ashkelon
(JUDG 14:11-20)

Traditions like those in the Saga of Samson were told at weddings by men celebrating their own sexual conquests. During the first six days of the wedding, the household of the groom displayed the bride-price that it was investing in the household of the bride. Likewise, the household of the bride displayed the dowry that it was investing in the household of the groom. The guests looked over the bride-price and the dowry to be sure that they met the stipulations of the covenant that the two households had negotiated. Then, on the seventh day of the wedding feast, the guests witnessed sexual intercourse between the bride and groom to officially consummate the covenant.

Riddles were also part of the wedding ritual. Riddles are sexual word games that men used at weddings to determine their rank in the household. The groom ran a gauntlet of riddles before going in to have intercourse with the bride. Samson Kills the Warriors of Ashkelon (Judg 14:11-20) begins when Samson loses a riddle contest, which renders him impotent and, therefore, unable to consummate his marriage.

To redeem the honor of his household, Samson kills and strips thirty Philistine warriors to shame them. Exposing the genitals of a warrior was comparable to castration. Only children played naked. Clothing was the uniform of a sexually active adult. To remove the clothing of sexually active adults returns them to the status of children. Hanun cuts off the tunics of the men whom David dispatched to the funeral of Nahash, Hanun's father (2 Sam 10:4). By symbolically castrating David's messengers, Hanun declares that Israel is impotent in Rabbath-Ammon.

In the world of the Bible, marriage was almost always patrilocal. Women left the households of their fathers and moved to the households of their husbands. In this story there is no marriage. Samson leaves the wedding feast unable to consummate his marriage, so the woman of Timnah returns to the household of her father unmarried.

Samson Burns the Crops of Timnah
(JUDG 15:1-8)

The story of how Samson Burns the Crops of Timnah begins when Samson returns to have intercourse with his wife. The father of her household, however, has already abrogated the covenant that he negotiated with the household of Samson, and turns Samson away. Again Samson is shamed.

To recover his honor, Samson runs three hundred foxes through the fields, orchards, and vineyards of Timnah, setting them on fire. Foxes are often associated with sexual revenge. Men frustrated in their desire for sexual intercourse shift into the shape of a fox to seduce the women. These traditions are especially popular during the grain harvest when foxes, whose burrows have been disturbed by workers in the fields, appear everywhere. As the book of Ruth reflects, men and women sleep in the fields during the long hours of harvesting. Harvesters take advantage of being away from their homes for days at a time to make love in the field, as undetected as foxes digging burrows in the grain. The land whose grain is abundant at the harvest is imitated by harvesters sowing their own seed. In Samson Burns the Crops of Timnah, Samson himself is the fox, and the fields into which the fox burrows are the women of Timnah. Denied intercourse for a second time with his wife, he stealthily ravages every other woman in the village.

Samson Massacres the Garrison of Lehi
(JUDG 15:9-17)

The stories of how Samson Massacres the Garrison of Lehi (Judg 15:9-17) and How Samson Raids the Spring at Hakkore (Judg 15:18-20) use mnemonics to help their audiences remember where the stories take place, the cry that Samson lets out, and the

unorthodox weapon with which he massacres the Philistines. The Hebrew letter 'ayin
appears in the word that means "to cry out." Each of the seven stories that make up
the climax of the saga expand the two parts of the episode in a standard hero story,
where enemies oppress Israel for years until the Hebrews cry out to Yahweh for help.
The tradition names Lehi "Jawbone Springs." The name reminds the Hebrews where
Yahweh began their deliverance from the Philistines, because at this spring Samson cried
out for independence.

The same Hebrew letter also appears in the Hebrew word that means a "spring of
water." It is shaped like a fork with two tines. These prongs represent the crack in the
face of a rock through which the water, here portrayed as the handle of the fork, trick-
les like tears from a human eye. By drinking water from the spring shaped like the sound
of a cry for help, Samson cries out. The shape gives birth to a sound.

Finally, the letter 'ayin and the jawbone of an ass have the same shape. Again, the
association between the shape of the spring leads Samson to the shape of his unorthodox weapon. Traditional people strongly believe in the desire of creation to harmonize.
Nothing likes to stand out or create discord. In the Stories of Jacob, Leah, and Rachel,
Jacob exploits nature's penchant for harmony, when he breeds Laban's sheep and goats
in pens constructed with spotted fence poles (Fig. 36). In order to harmonize with their
surroundings, the ewes and nannies give birth to lambs and kids with spotted coats (Gen
30:25-43).

Laban said, "How will I pay you?" Jacob said, "You will not pay me anything. I will
continue to graze and herd your sheep and goats as long as you give me every speckled and spotted sheep and every black lamb, and the spotted and speckled among
the goats. My honesty will speak for itself, when you inspect your sheep and goats
and not one which is not speckled and spotted among the goats and black among
the lambs is missing." Laban said, "Agreed!" But that day Laban removed the male
goats that were striped and spotted, and all the female goats that were speckled
and spotted, every one that had white on it, and every lamb that was black, and
put them in charge of his sons. He moved their herds three days away from the
herds of Jacob.

Then Jacob cut fresh poles from poplar and almond and plane trees. He peeled
white streaks in them, exposing the white of the poles. He set up the poles, which
he peeled at the watering troughs in front of the sheep and goats. Since the sheep
and goats bred when they came to drink, they produced kids and lambs that were
speckled and spotted.

FIGURE 36   Stories of Jacob, Leah, and Rachel (Gen 30:31-39)

Samson Raids the Spring at Hakkore
(JUDG 15:18-20)

The formula: "Samson judged Israel for twenty years in the days of the Philistines" (Judg 15:20) at the end of the story of how Samson Raids the Spring at Hakkore originally concluded the Saga of Samson. As the saga continued to develop, its literary conclusion was moved from here, even though the formula remained.

Samson Wrecks the Gates of Gaza
(JUDG 16:1-3)

Striking natural phenomena invite interpretations handed on as etiologies. The gates orf Gaza are stone, not wood or metal. The story of how Samson Wrecks the Gates of Gaza provides an interpretation for an unusual rock formation on a hill outside the city that people nicknamed "The Gates of Gaza." Etiologies appear today in the names of natural formations like the "Devil's Post Pile" or "Camelback Mountain."

The gates of a city and the doors of a house are also metaphors for the vagina of a woman. The metaphor appears in Egyptian love songs (Fig. 37) and in the Song of Solomon (Song 5:2-6). When Samson goes into the woman and comes out through the gates of the city, he shames the Philistines of Gaza, who cannot protect either their women or their city. The interplay between the woman and the gates of the city in this hero story is comparable to the interplay between the woman of Timnah and the lion.

> *The woman whom I love is the lady of a great house.*
> *You enter her house in the center.*
>
> *The doors are wide open, the bolt is unfastened*
> *Because she is angry with her lover . . .*
>
> *If she hired me to guard her door,*
>
> *At least when I made her angry,*
>
> *I would get to hear her voice,*
> *Even as I tremble like a child.*

FIGURE 37   Egyptian Love Song (Matthews and Benjamin 1997: 300–01)

Samson Terrorizes the Wadi Sorek
(JUDG 16:4-22)

In the story of how Samson Terrorizes the Wadi Sorek (Judg 16:4-22), Samson delivers Israel from Philistia three times, before Delilah delivers Philistia from Israel by shaving his head. A man's hair and his beard were comparable to his pubic hair because they appear together during puberty. By shaving Samson's head, Delilah castrates him, and leaves him as weak as a child.

Other aspects of the story also describe the transformation of Samson from powerful to powerless. In a Hymn to Yahweh celebrating the deliverance of Israel from Harosheth-ha-goiim, Sisera "sank, he fell, he lay still at Jael's feet; at her feet he sank, he fell; there he sank, there he fell dead" (Judg 5:27). Similarly, Delilah "let Samson fall asleep on her lap" (Judg 16:19). Both gestures are reversals. Sisera tries to fall between the legs of Jael and rape her, but instead he falls between her legs dead. Samson tries to fall between the legs of Delilah and have intercourse with her as an adult, but instead falls asleep on her lap like a child.

When the Philistines take Samson prisoner, they gouge out his eyes. The tactic renders warriors powerless. Blinding was also equivalent to castration because the eyes of warriors were equivalent to their testicles. To be blind was to be impotent. The Middle Assyrian Code (1115–1077 B.C.E.) reflects this equivalence: "If a woman ruptures a man's testicle during a fight and, even after medical treatment, his other testicle also ruptures, then both of the eyes of the woman are gouged out" (Art. 8).

Mutilating prisoners of war also disabled them from bearing arms. The Babylonians blind Zedekiah after destroying Jerusalem and executing the members of his household before his eyes (2 Kgs 25:7; Jer 39:7; 52:11). The king is powerless to protect the land and its children. Mutilated warriors could work, but they could not fight. Adoni-bezek the Perizzite cuts off the thumbs and toes of seventy rulers he defeats, before the warriors of Judah cut off his thumbs and toes (Judg 1:4-7). Without their big toes, warriors could not balance. Without thumbs it was virtually impossible for warriors to grasp their weapons. Mutilation also clearly identified convicts and served as a warning to others.

The Philistines sentence Samson to grind at a mill. The great warrior is forced to do the work of a woman. Grinding grain for bread was a metaphor for sexual intercourse. Job testifies that his wife never ground grain for another while he was father of the household (Job 31:9-10). During intercourse a woman grinds the semen of a man to create a child, just as at the mill she grinds grain to bake bread. With the same motion she draws life from the land and from its men.

Samson Destroys the House of Dagon
(JUDG 16:23-31)

Prisoners of war were brought back from the battlefield as evidence to the people at home that the warriors had fulfilled their obligation to protect them from their enemies. Some prisoners were sold as slaves. Others, like Samson, are publically tortured and executed in mock battles in order to shame them. Pharaohs would use conquered rulers as footstools, or they would have them lashed beneath the anuses of the horses on the tongue of their war chariots. As the pharaohs entered the city with their victorious troops, crowds waited for the horses to shower their enemies with excrement. During the festival of Dagon, the Philistines sexually abuse Samson by striking or fondling the blind man's genitals (Gen 26:8-9).

Samson puts out the "eyes," or twin pillars, of the Philistine sanctuary in retaliation for the loss of his eyes. The pillars mark the place where the divine patrons of the community enter and leave the human plane. The Philistine sanctuary at tel Qasile just north and east of the mouth of the Yarkon River likewise rests on two pillars. Through these eyes of the Philistine temple Dagaon enters Philistia. Blindness closes the vent, cutting Philistia off from its divine patron. The Philistines have left Israel powerless by blinding Samson. Samson has left Philistia powerless by blinding Dagon.

The Saga of Samson does not celebrate Samson. The stories make fun of him in order to question whether heroes really protect Israel from its enemies. Similarly, the book of Jonah does not celebrate Jonah, but makes fun of him in order to question whether the death sentence that the prophets imposed on the enemies of Israel will be carried out. In all his glory, Samson is a fool. Only blind and powerless does he become a hero. The hero stories with which the book of Judges opens (Judg 1:1— 12:15) are told only to argue in the Saga of Samson that Yahweh does not need great warriors like Othniel, Deborah, Jael, or Gideon to deliver Israel from its enemies, but can use a blind man like Samson. It is Yahweh, and Yahweh alone, who feeds and protects the land and its people.

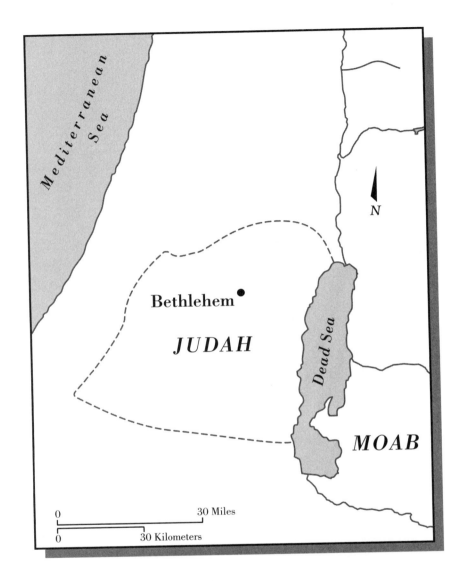

Points of Interest (Chapter 5)

5

BOOK OF RUTH

(RUTH 1:1—4:22)

The book of Ruth (Hebrew: *Ruth*) combines a Parable of a Persevering Widow (Ruth 1:1-22) and a Parable of Workers in a Wheat Field (Ruth 2:1-23) with two ancestor stories (Ruth 3:1-18; 4:1-21). Naomi is the protagonist in one parable; Ruth in the other parable. Ruth is the protagonist in one ancestor story; Boaz is the protagonist in the other ancestor story.

There are four changes of scene in the book of Ruth: the road to Bethlehem, the field of Boaz, the threshing floor, and the gates of Bethlehem. Action, however, marks the most significant divisions in the book of Ruth. The action that causes the greatest conflict in a plot is the climax episode (Ruth 3:1-18). Actions that lead up to the climax are crisis episodes (Ruth 1:1-21; 2:1-23). Actions that restore shalom are in the denouement episode (Ruth 4:1-22). At the outset, the household of Elimelech leaves the dying land of Judah for Moab only to be ambushed there by epidemic. Naomi and Ruth come back to Judah, and initiate legal action to reclaim their land when Ruth exercises the widows' right of gleaning. The action reaches a climax when Naomi sues Boaz to restore full legal status to the household of Elimelech by marrying Ruth, thus reclaiming the land and children of her household.

Parable of a Persevering Widow
(RUTH 1:1-22)

The coherence of the book of Ruth does not deprive the parables and ancestor stories on which it builds of their independence as traditions in their own right. Parables challenge the values of the establishment, who are people with land and children, the two things widows, orphans, and strangers lack. Being without the political and economic power that land and children conferred on members of the establishment, widows, orphans, and strangers were easy targets for discrimination (Exod 22:20-23). The intention of the Parable of a Persevering Widow (Ruth 1:1-22) is to help its audience think about: "What are the advantages of believing in Yahweh if it does not get you land and children?" (Ruth 1:21).

Crisis Episode
(RUTH 1:1-7)

The words with which parables begin are as predictable as the questions with which they end. "In the days when the judges ruled" (Ruth 1:1) is a good example. Like "once upon a time" and "many years ago in a far off place," this introduction makes no reference to particular dates, times, or places. It is a broad, universal orientation that is as sweeping and inclusive as possible. Parables catch audiences in the most ecumenical moments of their lives, moments that they have in common with people of any time and place.

Characters in parables are also generic rather than specific. Because parables are a class-action form of tradition, they introduce their audiences to "a certain man of Bethlehem in Judah . . . and his wife" (Ruth 1:1). Although later storytellers gave the man and his wife names such as "Elimelech" and "Naomi," the typecasting remained. They named the characters in this parable for virtues and vices, like characters in medieval morality plays in western Europe. Naomi is "Blessed," Mahlon is a "Critical Patient," Chilion is a "Terminal Patient," Ruth is a "Companion," and Orpah is "One Who Returns Home."

Parables also regularly employ hyperbole, a literary technique that uses exaggeration for emphasis. The Parable of a Persevering Widow uses hyperbole to exaggerate the suffering of the household of Elimelech. Even in Bethlehem, the breadbasket of Judah, famine was a predictable part of life. Just as famine drives the household of Jacob south into Egypt in the book of Genesis, famine drives the household of Elimelech east into Moab in the book of Ruth. Hungry households in ancient Israel went to Egypt or Moab as easily as hungry households today go to the store. Hyperbole, however, turns hunger into a hound that relentlessly pursues the household of Elimelech. Famine, migration, and then death after death changes the status of Elimelech and Naomi from powerful to powerless.

Climax Episode
(RUTH 1:8-18)

In the climax of the Parable of a Persevering Widow, Naomi ritually degrades herself. Although Orpah and Ruth attempt to console Naomi, she abrogates the covenant that binds them to her. Naomi uses a variation of the divorce formula to dismiss her daughters-in-law: "you are not my clients and I am not your patron" (Hosea 1:8).

Naomi's dispensation of Ruth and Orpah directs them "to go back . . . to your mother's house" (Ruth 1:7). The standard formula is "to your father's house" (Gen 38:11; Lev 22:13; Num 30:16; Deut 22:21). "Your mother's house" appears only four times in the Bible, and always in reference to the ability to bear a child (Gen 24:28; Ruth 1:7; Song 3:4; 8:2). Ruth and Orpah can have children only if they leave behind their condition as liminal women in the household of Elimelech and remain in Moab. With this ritual degradation, Naomi strips herself of every last vestige of power and authority. She stands powerless on the border between Moab and Judah. She is a woman without a household. Without land and children she stands alone in no-man's-land.

Both Ruth and Orpah obey Naomi when she annuls the covenant obligations that they assumed by marrying her sons. Orpah returns home to Moab as Naomi tells her to do. Ruth obediently accepts her annulment, but instead of leaving Naomi, Ruth negotiates a new covenant with her. Ruth clings to Naomi (Ruth 1:14-16) as a husband is expected to cling to his wife (Gen 2:24; Prov 18:24). The strength of these women is in their sisterhood with one another.

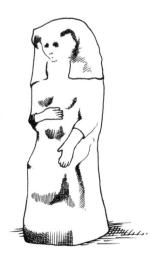

Expectant Mother
(Akhziv 700–600 B.C.E.; ceramic 23.5 cm)

Covenants were negotiated by rulers. For Ruth, a widow from Moab, to negotiate a covenant with Naomi, a widow from Judah, is ironic. Ruth professes her faith in the life-giving power of someone who is, for all intents and purposes, lifeless. The parable teaches that it is not the power of rulers, but the perseverance of widows that blesses Judah and Moab with land and children (Sir 35:5-15). Yahweh does not deliver Naomi the widow from suffering, but, like Ruth, Yahweh simply shares her suffering. Yahweh sends Ruth only to accompany the suffering Naomi, not to deliver her from suffering. Yahweh does not march with the powerful, but travels instead with the poor who clog the roads and glean the fields. The powerful put the land and children to death; the perseverance of widows raises them to new life.

Only two components of a standard covenant appear here. They are the stipulations (Ruth 1:15-17) and the litany of blessings and curses (Ruth 1:17-18). The credential (Exod 20:2), the story (Exod 20:2), the list of witnesses (Exod 24:1-2), and the promulgation and documentation (Exod 24:3-11) are missing. In the stipulations, Ruth describes her obligations to Naomi. The opening stipulations in a covenant are often arranged in a decalogue (Exod 20:3-17). Here there are only five components, not ten. In the covenants in the books of Exodus and Deuteronomy, the stipulations in the decalogue are directives like "Remember the Sabbath day, to keep it holy" and "You shall not kill." In the Parable of a Persevering Widow (Ruth 1:15-17), the stipulations are promises patterned on the words of Yahweh to Israel: "I will be your divine patron, and you shall be my people" (Lev 26:12). In the litany, Ruth describes both the blessings that her household will enjoy if she fulfills her obligations to Naomi, and the curses that it will experience if she does not.

Denouement Episode
(RUTH 1:19-22)

Parables are stories without a denouement. In place of a standard denouement that restores the shalom interrupted by the crisis, the denouement in the parable simply asks the audience a question. In the crisis episode of the Parable of a Persevering Widow, Naomi begins her exodus deprived of land by a famine in Judah and of children by an epidemic in Moab. In the climax, Naomi completes her divestiture by emancipating the widowed Ruth and Orpah. In the denouement, Naomi asks: "Why call me Naomi, when Yahweh has afflicted me and the Almighty has brought calamity upon me?" (Ruth 1:21). Is this what it means to be chosen by Yahweh? To have no land and no children? How can a woman whose name means "Blessed" be cursed with the loss of her land and her children? How can Yahweh's chosen people lose their land and children?

The loss of land and children creates worry and doubt. It raises questions, and turns faith into cynicism. Yahweh promised to bless the Hebrews with land and children (Gen 12:1-8; Deut 30:15-20). When Yahweh is in the land, children are born and harvests are full. So, when Yahweh is the guest of Abraham and Sarah, they conceive a child (Gen 18:1-15). When Yahweh leaves the land, famine and epidemic cripple its children and weaken its harvests. The Parable of a Persevering Widow struggles both with the question of why the innocent suffer, a classic theme in the teaching traditions of Mesopotamia, Syria-Palestine, and Egypt, and with the question of how the Covenant between Yahweh and Israel will be fulfilled, a classic theme in the Bible.

For the Parable of the a Persevering Widow, the powerful cannot permanently deprive the powerless of land and children. By continuing to tell the story and ask the question, parables deny the powerful of an uncontested claim to the land and its children. The perseverance of the storytellers is like the perseverance of the widows in their parables. They continue to ask: "When will the promises of land and children be fulfilled?" They ask, not because they doubt, but because they are absolutely confident that now is a good time for those promises to be fulfilled.

Parable of Workers in a Wheat Field
(RUTH 2:1-23)

A Parable of Workers in a Wheat Field heightens the crisis initiated by the Parable of a Persevering Widow. The Parable of a Persevering Widow wants its audience to think about whether Yahweh delivers the Hebrews from evil, or simply shares their suffering. The Parable of Workers in a Wheat Field asks its audiences to consider whether the hospitality of Yahweh and Boaz to strangers is a blessing or a curse for the households of Judah. "Why should the last, like Ruth from Moab, be first, and the first, like the harvesters from Judah, be last?" The book of Jonah is a parable with much the same intention.

Crisis Episode
(RUTH 2:1-3)

Ruth is the protagonist (Ruth 2:2). By gleaning, without being clearly eligible to do so, she provokes a crisis among the other workers. They react to Ruth as a stranger. This woman from Moab should not be entitled to gather the grain left in the field by the harvesters. Only the widows of Judah are entitled to food from the land of Judah.

Climax Episode
(RUTH 2:3-7)

By continuing to glean (Ruth 2:7), Ruth aggravates the crisis into a climax when workers report her to the owner of the field, but this "man of honor" (Ruth 2:1) treats Ruth like his heir, instead of his enemy. Ruth meets Boaz in a wheat field, at a threshing floor, and at the city gate. Each is a threshold that leads to fertility. At each site, Ruth and Boaz ritually anticipate the intercourse that will bless the household of Elimelech and Naomi with an heir. When a man "comforts" and "speaks kindly" to a woman, as Boaz does with Ruth in the wheat field, he is courting her. When a man feeds a woman as Boaz feeds Ruth in the wheat field, he is marrying her. Today when the bride and groom give each other wine to drink or feed each other wedding cake, they continue a tradition in which feeding one another was the ritual by which a man and woman consummated the marriage vows that they had spoken.

After a remarkably short bargaining session, Boaz grants Ruth three employee benefits. First, Boaz is legally obligated to allow Ruth the privilege of gleaning for only one day, but he extends her privileges for the duration of the harvest. Second, Boaz guarantees Ruth's security. Third, Boaz agrees to allow Ruth water breaks and even agrees to provide the water.

Denouement Episode
(RUTH 2:8-23)

Cultures define strangers or outsiders in a variety of ways. In the Parable of Workers in a Wheat Field, Ruth asks: "Why have I found favor in your eyes, that you should take notice of me, when I am a stranger?" (Ruth 2:10). Like the question in the Parable of a Persevering Widow, the question in this parable asks: "Am I an insider or an outsider? Am I blessed or cursed?" (Ruth 2:10).

The commentary on the benefits that Ruth negotiates from Boaz stresses that no act of kindness is forgotten. Ruth's compassion toward Naomi is repaid by the compassion of Boaz to Ruth. Ruth treats Naomi as she does not deserve. Despite the fact that Naomi dispenses Ruth from any legal obligation to her, Ruth continues to care for her mother-in-law in excess of what even the law itself would require. Likewise, despite the fact that Boaz fulfills his legal obligation to Ruth as a widow, he continues to care for her in excess of what even the law itself would require. Loving-kindness exceeds the law.

Boaz grants Ruth more generous privileges in his fields than the law obligates him to grant. He adds a fourth, fifth, and sixth benefit to the three he has already granted Ruth. Fourth, Ruth eats a hot meal with Boaz, rather than parched grain with the other workers. Fifth, Ruth gets to gather not only the gleanings to which the law entitles her, but also from the standing sheaves. Sixth, the harvesters are to show Ruth which is the good grain. With these gestures, this parable reminds audiences that Israel does not deserve Yahweh's favor any more than Naomi deserves the favor of Ruth, or Ruth deserves the favor of Boaz.

In the wheat field, Boaz promises Ruth: "may you have a full reward from Yahweh, the divine patron of Israel, under whose wings you have come for refuge" (Ruth 2:12). At the threshing floor, Ruth asks Boaz to keep his promise and "spread your cloak over your servant" (Ruth 3:9). The book of Deuteronomy uses the same idiom. "A man shall not marry his father's wife, and lift up the cloak that his father spread over her" (Deut

22:30). "Cursed be anyone who lies with his father's wife and lifts up the cloak that his father spread over her" (Deut 27:20). The imagery is sexual. A woman's dress or cloak are like the wings of her husband. Boaz promises to take Ruth under his wing. He will cover her body with his cloak when he has intercourse with her.

Story of Ruth as a Persevering Widow
(RUTH 3:1-18)

Having used two parables to create a crisis, the book of Ruth uses an ancestor story to reach a climax.

Crisis Episode
(RUTH 3:1-9)

The Story of Ruth as a Persevering Widow (Ruth 3:1-18) ends with the same question found in the Parable of Workers in a Wheat Field. In the parable, Boaz asks: "Whose woman is this?" (Ruth 2:5). Here Boaz asks: "Who are you?" (Ruth 3:9).

The Story of Ruth as a Persevering Widow that serves as a climax for the book of Ruth celebrates this woman of Moab who continues to embrace Judah until it bears a child to enjoy its harvest. Ruth is tenacious. She holds on to Naomi, and she holds on to Boaz as the household of David holds on to Judah. In the end there is a harvest, and there is a child. Like Naomi, Ruth is a persevering widow.

Ruth is a "woman of honor" (Ruth 3:11). She is a "woman, who . . . like Rachel and Leah . . . built up the house of Israel" (Ruth 4:11). The power of an ancestor is not based on land and children, but rather on some virtue that compensates for land and children. As an ancestor, Ruth has neither land nor children, but she compensates for her lack of land and children by her perseverance, which the clan telling her stories wants its households to imitate.

The story portrays Boaz as one of two legal guardians of the household of Elimelech (Ruth 3:12). Boaz and the other legal guardian are elders, who oppose the "young men, whether poor or rich" (Ruth 3:10), who were the warriors in the village. Ruth must decide which of these elders would be a better legal guardian for the household of Elimelech.

The threshing floor is not only a place where grain is processed, but where rulers are chosen. Since it is the responsibility of the ruler to provide food for the people, the question: "Who will feed Israel?" is decided at this location where food is processed.

Climax Episode
(RUTH 3:9-13)

Ruth dresses not to be seductive, but so that she can act officially as the representative of the household of Elimelech (Ruth 4:3). Clothes were not a personal accessory; they were a uniform indicating social status.

Ruth goes to the threshing floor and uncovers the feet of Boaz. In the story that follows, Ruth pulls the sandal off the foot of her legal guardian. In both passages, the word "foot" is a euphemism for a man's penis. By placing herself in the physical position for intercourse with Boaz, she challenges him to fulfill his obligation, as the legal guardian of the household of Elimelech, to have a child with her. By removing the sandal of the other legal guardian, she abrogates the covenant between his household and the household of Elimelech. The sandal is a symbol both of the land, which Elimelech walked, and of the women who would bear the children of his household. The foot of her legal guardian is removed from the sandal, symbolizing a man's withdrawal from the vagina of a woman during intercourse. The act is terminated, and there will be no child. Boaz remains as the only legal guardian of the household. Both rituals are legal, not romantic.

Denouement Episode
(RUTH 3:14-17)

Boaz accepts his responsibility as the legal guardian of the household of Elimelech by sending Ruth home with his grain. The grain, which is his return of the land to the household of Elimelech, will be matched soon by the semen, which will be his return of children to the household. The association between the seed that will give birth to a child and the seed that will produce a harvest is further strengthened when Boaz pours barley into Ruth's apron. She pulls the apron full of heavy with grain to her body, making her look like a woman who is heavily pregnant.

Ruth functions at the threshing floor the way Tamar functions at the sanctuary of Timnah (Gen 38:1-30). Both use alternative means to access the power of their legal guardians. There are strong parallels between this a Story of Ruth as a Persevering Widow and the Story of Tamar as a Persevering Widow. Both Elimelech and Judah move their households to strange lands. In both stories, two sons die. Both Ruth and Tamar become liminal women who leave their households, and go above and beyond the call of duty to preserve the households of their husbands from extinction.

The Story of Ruth as a Persevering Widow also serves as an apology. It admits the accusation and then carefully reinterprets it as a compliment. Granted, Ruth was from Moab and, therefore, an outsider, but it is precisely the widow, the orphan, and the stranger whom Yahweh favors and through whom Yahweh delivers Israel. Even traditions as fearful of strangers as those in the book of Deuteronomy admit that the widow, the orphan, and the stranger are under the protection of Yahweh.

Story of Boaz as Legal Guardian
(RUTH 4:1-22)

The book of Ruth concludes with a Story of Boaz as Legal Guardian, to argue that Yahweh returns to Judah when David becomes its monarch. When a poor woman like Naomi recovers her land, and a barren woman like Ruth gives birth to a child, the land is alive and Yahweh is present. This Story of Boaz is also an ancestor story. It answers the question so painfully raised in the Parable of a Persevering Widow by asserting that widows are blessed, not cursed, by legal guardians like Boaz and kings like David (Ruth 4:14-16).

Crisis Episode
(RUTH 4:1-4)

When the father of a household died without designating an heir, the tribe appointed a legal guardian to look after the household. The tribe could not interfere in the internal affairs of a household unless these two conditions were fulfilled: the father of the household must have died and, and the household had must have no son (Deut 25:5). Most English translations render the word for this legal guardian as "brother-in-law" or "redeemer." Provisions for the appointment of legal guardians are found throughout the ancient Near East. The Hittite Code, which represents a legal tradition in the Empire of Hatti between 1450 and 1200 B.C.E., establishes provisions for the appointment of a legal guardian similar to those found in the Bible (Gen 38:1-30; Lev 25:25-38; Deut 25:5-10; Jer 32:6-44). These traditions are comparable, but not identical. In some cases, the guardian is delegated to take over only the land of the household,, whereas in others he must father an heir with the widow as well. Legal guardians represent the larger interests of the tribe in preventing a leaderless household from losing the ability to feed and protect its members. The story opens when Boaz asks the primary other legal guardian of the household of Elimelech if he is able to fulfill his legal obligations. Legal guardians were expected to feed and protect the households for which they were legal guardians with the resources of their own households. The primary legal guardian of the household of Elimelech publically affirms his ability to work the land.

Climax Episode
(RUTH 4:5-12)

Boaz then challenges the primary legal guardian of the household of Elimelech to assume responsibility for both the land and the children of the household. Although the liabilities of a household without a father were generally greater than its assets, a legal guardian did enjoy the use of the property and the people of the household as long as there was no heir. He could keep any profit realized while he was guardian.

While rebuilding the ability of the household to work its land and tend its herds, for which it was responsible to the village, the guardian was also to have intercourse with the widow until she had a son. He did not marry the mother of the household (Lev 18:16; 20:21). He simply carried out the physical and economic commitments that her husband had failed to complete before his death. The guardian was authorized to care for her only until she had an heir, and the household could once again care for its own land and children.

For financial reasons, the primary legal guardian of the household of Elimelech waives his right to father a child with Ruth, and, consequently, to farm her land as well. By removing his sandal, he abrogates his covenant with the household of Elimelech. He may no longer walk the land which for which the sandals are his title. He also may no longer have intercourse with the mother of the household of Elimelech in order to sire an heir for him. Removing the sandal ritually enacts coitus interruptus, and thus terminates the social status of the legal guardian. Boaz remains the only legal guardian of the household of Elimelech.

Denouement Episode
(RUTH 4:13-22)

According to the ritual for legal guardians, the natural child of Boaz and Ruth should be the legal child of Mahlon, Ruth's husband. Nonetheless, the women of Bethlehem celebrate the birth of the child, singing: "Praise Yahweh . . . a son has been born to Naomi" (Ruth 4:14-17). Like the words "go back . . . each of you to your mother's house" (Ruth 1:8), these words are both unexpected and surprisingly feminist. The use of words so emphatically women's words may be characteristic of the liminal condition of widows, who are operating without any relationship to the households of a father, a husband, or a son. It is unlikely that the women, or even the storytellers, name Naomi as the mother of the child in order to erase the memory of Ruth as a sexually forward stranger. The traditions consistently celebrate both Naomi and Ruth as widows, who use their status as liminal women to restore the honor of their common household.

Throughout, these women act together, and they act honorably. The names of Ruth and Naomi are interchanged without prejudice to either of them. As liminal women they are entitled to act aggressively to restore the honor of their households. Ruth is a surrogate mother for Naomi. She carries the child for Naomi, who then adopts it from Ruth at birth. Sarah made a similar arrangement with Hagar (Gen 16:1-16).

Audiences in different periods of ancient Israel have heard the traditions that make up the book of Ruth differently. In the villages of early Israel, households in jeopardy of losing their land and children asked: "Who will enjoy the blessings of land and children?" In the book of Ruth, they heard that land and children belong to persevering widows like Naomi, to fearless strangers like Ruth, and to decisive legal guardians like Boaz. By challenging the powerful, who curse Israel with famine, epidemic, poverty, and infertility, the book of Ruth championed the quiet rights of the powerless celebrating their harvests of barley and wheat. Jews today continue this tradition of harvest storytelling. The Song of Solomon is read on Passover in March, the book of Ruth is read during Pentecost in April, and the book of Ecclesiastes is read during Booths in September.

The household of David heard the traditions in the book of Ruth as supporting its right to rule Israel as a state. These traditions showed how Yahweh saved Israel with the help of Ruth, a foreign woman who was the grandmother of David.

When Ezra and the household of David were repatriated to Judah by the Persians after 537 B.C.E., the people of Judah who had not been deported heard the traditions in the book of Ruth as a challenge to the right of the household of David to resume its rule of Judah. After its repatriation, the household of David prohibited marriage with women outside the household. For the people of the land, the book of Ruth shows that Ruth, though not a member of the household of David, was more faithful to the covenant between Yahweh and Israel than those who were.

For generation after generation the book of Ruth captured the hearts of the people on the margins of ancient Israel. They fondly remembered Naomi and Ruth precisely because they were not conquering warriors claiming colonies for an emperor, or riding triumphant into the cities of their enemies. Widows, orphans, and strangers remembered Naomi and Ruth as being as powerless as themselves. But they also remembered them as signs of hope, those whose persevereance would allow them to inherit the earth. For the book of Ruth, David was not the ruthless descendant of the rulers of Egypt and Mesopotamia, but rather the grandson of widows and strangers.

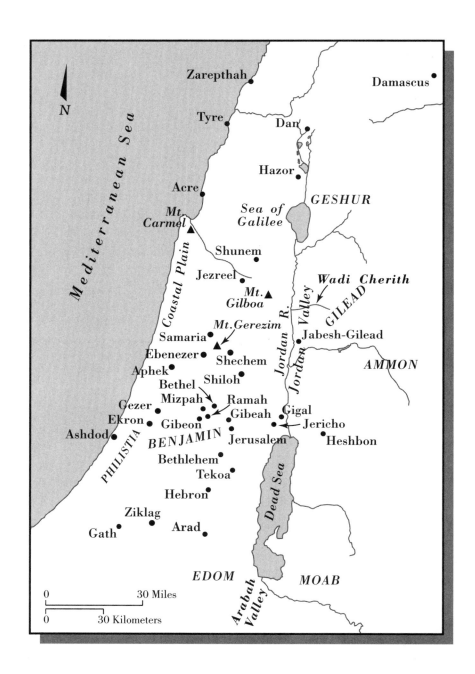

Points of Interest (Chapter 6)

6

BOOKS OF SAMUEL AND KINGS

(1 SAM 1:1—2 KGS 25:30)

The books of Samuel (Hebrew: *Shemu'el*) and Kings (Hebrew: *Melakim*) in the Bible today preserve at least four major traditions. There are the Stories of Samuel (1 Sam 1:1—8:3), the Stories of David's Rise to Power (1 Sam 8:4—2 Sam 8:13), the Stories of David's Successor (2 Sam 9:1—20:26+1 Kgs 1:1—11:43), and a Review of the Annals for the Monarchs of Israel and Judah (1 Kgs 11:44—2 Kgs 25:30).

The Stories of Samuel, which include the Ark of the Covenant Stories (1 Sam 4:1—7:2), hand on the idealism of early Israel (1200–1000 B.C.E.). The villages of early Israel depended upon Yahweh to lift up a chief to defend them from their enemies. There were no monarchs, no taxes, no soldiers, no slaves, and no cities in early Israel.

The Stories of David's Rise to Power, which include the Stories of Saul (1 Sam 8:4—15:35), defend David for betraying his patron Saul. David's enemies also labeled him a heretic for declaring himself to be king of Israel where only Yahweh was king. These stories argue that both Saul and Jonathan adopted David as heir to the household of Saul, and that Yahweh lifted up David to rule Israel just as Yahweh had lifted up Saul and all the other chiefs in Israel.

Although today Solomon is known and honored, in ancient Israel he was virtually unknown before he became king of Israel. Amnon (2 Sam 13:1—14:33), Absalom (2 Sam 15:1—24:25), and Adonijah (1 Kings 1–10) were the leading candidates to become heir to the household of David. The Stories of David's Successor review the credentials of these three sons and disqualify each from becoming king. Only Solomon, with the endorsement of Bathsheba and Nathan, remains eligible to succeed David.

A Review of the Annals for the Monarchs of Israel and Judah, with which the books of Samuel-Kings conclude, is a lengthy answer to a single question: "Why did the

Hebrews lose the land and children that Yahweh had promised to Abraham and Sarah?" This review of the yearly reports that the monarchs of Israel and Judah made to Yahweh shows that every ruler but David (1000 B.C.E.), Hezekiah (715–687 B.C.E.), and Josiah (640–609 B.C.E.) failed as stewards of the land and its children. The review evaluates these rulers on a single issue promulgated in the book of Deuteronomy: Yahweh blesses the Hebrews with land and children only when, as one people, they worship Yahweh in one way in one sanctuary, Jerusalem. The review indicts Israel and Judah for worshiping Yahweh with various liturgies in various communities at various sanctuaries throughout their land. Therefore it sentences the land and children of Israel to be taken away by Assyria (721 B.C.E.), and the land and children of Judah to be taken away by Babylon (587 B.C.E.).

Stories of Samuel
(1 SAM 1:1—8:3)

Annunciation to Hannah
(1 SAM 1:1—2:11)

Annunciation stories are a particular kind of ancestor story which teaches that children are divine gifts, not human accomplishments. The Annunciation to Hannah (1 Sam 1:1—2:11) celebrates Hannah for her perseverance. She is the protagonist. Eli the priest is the antagonist. She sets out to have a child. He attempts to prevent her. In both this annunciation and in a Trial of Eli and His Sons that follows, Hannah and her son, Samuel, are wise. Eli and his sons, Hophni and Phinehas, are fools.

At the beginning of the annunciation and at the end of the trial, Eli is sitting at the gate of Shiloh where he can watch the two courtyards between the gate and the holy of holies. During the day Eli determines who may enter the sanctuary. At night he guards it. He is responsible for maintaining order within the sanctuary. Before the story ends, it will be clear that this priest of the gate cannot tell who should enter the sanctuary from those who should not. Eli is even powerless to stop the inappropriate behavior of his own sons within the sanctuary.

When the story opens, Hannah is infertile. Since she cannot conceive a child, she does not eat. The blessing of the child and the blessing of the land are interdependent. While her household is eating, Hannah steps quietly into the courtyard reserved for priests. Eli sees her, mistakenly labels her a drunk, and tries to throw her out. Drunks

Ships of Tyre Unload Cedar for Palace of Sargon II
(Khorsbad 721-705 B.C.E.; Alabaster 2.83 m)

are fools who do not ration their wine. Households that eat too much and drink too much deprive others of the food and drink they need to survive. Rationing is the virtue of the wise.

Ironically, Eli does not hear Hannah pray for a child who will not drink at all so that he can serve Yahweh worthily in the very courtyard where Hannah is praying. Eli is sober, but still so blind that he cannot tell this woman of honor from a fool. The sentence that Eli tries to impose on Hannah and her son will be imposed on him and on his sons. Consequently, he and his sons will be expelled from the sanctuary.

Before she leaves the sanctuary, Hannah explains her prayer to Eli and asks him to approve the favor she seeks. Her prayer plays on her name. She tells Eli: "Yahweh's 'favorite' needs a 'favor.'" Eli reverses himself and declares Hannah to be in good standing.

Originally Hannah names her child "Saul" because he is was "the answer to a prayer." Curiously, Hannah now calls him "Samuel." Leaders were often honored with stories telling of the events that marked their births. Moses is a newborn saved from death by a daughter of Pharaoh, and Gideon is the only child of a woman who, like Hannah, was infertile. In the beginning, the clan of Saul and the clan of Samuel told distinct stories celebrating the birth of each leader. In the struggle between Samuel and Saul, however, the clan of Samuel looted the birth story of Saul. Today the Bible explains the name "Samuel," which means "the name of our Creator," as if it were "Saul," which means the "answer to a prayer."

Trial of Eli and His Sons
(1 Sam 2:12—4:22)

A Trial of Eli and His Sons is made up of an indictment (1 Sam 2:12-17) and three sentences (1 Sam 2:18—4:22). Because Eli was Samuel's patron, the Stories of Samuel also want to make it clear that Samuel did not betray his patron, but that it was Yahweh who removed Eli and his sons from office. Samuel took their place because he knew how to guard the gate, and how to collect sacrifices properly.

Eli and his sons are indicted for abusing the land by taking more than their share of the sacrifices and for abusing the children of Israel by having intercourse with "the women who served at the entrance to the tent of meeting" (1 Sam 2:22). At Shiloh priests stuck a fork into the pot to draw out their portion "whether it be bad or good" (4QSam^a). By using a fork, they did not always receive the prime cuts of meat reserved for the priests at other sanctuaries (Lev 7:28-36; Deut 18:3). Hophni and Phinehas not only take too much, but also do not wait their turn. They take the first part of the sacrifice, which at most sanctuaries was reserved for Yahweh (Lev 3:16; 7:23-31; 17:6; Ezek 20:40). Finally, Hophni and Phinehas do not just steal meat occasionally, but every time the households of Israel come to offer sacrifice. They are fools. The same label that Eli imposed on Hannah is now imposed on him and his sons.

Both as the priest of the gate, and as the father of the household, Eli places Hophni and Phinehas on probation. They do not, however, honor their father. The household of Eli is shamed. The first sentence is announced by Samuel (1 Sam 2:18-21 + 3:1—4:1). Hophni and Phinehas are stripped of their position as priests (Jer 33:18). For as long as they live they are forbidden to go up to the altar, to offer incense, and to wear their ephod aprons. The second is announced by an unnamed "member of the household of our Creator" (1 Sam 2:27) and is nested inside the sentence announced by Samuel. They are no longer entitled to any community support, and they are no longer exempt from communal labor. The third is included in the story of how the Ark Delivers Israel from Philistia (1 Sam 4:1—7:2). Finally, Eli and his sons are sentenced to die without heirs.

The Ark Delivers Israel from Philistia
(1 SAM 4:1—7:1 + 2 SAM 6:2-23)

The sentence in the Trial of Eli and His Sons concludes with the Ark of the Covenant Stories (1 Sam 4:1—7:1). There are three important arks in the Bible: the ark of Noah, the ark of Moses, and the Ark of the Covenant. The ark of Noah is the great barge in which his household survives the flood. The ark of Moses is the basket in which Jochebed places her child before exposing him on the banks of the Nile. The Ark of the Covenant is a portable pedestal on which Yahweh stands. Jews today also refer to the cabinet where the Torah scrolls are stored in the synagogue as an ark.

Cultures throughout the world of the Bible carried their divine patrons on pedestals in processions to visit the land and their people. These pedestals were not images but vehicles. In Egypt, the pedestals were shaped like boats. In Syria-Palestine they were great lions or bulls. Yahweh rode on two different pedestals. One was the Ark of the Covenant, the other a great bull, which a Trial of Aaron (Exod 32:1-35) calls a "Golden Calf."

Aaron uses the jewelry of the Hebrews to gold-plate a wooden statue of a great bull on whose back Yahweh will ride into battle against their enemies. Jeroboam, who won independence for the northern Hebrew villages from the household of David and Solomon after 932 B.C.E., commissioned two bull pedestals for Yahweh. He erected one in the sanctuary at Dan and the other in the sanctuary at Bethel. The Ark of the Covenant was shaped like a high place. It was a gold-plated dias dais or platform. Yahweh stood invisible between two cherubim or sphinx, with the faces of humans, the bodies of lions, the feet of oxen, and the wings of eagles. The spot where Yahweh stood was called the "mercy seat."

Philistines and Hebrews appeared in Syria-Palestine for the first time at the end of the Late Bronze period (1400–1200 B.C.E.), when the empires of Mycenae, Hatti, and Egypt collapsed. The Philistines and the Hebrews were peoples brought together in the same land, at the same time, by Egypt, their common enemy. The Philistines emigrated from Cyprus and settled onto the southern end of the coastal plains, which became known as "Philistia" or "Palestine." The walls of the funeral chapel of Ramses III (1194–1163 B.C.E.) describe a fierce battle between the Philistines and the Egyptians for the control of the region. The Hebrews emigrated from the coastal plains into the hills above the Jordan River. The called their new land "Israel." The Death of the First-born of Egypt (Exod 1:7—13:16) tells how the Hebrews escaped from Egypt. Hebrews and Philistines shared a common border in a common land, which led to both competition and conflict for 250 years. In the Ark of the Covenant Stories, Yahweh alone leads the Hebrews into battle. In hero stories, Yahweh lifts up chiefs like Joshua, Samuel, Saul, and David to deliver the Hebrews from their enemies.

The episodes in the hero stories are punctuated with formulas. In the crisis the Hebrews "forget Yahweh," who then abandons them to their enemies. In the climax, Yahweh "lifts up" a chief after the Hebrews "cry out" for deliverance. In the denouement, the land is "at rest." The Ark of the Covenant Stories follow the same pattern, but without the formulas.

The covenant between Yahweh and Israel stipulates that Yahweh, and only Yahweh, may feed and protect the Hebrews. Nonetheless, the Hebrews continually tried to protect themselves by going out to battle against the Philistines. Yahweh does not punish the Hebrews with defeat, but simply allows them to suffer the consequences of their actions.

When the Philistines defeat the Hebrews on the battlefield between the villages of Ebenezer to the west and Aphek to the east, the Hebrews try to force Yahweh to defend them by carrying the Ark of the Covenant into battle. By trying to force Yahweh into battle, the Hebrews forget that Yahweh leads the Hebrews, but Yahweh will not be led by them. As priests, Eli, Hophni, and Phinehas are expected to see what Yahweh is doing in Israel, but Eli is blind (1 Sam 4:18). Neither he nor his sons see that when they fight to defend themselves they fight without Yahweh.

Hophni and Phinehas are killed. The Hebrews retreat. Eli is not only too blind to see what Yahweh is doing in Israel, but also too blind to see the stool where he sits day after day. He stumbles over it, and breaks his neck, just as the wife of Phinehas goes into premature labor. Before she dies in childbirth, she names her child "Ichabod," because she thinks that Yahweh "has departed" (1 Sam 4:21). "Ichabod" also means that, at the same moment that this child was born, Yahweh "broke out" of the hills of Israel "like a flood" to invade Philistia. Yahweh is not departing Israel as a prisoner of the Philistines. Yahweh is breaking out of Israel and invading Philistia. Finally, the Hebrews cry out to Yahweh for deliverance.

The Philistines place the Ark of the Covenant, like a prisoner of war, at the feet of the statue of Dagon, their divine patron. During the night, however, the statue of Dagon prostrates itself before the Ark of the Covenant, acknowledging Yahweh as its patron. The people of Ashdod are outraged and hurriedly reerect the statue of Dagon. The next night the statue again prostrates itself before the ark, breaking off his its hands and head in the process. Statues of the divine assembly were dedicated by placing a weapon in their upraised hand or inlaying their eyes with semiprecious stones. When warriors overran a city, they executed the statue of its divine patron by cutting off its hands or its head. For example, archaeologists have recovered a decapitated basalt statue of the divine patron of Hazor, a city overlooking the Huleh plain north of the Sea of Galilee.

Once Dagon surrendered, Yahweh "dealt severely with the people of Ashdod. He ravaged and afflicted the city and its vicinity with hemorrhoids; he brought upon the city a great and deadly plague of mice that swarmed in their ships and over their fields"

(1 Sam 5:6 NAB). It is unlikely that the weapons of Yahweh against Ashdod, Gath, and Ekron are either hemorrhoids or bubonic plague. Bubonic plague is spread by rats, not mice. Furthermore, bubonic plague had not yet appeared in the coastal cities of Syria-Palestine during the Late Bronze period. It is more likely that Yahweh sends mice, not rats, to eat the grain of Philistia. Similarly, it is more likely that Yahweh does not strike the Philistines with hemorrhoids, but prolapses the uteruses of their women. The harvests of Philistia are destroyed, and the women of Philistia become infertile. Yahweh is the divine patron of both land and children, even in Philisitia.

By casting a mouse and a diseased or prolapsed uterus in gold, each of the five cities of Philistia acknowledges that only Yahweh can bless them with land and children. These figurines are fetishes, which are images of the causes or of the symptoms of a disease. Shamans use fetishes like magnets to draw disease out of their patients. Once the disease has left the patient and entered the fetish, the fetish can be isolated or destroyed. Isolating or destroying the fetish isolates or destroys the disease.

The Philistines load their fetishes on an ox-drawn cart and send them with the Ark of the Covenant back across their border into Israel. By returning the Ark of the Covenant to the Hebrews, the Philistines renounce their title as conquerors of Israel. By placing the fetishes on the cart with the Ark of the Covenant, they hope to lure the plague out of Philistia and into Israel. The Philistines hope that the Hebrews, in their excitement to recover the ark, will not realize that they are also infecting themselves with plague. The Philistine strategy is comparable to that used by the Greeks in Homer's *Iliad*. The Greeks leave the Trojans a great wooden horse on the beach as they sail away from the coast. By offering the Trojans this gift, the Greeks renounce their title as conquerors of Troy. The Greeks also hope that the Trojans, in their excitement to take possession of the great horse, will not realize that they are also bringing the Greek warriors hiding inside the statue through the gates and into the city, and sentencing Troy to death.

Ironically, the Hebrews of the village of Beth-Shemesh on the border between Israel and Philistia are harvesting grain. The Philistines are starving, but the Hebrews are eating. As the Philistines had hoped, the Hebrews accept the Ark of the Covenant. Only the household of Jeconiah is aware of the impending disaster that the fetishes bring into Israel. When seventy warriors of Beth-Shemesh die while celebrating their victory over Philistia, the Hebrews exile the ark to the village of Kiriath-Jjearim, which is a Gibeonite, not a Hebrew village. The ark remains outside Israel until David repatriates it to Jerusalem years later. The ark would not vindicate either the Philistines or the Hebrews for their parts in a war that the divine assembly did not call. Both Philistines and Hebrews learn from the experience that fertility is a divine blessing, not a human achievement.

Stories of David's Rise to Power
(1 SAM 8:4—2 SAM 8:13)

After 1000 B.C.E., David united most Hebrew villages into a state. The Stories of David's Rise to Power present David as both a traditional chief and an innovative monarch. David is portrayed not so much as a real person in a biography, but as a silent and motionless ideal chief and ideal monarch. These traditions create a general series of associations and attitudes about who should be a chief and who should be a king. In one tradition David is romantic (1 Sam 16:14-19+23); in another he is competitive (1 Sam 13:1—14:15), humble or persecuted (1 Sam 16:20-22), popular (1 Sam 14:24—15:35), fearless (1 Sam 13:23—14:52), merciful to his enemies, magnanimous with his followers, or well advised.

Stories of Saul
(1 SAM 8:4—15:35)

The Stories of David's Rise to Power begin with the Stories of Saul (1 Sam 8:4—15:35). Once they celebrated how Saul delivered Israel from its enemies. Now, as part of the Stories of David's Rise to Power, the Stories of Saul explain that Yahweh "was sorry that he had made Saul to be king over Israel" (1 Sam 15:35).

Initiation of Saul at Ramah
(1 SAM 8:4-22)

The Hebrews understood Yahweh as all-powerful. Yahweh caused everything, good and bad. Therefore, as much as they loved Saul, when he ultimately failed to deliver Israel from the Philistines, they assumed that he failed because Yahweh had abandoned him. As little as they loved the state that David founded, they believed Yahweh had helped him to do so. The Stories of Saul show a reverence for Saul, but indict him on a variety of charges in order to explain why it was necessary for David to replace him. The Initiation of Saul at Ramah portrays Saul as the ruler whom the Hebrews chose to replace Yahweh (1 Sam 8:7) and who taxed the blessings of land and children that Yahweh had bestowed upon their households for himself (1 Sam 8:10-22). Yahweh approved the anointing of Saul, but only with regret.

Initiation of Saul at Zuph

(1 SAM 9:1 — 10:16)

More than one story in the Bible tells how Saul came to rule Israel. The Initiation of Saul at Zuph (1 Sam 9:1—10:16) and the Initiation of Saul at Mizpah (1 Sam 8:4-22 + 10:17-27) are not two different events, but two performances of the same story in which Samuel anoints Saul. The authorization of a chief by a prophet is one episode in the hero stories common in the books of Joshua and Judges. Initiation stories expand this episode into an independent genre with a crisis, climax, and denouement of its own. The episodes of the initiation story are developed much like those in the inauguration stories that celebrate Yahweh's call of a prophet.

When Samuel initiates Saul at Zuph, there are two episodes in the crisis (1 Sam 9:1-19). In the first, Yahweh lures Saul away from his village by hiding its livestock. Saul investigates their disappearance by going in search of them. The episode emphasizes the humility of Saul. He is not a man who would be king. Like David, Saul is a good herder who becomes a good ruler. Here asses are not simply livestock, they are the animals on which rulers ride. Saul sets off in search of an ass and finds a throne.

In the second episode, Saul meets Samuel, a seer who channels from the human to the divine plane. Samuel announces that Yahweh will return the livestock, and that all Israel wants Saul to be its chief. Saul demurs to Samuel's greeting. His household does not merit such divine notice (Judg 6:1—8:35). The episode certifies Saul as humble enough to exercise authority.

In the climax, Samuel serves Saul a prime portion of the sacrifice and anoints him with oil (1 Sam 9:22—10:1). Both gestures designate him as ruler of Israel.

Finally in the denouement, Saul's initiation is confirmed when the fathers of three households present him with their sacrifices, and the prophets teach Saul how to induce ecstasy with music and dance (1 Sam 10:2-16). Saul leaves Zuph to walk off the boundaries of the land he is to rule. He travels north to Bethel and then to Mt. Tabor. Then he turns southeast to Gibeah. Zuph, Bethel, Gibeah, and Mizpah mark the frontiers of Israel. At each landmark Saul's leadership is officially acknowledged. Two of the three households en route to Bethel recognize Saul as their leader by leaving their sacrifices with him. As he approaches, the prophets of Gibeah become ecstatic. Yahweh takes possession of them and they play music, dance, and sing to greet the new ruler of Israel who joins their celebration.

Saul Delivers Jabesh-Gilead from Ammon
(4QSam^A + 1 Sam 11:1-15)

Gilead is a region twenty-five miles wide and one hundred miles long between the Jordan River and today's city of Amman. Amman was once the Rabbath-Ammon, the great city of the Ammonites. On this great plateau there were forests, fields, and pastures. Through the land ran the Royal Highway connecting the Red Sea and Damascus. Less than twenty-five miles north and west of Rabbath-Ammon the Wadi Yabis joins the Jordan Valley. Here stood Jabesh-gilead, where they told a story of how Saul delivered them from Nahash, king of Rabbath-Ammon (1 Sam 11:1-15). A longer version of the story, recovered by archaeologists between 1947 and 1967 from Qumran on the west coast of the Dead Sea, describes in greater detail than the Bible just how the war between Rabbath-Ammon and Jabesh-gilead began (Fig. 38). The tradition from Qumran also makes it clear that the maneuvers of Nahash are part of a sophisticated strategy and not simply unprovoked acts of mayhem.

The Ammonites enjoyed the same monopoly on transit trade along the Royal Highway east of the Jordan River as the Philistines did along the Coast Highway to the west. Both profited greatly from guarding the caravans; feeding, watering, and restocking their animals; and bedding and boarding the caravan workers. Hebrew villages both east and west of the Jordan plundered caravans to supplement their herding and farming (Judg 5:6-7). Raids cost the Philistines and the Ammonites dearly, and both eventually mounted campaigns against Hebrew villages suspected of raiding.

When the story opens, Nahash and his soldiers have swept through all the Hebrew villages in southern Gilead and halfway through those in northern Gilead. Nahash does not want to exterminate the Hebrews. He simply wants to destroy their ability to raid caravans along his section of the Royal Highway. Nonetheless, the tradition emphasizes the cruelty of Nahash with a play on words. In Hebrew *nahash* can mean either "fortune" (Num 23:23; 24:1) or "snake" (Gen 3:1; Amos 9:3). Although this king of Rabbath-Ammon, no doubt, carried the throne name of "Good Fortune," Hebrew storytellers always refer to him as the "Snake."

Mutilating prisoners of war was standard. The Philistines blinded Samson (Judg 16:21) and the Babylonians blinded Zedekiah (2 Kgs 25:7; Jer 39:7; 52:11). Blinding both eyes completely destroyed a warrior's vision, but it also destroyed his usefulness as a farmer or herder. Blinding his right eye severely limited his ability to fight, but it did not deprive him of the ability to farm and herd. Without a right eye, it was difficult to aim a bow, a spear, or a sling, and without full peripheral vision the warrior became an easier target on the battlefield. The wound also clearly identified those convicted of raiding. Furthermore, blinding the eyes of a man was equivalent to castrating him.

When Nahash, king of Rabbath-Ammon, conquered the tribes of Gad and Reuben, he gouged out the right eyes of their warriors. When he had conquered all Israel, Nahash gouged out the right eye of every Israelite warrior east of the Jordan, except for seven bands of warriors who escaped to Jabesh-gilead.

About a month later Nahash laid siege to Jabesh-gilead. The elders of the city sued for peace. "Negotiate a covenant with us and we shall become your slaves." But Nahash issued an ultimatum. "If I negotiate a covenant with you, you must gouge out the right eyes of the Hebrew warriors in your city, so that I may shame all Israel." The elders of Jabesh-gilead agreed to consider his terms. "Give us seven days to send messengers throughout all Israel. If there is no one to deliver us, we shall surrender them to you."

FIGURE 38 Saul Delivers Jabesh-gilead from Ammon (4QSam^a + 1 Sam 11:1-3)

For Nahash, caravans crossing through Ammon would be safe only when every Hebrew warrior had been mutilated. Allowing any able-bodied Hebrew to remain east of the Jordan left caravans on the Royal Highway at risk. Therefore, Nahash crosses the Wadi Yabis and lays siege to Jabesh-Gilead. The elders of Jabesh-gilead offer to negotiate a covenant with Nahash. He demands that his new covenant partners extradite the Hebrews who are his enemies. Joab imposes the same terms on Abel of Beth-maacah where Sheba and his warriors seek asylum (2 Sam 20:20-21). Such terms are standard in covenants like the Treaty of Ramses II and Hattusilis III.

Before ratifying their covenant with Rabbath-Ammon and blinding the Hebrew warriors, the elders of Jabesh-gilead send out a call to arms. Nahash does not expect Jabesh-gilead to be able to field a chief to meet his challenge. While establishing a covenant with Jabesh-gilead would give him an investment in the village, winning a war against it would give him complete control of all its land and resources. Invaders like Nahash or Ben-hadad of Syria (1 Kgs 20:5-7) care little whether their enemies fall by covenant or conquest.

The crisis not only locks Rabbath-Ammon and Jabesh-gilead in a duel to the death, but also brings Milcom, the divine patron of Ammon, into direct confrontation with Yahweh, the divine patron of Israel. If the people of Jabesh-gilead become a covenant partner of Rabbath-Ammon, they become the people of Milcom. If Milcom can conquer the people whom Yahweh cannot protect, then Milcom is the divine patron of Israel, and Yahweh is not. The response of the tribe to the elders' call to arms will determine whether Jabesh-gilead are the people of Yahweh or the people of Milcom.

When the call to arms reaches Gibeah, the messengers mourn for Jabesh-gilead as if it were already destroyed. They use laments like the Laments for Ur, the Laments for

Deir 'Alla or the Laments for Jerusalem (Lam 1:1—5:22). This story is the first in which Saul demonstrates his ability to fulfill his initiation as ruler of Israel. Since there was no immediate action taken by Saul after being anointed, the story of Saul told at Jabesh-gilead now functions as the labor confirming his anointing.

The reaction of Saul the villager to the call to arms from Jabesh-gilead designates him as Saul the chief, commissioned by Yahweh to deliver the people from their enemies. The call tests Saul, who proves himself a chief by reacting appropriately to the crisis. In some stories the spirit of Yahweh marks Saul as ecstatic (1 Sam 9:10; 16:14). Here the spirit of Yahweh marks Saul as physically huge: "he stood head and shoulders above everyone else" (1 Sam 9:2). By butchering the oxen, Saul demonstrates the great physical strength that distinguishes him from other villagers.

Saul's sacrifice emphasizes the commitment that Gibeah is making to deliver Jabesh-gilead. Saul and the other warriors swear that if they do not deliver Jabesh-gilead from Rabbath-Ammon, they wish their own bodies to be quartered just as Saul quarters his oxen. "Whoever does not come out after Saul and Samuel, so shall it be done to him" (1 Sam 11:7).

Saul sends the pieces of the oxen with the messengers to muster warriors from other villages. The raw meat serves as gruesome physical evidence that Saul and the warriors of Gibeah will spare nothing to fulfill their covenant with Jabesh-gilead. During the seven-day waiting period, warriors from both Gibeon and Benjamin respond to Saul's call to arms. The sheer number who come further indicates that Saul is Yahweh's designated leader.

Samuel the prophet appears in the story. Typically, a prophet confirmed the designation of the chief before the battle. Here the story assumes that Samuel has designated Saul as chief in stories that precede his deliverance of Jabesh-gilead.

There is also no mention of the oath that Saul and his warriors took before the battle, promising to sacrifice all or a portion of their prisoners and plunder to Yahweh. Saul and his warriors simply "scatter Nahash and his warriors so that no two of them were left together" (1 Sam 11:11). Nahash is punished according to the principle of reciprocity. What he had intended to do to the Hebrews was done to his soldiers. He had hoped to eliminate the military effectiveness of the Hebrews by separating one eye from the other. Saul destroys the military effectiveness of the Ammonites by separating one soldier of Ammon from the other.

Saul shows his skill as a chief not only in his ability to recruit warriors, but through his use of military tactics as well. He boosts the morale of Jabesh-gilead by sending messengers to tell them they would be delivered the next day. Subsequently, they send a carefully worded message to Nahash: "tomorrow we will come out to you" (1 Sam 11:10). Their message confirms that the full seven-day waiting period will be observed, and gives Saul's warriors enough time to arrive and lift the siege. The message also makes a brilliant use of irony to threaten Nahash. Throughout the negotiations, the elders of Jabesh-gilead stress their willingness to "come out." The verb can mean either "surrender" (Gen 38:24; Josh 2:3) or "attack" (Deut 20:1; Prov 30:29; 1 Sam 29:6). Ostensibly, they offer to surrender to the Ammonites and become their clients. Now they reiterate that offer, but the double meaning here allows for their intention to attack the Ammonites, scissoring them between Saul's warriors and the warriors of Jabesh-gilead.

After their victory over the Ammonites, the Hebrews begin to fight among themselves. Saul's supporters want Saul to execute his opponents. Nonetheless, Saul magnanimously grants his opponents a pardon. "No one shall be put to death today, for today Yahweh has delivered Israel" (1 Sam 11:13). Saul's actions have been vindicated by Yahweh. Magnanimity itself is a quality that makes Saul eligible to be a ruler in Israel. Rulers who do not execute their opponents treat them as divine messengers. David exercises magnanimity when he refuses to have Shimei executed for opposing his right to the throne (2 Sam 16:5-13).

Saul's opponents want Samuel to challenge Saul, but Samuel refuses. Instead he assembles the Hebrews at Gilgal, the sanctuary of Jericho. It was at Gilgal that the Hebrews entered the promised land and it was here that they designated Joshua to lead them. Samuel goes to Gilgal to reconfirm the covenant that joins the villages into a tribe and designates Saul as its chief.

The use of words like "king" and "kingdom" in the story shows how later tellers considered the deliverance of Jabesh-gilead to be a turning point in the career of Saul, and the evolution of Israel from villages into a state. Samuel is not simply celebrating Yahweh's deliverance of the people from their enemies, but is proclaiming Israel a state, and acclaiming Saul to be king of all Israel. Saul's victory allowed him to extend his leadership from the villages of Benjamin northward, and Samuel's celebration at Gilgal was, in effect, Saul's coronation. Yet, there was still no royal army, no royal sanctuary, and no royal priests. Saul was Israel's last great chief; David was its first real monarch.

Saul Delivers Jabesh-gilead from Ammon demonstrates how tribes select a chief in a time of crisis. This social institution was not only a practical strategy for protecting the villages in early Israel, it was also an important theological statement that only Yahweh fed and protected Israel. Early Israel considered states ruled by monarchs and protected by standing armies to be "houses of slaves," whose people had too much confidence in themselves, and too little faith in their divine patrons. For almost 250 years, these Hebrew villages maintained their commitment to a society without monarchs, without taxes, without soldiers, without slaves, and without cities. Then they had to choose between accepting a monarch and becoming a state, or facing annihilation altogether. It was a difficult choice with which Israel was never completely satisfied.

Jonathan Delivers Israel from Philistia
(1 SAM 13:15—14:23)

The Stories of David's Rise to Power incorporate the Stories of Jonathan, which demonstrate that anyone who would be chief must be competitive. To be competitive, candidates must strive against a worthy opponent. Jonathan is portrayed as a worthy opponent who, in the end, endorses David, his rival.

In the Stories of Jonathan, he is not only the worthy rival of David, but also David's trusted adviser. Good rulers must be well advised by those they can trust and who will be loyal to them. Jonathan is David's twin. Twin heroes like David and Jonathan are a motif in the Bible. New worlds are founded by twins, who reflect that this new world is both fertile and flawed. Multiple births from a single pregnancy are a sign of extraordinary fertility. Twins are also the source of sibling rivalry, which eventually curses the new world with violence. Not all the twin characters in the Bible are natal siblings, or even human siblings. In the Creation of the Heavens and the Earth, light and darkness are twins (Gen 1:4), the waters above the dome and the waters below the dome are twins (Gen 1:7), the earth and the sea are twins (Gen 1:10), day and night are twins (Gen 1:14), and the sun and the moon are twins (Gen 1:15-18). Likewise in the Stories of Adam and Eve, the man and the woman are twins (Gen 1:27), and in the Stories of Cain and Abel, Cain and Abel are twins. In the Stories of Jacob, Leah, and Rachel, Jacob and Esau are twins.

Jonathan Delivers Israel from Philistia (1 Sam 13:2-22) also portrays him as a fearless chief. By going into battle with only his shield-bearer, Jonathan shames the Philistines, just as Saul shames Goliath by sending the boy David out to do battle with him. Jonathan goes into battle against the Philistines as the underdog to demonstrate that it is Yahweh, and not Jonathan, who delivers Israel. Storytellers regularly portray Yahweh with what psychologists today call a "Florence Nightingale complex." Like Florence Nightingale (1820–1910), the English nurse who tended even the hopelessly wounded in the Crimean War, Yahweh is the patron of hopeless cases. Yahweh always reaches out to rescue the underdog. Therefore, like Gideon, Jonathan consciously goes into battle below strength to win Yahweh's support (Judg 7:4-7; 2 Sam 16:1-14).

Until the time of David, Hebrew warriors were no match for Philistine soldiers. They compensated for their powerlessness by using guerrilla tactics (Gen 34:1-31; Josh 8:1-29; 9:3-27; Judg 7:16-22; 9:34-45). Jonathan and his shield-bearer approach the Philistine checkpoint as if they are deserters (1 Sam 14:11-12). Here, the term "Hebrews" (1 Sam 14:11) means "mercenaries," not "Israelites." The Philistine chariot warriors assume Jonathan and his shield-bearer are Philistine infantry who deserted during a previous battle with Israel and are now being starved out. Because so many infantry deserted during battles, the word "Hebrew" was also used by the Philistines to mean both "foot soldier" and "deserter."

Trial of Saul
(1 SAM 14:24—15:35)

A Trial of Saul portrays a chief like Jonathan as popular. The trial is a complex of three traditions. The Annals for Saul, which report to Yahweh on his care of the land and children of Israel (1 Sam 14:47-52), are nested between a trial that indicts him for endangering the land (1 Sam 14:24-46) and a trial that indicts him for endangering the children (1 Sam 15:1-15).

To some extent, the indictments of Saul are frivolous. They strain to provide an explanation for the painful reality that this chief, lifted up by Yahweh and loved by the people of Israel, had been rejected by both. There is sensitivity in the traditions, which say to their audiences that there were reasons for Saul's downfall, but they were not good reasons.

Curiously, Samuel first indicts Saul for ordering the warriors of Israel to fast until after their victory over the Philistines. Warriors always fast. They eat only rations, and they remain celibate, until victory (2 Sam 11:1-27). Just as eating and sexual intercourse are interchangeable, so are fasting and celibacy.

When rulers could not reach a decision, their priests used two rituals to help them "draw near to Yahweh" (1 Sam 14:36) and resolve the crisis. One was the ephod apron. The other was the urim and thummim. The urim and thummim were dice that were rolled to answer a question put to Yahweh. The urim and thummim were kept in a pocket of the ephod apron that priests wore. Priests were cooks who prepared food or sacrifices for Yahweh to eat (Gen 8:21). Rulers in ancient Israel who wanted to know the will of Yahweh summoned a priest wearing an ephod-apron and ordered him to roll the urim and thummim. This game of chance solves problems much like "cutting the Bible" to answer life questions today or using a Ouija board. Saul tells the priest: "withdraw your hand" (1 Sam 14:19).

The hero story closes with a report that Israel was at peace. "Then Saul stopped pursuing the Philistines, and let them retreat to their own cities." (1 Sam 14:46).

Stories of David
(1 SAM 16:1—2 SAM 8:13)

Inauguration of Samuel
(1 SAM 16:1-13)

Inauguration stories establish the credentials of prophets to advise the monarchs of Israel and Judah. An Inauguration of Samuel commissions him to initiate David as a chief in Israel. The role of prophets designating chiefs is analogous to the role of midwives delivering children. Like midwives, prophets bathed, anointed, dressed, and named their candidates to designate them as chiefs.

The Inauguration of Samuel was retold by the household of David to establish its authorization to rule Israel, even though the protagonist in the tradition is Yahweh, not David. It is Yahweh who leads Samuel through a conversion from Saul to David after interviewing seven other candidates. David does not play a character role.

The inauguration assumes, but does not retell, the crisis and climax episodes of the Inauguration of Samuel that appears in the Trial of Eli and His Sons (1 Sam 2:12—4:22). Here the inauguration begins with the denouement, which elaborates Samuel's demurral to and then compliance with Yahweh's commission.

Samuel demurs because Saul would consider anointing a new chief as treason. Bethlehem was the Iowa or New Hampshire of the political world of ancient Israel. Here in Bethlehem, only ten miles from Jerusalem, revolutions began, and new leadership was designated. Yahweh coaches Samuel to distract Saul and the elders of Bethlehem by offering sacrifice.

The spirit of Yahweh alters the appearance of a chief. Ehud is left-handed; Samson has powerful hands; Saul stands head and shoulders above other warriors. A chief is physically unique. What Yahweh tells Samuel here is that human beings should not try to understand how the divine patron of Israel works. Yahweh does not choose or reject leaders according to the standards that humans use. Not even a seer can see what Yahweh does. David is not a leader because he is "ruddy, and had beautiful eyes and was handsome" (1 Sam 16:12), but in spite of it. Yahweh will use this eighth child to deliver Israel from the Philistines. This Cinderella motif calls powerless candidates to act powerfully, so that it is clear the real actor is divine, not human.

Saul Adopts David as His Musician
(1 SAM 16:14-23)

The stories of the first meeting of the two rivals are apologies that argue that competition does not destroy continuity. The winner and the loser are one. The winner is not an outsider, but an insider. In three, originally separate, stories about David and Saul, each stresses not only that David is a native, but also that he is a shaman, that he is powerless, and that he is fearless.

In Saul Adopts David as His Musician (1 Sam 16:14-19+23), David is a shaman whose music treats Saul for spirit possession. The spirit that at first empowered Saul as a chief now torments him. The spirit of a chief is trapped in the body of a man who is no longer a chief. David draws the spirit out of Saul and into himself. The tradition also identifies David as a gentle man who effects change without violence. He is romantic.

In Saul Adopts David as His Shield-Bearer (1 Sam 16:20-22), David is powerless. He is the youngest son in a household full of sons, and therefore an underdog. David is left at home while his older brothers are off in search of their fortunes as warriors in the service of Saul. David is the youngest of eight sons. Eight is one too many. The perfect household has seven sons (2 Macc 7:1-41). The youngest are spoiled by their parents and persecuted by their siblings. Youngest children lead sheltered lives and are often unable to cope with the real world. It is also difficult for the fathers of a household to find work for their youngest children. Often, there is no land left in the household for its youngest children. Therefore, in the medieval cultures of western Europe, sons left-over after household resources are were exhausted were offered to the state as soldiers and to the church as clergy.

Monarchs are called "shepherds." Monarchs keep states the way shepherds keep sheep. The responsibilities of both are to feed and to protect (Ezek 34:1-31). Monarchs feed their people by maintaining a healthy economy, and they protect their land by maintaining a strong defense. David, here, moves from keeper of sheep to keeper of the state.

Shepherds also know animals. In contrast to Balaam (Num 22:1—24:25), who does not know his animal, most herders have a highly developed ability to commune with nature and to understand humans. As the father of the household, Jesse is anxious for Samuel to evaluate the potential of his sons.

Jesse also carefully prepares food for his sons who are serving Israel as warriors. This food, which Jesse sends to Saul, is more than groceries. It is a portfolio reflecting the honor of the household, and a letter of recommendation for David, his youngest son. The gifts encourage Saul to remember David favorably and to give him a job. When Saul adopts David as shield-bearer, he becomes his patron, and David becomes a client of Saul.

David Delivers Israel from Goliath
(1 SAM 17:1-58)

The story of how David Delivers Israel from Goliath (1 Sam 17:1-58) portrays David as fearless. It places Saul and David together on the battlefield as David visits his brothers serving with Saul. In a parallel tradition describing David's visit to the front, Jesse's gifts (1 Sam 17:17-18) are for his sons' commanding officer, and not for Saul. In one telling, Saul meets David before his duel; in another Saul meets David only after watching him kill Goliath. Both traditions want to show that David did not revolt against Saul, but that Saul accepted David as his heir.

The crisis in the story begins when Goliath taunts the warriors of Israel. Taunts (2 Kgs 2:23-25) are a common strategy in making war in the world of the Bible. Tiamat taunts Marduk (Enuma 4:63-74). Gilgamesh taunts Ishtar (Gilg 6:31-78). Aqhat and Anat taunt each other, taunt Yamm, or taunt Baal (Aqhat 6:35-49). Although the word "taunt" appears only four times in the Bible (Deut 28:37; 1 Kgs 9:7; 2 Chr 7:20; Jer 24:9), taunting is widely used. Jacob taunts Laban (Gen 31:36-44). Ga'al taunts Abimelech (Judg 8:28-29). Ahab taunts Ben-hadad (1 Kgs 20:11). Jezebel taunts Jehu (2 Kgs 9:31-32). The Rabshakeh taunts Hezekiah (2 Kgs 18:19-37). The Jebusites taunt David (2 Sam 5:6). Goliath (1 Sam 17:8-10) and Nabal taunt David (1 Sam 25:10-11).

The warriors of Israel respond to Goliath by crying out. The crying-out formula in hero stories acknowledges the complete dependence of the victims on Yahweh for victory. Here, however, the warriors of Israel cry out because they fear Goliath, not because they have faith that Yahweh will deliver them from Goliath. They cry out in impotence.

David is fearless. He has no question that Yahweh will deliver him from Goliath. David shames Goliath by calling him "uncircumcised" (1 Sam 17:26). Western Mediterranean cultures, like the Philistines, did not circumcise their sons; Semitic and African cultures, like the Hebrews, did. Circumcision, despite the Hebrew practice of circumcising newborns, was originally a sign that males had reached puberty, and were now sexually active adults. They were men. David calls Goliath an impotent child, and shames the warriors of Israel for being afraid of a "little boy."

The armor of Goliath is characteristic of the Sea Peoples on Egyptian monuments. This armor and the size of Goliath contrast the power of surplus state economies like Philistia with the powerlessness of subsistence village economies like Israel. Attempting to dress David in the same armor as Goliath portrays Saul as trusting in the armor of his military policies for protection. David trusts only in Yahweh. Saul and his soldiers go into battle fully armored, which demonstrates that they depend on themselves for victory. David goes into battle unarmed, which demonstrates that he depends on Yahweh for victory.

Now Goliath taunts David: "Am I a dog, that you come to me with a stick?" (1 Sam 17:43). Although there is a long-standing tradition that David kills Goliath with a slingshot, he may have used an atlatl or throwing stick. The bow, the sling, and the throwing stick are all unorthodox weapons. They are weapons that no honorable warrior would use. Weapons of honor allow fighters to come face to face with one another. The bow, the sling, and the throwing stick kill their victims anonymously, and therefore, shamefully. They were considered the weapons of cowards, who do not fight their enemies face to face, but ambush them from a distance. Goliath asks David if he thinks the Philistines are dogs ready to play fetch.

The story also indicts Saul for his ambition to be a monarch (1 Sam 13:2-14) and for wanting to negotiate covenants between Israel and other states (1 Sam 15:10-23). His policies threaten the land and children of Israel (1 Sam 16:4).

Shepherds whose flocks were attacked had to recover at least an ear or a tail of the sheep destroyed to prove they did not rustle the animals (Amos 4:12). These trophies proved that they had done their jobs. David returns with Goliath's head as proof that Goliath was dead.

Jonathan Adopts David
(1 SAM 18:1-5+19:1-7+20:1-42)

Jonathan Adopts David is a tradition that portrays David as a chief who is well-advised (1 Sam 18:1—23:28). Jonathan adopts David and becomes his patron, advising him how to succeed in becoming a chief in Israel. David is wise to seek out Jonathan as his covenant partner. Jonathan, loved by David and by Saul, is well suited to advise David, the outsider, how to become an insider.

Jonathan adopts David by clothing him. The same ritual is used by midwives and husbands. Midwives swaddle newborns as a sign that they have been adopted into a household (Ezek 16:4). Husbands dress their wives as a sign that they have negotiated a marriage covenant with them (Ezek 16:10). Ruth proposes marriage to Boaz by asking: "spread your cloak over me, for you are my legal guardian" (Ruth 3:9).

When Saul decides to execute David for treason, it is Jonathan who convinces him that David has always been, and is still, loyal to Saul (1 Sam 19:1-7). Were it not for the loyalty of David, Jonathan argues, Saul himself would never have defeated Goliath and routed the Philistines at Azekah.

Saul Adopts David
(1 SAM 18:17-30 + 24:1-22 + 26:1-25)

Just as there are three traditions describing how David and Saul meet, there are three
traditions describing how Saul adopts David as his heir. In one tradition, Saul allows David
to marry his daughter Michal (1 Sam 18:17-30). The other two traditions characterize
Saul as a fool who inadvertently exposes himself to his enemies. In one tradition (1 Sam
24:1-22), Saul is relieving himself in the same cave where David and his warriors are
hiding. For Saul to die in battle would be honorable. For him to die while relieving himself would be shameful. David's warriors consider Saul's foolishness to be a sign that Yahweh has put Saul into the hands of David. David, however, refuses to kill Saul. Instead
he ritually castrates him by cutting the tassels, which are the symbols of his status, off
his cloak. David's action is comparable to the *coup* stick used by the Sioux peoples of
North America. Rather than kill their enemies, they would touch them with a stick to
shame them. A live enemy who has been shamed brings more honor to the victor than
an enemy who has been slain. David touches Saul, but does not kill him, and the action
makes Saul a client of David.

   In another tradition (1 Sam 26:1-25), David and Abishai slip into the camp of Saul
and find him and Abner, his bodyguard, sound asleep. Here it is Abishai who pronounces
the death sentence on Saul. Again David carries out the sentence by shaming Saul, rather
than by killing him. David takes Saul's spear and his water gourd, which are phallic symbols for Saul's penis and testicles. When David and Abishai are safely out of the camp
of Saul, David shouts to Saul and then dangles his trophies in front of him.

David Delivers Gath from Amalek
(1 SAM 27:1—28:2)

In David Delivers Gath from Amalek, Saul rescinds his adoption of David and drives
him into exile. Undaunted, David courts Saul's opponent, Achish, Philistine ruler of
Gath, by delivering Gath from Amalek (1 Sam 27:1—28:2). Achish becomes David's
patron and appoints him governor of the Philistine province of Ziklag (1 Sam 27:5-6).
The capital of the province is Ezion-geber, about twelve miles northwest of Beersheba.
Ezion-geber governs a number of villages and forts like Horvat 'Uzza (Josh 19:2-6; 1
Chr 4:28-31).

   David cleverly governs Ziklag to the advantage of both the Philistines and the
Hebrews. Although Achish expected David to use Ziklag as a base to raid Judah to the
north, David actually raids Amalekite caravans to the south (Josh 15:24; 1 Sam 15:4;

27:8). The raids enrich Achish and build support for David in Judah. After one raid against the Amalekites, David distributes a share of his plunder to every village in Ziklag.

When David becomes king of Israel, he annexes the province of Ziklag (1 Sam 27:10; 30:14; 2 Sam 24:7). This whole area along Judah's southern border, which runs from Beersheba in the north to the Gulf of Aqaba or at least to the oasis of Kadesh in the south, is called the "Negeb." In contrast to the Sinai, which is deep desert, the Negeb is near desert. Rainfall in the Negeb is minimal, but there are a series of wells along the Edom Highway, which runs east and west from Arad north of the Jebel Usdum Mountains before descending into Arabah valley. Forts were located about every twenty miles along the Edom Highway (2 Kgs 3:20). After David annexed Ziklag, the commander of Arad became responsible for protecting the southeast section of the Edom Highway.

Covenant between Abigail and David
(1 SAM 25:2-43)

A Covenant between Abigail and David seals his takeover of the household of Nabal. The tradition is parallel to the Covenant between Bathsheba and David, which seals his takeover of the household of Uriah. When Nabal dies, David marries Abigail, just as when Uriah dies, David marries Bathsheba. Neither tradition describes only simply romantic pursuit, but, more importantly, political victory. David challenges Nabal and Uriah for their households and finalizes his victories by marriage.

Sheep shearing and grain threshing were comparable to a stock show or a rodeo today. These were times when debts from the previous grazing and growing seasons were paid, and new covenants for the upcoming seasons were negotiated. Here negotiations begin when David sends his warriors to demand payment for the protection that they have provided to the household of Nabal. Nabal refuses to pay, and indicts David's warriors as slaves who have run away from Saul. David orders reprisals to collect payment.

Abigail now replaces Nabal. Whereas Nabal was "harsh and ungenerous," she is "intelligent and attractive" (1 Sam 25:3). Abigail abrogates her marriage covenant with Nabal, and negotiates a marriage covenant with David. She not only offers to pay the household of David for his services (1 Sam 25:27-28), she also offers to become his covenant partner against Saul (1 Sam 25:28) and to join David's campaign to become "the commander over Israel" (1 Sam 25:29-30). In return she wants a political appointment in David's Israel (1 Sam 25:32).

David cuts a covenant with Abigail, when he says: "Go up to your village in peace" (1 Sam 25:35). When there is peace between two households, a covenant is in place. The marriage of David and Abigail is the public ratification of the covenant that they negotiated.

The covenant between David and Abigail gives him a significant advantage over Saul. Abigail controls the northern coast, including the Carmel Mountains and the strategic pass leading from the Coast Highway through the Wadi Ara onto the plain of Megiddo. Saul only controls the land around Gibeah, just north of Jerusalem, which is now surrounded by David.

Creation of the City of David
(2 SAM 5:6-16)

In the Creation of the City of David, David says: "Anyone who conquers the Jebusites will have to use the *tsinnor* to reach those lame and blind who are David's enemies" (Fig. 39). That is why they say, "The blind and lame will not enter the palace" (2 Sam 5:8). *Tsinnor* is generally translated as "water shaft" and identified with Warren's Tunnel, although the word can also mean a weapon like a dagger, a hook, a trident, or a shield, or a part of the human body, like the arm, leg, throat, neck, or genitals.

The entrance of Warren's Tunnel inside the walls of Jerusalem is cut into solid rock. It leads to steps that descend twenty-six feet to the beginning of a sloping path ninety-two feet long. The path leads to a vertical, oval shaft that drops forty feet down to an aqueduct bringing water from the Gihon spring some seventy-two feet away.

From 1977 until 1987, Yigal Shiloh (Hebrew University, Jerusalem) directed excavations of the City of David on Mt. Ophel. His team made some fascinating discoveries

crisis (2 Sam 5:6)

> *When King David and his soldiers attacked Jebus,*
>   *They went up against Zion.*
>
> *The people of Jebus and their ruler taunted David:*
>
> *"The blind will see*
>   *Before David looks inside Zion,*
>
> *The lame will walk*
>   *Before David marches through the gates of the city."*
>
> *David retorted:*
>
> *"Yes, but my warriors will crawl through the tsinnor,*
>   *Before the lame can stop them.*

(continued)

> *David will come up behind his enemies,*
> *Before the blind can see him."*

climax (2 Sam 5:7-9)

> *Then David conquered Zion.*

> *He renamed it "City of David."*

> *Where the lame never walk through its gates,*
> *Where the blind never see its palace.*

> *David conquered Jebus,*

> *He renamed it "City of David."*

denouement (2 Sam 5:9-16)

> *Finally, David constructed a millo,*
> *He built the City of David on a great foundation.*

> *David grew more and more powerful,*
> *Yahweh Sabaoth was with him.*

> *Hiram sent messengers to David,*
> *Hiram furnished cedar wood for David.*

> *The ruler of Tyre sent carpenters and masons,*
> *He built a palace for David.*

> *Hiram saw that Yahweh had enthroned David,*
> *He recognized David as ruler of all Israel.*

> *Tyre saw that Yahweh had extended David's rule,*
> *Tyre recognized David's reign over Yahweh's people.*

> *David negotiated more great covenants in Jerusalem,*
> *He cut more lesser covenants than in Hebron.*

> *David had more sons and daughters in Zion,*
> *He sired eleven new children:*

> *Shammua, Shobab, Nathan, Solomon, Ibhar, Elishua,*
> *Nepheg, Japhia, Elishama, Eliada, and Eliphelet.*

FIGURE 39 Creation of the City of David (2 Sam 5:6-16)

about the engineers who developed the city's water supply, and make it very unlikely that *tsinnor* here refers to Warren's Tunnel. The structural concept and design of Warren's Tunnel, as well as the pottery associated with it, are Israelite, not Jebusite. It was built according to the plan for underground water systems in royal cities used by Israelite monarchs. Therefore, it is more likely that the Hebrews built Warren's Tunnel than that David ordered Joab and his warriors to climb it. Even if Warren's Tunnel had been built before David's conquest of Jerusalem, it is physically unlikely his warriors could have climbed through it and into the city. The engineers who planned Warren's Tunnel cut the shaft connecting the well cap with the aqueduct to make it virtually impossible for warriors to scale. During the Shiloh excavations, Swiss alpine climbers had to use highly technical equipment to work their way up the sheer vertical shaft.

David wanted Israel to take its place in the family of nations. Consequently, the household of David created a portfolio of traditions comparable to those of other states. These creation stories may be more helpful than archaeology in understanding David's words to his warriors. The Creation of the City of David is similar in many ways to other creation stories like the Enuma Elish Stories from Mesopotamia. Two common episodes in these stories are a great battle and the building of a great house. Like Marduk in the Enuma Elish Stories, David defeats Jebus and its blind and lame covenant partners, who play the role of Tiamat and her allies. David sentences the blind who cannot see the great work of Yahweh, and the lame who cannot walk in the way of Yahweh, to the gates of the new world before building a great house. The victory designates him as ruler of all Israel and gives birth to a new people for this new world. Tyre leads the nations in acknowledging David as the unchallenged ruler of the people of Yahweh (2 Sam 5:11).

The crisis is a modest declaration of war. Its parallelism is artistically balanced and the language is carefully Israelite. The words "King David and his warriors" in the first line are balanced by "the people of Jebus and their ruler." "King" is a carefully chosen title for David. He is no longer just a chief who leads part-time warriors, but a king who commands full-time soldiers. Therefore, the conquest of Jerusalem is an achievement of the household of David, and not the legacy of Israel. David "goes up" to Jerusalem, which is a Hebrew idiom for "makes a pilgrimage." He is summoned to his campaign by Yahweh, as subsequent pilgrims will be summoned to make their regular visits to the temple in Jerusalem.

The refrain: "David conquered Zion. He renamed it 'City of David'" frames the climax. This refrain is only a digest of the elaborate cosmogony in the Enuma Elish Stories (Enuma IV:87-104). Just as Tiamat commissions her covenant partners to be the first line of defense against Marduk, Jebus commissions the lame and the blind to defend the city against David. Some rabbinic interpretations arrive at almost this sense of the tradition, although not on the basis of any ancient Near Eastern parallels. For these rabbis "Lame" and "Blind" are the names of two members of the divine assembly of Jebus whose statues, like gargoyles, protected the city walls. The interpretation developed from reading a hymn in the book of Psalms (Ps 115:4-8) as David's personal reflection on the battle of Jerusalem.

Like Tiamat defying Marduk, Jebus defies David to march through the gates of the city in victory. Jebus contends that even the blind and the lame can defend Jerusalem against him. In David's retort, there is not any prejudice against persons with disabilities in general, or the disabled of Jerusalem in particular. Jebus taunts that David could not capture Jerusalem from the blind and the lame, much less an able-bodied army. David retorts that he will take Jerusalem from anyone, handicapped or healthy. Jebus taunted: "the blind and the lame will see to it that David will not march through the gates of Jerusalem." David retorts: "the blind and lame will not see David crawl through the *tsinnor* either." David's retort grants the claim of the people of Jebus that he cannot walk, but switches it from a handicap to an asset. The blind and the lame may be able to defend their city against walkers, but not against crawlers. The blind can stare out from the gates of Jerusalem all they want, but they will miss seeing his warriors entering the city from behind them. They may be able to see the gates, but that will not save the city. The Hebrews will not capture Jerusalem by marching through its gates, but will capture it by crawling through its *tsinnor*. If the powerful enter the city through the gates, the powerless enter through the *tsinnor*. David grants his victory will not be glamorous, but it will be decisive. He is not leading a procession; he is waging a war. David boasts of his ability to use unorthodox tactics to defeat the enemies of Israel, who outnumber his warriors and are better armed.

In the Enuma Elish Stories, Marduk turns the covenant partners of Tiamat into statues which he erects at the door of the Apsu Palace to remind all who enter of his victory (Enuma 4:105-18). The blind and the lame outside the gates of Jerusalem are also a reminder of David's victory. The blind remind all who enter that the attack on Jerusalem was led by Yahweh himself, whose glory blinded its defenders.

The denouement of the Creation of the City of David begins with the construction of the *millo*. Kathleen Kenyon (British School of Archaeology, Jerusalem) pioneered the identification of the *millo* as stone retaining walls creating agricultural terraces on the slopes of the Kidron valley (2 Sam 5:9; 1 Kgs 9:15-24; 11:27; 1 Chr 11:8; 2 Chr 32:5). Lawrence E. Stager (Harvard University) argued that these terraces were not the *millo*, but the "Slopes of Kidron" (2 Kgs 23:4). For Stager the *millo* is a massive five-story-high stone footing first uncovered by R. A. Macalister (Palestine Exploration Fund). Kenyon also partially excavated this foundation, but mistakenly dated it to the Hasmonean period (170–64 B.C.E.). Following 1977, Shiloh excavated this foundation more completely and suggested that what Kenyon dated to the Hasmonean period was merely a stone tower built on top of an earlier, massive, stepped-stone foundation that is the largest human-made structure in Israel. Nonetheless, Shiloh himself was not ready to identify it as the *millo*, but rather as an *ophel* that marked the acropolis in a royal city. Similar ophels have been excavated at Samaria (2 Kgs 5:24), and the stele on which the Annals of Mesha were carved may have been erected on the acropolis of Dibon.

The *millo* in the Creation of the City of David serves the same purpose as the Apsu Palace (Enuma I:71-77) and the Esagila ziggurat (Enuma VI:45–66) in the Enuma Elish Stories. "*Millo*," "Zion," and "City of David" are all names for the Great House that David constructs to ratify his victory as the divine warrior over Jebus. A similar use of *millo* appears in Abimelech Delivers Israel from Shechem: "all the elders of Shechem and all Beth-millo came together, and they went and made Abimelech king, under the Oak of Shechem" (Judg 9:6). Other creation stories in the Bible include similar building programs. In the Creation of the Heavens and the Earth, Yahweh builds Eden. In the Stories of Cain and Abel, Enoch builds Irad. In the Flood Stories, the descendants of Noah build Babel. In the Creation of the Firstborn of Israel, the Hebrews build the Great Tent. Building a new world, a new house, a new altar, a new temple, or a new city celebrates the victory of the divine warrior over the conspirator. Therefore, both the Stories of David's Rise to Power and the Stories of David's Successor describe the great monarchs of Israel as the builders of sacred dwellings. The construction ratifies their right to rule.

Besides serving to ratify a monarch's right to rule, these building projects teach the citizens of the new world all the important crafts and trades necessary for survival. Guilds of artists and craftspeople consider their skills to be divine gifts. They were taught their trades by a divine patron so that they could make a living and so they could make a difference in their world. The guilds considered their apprenticeships to have taken place while building the Great House. According to the rabbis, thirty-nine different guilds of Hebrew weavers, tailors, metalworkers, and carpenters traced the origins of their crafts to the days when Yahweh taught them how to build the Great Tent.

The structure of a Great House also outlines the structures of the society at whose center it is erected. Houses are microcosms that model the worldview of those who build them. The temple in Jerusalem, the African dogon, the Pueblo kiva, and the Zuni village are all models of the cosmos celebrated in the creation stories of their respective cultures.

The use of first-growth cedar from the forests covering the Lebanon mountains is an indication that David's Great House is sacred. The cedars of Lebanon were harvested only for the building of houses for members of the divine assembly. One thousand years before David, Gudea of Lagash boasts: "From the cedar forests on the Amanus Mountains, I harvested raft after raft of logs" to construct the House of Ningursu.

Just as the members of the divine assembly convene at the Esagila ziggurat to celebrate the coronation of Marduk as a world ruler (Enuma VI:67-120), the Creation of the City of David recounts how Hiram the monarch of Tyre sends messengers to Jerusalem to celebrate the coronation of David as the ruler of the people of Yahweh. According to Josephus and Menander, Hiram was king of Tyre at the end, and not at the beginning, of David's reign. Furthermore, Hiram helps Solomon, and not David, with his royal building projects. Abibaal was monarch of Tyre during David's time. Therefore, the story telescopes the reigns of David and Solomon and their counterparts from Tyre.

Just as the celebration of Marduk's coronation concludes with the bestowal of fifty titles, the last of which is "Ruler of Earth" (Enuma VII:121—44), the Creation of the City of David concludes by bestowing the titles of Jerusalem on David. To take possession of Jebus, the household of David and the households of Jebus would have intermarried. These women are David's title to Jerusalem. The names of his children are the names by which David exercises title to the land and children that their mothers represent.

David Delivers Israel from Baal-perazim
(2 SAM 5:17-25)

David Delivers Israel from Baal-perazim actually contains two hero stories as well as components of a Trial of Baal-perazim. Yahweh imposes sentence on Baal-perazim, which David then executes.

Few villages in ancient Israel told as many stories celebrating Yahweh as the divine warrior as Gibeon. Jonathan Delivers Israel from the Philistines (1 Sam 13:23—14:23), David Delivers Israel from Baal-perazim (2 Sam 5:17-25), and the Ark of the Covenant Delivers Israel from Benjamin (Judg 20:1-48) all involve Gibeon. In each story a chief requests Yahweh's approval and participation in the action. Consequently, it is Yahweh, and not Jonathan, and not David, who receives credit for the victory.

Just how David speaks to Yahweh, and or how Yahweh speaks to David, is not explained (2 Sam 5:19+23-24). Priests normally serve as intelligence officers for a chief and speak for Yahweh to the chief. The priests interpret their intelligence to the chief, who makes the final decision. Priests could use the urim and the thummim dice to answer David's first question, because it requires only a simple "yes" or "no" (2 Sam 5:19). David's second question is too complex (2 Sam 5:23-24). The priest tells David to attack when he hears the wind in the trees (Fig. 40).

The Hebrews never lead an attack. They fight only in support of the divine warriors commanded by Yahweh. In Samuel Delivers Israel from Philistia, Yahweh's thundering voice is the signal that the divine warriors have already attacked, and that the Hebrews can come forward (1 Sam 7:3-17). Here, the Hebrews listen for the wind created by chariots of the divine warriors as they rush into battle as their sign to move forward.

> The Philistines came up, and deployed in the valley of Rephaim. When David asked Yahweh if he should attack, Yahweh answered: "Do not attack the Philistines from the front. Flank them behind the balsam trees. When you hear the wind whistling through the branches of the balsam trees, then prepare to attack, for Yahweh has led the divine warriors ahead of you to attack the Philistines." David obeyed Yahweh, and did what Yahweh had ordered him to do, and drove the Philistines from Geba all the way to Gezer.

FIGURE 40   Stories of David's Rise to Power (2 Sam 5:22-25)

Stories of David's Successor
(2 SAM 9:1—20:26 + 1 KGS 1:1—11:43)

The Stories of David's Successor were developed by the household of David to authorize Solomon's right to rule Israel. The stories begin with a Trial of David (2 Sam 9:1—12:31), which indicts the king for failing to protect and provide for the land of Israel and for its people by abusing his power in taking over the household of Saul and the household of Uriah. In each case David fails to negotiate an effective covenant for his succession, and instead uses force to implement his claim. The trial indicts David for no longer being a chief ruling with the consent of the households of Israel. David had become a monarch who wielded the absolute power of a pharaoh. He had lost the approval of Yahweh in much the same way Saul did.

Stories of Merib-baal
(2 SAM 9:1-13; 16:1-4; 19:24-30)

The Stories of Merib-baal were also part of the argument in the books of Samuel-Kings that Solomon, rather than Absalom, should rule Israel (Fig. 41). Merib-baal is the father of the household of Saul to which David once belonged, and which supported the household of Absalom against Solomon for control of Israel. The first of these Stories of Merib-baal (2 Sam 9:1-13) complements a Trial of David by Nathan (2 Sam 10:1—12:31). It indicts David for a domestic policy that exploits the land, rather than developing it. The trial also indicts David for a foreign policy that creates war, rather than prevents it.

In some of the Stories of Merib-baal, the name "Merib-baal," which is a label of honor, has been changed to "Mephibosheth," which is a label of shame. Jonathan named his son "Word of Yahweh" or "Messiah of Yahweh." Because the household of Saul sided with the household of Absalom in its revolt against David, later storytellers labeled Merib-baal as "Mephibosheth," or a "Death Sentence" for the household of Saul. The label deprived the household of Saul of all its rights and privileges in Israel.

The Stories of Merib-baal begin when David decides to review the status of the household of Saul. David tells Ziba that he wishes "to show kindness to Saul," using a technical expression for his determination to renegotiate the covenant between their households (Gen 21:22-24; 1 Sam 20:8; 2 Sam 9:1-7; 10:2; 20:14-16).

The struggle between the households of Saul and David for control of Israel was suspended after the battle of Gilboa where the Philistines massacred Saul and Jonathan. Long before his death, Jonathan transferred his status as heir of the household of Saul to David (1 Sam 18:1-5). Saul initially confirmed the transfer by allowing David to marry his daughter Michal (1 Sam 18:20-29). At the time of the death of Saul and Jonathan, however, David had neither the need nor the power to take over the household, so he simply froze its assets. Therefore, the stories describe Merib-baal as "crippled in his feet" (2 Sam 9:3), "a dead dog" (2 Sam 9:8), and "lame in both his feet" (1 Sam 24:6). Since "feet" is a euphemism for male genitals and a phallic symbol of power, Merib-baal is not simply unable to walk, but the household of Saul can no longer work its land and give birth to children.

David questioned a slave from the household of Saul whose name was Ziba. "Are you Ziba, the slave of Saul?" "I am," he testified.

The king asked: "I wish to renegotiate the covenant between the household of David and the household of Saul. Who is father of the household now?" Ziba testified: "The son of Jonathan, but he is powerless."

The king asked: "Where is he?" "Under the protection of the household of Machir, son of Ammiel at Lo-debar," Ziba testified.

So King David ordered the household of Machir to extradite the son of Jonathan from Lo-debar to Jerusalem. The son of Jonathan was brought before David, and he put his face to the ground and put David's foot on his neck. "Are you Merib-baal?" David asked. "I am," he testified.

So David decreed: "Do not be afraid! For the sake of Jonathan, I will restore the household of Saul to you as long as you eat at my table." Again, Merib-baal put his face to the ground and David's foot on his neck, and accepted the covenant with the words: "This dead dog is not worthy to be your slave."

Then David ordered Ziba to appear before him. "I have restored the household of Saul to your patron's heir. But you shall work the land with your sons and your slaves, and bring the produce to me as along as Merib-baal shall eat at my table." Now Ziba had fifteen sons and twenty slaves. Then Ziba said to the king: "Your word is this slave's command."

FIGURE 41   Stories of Merib-baal (2 Sam 9:1-13)

David interrogates Merib-baal to determine if he is supporting Absalom or another of David's sons for the throne. When David calls Merib-baal by name at the beginning of his hearing, he wants to know whether Merib-baal answers to him or to one of his sons. Merib-baal answers David's call, which pledges the household of Saul to support only the heir designated by David.

David then confirms Merib-baal as the heir to the household of Saul. This decree not only acknowledges Merib-baal's pledge of allegiance, but also preempts his campaign to increase control of the household by conspiring with one of David's sons. David does not permit him to exercise his authority immediately, but assigns Merib-baal to "eat at my table" (2 Sam 9:7).

Monarchs brought leaders to eat at their tables for two purposes: location and indoctrination (Dan 1:1-10; Fig. 42). With Merib-baal at his table, David always knows where he is, and has regular opportunity to teach Merib-baal how to support state policy. Patron states today still bring the best and the brightest from client states to the mother country for education and military training. As in David's time, the policy facilitates the control that patrons exercise in the states of their clients.

Until David is satisfied that Merib-baal is loyal enough to exercise the actual authority of father of the household, Ziba acts as his legal guardian to "till the land for him" and "bring in the produce" (2 Sam 9:10). In the villages of Israel, when the father of a household died without an heir, the tribe appointed a legal guardian. By appointing Ziba to administer Saul's property, David uses the tradition of the legal guardian to confiscate the land of Saul (Joshua 21; 1 Chr 6:39-66; 1 Kgs 10:28). Consequently, Ziba works for David, not Merib-baal. To carry out his responsibility, Ziba negotiates fifteen primary labor contracts with his sons and twenty secondary contracts with his slaves. By reorganizing the household of Saul, David is not a philanthropist granting Merib-baal a benefice whose revenue will pay for his upkeep. David is a monarch renegotiating his covenant with a household to put it back into production by transferring it to the state. Despite his sus-

King Nebuchadnezzar of Babylon . . . ordered his palace master Ashpenaz to bring some of the Israelites from the royal household and the households of Judah. They were to be young men who had not been wounded and were handsome. They were to be educated in every branch of wisdom, endowed with knowledge and insight, and competent to serve in the king's palace. They were to be taught the traditions and language of Babylon. The king assigned them a daily ration of the royal food and wine. They were to be educated for three years, so that at the end of that time they could be stationed in the royal court.

FIGURE 42   Four Friends Thrive on Vegetables and Water (Dan 1:1-5)

picions that Merib-baal is conspiring against him, David himself does not shame Merib-baal, but instead allows him to remain father of the household under the supervision of a legal guardian. He wants to bring Saul's covenant partners to his side.

David also assumed the role of legal guardian for the household of Uriah in order to confiscate the land and children of this rival. Subsequent monarchs in Israel and Judah followed suit. Ahab and Jezebel appointed themselves legal guardians to confiscate the land of Naboth (1 Kgs 21:1-29). A trial in the book of Ezekiel (Ezek 34:1-31) indicts the monarchs of Israel and Judah for this abuse of power. It indicts monarchs who foreclose on the property of households in financial difficulty, not to reorganize them, but to seize their lands for the state.

When David renegotiates his covenant with the household of Saul in the opening episodes of the Stories of Merib-baal, he carries out only one stage of the strategy used by monarchs to centralize production and distribution in the state. The stories also reflect the subsequent steps that David takes to tighten his control.

Amnon, Absalom, and Adonijah, among others, try to overthrow David. Absalom almost succeeds. When Absalom marches on Jerusalem, David orders a strategic retreat from the city. Since David does not know who in Jerusalem remains loyal to him, he withdraws from the city assuming that only those loyal to him will follow. Merib-baal is one of those whose loyalties are unmasked (2 Sam 16:1-4). He remains in Jerusalem, while Ziba departs. Ziba not only follows David into the field, but also pays the taxes due to the state from the household of Saul at the precise moment when David and his soldiers need them most (Fig. 43).

When David had passed a little beyond the summit of the Mount of Olives as he retreated from Jerusalem, Ziba the slave met him with two asses, carrying two hundred loaves of bread, one hundred bunches of raisins, one hundred strings of dried summer fruit, and one skin of wine.

The king asked, "What is all this?" Ziba replied, "The asses are for the king's chariot, the bread and summer fruit are for his warriors to eat, and the wine is medicine for casualties who faint in the desert to drink."

Then the king asked, "And where is Merib-baal?" "He stayed in Jerusalem," Ziba replied, "for he said, 'Today Israel will once again belong to the household of Saul.'"

Then the king said to Ziba, "The household of Saul is yours." And Ziba said, "I put my face to the ground and your foot on my neck. You are my patron and my king. Your wish is my command."

FIGURE 43   Stories of Merib-baal (cont.) (2 Sam 16:1-4)

States taxed their villages in order to defend them and to maintain strong markets for their produce. Tax rates were variable. During wartime, states assessed their households on the basis of how many rations were needed to feed the soldiers necessary to protect the households (1 Chr 12:41; 2 Chr 11:11). The register of rations that Ziba delivers to David invoices typical commodities taxed by the state: "loaves of bread, bunches of raisins, strings of summer fruit, and a skin of wine" (2 Sam 16:1-2). Grain, wine, and olive oil were the most common items taxed and traded because they could be stored, transported, and rationed. The same commodities appear elsewhere in the Bible (1 Sam 25:18; 1 Kgs 5:25; Ezek 27:17; 1 Chr 12:41; 2 Chr 11:11). Asses were not typical tax commodities. For farmers livestock was an asset; for tax collectors it was a liability. Farmers herded livestock to insure their households against crop failure, and to supplement available human labor. Livestock was too inconvenient for tax collectors to store, transport, and ration. Nonetheless, the tax-stamp formula "for the king's household" identifies the team as a tax payment, not simply transportation for the payment. This formula also appears on storage jars used by villages of Hebron, Ziph, and Socoh to transport their grain, wine, or olive oil to the state during the reign of Hezekiah (715–687 B.C.E.).

David listened to the testimony of Ziba and rewarded him by removing Merib-baal as father of the household of Saul and designating Ziba to replace him. David's decision has precedents in traditions from states like Alalakh and Ugarit where the lands of traitors were also taken over by the monarch.

In the final episode David makes another attempt to stabilize the relationship between his household and the household of Saul (2 Sam 19:24-30). During his hearing, Merib-baal accuses Ziba of treason, and professes his own loyalty to David. Merib-baal testifies that he had not conspired with Absalom, that he planned to leave Jerusalem and work for David, but had been deceived into staying behind by Ziba (Fig. 44).

David offers to divide the property between Merib-baal and Ziba. With two fathers working the land of Saul, David could double the harvests. Saul's farmers would work harder for Merib-baal and Ziba together than for Ziba alone. Merib-baal points out that such a reorganization is pointless, since the revolt is over. He declines David's offer, not simply out of piety, but because doubling the number of harvests would overwork the land and the farmers. In wartime, overworking farmland was a military necessity; in peacetime, it was economic and political suicide. When farmers planted too many crops, the quantity and quality of the harvest dropped off. The work doubles; the yield does not. Overworked and underpaid farmers murder their overseers. Merib-baal refuses to turn Saul's farmland into a dust bowl and to drive his farmers into rebellion. The policy risks destroying David, and Merib-baal along with him.

As David was returning to Jerusalem after putting down the revolt of Absalom, Merib-baal came to meet the king. He was dressed as if he had been in mourning since the day David evacuated the city..

The king questioned him: "Why did you not go with me, Merib-baal?" He testified: "Ziba, my slave left without me. Because I am powerless, I ordered him to saddle an ass for me, so that I might ride out with you, my lord and king. But the slave tricked me and then lied to you. But you are the messenger of Yahweh to me. Do what seems good to you. The household of Saul was sentenced to death, but you set your slave among those who eat at your table. What further right have I, then, to appeal to you again for mercy.?"

So the king decreed: "These charges and countercharges must stop. You and Ziba will divide the household of Saul." But Merib-baal declined. "As a sign of my gratitude that you have come back to Jerusalem safely, let Ziba keep the household."

FIGURE 44 Stories of Merib-baal (cont.) (2 Sam 19:24-30)

Trial of David
(2 SAM 10:1—12:31)

In his Trial of David, Nathan charges David with unnecessarily getting Israel into a war with Ammon, and with sexually assaulting Bathsheba to take over the household of Uriah. David unwittingly hears a case against himself that Nathan brings before him as ruler of Israel. David finds himself guilty as charged, but repentant.

The trial indicts David for abuse of power in conducting foreign policy and in conducting domestic policy (2 Sam 10:1-19). His foreign policy bungles his negotiations with Ammon and leads to war. The Ammonites lived in what is Amman, Jordan, today. The Arameans lived in Aram, which is Damascus, Syria, today. "Arameans" can also simply mean "westerners," and refer to any of the peoples who lived west of the Euphrates River in Syria-Palestine.

The messengers that David sends to the funeral of Nahash in Ammon are denounced as spies by Hanun, who considers David ready to challenge his right to be the heir of Nahash. The messengers taunt Hanun, who retorts by claiming that David will not "deal loyally with Hanun son of Nahash" (2 Sam 10:2). Then Hanun ritually castrates David's messengers by cutting their tunics in half, exposing their genitals, and by shaving off half of their beards. The actions proclaim that David is powerless in Ammon.

What Hanun does to the messengers of David is done to David himself. Messengers were an incarnation of those whose words they carried, and they were honored or shamed accordingly by those to whom they were sent. Hosts lavished food, clothing, and slaves on messengers who delivered them good news. They also provided them with body-guards and escorts both to protect them from harm while they were in their land and to prevent them from spying on it. Hosts abused messengers who delivered bad news.

Nathan's indictment of David basically agrees with Hanun. David's Ammon policy was an unnecessary and costly failure. It is Joab, not David, who faces the consequences of David's ill-advised actions, and it is Joab who restores the honor of Israel by conquering Rabbath-Ammon. David's role in the campaign is purely ceremonial. He is impotent not only in Israel, but in Ammon as well.

David is also indicted for a failed domestic policy (2 Sam 11:1—12:9). David is indicted on two charges of conduct unbecoming of a ruler in Israel. He sleeps in his own bed in the palace instead of with his soldiers in the field, and he sleeps in the bed of Uriah, instead of protecting the household of his covenant partner.

War was a time of transition between an old world and a new world. Warriors and soldiers who entered this liminal space abstained from life-sustaining activities. They fasted and they were celibate. They did not farm and they did not sleep in houses. Battle was the only passionate activity permitted soldiers and warriors. Uriah and the rest of the soldiers had vowed to abstain from sexual intercourse and from wine until Israel conquered Rabbath-Ammon.

Uriah was a one of the thirty members of David's royal guard (2 Sam 23:34). His Hebrew names means "Yahweh is my Light." He is not a Hebrew, but a Hittite. The Hittites were a people from what is today central Turkey. Until 1280 B.C.E., Hatti competed with Egypt for control of Syria-Palestine. Although the Hittites were not a political power in Israel during the time of David, they did play an important role in its economy. The trial contrasts the faithfulness of Uriah, the outsider, with the unfaithfulness of David, the insider. In stark contrast with the monastic lifestyle adopted by Uriah and the soldiers of Israel, David is sleeping in the royal palace, and sleeping with the wife of Uriah.

Uriah is a covenant partner of David who is fighting for Israel against Ammon. David's rape of Bathsheba not only destroys the household of Uriah, but threatens the land and children of every household in Israel. David is intent on taking over the household of Uriah, who tries unsuccessfully to defend it. Bathsheba is a woman of honor, who is raped and then witnesses the torture and execution of Uriah, who is a man of honor.

Today, sexual activity carries personal and romantic connotations. In the world of the Bible, sexual activity carried economic and political connotations. Sexual relationships were a measure of the honor and shame of households. Women like Bathsheba were important in the distribution of power. The Hebrews rated a father's fulfillment of his responsibility to feed and protect his household on the basis of how well he cared for and protected its women. The women of a household were living symbols of its honor, and a measure of the fixed assets of a household. If the father of a household could protect the women of his household, then he could protect all its members. If he left them in harm's way, then he was impeached and someone else took over the land and children of his household.

To test the stability or honor of a household, a man from another household attempted to rape one of its women. Rape was not simply an act of sexual violence, but a political challenge to the father of the household to which the woman belonged. It was a hostile takeover bid. Stories involving rape or adultery, like those of Shechem and Dinah, David and Bathsheba, or Amnon and Tamar, are not soap operas describing how men and women feel for each other, or explaining why they hurt each other. Like war, rape was a violent social process for redistributing the limited goods that a society possessed so that it was not destroyed by the weakness of a single household. If a household could not protect its women, rape declared the household to be insolvent or shamed, and unable to fulfill its responsibilities to the community as a whole.

Not every wanton act of sexual violence by any man against any woman was a challenge to the honor of a household. For a challenge to be set in motion, the woman had to be either *married* like Rizpah (2 Sam 3:6-11), Michal (2 Sam 3:12-16), Bathsheba, David's secondary wives (2 Sam 16:21-22), and Abishag (1 Kgs 1:1-4), or *marriageable* like Dinah and Tamar. The woman could not be a widow or a child. The man could not be just any male, but needed to be the father of the household or his heir. Rape had to take place in the context of some activity connected with fertility such as harvesting (Gen 34:1-2; Judg 21:17-23), sheep shearing (2 Sam 13:23-28), eating (2 Sam 13:5-6), or menstruating (2 Sam 11:4). Otherwise, it was treated like any other crime (Deut 22:23-27). Tying the aggressive act to fertility clearly identified it as a legal test of the economic stability of the household. If the rape was successful, then the rapist became the legal guardian for the shamed household while negotiations to realign its resources and responsibilities took place (Gen 34:4-24; 2 Sam 11:6-26; 13:15-22).

The steps that a shamed household followed to reestablish its honor were parallel to those followed to challenge it. The father of the shamed household or his heir needed to assassinate the challenger who had taken over the household, and this avenger had to carry out the assassination while the challenger was exercising the power that he had seized.

David orders Bathsheba to the palace. Bathsheba is not seductive. She is modest and obedient both to the tradition of bathing after menstruating and to the command of the ruler of Israel. She is not conspicuously bathing in sight of David. The roof was a private, not a public, place to bathe. It was out of sight of all those on the ground floor of a pillared house. Furthermore, like the rest of Israel, she assumes that David is in the field with his soldiers.

When Bathsheba conceives a child, David orders Uriah back to Jerusalem. David wants Uriah to fight for his household. David wants Uriah to break his vows as a soldier, and to accuse his patron of adultery, so that David can execute Uriah as a traitor. David tries three different strategies to tempt Uriah to break his vow of celibacy. First, David orders Uriah to eat a full meal and have intercourse with his wife. Second, David dispenses Uriah from his vow of celibacy because he has made a journey from the battlefield to Jerusalem (2 Sam 11:10-12). Third, on the assumption that in wine there is truth, David gets Uriah drunk (2 Sam 11:12-13).

Uriah frustrates David by remaining loyal both to his vows as a soldier and to his covenant with David. He will not fight the king for whom he is fighting. He counters each of David's moves with a countermove. Uriah is both an honorable and a talented match for his patron intent on taking over his household.

Finally, David orders Uriah to carry his own death sentence back to Joab. Uriah does not have to open the message to know its contents. He is well aware of David's decision that if he insists on remaining a soldier at war, David will sentence him to die in battle, but without honor. Joab's order to rush the wall of Rabbath-Ammon is suicidal. Uriah understands it to be so, but he carries out the order nonetheless. Only fools, like Abimelech who rushed the walls of Thebez (Judg 9:22-57), rush the wall of a city during a siege (Fig. 45). Like Abimelech, who was killed by a grinding stone thrown by a woman, fools, who get too close to the wall, die a shameful death. David sentences Uriah to a death without honor.

Joab carefully coaches the messenger who will report Uriah's death to David. Even though the messenger from Joab was delivering the news that David's orders had been obeyed, he might still be in harm's way and be put to death like the messenger who brought David the news that Saul and his sons were dead (2 Sam 1:1-27).

Since David had preempted the covenant obligations of Yahweh, and tried to protect and provide for Israel himself, Nathan announces that Yahweh has sentenced his

Then Abimelech went to Thebez, laid siege to the city and captured it. There was a battle tower inside the city. All the men, women, and rulers of Thebez took refuge on the roof of the tower. Abimelech fought his way to the gate of the tower and tried to set fire to it. But a certain woman hit Abimelech with a grinding stone and crushed his skull. Immediately he called to the warrior who carried his shield and ordered him: "Draw your sword and kill me, so people will not say, 'A woman killed him.'" So the warrior thrust him through, and he died. When the Israelites saw that Abimelech was dead, each returned to his own village. In this way Yahweh repaid Abimelech for the crime he committed against his father in killing his seventy covenant partners. Yahweh also punished the people of Shechem for their crimes and for the crime of Jotham, son of Jerubbaal.

FIGURE 45   Abimelech Delivers Israel from Thebez (Judg 9:50-57)

foreign and domestic policies to failure (2 Sam 12:10-12). The household of David will be continually at war trying to defend Israel against its enemies: "the sword shall never depart." The household of David will also never enjoy economic stability, but will consistently be challenged by other households for the right to rule Israel. Yahweh "will take your wives before your eyes, and give them to your neighbor."

David appeals the sentence, and, surprisingly, Yahweh mitigates it (2 Sam 12:13-31). The mitigation sentences only the first child of David and Bathsheba to death, and promises that they will have a child to replace it. Solomon's name means: "The Replacement." The mitigation also promises that despite the death of Uriah beneath its walls, Israel will conquer Rabbath-Ammon. In the short term, the household of David suffers the loss of this royal child and a loyal covenant partner. In the long term, the land and children of the household of David are restored.

Trial of Amnon
(2 SAM 13:1—14:33)

Following the Trial of David are the trials of his three sons: Amnon (2 Sam 13:1-22), Absalom (2 Sam 15:1—24:25), and Adonijah (1 Kgs 1:1-10). Each son campaigns to become the heir of David and fails. The first crisis episode (2 Sam 13:1-2) in the Trial of Amnon portrays Tamar as fertile. There were certainly sexual relationships that reflected deep personal and emotional love of one person for another in the world of the Bible. There was certainly romance in the world of the Bible, just as there is romance in every other world (Gen 24:67; Exod 21:7-11; Song 8:1-4). There is, however, more politics and economics than romance in these sexual relationships. The Hebrew word describing Tamar does not refer simply to a pleasing physical appearance, but to her economic potential. In the Song of Solomon, the same Hebrew word that describes Tamar describes the lips that can stimulate every taste of one's lover (Song 4:10), and the feet of the dancer, which are graceful (Song 7:1; Fig. 46). The same word also describes Jerusalem maturing from a girl into a woman in the book of Ezekiel (Ezek 16:1-63). Here, the word describes Tamar as a woman coming of age, fully capable of fulfilling her role as mother of a household. She is physically capable of sexual intercourse, and the conception of a child, and has learned well from the mother of her own household the skills that she will need to manage a household of her own. Tamar is wise and will demonstrate just how wise a mother she will be. Tamar will endow her husband with the resources of the household of Absalom, and virtually guarantee him the throne of David.

Tamar arouses not only the passion of Amnon, but also his ambition. His actions are political, not simply personal. When he falls in love with Tamar, and is so tormented

How graceful are your feet in sandals,
*   You, fit to marry a king!*

Your rounded thighs are like jewels,
*   The work of a master hand.*

Your navel is a rounded bowl,
*   Full forever with wine.*

Your belly is a heap of wheat,
*   Wreathed with lilies.*

Your breasts are like matched fawns,
*   Twins of a gazelle.*

Your neck is like an ivory tower.
*   Your eyes are like sacred pools at the gate of Heshbon.*

Your nose is like a tower of Lebanon overlooking Damascus.
*   Your head crowns you like the Carmel Mountains,*

Your hair flows like drapes of royal purple.
*   A king is the prisoner of your braids.*

FIGURE 46   Tour-Burlesque of the Woman's Body (Song 7:1-5)

that he makes himself ill because of her, Amnon is dealing not just with unrequited love, but with political ambition. He is a man who would be king in Israel. Amnon loves Tamar as David loved Michal, the daughter of Saul, and Bathsheba, the wife of Uriah. Their actions do not just reflect personal passion or pain, but distinct strategies in a political campaign.

Similarly, the titles by which Amnon, David, Tamar, and Absalom address each other reflect more than their kinship. In English, "brother" and "sister" are used almost exclusively for people related by blood kinship. Here, they identify people related by covenant, who call each other "father," "son," and "brother." The issue in the story is power.

Amnon is tormented, but impotent. He finds Tamar marvelous to admire, but difficult to possess. Amnon is portrayed like the pharaoh who cannot have intercourse with Sarah (Gen 12:9—13:1); Abimelech, who cannot have intercourse with Rebekah (Gen 26:6-11); and David, who cannot have intercourse with Abishag (1 Kgs 1:2-4). Amnon looks at Tamar but cannot hold her. Voyeurs cannot be kings, because they are impotent.

The second crisis episode (2 Sam 13:3-9) portrays Amnon as a fool who chooses a fool for a friend and follows the fool's advice. Jonadab is introduced as a wise man who becomes a friend of Amnon. "Friend" is the title for a royal adviser (1 Kgs 4:5; Ps 45:14). Jonadab is anything but wise. His advice destroys the household of Amnon. Amen-em-ope, who taught in Egypt between 1200 and 1000 B.C.E., considered the choice of friends to be a defining test for the wise. In his teachings he cautions against just the kind of flawed judgment that Amnon demonstrates in choosing Jonadab to be his friend. The appointment reveals that Amnon cannot tell a wise man from a fool (Fig. 47).

Jonadab is also not a trickster. Tricksters are outcasts without land and children who manipulate the powerful into endowing them with land and children. When Abraham and Sarah negotiate with Pharaoh, they are tricksters. They are powerless, but use fast talk and good looks to trick the pharaoh into giving them land and children. Jonadab is not an outcast, but a member of the royal household. His actions are not shrewd; they are incompetent. He acquires nothing by the end of the story that he did not possess at the beginning of the story.

Absalom may have dispatched Jonadab to the household of Amnon to seed it with bad advice. David uses the same strategy against Absalom, and forces him to choose

Do not take counsel with fools,

 Do not seek their advice.

Do not speak back to superiors,

 Do not insult them.

Do not let superiors discuss their troubles with you,

 Do not give them free advice.

Seek advice from your peers,

 Do not ignore your equals.

More dangerous are the words of fools,

 Than storm winds on open waters. . . .

Do not rush to embrace fools,

 Lest their advice drown you like a storm.

FIGURE 47 Teachings of Amen-em-ope (Matthews and Benjamin 1997: 278)

An *arzawa* woman takes her impotent client into the temple of Uliliyassis. There she prepares one day's rations, enriched with "three sweet sacrificial loaves of flour, one *tarnas* weight of water, figs, grapes . . . a little of everything; the fleece of an unblemished sheep, a pitcher of wine. . . ."

They remain in the temple for three days. Three times a day she prepares a meal for Uliliyassis, her divine patron, and for her impotent client, and then has intercourse with him.

FIGURE 48   Hittite Cure
for Impotence
(KUB, vii, 5; KUB, vii, 8; KUB ix, 27)

between a friend who is wise and a friend who is a fool (2 Sam 15:32-37). Jonadab advises Amnon to launch his campaign to succeed David by asking him to assign Tamar to feed him. Amnon is not simply asking for some tender loving care while he is not feeling well. His request implies that he needs a hostage to protect him from his enemies.

Food plays a significant role in the trial. The story begins when Amnon asks for food, and ends when he is murdered while eating (2 Sam 13:23-29). Amnon, who could neither feed nor protect himself, should not become a monarch who must feed and protect Israel. The bread, which Tamar prepares, says more about the relationship between the people who eat it together than about its nutritional or medicinal value. Tamar and the bread she bakes are samples of the children and the land that the household of Absalom provides in Israel (Fig. 48).

David is not simply a concerned parent coming to the bedside of a sick child. He is a royal magistrate hearing Amnon's petition in a court of law. Unlike a village assembly, which listens to many witnesses and discusses a case until the elders reach a consensus, royal magistrates simply hear a plaintiff and then render a decision. Tamar belongs to the household of Absalom, which may have already made an attempt on Amnon's life, so Amnon asks David to make it directly responsible for his safety, which also makes the household of Amnon directly responsible for her safety.

The third crisis episode portrays Amnon as a fool who cannot negotiate a covenant for land and children. Amnon tries to impose a covenant on the household of Absalom by ordering Tamar to have intercourse with him. Amnon exploits Tamar's vulnerability by telling her to bake bread for him, and to have sexual intercourse with him. The request invites Tamar to commit Absalom's resources to Amnon's campaign to become monarch in David's place. She tells Amnon that if he wants a covenant between his household and the household of Absalom, he needs to negotiate for it. Amnon is a fool who acts on impulse (Prov 15:5). Tamar is wise because she is patient. The wise know when to talk and when to listen. Fools are hot-tempered because they let passion run or ruin their lives. Tamar's words shame Amnon, just as the woman from Shunam shames Elisha

(2 Kgs 4:8-37), Michal shames David (2 Sam 6:20-23), and Jezebel shames Jehu (2 Kgs 9:30-37). Three times Tamar appeals to Amnon, assuring him that if he can be patient and negotiate with David, their marriage could ratify a covenant between the households of Amnon and Absalom.

In the climax, Amnon ignores Tamar's refusal and rapes her (2 Sam 13:14-19). With this act of sexual violence Amnon lays claim to the land and children that she represents, and issues a political challenge to Absalom.

In clear violation of his newly acquired responsibility as the legal guardian of her household, Amnon divorces Tamar instead of having a child with her. Again Tamar protests. Once a household is challenged, it is entitled to redeem its honor. Tamar demands this right. She has been shamed, but her household should not be politically destroyed. The Middle Assyrian Code outlines the due process for which Tamar appeals (Fig. 49). Amnon is unrelenting. Tamar tears her clothes to mourn the lost honor of Absalom's household (2 Sam 13:19). As the physical symbol of the fertility and honor of the household, Tamar now becomes the physical symbol of its impotence and shame (Gen 37:29-35; 39:11-15).

In the denouement (2 Sam 13:20-38) Tamar cries out, and Absalom hears her cry, but refuses to avenge her without deliberation. In the meantime, his household remains shamed. Only after two years is Absalom ready to restore the honor of his household by challenging Amnon to a duel at the sheepshearing. David delays sending Amnon to the sheepshearing, hoping to avoid admitting that Absalom has challenged the honor of Amnon by inviting him. Eventually Absalom convinces David to offer Amnon a chance to defend his honor.

If a marriageable woman, who is the daughter of a citizen, who is living in her father's house, who is not engaged or married, and who is not collateral for any of her father's debts, is kidnaped and raped by another citizen, within the city, in the country, in the street at night, in a granary, or at a city festival, then the father of her household is to kidnap and rape the wife of his daughter's assailant.

If the assailant has no wife, the father of the daughter who was kidnaped and raped may also give his daughter to her assailant in marriage, and the assailant is to pay one-third more than the standard bride price in silver to her father as the bride price for a marriageable woman, and marry her without the opportunity for divorce.

If the father does not wish to marry his daughter to her assailant, he is to accept one-third more than the standard bride price in silver as a fine and marry his daughter to whomever he wishes.

FIGURE 49   Middle Assyrian Code, art. 55 (Matthews and Benjamin 1997: 122)

Absalom assassinates Amnon at Baal Hazor, which is six miles northeast of Bethel. David's other sons flee back to Jerusalem along the road from the twin villages of upper Beth-Horon and lower Beth-Horon, which are northwest of Gibeon. By assassinating Amnon, Absalom makes his own bid to be David's heir and invites David's other sons to endorse him. Not one of the sons of David stands by either Amnon or Absalom.

Absalom takes refuge in his mother's household, with Talmai in Geshur northeast of Galilee (2 Sam 3:3). By leaving Absalom in the household of his mother, David refuses to confirm him as his heir. Even after the wisewoman of Tekoa convinces David to allow Absalom to return, he still refuses to grant Absalom's claim to become David's heir (2 Sam 14:1-33).

The Trial of Amnon itself says nothing of Tamar after the assassination of Amnon. A genealogy of Absalom lists: "three sons, and one daughter whose name was Tamar; she was a beautiful woman" (2 Sam 14:27). By naming his daughter Tamar, Absalom may have celebrated the restoration of his sister's honor in the household. A genealogy of Abijam identifies his mother and father as Rehoboam and Maacah, "the daughter of Abishalom," or Absalom (1 Kgs 15:2; 2 Chr 11:20-22). Consequently, some Septuagint Greek and Old Latin manuscripts read "Maacah" instead of "Tamar" in the genealogy (2 Sam 14:27). Abishalom is probably not Absalom, and therefore, Maacah is not Tamar. Nonetheless, the identification of the two women and their fathers reflects an ancient conviction that eventually a namesake of Tamar became the mother of a household, thus fully restoring the honor of her ancestor, and the honor of the household of Absalom in Israel.

Trial of Absalom
(2 SAM 15:1 — 20:23)

A Trial of Absalom indicts him for failing to honor David his father. To force David to designate him as heir, Absalom takes his campaign to the people. He plans to trick the people of Hebron, where David began his political career, into proclaiming him king of Israel, and to trick David into thinking that the people have acclaimed him as their king. Hebron was the New Hampshire primary or the Iowa state caucus of ancient Israel. Absalom begins his campaign by promising the people that he will expedite courts martial. The court was an important part of domestic policy in resolving disputes between households. Then Absalom attempts a military coup d'état. War was an important part of foreign policy in protecting the land from its enemies. Absalom wants to demonstrate his skills in both domestic and foreign policy. David does not arrest Absalom, because it is important for him to remain as neutral as possible while his sons compete with one another for the right to succeed him.

Like Don Quixote in *Man of La Mancha*, David regains his vision in the darkest moment of his political career. David is a failure in peace, but a master at war. By provoking David into battle, Absalom foolishly challenges David in the area of his greatest competence. In a masterful strategy, David plans to uncover Absalom's plot by evacuating Jerusalem. Only those loyal to David will follow him into exile, and then the people will recognize that Absalom is a rebel and not an heir.

David began his own rise to power by using mercenaries. Now David has only mercenaries with whom to reestablish his claim to power. The stark contrast between the loyalty of Ittai and his Philistines and the disloyalty of Absalom is striking. It is equally ironic that the same David who delivered the Israelites from the Philistines must be delivered from the Israelites by Philistines.

Although Zadok and Abiathar join the retreat from Jerusalem carrying the Ark of the Covenant, David sends them back (2 Sam 15:24-29). The ark is David's ensign. He wants to leave it in the city to show that he does not relinquish his claim to Jerusalem to Absalom. He is not surrendering, but preparing to fight.

Shimei from the household of Saul also joins David as he retreats, but to taunt David, not to support him (Fig. 50). Abishai asks David to sentence Shimei to death, but David refuses (2 Sam 16:5-14). David tells Abishai that Shimei may be the prophet that Yahweh has sent to sentence David. To kill him would be heresy. Furthermore, David continues, even if Shimei is a traitor, for a king to be cursed by a fool is so humiliating that it will convince Yahweh to enter the conflict on David's side. Yahweh regularly supports the powerless against the powerful.

When David came to Bahurim, a man of the household of Saul attacked him. Shimei, son of Gera threw stones at David and his soldiers, and taunted them: "Who is this traitor you follow? Who is this runaway slave who is your chief? David is nothing but a murderer and a thief. Yahweh is punishing you for betraying the household of Saul, whose land and children you stole. Yahweh is giving your kingdom into the hand of your son Absalom. Disaster has overtaken you, because you murder the innocent."

Then Abishai . . . said to the king, "Why should this dead dog curse my king? Let me cut off his head." But the king said, "If he is cursing me because Yahweh has ordered him to curse David, who can question Yahweh's judgement? My own son seeks my life. This member of the household of Saul is doing nothing more. Let him alone. Let him continue to curse me if Yahweh has ordered him to curse me. Maybe Yahweh will notice my suffering, will repay me with good for this cursing of me today."

FIGURE 50   Stories of David's Successor (Sam 16:5-12)

David also leaves his ten of his secondary wives in Jerusalem. His marriages to these women ratified the ten major covenants on which David built his state. The Ark of the Covenant is David's legal claim to the land of Israel; the ten wives are his claim to its children. When Absalom enters the city he publicly rapes David's wives to demonstrate that he is now king of Israel, who will fulfill the terms of the covenants that the household of David has with their households.

Finally, David sends Hushai back to Jerusalem to serve as his an agent-in-place with the mission of undermining the relationship between Absalom and Ahithopel, who is as capable a strategist as David (2 Sam 16:32-37). Absalom must choose between Hushai and Ahithopel, just as David must choose between Ziba and Merib-baal. Unlike David, Absalom cannot choose wisely. Absalom chooses the fool Hushai, and rejects the wise Ahithopel (2 Sam 17:23).

The warriors that each household sends to David are assigned to three detachments commanded by Joab, Abishai, and Ittai. David attacks Absalom in a forest, a terrain favoring David the chief rather than Absalom the monarch. By having a the branches of a sacred oak (2 Sam 18:9) capture Absalom, nature is portrayed as David's covenant partner. In the Enuma Elish Stories (Enuma IV:34-104) nature also joins Marduk against Tiamat.

The Obituary of Absalom (2 Sam 18:9-18) shames Absalom for seeking power illegitimately. Absalom shares the fate of Abimelech (2 Sam 11:21), Eglon (Judg 3:21-25), and Sisera (Judg 4:21-22). Each seeks power, that belongs to Yahweh alone. Absalom swings by his hair awaiting judgment. Joab orders an ordinary soldier to kill Absalom, but this fails. The soldier reminds Joab that David has ordered Absalom be spared. Absalom is not simply to be killed; he must be formally executed. Therefore, Joab drives three javelins into Absalom's body. The javelin is an officer's weapon. Here they represent the consent of Joab, Abishai, and Ittai to Absalom's execution. After they condemn Absalom, ten soldiers representing David's covenant partners vote to kill him. These ten soldiers represent the same ten covenants as the wives whom David had left in Jerusalem. Absalom's executioners would then have cut his hair, but not just to free his body. Like Samson before Delilah, like Saul before David, and like David's messengers before Hanun, Absalom is powerless. His hair has been cut. He has been castrated.

Ahima'az, hoping for a reward, wants to be the messenger to tell David that the revolt has been put down and that Absalom has been executed. Joab, however, knows that David will be outraged by the news, and will kill this messenger, just as he did to the messenger who informed him of Saul's death. Therefore, Joab orders an Ethiopian, a black African, to carry his own death sentence to David. David's inability to consolidate his victory over Absalom still leaves his household without an heir.

Trial of Adonijah
(1 KGS 1:1-53)

A Trial of Adonijah sentences the last of the three unsuccessful candidates in the struggle for the succession. The trial opens with David both old and impotent. In his youth, David was a womanizer. As an old man he cannot have intercourse even with the most seductive woman in Israel. He is no longer fit to be king, but he still has not adopted an heir.

Aware of the danger that David's impotence, and indecisiveness, poses to Israel, Adonijah attempts to usurp David's authority as father of the household, and appoints himself heir. He opens his bid for the throne by appointing a bodyguard (1 Kgs 1:5). Presidents of the United States often assign Secret Service agents as bodyguards to their opponents who have not formally declared their candidacy to preempt them and officially designate them as candidates. Adonijah also throws a fund-raising dinner. His guest list includes Joab and Abiathar, but not his father's advisers or Solomon (1 Kgs 1:6-8).

Even in the face of Adonijah's direct challenge to his authority, David remains helpless, until Bathsheba and Nathan convince him to adopt Solomon. Solomon consummates his adoption by demanding the resignation of Adonijah, who complies. The household finally has a successor.

Trial of Solomon, 1000–925 B.C.E.
(1 KGS 2:1—11:43)

The annals of Solomon record striking examples of his ability to feed and protect Israel. One of the most striking reports that Solomon makes to Yahweh is the construction of a house for the divine patron of Israel. By building a temple for Yahweh, Solomon officially takes possession of the land that Yahweh promised to Abraham and Sarah. Yahweh has a house, and Israel is a state.

Few architectural remains of the Temple of Solomon, which was destroyed by the Babylonians in 587 B.C.E., have been recovered. Nonetheless, archaeologists are able to reconstruct the temple from similar temples excavated elsewhere in the world of the Bible. Descriptions of the Sanctuary and the Temple in the Bible itself, like those in the book of Exodus, the books of Samuel-Kings (1 Kgs 6:1—7:51), and the book of Ezekiel, however, are not much help in reconstructing the temple. These biblical traditions were not intended to be blueprints of the temple. Furthermore, crafts in traditional societies like ancient Israel are handed on through deliberately long and carefully guarded apprenticeships. Guilds do not develop how-to handbooks for their members.

The description of the Sanctuary and the Temple, like the description of the ark of Noah, affirms what was done, not how to do it.

The annals also include an evaluation of Solomon by the Queen of Sheba, who ruled the most ancient state in the world of the Bible, where Yemen is today (1 Kgs 10:1-13). When the Assyrians conquered Sheba after 800 B.C.E., the land was still ruled by queens. The people of Sheba, the Sabeans, were actively involved in trade along the caravan routes of Arabia. Solomon's maritime activities in the south brought him to the attention of those who had their own trading interests in the region. Therefore, an accreditation of Solomon by Sheba has been included in the annals (1 Kgs 9:26—10:29). The queen comes to Jerusalem to test Solomon. She leaves praising his wisdom and the good fortune of his subjects. Her approval of Solomon is all the more significant because like the praise of Jethro, Balaam, and Rahab for Israel, it comes from an outsider.

Review of the Annals
for the Monarchs of Israel and Judah
(1 KGS 11:44—2 KGS 25:30)

The destruction of Jerusalem and the deportation of the household of David by the Babylonians between 597 and 587 B.C.E. affected the people of Judah in much the same way as the mass murder of European Jews and the destruction of Jewish culture by the Nazis in the twentieth century affects Jews today. Attempts to understand these crimes are mocked by their enormity. Holocausts test the limits of justice to react, no less than they test the limits of tradition to interpret them. A Review of the Annals for the Monarchs of Israel and Judah (1 Kgs 11:44—2 Kgs 25:30) tries to explain how something like this could happen, and how the Babylonians could take away the land and people that Yahweh promised to Abraham and Sarah. Royal annals were published by monarchs as yearly reports to Yahweh of their stewardship of Israel's land and people. The review uses these annals to put each monarch on trial in absentia. On the assumption that the Hebrews could be one people only if they worshiped one divine patron in one particular sanctuary, the review investigates whether or not each monarch limited the worship of Yahweh to the temple in Jerusalem. With the exception of David, Solomon, Hezekiah, and Josiah, the review finds each monarch guilty of breach of covenant and punishes them with the loss of land and people. Therefore, the review concludes that the Assyrians and the Babylonians simply executed a divine sentence.

Trial of Ahab and Jezebel

(1 KGS 16:29—22:40)

Indictment: Annals for Ahab and Jezebel of Israel, 875–854 B.C.E.

(1 KGS 16:29-34)

Many trials in the review simply annotate royal annals with formulas like: "he did what was evil in the sight of Yahweh, and followed the sins of Jeroboam son of Nebat." Some trials, however, expand the annals to explain how a royal household failed to fulfill its covenant with Yahweh. The Trial of Ahab and Jezebel (1 Kgs 16:29—22:40) explains their failures by converting the four most significant accomplishments reported in their annals into indictments.

First, Ahab and Jezebel are indicted for negotiating a covenant between Israel and Tyre (1 Kgs 16:31). Ahab was more successful than any other monarch of Israel in negotiating covenants with other states. Israel's covenant with the state of Tyre was his most important diplomatic accomplishment (Fig. 51). It was ratified by his marriage to Jezebel, who was a daughter of the household of Ethbaal, ruler of Tyre. Like the marriage of Solomon to a daughter of Pharaoh, the marriage of Jezebel and Ahab gave Israel the recognition of one of the most powerful states (1 Kgs 16:31; Psalm 45). Ahab and Jezebel considered the negotiation of covenants for food and for protection to be their responsibility as the heirs of Yahweh. All the monarchs of Israel and Judah saw themselves as stewards of the land and its people. Consequently, these rulers negotiated covenants with other states to invest the land and its people abroad in return for food in times of famine and for soldiers in time of war. The Review of the Annals for the Monarchs of Israel and Judah, however, considers negotiating covenants with other states

Founded during the Early Bronze period, Tyre was a significant economic power in Syria-Palestine until 640 C.E. It is about thirty miles north of the city of Acre and the Carmel Mountains. Today, Tyre is on a peninsula. Originally it was built on two islands about one-half mile from the coast. Alexander the Great conquered Tyre by building a causeway to the island in 332 B.C.E. Eventually, the currents piled enough silt against it to create the peninsula. Tyre covered almost 150 acres and had a population of 35,000. Cloth dyed deep purple was a major trade commodity for Tyre. Piles of murex snail shells, from which the dye was harvested and a dye factory have been excavated just outside the city walls. The murex shell also represents Tyre on its coins, and the pungent smell of dye manufacturing became the city's characteristic aroma.

FIGURE 51   City of Tyre

to be a complete lack of confidence in the ability or in the willingness of Yahweh to feed and protect the people of Israel and Judah.

Ethbaal (887–855 B.C.E.) expanded the borders of Tyre south as far as the Carmel Mountains, and negotiated covenants with states throughout Syria-Palestine. A Lament for Tyre in the book of Ezekiel chronicles the sprawling empire of Tyre on both land and sea (Ezek 27:1—28:26). The city became "the bestower of crowns, whose merchants were princes, whose traders were the honored of the earth" (Isa 23:8).

Second, Ahab and Jezebel are charged with renovating the sanctuaries to Yahweh in Dan and Bethel, where Yahweh stood invisible on the back of a golden bull (1 Kgs 16:31). These sanctuaries were dedicated to Yahweh as the divine patron of Israel. Nonetheless, the review considers these sanctuaries to be sacrilegious because Yahweh was to be worshiped only in Jerusalem. Although bulls were common pedestals for the divine patrons of peoples throughout Syria-Palestine, the review considers the only suitable pedestal for Yahweh to be the Ark of the Covenant.

Third, Ahab and Jezebel are charged with constructing a new temple to Yahweh in Samaria (1 Kgs 16:32-33). Ahab and Jezebel built this spectacular royal sanctuary in their capital city to honor Yahweh as both the Godmother who feeds the Hebrews and the Godfather who protects them. It was a showplace. The "House of Yahweh" in Samaria was a sign of their devotion to Yahweh. For the review it is an "outhouse," whose sacrifices, like human excrement, attracted flies. This House of Yahweh had turned the "Lord of Hosts" into the "Lord of Flies."

Fourth, Ahab and Jezebel are charged with reconstructing the ancient city of Jericho to fortify Israel's borders to the south and to the east (1 Kgs 16:34). They pointed to this undertaking as the fulfillment of their roles as protectors of the land. As an act of humility before beginning the reconstruction, Hiel of Bethel sacrificed his oldest son, and then sacrificed his youngest son upon completing the reconstruction. Human sacrifice, by depriving a household of its heir, placed it completely in Yahweh's care. Once the heirs of a household were dead, no one but Yahweh could feed and protect it. Jericho was to be the city of Yahweh, not the city of Hiel or the city of Ahab.

Sentence: Stories of Elijah
(1 KGS 17:1—22:40)

The Stories of Elijah were once independent from the Annals for Ahab and Jezebel, Ahaziah, and Jehoram. Here they elaborate both the indictments and the sentences that are brought against these three monarchs from the household of Omri, which ruled Israel from 886 to 844 B.C.E. The stories originally developed among Hebrew clans in Gilead east of the Jordan River. Opposition to the household of Omri was the catalyst, that gave them their present shape. In the Trial of Ahab and Jezebel, the Annals for Ahab and Jezebel serve as the indictment (1 Kgs 16:29-34) and the Stories of Elijah announce the sentence (1 Kgs 17:1—22:40).

Elijah and Elisha, like Amos, Hosea, Isaiah, Jeremiah, and Ezekiel, were prophets. Today, prophets are psychics who read the future, activists who bring about social change, poets who warn of impending doom, precursors who identify Jesus as the Messiah, or theologians who emphasize individual responsibility and social morality. In the world of the Bible, however, prophets monitored covenants that the rulers of Israel and Judah negotiated with their neighbors (1 Sam 12:14-15; 2 Sam 15:3-5; Hosea 11:1; Amos 5:15). Prophets were sentries or watchdogs doing for the state as a whole what lookouts on the walls did for their cities (Jer 1:11-13; Ezek 3:17-21; 33:1-9). They did not predict crises. They responded to them. Prophets announced the significance of present decisions by rulers for the near future.

The Bible does not canonize prophets and condemn monarchs. Monarchs and prophets were both committed to fulfilling Yahweh's covenants with Israel and Judah. Likewise, confrontations between monarchs and prophets like David and Gad (2 Sam 24:1-25) were not simply personality conflicts or unavoidable political tension. These confrontations reflect two different understandings of the terms of the covenant. Monarchs understood the covenant one way; the prophets understood it in another. The monarchs understood the covenant as an mandate to create a surplus, centralized economy. The prophets understood the covenant as a mandate to preserve a subsistence, decentralized economy that characterized Israel as villages between 1200 and 1000 B.C.E.

The books of Deuteronomy, Joshua, Judges, Samuel, and Kings portray prophecy as a single, homogeneous movement from the time of Abraham and Sarah in the Middle Bronze period (2000–1500 B.C.E.) to the time of Haggai, Zechariah, and Malachi in the Persian period (539–323 B.C.E.). Therefore, Abraham, Moses, Aaron, Miriam, Deborah, and Samuel are all honored as prophets (Exod 4:14-16; 7:1-2; 15:20; Deut 18:18; Judg 4:4; Hosea 12:13). Similarly, the books of Chronicles (1 Chronicles 25; 2 Chronicles 12–20) describe the Levites in the Jerusalem temple after 537 B.C.E. as prophets. Nonetheless, Abraham, Moses, Aaron, and Miriam were ancestors, not prophets; Deborah and Samuel were chiefs; and Daniel, Haggai, Zechariah, and Malachi were seers. Only men and women, like Elisha, Huldah, Hosea, and Ezekiel, who functioned during the time when Israel and Judah were states ruled by monarchs are officially prophets. For there to be prophets, there need to be monarchs. Prophets and monarchs created a balance of power in ancient Israel from 1000 to 587 B.C.E.

Some prophets, like Nathan and Isaiah, were closely aligned with their monarchs; others, like Elijah, Elisha, and Amos, were peripheral and were aligned with village elders. Nonetheless, all prophets exercised power as the monarchs' loyal opposition, and evaluated the domestic and foreign policies of their monarchs.

There were similarities between the messengers and the prophets in the world of the Bible, but the role of the prophet was more judicial than administrative. Although the books of Samuel-Kings refer to messengers more than twenty times, only the books of Haggai and Malachi refer to prophets as messengers (1 Sam 23:27; 2 Sam 11:19-24; Hag 1:13; Mal 3:1). Both messengers and prophets were representatives. Messengers represented monarchs; prophets represented the divine assembly. Both the divine assembly and the monarchs commissioned their representatives with the formula: "Go to . . . and say: . . ." Messengers carried information; prophets delivered legal verdicts. Both messengers and prophets were treated with the same respect, or disdain, due those they represented. Messengers, however, played no role in the development of or response to the communications they carried. Prophets took an active part in both the deliberations of Yahweh and the divine assembly that led to the verdicts they announced, and in working out Israel's response (Fig. 52).

The Stories of Elijah highlight important moments in his campaign to abrogate the Covenant between Israel and Tyre, and to recommit Israel to economic self-sufficiency. Prophets considered covenants between foreign states and Israel to be violations of the Covenant between Yahweh and Israel. For the prophets, these covenants called into question the stipulation that only Yahweh was to feed and protect Israel. Prophets also opposed these covenants because of the sweeping economic changes that they set into motion. The covenants made royal administrators in Israel very rich and its villagers miserably poor. Taxes ballooned. Corruption spread (Mic 6:9-16; 1 Kings 21). The rich had never been richer, and the poor had never been poorer.

Elijah considers the temple in Samaria, built of dressed limestone, and its sacred tree to be sacrilegious. For Elijah, altars to Yahweh were to be built of natural, not worked stones, and Yahweh could not be honored as a Godmother with a Tree of Life. Likewise, for Elijah, the new Jericho rebuilt by Hiel could not protect the borders of Israel. Only Yahweh could protect Israel from its enemies. Furthermore, prophets opposed human sacrifice, because they considered it to be a ritual for reminding Yahweh to feed and protect the land and the people. Yahweh did not need to be reminded, by human sacrifice, to protect and to feed the people. Yahweh always remembered; it was the people who forgot.

Elijah Divines Water from the Wadi Cherith (1 Kgs 17:1-7)

Soldiers were fed before farmers. The first harvest was called the "King's Harvest" (Amos 7:1) because it was taxed 100 percent. Monarchs used the entire first harvest to pay their soldiers, their priests, and all the other members of the royal household. They also used this harvest to pay the premiums on their covenants negotiated with other states

When people of Judah living in Alexandria, Egypt, translated the Hebrew Bible into Greek sometime after 300 B.C.E., they labeled some of the prophets as "false prophets." For example, although the Hebrew Bible simply refers to Hananiah as a "prophet" (Jer 28:1), the Greek translation introduces him as a "false prophet" (Jer 35:1). Therefore, "false prophets" in English translations of the Bible today were not necessarily morally degenerate or politically corrupt officials. They were prophets retained by the monarchs of Israel and Judah.

FIGURE 52   False Prophets

for food and protection. Nevertheless, not even these covenants could protect the people of Israel from starvation, when a yearlong drought struck. Ahab and Jezebel could not even feed their soldiers (1 Kgs 18:2b-5), much less their people (1 Kgs 17:1-24).

The Stories of Elijah argue that only widows and prophets will survive the drought, because only the poor in Israel recognize that "Yahweh is our Creator," which is the meaning of the name "Elijah." Only widows and prophets rely on Yahweh to feed and to protect them. Monarchs, like Ahab and Jezebel, starve, because they negotiate covenants with others for food and for protection.

Ahab is not a pagan. Ahab and Elijah are both followers of Yahweh. Ahab is not a pagan. Both agree that Yahweh is the divine patron of Israel. They disagree, however, on how Israel should honor Yahweh. For Ahab and Jezebel, Yahweh is a Great King like Melqart, the divine patron of Tyre (1 Kgs 16:32; 2 Kgs 11:18). For Elijah, Yahweh is a Good Shepherd, who has promised to feed Israel forever. In the Bible, these divine titles have been abbreviated. "Yahweh, the Great King" has been shortened to "Baal"; "Yahweh, the Good Shepherd" has been shortened to "Yahweh." Nonetheless, both titles refer to the same divine patron God, not two different divine patrons. "Baal" honors Yahweh as triumphant; "Yahweh" honors the divine patron of Israel as humble. Ahab and Jezebel consider Elijah's theology of a humble Yahweh to be archaic. Elijah considers Ahab and Jezebel's theology of a triumphant Yahweh to be heretical. Therefore, Elijah does not indict Ahab and Jezebel for worshiping the wrong divine patron, but for worshiping Yahweh wrongly.

In the Stories of Elijah, Elijah and Moses are parallel. Moses leads the Hebrews from slavery in Egypt into freedom at Mt. Sinai. Elijah leads the Hebrews from slavery in the Israel of Ahab and Jezebel into freedom at the Carmel Mountains. Moses and Elijah each rehearse significant aspects of their exodus experiences. Moses goes into the Nile River as a newborn and is drawn out by the daughter of Pharaoh to rehearse his role in leading the Hebrews into the Red Sea. Elijah goes to Mt. Horeb as a dead man and is raised up by Yahweh as a new man to rehearse his role in leading the starving Israelites to the Carmel Mountains so that Yahweh can raised them up with rain (Fig. 53).

The story of how Elijah Divines Water from the Wadi Cherith (1 Kgs 17:1-7) is a miracle story. Like all miracle stories, it contrasts the ease with which Yahweh feeds the poor with the crushing labor with which Ahab and Jezebel feed the rich. Yahweh effortlessly feeds the prophet at the Wadi Cherith, and the widow of Zarephath. Their poverty makes it perfectly clear that they know it is Yahweh who feeds them, and that they do not feed themselves.

The Wadi Cherith, like the Wadi Kishon, is a sacred river that flows from the base of a sacred mountain. The Wadi Kishon flows from the base of the Carmel Mountains. The Wadi Cherith flows from the base of one of the many mountains in Gilead overlooking the Jordan River and north of Amman today. Gilead is the most eastern province in Israel, and it is the most fertile. If there are no harvests in Gilead, then the drought is severe. Elijah comes to this sacred place to pantomime the execution of Yahweh's verdict against Ahab and Jezebel. The powerless in Israel will eat; the powerful will starve.

There has been no rain to for planting and no rain at harvesttime. Ahab and Jezebel have appealed to Yahweh as a Great King to send the rain by negotiating covenants with Tyre and Sidon. Elijah appeals to Yahweh as a Good Shepherd who sends ravens to feed him.

The stories call Elijah and Elisha "seers" or "prophets." Anthropologists would call them "shamans." Shamanism developed around 4000 B.C.E. among the Aryan peoples in southern Iran. After 2000 B.C.E., Aryans began to migrate across the Hindu Kush into northwest India and later onto the Ganges Plain. Their language became Sanskrit, and their way of life Hinduism. Consequently, shamanism figures prominently in the Rigveda traditions. From India, shamanism swept eastward to the shores of the Pacific.

For shaman cultures the visible world is only a portion of a much larger cosmos populated by invisible spirits. Although these invisible and visible planes are distinct, they are joined. Spirits can pass through the human plane, and shamans can cross into the divine plane. Shamans keep the human and the divine planes in balance. Like shamans, Elijah and Elisha use various implements to channel into the divine plane in order to feed and protect Israel. Their ability to trance, and to become clairvoyant, allows them to work miracles like divining water, multiplying food, finding lost objects, knowing what is going on in a faraway place, healing the sick, and raising the dead.

FIGURE 53 Shamans

Elijah Feeds a Widow and Her Son (1 Kgs 17:8-16)

The story of how Elijah Feeds a Widow and Her Son is a miracle story. Its crisis is a damage report (1 Kgs 17:8-12); the climax is a ritual (1 Kgs 17:13-14); and the denouement is an affidavit (1 Kgs 17:15-16).

The story takes place in the land of Tyre, Israel's covenant partner. The Wadi Cherith is on the eastern border of Israel; Tyre is on the west. The drought affects Israel from border to border. Tyre is the homeland of Jezebel. Even the people of these great states are starving. They cannot feed Israel, and they cannot even feed their own households. Tyre was a model state. Its people were safe and fed, even when other states were destroyed by war and drought. Nebuchadnezzar, great king of Babylon, laid siege to Tyre for thirteen years (585–573 B.C.E.) without being able to conquer it. Yahweh cripples it with a single drought.

All the characters in the story are powerless. Elijah is a stranger, his host is a widow, her son an orphan. They are the protégés of Yahweh because they cannot feed themselves. Consequently, Elijah, like a shaman, calls flour and olive oil out of empty jars and turns the widow's last supper into her daily bread.

Elijah Raises a Household's Heir from the Dead (1 Kgs 17:17-24)

Stories of shamans raising the dead to life are found in many cultures, but in ancient Israel are preserved only in the Stories of Elijah and Elisha. In the story of how Elijah Raises a Household's Heir from the Dead, his host is the mother of the household. Her son is not a minor, but a young man, twenty-some years old and able to go to war (Num 1:3; 2 Kgs 3:23; Gen 14:14).

The story does not describe the son's illness. The Bible has few detailed descriptions of either the causes of illness or their cures. Miracle stories are intended to demonstrate that Yahweh feeds and protects Israel with ease, in contrast to the monarchs whose covenants for food and soldiers are labor-intensive and ineffective. Therefore, the woman's son may have been drafted by Ahab to serve as a soldier, and sent home from the army dying from his wounds. She is angry with Elijah for rescuing her son from hunger, only to have him die as a soldier. Ahab leaves the widow to starve, and her son to die. Elijah feeds them both, and raises the son from the dead.

Elijah repeats directly to Yahweh the complaint that the mother of the household brings to him. She says to Elijah: "What have you against me? You have come to me to bring my sin to remembrance, and to cause the death of my son!" Elijah says to Yahweh: "Yahweh, my divine patron, have you brought calamity even upon the widow with whom I am staying, by killing her son?" Even though it is Ahab's military policy that has led to the death of her son, everything is attributed to Yahweh. Yahweh is the cause of all things, good and bad.

Elijah does not "cry out" as an admission of sin, as the term is used in hero stories. Elijah calls on Yahweh as a covenant partner to carry out the responsibility of protecting Israel.

Elijah is not simply using cardiac pulmonary resuscitation to raise the widow's son from the dead. Like a shaman, Elijah follows the dead from the human plane into the afterlife. Elijah hurries to chase the disoriented spirit into the afterlife where it has fled after colliding with the widow's son. If a person has been dead too long, a shaman cannot find the spirit and reorient it. Elijah finds the spirit, and directs it back into its channel so that it can continue its passage through the human plane. The spirit's host is then brought back to life. Like a midwife, the prophet announces that the son as a newborn is viable or alive. The mother of the household renews her covenant with Yahweh, whom she acknowledges as the divine patron who feeds and protects her household.

Elijah Divines Rain on the Carmel Mountains (1 Kgs 18:1-2+17-39)

Elijah Divines Rain on the Carmel Mountains is a miracle story in which royal prophets, who worship Yahweh as a Great King, duel with Elijah, who worships Yahweh as a Good Shepherd. The story, which takes place on the Carmel Mountains, was originally independent from the story of how Elijah Divines Lightning against Obadiah (1 Kgs 18:2b-16+41-46), which takes place at Jezreel.

Worship mirrors the economy. States with a centralized, surplus economy, like the Israel of Ahab and Jezebel, worship Yahweh as a Great King. Villages with a decentralized, subsistence economy, like the Israel of Elijah, worship Yahweh as a Good Shepherd. The lightening of Yahweh will only protect the land of the true Israel from the curse of storms and floods. Rain will identify which worship is fitting for the divine patron of Israel. The rain of Yahweh will only bless the land of the true Israel with harvests and children. The Stories of Elijah endorse the simple worship of Yahweh as a Good Shepherd, and condemn the triumphal worship of Yahweh as a Great King.

The site where Elijah demonstrates the power of Yahweh is the Carmel Mountains. "Carmel" is not a single mountain, but a range jutting north and west into the Mediterranean Sea. These mountains create a natural barrier across the Coast Highway. Armies and caravans either detoured inland through the narrow Wadi 'Ara to Megiddo or negotiated the treacherous cliffs of the Carmel Mountains overlooking the Mediterranean Sea.

The Carmel Mountains are the Garden of Eden. They mark a sacred center. They also marked the frontier between Israel (2 Sam 5:11; 1 Chr 14:1) and Tyre (1 Kgs 9:11-13). Ethbaal gave the Carmel Mountains to Jezebel as a dowry when she married Ahab (1 Kgs 18:19).

The Carmel Mountains were also a weather-maker. The winds that blew out of the west climbed the mountains and blessed their slopes with as much as thirty-five inches of rain each year (Amos 1:2). To prevent crop failure, these rains had to come at the right time and in the right quantity. Therefore, this is a story about rain, not fire (Exod 3:2; Lev 20:14; Zech 2:5; Mal 3:2). The fire that consumes Elijah's offering is a flash of lightning that announces the rain (Judg 6:21; 13:20; Ezek 1:13; Job 1:16; 2 Kgs 1:10-14). Lightning was not something to fear, but a reminder that Yahweh is present to protect the people and punish their enemies. By referring to the lightning as "the fire of our Creator" and Elijah as "a member of the household of our Creator," the story achieves a masterful play on words. Elijah is a fire man who carries the lightning of his Godparent. His special relationship to Yahweh entitles him to summon his divine patron's own lightning. Therefore, Elijah is a rainmaker.

The Carmel Mountains were a fitting location to for telling a story that asks: "Who makes it rain?" The connotations of this challenge are lost in translations that ask: "How long will you waver or limp between two opinions?" (1 Kgs 18:21-26). This translation conveys the image of traveler lost at an intersection or a bird hopping through a tree from one branch to the other. A better translation is: "How long are you going to dance for Yahweh as a Great King?" In the world of the Bible, dancing is not simply recreation, it is a sign of faith (Ps 26:6). Divine patrons are musicians. Creation is a melody

---

The royal prophets of Ahab and Jezebel dance to induce ecstasy, which disconnects the senses from the human plane and focuses them on the divine plane.

Similarly, Aryan shamans ate the "fly agaric," a hallucinogenic mushroom, to induce ecstasy. Hindu shamans or brahmins induced ecstasy with a *soma* liquor. In Mexico, Huichol shamans eat peyote, a tiny, bulbous hallucinogenic cactus. Native American shamans smoke, snuff, lick, chew, and even use a high-nicotine tobacco as an enema. Carib shamans in Suriname eat *takini* fig juice, a relative of marijuana. Tirios shamans in the Amazon drink a tea made from the *ku-pe-de-yuha* Brunfelsia plant.

Witches were the shamans of medieval Europe. In the opening scene of Shakespeare's *Macbeth,* witches brew "toe of frog" and "root of hemlock" to induce ecstasy. The brew induced a trance that allowed the witches to fly from the human plane to the divine. Witches also induced ecstasy by rubbing themselves with alkaloid-rich plants such as hemlock, aconite, belladonna, mandrake, and henbane to cause mental confusion, irregular heartbeat, delirium, and erotic dreams.

Like the prophets of Ahab and Jezebel, shamans dance, chant, beat on a drum, or shake a rattle to induce ecstasy.

FIGURE 54 Dancing

to which humans must dance. Elijah wants Israel to decide to dance either with the Good Shepherd or with the Great King (Fig. 54).

In the story of how Elijah Divines Lightning against Obadiah, Ahab taunts Elijah when they meet (1 Kgs 18:17-18), and in the story of how Elijah Divines Rain on the Carmel Mountains, Elijah taunts the prophets of Ahab and Jezebel while they pray (1 Kgs 18:27). In the standard taunt, "who" introduces the first line and "that" introduces the second. "Who is David the son of Jesse, that I should feed his runaway slaves with my wine, my bread, my meat?" (1 Sam 25:10) catches the sense, if not the precise grammar, of the genre.

Elijah does not taunt the royal prophets directly, but teaches the people to taunt them. The words "call louder," like "come here" (1 Kgs 18:30) and "seize the prophets" (1 Kgs 18:40), are addressed to the people. Elijah is teaching the people to outshout the singing and dancing prophets with his taunt.

Elijah's taunt is brimming with double entendre. On the surface the taunt echoes the liturgical language of the royal prophets. They addressed Yahweh as a Great King, as the people of Tyre addressed Melqart, whose statues they transported from one end of the Mediterranean to the other as they worked the trade lanes for which their city became famous. If a statue of Melqart did not board every freighter that sailed from Tyre, and accompany every inland caravan, the commercial world of Tyre would collapse. Likewise, at the onset of the dry season, statues of Melqart would be taken to the border, where farms end and dry wasteland begins, to do battle with the heat of summer. The heat of the long, hot summer drove the life-sustaining moisture of Melqart to sleep, deep in the earth, only to be reawakened when the planting rains began in the fall. With only subtle changes in spelling, accent, or meaning, Elijah's taunt conjures up the image of Melqart as an impotent old fool unable to perform the routines of daily living, such as getting in or out of bed and using the toilet, without assistance. Simply by shifting the pronunciation of a single letter, the taunt converts a liturgical expression meaning "to travel on business" to the vulgar expression "to go out into a field to relieve oneself" (Gen 24:61-67; Fig. 55).

Pantomime is the art of gesture. First celebrated in the cave paintings and dances of the Stone Age, pantomime is a "movie" whose medium of action appeals to the sense of sight. It is quite distinct from story, whose medium of sound appeals to the sense of hearing. Pantomimes use gestures to address those human realities whose profundity demands silence. Pantomime is not solely a representational art describing events, but also a sympathetic art that brings about events. Therefore, it is a genre of social change that highlights and ridicules the faults of the powerful.

The prophets of ancient Israel were masters not only of the sounded art of word, but the silent art of movement as well. Therefore, the symbolic actions of Elijah here,

Rebekah and her slaves mounted their camels, and followed the slave of Abraham.

Isaac had gone out into a field to relieve himself. He looked up and saw camels coming. At the same moment Rebekah looked up and saw Isaac. She dismounted quickly from the camel and said to a slave, "Who is the man over there in the field?" The slave said, "It is my master." So she took her veil and covered her face. The slave told Isaac everything he had done. Then Isaac brought Rebekah into his mother Sarah's tent. He had intercourse with Rebekah, and she became his wife, and he was faithful to her.

FIGURE 55 Stories of Abraham and Sarah (Gen 24: 61-67)

like those of Isaiah, Jeremiah, and Hosea (Isa 20:1-6; Jer 13:1-11; Hosea 1:1—3:5), are best understood as pantomimes.

On the Carmel Mountains Elijah retells a story of creation both in words and in pantomime. Just as the royal prophets mime their prayer in dance (1 Kgs 18:26), Elijah mimes his story with two symbolic acts. He begins by rebuilding the altar as the primeval mountain representing the dry land. Then, he digs a great circular reservoir that will hold the primeval sea, just like the huge round cauldron called "the sea" (2 Kgs 16:17), "the bronze sea" (2 Kgs 25:13), or "the molten sea" (1 Kgs 7:24) outside the temple. The dirt that Elijah piles along the edges of his trench creates the great dikes or horizons that will hold in the sea.

There are two kinds of water in creation stories. The seas and great rivers threaten the cosmos (Gen 1:1; 2:6). Springs and rains sustain it (Ezekiel 31, 37; Ps 36:8-9). Elijah floods his model of the cosmos with the waters of the chaos. Elijah has created a model of chaos.

Now, Elijah tells a creation story. The Bible no longer preserves the story but only the prayer with which he draws it to a close precisely at noon (1 Kgs 18:36). At that moment Yahweh strikes the waters of chaos with lightning. The waters recede and the dry land of the altar emerges. A new world has been created. Israel is free once again. Elijah sets the stage and tells the story that Yahweh acts out.

Elijah's pantomime and story were easily understood by the people gathered on the Carmel Mountains. A parallel appears on a limestone stela from Ugarit cut after 2000 B.C.E. On the stela a divine patron stands poised with a spear of lightning over the primeval sea. Two other parallels from Ugarit also portray divine patrons wielding lightning bolts to drive off the waters of chaos and bring on the life-giving rain. Elijah celebrates Yahweh as a divine warrior who conquers the primeval sea and is then enthroned as creator of the cosmos (Ps 29:1-11; Fig. 56).

call to worship

> Sing to Yahweh, all you members of the divine assembly,
>> Sing to Yahweh: "You are glorious and powerful!"
>
> Sing to Yahweh the glory due the name,
>> Worship Yahweh who is holy.

creation story

> The voice of Yahweh rules over the waters of chaos,
>> The Glorious Godparent thunders.
>
> Yahweh subdues the great waters,
>> The voice of Yahweh is powerful,
>> The voice of Yahweh is majestic.
>
> The voice of Yahweh splits the cedar trees,
>> Yahweh snaps the cedars of Lebanon.
>
> Yahweh makes the Lebanon mountains dance like a calf,
>> Yahweh makes the Sirion mountains shake like a young
>> wild ox.
>
> The voice of Yahweh strikes with bolts of lightning,
>> The voice of Yahweh shakes the desert.
>> Yahweh makes the desert of Kadesh tremble.
>
> The voice of Yahweh causes the oaks to mourn,
>> The voice of Yahweh drops the leaves from the trees.

call to worship

> Let all those in the Temple sing: "Yahweh is Glorious!
>> Yahweh sits enthroned above the waters of chaos,
>> Yahweh sits enthroned as the eternal ruler.
>
> Yahweh strengthens the people!
>> Yahweh blesses the people with peace!"

FIGURE 56   Hymn (Ps 29:1-11)

Elijah Tests the Royal Prophets at the Wadi Kishon (1 Kgs 18:40)

The Trial of Ahab and Jezebel actually preserves two parallel traditions describing the duel between Elijah and the royal prophets. Elijah Divines Rain on the Carmel Mountains describes the day of creation. Elijah Tests the Royal Prophets at the Wadi Kishon (1 Kgs 18:40) describes the day of judgment. The first story is long; the second is short.

Judgment takes place at a raging river that flows from the foot of the mountain where the divine assembly meets (Deut 32:34-36; Ps 18:7; 32:6; Job 21:30). The river decides who lives, and who dies (Ps 124:2-5; Zech 14:8). Defendants were thrown into the river as they cried out for deliverance (Ps 18:7; 69:15-16; Jonah 2:3). If they survived, they were innocent; if they drowned, they were guilty and their property was confiscated (Job 21:17; CH art. 2).

In some translations Elijah "had the royal prophets brought down to the brook Kishon and there he slit their throats" (1 Kgs 18:40). The Hebrew would be better read: "Elijah ordered the people to throw the royal prophets into the Wadi Kishon as they cried out to Yahweh as their Great King for judgment."

In both Elijah Divines Rain on the Carmel Mountains and Elijah Tests the Royal Prophets at the Wadi Kishon there is a mountain, water, and a judgment. The altar in the first tradition and the Carmel Mountains in the second are parallel. The waters in the trench in the first tradition and the Wadi Kishon in the second are parallel. In the first tradition, Elijah stands at the foot of the altar drowned in water and cries out to Yahweh as a Good Shepherd for judgment. In the second, the royal prophets are thrown into the wadi and cry out to Yahweh as a Great King for judgment.

Inauguration of Elijah at Jezreel (1 Kgs 18:41-46)

In an Inauguration of Elijah at Jezreel, the prophet draws rain from the sky like a shaman. The story opens when Elijah promises Ahab that the rain is coming. "I hear thunder" (1 Kgs 18:41), says Elijah. He orders Ahab to prepare to celebrate the end of the drought with a feast. The fast imposed by the drought is over.

To summon the rain Elijah takes the fetal position, and then stands. The gesture mimics a human birth. Elijah repeats the gesture until, on the seventh time, a rain cloud appears on the horizon. Although the cloud is small, Elijah promises that the rain will flood the Wadi Kishon and trap Ahab in the mountains if he does not leave immediately for his palace at Jezreel.

Elijah runs the seventeen miles between the Carmel Mountains and Jezreel in front of Ahab's chariot. The prophet's strides mark him here as more divine than human. In the stories of Aqhat, Dan'il and Danitiya recognize the approach of Kothar-wa-hasis as a divine messenger by his giant strides.

Inauguration of Elijah at the Great Mountain (1 Kgs 19:9-18)

An Inauguration of Elijah at the Great Mountain describes the prophet as "very zealous for Yahweh Sabaoth" (1 Kgs 19:10). With this profession of faith, Elijah reports for duty like a warrior answering a call to arms who addresses Yahweh as commander of the warriors of the divine assembly.

Not one other warrior reports for duty, which emphasizes the power of Yahweh, not the cowardice of the Hebrews. Typically, the Hebrews go into battle as underdogs to make it clear that human warriors fight only in support of the warriors of the divine assembly commanded by Yahweh. Too many human warriors might lead to the mistaken conclusion that the Hebrews delivered themselves from their enemies.

The warriors of the divine assembly muster at a great mountain. Great mountains are places where the earth is pregnant, and about to give birth to a new world. In the traditions of Ugarit, the great mountain is Saphon. In the Bible, the Carmel Mountains, Mt. Tabor, Mt. Gerazim, Mt. Zion, Mt. Sinai, and Mt. Horeb are all divine mountains from which new life spreads out in concentric circles to the world beyond. Elijah takes his place in the cave or womb of the great mountain and waits like a fetus to be born.

Like the royal prophets in Elijah Divines Rain on the Carmel Mountains, Elijah here prays to Yahweh as a Great King. He wants Yahweh to show power by destroying the household of Ahab and Jezebel (1 Kgs 19:9-10+14-18). The Yahweh who answers, however, is Yahweh the Good Shepherd (1 Kgs 19:11-13). Elijah's call for Yahweh to display power goes unanswered. A great wind roars across the mountain, but "Yahweh was not in the wind" (1 Kgs 19:11). An earthquake shakes the mountain, but "Yahweh was not in the earthquake" (1 Kgs 19:11). Lightning strikes the mountain, "but Yahweh was not in the lightning" (1 Kgs 19:12). When Yahweh does answer Elijah's prayer, it is in the "still small voice" of a mourner, working her way through the canyons of the great mountain like "a gentle breeze" (1 Kgs 19:12). Yahweh is not the monarch who marches powerfully into battle against Ahab and Jezebel, but the mourner who laments those whom the powerful have slain.

Trial of Ahaziah
(2 KGS 1:1—2:25)

Indictment: Annals for Ahaziah of Israel, 854–853 B.C.E.
(2 KGS 1:1-18)

A Trial of Ahaziah (2 Kgs 1:1—2:25) indicts Ahaziah for trying to heal himself with the help of the divine patron of the Philistine city of Ekron (2 Kgs 1:1-8). He is also indicted

and for trying to protect Israel with his own soldiers (2 Kgs 1:9-15). He is convicted and sentenced to death (2 Kgs 1:16-18).

Sentence: Stories of Elisha
(2 KGS 2:1-25)

After the household of Omri had fallen from power, the Stories of Elijah were told and retold over the next two hundred years. Some six major stories about Elijah developed.

Eventually, tellers incorporated the Stories of Elisha (1 Kgs 16:29—17:1; 2 Kgs 4:1-7) into the cycle. Many of the Stories of Elisha are parallels to the Stories of Elijah. Elisha was a powerful player in the events that brought Jehu to the throne of Israel (842–815 B.C.E.), and engineered some of the major foreign and domestic policy shifts that took place at the time.

Inauguration of Elisha at the Jordan River (2 KGS 2:1-18)

An Inauguration of Elisha at the Jordan River stresses that the triumphant foreign policies of Ahaziah are powerless to protect the royal household and the land of Israel, whereas the isolationist policies of Elijah and Elisha are a powerful deterrent to both famine and war. The prophets are absolutely confident that Yahweh, and Yahweh alone, will feed and will protect Israel.

The transfer of authority from Elijah to Elisha is parallel to the transfer of authority from Moses to Joshua (Num 27:18-23; Deut, 34:9). Neither Moses nor Elijah has a grave. The Inauguration of Elisha takes place away from the ordinary world. He undertakes a heroic journey across the Jordan River and into the divine plane. Ordinary human beings, like the prophets at Jericho, do not follow. The ascension of Elijah occurs once the Jordan has been crossed. The journey of Elisha across the Jordan and into the desert also parallels the journey of Elijah out of Beersheba and into the Negeb.

The whirlwind and the burning chariot that take Elijah away from Elisha are storm clouds and lightning. Both are symbols of Yahweh's ability to protect Israel from its enemies. Fierce winter storms ravaged the coast of the Mediterranean. Ships went down, crops were leveled, cities and villages were destroyed by the raging seas. For meteorologists today, clouds and lightning cause sea storms. Clouds and lightning protected the land against these storms. Clouds were the dust churned up by the chariot of Yahweh, who rode to Israel's defense against the sea. Lightning bolts were the arrows that Yahweh fired at the sea to make it retreat.

As Elijah departs, Elisha celebrates him as "father, father! The chariots of Israel and its cavalry!" (2 Kgs 2:12). The Assyrians dedicated horses and chariots to the sun (2 Kgs 23:11), whose title was "the charioteer." In traditional cultures, calling anyone by a given name exercises power over them. Therefore, shamans like Elijah are commonly addressed by their apprentices like Elisha as "father" or "grandfather." The titles acknowledge the shaman's wisdom.

Elisha tears his cloak, not just to mourn a dead Elijah, but to bring the old world of the household of Omri to an end. Similarly, in the Stories of David's Successor, Ahijah tears the cloak of Jeroboam to bring the old world of the household of David to an end (1 Kgs 11:19-39).

The waiting prophets witness Elisha's demonstration of his succession when he wields the cloak to duplicate Elijah's final miracle, which is modeled on Moses' actions at the Red Sea (Exod 14:15-18), and the actions of Joshua at the Jordan River (Josh 3:7-17). Moses parts the Red Sea with a staff. Elijah and Elisha part the Jordan with a rolled cloak. Both are phallic symbols inserted into the watery uterus of the Red Sea and the Jordan River. The result of this intercourse is the birth of a people. The Hebrew slaves emerge from the sea, and the prophet Elisha comes out of the river. Both are the newborn who will populate the new world that is being created.

Unlike Joshua, who marches across the Jordan River with many warriors, Elijah crosses with only a single disciple. Likewise, Elisha also crosses the Jordan as the new Israel. Unlike Joshua, who leads many, Elisha is alone. This new Israel does not need warriors to be saved from its enemies. Yahweh will protect it, the way Yahweh has protected Elijah and Elisha.

Elijah and Elisha continually challenge the monarchs of Israel such as Ahab and Jezebel to allow Yahweh to protect Israel, and to stop negotiating covenants with other states to defend the land. The soldiers of Ahab and Jezebel cannot even protect Israel from a single prophet, much less from an invading army. Miracle stories demonstrate that Yahweh can feed and protect the people and land of Israel, while its monarchs cannot. Monarchs laboriously negotiate covenants that impose crushing tax burdens on the people of Israel. Yahweh designates the prophets to effortlessly use divine power to feed and to protect the people virtually without cost. Every miracle is Yahweh's challenge to a monarch.

Elisha Sweetens the Spring at Jericho (2 Kgs 2:19-22)

The Inauguration of Elisha is followed by two stories that ratify his call to be a prophet. In Elisha Sweetens the Spring at Jericho, he feeds the people. In a Trial of the Warriors of Bethel, he protects the land.

In the miracle story, Elisha Sweetens the Spring at Jericho, a damage report describes the crisis (2 Kgs 2:19), a ritual takes place during the climax episode (2 Kgs 2:20-21), and there is an affidavit in the denouement (2 Kgs 2:22). The quantities of snail shells that appear in the excavation debris of Jericho today may provide a key to the cause of the pollution of Ein es Sultan spring. Snails are a common carrier of a blood fluke parasite that infects humans with schistosomiasis. Schistosomiasis, which like malaria is a life-threatening parasitic infection for humans, still affects tens of millions of people today. The recurrence of the disease at Jericho may explain the surprisingly frequent periods of vacancy at this ancient city (Fig. 57).

Trial of the Warriors of Bethel (2 Kgs 2:23-25)

The Trial of the Warriors of Bethel is a companion case to the Trial of Ahaziah (2 Kgs 1:1-8). Both contrast the power of Yahweh to protect the land with the power of the monarchs and their soldiers. In the Trial of Ahaziah, he sends soldiers to arrest Elijah, and twice Elijah destroys them with lightning, which is Yahweh's own weapon.

The Trial of the Warriors of Bethel contains an indictment (2 Kgs 2:23) and a sentence (2 Kings 24–25). In the indictment Elisha is not challenged by "small boys," but by young warriors (Gen 14:14). The two most important groups of men are the warriors, who are young, and the elders, who are old (Gen 19:4). The young have the courage

Shamans in the Amazon and south Africa use species of the *pah-nah-ra-pah-nah* vine, a relative of the North American pokeweed, to kill fleas, lice, and the bilharzia larvae, which causes schistosomiasis in humans. The vine has a scarlet stem on which grow rows of lime-green fruit about the size of small blueberries. Amazon shamans crush the entire plant and rub it into their hair.

Illnesses like schistosomiasis are considered by shamans to be symptoms that the divine plane and the human plane are out of balance. Spirits channeling the human plane have become disoriented, or have been consciously distracted by rival shamans, and have become trapped in the bodies of those who are sick. Therefore shamans not only treat disease with prescriptions like *pah-nah-ra-pah-nah* salt, but also enter the divine plane to diagnose illnesses and to determine what special plants might be needed to treat them. Spirits teach shamans which plants, animals, and water sources aid or threaten human life. Consequently, shamans possess detailed knowledge of the healing properties of a wide variety of local plants.

Channeling the divine plane also teaches shamans how to redirect spirits who have become disoriented while channeling the human plane. Medicating patients with plants is supplemented with relaxation, massage, hypnosis, aromatherapy, and visualization to draw the trapped spirits out of their human hosts and return them to their proper frequencies.

FIGURE 57   Healing

to fight for their villages; the old have the wisdom to negotiate for them. Warriors are "those who go out" of the gate of the city. Elders are "those who come in" through the gate (Josh 6:1). These forty-two warriors of Bethel are comparable to the fifty soldiers of Ahaziah. They are indicted for slandering Elisha with the words "Go away, bald head! Go away, baldhead!" (2 Kgs 2:23). The warriors are not simply guilty of mocking an old man whose hairline is receding. Body hair is a sign of virility. The warriors are saying that Elisha is too impotent to protect Israel.

In the sentence, Elisha summons two female bears from the forest beyond the village to execute the warriors. Shamans are particularly proud of their ability to imitate the call of wild birds and animals well enough to summon them at will. Elijah summons ravens who feed him (1 Kgs 17:1-7), and Elisha summons bears who protect him. Some shamans are also shape-shifters who can enter the bodies of their patron spirits to compensate for the limitations of their human bodies. As a raven, Elijah can fly. As a bear, Elisha can fight. The jaguar, which is the most intelligent, mysterious, and powerful creature in Brazil's jungles, is a favorite shape into which shamans in the Amazon shift. Elisha uses divine power to demonstrate that he is not impotent, and certainly does not need warriors to defend Israel. When Israel needs to be defended, Yahweh will summon the beasts of the forest.

Trial of Jehoram
(2 KGS 3:1—8:24)

Indictment: Annals for Jehoram of Israel, 849–842 B.C.E.
(2 KGS 3:1-3)

The Trial of Jehoram of Israel, 849–842 B.C.E. (2 Kgs 3:1—8:24), indicts him for continuing to subsidize the temples to Yahweh at Dan and Bethel. He is commended for having removed a large stone column dedicated to Yahweh as a Great King, which had been erected at the sacred center of the sanctuary by Amaziah, his predecessor. The stone was a phallic symbol liturgically celebrating the intercourse between the land and its divine patron, which brought the land and its people to life.

Sentence: Stories of Elisha
(2 KGS 3:4—8:24)

Jehoram is sentenced to rule an Israel racked by war and famine. The Stories of Elisha describe his punishment.

Elisha Ransoms a Widow from Debt (2 Kgs 4:1-7)

In Elisha Ransoms a Widow from Debt, Elisha comes to the aid of a household whose land and people are threatened by an abuse of power by the household of Jehoram. Because the widow's household cannot pay its taxes to the monarch, her sons become state slaves. The miracle by which Elisha resolves the crisis is not intended simply to inspire awe, either in the ability of the prophet or in the power of Yahweh to suspend the laws of nature. The contrast that the miracles establish is between the ease with which Yahweh feeds and protects the poor, and the difficulty and suffering that the complicated systems for the distribution of goods designed by rulers like Jehoram impose upon the poor. Yahweh feeds effortlessly. Human rulers Llike Jehoram feed their people only by inflicting suffering on the poor. Elisha questions the policies that drive the widow into slavery. Prophets participate in society in order to improve it, not to destroy it. They are neither silent nor compromised. They are outspoken and they are committed.

Elisha Raises the Son of a Stranger from Shunem from the Dead (2 Kgs 4:8-37)

Elisha Raises the Son of a Stranger from Shunem from the Dead is parallel to Elijah Raises a Widow's Son from the Dead (1 Kgs 17:17-24). Each story celebrates the persistence of the widows, who will not depart until their people are well.

Shamans use special instruments, like a hand mirror, and special clothing to open a window into the divine plane. Siberian shamans wear a parka connected to a chain so that helpers can pull them back into the human plane if they become disoriented on the divine plane. Elisha uses a staff (2 Kgs 4:29-31).

Apprentices like Gehazi assist shamans while they are in a state of trance. Sometimes they run errands for their shamans or serve as informants to interpret the words and actions of their shamans for the community. A variety of Hebrew terms identify apprentices like Gehazi, Elisha, and the other "sons of the prophets" in the Stories of Elijah and Elisha.

Elisha Changes Bad Vegetables into Good Vegetables (2 Kgs 4:38-41)

Like most miracle stories, Elisha Changes Bad Vegetables into Good Vegetables contains a damage report in the crisis episode (2 Kgs 4:38-40), a ritual in the climax (2 Kgs 4:41), and an affidavit in the denouement (2 Kgs 4:41). Again, this story stresses the ease with which Yahweh feeds the people in contrast to the labor-intensive economic systems devised by the monarchs, which only end up destroying the land and its people rather than enriching it. The announcement of the prophets that "there is death in the pot" (2 Kgs 4:40) is as much an analysis of the economy of Israel as it is a description of the food cooking in the wide-mouthed jar over the fire. The economic policies of the monarchs have ruined the land, which now produces only inedible plants. The fields of grain, rows of vines, and orchards of olive trees are taxed, and the produce is shipped out of Israel to the states with which the monarchs have negotiated covenants. All that is left for the people of Israel is weeds and death by starvation.

The scent or sight of certain plants can also distract spirits from their channels (Fig. 58). Anyone who tries to eat from a plant where a spirit is feeding is poisoned. Here,

---

The ritual that Elisha uses to change bad vegetables into good assumes a view of the world common among shamans. For shamans, spirits follow assigned channels when crossing through the human plane. The channels are invisible unless, for example, smoke rising from a cooking fire makes them visible. Most traditional cultures are quite careful to orient the smoke holes in the roofs of their houses to grant the spirits safe conduct. Steam rising from a cooking pot is another technique for making channels visible. Shamans also use water, mirrors, and crystals to locate and follow these channels into the divine plane.

Because the channels that spirits use are invisible, humans can inadvertently block a channel by stepping into the path of a spirit. A spirit cannot simply leave a blocked channel and go around the human, but becomes trapped in the human body. The efforts of the spirit to break out and continue on its way cause its human host discomfort and pain. Shamans are experts at drawing trapped spirits out of the human body and allowing them to continue on their way.

Spirits channeling through the human plane can also be distracted by a beautiful woman and leave their channels to make love. While the spirit is making love, it protects itself with a shield. Any man who tries to make love to a woman with a spirit lover dies. In the book of Tobit, for example, "Sarah, the daughter of Raguel . . . had been married to seven husbands, and the wicked demon Asmodeus had killed each of them before they had been with her as is customary for wives" (Tob 3:7-8).

FIGURE 58 Channeling

"when Elisha returned to Gilgal, there was a famine in the land. As the company of the prophets was sitting before him, he said to his servant, 'Put the large pot on, and make some stew for the company of the prophets.' One of them went out into the field to gather vegetables; he found a wild vine and gathered from it a lapful of wild beans, and came and cut them up into the pot of stew, not knowing what they were. They served some for the men to eat. But while they were eating the stew, they cried out, 'there is death in the pot!'" (2 Kgs 4:38-40).

Clinically, when some Mediterranean people eat broad beans, which are a common food crop in China, they suffer from a condition known as favism, which causes fever, vomiting, and acute hemolytic anemia. In the worldview of shamans, however, as Elisha's slave foraged for food in the drought-stricken land around Gilgal, he collected beans from which a spirit was eating. Beans are typically the food of the very poor. The shield that the spirit erected to protect itself while it was feeding was poisonous to humans like the prophets. They could not eat until the spirit had finished. To entice the spirit to release its hold on the beans, Elisha crumbles a pastry and scatters it on top of the stew. The spirit stops eating the beans when it begins to eat the cake, and the prophets can safely get on with their meal.

Elisha Heals Na'aman the Leper (2 Kgs 5:1-27)

In Elisha Heals Na'aman the Leper, Na'aman is a high-ranking military official, an adviser to the monarch of Syria, and a leper (1 Kgs 15:5). The juxtaposition of these labels of honor with a label of shame is shocking. Na'aman is a mighty one who has fallen. He can no longer command the army and advise the monarch. The adviser to the monarch now seeks advice from a slave.

The Hebrew slave tells Na'aman that the prophet Elisha can cure him. So Na'aman goes into exile in the land of his enemy (2 Kgs 5:3-5). He takes a letter for the monarch of Israel and gifts for the prophet Elisha.

Na'aman presents a letter from the ruler of Syria to the ruler of Judah, who considers it to be a taunt. "Does the ruler of Syria think I can wield divine power and cure this man of his leprosy? He is trying to start a war with me" (2 Kgs 5:7). For a leper, even the letter of one monarch to another is of no value.

Na'aman continues his pilgrimage from the monarch to the prophet. There is tension in this story not only between the clean and the unclean, but between the prophet and the monarch as well. Again, Na'aman presents himself and his gifts to the prophet and asks to be healed. The prophet grants his request, but returns his gift. The cure is not what Na'aman expected. He does not even see Elisha. Na'aman is taught by a slave of Elisha just as he had from been by his own slave. Gehazi tells Na'aman to wash seven times in the Jordan River.

Elisha Recovers an Axe (2 Kgs 6:1-7)

Elisha Recovers an Axe is a miracle story. There is a damage report in the crisis (2 Kgs 6:1-5), the climax describes a ritual (2 Kgs 6:6), and there is an affidavit in the denouement (2 Kgs 6:7). The damage report recounts that the household of Elisha, which called itself "the sons of the prophet," had outgrown its village. Therefore, it decided to build a new village near the Jordan River. The sons of the prophet borrowed tools to build new houses. During the construction, a prophet loses a borrowed axe. While he is using it, the iron or stone head comes off and flies into the river. If it cannot be recovered, the household will have to reimburse the owners, and borrow another. These conditions reflect the kind of economic slavery that the rulers of Israel imposed upon villagers. These taxes were impossible for households to meet. When households could not pay their taxes, monarchs confiscated their land. The members of the household became refugees, overcrowding existing villages, and pioneering new ones on the rugged and inhospitable land in the Arabah Valley cut by the Jordan River. Pioneering was costly. Households mortgaged everything they owned to pay for the expenses of moving. There was little or nothing left to pay for something as costly as a new axe. If it could not be recovered, then the sons of the prophet would become debt slaves working for the state.

Like a shaman, Elisha draws the axe head out of the water. He uses a wooden stick, which knows how to float, to teach the stone axe head how to float.

The prophets did not tell miracle stories to prove the existence of Yahweh, because no one, neither rulers, nor prophets, nor villagers, questioned the existence of Yahweh. The prophets also did not tell miracle stories to legitimate their own authority. The intention of miracle stories was to celebrate Yahweh as the divine patron who frees Hebrews from slavery, whether in Egypt or in Syria-Palestine. Unlike the other divine patrons who protected slave owners, Yahweh emancipated slaves and sent prophets to confront their owners. Elisha recovers the axe to demonstrate that Yahweh protects the sons of the prophets from the slavery that the taxes of the rulers of Israel, like Ahab, Ahaziah, and Jehoram, impose.

The Stories of Elijah and Elisha reflect how villagers in ancient Israel worshiped Yahweh as a Good Shepherd. The miracles of these prophets demonstrate the simplicity with which Yahweh feeds and protects the land and its people, in contrast to the destructive and labor-intensive economy of the rulers of Israel, who worship Yahweh as a Great King. Only the poor survive. Their poverty makes it perfectly clear that they are dependent upon Yahweh to feed and protect them. It is the power of rulers like Ahab and Jezabel that leads them to assume that they feed and protect themselves. What the Hebrews learned from listening to these stories, and what they taught in telling them, was that, as often as humans remember that only Yahweh can feed and protect, a new world is born. The words and deeds of Elijah and Elisha captured the essence of what it meant to be the people of Yahweh.

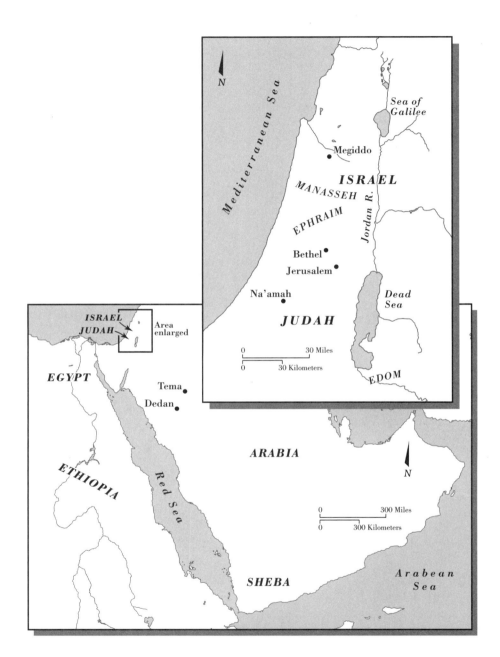

Points of Interest (Chapter 7)

7

Book of Job

(Job 1:1 — 42:17)

The book of Job (Hebrew: *'Iyyov*), the book of Ecclesiastes, and the book of Proverbs are the core of the wisdom traditions in the Bible. The book of Proverbs establishes the standards for wisdom and foolishness. The books of Job and Ecclesiastes review and evaluate these standards to maintain their quality.

Wisdom traditions reflect the worldview of the powerful, not only in ancient Israel, but in Egypt and Mesopotamia as well. When the Hebrew villages united to create the state of ancient Israel, they faced the challenge of learning how to take their place in the family of nations. They needed to learn how to govern their public and private lives like the citizens of the great states of Egypt and Mesopotamia. The sages in ancient Israel, whose teaching traditions are preserved in the books of Proverbs, Job, and Ecclesiastes, patiently engineered this transition. Like Joseph in the book of Genesis (Gen 37:2—Exod 1:7), who goes from the life of a shepherd in the villages of Syria-Palestine to the life of a vizier in the palaces of Egypt, these teachers guided Israel from its life as a village people to a new life in the great cities of Jerusalem, Samaria, Meggido, Gezer, and Hazor.

During the time of early Israel (1200–1000 B.C.E.), "Joseph" was the name of a people who lived in the regions of Ephraim, Manasseh (Judg 1:22-35), and Benjamin (2 Sam 19:21), between the cities of Bethel and Megiddo. After the death of Solomon (925 B.C.E.), these cities and villages seceded from Judah to become a separate state called "Israel" (Amos 5:6-15). These Israelites developed traditions like the Stories of Jacob, Leah, and Rachel (Gen 25:19—37:2), the Death of the Firstborn of Egypt (Exod 1:7—13:16), the Creation of the Firstborn of Israel (Exod 13:17—27:1), the Ark of the Covenant Stories (1 Sam 4:1—7:2), and the Teachings of Joseph (Gen 37:2—Exod 1:6).

Although the same characters that appear in the Stories of Abraham and Sarah (Gen 11:27—37:20) and in the Stories of Jacob, Leah, and Rachel also appear in the

Teachings of Joseph, these teachings develop as part of a different kind of tradition altogether. These traditions are not ancestor stories, but wisdom or teaching stories. Joseph is not an ancestor, but a wise man. Unlike other biblical traditions, the wisdom tradition was based on human observation, not divine revelation. The wise used analogy to hand on their judgments. Analogies could be as short as an adage (Prov 9:17) or a proverb (Prov 10:1), or as long as the essays that make up the Teachings of Joseph. The wise, like Joseph, follow these teachings and excel in every aspect of life (Prov 31:10-31). Joseph knows his strengths (Gen 45:8-9) and his weaknesses (Gen 41:16). He knows when to speak (Gen 41:22) and when to keep silent. He knows the significance of meals (Prov 23:1; Sir. 8:1; 31:12) and how to deal with women (Prov 6:24; Sir 9:1). He makes the right friends (Sir 6:7), to whom he is loyal (Gen 39:9; Prov 25:13) and from whom he solicits advice (Prov 2:4). Consequently, Joseph governs with subtlety (Gen 42:9; 44:15) and pleases his patron, the pharaoh.

The wise learn from their experiences, even when those experiences are painful. Joseph is repeatedly put down and raised up—put to death and raised from the dead. When his brothers throw him down into a cistern (Gen 37:24), nomads raise him up. When the nomads sell him into slavery (Gen 37:25-28; 39:1), Potiphar raises him up. When Potiphar throws him into prison (Gen 39:20), Pharaoh raises him up to serve as vizier of Egypt. Joseph does not judge by appearances. He does not act with cynicism or betrayal, but looks beyond the superficial crisis and observes a divine plan for deliverance.

Wisdom guides the observant Joseph safely through one life-threatening situation after another. The Teachings of Joseph meticulously weave and reweave events, symbols, and dialogue around him to demonstrate how wisdom can turn strangers into covenant partners, the least into the greatest, famine into plenty, and death into life. These teachings became a textbook for monarchs in Israel, especially those who, like Joseph, rose to power over older candidates and who, like Joseph, struggled to build and maintain unity in the face of famine and war.

Like the books of Daniel (Daniel 1–6) and Esther, the Teachings of Joseph also became an inspiration for Jews living in foreign lands who wanted to survive, to succeed, to understand their exile as a call to take Yahweh's blessings to foreign lands.

The books of Proverbs, Ecclesiastes, and Job are timeless traditions with no fixed dates or places. Some teachings in the book of Job are as old as A Sufferer and the Soul from Egypt (2050–1800 B.C.E.) and Man and God from Sumer (2000 B.C.E.). In these traditions, the protagonist is innocent, yet suffers painful losses. These traditions are permeated with complaints about innocent suffering and about how to square belief in a Creator who is good with the existence of a world that is evil. None of the traditions answers the question of why the innocent suffer. Each is a theodicy that laments the suffering of the innocent, and how much such suffering affects the way humans understand their divine patrons. The book of Job reflects the way this tradition was told after the destruction of Jerusalem in 587 B.C.E. Like the Servant of Yahweh traditions (Isa

Hippopotamus Grazing Riverbank
(Dra Aboul Naga 2040–1640 B.C.E.; Faience 12.7 cm)

42:1-9; 49:1-6; 50:4-11; 52:13—53:12), the book of Job may have been an attempt to understand why Yahweh failed to protect Israel and Judah from their enemies.

The household of Job is from Uz (Gen 10:23; 22:21; 36:28; 1 Chr 1:17+42). Uz was a state in present-day Saudi Arabia, east of Edom in Jordan, and north of Sheba in Yemen. Uz may have been an important covenant partner of both Edom and Sheba between 1200 and 587 B.C.E. (Jer 49:8; Ezek 25:13). South of Uz lay Tema (Job 6:19) and the Dedan oasis along the Gulf of Aden on the Indian Ocean (Isa 21:13-14; Jer 25:23; Gen 10:7; 25:3). The people of Tema and Dedan were Sabeans from Sheba. After 750 B.C.E., the Sabeans migrated north into the desert. They operated a very productive trade route that exported incense from Sheba throughout the world of the Bible and into the western Mediterranean. The raids that destroyed the lands and herds of the household of Job may have resulted from a campaign mounted by Nabonidus of Babylon (555–539 B.C.E.) to conquer the Sabean trade highway between the Dedan oasis and Tema (Job 1:15-17).

Sometimes, the book of Job is called a "drama" or a "soliloquy." Denis Diderot (1713–84) and Pierre Augustin Caron (1732–99) first use the French word *drame* to describe their plays dealing with the life of the middle class. Today, a drama is any play that deals with significant human problems. A soliloquy is a speech in which characters, who are alone on stage, express their open and honest feelings. The soliloquy appears first in Greek and Roman plays, but playwrights in the England of Elizabeth I (1533–1603) fully developed the genre. Some of the most famous are the soliloquies of William Shakespeare (1564–1616) in *Hamlet*: "To be or not to be" and "How all occasions do inform against me," and in *Richard III*: "Now is the winter of our discontent." Although powerful renditions of the book of Job, like "J. B." by Archibald MacLeish (1892–1982) and "Masque of Reason" by Robert Frost (1874–1963), have appeared in western European cultures, the book of Job itself is neither a drama nor a soliloquy. Drama and soliloquy are western Mediterranean genres from the cultures of Greece and Rome. The book of Job is an eastern Mediterranean genre from the world of the Bible. The setting of the book of Job is not theatrical, it is judicial.

Technically, the book of Job is not a full-blown trial before the divine assembly, but a series of pretrial hearings. Job argues with Eliphaz, Bildad, and Zophar about whether or not to impeach Yahweh for breach of covenant. Impeachments charge public officials with misconduct. (Fig. 59)

The pretrial hearings open with a review of Job's credentials as an attorney (Job 1:1—2:13) followed by a review of the merits of Job's proposal to indict Yahweh (Job 3:1—42:6). The argument between Job, Eliphaz, Zophar, and Bildad is only over how to file the case. Job wants to indict Yahweh for breach of covenant. Eliphaz, Zophar, and Bildad want Job to confess to treason.

The book of Ezekiel (Ezek 14:12-20) considers Ezekiel, Job, Daniel, and Noah to be peers, even though Ezekiel is a prophet, Job is a teacher, Daniel is a seer, and Noah is a person primeval. After pronouncing sentence on Jerusalem, Yahweh warns Ezekiel not to appeal the ruling. Yahweh warns that even if Job, Noah, and Daniel went before the divine assembly to seek a mitigation of Jerusalem's sentence, they would be able to save only themselves, not even their households. As a peer of Daniel and Noah, Job is eminently qualified to serve the divine assembly in a trial of impeachment.

Every year the cosmos has to be re-created. As part of the celebration of the Akitu New Year, the divine assembly would meet and review the status of its covenant with each state. The struggle between the creator and chaos represented by creatures like the ostrich, the hippopotamus, and the crocodile took place, not only once at the beginning of time, but also at the beginning of each new year. The book of Job reminds its ancient audiences of the traditions that celebrate the Akitu New Year in order to question whether the new world coming into being will truly be a kinder and gentler place for the powerless than the old world that is coming to an end.

During the meetings of the divine assembly, the standard question is: "Have the people of Israel and Judah been faithful to their covenant with Yahweh?" Surprisingly, the question in the book of Job is: "Has Yahweh been faithful to the covenant with Israel and Judah?" The prophets always found the Hebrews guilty of failing to allow Yahweh to feed and to protect them. Famine and war were the consequences of their exaggerated self-reliance. Job, however, impeaches Yahweh for failing to feed and protect even the faithful like his own household, and proposes to sentence Yahweh to be deprived of all the faithful (Job 3:1-10).

The use of a judicial genre in the book of Job also indicts the prophets as coconspirators with Yahweh. The prophets taught the people of Israel and Judah that Yahweh protects the faithful. Job argues that Yahweh does not.

Credential Hearings
(JOB 1:1—2:13)

The Credential Hearings open with a reading of Job's portfolio (Job 1:1-5). The portfolio describes three qualities of Job: he is a stranger, he is wealthy, and he is liturgically observant.

First, Job is a stranger; he is from Uz, and not from Israel or Judah. The status of Job as an outsider gives him greater latitude than if he were a prophet in Judah like Isaiah or a teacher in Jerusalem like Qoheleth (Eccl 1:1). Job can discuss sacred subjects without being branded as a heretic. When Job brings up a subject such as the unfaithfulness of Yahweh, audiences would assume that Job simply does not know better. Nonetheless, they would applaud his willingness to voice their own unspoken concerns. Strangers can be outspoken with more impunity than members of the household. The book of Job also insulates Job from the repercussions of his prosecutor's role by only referring to the defendant as "Yahweh" three times (Job 1:22; 38:7; 40:2). Instead it refers to the defendant generically as "our Godparent."

Second, Job is wealthy. His household has strong fixed assets and potential for growth. The daughters and sons of the household are its potential for growth. They measure the household's ability to negotiate covenants that will be ratified by their marriages. The livestock and draft animals are its fixed assets. Both these fixed assets and the potential for growth are perfectly balanced. There are ten children: seven sons and three daughters. There are ten thousand livestock: seven thousand sheep and three thousand camels. There are one thousand draft animals: five hundred teams. These oxen are an indication of just how many heavy wagons the household of Job operates along its caravan routes. There are too many slaves to count. Slaves are an indication of just how many households are working off their debts to the household of Job. Each number is not so much an inventory, but a perfect number. This material abundance marks the household of Job as perfectly positioned to audit the worldview according to which it has succeeded.

Third, Job is liturgically observant. He offers sacrifice each day for his household. Material prosperity was the mark of a wise household for the teachers whose traditions are preserved in the books of Proverbs and Wisdom of Solomon. Liturgical observance was the mark of a clean household for the priests whose traditions are preserved in the books of Exodus, Leviticus, and Numbers (Lev 4:1-35). The labels "wise" and "clean" both identify households with honor, which not only feed and protect their own members, but contribute to the support of the village. Certifying the household of Job according to the traditions of both the teachers (Job 1:2-4) and the priests (Job 1:5) emphasizes that Job is qualified to serve as an attorney in an impeachment, regardless of what standard of evaluation the divine assembly employs. Like Louisiana lawyers

a. Credential hearings (Job 1:1—2:13)

  1) Job's portfolio (Job 1:1-5)

  2) hearings (Job 1:6—2:13)
    (a) first hearing (Job 1:6-22)
    (b) second hearing (Job 2:1-13)

b. Indictment hearings (Job 3:1—42:6)

  1) lament (Job 3:1-28)
    (1) petition (Job 3:1-19)
    (a) creation-story parody (Job 3:1-10)
      i. certificate for "man–child" (Job 3:3)
      ii. certificate for "darkness–light" (Job 3:4)
      iii. certificate for "gloom–darkness" (Job 3:5)
      iv. certificate for "days–months" (Job 3:6-7)
      v. certificate for "sea–Leviathan" (Job 3:8)
      vi. certificate for "stars–light" (Job 3:9-10)
    (2) complaint (Job 3:19-26)

  2) *legal arguments* (Job 4:1—42:6)
    (1) *first session* (Job 4:1—14:22)
    (a) first argument (Job 4:1—7:21)
      i. Eliphaz's opinion (Job 4:1—5:27)
      ii. Job's opinion (Job 6:1—7:21)
    (b) second argument (Job 8:1—10:22)
      i. Bildad's opinion (Job 8:1-22)
      ii. Job's opinion (Job 9:1—10:22)
    (c) third argument (Job 11:1—14:22)
      i. Zophar's opinion (Job 11:1-20)
      ii. Job's opinion (Job 12:1—14:22)
    (2) *second session* (Job 15:1—21:34)
    (a) first argument (Job 15:1—24:25)
      i. Eliphaz's opinion (Job 15:1-35)
      ii. Job's opinion (Job 16:1—17:16)
    (b) second argument (Job 18:1—19:29)
      i. Bildad's opinion (Job 18:1-21)
      ii. Job's opinion (Job 19:1-29)
    (c) third argument (Job 20:1—21:34)
      i. Zophar's opinion (Job 20:1-29)
      ii. Job's opinion (Job 21:1-34)
    (3) *third session* (Job 22:1—28:28)
    (a) first argument (Job 22:1—24:25)
      i. Eliphaz's opinion (Job 22:1-30)
      ii. Job's opinion (Job 23:1—24:25)

(continued)

(b) second argument (Job 25:1—27:21)
  i.   Bildad's opinion (Job 25:1-6)
  ii. Job's opinion (Job 26:1—27:21)
(c) third argument (Job 28:1—31:37)
  i. [Zophar's] opinion (Job 28:1-28)
  ii. Job's opinion (Job 29:1—31:39)

Colophon (Job 31:40b)
  (4) *fourth session—supplementary* (Job 32:1—42:6)
  (a) first argument (Job 32:1—37:34)
    i.   Elihu's opinion (Job 32:1—37:34)
    ii. Job's opinion (missing)
  (b) second argument (Job 38:1—40:5)
    i.   Yahweh's opinion (Job 38:1—39:30)
    ii. Job's opinion (Job 40:1-5)
  (c) third argument (Job 40:6—42:6)
    i.   Yahweh's opinion (Job 40:6—41:26)
    ii. Job's opinion (Job 42:1-6): Job withdraws his indictment with
         the words "therefore I despise myself and repent in dust and
         ashes" (Job 42:6).

  c. Endowment: Job's land and children, placed in a blind trust during the
     hearings, are returned to him (Job 42:7-17)

FIGURE 59   Patterns in the Book of Job: A Pretrial Hearing (Job 1:1—42:17)

today, who must know both Roman Law or the Napoleonic Code, which sets the standards in Louisiana courts, and the English Common Law, which governs jurisprudence
in the other states, Job knows and practices both what the teachers and the priests
expect of the faithful.

Job's status as a stranger, as wealthy, and as liturgically observant establishes his
credentials as an attorney immune from prosecution, and eminently qualified to appear
before the divine assembly to argue that Yahweh does not protect the faithful.

Once the divine assembly hears the portfolio of Job, it hears from the Satan who
"goes to and fro on the earth . . . walking up and down on it" (Job 1:7), in order to evaluate the covenants that the divine assembly has negotiated. The Satan is not the devil,
but a member in good standing of the divine assembly. Only after the conquest of the
world of the Bible by Alexander in 332 B.C.E. did both biblical and nonbiblical traditions begin identifying the snake in the Stories of Adam and Eve (Gen 2:25—4:2) and
the Satan here and in the book of Zechariah (Zech 3:1-2) as the devil. Originally, the
snake and the Satan are quality-control engineers, like Qoheleth (Eccl 1:12-13) and the

"riders" (Zech 1:7-17). They continually audit the cosmos, not to tempt and to destroy it, but to see that the stipulations of the covenant are met. They guarantee the quality of Yahweh's estate. The Satan proposes to audit the household of Job to see if its faithfulness is genuine or simply self-serving.

The standard audit has a mandate, which describes the purpose of the investigation, a report on the sample taken or spot-check conducted (Eccl 3:1-8), and an evaluation of the results (Eccl 3:9-15). The report often cites a proverb from the wisdom tradition that the evaluation grades by stressing its limitations. Here the Satan proposes a wager. The metaphor is not irreverent; it is anthropomorphic.

Gambling is a form of divination that appears in virtually every culture. Gambling allows humans and their divine patrons to communicate with one another. The game is not a diversion. Gambling is a microcosm for the creative tension that characterizes the relationship between human beings and their divine patrons. The hearing on the credentials of Job portrays Yahweh gambling with the other members of the divine assembly as if they were the men of a village in Israel or Judah. The players in the game are Job, his wife, and the Satan.

The wife of Job and the Satan are the prosecuting attorneys, who call the worldview in the book of Proverbs into question. The prosecutor during these credential hearings is Job's wife. She advises Job to curse (Job 2:9; 1 Kgs 21:10-13; Ps 10:3) his divine patron, and to die as a punishment for the sacrilege (Job 2:7-10). Her advice reflects one tradition on suffering, which teaches that sufferers bring suffering on themselves. Therefore they can stop suffering if they wish.

The most painful aspect of suffering for human beings is losing control. To some extent, suicide gives the suffering an illusion of regaining control of the situation. Job defends the worldview in the book of Proverbs, in which the wise prosper and fools perish. Job's performance as a defense attorney demonstrates his thorough understanding of the worldview that he will prosecute in the hearings on his indictment of Yahweh. Job responds to his wife and the Satan by wisely saying that humans must accept evil from their divine patron just as they accept good.

Three of Job's covenant partners come to mourn for him (Job 6:15). Here in the credential hearings they are silent. They share his suffering without trying to explain it.

The first audit evaluates the proverb: "Households bless a divine patron who blesses their land and children, but they curse a divine patron who curses their land and children" (Job 1:9-11). Job witnesses the loss of all his land and children in four attacks. In the world of the Bible, "four" is the number of misfortunes similar to "three strikes, and you're out" in North America (2 Sam 24:10-17; Prov 30:15). Bad news in the Bible comes from every direction—north, south, east, and west—all at once.

Yahweh is the agent of two of the attacks against the household of Job; humans are the agents of the other two. The lightning of Yahweh strikes Job's herders, scattering his sheep, and a windstorm destroys a house of Job, killing his sons and daughters. Rustlers murder Job's cattlemen to steal his oxen and asses, and kill Job's drivers to rustle his camels.

One of the traditional ways of coping with suffering is to develop an attitude of stewardship rather than ownership. Job prostrates himself before Yahweh to show that he is a steward, not an owner. His children and property belong to Yahweh. Yahweh only gives humans land and children temporarily. Eventually, all land and children must be returned to Yahweh.

The Satan proposes another audit of Job. The Satan tells the divine assembly that the reason Job has not sinned is because he himself was spared. The second audit evaluates the proverb: "Fathers of a household continue to bless a divine patron who curses only their land and children, but they curse a divine patron who curses them personally" (Job 1:4-5).

The second audit is different from the first audit, but not necessarily more difficult. It is not necessarily easier to suffer than to watch a loved one suffer. Therefore, the first audit may, in fact, be more difficult than the second. Job's response to this second audit is parallel to his response to the first. He observes that all humans are born helpless, and that they die helpless. Health is gift, not a right.

Indictment Hearings
(JOB 3:1 — 42:17)

Indictment
(JOB 3:1-28)

The hearings on Job's proposal open with his statement of the indictment. Job argues that, contrary to the assurances of the wisdom tradition as expressed in the book of Proverbs, Yahweh in fact allows the innocent to suffer.

Here Job is no longer a defense attorney as he was in the credential hearings. Now he is the prosecutor, who reviews his case with Eliphaz, Bildad, Zophar, and then with Elihu and with Yahweh, the defendant.

The roles of Eliphaz, Bildad, and Zophar here are also different from their roles in the credential hearings. In the credential hearings they are mourners; in the indictment hearings they are auditors like Qoheleth (Eccl 1:12-18) or the Queen of Sheba (1 Kgs 10:1-10), who "seek and search out by wisdom all that is done under heaven" (Eccl 1:13). Bildad comes from Shuah in eastern Arabia, Zophar from Naamah in southern Arabia, and Eliphaz from Tema in western Arabia. As a three-member, blue-ribbon commission, Eliphaz, Bildad, and Zophar now have the responsibility of auditing Job's charge that Yahweh is guilty of breach of covenant. They bring to their task a world of wisdom.

Lament
(JOB 3:1-26)

Job argues that Yahweh and the divine assembly commissioned humans as their "image" (Gen 1:24-31), but then abandoned them to lives of slavery like the aborigines in the Enuma Elish Stories or the *lullu* in the Atrahasis Stories from Mesopotamia. Job places this indictment before his covenant partners in a powerfully worded lament like those in the book of Psalms. The lament portrays Yahweh as inhospitable for not welcoming Job and other humans into the world. Job then petitions the divine assembly to relieve his suffering by removing his birth date from the calendar. Jeremiah (Jer 20:14-18), Elijah (1 Kgs 19:4), and Jonah (Jonah 4:3-8) also curse the days of their birth. Similarly, Ben Sira teaches students to behave as if their parents are always present, "lest you be deemed a fool on account of your habits; then you will wish that you had never been born, and you will curse the day of your birth" (Sir 23:14).

Laments have five parts. There is a petition to Yahweh for a hearing before the divine assembly (Ps 3:7). There is a complaint explaining the injustice suffered by the household (Ps 44:10-17). There is a vow that the household makes to publicly recommit itself to Yahweh as its divine patron if the loss is restored (Ps 137:4-6). There is a declaration of innocence that explains why the household should not continue to suffer (Ps 22:9-10). There is a confession of faith in Yahweh as the divine deliverer of the household (Ps 22:3-50). Few laments have all five components, and there is no standard sequence for the components. The Lament of Job contains only two components. There is a petition (Job 3:1-19) and a complaint (Job 3:20-26).

Job wants to be delivered stillborn, or to be offered as a child sacrifice. Job repeats the petition in more than one way. Job petitions Yahweh to tell his life story backwards. When the story reaches his birthday, Job wants Yahweh to abort it. Job never wants to see light (Jer 20:14-18; 1 Kgs 19:4; Jonah 4:3, 8; Sir 23:14). Job does not want to hear: "A child is born!" (Job 3:3), but to have a birthday with "no shout of joy . . . heard in it" (Job 3:7). Job does not want to hear: "Let there be light" (Gen 1:3), but to have a birthday that is dark (Job 3:5).

Life begins not with the physical process of birth, but rather with the legal process of adoption. Only those for whom a midwife announces "A child is born!" (Job 3:3), and who are laid in the lap of their adoptive parent to nurse (Job 3:12) are alive. Regardless of the clinical status of the fetus at the moment of delivery, without adoption it is stillborn (Ezek 16:4-5). The lament evokes powerful feelings of pity, tenderness, and sympathy in its audience. Job complains that the adoption covenant was not fulfilled.

Although the sequence of events described in the Lament of Job is similar to the sequence of events in the Creation of the Heavens and the Earth, the two are not identical. The birth certificate for humans concludes the sixth day in the book of Genesis, whereas the death certificate inaugurates the first day in the book of Job. There are other differences. The Lament of Job does not refer to the birth of earth and sea (Gen 1:9-13), and the Creation of the Heavens and the Earth alludes to the birth of stars and light (Gen 1:16), but does not assign them a separate birthday comparable to day six in the book of Job (Job 3:9-10).

Although pregnancy is universally a time of happiness, the parody in the Lament of Job turns his mother's pregnancy into a time of suffering. The same reversal appears in the sentence that Isaiah pronounces on Ahaz (Isa 7:1-25), who must watch the pregnancy of his wife, and then the birth and rearing of his son, Immanuel, not with joy, but with sadness.

The Creation of the Heavens and the Earth concludes six days of labor by endowing the cosmos with the Sabbath on the seventh day. Job concludes his petition to reverse the six days of creation with a request that the cosmos be endowed, not with the Sabbath, but with Sheol. "Sheol" is the Hebrew word for the depths of the earth where the dead assemble (Deut 32:22; Amos 9:2; Prov 9:18). It is the counterpart of Hades and Tartarus in the western Mediterranean traditions. Sheol is the antithesis of Sabbath. The rest characteristic of Sabbath is creative; the rest of Sheol is abortive. It is a sensual vacuum. There is no joy, and there is no sadness. Death makes no distinctions. It is the absolute democracy. The Lament of Job does not romanticize a political system. It simply petitions Yahweh to stop the violence so that powerful rulers, teachers, chiefs, and slave owners will no longer be able to hurt their powerless citizens, students, warriors, and slaves.

Legal Arguments
(JOB 4:1 — 42:6)

First Session
(JOB 4:1 — 14:22)

In the legal arguments (Job 4:1—31:40) that follow the Lament of Job, Eliphaz, Zophar, and Bildad object strongly to his proposal to indict Yahweh for breach of covenant. Today, attorneys are expected to answer one another directly. The logic of trials today is linear. Linear logic proceeds like snapping one Lego to another. Linear logic, however, can be provocative. The logic in the book of Job is circular. It proceeds like rolling up a hose. During these pretrial depositions, Eliphaz, Zophar, and Bildad argue past one another. Although English translations say: "then Eliphaz answered" or "then Job answered," there is often no direct connection between the remarks of one and the remarks of the other. Nonetheless, by the time the hearing has ended, they have thoroughly discussed whether or not the innocent suffer and, consequently, whether or not Job should impeach Yahweh for breach of covenant.

In the first session (Job 4:1—7:21), Eliphaz argues that Job suffers because of his sins, and that his only hope is in repentance (Job 4:1—5:27). Job is equally passionate that his suffering is not phantom pain. It is real pain, and it is caused by Yahweh. What Job does not know is why Yahweh is causing his suffering (Job 6:1—7:21). Bildad argues that Job's hope lies in confessing his guilt to a lesser offense and plea-bargaining with Yahweh for the greater offenses (Job 8:1-22). The objections of Eliphaz, Zophar, and Bildad reflect the wide range of traditions in the world of the Bible that developed to explain the suffering of the innocent. Job is quite clear that all of these explanations for the suffering of the innocent are inadequate.

Second Session
(JOB 15:1—21:34)

In the second session, Eliphaz, Bildad, and Zophar remind Job that the guilty are punished, if not immediately, then in due time. Eliphaz argues that Job is shortsighted (Job 15:7-10). He is too young, too inexperienced to have seen that, eventually, the guilty suffer. Eliphaz wants Job to wait and see that, in fact, the guilty get what is coming to them. Bildad seconds the argument of Eliphaz. It is the guilty, and not the innocent, who suffer (Job 15:8-21). Zophar concedes that the wicked are successful, but then points out that their success is temporary (Job 20:4). Only the success of the innocent lasts.

Job argues that the innocent do not become guilty when they protest their suffering. Job points out that he continues to suffer, whether or not he protests (Job 16:6). Job also argues that whether or not he personally protests, his suffering itself cries out to the divine assembly for justice (Job 16:19). Furthermore, he indicts Eliphaz, Bildad, Zophar, and even his wife (Job 19:17) for making him suffer rather than helping him understand his suffering.

Third Session
(JOB 22:1—28:28)

When Zophar speaks the third time, he sings a hymn praising Yahweh for the wisdom of creation (Job 28:1-28). This hymn is not a later insertion into the book of Job, but yet another perspective on why the innocent suffer. The hymn is an almost unique contribution to the survey of traditions that explain the suffering of the innocent. The hymn does not refer to the personal experiences of Job, but simply argues that wisdom is accessible only to Yahweh. "Where does wisdom live? Where is the sanctuary of understanding?" (Job 28:12). Yahweh makes a similar assumption during the fourth session (Job 38:2—40:2). The other explanations discussed consider wisdom accessible to humans.

The hymn reminds its audience that humans can mine metals and gems hidden deep in the earth, but still find no trace of wisdom. To understand wisdom would be to understand Yahweh, and Yahweh cannot be understood by humans. Therefore only Yahweh knows why the innocent suffer. It is not a problem to be solved, but a mystery with which humans must live. For the book of Job, the paradox of innocent suffering is only one example of the paradox in all life. Therefore, the wise must search for Yahweh in nature and beyond it; encounter Yahweh directly and through messengers; and realize that Yahweh never changes, and yet is moved by human prayers.

Fourth Session
(Job 32:1—42:6)

Originally, there were only three sessions in the indictment hearings (Job 4:1—31:37). Now, there are four (Job 32:1—42:17). The speeches of Elihu (Job 32:1—37:24) and the speeches of Yahweh (Job 40:7—41:26) developed separately from the speeches of Eliphaz, Bildad, and Zophar. Unlike Eliphaz, Bildad, and Zophar, who are from Edom, Elihu is from Israel. In the first three sessions, Eliphaz, Bildad, and Zophar take turns giving opinions on Job's proposal to impeach Yahweh. In the fourth session, Elihu renders an opinion (Job 32:1—37:34). Yet neither the advice of the wise outside Israel nor the wise inside Israel adequately explains why the innocent suffer. Even though the book of Job assembles a team of experts with impeccable credentials, the question remains inscrutable.

Job does not respond to Elihu, but Yahweh immediately gives the second (Job 38:1—39:30) and third opinions (Job 40:6—42:17) in the fourth session. Yahweh does not explain why the innocent suffer, but teaches Job how to understand the cosmos by using an in-depth study of a single creature (Job 40:6—41:26). Yahweh teaches Job that humans are not the center of the universe, but that the wise carefully observe creation to understand its creator. Every creature is a microcosm of the cosmos. No one can observe the cosmos as a whole, but everyone has an observable universe in a single creature like the hippopotamus (Job 40:15) or the crocodile (Job 40:25), two creatures representing the once fearsome Mesopotamia and Egypt. The wise can see that these creatures, which were once out-of-control or chaos, are now in-control or cosmos. If the hippopotamus and the crocodile are in good order, then the rest of the cosmos must be in good order. The lesson does not explain why the innocent suffer, but simply argues that if everything else in the cosmos makes sense, surely the suffering of the innocent must make sense.

After very gently advising Job, Yahweh is unexpectedly harsh with Eliphaz, Bildad, and Zophar for their uncritical loyalty to the tradition in the book of Proverbs, and for their hostility to Job. In the book of Proverbs, the wise are unquestioning. In the books of Job and Ecclesiastes, the wise ask good questions. The books of Job and Ecclesiastes do not destroy the book of Proverbs, but they do want to put it into perspective. The wise, like Job, who ask questions, are neither disloyal nor destructive. They want the tradition in the book of Proverbs to do what it promised: to help humans meet the challenges of remaining alive. The blind obedience of Eliphaz, Zophar, and Bildad is a living death.

The book of Job never explains why the innocent suffer, but it does present an experience of how many questions the suffering of the innocent raises for people of faith. A variety of traditions dealing with the suffering of the innocent is carefully audited. All are valuable. None is definitive. By charging Yahweh with breach of covenant, Job clearly demonstrates that the worldview of the Bible is only a partial, not a definitive, answer to the questions that the suffering of the innocent raises. This audit prevents both presumption and despair. Too much confidence in the assumptions on which any culture exists is reckless. Too little confidence creates hopelessness.

Eliphaz, Zophar, and Bildad argue that if the innocent suffer, then Yahweh is neither good nor powerful. Job argues that the innocent suffer, and that Yahweh knows why. He does not question the goodness or the power of Yahweh, but the silence of Yahweh. Suffering is part of human life. Fools like Eliphaz, Zophar, and Bildad argue that the innocent do not suffer. The wise like Job recognize that the innocent do suffer. Suffering does not distinguish the innocent from the guilty. Suffering is the experience of both the innocent and the guilty.

Having completed his argument, Job withdraws his charges against Yahweh (Job 42:1-6). Eliphaz, Bildad, Zophar, Elihu, and Yahweh have all listened to Job's complaint. The suffering of the innocent has been fully discussed, even though the question remains unresolved. Nothing more can be accomplished by taking the matter to trial. Job has had his say, and is satisfied.

Job rests his case with a prayer in which he and Yahweh speak to one another. The words clearly characterize Job as a believer, not a cynic. His argument complete, Job revokes his status as a special prosecutor.

Job:

I believe that you, our Creator, can do all things,
No purpose of yours can be thwarted.

Yahweh:

Who do you think you are?
Why hide the wisdom of my creation behind such foolish questions?

Job:

I have tried to explain the inexplicable.
I have tried to describe the indescribable.

Yahweh:

> Listen to me, I will teach,
> You will learn.

Job:

> My ears have heard of you,
> Now my eyes see you.
> Therefore, I humble myself,
> I repent in dust and ashes. (Job 42:1-6)

Yahweh accepts Job's decision as a wise decision. Job knows when to speak out and when to be silent. In contrast, Eliphaz, Bildad, and Zophar are fools who try to explain the suffering of the innocent. The virtue of Job is not in his wealth, but rather in being able to discipline his speech. Job knows when to speak and when to listen.

Entitlement Hearing
(JOB 42:7-17)

In preparation for the hearings, Job's land and children were not so much "killed," "stolen," or "destroyed," but rather "taken away" from him and placed in a blind trust. By placing them in this trust, Job waives control of these assets in order to avoid a conflict of interest while prosecuting Yahweh for breach of covenant. Once the hearings are over, and once Job has decided not to proceed with a formal trial, the land and children of his household are restored with interest (Job 42:12-16). Admittedly, the land and children that Job loses during the hearings on his credentials are not identical with the land and children that Job recovers after the hearings.

Job may have used his own three-point strategy to survive the loss of his land and children. First, Job argues that humans can survive suffering by understanding their lives as a blessing, rather than a wage (Job 1:21). Second, Job argues that humans can also survive suffering by understanding human responsibility for land and children as stewardship, rather than ownership (Job 2:10). Third, Job argues that humans can survive suffering only by admitting that the innocent suffer. Suffering does not call into question the goodness or the power of Yahweh, and suffering is not a symptom of guilt. Suffering is the inevitable experience of being human.

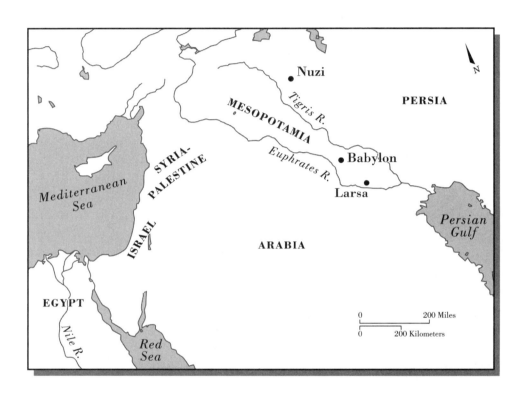

Points of Interest (Chapter 8)

8

BOOK OF PSALMS

(Pss 1:1—150:6)

The book of Psalms (Hebrew: *Tehillim*) is a summary of the Bible. The psalms reflect all of the major traditions that developed in ancient Israel. Some psalms summarize creation stories in the books of Genesis and Exodus. Some retell the hero stories in the books of Joshua-Judges. Others reflect the Stories of David's Rise to Power from the books of Samuel-Kings. There are psalms that teach like the book of Proverbs, and there are psalms that revisit the trials of the prophets. Finally, there are apocalyptic psalms that describe the death of an old world and the creation of a new world from the books of Isaiah and Ezekiel and Daniel. Rabbis emphasized the character of the book of Psalms as a summary of the Bible by dividing it into five parts (Pss 1–41; Pss 42–72; Pss 73–89; Pss 90–106; Pss 107–50) just as the Torah is divided into five parts—Genesis, Exodus, Leviticus, Numbers, Deuteronomy (*Midrash Tehillim* on Psalm 1).

One psalm in the book of Psalms is dedicated to Moses (Psalm 90), one to Heman (Psalm 88), and one to Ethan (Psalm 89). Two psalms are dedicated to Solomon (Pss 27, 127). Nine psalms are dedicated to Asaph (Psalms 74–82). Twelve psalms are dedicated to Korah (Ps 42, 43, 44, 45, 46, 47, 48, 49, 84, 85, 87, 88). Seventy-three psalms are dedicated to David. David's patronage of the book of Psalms develops from the story of his rise to power in the books of Samuel-Kings, where David is introduced as a harp player, whose skill relaxes Saul, his volatile patron. David also sings a psalm as his last will and testament (2 Sam 23:1-7).

There are 150 psalms in the book of Psalms. Just as the twelve tribes are named in more than one way, the psalms are also combined and divided in more than one way. For example, four of the five hymns that conclude each part of the book of Psalms are attached to the psalms that precede them, and are not separately numbered. Only the final hymn is numbered separately (Psalm 150). Some numbered psalms are made up of more than one psalm (Ps 9, 66, 147). Some psalms are repeated and are numbered separately (Psalms 14, 53). Sometimes a single psalm is divided into two psalms (Psalms 1–2; 9–10).

Technically, the words "psalm," "song," or "poem" do not refer to a genre or literary pattern, but rather to a literary technique that can be used in any genre. The language in every genre has tempo or sound quality. A psalm, song, or poem is a tradition in which the tempo is pronounced. English increases the tempo by rhyming the ends of lines. Semitic languages increase tempo with a type of repetition called "parallelism." There are two basic kinds of psalms: hymns and laments.

The book of Psalms is not the only collection of psalms in the Bible. There is a wonderful collection of psalms in the book of Isaiah (Isa 56:1—66:24), and there is a powerful series of seven laments in the book of Jeremiah (Jer 11:18-23; 12:1-6; 15:10-21; 17:14-18; 18:18-23; 20:7-13; 20:14-18). Individual psalms also appear elsewhere throughout the Bible (Genesis 49; Deuteronomy 33; 1 Sam 2:1-10; 2 Sam 22:2-51; Isa 63:7—64:12; Sir 51:1-30; Proverbs 1–9; Jonah 2:3-9). The Greek Bible (LXX) and the Dead Sea Scrolls include not only the 150 psalms in the Hebrew Bible, but also an additional hymn in which David praises Yahweh for his victory over Goliath (Psalm 151).

Teachings

Teaching on Prayer
(Ps 1:1-6)

In the world of the Bible, prayer never began abruptly. There was always a short, formal instruction, admonishing those who wished to pray on the seriousness of the work that they were about to begin, and the behavior that they must carefully observe when they crossed the threshold into the sanctuary. Today, the Liturgy of the Hours prepares Christian monks and nuns for prayer with the words: "O Lord, open my lips, and my mouth will proclaim your praise. God, come to my assistance. Lord, make haste to help me." The Qur'an prepares Muslims for prayer with the words of the *Al-Fatihah:* "In the name of Allah, the beneficent, the merciful. Praise be to Allah, Lord of the worlds, the beneficent, the merciful, owner of the day of judgment. You alone we worship. You alone we ask for help. Show us the straight path, the path of those whom you have favored, not the path of those who earn your anger, nor of those who go astray." In part one of the book of Psalms, there are three psalms that prepared the Hebrews for prayer and taught them how to pray (Ps 1:1-6; 15:1-5; 24:1-10). The book of Psalms opens with

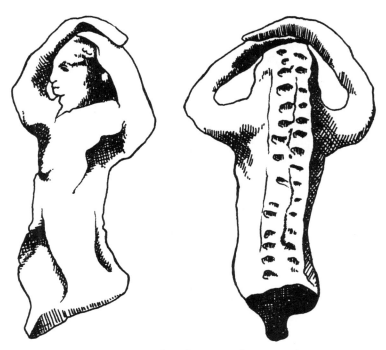

Mourners Strike Their Heads in Grief
(Tell 'Aitun 1200–1100 B.C.E.; terra cotta)

the first of these teachings on prayer. This teaching is composed of three analogies. One analogy is an adage; two are proverbs (Fig. 60).

An analogy is a genre in which something known is used to teach something unknown. It is the most common genre in the book of Proverbs. An analogy that compares the known with the unknown is an "adage." An analogy that contrasts the known with the unknown is a "proverb."

Each line in an analogy is called a "colon." These lines are combined like a child's Legos into sets of two or three. The lines mirror or parallel one another by comparison or contrast. Parallelism is the identifying characteristic of all psalms in Hebrew and other Semitic languages.

The adage in the Teaching on Prayer is composed of five beatitudes (Ps 1:1-2). There are three beatitudes in the first line, and two in the second. The first three beatitudes are expressed negatively: "Wise are those who do not walk with the wicked" (Ps 1:1). The second three are expressed positively: "Wise are those who obey the law of Yahweh" (Ps 1:2).

"Blessed" or "happy" are the words that most translations use in beatitudes that are expressed positively. To be "blessed" is to be "wise." The wise have status or honor. Only

adage

> *Wise are those who do not walk with the wicked . . .*
> > *Wise are those who do not stand with sinners . . .*
> > *Wise are those who do not sit with fools . . .*
>
> *Wise are those who obey the law of Yahweh.*
> > *Wise are those who meditate on it day and night.*

proverb

> *The wise are like trees planted by water.*
> > *They yield fruit every season.*
>
> *Their leaves do not wither.*
> > *They thrive year after year.*
>
> *Not so fools,*
> > *Not so.*
>
> *Fools are like chaff.*
> > *They are blown away by the wind.*

proverb

> *Fools never stand in the gates of the city,*
> > *Sinners never sit with the village assembly.*
>
> *Yahweh protects the way of the wise.*
> > *Neither fools nor sinners shall stand in their way.*
>
> *Yahweh protects the way of the wise,*
> > *The way of fools Yahweh leaves unguarded.*

FIGURE 60   Teaching on Prayer (Ps 1:1-6)

the wise can survive and are admitted to the sanctuary where all the households in the clan come to pray. The adage reminds those about to pray that they should not "walk with the wicked . . . stand with sinners," or "sit with fools" (Ps 1:1). Only those who "obey the law of Yahweh" and "who meditate on it day and night" (Ps 1:2) are prepared to pray (Mic 6:8). The same motif appears in the book of Deuteronomy and in other psalms (Deut 30:15-20; Ps 19:7-13; 119:1-176).

The first proverb in the teaching contrasts the wise, who are "trees planted by water" (Ps 1:3) with fools, who are "chaff . . . blown away by the wind" (Ps 1:4). The wise are blessed. Fools are cursed. Because fools have no status and are shamed, they cannot survive. They cannot feed and protect their own households, and they cannot contribute to the support of households at risk in the tribe. The teaching does not say that fools will not prosper, but rather that the prosperity of fools will not last. The prosperity of fools appears quickly, but disappears as soon as the wind blows. The prosperity of the wise is slow in coming. It takes time for their roots to reach the water table. Yet, when they begin to bloom, they bloom season after season.

The second proverb contrasts fools who cannot stand, sit, or walk with the wise, who have Yahweh as a companion to watch over them wherever they go. It uses a chiasm or frame. "Yahweh protects (A), the way of the wise (B), the way of fools (B'), Yahweh leaves unguarded (A')." The first phrase in the first line is parallel to the second phrase in the second line, and the second phrase in the first line is parallel to the first phrase in the second line.

Hymns

Most hymns have two components. There is a call to worship and a creation story. There are, however, hymns in which the call to worship is repeated like an antiphon or chorus throughout the creation story (Psalm 66), or at the beginning and the end of the creation story (Psalm 136). There are also hymns that have only a call to worship, and no creation story (Psalm 150:1-6), or a creation story and no call to worship (Psalm 23).

Calls to worship challenge their audiences to praise and acknowledge Yahweh as their divine patron who delivered them from slavery and endowed them with land and children. The standard call is "Praise Yahweh!" or "Alleluia." These calls are best translated in the imperative. Therefore, "Bless Yahweh!" captures the sense of a call to worship better than "Blessed be Yahweh!" When it appears in a call to worship the Hebrew word "bless" does not mean something that the Hebrews do for Yahweh, but rather calls on the Hebrews to acknowledge what Yahweh has done for them. Other verbs like "Come!" "Sing!" "Shout!" "Give thanks!" "Extol!" are also calls to worship.

Hymn
(Ps 8:1-9)

The creation story in a hymn offers a rationale or explanation why the community should acknowledge Yahweh as its divine patron. It is Yahweh who acts, but it is the

Hebrews who must tell the story. The two most common creation stories describe Yahweh as creator and as warrior. As creator, Yahweh builds the cosmos. As warrior, Yahweh delivers the Hebrews from slavery. For the Hebrews, Yahweh was ruler both of nature and of history.

A hymn in part one of the book of Psalms (Ps 8:1-9) calls on the heavens and the earth to worship Yahweh as their divine patron (Fig. 61). This call to worship frames (Ps 8:1+9) a story of Yahweh creating the heavens, creating humans, and creating the animals (Ps 8:2-8).

The story contrasts the power of Yahweh with the powerlessness of the creatures that Yahweh uses. The battle cry of the enemies of Israel is silenced by a newborn's wailing to be nursed. Yahweh gently slides the planets, the moon, the sun, and the stars into place with only the tip of a finger. Then the hymn asks: "Given this penchant of Yahweh to use the powerless to do works requiring such great power, should it surprise anyone that Yahweh creates humans from clay to steward all creation?" Yahweh entrusts creation to the care of humans not because of their power, but precisely because of their powerlessness (Gen 1:26).

Hymn
(Ps 23:1-6)

Perhaps the most often prayed psalm in the Bible today is a Hymn to Yahweh as a Shepherd (Ps 23:1-6). This hymn is a powerful reminder that Yahweh is a companion whose "goodness and kindness" (Ps 23:6) are close at hand, not just in good times, but at all times (Fig. 62). The hymn also reminds those who sing it that human life is both a challenge or "valley of darkness" (Ps 23:4), and a paradise or "green pastures" (Ps 23:1). Human life is neither all bad nor all good.

Those who sing the hymn are not a herd of sheep, but the fathers of the households in a clan. The hymn is not a fable, which casts nonhuman characters like plants and animals as if they were humans. It is missing one important characteristic of fable, which is satire. The standard fable technique not only gives plants and animals human qualities, but also develops its plot as a quarrel or dispute. Although fables were very popular in Egypt and Mesopotamia, only a few appear in the Bible. A Trial of Jotham (Judg 9:8-15) casts the Hebrews as trees in search of a ruler. Their candidates are an olive tree, a fig tree, a grapevine, and a thornbush (Deut 8:8). The fable is a satirical portrayal of monarchs as being as useless as thornbushes. No tree with any socially redeeming value, like the olive, the fig, or the grape, would consider becoming a monarch in Israel. The fable technique is simply too rare in the Bible, and virtually unparalleled in the book of Psalms, to assume that it appears in this hymn.

call to worship

> Proclaim Yahweh on earth!
> > Glorify our divine patron in the heavens!

creation story

> Powerless newborns cry out like warriors against
> > your enemies,
> > The wail of helpless infants silences your foes.

> The heavens are the work of only your little finger,
> > The moon and the stars you set effortlessly in place.

> Is it surprising that you choose humans?
> > Should any be amazed that you should shape
> > creatures of clay?

> To be second only to the divine assembly,
> > To be crowned with glory and honor?

> That you made them stewards over the works of your hands,
> > That you put all things under their feet:

> All sheep and oxen,
> > All the wild beasts.

> The birds of the air,
> > The fish and everything which swims in the sea?

call to worship

> Proclaim Yahweh on earth!

FIGURE 61   Hymn (Ps 8:1-9)

The fathers celebrate Yahweh as a contract herder whose household faithfully fulfills the covenant that it has negotiated to care for the sheep, even when they are being grazed, out of sight, at their dry-season pastures. The Bible regularly describes Israel's relationship with Yahweh as a covenant.

The hymn catalogs the same kind of responsibilities described in the covenants between households and shepherds that archaeologists have recovered at Larsa and Nuzi.

creation story

> When Yahweh is shepherd of my household, I shall not want.
>   Yahweh grazes its sheep in green pastures;
>
> Yahweh leads them to still waters;
>   Yahweh restores my life.
>
> Yahweh leads the sheep in right paths
>   For the sake of the name of Yahweh.
>
> Even though the sheep walk in the valley of darkness,
>   I fear no evil;
>
> For Yahweh is always with me;
>   Your rod and your staff protect me.
>
> You prepare a table before me;
>   You set a table in the presence of my enemies;
>
> You anoint my head with oil;
>   My cup overflows.
>
> Surely goodness and kindness shall follow me
>   All the days of my life;
>
> My household shall dwell in the house of Yahweh
>   My whole life long.

FIGURE 62   Hymn (Ps 23:1-6)

Larsa was a Middle Bronze period (2000—1550 B.C.E.) city in southern Mesopotamia. It was located near Ash Shatrah on the Euphrates River about two hundred miles south of Baghdad. Nuzi is a Late Bronze–period city (1550—1200 B.C.E.) near Kirkuk, about 150 miles north of Baghdad.

Yahweh is a faithful herder with "goodness and kindness." Yahweh does not run at the first sign of trouble, but remains with the sheep. Yahweh skillfully grazes the hungry animals and "restores life." Yahweh knows "the right paths" from the village to pasture and water during the dry season. Yahweh knows how to feed the hungry. The hymn also celebrates Yahweh for knowing how to protect the animals from harm. Unlike Abel, whom Cain accuses of getting lost and therefore not being worthy of the name "shepherd," Yahweh does not wander off (Gen 4:9-10). The "valley of darkness" through which Yahweh leads the animals describes the dangers that can lead to the loss of herd animals. As long as Yahweh is the herder, the sheep are safe. They "dwell in the house of Yahweh," not because they are in the temple, but because they are cared for by Yahweh, who is a good shepherd.

Hymn
(Ps 150:1-6)

A Hymn to Yahweh as Creator and Warrior, which closes part five in the book of Psalms (Ps 150:1-6), creates a litany of calls to worship. Twelve times the hymn calls on its audience to "Praise Yahweh!" Each of the tribes of Israel is challenged to acknowledge Yahweh as its divine patron (Fig. 63). The opening and closing lines of the hymn, "Praise Yahweh!" (Ps 150:1), "Let every living creature praise Yahweh" (Ps 150:6), frame the other five sets of parallel lines in the hymn.

The creation story in the hymn celebrates Yahweh for making a home or sanctuary in the land with the people, and for pitching the heavens like a tent over the heads of the people. It then celebrates Yahweh for the great works that delivered the Hebrews from slavery. The books of Exodus and Deuteronomy describe the great works of Yahweh in Egypt, the books of Joshua and Judges the great works of Yahweh in Syria-Palestine, and the book of Isaiah the great works of Yahweh in Mesopotamia. In each, Yahweh delivers the Hebrews from slavery to their enemies and blesses them with land and children. This hymn challenges the Hebrews to retell these great stories, not just in words, but in music and in dance as well. The same eight wind, string, and percussion instruments that led the Hebrews into battle against their enemies are to be played in victory.

Although rulers and their priests led their people in the singing of psalms during worship in ancient Israel, hymns may have originally been sung by midwives during birth. These women were the guardians of the threshold that newborns crossed to enter the human plane. Midwives marked the transition with a hymn. Midwives washed, anointed, and swaddled children, after which they placed them on the lap of the mother of the adopting household. As mothers accepted their newborns, midwives affirmed the adoption by intoning a hymn inviting the household to praise Yahweh, who created the earth, who delivered the Hebrews from slavery, and who had now endowed this child with land and children.

call to worship

> Praise Yahweh!
>
> Praise Yahweh inside the sanctuary,
>   Praise Yahweh out-of-doors.
>
> Praise Yahweh who delivers us from slavery,
>   Praise Yahweh for blessing us with land.
>
> Praise Yahweh with trumpets,
>   Praise Yahweh with lyres and harps.
>
> Praise Yahweh with timbrels and in dance,
>   Praise Yahweh with strings and pipes.
>
> Praise Yahweh with castanets,
>   Praise Yahweh with cymbals.
>
> Let every living creature praise Yahweh!

FIGURE 63   Hymn (Ps 150:1-6)

Laments

Mourners were the midwives of the dead. Like midwives, mourners washed and anointed the bodies of the dead. Like midwives who swaddled the newborn, mourners shrouded the dead. Like midwives who celebrated the birth of the newborn with hymns, mourners announced the passage of the dead with laments. The lamenting of mourners was not simply a clinical symptom of pain, but a legal petition for admittance into the afterlife. As the legal representatives of the dead, mourners used laments to petition the long dead to accept the newly deceased as members of their household. Just as the primal scream of the newborn was understood as a legal petition to enter a household in the clan, the lament of mourners was considered to be a primal scream on behalf of the dead. It was a legal petition for admittance to the world of the dead.

Lament

(Ps 44:1-26)

Most psalms are laments. Standard laments have five components: a complaint, a petition, a vow, a declaration of innocence, and a confession of faith. The core of most laments is a complaint describing the suffering of the household. Complaints express the anger of a clan at Yahweh for breaking the covenant in which Yahweh promised to protect its villages from their enemies. This anger is not simply an internal emotion. It is a legal protest filed in a public forum. Complaints do not simply help the households vent their feelings. Complaints are a form of judicial outrage. The clan has suffered a loss, and it is demanding that Yahweh compensate it for its loss.

A lament in part two of the book of Psalms (Ps 44:1-26) complains that Yahweh has allowed the enemies of a household to defeat its warriors in battle, plunder its land, and sell its women and children for virtually nothing as slaves (Fig. 64). Mourners blame Yahweh for allowing the people delivered from slavery to be sold back into slavery. Such a tragic reversal leaves the household without honor, hunted and hated, not just by their enemies but by everyone. No one grants them status. No one allows them to participate in daily life. Everyone considers the household to be such a fool that they taunt it with jokes and stories.

Complaints in most laments are not only painfully outspoken, but shockingly frank in blaming Yahweh for suffering. Few today pray with such unrestrained anger at God. Nonetheless, these ancient people were not heretics who had lost their faith, they simply expressed their faith differently than most people in biblical religions today. They considered themselves to be full partners with Yahweh in determining what happened and how it happened. Believers today are much more passive and in some ways more fatalistic than their ancestors in the Bible. They more often pray with resignation rather than with outrage. They pray to accept the will of God. The laments in the book of Psalms pray to change it.

Lament
(Ps 3:1-8)

Laments are the traditions of a people in process, not a fully defined theology of suffering. Therefore, petitions for help from Yahweh, which appear in many laments, can represent both healthy and unhealthy reactions in a household to its loss of land and children.

Petitions reflect a healthy human participation in developing divine will when they remind Yahweh to protect and provide for a household whose land and children are threatened. Petitions are a form of denial when they are prayed without passion or pain or anger. The denial in unhealthy petitions pretends that loss has not occurred at all, or that the loss is only temporary. Denial not only postpones the beginning of recovery, it also prolongs the time during which unchallenged loss continues to drain the resources of a victim. In contrast, the acceptance in healthy petitions that angrily call upon Yahweh to come to the aid of a household in crisis allows victims of loss to begin recovery.

complaint

> *You disown us and shame us;*
> *You do not march into battle with our soldiers.*
>
> *You let our enemies drive us back;*
> *Our foes plunder us without opposition from you.*
>
> *You mark us as sheep to be slaughtered;*
> *Among strangers you scatter us.*
>
> *You sell your people at a loss;*
> *You make no profit.*
>
> *You make us fools in the eyes of our enemies;*
> *Our foes laugh at us.*
>
> *You make us a proverb among strangers.*
> *Outsiders tell jokes about us.*
>
> *All the day my shame is before me;*
> *Every day shame covers my face*
>
> *When my foes taunt me,*
> *When my enemies make fun of me.*

FIGURE 64   Lament (Ps 44:10-17)

The petition in a lament from part one of the book of Psalms (Ps 3:1-8) is a healthy petition that wakes up Yahweh and angrily petitions Yahweh to attack the enemies of the household (Fig. 65). Mourners in ancient Israel assumed that in times of peace Yahweh rested or slept. Sleep was the normal state of a divine patron whose people were secure. Sleep was a sign of peace. At a moment of crisis, the people wake up their divine patron.

The petition also asks Yahweh to attack the enemies of Israel like a boxer. The lament pleads: "land a blow with your fist right on the jaw of my enemies. Hit them in the mouth and break their teeth." The lament wants Yahweh to wake up and come out fighting.

petition

> *Awake from your sleep, Yahweh!*
> *Deliver me, my divine patron!*
>
> *Land a blow with your fist right on the jaw of my enemies.*
> *Hit them in the mouth and break their teeth.*

FIGURE 65   Lament (Ps 3:7)

Lament
(Ps 137:1-9)

There is a lament in part five of the book of Psalms whose last two lines contain one of the most painful petitions in the entire Bible: "You are a monster, Babylon. Blessed are they who do to you what you did to us. Blessed are they who grab your children by the ankles. Blessed are they who smash their skulls against a rock" (Ps 137:8-9; Fig. 66). Nothing in the opening lines of the lament prepares today's audiences to hear such scandalizing words spoken by the people of Yahweh.

The lament opens with a complaint in which the mourners indict the Babylonians for not only destroying Jerusalem, but also ordering their prisoners of war from Judah to celebrate the Babylonian victory by singing hymns celebrating Yahweh as the builder and the protector of Jerusalem (Psalms 46, 48, 76, 84). The more exalted and heroic the descriptions of Yahweh in these hymns, the more exalted and heroic the victory of Babylon over the people of Yahweh. Raping the culture of captives was a common practice. War was not simply a matter of victory on the field of battle, but the victory of one way of life over the other.

The mourners then describe the vow of the people of Judah not to sing songs celebrating Yahweh, and not to forget this city that Yahweh built. "We hung our harps in the weeping willows. How could we sing hymns to Yahweh in a strange land? If I forget you, Jerusalem, paralyze the hand with which I play. Let my tongue stick to the roof of my mouth, if I do not remember Jerusalem above everything else" (Ps 137:4-6). The people of Judah would not betray Jerusalem as the people of Edom had done (Obad 8-14; Ezek 25:12-14; 35:2-9). The mourners then recall with bitterness how these Semitic people from southern Jordan betrayed their covenant with the people of Judah and joined wholeheartedly in the Babylonian campaign against Jerusalem, and then sang enthusiastically to celebrate its destruction.

complaint (Ps 137:1-3)

> We mourned by the Rivers of Babylon,
>> We prostrated ourselves to remember Zion.
>
> Our enemies told us to sing hymns,
>> Our conquerors ordered us: "Sing the hymns of Zion!"

vow (Ps 137:4-6)

> We hung our harps in the weeping willows.
>> How could we sing hymns to Yahweh in a strange land?
>
> If I forget you, Jerusalem,
>> Paralyze the hand with which I play.
>
> Let my tongue stick to the roof of my mouth,
>> If I do not remember Jerusalem above everything else.

petition (Ps 137:7-9)

> Remember, Yahweh, how Edom sang when Jerusalem fell:
>> "Pull down its walls.
>> Raze the city to its foundations."
>
> You are a monster, Babylon.
>> Blessed are they who do to you what you did to us.
>
> Blessed are they who grab your children by the ankles.
>> Blessed are they who smash their skulls against a rock.

FIGURE 66   Lament (Ps 137:1-9)

The complaint and the vow in the lament elicit respect for households that reflect such grace under fire. The petition that follows, however, completely destroys the sympathy of most audiences today, who hold Jews, Christians, Muslims, and their biblical ancestors to an ethic of forgiveness rather than vengeance. The words were strong in the world of the Bible as well, but not as outrageous as they sound now.

For its military and civilian victims alike, war is hell in any time and place. Even the signing of the Geneva Convention in 1864, which sought to convert war into a sport played by rules of conduct, did not eliminate the barbaric and, oftentimes, sadistic cruelty of war. No war has ever been simply a game. The petition is an unvarnished description of one of the cruel and common practices of war in the world of the Bible.

War was waged on four fronts. First, warriors confronted one another on the field of battle. Victory here, however, was only a prelude to three other confrontations. A battlefield victory was only a victory over the present generation. Second, warriors were expected to rape childbearing women, disembowel pregnant women (2 Kgs 15:16), and massacre newborn infants. Third, warriors laid siege to the past generation by desecrating graves and sanctuaries. The dead and the divine were the third and fourth fronts in a war. Human remains were exhumed and burned or scattered to prevent the ancestors of a village from coming to its defense from the land of the dead. Sacred furniture from sanctuaries was smashed and burned, and sacred images were decapitated or taken into exile to prevent the divine patrons of a tribe from restoring its households to life, either in the land of the living or in the land of the dead. The petition in this lament reflects the simple and harsh reality that war was always total war.

The petition is not lawless. It carefully asks that the punishment of Babylon fit its crime. The principle of reciprocity, an eye for an eye and a tooth for a tooth, exercised a civilizing control against unrestrained vengeance of one tribe against another.

Admittedly, believers today can pray the petition only with contrition for this dark side that lurks in every culture, and never as a justification for violence, even against oppressors. Nevertheless, even today parents cannot witness the murder of their children with serenity. The petition voices the pain of all those who watch the innocent suffer, and cries out to believers to be their companions in suffering the loss.

A Hymn and a Lament
(Ps 66:1-20)

In some laments, households vow to tell the story of how Yahweh delivered them from slavery, if their losses are restored (Ps 22:22-31; 50:14; 61:4-8; 66:13-17; 116:14-18). Vows reflect the efforts of households to bargain with Yahweh to relieve suffering. Vows are the "let's make a deal" component of a lament. Complaints, petitions, and bargaining with Yahweh by making a vow all reflect the respect that traditional cultures have for the responsibility of humans in determining the course of events. Admittedly, bargaining is an anthropomorphic way to describe Yahweh. Nonetheless, it does not intend to reduce Yahweh to a merchant haggling over the price of a sale. The Hebrews considered what happened to have been the result not simply of divine action, but also of human reaction. Yahweh did not act unilaterally, but interacted with humans. Bargaining reflects the understanding that different human reactions to divine initiatives produce different results.

Some laments in the book of Psalms lack a complaint or a petition, and have only a vow. These laments have been labeled "songs of thanksgiving." One psalm with such a vow is preserved in part two of the book of Psalms. This numbered psalm in the Bible today actually combines two psalms: a hymn (Ps 66:1-12) and a lament (Ps 66:13-20).

The hymn alternates three calls to worship with three creation stories (Fig. 67). The initial call to worship and the final creation story are long; the calls to worship and creation stories in the middle of the hymn are short. The initial call to worship summons the community ten times to acknowledge Yahweh as its divine patron. "Make a joyful noise! Sing! Praise! Say! Prostrate yourselves! Worship! Praise! Praise! Come! See!" (Ps 66:1-5).

The first creation story reminds the households that Yahweh delivered them from slavery in Egypt. "Yahweh turned the sea into dry land" (Ps 66:6). The second creation story reminds them that Yahweh delivered them from slavery in Syria-Palestine. Yahweh "watches over the nations" (Ps 66:7). The third creation story reminds them that Yahweh delivered them from slavery in Babylon. Yahweh "tested us . . . tried us as silver is tried" (Ps 66:10).

The lament is made up of a vow (Ps 66:13-17), a declaration of innocence (Ps 66:18-19), and a confession of faith (Ps 66:20). In the vow, mourners promise that the shamed household will do something, and will say something. It will offer sacrifice to Yahweh: "I will come into your house with burnt offerings" (Ps 66:13). And it will tell all those from the clan who are eating the sacrifice how Yahweh delivered it from its enemies: "I will tell what he has done for me" (Ps 66:16).

The vows that appear in laments are not promises made by unbelievers to become converts. Vows are the promises of believers to assemble the community, to eat a sacrifice, and to tell the story. Those whom Yahweh delivers will not forget to celebrate their salvation from their enemies.

Lament
(Ps 22:1-31)

Some laments have declarations of innocence that explain why a household should not suffer. These declarations can express both healthy and unhealthy reactions to loss. As a healthy reaction, declarations of innocence place in evidence the public record of a household that has fulfilled the stipulations of its covenant with Yahweh, in order to argue that it has kept its part of the covenant and that it expects Yahweh to do the same. As an unhealthy reaction, declarations of innocence can reflect the depression of a household that acknowledges its loss, but cannot express its anger over the loss. Therefore, the household simply represses the anger as if the loss of its land and children were without consequences for the honor or survival of the household, which the declaration of innocence describes as if it were still intact.

A lament in part one of the book of Psalms (Ps 22:1-31) contains each of the five standard components of a lament. There is a complaint, a petition, a declaration of innocence, a vow, and a confession of faith (Fig. 68).

The complaint is divided into three parts (Ps 22:1-2, 6-8, 12-18). Mourners grieve that both humans and animals, and even Yahweh, shun the household as if it were a maggot (Ps 22:6; Isa 41:8-13). The household is not only excommunicated from all divine, from all human, and from all animal companionship, but it is also attacked by bulls, lions, dogs, and oxen. The array of creatures in the lament is striking. Its enemies knock the members of the household to the ground. They lie there dying like water soaking into the land as it runs out of a jar, or like wax cooling on the earth as it runs out of a mold. They are so helpless that their enemies loot even the clothes they are wearing.

The petition is divided into two parts (Ps 22:11, 19-21). In the first petition, mourners cry out to Yahweh to stay close, so that Yahweh can come quickly to the aid of the household when its enemies attack. Many Muslims, Christians, and Jews today consider suffering as a sign that God has abandoned them, or is far away from those who suffer. This petition, however, reflects the standard biblical belief that Yahweh is always close at hand. In good times or in bad, in sickness or in health, in poverty or in riches, Yahweh is Immanuel (Isa 7:14), the "Godparent who is with us." In the world of the Bible, suffering did not separate divine patrons from their people.

In the second petition, the mourners address Yahweh with the same title that the Stories of Adam and Eve use for the woman (Gen 2:20). Both are "helpers." In neither tradition do the titles carry connotations of inferiority or subordination. They are the titles of the mothers on whom households depend for food and protection.

The mourners address Yahweh not only as the mother of a household, but as its midwife as well. The declaration of innocence in the lament affirms: "You were my midwife. You showed me to my mother's breast. I have depended upon you since I was born, since my mother bore me you have been my divine patron" (Ps 22:9-10). The declaration certifies that at no time in its life has the household ever forgotten who feeds it and who protects it. It has always known, and publicly acknowledged, Yahweh as its mother and midwife (Jer 1:5). Like all declarations, this declaration puts Yahweh on notice that Yahweh's reputation as a divine patron is completely dependent upon the fate of the household. If the household falls victim to its enemies, everyone in the clan will know that Yahweh was either powerless or unwilling to save it.

As in other laments, the vow promises that when the clan gathers at the sanctuary the household will sacrifice enough to feed everyone, and while they are eating, it will retell the stories of the great works that Yahweh used to deliver it from its enemies. The household also promises that these stories will be told not only during the lifetimes of those whom Yahweh actually saved, but also by the future generations of the household: "Our descendants will serve Yahweh. Future generations will hear of Yahweh. They will hand on the stories of the great works of Yahweh to a people yet unborn. They will tell future generations everything Yahweh has done" (Ps 22:30-31). The entire Bible, not just this lament, is the fulfillment of vows like these: not to forget what Yahweh has done. Storytelling transcends the boundaries of time, and endows divine works with immortality.

Confessions of faith are spoken by the mourners singing a lament (Ps 22:3-5). Words of assurance are spoken by someone else in the clan on behalf of Yahweh. The intention of both confessions of faith and words of assurance is to express a household's acceptance of its loss without losing its faith in Yahweh as its creator and deliverer. Mourners affirm that suffering is real, and that land and children have been lost, but they also affirm that the loss does not prove that "Yahweh is not our divine patron."

The confession of faith here affirms, first of all, that Yahweh is holy, which is the distinguishing characteristic of Yahweh. It describes Yahweh as a mystery that human beings must learn to respect, and not a problem that human beings can solve. There are no metaphors that can accurately and completely explain Yahweh to Israel. The Bible is only a limited reflection on the Yahweh whom the Hebrews encounter. Suffering is the experience of human limitations. The greatest limitation for human beings, and consequently their greatest suffering, is their inability to understand their divine patrons. Therefore, this confession of faith reminds the clan that it suffers, ultimately, because it can never fully understand Yahweh, who is holy.

Secondly, the confession of faith reminds the clan that its ancestors cried out to Yahweh in laments, and that they survived their suffering. "Our ancestors had faith in you. They had faith, and you delivered them from their enemies. They cried out to you, and were saved. They had faith in you, and were not shamed" (Ps 22:4-5). Today, people in western European cultures look forward to find answers to problems. Research and development define their lifestyles and their worldviews. In contrast, the Hebrews looked backward to find answers to problems. In the world of the Bible, there was nothing new to discover. Problems resulted when people forgot something. The world came with a complete set of instructions. Problem solving was simply taking the time to reread them. To a large extent the Bible is the legacy of remembering of the past that this confession of faith reflects. "Our ancestors suffered, and so we suffer. Our ancestors cried out to Yahweh, and so we cry out to Yahweh. Our ancestors survived, and so we will survive."

The emphasis in the confession of faith is not that the ancestors cried out to Yahweh and the suffering stopped. The ancestors cried out to Yahweh and they survived the suffering, which, in due time, ran its course. Laments were not intended to help the Hebrews to avoid pain, but to survive it.

Today, it is common enough for people to embrace a faith tradition as an insurance policy against suffering. Believers often think that they cannot, or at least that they should not, suffer. When they do suffer, some Muslims, Christians, and Jews revoke their faith. Suffering in ancient Israel was no different than suffering today, but suffering was not an argument against the existence of God. The Hebrews did not expect to lead a life without suffering, but unlike many today who suffer alone, they suffered as a community and with their divine patron at their side. Laments did not create a pain-free world, but rather assembled the clan and Yahweh to support the household whose land and children were at risk. Like the mourners themselves, Yahweh and the clan did not take away the pain of the household; they simply stood with it in its pain, and that made it possible for the household to survive.

Hymn (Ps 66:1-12)

call to worship (Ps 66:1-5)

> *Make a joyful noise to Yahweh, all the earth.*
> > *Sing the glory of the name of Yahweh.*
>
> *Give to Yahweh glorious praise.*
> > *Say to Yahweh, "How awesome are your great works.*
>
> *Because of your great power, your enemies are prostrate*
> > *before you.*
> *All the earth worships you;*
>
> *They sing praises to you,*
> > *They sing praises to your name."*
>
> *Come and see what Yahweh has done;*
> > *Come and see the great works Yahweh does for the*
> > *powerless.*

creation story (Ps 66:6)

> *Yahweh turned the sea into dry land;*
> > *They passed through the river on foot.*

call to worship (Ps 66:6)

> *Let us rejoice in Yahweh,*
> > *Let us rejoice in Yahweh, who rules by might forever,*

creation story (Ps 66:7)

> *Who watches over the nations,*
> > *Who humbles the rebellious.*

call to worship (Ps 66:8)

> *Bless Yahweh, O peoples,*
> > *Let the sound of praise be heard,*

creation story (Ps 66:7-12)

> *Who kept us alive,*
> > *Who did not let our feet slip.*

(continued)

Who tested us;
> *Who tried us as silver is tried.*

Who brought us into the net;
> *Who laid burdens on our backs;*

Who let strangers rule over us;
> *Who led us through fire and through water;*

Who, finally, brought us into this fertile land.

Lament (Ps 66:13-20)

vow (Ps 66:13-17)

I will come into your house with burnt offerings;
> *I will pay you my vows,*

The vows that my lips uttered,
> *The vows that my mouth promised when I was in trouble.*

I will offer you burnt offerings of yearlings;
> *I will offer you the smoke of the sacrifice of rams;*
> *I will offer you bulls and goats.*

Come and hear, all you who fear Yahweh,
> *I will tell what he has done for me.*

I cried aloud to him,
> *Yahweh was extolled with my tongue.*

declaration of innocence (Ps 66:18-19)

If I had cherished iniquity in my heart,
> *Yahweh would not have listened.*

But Yahweh has listened;
> *Yahweh has given heed to the words of my prayer.*

confession of faith (Ps 66:20)

Bless Yahweh, who has not ignored my prayer.
> *Bless Yahweh, who has not stopped loving me.*

FIGURE 67   A Hymn and a Lament (Ps 66:1-20)

My Creator, My Creator, why have you forsaken me?

complaint (1-2)

> *Why are you not helping me?*
> *Why are you not listening to the words of my lament?*
> > *My Creator, I cry out during the day, but you do not*
> > *answer;*
> *I cry out at night, but I find no peace.*
> > *You are holy.*

confession of faith (3-5)

> *The hymns of Israel rise up to your throne.*
> > *Our ancestors had faith in you.*
> *They had faith, and you delivered them from their enemies.*
> > *They cried out to you, and were saved.*
> *They had faith in you, and were not shamed.*
> > *I am a maggot, not a man.*

complaint (6-8)

> *Scorned by animals, despised by humans.*
> > *All who see me mock me,*
> *They make faces at me,*
> *They shake their heads.*
> > *"What good is your faith in Yahweh?*
> *Why cannot Yahweh deliver you?*
> *Why cannot Yahweh rescue a beloved heir?"*
> > *You were my midwife.*

declaration of innocence (9-10)

> *You showed me to my mother's breast.*
> > *I have depended upon you since I was born,*
> *Since my mother bore me you have been my divine patron.*
> > *Do not be far from me.*

petition (11)

> *Trouble is near.*
> *No one else can help me.*
> > *Herds of bulls encircle me.*

complaint (12-18)

> *Powerful bulls from Bashan surround me.*
> > *They roar at me like hungry lions,*

(continued)

They bawl like lions on the prowl.
    I am poured out like water,
All my bones are out of joint.
    My heart is like wax,
My heart melts within my breast.
    My mouth is as dry as clay,
My tongue sticks to my cheek.
    You let death return me to clay,
Dogs are all around me.
    Evildoers encircle me.
My hands and feet have shriveled.
    I can count all my bones.
They stare and gloat over me.
    They divide my clothes among themselves,
They gamble for my clothing.
    Yahweh, do not stay so far away.

petition (19-21)

My helper, come quickly.
    Deliver me from the sword,
Save me from powerful dogs.
    Protect me from the mouths of lions,
Rescue me from the horns of wild oxen.
    I will praise your name in my household.

vow (22-31)

At the sanctuary I will sing hymns to you. . . .
    I will praise Yahweh in the assembly,
My vows I will pay before the people of Yahweh,
    I will feed the hungry until they are satisfied. . . .
Our descendants will serve Yahweh.
    Future generations will hear of Yahweh.
They will hand on the stories of the great works of Yahweh to
    a people yet unborn.
They will tell future generations everything Yahweh has done.

FIGURE 68   Lament (Ps 22:1-31)

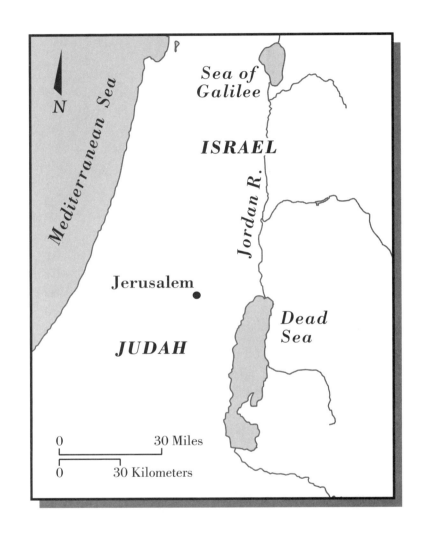

Points of Interest (Chapter 9)

9

BOOK OF PROVERBS

(PROV 1:1 — 31:31)

In the world of the Bible, teachers carried the title "father" or "mother" (Prov 1:8). There are two teachers in the book of Proverbs (Hebrew: *Mishle*). One teacher is wise; the other is foolish. Both are women. The wise woman is described as a "wife" or "mother" (Prov 2:1-22; 3:1-35; 4:1-27). The foolish woman is described as an "adulterer." These metaphors for teachers are modeled on the role of the mother of the household in village cultures like early Israel (1200–1000 B.C.E.).

Mothers were not only the child-bearers and the managers of the household; they were also the teachers of its women and children. Once boys became young men and were old enough to participate in the communal labor of the village, the fathers of the household became responsible for their education, but even when girls became young women, and were old enough to conceive children, they continued to be educated by the mothers of their households.

The role of mothers as teachers was a development of the close physical contact between mother and child, which lasted not simply during the months of pregnancy, but for as long as three years during which infants were nursed (1 Sam 1:22-23). Teachings in the Mishnah (200 C.E.) and the Talmud (400 C.E.) continued to emphasize the connection between childbearing and teaching found in the Bible. Nonetheless, childbearing and teaching were comparable but not identical roles. Not every child-bearer was the mother of a household, and not every woman who was physically close to her children during pregnancy and nursing became their teacher. The book of Proverbs honors the mother of the household almost exclusively as a teacher (Prov 1:8; 4:1-3; 6:20; 10:1; 15:20; 23:22-25), and says virtually nothing about women as child-bearers.

Mothers handed on the traditions of the Hebrews in both words and actions. Each time a mother taught a child to dress, she explained the meaning of the clothing. Each time she showed her children how to wash their hands and comb their hair, she told them how washing and combing set them apart. When mothers taught their children how to help with gardening and cooking, they explained to them why the foods they ate at harvest times were different from those the household enjoyed every day; why certain plants and animals were eaten and others were not; why some foods were consumed and others were shared. Washing, dressing, combing, gardening, herding, cooking, weaving, and making pottery were not simply skills to be learned; they were rituals that enacted the traditions that distinguished one people from another.

Mothers not only taught children their roles, but also explained to children the roles of everyone else in the household and in the village. A household that fulfilled its role in the village had honor. A household was shamed when it did not. The mother of a household who wisely fulfilled her role as teacher had honor. The mother of a household who fulfilled her role as teacher foolishly was shamed. The wise woman taught her students that wisdom demands labor. When there is no pain, there is no gain. The foolish woman taught her students to think that they could get something for nothing. The book of Proverbs preserves the teachings of wise women on how to acquire honor and how to remove shame (Prov 1:7-19). This wisdom was a legacy of the household to its members.

Over time, the teachings of the mothers of households in the villages were canonized by the men who trained the rulers of Mesopotamia, of Egypt, and of Israel. The book of Proverbs preserves the traditions of both the mothers of households in villages and the royal teachers in the palaces. Both men like Ptah-hotep, Amen-em-ope, and Ben Sira, and women like Ma'at, Bathsheba, and Jezebel were teachers who taught those who would be rulers.

Although the mothers of households educated both sons and daughters, royal teachers trained, with some few exceptions, only sons. These sons were adult, but the book of Proverbs refers to these students as "son," "child," "youth" (Prov 1:4) or "heir" (Prov 1:8).

Most traditions in the Bible reflect a direct encounter, between the Hebrews and Yahweh, which is called "revelation." Wisdom traditions, like those in the books of Proverbs, Job, and Ecclesiastes, develop from observation of the world and human behavior. The wise sought to know the creator by observing creation. They taught their students to observe, to judge, and to act.

Teachers used the genre "saying" to hand on their observations (Prov 1:17), and the genre "analogy" to hand on their judgments (Prov 9:17; 10:1). There are two kinds of analogies. One is an adage; the other is a proverb. Both the adage and the proverb are analogies. The adage is an analogy built on the similarity of the images. The proverb is an analogy built on contrast. The subsequent lines of both the adage and the proverb intensify the first line. Each line contains very concrete and practical images. Subsequent lines do not spiritualize the image in the first line.

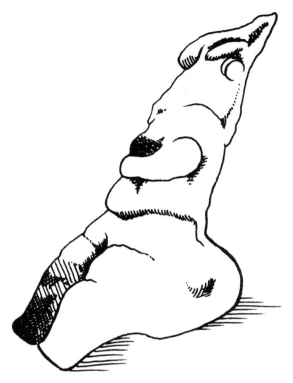

Godmother with Great Hips, Full Breasts and a Pointed Crown
(Horvat Minha 6000 B.C.E.; terra cotta 11 x 65cm)

The wise in the world of Greece and Rome taught their students internal or mental virtues. The wise in the ancient Near East taught their students behavior. Every action has consequences. Some consequences are good; some are bad.

Teachers linked sayings and analogies together, creating teachings. Teachings that provide advice on how to avoid pride, get good advice (Prov 2:4), practice table manners (Prov 23:1; Sir 8:1; 31:12), be reliable (Prov 25:13), make friends (Sir 6:7), and deal with women (Prov 6:24; Sir 9:1) are often framed by teachings that encourage students to excel in life.

Sayings and analogies are only as good as those who use them. They have no value in themselves. Competent or wise students can apply teachings. Incompetent or foolish students cannot apply the sayings and analogies that they have memorized. Only in the hands of the wise, who can locate the proper saying or analogy to apply to the proper challenge, do sayings or analogies become "apples of gold in a setting of silver" (Prov 25:11). In the hands of fools, who can neither adequately recover the appropriate sayings or analogies from a tradition like the book of Proverbs, nor make satisfactory use of them, these sayings and analogies are "like the legs of a cripple" (Prov 26:7) or "a thorn branch that a drunk tries to use for a cane" (Prov 26:9). They are useless.

The patterns that teachers used to group the teachings in the book of Proverbs are often no longer clear. Sometimes a catchword is repeated in each saying or analogy. Sometimes there is a common theme. Sometimes it is the word patterns in analogies that draw them together. Ultimately, it is the wise who must pattern the sayings and analogies by applying them to particular situations.

The book of Proverbs contains all those things that the experience of a particular culture has identified as potentially valuable. It contains information that at some point made a significant difference in the quality of its life. Travelers must expect the unexpected and prepare to respond. Human lifetimes are no more than extended journeys, and human beings are all travelers who carry traditions, like the book of Proverbs, in order to face life's challenges better. Teachers possessed a special sensitivity for the thresholds of human life, and designed the book of Proverbs to send along with their students on life's journey.

Part One: Courtyard Teachings
(PROV 1:1—9:18)

The shape of the physical text on the Proverbs scroll and the shape of the Temple of Solomon may have some intentional similarities. Temples were microcosms or models of the worldview of a culture, and the book of Proverbs is a handbook for living in that world. This relationship between the significance of the temple and Proverbs in the world of ancient Israel may have influenced the way in which the text of the book of Proverbs was divided.

The Temple of Solomon was a rectangular building some 140 feet long and eighty-five feet wide. It was divided into three parts. The entrance was a courtyard about thirty-five feet long. The great room was about seventy feet long. The holy of holies was thirty-five feet long. The sizes of these rooms in the temple were roughly in the same proportion to one another as the lengths of the three parts of the scroll that preserved the book of Proverbs. The length of the first part may be comparable to the courtyard of the temple (Prov 1:1—9:18). The second is comparable to the length of the great room (Prov 10:1—22:16). The third is comparable to the holy of holies (Prov 22:17—31:31).

By using the ground plan of the temple for its pattern, the book of Proverbs also visibly acknowledges Solomon's patronage, and indicates its intention to help students learn how to serve their monarchs well (Fig. 69). The Courtyard Teachings (Prov 1:1—9:18) make these candidates a promise (Prov 1:1-7). The Great Room Teachings (Prov

Courtyard Teachings of Solomon (Prov 1:1—9:18)

Prov 1:8-19

Prov 1:20-33

Prov 2:1-22

Prov 3:1-12

Prov 3:13-24

Prov 3:25-35

Prov 4:1-9

Prov 4:10-27

Prov 5:1-23

Prov 6:1-9

Prov 6:20-35

Prov 7:1-27

Prov 8:1-36

Prov 9:1-18

Great Room Teachings of Solomon (Prov 10:1—22:16)

Prov 10:1—15:33

Prov 16:1—22:16

Holy of Holies (Prov 22:17—31:31)

Teachings of Amen-em-ope (Prov 22:17—24:22)

Teachings of the Wise (Prov 24:23-34)

Teachings of Solomon (Prov 25:1—29:27)

Teachings of Agur (Prov 30:1-33)

Teachings of Lemuel (Prov 31:1-31)

FIGURE 69   Patterns in the Book of Proverbs

10:1—22:16) outline a program for students to follow. The Holy of Holies Teachings (Prov 22:17—31:31) describe their rewards. The promise is a well-integrated and successful life; the program is a disciplined commitment to the advice of their teachers; and the reward is a life free from anxiety (Prov 31:10-31).

Titles dedicate the Courtyard Teachings and the Great Room Teachings of the book of Proverbs to Solomon. One section of the Holy of Holies Teachings (Prov 25:1—29:27) is also dedicated to him. One section of the Holy of Holies Teachings is parallel to Amen-em-ope (Prov 22:17—24:22). Two sections are dedicated to teachers named Agur (Prov 30:1-33) and Lemuel (Prov 31:1-31). Ptah-hotep taught about 2450 B.C.E. in Egypt. Amen-em-ope taught in Egypt about 1000 B.C.E. The Teachings of Ptah-hotep and the teachings of Amen-em-ope demonstrate both the consistency and the important changes that took place in Egypt's worldview over two thousand years. Both Ptah-hotep and Amen-em-ope contrast the wise and the foolish. The wise are soft-spoken or silent. Fools are hot-tempered or hotheaded. The wise know when to talk and when to listen. Fools let anger run or ruin their lives. Ptah-hotep teaches that the wise prosper, and should share the fruits of their success with others. Amen-em-ope, however, teaches that the wise seldom prosper; nonetheless they should remain self-controlled, modest, thoughtful in speech, considerate of others, and humble servants of their divine patrons.

Teaching on Wisdom
(PROV 1:1-7)

The Hebrew title for the book of Proverbs is "Teachings of Solomon, heir of David, ruler of Israel" (Prov 1:1). The title identifies Solomon as a wise ruler to whom this teaching tradition is dedicated. Solomon is not the author of the book of Proverbs, but rather its patron (Fig. 70). These traditions do not reflect the genius of a single individual, even one as great as Solomon, but rather the way in which an entire culture understood the world and looked at life.

The purpose of the book of Proverbs is explained by a Teaching on Wisdom composed of an adage (Prov 1:2-6) and a proverb (Prov 1:7). The adage uses seven different Hebrew synonyms for "wisdom." For example, wisdom is a disciplined life. Wisdom is sound moral judgment. Wisdom is the art of compromise. Wisdom is the ability to apply analogies properly. Wisdom is a life of gratitude to Yahweh.

The teaching ends with the proverb: "The fear of Yahweh is the beginning of wisdom. Fools despise wisdom" (Prov 1:7). In ordinary speech today, "fear of God" describes people who are good, so that God will not harm them. In the books of Deuteronomy (Deut 6:13), Joshua (Josh 24:14), and Samuel-Kings (1 Sam 12:14), however, "fear of Yahweh" describes households who love and serve Yahweh by fulfilling their obligations

> ## The Teachings of Solomon
>
> The Wisdom of a Son of David and Ruler of Israel (Prov 1:1):
>
> Provide wisdom and discipline (Prov 1:2);
>   Good conduct; right, just, and honest manners (Prov 1:3);
>   Guidance for the young;
>   Education and good judgment for students (Prov 1:4),
>
> Understanding for listeners;
>   A key to proverbs, parables, teachings, riddles (Prov 1:5-6).
>
> The wise are zealous for Yahweh,
>   Fools despise discipline (Prov 1:7).

FIGURE 70 Teaching on Wisdom (Prov 1:1-7)

to the covenant (Deut 5:29). They cling to Yahweh (Deut 10:20) and walk in the way of Yahweh (Deut 8:6). In the book of Psalms (Ps 15:4; 22:24-26; 31:20; 65:6-9; 66:16), "fear of Yahweh" describes those who celebrate Yahweh as the creator of the cosmos and the divine patron of Israel. "Fear of Yahweh" means that the wise were aware that Yahweh was always ready to provide for their households. They never forget that Yahweh feeds and protects their households.

Teaching on Foolishness
(PROV 1:8-19)

A Teaching on Wisdom with which the book of Proverbs opens is followed by a Teaching on Foolishness. In the opening proverb (Prov 1:8), the second line contrasts with the first. Together they relate the book of Proverbs to the stipulation from the decalogue: "honor your father and your mother, so that your days may be long in the land that Yahweh, your divine patron, is giving to you" (Exod 20:12). This comparison of the observation-based traditions in the Bible with its revelation-based traditions is unusual (Fig. 71).

In the adage (Prov 1:9) linked to the opening proverb, the second line mirrors the first line to describe wisdom as jewelry. Wisdom highlights the natural beauty of human nature just as jewelry highlights the natural beauty of the human body.

The teaching is a complex proverb. The simple proverb and adage with which it opens (Prov 1:8-9) are contrasted with a complex adage describing foolishness with seven

> My child, honor the instruction of your father,
>   Do not ignore the teaching of your mother.
>
> They are crown of flowers for your head,
>   They are a string of precious stones for your neck.
>
> Students, when fools invite you in, do not accept.
>   Students, do not walk in their way.
>
> If they say, "Follow us!—
>   Let us lie in wait for blood,
>
> Let us wantonly ambush the innocent,
>   Let us swallow them like Sheol,
>
> Let us engulf them like the Pit.
>   We shall find treasure,
>
> We shall fill houses with riches.
>   Throw in your lot with us, we will all get rich."
>
> Don't bait a trap while the prey watches!
>
> Fools lie in wait to kill one another,
>   One sets an ambush for the other!
>
> They are their own worst enemies.
>   Greed puts the greedy to death.

FIGURE 71   Teaching on Foolishness (Prov 1:8-19)

different Hebrew terms (Prov 1:10-14), just as wisdom is described with seven different Hebrew terms in the preceding teaching (Prov 1:1-7). Fools follow the crowd (Prov
1:10), and think they can deprive their neighbors of their honor (Prov 1:11), commit
the perfect crime (Prov 1:12), and get everything for nothing (Prov 1:13).

Teaching on Wise Teachers
(PROV 3:13-18)

Some adages are macarisms or beatitudes. Each line of the adage begins with the word
"blessed," which is a synonym for "wise" rather than "happy." A Teaching on Wise

Teachers (Prov 3:13-18) is framed with beatitudes. It opens with the adage: "Blessed are those who find a wise teacher. Blessed are those who discover a discerning wife" (Prov 3:13). It closes with the adage: "A wise teacher is a tree of life to those who find her. Blessed are those who follow her faithfully" (Prov 3:18).

The tradition compares a wise teacher with a tree. The date palm, the grapevine, and the olive are the most common trees in the world of the Bible. Each requires years of care before it bears edible fruit. Likewise, students require years of discipline before they become wise. Nonetheless, once trees and students mature they provide fruit year after year. The Bible also portrays the wise as eating from a tree or sleeping under a tree. Adam and Eve eat from a tree. Elijah (2 Kgs 19:5) and Jonah (Jonah 4:6-7) sleep beneath trees. For the Hebrews and other cultures the branches of a tree were like the uterus of the Godmother, and its trunk her birth canal through which creatures left the divine plane and entered the human plane. The spot at which the trunk entered the earth created a sacred center or navel. Here the creator, like the mother of a household, taught humans how to have a child and have a harvest. A sacred tree marked the spot where humans became wise and truly understood the cosmos and its creator.

Teaching on Foolish Teachers
(PROV 5:1-23)

A Teaching on Foolish Teachers tells students that a foolish teacher is an adulterer who promises students something for nothing (Fig. 72). A wise teacher is a wife who stays with her students for a lifetime to help them learn that there is no gain without pain. A wise teacher is faithful and demands discipline from students. A foolish teacher is unreliable and allows students to run wild.

The words of a foolish teacher are smooth or easy (Prov 5:3). Like honey, they intoxicate students into believing that all things are simply there for the taking. Consequently, her students lack discipline and wander thoughtlessly from their household and village into the households and villages of others. "She does not stay on the path of life. She wanders around lost" (Prov 5:6). The students of a foolish teacher do not know their place, and they do not stay in place.

Teaching of the Wise Woman
(PROV 8:1-36)

A Teaching of the Wise Woman begins with the adage: "Does not the wise woman cry out, does not the understanding woman raise her voice?" (Prov 8:1). "Understanding"

Students, pay attention to my teaching.
    Listen to my instruction.

Act prudently.
    Talk sensibly.

The lips of a foolish woman drip honey,
    Her words are smoother than oil.

In the end her lips taste bitter as wormwood,
    Her words cut like a two-edged sword.

Her feet lead to death,
    Her steps follow the path to Sheol.

She does not stay on the path of life.
    She wanders around lost.

Students, listen to me,
    Do not depart from the words of my mouth.

Keep away from the foolish woman.
    Do not go near the door of her house.

You will give your honor to others,
    You will give your years to the merciless.

Strangers will take your wealth,
    Households of strangers will use your labor.

At the end of life you will groan.
    When flesh and blood dry you will lament.

"How I hated discipline,
    How my heart despised reproof.

I did not listen to the voice of my teacher,
    I did not obey the wise woman.
    Now I am a fool in the village assembly."

Drink water from your own spring.
    Draw living water from your own oasis.

(continued)

> *Do not drink from the springs of others.*
> *Do not draw water in the streets.*
>
> *Keep your spring for your household.*
> *Do not let strangers drink from your oasis.*
>
> *Bless your spring.*
> *Rejoice in the wife of your youth.*
>
> *Enjoy the lovely deer.*
> *Delight in the graceful doe.*
>
> *May her breasts always satisfy you.*
> *May her love always intoxicate you.*
>
> *Students, do not be fooled by a strange woman.*
> *Do not embrace a foolish woman.*
>
> *Yahweh knows the ways humans walk.*
> *Yahweh examines all their paths.*
>
> *Foolishness is a trap.*
> *Sin has consequences.*
>
> *Fools die for lack of discipline.*
> *Foolishness leads them astray.*

FIGURE 72   Teaching on Foolish Teachers (Prov 5:1-23)

and "raise her voice" in the second line create an analogy with "wise woman" and "cry out" in the first line. The teaching continues to elaborate this simple adage with a hymn (Prov 8:2-36).

The wise woman in the teaching is celebrated as Yahweh's midwife when the world was born (Fig. 73). She is "the firstborn of the ways of Yahweh, the forerunner of the great works of Yahweh" (Prov 8:22), and the "master worker" (Prov 8:30). She celebrates, "delights," or "rejoices" in each new creature by singing hymns praising Yahweh for having given birth to such magnificent children (Prov 8:31). In the world of the Bible, cultures often celebrated creators like this wise woman as Godmothers. They portrayed them with great hips from bearing many children and with full breasts for nursing them.

When Yahweh began to create, I was there.
    Yahweh called me on the first day of labor.

In the beginning, I opened the womb,
    On the first day, before the world took shape, I was there.

Before the seas of saltwater were born, I was there.
    Before the springs of freshwater were born, I was there.

Before the mountains at the horizons took shape, I was there.
    Before these eternal hills were created, I was there.

Before there was soil to work, I was there.
    Before there was anyone to work the soil, I was there.

When Yahweh created the heavens, I was there.
    When Yahweh drew the shorelines of the earth,
    I was there.

When Yahweh pitched the skies like a tent over our heads,
    I was there.
    When Yahweh capped the geyser flooding the earth,
    I was there.

When Yahweh called the sea together in one place,
    I was there.
    When Yahweh set the pillars of the earth in place,
    I was there.

I was beside Yahweh as midwife,
    I sang at the birth of each day of creation.

I sang a hymn when the world was created.
    I sang praise when the human race was born.

Now, students, listen to me.
    Blessed are those who follow a life of learning.

Listen to my teachings and become wise,
    Do not ignore wisdom.

(continued)

> *Blessed are those who listen to me,*
>   *Blessed are those who meet me every morning at the gate,*
>   *Blessed are those who wait for me at the door.*
>
> *Those who meet me find life,*
>   *Those who meet me receive blessings from Yahweh.*
>
> *Those who miss me take their own lives,*
>   *Those who break their promises to me make a covenant*
>   *with death.*

FIGURE 73   Teaching of the Wise Woman at Creation (Prov 8:1-36)

These divine women often wore pointed caps like the pharaoh's double crown or a bishop's miter.

The Teaching of the Wise Woman parallels the Creation of the Heavens and the Earth (Gen 1:1—2:4), building an analogy between creation, birth, and learning. Creators, like midwives, and teachers, draw their protégés from darkness to light, and from death to life. Therefore, "when Yahweh began to create" (Prov 8:22) can also mean "when Yahweh began to give birth" (Prov 8:24-25), or "when Yahweh began to teach" (Prov 4:5-7). As in the Creation of the Heavens and the Earth, this teaching describes creating as separating or organizing. Yahweh separates the depths, or the saltwaters, from the springs or freshwater (Prov 8:24). Then the mountains at one horizon are separated from the mountains at the other (Prov 8:25). These mountains on the horizons worked like a seal or O-ring to join the sky above to the earth below, and to keep the waters beyond from flooding the earth. Yahweh separates humans from the humus. The "earth and fields" are the farmlands from which Yahweh separates the farmers who are the "world's first bits of soil" (Prov 8:26) and "first clods of the world." Yahweh places the heavens over the earth to separate the waters above the dome from the earth and water below it (Prov 8:27). The Hebrews thought of the dome as a translucent sheet of hammered metal. Yahweh also separates the sky from the land (Prov 8:28). Yahweh pushes up the sky like the mother of a household pitching her tent.

The Story of the 'Adam as a Farmer (Gen 2:4-17) describes chaos, in part, as a "stream rising from the earth" (Gen 2:6). The world flooded with water is a common description of the chaos that precedes creation. To control the flood, Yahweh caps off the great geyser deep under the earth (Prov 8:28). The underground swell of water is a motif in the Stories of Gilgamesh and the Stories of Atrahasis. This powerful source of water can only be tapped with divine power (Job 36:27). Yahweh "draws a circle on the face of the deep, sketching a shoreline to separate the sea from the land" (Prov 8:29). As in the Creation of the Heavens and the Earth, Yahweh speaks and the sea responds by taking its place, where it will not threaten life on the land. This image of the sea over its banks was drawn from the raging winter storms on the Mediterranean, which caused it to jump the shore and flood the cities and villages built along its east coast. The surface of the earth is mounted above the waters beneath it on legs or pillars like an offshore drilling platform. These pillars are the "foundations of the earth" (Prov 8:29).

Because the wise woman is such a close collaborator with Yahweh in the creation of the world, she is the teacher of choice when human beings want to know how they work, and how the world where they live works. The wise woman can maintain and repair the world she helped build (Prov 8:32-36).

Part Two: Great Room Teachings
(PROV 10:1 — 22:16)

The Great Room Teachings of the book of Proverbs are divided into two sections (Prov 10:1—15:33; 16:1—22:16). These teachings contain 375 sayings and analogies, which is the sum of the numerical values of the Hebrew letters in its title: "Teachings of Solomon."

Sayings, Adages, Proverbs about Mothers of Households

The world of the Bible was a patriarchy. Patriarchy is a patrilocal and patrilinear social system. Women live in the households of their husbands, not their fathers, and heirs of households are designated by their fathers, not their mothers. Nonetheless, the mother of a household had significant authority over its land and children.

The authority of the mother of the household was distinct from the authority of the father of the household. Not every female, however, was subordinate to every male, and not every man became the father of a household. The status of mothers of households was equal to or greater than the status of many men in the village. Sayings, adages, and proverbs carefully distinguish between women who honor their households and those who shame them.

"The mouth of the mother of a household who is a fool is a pit where Yahweh traps those sentenced to death" (Prov 22:14) is a saying. There is no parallelism between the lines. It is a short statement handing on an observation and a judgment. There is no attempt to apply the known of the observation to any unknown. Pits are dug to trap wild animals. The teaching of a mother who is a fool sentences the members of her household to death as surely as a trap sentences its prey to death. The danger of foolish women is not their sexual promiscuity, but their teaching. A dangerous woman is a stranger or a fool, not a prostitute.

"Like a gold ring in the snout of a pig, is a beautiful, but foolish, woman" (Prov 11:22) and "Blessed is he who finds a wise wife, he finds favor with Yahweh" (Prov 18:22) are adages. The lines are parallel and they are synonymous. In western European cultures "clothes make the man." Externals are windows to the soul. The world of the Bible, however, was suspicious of externals, which camouflage as well as reveal. The value of the gold disguises the value of the sow. The physical attributes that allow a woman to bear children for her household disguise her intellectual limitations for rearing them wisely. Finally, a wise wife makes the land and children, which Yahweh promised in the covenant, a reality for a household. She is not a wage that has been earned, but a blessing freely received.

"The words of the mother of a household who is a fool torture like drops of water" (Prov 19:13) and "Better to live outside on a cramped rooftop in silence, than to live inside a great house with the mother of a household who is always talking" (Prov 21:9) are also adages. The wise and the fools are marked by their use of words. Fools nag and complain, argue and criticize. The wise counsel, reconcile, teach, and inspire. The words of a foolish mother physically destroy a household as inevitably as water dripping through its roof. The words of a fool are many; the words of the wise are few. The avalanche of words from a foolish mother is as deadly to the members of her household as the isolation and exposure of exile.

"Wise mothers earn honor for their households. Foolish mothers cover their households with shame" (Prov 11:16) and "Wise mothers of households are crowns for their husbands, foolish mothers are a cancer" (Prov 12:4) are proverbs. The two lines are parallel, and they are antithetical. Wise mothers teach their children discipline; foolish mothers promise them something for nothing. Wise mothers develop their households externally in the village. Foolish mothers destroy their households from within.

The Great Room Teachings consider foolishness to be a fierce instinct in mothers of households. "Better to take a cub from a bear, than to take foolishness from the mother of a household" (Prov 17:12). Once a fool became mother of a household the damage was irreparable. Mothers who are wise bless their households with the land and children that Yahweh promised in the covenant. Households do not earn wise mothers; they are a divine blessing: "Blessed is the father of a household who finds a wise wife to be mother of his household. His household finds favor with Yahweh" (Prov 18:22).

Part Three: Holy of Holies Teachings
(Prov 22:17—31:31)

Hymn
(Prov 31:10-31)

A hymn concludes the book of Proverbs. It contains a teaching on wisdom and a call to worship. The teaching serves as the hymn's creation story and describes all the ways in which wisdom enriches human life. Its adages and proverbs are arranged like a litany or acrostic following the twenty-two letters of the Hebrew alphabet beginning with 'alef (Prov 31:10), beth (Prov 31:11), gimel (Prov 31:12), and ending with resh (Prov 31:29), shin (Prov 31:30), and tav (Prov 31:31). This hymn and the Teaching on Wisdom (Prov 1:1-7) with which the book of Proverbs opens frame the Courtyard Teachings, Great Room Teachings, and Holy of Holies Teachings. The teaching mirrors the hymn and the hymn mirrors the teaching. Everything that the opening teaching promises, the closing hymn delivers. The teaching promises to endow students with discipline and judgment, and the hymn identifies all the aspects of human life that wisdom creates.

Just as the mother in other teachings (Prov 1:8-19) is not the woman who gave birth to a student, the wife in the hymn is not the woman whom a student will marry (Fig. 74). Both are teachers. The 'alef and beth adages and the gimel proverb in the teaching observe how few students actually succeed in learning from a good teacher. "Who can find a wise woman? How few uncover this priceless treasure. Yahweh entrusts his heart to her. She knows all things. A wise woman blesses the days of the learner with good. She does not curse her disciple with evil" (Prov 31:10-12). Yet those who persevere are blessed whether they are women who weave (Prov 31:13) or men who sail (Prov 31:14),

> *Blessed is the husband of a wise wife.*
> *The number of his days will be doubled.*
>
> *A faithful wife brings joy to her husband,*
> *He will complete his years in peace.*
>
> *A good wife is a great blessing.*
> *She is a gift for a husband zealous for Yahweh.*
>
> *Whether rich or poor, his heart is content,*
> *His face is always cheerful.*

FIGURE 74   Teaching on the Mother of a Household (Sir 26:1-4)

fathers who work the land (Prov 31:16) or mothers who manage households (Prov 31:15). Wherever they go and whatever they do, the students of a wise teacher bring life to their households.

The *samek* proverb in the teaching addresses the wise woman with her Greek title "Sophia." "The household of a wise woman is hardworking. Fools do not eat her bread" (Prov 31:27).

The *shin* proverb reminds students that wisdom resides not in how they look, but in what they do. "Physical appearance disguises. Beauty does not last. True wisdom is zeal for Yahweh" (Prov 31:30). The proverb introduces the Hebrew word that is the signature of the book of Ecclesiastes: "Vanity of vanities, all is vanity" (Eccl 1:2). The connotation of the Hebrew word, however, is not "useless," but "limited." A breath of air has limited value. The wise inhale, but do not "chase after the wind" (Eccl 1:7) or hold their breath. Physical appearances have limited value. They are to be used and then discarded. Lasting wisdom is the work of the hands.

The *tav* adage that ends the teaching is a call to worship: "Give thanks to Yahweh for the wise work of our hands. Let the gates of the city praise Yahweh for wisdom that lasts!" (Prov 31:31). Wisdom is not a human wage, but a divine gift.

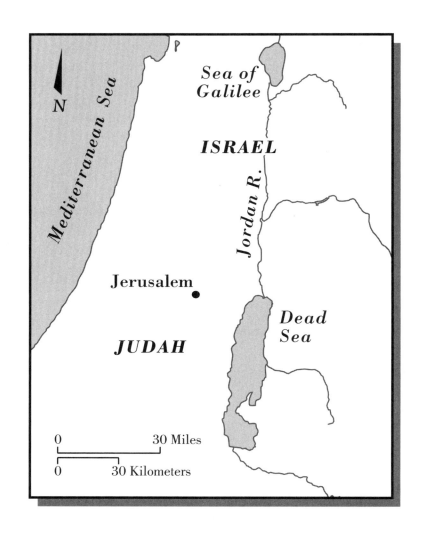

Points of Interest (Chapter 10)

10

BOOK OF ECCLESIASTES

(ECCL 1:1 — 12:14)

The wise woman in the book of Ecclesiastes (Hebrew: *Qoheleth*) audits the traditional teachings of the wise in the world of the Bible, like those preserved in the book of Proverbs (Deut 31:30; Ezek 23:47; Prov 26:26). The wise continued to review and evaluate their teachings. Like the wise woman in the book of Proverbs, who was there when Yahweh created the cosmos (Prov 8:27), Qoheleth is the wise woman who was there when David ruled Jerusalem (Eccl 1:1).

For the books of Job and Ecclesiastes, blind obedience was disloyal. Unquestioning loyalty was treason. Untested faith was heresy. The only true faith was a questioning faith. The only real loyalty was a tested loyalty. The only genuine obedience was an obedience given by students who had passed through the novitiate of doubt. The wise woman is not a skeptic. She is a quality-control engineer like the snake in the book of Genesis or the Satan in the book of Job. This wise woman is responsible for assembling and evaluating traditions like those in the book of Proverbs, not to destroy them, but to improve them. The title page assures audiences that the book of Ecclesiastes is an official audit of Israel's teaching traditions, and not an eccentric rejection of them.

The wise woman reviews the book of Proverbs in order to remind students that its teachings are wise, but not all-wise. Discipline and learning and material possessions have value, but they do not always bring happiness. The wise woman formulates her assessment of the book of Proverbs with the words "Vanity of vanities, all is vanity" (Eccl 1:2). In Hebrew "vanity" does not mean "useless," but "limited." Like a breath of air (Isa 57:13; Job 7:16; Ps 39:5-6, 11; 62:9; 78:33; 94:11; 144:4; Prov 21:6), wisdom has important, but limited, uses. This "wind" (Eccl 1:17) is absolutely necessary for life, but it is hopeless to try and save or "chase after" it. Humans must inhale one breath at time, then exhale and discard it. The teachings in the book of Proverbs are not useless, but they are limited.

The most common genre in the teaching of the wise woman is an audit. Audits have four parts: a citation, a mandate, a research report, and an evaluation. The mandate explains how the Proverbs tradition will be evaluated: "I said to myself, 'I will test pleasure.'" The research report explains the method that the wise woman used to test the Proverbs tradition: "I cheered my body with wine . . . I acted like a clown to see if this is how humans should live their lives" (Eccl 2:1-3). The evaluation presents the wise woman's conclusions: "laughter is insanity and pleasure is foolishness" (Eccl 2:2).

In the book of Proverbs the wise enjoy sensual pleasures. They "laugh at the days to come" (Prov 31:25) because they can anticipate the future without anxiety. The wise woman tests this teaching by satiating the senses in search of laughter, only to discover laughter is not happiness, but lunacy. Those who laugh are not wise, but fools whose overindulgence destroys their ability to learn.

Audit of Work
(ECCL 1:2-11)

An Audit of Work evaluates repetition and reliability. The audit cites the creation story from a hymn that praises Yahweh for the reliability in nature (Eccl 1:4-8). The sun always rises. The wind always blows. Rivers always run. Human conversation goes on. Eyes always see. Ears always hear. The book of Proverbs encourages the wise to imitate the reliability of nature, to do today what they did yesterday.

The audit catalogs the shortcomings of repetition (Eccl 1:9-11). Repetition, for the wise woman, is not always wise. Often it is boring. "All things are more wearisome than one can express. The eye is not satisfied with seeing, nor the ear filled with hearing" (Eccl 1:8). Taken to an extreme, repetition creates anonymity because one generation is no different from the next. "What has been is what will be. What has been done is what will be done. There is nothing new under the sun. Is there anything new? Everything has already been, in the ages before us" (Eccl 1:9-10). Finally, every generation doing exactly what preceding generations have done destroys the need for storytelling to celebrate the survival skills of a clan's ancestors. "The people of long ago are not remembered. There will be no remembrance of a people yet to come by those who come after them" (Eccl 1:11). There are limits to the repetition in nature as a model for human behavior.

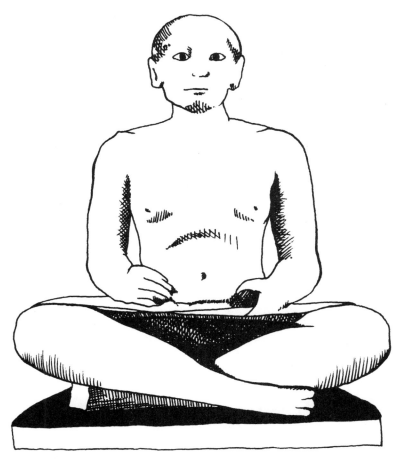

Teacher like Amen-em-ope Whom Ecclesiastes Audits
(Saqqara 2575–2134 B.C.E.; limestone 53.7 cm)

Audit of Wisdom
(ECCL 1:12-18)

An Audit of Wisdom evaluates how the world works. While it is admirable to "study all that is done under heaven" (Eccl 1:13), the wise cannot change the world. "What is crooked cannot be made straight. What is missing cannot be replaced" (Eccl 1:15). Furthermore, when understanding the world creates a desire to change the world, the wise are frustrated rather than fulfilled. "In much wisdom there is much vexation. Those who increase knowledge increase sorrow" (Eccl 1:18). Wisdom gives the wise an opportunity to live in harmony with creation. It does not give them the power to change it.

Audit of Possessions
(ECCL 2:4-11)

An Audit of Possessions evaluates material goods. This audit has three parts. One part cites the Proverbs tradition, where those who live wisely acquire and enjoy material goods. "My heart found pleasure in all my toil, and this was my reward for all my toil" (Eccl 2:10).

Another part reports that the wise woman has immersed herself in material goods in order to research the Proverbs tradition. "I built houses and planted vineyards for myself. . . . Whatever my eyes desired I did not keep from them" (Eccl 2:4-10).

Another part is the wise woman's evaluation: "Then I considered all that my hands had done and the toil I had spent in doing it, and again, all was vanity and a chasing after wind, and there was nothing to be gained under the sun" (Eccl 2:11). Generally, the word "toil" refers to slave labor (Deut 26:7; Jer 20:18; Job 3:10; 4:8; 5:6; Ps 73:16; 140:9). In the book of Ecclesiastes "toil" is a synonym for human life. Toil produces goods, yet cannot protect humans from death. Toil produces houses, vineyards, gardens, parks, orchards, pools, forests, slaves, herds, flocks, silver, gold, singers, and sexual partners, but cannot prevent suffering. The wise can enjoy their material possessions, but not even all the material possessions that the wise woman amasses constitute insurance against suffering and death. The value of material possessions is limited.

Audit of Harmony
(ECCL 3:1-15)

In an Audit of Harmony the wise woman cites the Proverbs tradition (Eccl 3:1-8). Then she states her mandate (Eccl 3:9), and reports her research (Eccl 3:10), before making an evaluation (Eccl 3:11-15). The creation story that opens the audit praises Yahweh for the harmony in creation: "For everything there is a season, and a time for every matter under heaven. A time to be born, and a time to die . . . a time to love, and a time to hate" (Eccl 3:1-8). The hymn praises Yahweh for establishing an appropriate occasion for every human endeavor. In Western industrial cultures today, time is neutral. Those who use calendars must assign each month, day, and hour its task. In the world of the Bible, time was predetermined. Each day and each hour of the day had an assigned task. The wise identify the purpose assigned for each month and day and hour and harmonize their lives with the tasks to which each time was dedicated. Fools embrace when it is time to refrain from embracing, keep when it is time to throw away, and are silent when it is time to speak.

The hymn also praises Yahweh for the balance in creation. Birth is balanced with death. Planting is balanced with harvesting. Killing is balanced with healing. This twin-motif also appears in the yin-yang teaching from the *Tao te Ching* of Chinese philosopher Lao-tzu (570–490 B.C.E.). The yin feminine balances the yang masculine. The yin darkness balances the yang light. The yin cold balances the yang heat. The yin wet balances the yang dry. The wise know that life is not all laughing, dancing, and gathering stones together. They know that life is also weeping, mourning, and throwing stones.

The books of Ecclesiastes and Proverbs agree that Yahweh blesses creation with harmony and with balance. For the wise woman, however, humans are always out of tune and out of balance. Creation is ordered; human beings are not. They are forever tearing apart when they should be sewing together, hating when they should be loving, and making war when it is time for peace. Living in harmony with creation and with the creator is impossible for human beings. "Yahweh, our Creator, has created a time for everything . . . yet humans never know what our Creator is doing" (Eccl 3:11).

The audit concludes with two recommendations (Eccl 3:11-15). First, the wise woman recommends that her students eat and drink and enjoy their lives (Eccl 3:13) as a divine gift, not as a human wage. Human toil produces nothing. Food and drink and pleasure are the blessings of Yahweh (Eccl 3:9). Second, the wise woman recommends that her students let Yahweh take care of the cosmos. Human work cannot keep anything in place. Only Yahweh can repair and replace things in the world. Work does not impact the ongoing cycle of creation. Whatever motivates humans to work, it cannot be the desire to keep the cosmos going.

Audit of Students
(ECCL 7:23-29)

Again and again, the wise woman audits learning (Eccl 7:19-22; 8:1-9). In an Audit of Students (Eccl 7:23-29), the wise woman asks why there are so few good students. Her mandate (Eccl 7:23) is framed by two research reports (Eccl 7:23+25), which introduce the evaluation (Eccl 7:25-29). The wise woman agrees with the Proverbs tradition that foolishness is a death wish: "I recognized that wickedness is foolish and folly is madness" (Eccl 7:25).

Nonetheless, the life of learning traps students like death (Eccl 7:26). The death to which foolishness leads is bitter, but not necessarily more painful than living in the clutches of learning. Learning is consuming, but not fulfilling. Learning seizes students like a leg trap. She restrains them like handcuffs. No matter how violently students struggle to set themselves free from learning, they are trapped.

Consequently, the father of a household who is wise is rare. The mother of a household who is wise is even rarer. "See, this is what I found, says the wise woman, adding one thing to another to find the sum, which my mind has sought repeatedly, but I have not found. One man among a thousand I found, but a woman among all these I have not found" (Eccl 7:28-29). The point here is not that men are wise and women foolish, but that wisdom is rare. Only one—or not even one—person in a thousand is wise.

Audit of Learning
(Eccl 11:7—12:8)

The books of Proverbs and Ecclesiastes both close with superb traditions on learning. Unfortunately, the tradition in the book of Proverbs is often understood as an exhortation to men to choose wives with a staggering list of abilities, ranging from purchasing only prize wool and flax to rearing grateful children (Prov 31:10-31). Likewise, the audit in the book of Ecclesiastes is often understood as a fatalistic allegory on aging (Eccl 11:7—12:8; Fig. 75). It is better to read the tradition in Ecclesiastes as an audit that provides a sober assessment of how important it is to learn before the harshness of life leaves humans with senses too dulled to learn anything. The foundation of the wisdom tradition is human observation, not divine revelation. The wise are those who see, hear, touch, smell, and taste. The wise woman's closing audit is not ageism, but an exhortation to learn before the senses harden, which is the result not of aging, but of cynicism.

The wise woman is grateful for each new day. "The light of each day is sweet. Every morning their eyes delight to see the sun" (Eccl 11:7). The wise woman admonishes her students to learn something every day, no matter how long they live. Only a fool postpones until tomorrow what could be learned today. "No matter how many years they live, the wise learn something from each day. Days without learning are many in a lifetime, so treat every day like a breath of air" (Eccl 11:8).

The human senses are the tools of learning, but they are fragile and quickly become calloused. Therefore the wise woman teaches the wise to use them early and often. "My student, if you indulge your senses while they are sharp, if you let your heart learn something every day, if you satisfy your curiosity, and if you study everything you see, then the creator will endow you with wisdom" (Eccl 11:9). Having audited learning, the wise woman teaches her students to develop supple senses and lengthen the days of their learning.

Fools fill their days worrying about how to make a living. They physically work themselves to death. The wise do not let a day pass without learning from it. "Do not fill your mind with anxiety. Do not rack your body with pain. Life is too short. The time to learn vanishes like a breath of air" (Eccl 11:10).

The wise woman teaches the wise to observe the sun and moon and stars before cataracts cloud their sight. "Use your eyes before the sun, the moon, and the stars are darkened. Use your eyes before daylight is shrouded by rain clouds" (Eccl 12:2).

The wise woman teaches her students to feel with their hands, before they are crippled with palsy. She teaches them to travel before their legs are so bowed they cannot walk. The wise woman wants them to eat heartily before their teeth decay.

Youth is not a matter of years, but a condition of the senses. The "young" are those who delight in seeing and hearing and tasting and touching and smelling and feeling. The "old" are those whose senses are dark and silent and bland. "Use your hands before the guardians of the house tremble. Use your legs before the strong men are bent. Use your teeth before the grinders are idle because they are few. Use your voice before the sound of the mill is low. Use your eyes before they who look through the windows grow blind. Use your ears before the doors to the street are shut. Use your ears before the chirp of a bird is silent. Use your voice before the daughters of song are suppressed" (Eccl 12:3-4).

The wise do not wait to make love until their beards are as white as the blossoms on the almond tree. The wise make love when the locusts sing, not when they are silent. The hum of locusts during their reproductive cycle was deafening. Silence signaled that the locusts were dying. The wise do not let their passions harden until even the strongest aphrodisiac is impotent. The berries on a caper bush were eaten to enhance sexual performance. "Make love before the almond tree blooms. Kindle passion before the locust grows sluggish. Indulge concupiscence before the caper berry is without effect" (Eccl 12:5).

In the world of the Bible, people ate from their own bowls and drank from their own cups. Eating utensils were not shared. When people died, the household broke their bowl and cup. Similarly, when the sense of taste was permanently destroyed, learning ended. The wise learned with passion, always aware that the time for learning was limited. "All of us are on a journey to the grave. All of us will be escorted by mourners through the streets. Learn before your umbilical cord is snapped. Eat before your bowl is broken. Drink before your cup is shattered at the spring. Quench your thirst before the pulley falls broken into the well. Breathe before your clay returns to the earth. Inhale before your breath returns to your Creator" (Eccl 12:6-7).

For the wise the light of each day is sweet.
    Every morning their eyes delight to see the sun.

No matter how many years they live,
    The wise learn something from each day.

Days without learning are many in a lifetime,
    So treat every day like a breath of air.

My student, if you indulge your senses while they are sharp,
    If you let your heart learn something every day,

If you satisfy your curiosity,
    If you study everything you see,

Then the creator will endow you with wisdom. . . .

Do not fill your mind with anxiety.
    Do not rack your body with pain.

Life is too short.
    The time to learn vanishes like a breath of air.

Pay attention when your creator teaches.
    Learn before the days without learning come.

Use your eyes before the sun, the moon, and the stars are
    darkened,
    Use your eyes before daylight is shrouded by rain clouds.

Use your hands before the guardians of the house tremble.
    Use your legs before the strong men are bent.

Use your teeth before the grinders are idle
    because they are few.
    Use your voice before the sound of the mill is low.

Use your eyes before they who look through the windows
    grow blind.
    Use your ears before the doors to the street are shut.

Use your ears before the chirp of a bird is silent.
    Use your voice before the daughters of song are suppressed.

(continued)

Explore the world before you become afraid of heights,
     Seek adventure before you are frightened by perils
     in the street.

Make love before the almond tree blooms.
     Kindle passion before the locust grows sluggish.
     Indulge concupiscence before the caper berry
     is without effect.

All of us are on a journey to the grave.
     All of us will be escorted by mourners through the streets.

Learn before your umbilical cord is snapped.
     Eat before your bowl is broken.

Drink before your cup is shattered at the spring.
     Quench your thirst before the pulley falls broken
     into the well.

Breathe before your clay returns to the earth.
     Inhale before your breath returns to your Creator.

We live life one breath at a time, says Qoheleth.
     Exhale and the lesson of that day is gone forever.

FIGURE 75   Audit of Learning (Eccl 11:7—12:8)

Audit of Learning
(ECCLES 12:9-14)

The Audit of Learning (Eccles 12:9-14) with which the book of Ecclesiastes closes is the signature of this wise woman. It summarizes her work, which was a legacy to her students. In due time these students awarded their teacher seven honors. The wise woman was a model of wisdom, they said. She taught well. She was a critical thinker and an avid scholar who continued to rework tradition. She knew how to explain things, and she wrote clearly (Eccl 12:9-10).

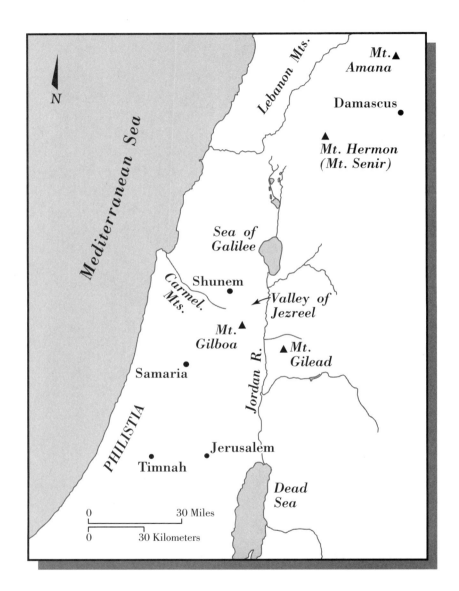

Points of Interest (Chapter 11)

11

SONG OF SOLOMON

(SONG 1:1—8:14)

E rotic propositions, tours-burlesque, flirts, boasts, and fantasies make up the Song of Solomon (Hebrew: *Shir Hashirim*). These traditions are joined to one another by motifs and catchwords. The Hebrew title "Song of Songs" (Song 1:1) is a superlative that means "the best song." "All the world is not worth the day that the Song of Songs was given to Israel. All the writings are holy, but the Song of Songs is the holy of holies" (Mishnah Yadaim 3:5)

Technically, however, the Song of Solomon is not a song. As in the book of Psalms, the words "song," "psalm," or "poem" describe a technique, not a genre. This technique enriches the sound and rhythm quality of the language in any genre. Language with little sound and rhythm quality is "prose" regardless of whether it is a creation story or a hymn. Language with highly developed sound and rhythm quality is a "song," "psalm," or "poem" regardless of whether it is a lament or an ancestor story.

There is a long-standing rabbinical tradition that understands the Song of Solomon as an allegory in which Yahweh courts Israel to an exalted spiritual union in the bond of perfect love. Similarly, during the Middle Ages, Bernard of Clairvaux (1090–1153) interpreted the Song of Solomon as a description of the union between Christ and the church, or of the union between Christ and the individual soul, or between Christ and Mary (2 Cor 11:2; Rev 19:6-8). These medieval interpretations became common in Christian hymns. Nonetheless, the Song of Solomon is not an allegory, which is not a genre, but a literary technique. Allegory assigns a particular moral value to each character, and develops the relationship between these values in order to teach the audience how to establish priorities. The technique can be applied to any genre.

The Song of Solomon is also not about marriage. The word "marriage" is mentioned only once when the woman is describing her lover: "Look, O daughters of Zion, at King

Solomon, at the crown with which his mother crowned him on the day of his wedding, on the day of the gladness of his heart" (Song 3:11). The characters in the Song of Solomon are lovers, but not husband and wife or even engaged to one another. When the man calls the woman "bride" (Song 4:8-12; 5:1) he is describing their intimacy, not their social status. Their relationship is sexual, but not marital.

The Song of Solomon is also not about Yahweh and Israel. It never mentions "Yahweh" or any other name for the divine patron of Israel. Even if the Song of Solomon were about Yahweh and Israel, prophetic traditions like the books of Isaiah, Ezekiel, Jeremiah, and Hosea use marriage to describe the covenant between Yahweh and Israel. Wisdom or teaching traditions like the books of Proverbs, Job, Ecclesiastes, and the Song of Solomon do not. For the prophets, Israel is the bride of Yahweh who has the exclusive right to provide for and protect Israel. When the rulers of Israel and Judah made covenants with other states for food and arms, the prophets indicted them for adultery. No such analogies appear in the books of Proverbs, Job, and Ecclesiastes. Therefore, it is unlikely that the Song of Solomon is describing the covenant between Yahweh and Israel, or using marriage to describe that covenant.

For the same reasons that the book of Job is not a drama, the Song of Solomon is not a drama. Drama presents conflicts and emotions through action and dialogue as a theatrical performance. It is a Greek genre, seldom used in the world of the Bible. Because they prohibited divine images, the Hebrews would have found the portrayal of Yahweh by a priest wearing a mask to be idolatry (Deut 5:6-10). Nonetheless, as early as 400 C.E. the Codex Sinaiticus understood the Song of Solomon to be a drama. Some verses in this Greek translation of the Bible are marked to be spoken or sung by the "bride (B)," some by the "groom (G)," some by the "daughters of Jerusalem (D)."

The Song of Solomon belongs to the genre erotica. Cultures develop erotic traditions to teach men and women how to make love, and to motivate them to make love. Lovemaking is unique to its culture of origin. Seldom are the patterns of behavior established by one culture transferable to another. Therefore, erotica, like the Song of Solomon and the love songs of Egypt, teaches adults in the expected patterns of sexual behavior (Fig. 76). Sexual behavior is also among the most fragile activities in any culture. Sexual behavior can be interrupted by any number of physical, emotional, or psychological factors. Erotica motivates adults to engage in sexual activity, or to return to regular sexual activity after it has been interrupted.

Erotica is not pornography. Erotic traditions focus on healthy and balanced physical relationships. Pornography promotes violence against one sexual partner by the other. Pornography promotes physical abuse, not sexual relationships. Erotica develops from the boy-talk and girl-talk that take place in every culture. When groups of boys and girls or men and women get together, they inevitably talk about the attributes of

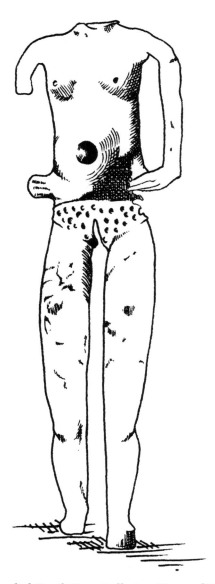

"Your Navel is a Rounded Bowl, Your Belly is a Heap of Wheat" (Song 7:2)
(Safadi 4300–3300 B.C.E.; ivory 10 cm)

the opposite sex. The daughters of Jerusalem who appear in the Song of Solomon are the women of the household with whom the singer speaks.

Propositions

The proposition is an invitation to make love, and a promise that it will be a sensual delight. There are at least ten propositions in the Song of Solomon (Song 1:2-4; 2:8-13, 14, 16-17; 4:8-9; 4:12—5:1; 7:11-14; 8:6-7, 11-12, 13-14). The structure of a proposition is similar to a hymn. The hymn invites its audience to praise Yahweh. The

Her song:

> I am still here with you,
>> But your heart is no longer here with me.
>
> Why have you stopped holding me?
>> What have I done?
>
> You no longer seek to caress my thighs. . . .
>> Would you leave me to get something to eat?
>> Are you that much a slave to your belly?
>
> Would you leave me to look for something to wear?
>> Would you leave me holding the sheet?
>
> If you are thinking about something to eat,
>> Then feast on my breasts, make my milk flow for you.
>
> Better a day in the embrace of a lover.
>> Than thousands of days elsewhere. . . .

His song:

> My lover is a marsh,
>> My lover is lush with growth. . .
>
> Her mouth is a lotus bud,
>> Her breasts are mandrake blossoms,
>
> Her arms are vines,
>> Her eyes are shaded like berries,
>
> Her head is a trap built from branches . . . and I am the gander.
>> Her hair is the bait in the trap . . . to ensnare me.

FIGURE 76   Egyptian Love Songs (Matthews and Benjamin 1997: 297–98)

proposition invites its audience to make love. Hymns use creation stories to remind their audiences of what Yahweh has done, to motivate them to accept the invitation to praise Yahweh. Propositions describe the pleasure of sexual intercourse, to motivate men and women to accept the invitation to make love.

The world of the Bible considers humans to be fully alive only when every sense has been stimulated. Sexual intercourse is one human behavior that brings the senses to life. Other human behaviors that fully engage the senses are eating, farming, learning, offering sacrifice, and waging war. Each of these activities demands the total involvement of every sense. Therefore, sexuality in the Song of Solomon is holistic, not genital. Only those who, with great deliberation (Song 2:16-17), involve the full attention of every sense enjoy fulfilling sexual relationships.

Woman's Proposition
(SONG 1:2-4)

The Song of Solomon opens with a proposition in which the woman invites the man to kiss her. She promises that the taste of her lips will exhilarate him like wine; that the sound of his name on her lips will arouse his ears; and that the smell of her perfume will excite his nostrils. "Let him kiss me. . . . For your love is better than wine, your anointing oils are fragrant, your name is perfume poured out" (Song 1:2-3). Then she invites him to embrace her, because he will feel her eagerness to make love: "Draw me after you, hurry" (Song 1:4). Finally, she propositions him to make love with her, because like wine she will intoxicate all of his senses. "My king has brought me into his chambers. We will celebrate your beauty. We will extol your love more than wine. Rightly do they love you" (Song 1:4). It specifically addresses the senses of taste, hearing, smell, and touch. The use of wine at the beginning and the end of the proposition creates a frame.

The woman addresses her lover as a king (Song 1:4), but he is neither a king nor King Solomon. Throughout the Song of Solomon, the man and the woman call each other by pet names: "sister," "brother" (Song 8:1), "bride," "shepherd," and "king" (Song 1:4). The names express affection. They do not indicate that the lovers are shepherds, monarchs, or related to one another by birth. The man and the woman also call each other by the names of animals like "fox" (Song 2:15), "gazelle" (Song 2:9), and "dove" (Song 2:14); by the names of plants like "flower of Sharon" (Song 2:1) and "palm tree" (Song 7:8); and by the names of foods like "quince" (Song 2:3), "pomegranate" (Song 4:13), "wine" (Song 5:1), and "milk" (Song 5:1). Lovers today still use titles of power, names of animals, plants, and foods as terms of endearment for one another. He is a "Prince." She is a "Lady." She calls him "Bull." He calls her "Kitten." He is "Forrest." She is "Rose." He is "Honey." She is "Sugar."

Solomon is the patron of the Song of Solomon. Like the identification of the books of Genesis, Exodus, Leviticus, Numbers, and Deuteronomy with Moses, the book of Psalms with David, and the books of Proverbs, Ecclesiastes, and Wisdom with Solomon, the identification of Solomon with the Song of Solomon is a long-standing tradition. Individual authorship in traditional societies is rare, if, in fact, it exists at all. The Song of Solomon is not the work of Solomon, but a legacy of generations of lovers. Solomon appears today in the title because ancient Israel honored him as a patron of the teaching traditions that Israel shared with Egypt and Mesopotamia. The dedication may also have sought the endorsement of such a revered figure in Israel to protect these sexually explicit traditions from being censored by those who found them unfit for the Bible. Therefore, it is better to understand the woman's use of "king" as a pet name for her lover (Song 1:4), and not a sign that she is being romanced by the ruler of Israel.

Man's Proposition
(SONG 2:8-13)

Both the man and the woman proposition each other. The proposition is not a gender-specific genre. In one proposition (Song 2:8-13) the woman describes the man "gazing through the windows, peering through the lattices" (Song 2:9). She is a feast for his eyes. Similar language in a story of Isaac and Rebekah is equally sensual: "Abimelech, ruler of the Philistines, looked out of a window and was surprised to see Isaac fondling his wife Rebekah" (Gen 26:8). The woman also describes the sound of his voice inviting her to have intercourse with him: "Arise, my love, my fair one, and come away" (Song 2:10). The invitation elicits the sense of touch as well as hearing. He will touch her hand, and her feet will touch the ground, as they find a place to touch one another.

The man endorses his invitation to the woman with the promise that their lovemaking will fill the senses like spring: "Flowers appear on the earth; and the voice of the turtledove is heard in our land. The fig tree puts forth its figs, and the vines are in blossom; they give forth fragrance as delightful as spring" (Song 2:11-13). They will see the flowers, hear the birds, and smell the grapes.

Woman's Proposition
(SONG 2:16-17)

Some translations render the verbs in propositions as indicative, rather than imperative. It would better preserve the form of the proposition if "my beloved is mine and I am his; he pastures his flock among the lilies" (Song 2:16) were translated: "be my lover and I will be yours, pasture your flock among my lilies." "Turn, my lover, be like a gazelle or a young stag on the cleft mountains" (Song 2:17) preserves the imperative necessary in an invitation. The deliberation with which goats graze elicits a touch image for the deliberation with which the man and woman make love. The contrast between the glimmering black sheen of the goats' wool and the stark white blossom of the lilies is a visual image. The gazelle or stag appearing on the mountainside at dusk is also a visual image of the capacity of the man to make love to the woman.

The tradition uses double entendre to compare grazing with lovemaking. The woman imagines her lover making love to her with the deliberation and thoroughness of a grazing animal. The breathing of the couple as they make love sounds like the breeze created as the heat of the day leaves the land at nightfall. "Until the day breathes and the shadows flee, turn, my beloved, be like a gazelle or a young stag on the cleft mountains" (Song 2:17).

Man's Proposition
(SONG 4:8-9)

The man compares his lover to a wildcat, whose power, grace, and color are sexually provocative visual images. Her eyes are particularly ravishing. The eyes are a very erotic part of the body. For a woman to look a man in the eye is like a cat sighting its prey. The eyes of one lover hypnotize the other as easily as the headlights of a car can paralyze an animal in the road. To look a person of the opposite sex straight in the eye was an invitation to have intercourse.

The man invites the woman to leave her den in the wilderness and make love with him. "Come with me from Lebanon, my bride. Come with me from Lebanon. Depart from the peak of Amana for the peak of Senir and Hermon, from the dens of lions, from the mountains of leopards" (Song 4:8). The woman is wild; the man is civilized. Their intercourse takes place on the boundary between these two worlds. In the Stories of Gilgamesh from Babylon, Enkidu is wild until the Wise Woman teaches him to make love (Gilg 1:3—3:7). Intercourse civilizes. It converts the people primeval into humans.

Man's Proposition
(SONG 7:1-6)

Cultures regularly identify one place in their world whose women are the most beautiful. In Syria-Palestine it was Shunem. Here at the foot of Mt. Gilboa, sixty miles north of Jerusalem and twenty miles southeast of the Carmel Mountains, where a pass leads north into the Valley of Jezreel, lived the most beautiful women in the world. After "they sought for a beautiful young woman throughout Israel," it was in Shunem that David's officials found Abishag, "who was very beautiful. She became the king's attendant and served him, but the king did not know her sexually" (1 Kgs 1:3-4). The woman in the Song of Solomon (Song 7:1-6) is a Shulammite. The words "Shulammite" and "Shunammite" both identify women from the village of Shunem. She is the most beautiful woman in the world.

The man sings: "dance, Shulammite, dance, that we may look at you" (Song 7:1). This proposition that appeals to the man's enjoyment of seeing the woman move is followed by a boast that brags: "is not the performance of this one woman from Shunem more exciting than two entire companies of dancers?" Together they introduce a tour-burlesque (Song 7:2-6).

Tour-Burlesque

The tour-burlesque is an erotic catalog for the parts of the human body, which it describes one feature at a time. At each stop on the tour, one lover describes a part of the other's anatomy using erotic analogies. Like the other genres in the Song of Solomon, the tour-burlesque appeals to one or more of the senses of the audience. One lover begins the tour at the head; the other begins at the feet (Song 5:11+16). There are at least nine tours-burlesque in the Song of Solomon (Song 1:5-6, 9-11; 3:6-11; 4:1-5, 10-11; 5:10-16; 6:4-7; 7:1-6, 7-10).

Tour-Burlesque of the Woman's Body
(SONG 1:5-6)

In the first tour-burlesque in the Song of Solomon, the woman describes her own body to the man. She begins with her head. "I am black and beautiful" (Song 1:5). The skin on her face is tanned because the sun has made love to her as she worked outdoors in the vineyards of her household. "I am dark, because the sun has gazed on me" (Song 1:6). In erotic traditions the sun is a voyeur who spends the day gazing on all the women on earth. The heavens are pitched like a tent overhead. At dawn the sun shoves its head into the tent and then lunges forward over the women of the earth (Ps 19:5-7). The women with whom the sun makes love wear his tan.

The woman's hair frames her face as naturally as "the tents of Kedar or the curtains of Solomon" (Song 1:5). Her face is dark. Her hair is black and radiant as the goat hair from which weavers fashion tents and curtains.

The third stop in the tour-burlesque is the woman's reproductive organs, which she describes as a vineyard. "My mother's sons were angry with me. They made me keeper of the vineyards, but my own vineyard I have not kept" (Song 1:6). The same imagery, which creates a parallel between farming and lovemaking, appears in a Trial of Jotham (Isa 5:1-7), where Yahweh and the farmers of Judah are not just working the vineyard, they are making love to it.

Sing of Yahweh as a lover.
Sing of Yahweh's love for the vineyard of Judah.
My lover built a vineyard.
Yahweh built it on a fertile hillside.
My lover spaded it, cleared it of stones.
Yahweh planted choice vines.
My lover built a tower to watch over it.
Yahweh hewed a wine press out of rock. (Isa 5:1-2)

Farmers make love to the land. The same words that describe farming in Hebrew also describe lovemaking. Fertility was the ability to have a child, which was the work of lovemaking, and to have a harvest, which was the work of farming.

The Stories of Tammuz and Ishtar model the parallel between farming and lovemaking throughout the world of the Bible. In 1845, Austen Henry Layard (1817–94) excavated Nimrud for the British Museum, where he located both the palace of Sennacherib (704–681 B.C.E.) and the library of Ashurbanipal (668–626 B.C.E.), containing one of two important copies of the Stories of Tammuz. Tammuz is also called "Dumuzi," and his lover, Ishtar, is also called "Inanna," "Astarte," "Ashtartu," and "Ashtoreth" (Fig. 77). The stories celebrated this divine couple as the patrons of herding, farming, and childbearing throughout the eastern Mediterranean. They were lovers separated by death, but reunited by love. In some traditions, it is Ishtar who descends into the land of the dead; in others it is Tammuz. In both, the widowed partner faithfully pursues and rescues the other from death. Their story of love and loss is also the story of the death of the earth during the long dry season, and its rebirth at the beginning of the wet season under the relentless labor of its farmers. These stories were told during a celebration at the end of the long dry season during June and July, on days 27–29 of the month of Du'uzu. Like the last drops of moisture that the parched soil sucks deep into the earth, Tammuz is drawn by stages into the land of the dead. Ishtar, however, will not forsake him. Like the rain that moistens the soil at the end of the dry season so that farmers can plow and plant, the words and actions of Ishtar in the land of the dead bring Tammuz back to life. She raises him from the dead like the first leaves of the crops that sprout through the soil under a farmer's care at the beginning of the growing season.

Words of anger inspire words of passion.
   Quarrels arouse a desire for love.

Let the farmer who plows between the boundary stones
   in his field,
   Let the farmer who plows between the boundary stones
   in his field,
   Plow between these boundary stones.

Dumuzi plows between the boundary stones in his field,
   He is the farmer who plows between the boundary
   stones in his field,
   Let Amaushumgalanna plow between
   these boundary stones.

Let the plower who fills his cistern with rain from the roof,
   Fill this cistern for her.

Let the plower who fills his cistern with rain off the walls,
   Fill this cistern for her. . . .

Plow between these boundary stones,
   Plow between these boundary stones.
   Who else will plow this field for her?

Dumuzi was created for me,
   Amaushumgalanna was made for me,
   With a beard as dark and rich as lapis lazuli.

Dumuzi was created for me by Anu, my Godparent,
   Amaushumgalanna was made for me,
   With a beard as dark and rich as lapis lazuli

With a beard as dark and rich as lapis lazuli
   With a beard as dark and rich as lapis lazuli.

FIGURE 77   Tammuz and Ishtar (Matthews and Benjamin 1997: 306–07)

Tour-Burlesque of the Woman's Body
(SONG 4:1-5)

In the tour-burlesque that opens the Song of Solomon, the woman describes her own body to the man. In a subsequent tour-burlesque it is the man who describes the woman's body (Song 4:1-5). He begins by describing the woman's eyes, then her hair, then her teeth, her lips, her cheeks, her neck, and finally her breasts.

The whites of the woman's eyes are shaped like doves drinking from pools that are the pupils of her eyes. "Your eyes are doves behind your veil" (Song 4:1). The analogy appeals to the sense of sight.

The tour moves from the woman's eyes to her hair, which is "like a flock of goats working its way down the slopes of Mt. Gilead" (Song 4:1). Like a goat's wool the woman's hair is black and has a rich and lustrous sheen. Like goats that follow the contour lines of the hills that they graze, the woman's hair perfectly complements the shape of her head.

The woman has a full and straight set of white teeth. None are crooked, none are rotting, and none are missing. Every upper tooth has a perfectly matched lower tooth. "Your teeth are like a flock of sheep just shorn coming up from the washing. Each has its twin. Not one of them is alone" (Song 4:2).

After the man celebrates the eyes, the hair, and the teeth of the woman, he describes her mouth. "Your lips are like a scarlet thread, your mouth is lovely" (Song 4:3). The curve of her mouth is as natural as the shape of a thread dropped on a cloth. Its color perfectly accents her face.

"Your cheeks behind your veil are like the halves of pomegranates" (Song 4:3). The shape of the pomegranate is full and healthy. Its cream-colored skin is lightly rouged.

Engineers who build battle towers must carefully place every stone so that the symmetry of the tower is perfect. The least flaw puts the tower out of balance and places its defenders at risk. The shape of the woman's neck is equally flawless. Its beauty is highlighted by a necklace. The shields of the warriors who defend a tower hang proudly from its parapet. The charms of every lover who has courted the woman hang proudly from her necklace.

The last stop on the tour of the woman's body is her breasts, which "are like the twin fawns of a gazelle grazing in lilies" (Song 4:5). The hide of the gazelles stands out from the lilies, and the tan of the woman's breasts contrasts with her white blouse. Her breasts are as soft as the coat of a fawn.

Tour-Burlesque of the Man's Body
(SONG 5:11-16)

The woman begins her tour-burlesque along the man's body with the skin on his face. Then she moves down his body toward his legs and returns to describe his mouth. Her tour-burlesque is a round trip.

"The skin of my lover is twenty-four karat gold" (Song 5:11), the woman sings. Like precious metal, his skin is smooth to the touch. Like gold, the skin of the man is a healthy bronze color that shines in the light. Like twenty-four karat gold, his skin is without imperfection.

The woman compares the hair of the man to the fruit of the palm that hangs curled beneath its branches. His hair is black and silky like the feathers of a raven (Song 5:12).

The whites of the man's eyes are like doves drinking from the pupils, which are like springs of water (Song 5:12). She describes him with the same metaphor he used to describe her.

The man's teeth are white as milk (Song 5:12). Each tooth is set as perfectly in his mouth as a jewel mounted on a ring.

The tour-burlesque then switches from analogies appealing to the sense of sight to an analogy that appeals to the sense of smell. "His cheeks are like beds of spice ready to be pressed into perfume" (Song 5:13). The scent of the man tells the woman that he is ready for making love just as the aroma of the spices tells the perfumer when it is time to harvest them.

The woman tastes the lips of the man. She compares them to the nectar that drips from the blossom of a flower ready to reproduce (Song 5:13).

The arms of the man are gold inlaid with semiprecious stones. His chest is ivory inlaid with sapphires (Song 5:14). The gold and ivory are smooth to the touch. These gem stones sparkle in the light, revealing the exquisite definition of his body.

The appearance of his legs, and his stature, are as firm as marble columns. They are rooted in the earth like the cedars of Lebanon (Song 5:15).

Finally, the mouth of the man is the epitome of sweetness (Song 5:16). He is a feast for the eyes and the nose and the tongue. His physical presence fully engages each sense.

Erotic Fantasies

The erotic fantasy is a story that anticipates or remembers a sexual encounter. Like all stories, it has a plot with a crisis, a climax, and a denouement. The crisis describes the foreplay between the man and the woman (Song 1:9—2:3). The climax describes their sexual intercourse (Song 2:3-6). The denouement of the erotic fantasy describes the afterglow (Song 2:7). There are at least seven fantasies in the Song of Solomon (Song 1:9—2:7; 3:2-8; 4:6-11; 5:2-8; 6:11-12; 8:1-4, 5).

Erotic Fantasy
(SONG 1:9—2:7)

In the first erotic fantasy in the Song of Solomon, the woman remembers making love with the man. The crisis episode describes their foreplay as a tour-burlesque (Song 1:9—2:3). The man arouses each of her senses. She hears the passion of the man like a stallion ready to mate, whose powerful breath causes his entire body to shudder, and his necklace to jingle like a harness (Song 1:9-11). She smells the aroma of his body and feels the gentle touch of his body against her breasts (Song 1:12-14). She looks deeply into his eyes (Song 1:15-16), and she sees the branches of the trees like ceiling beams over their heads as they make love on the grass (Song 1:16-17). She closes the crisis episode with a boast. She is a flower without equal (Song 2:1). He is the tree whose fruit is the quince, an erotic fruit that enhances sexual enjoyment.

The quince grows on a tree found throughout central Asia. It resembles a hard-fleshed yellow apple and is processed into marmalades, jellies, and preserves that were considered aphrodisiacs (Fig. 78). This is the tree that tradition, but not the Stories of Adam and Eve themselves, identify with the Tree of the Knowledge of Good and Evil. Those who eat from the quince tree are initiated into the sexual activity of adults.

In the climax episode of the erotic fantasy, the woman describes her intercourse with the man as a banquet (Song 2:3-6). His passion hangs like a banner over her (Song 2:4). Eating, like sexual intercourse, involves all five senses. She tastes their love. Raisins are not just a snack. Like the quince, they are an aphrodisiac that enhances sexual performance and enjoyment. She feels their love. "My lover caresses my head with his left hand. He fondles my body with his right" (Song 2:6).

> *My lover brings me into the banquet hall.*
> *He smothers me with love.*
>
> *My lover feeds me raisins so that I will not faint.*
> *He gives me quince to fire my passion.*
>
> *My lover caresses my head with his left hand.*
> *He fondles my body with his right.*

FIGURE 78   Erotic Fantasy (Song 2:4-6)

In the denouement, the woman tells the women in her household to let her enjoy the afterglow of intercourse: "I adjure you, daughters of Jerusalem, by the gazelles and hinds of the field, do not interrupt, do not end lovemaking prematurely" (Song 2:7). Wild deer are abundant because they relish mating. Humans likewise should let their lovemaking last.

Erotic Fantasy
(SONG 3:2-8)

In another erotic fantasy, the love of the man and the love of the woman are both unrequited (Song 3:2-8). In the crisis episode (Song 3:2-6), the man comes to the house of the woman at night while she is asleep (Song 3:2). He knocks, undresses, and reaches through a window in the wall to caress her (Song 3:3-4). By the time she is fully awake and opens the door, however, the man is gone (Song 3:5).

The climax of this erotic fantasy is not lovemaking, but violence (Song 3:7). The woman runs after him without her veil (Song 3:6; Fig. 79). The warriors guarding the city arrest the woman for not wearing a veil, strip her naked, and flog her (Hos 2:3, 10).

In the denouement (Song 3:8), the woman asks the women of her household to tell the man that the pain inflicted by the warriors is nothing. It is the pain of being unable to make love with him.

Teases

The tease is a riddle with two meanings. One meaning is always sexual. This technique of using language that carries at least two different levels of meaning is double entendre. There are, at least, five teases in the Song of Solomon (Song 1:7-8; 2:15; 6:1-3, 10; 8:8-10). Sometimes the Song of Solomon provides a solution to the tease (Song 1:8; 6:2 3; 8:10); sometimes it does not (Song 2:15; 6:10).

Tease
(SONG 2:15)

In the tease: "Who can catch the foxes? Who can catch the little foxes that damage the vineyard; that damage our vineyards when they bloom" (Song 2:15), the foxes carry the same connotations as they do in the Saga of Samson (Judg 15:18). The fox is a phallic symbol for the penis, the vineyard a symbol of the vagina. Just as the fox burrows into the vineyard, the penis buries itself in the vagina. The lover sings that she is "in bloom," or ready to make love, and every available male is ready to "damage her vineyard." To recover his honor, Samson runs three hundred foxes through the fields, orchards, and vineyards of Timnah, setting them on fire (Judg 15:1-8). Many traditional cultures associate foxes with sexual revenge. Men frustrated in their desire for sexual intercourse shift into the shape of a fox to seduce women. Like foxes digging burrows in the land, men have sexual intercourse with women. It is virtually impossible to prevent foxes from digging their burrows in the spring; similarly, it is virtually impossible to prevent men from making love with women.

A, art. 40

Mothers of households, widows, and other free women are to wear veils when they go out of their households. Marriageable women are to wear veils...when they go out of their households.

Secondary wives are to wear veils when they go out with the mothers of their households. *Qadiltu*-women, who are married priests, are to wear veils when they go out of their households.

Unmarried *qadiltu*-women are not to wear veils when they go out of their households. Prostitutes are not to wear veils.

If a citizen sees a prostitute wearing a veil, then she is arrested, witnesses are subpoenaed, and she is charged before the assembly at the palace gate. Her jewelry is not confiscated, but the plaintiff is to confiscate her clothing. She is flogged fifty times with staves, and tar is poured into her hair.

If a citizen sees a prostitute who is wearing a veil, and does not charge her at the palace gate, then he is flogged fifty times with staves, his clothes are confiscated, his ears are pierced and tied with a cord behind his head, and he is to serve as a slave for the state for one full month.

Slaves are not to wear veils.

If a citizen sees a slave wearing a veil, then she is arrested, charged before the assembly at the palace gate, her ears are cut off, and her clothes are confiscated by the plaintiff.

If a citizen sees a slave wearing a veil and does not arrest her and charge her at the palace gate, then, following due process, he is flogged fifty times with staves, his ears are pierced and tied with a cord behind his head, his clothes are confiscated, and he is to serve as a slave for the state for one full month.

FIGURE 79   Middle Assyrian Code (Matthews and Benjamin 1997: 119–20)

Tease

(SONG 8:8-10)

The tease: "What do we do with a sister whose breasts develop before it is time to betroth her?" is followed by the solution: "if she is chaste, build towers of silver over her breasts. If she is promiscuous, panel her breasts with cedar" (Song 8:8-10), that is, highlight the physical endowments of a chaste woman to enrich the honor to the household, or disguise the physical endowments of a promiscuous woman to protect the household from shame. One tease is a riddle about how to control men who want to make love; the other is a riddle about how to control women who want to make love. Both the fantasies that the riddles evoke and the solutions that they elicit erotically stimulate the senses by proposing extraordinary sexual behavior.

Boasts

Like a better proverb (Prov 17:1), a boast compares lovers and declares one to be unique. There are, at least, two boasts in the Song of Solomon (Song 5:9; 6:8-9).

Boast

(SONG 5:9)

The boast: "How can you, blessed woman, boast: 'My lover is unique.' How can you, beautiful woman, swear: 'My lover is different from all others'" (Song 5:9) invites the woman to specify the comparisons or the contrasts that set the man apart from all other men.

Boast

(SONG 6:8-9)

"My dove stands out from sixty mothers of households or eighty secondary wives. She is perfect. She is her mother's chosen. She is her father's beloved. Mothers of households and secondary wives sing: 'Who rises like the moon, dawns like the sun, and advances like soldiers with their banners flying?'" (Song 6:8-10). The man has compared the woman with all the mothers and wives in the city and declares her to be unique. The mother and the father of the woman endorse his boast, as do the mothers and wives with whom they compare her. No experience, human or divine, compares with the sight of this woman.

Sexual intercourse was not only a personal relationship, but also a public obligation. In the Stories of Ishtar and Tammuz, for example, the semen from the lovemaking of this divine couple pours down on the earth like rain and fertilizes it. When they
are separated, there is no semen to water the earth. Everything begins to dry up and
die. To end the drought, men and women in the villages, like the couple in the Song
of Solomon, engaged in sexual intercourse until they aroused Tammuz and Ishtar to make
love again and bring the earth back to life (Ezek 8:14).

The Hebrews opposed ritual intercourse. They were not sexual prudes. For the
Hebrews sexuality was characteristic of humans. They objected to appropriating human
sexuality to Yahweh. Yahweh was not sexual, but integral.

The Hebrews also objected to ritual intercourse because they considered it to be a
way of reminding Yahweh to keep them and their land fertile, and therefore irreverently
implied that Yahweh was forgetful. The Hebrews were to be patient and to have absolute
confidence in the promises that Yahweh made, even during the dry season when, for
all intents and purposes, the land was dead.

The Song of Solomon encourages human beings to cherish their sexual lives. Teachers studied the importance of sexuality in human life, just as they studied the role of
work, of learning, and of possessions. They use erotica like the Song of Solomon not
only to teach their students how to engage in sexual intercourse, but also to motivate
them to lead sexually active lives.

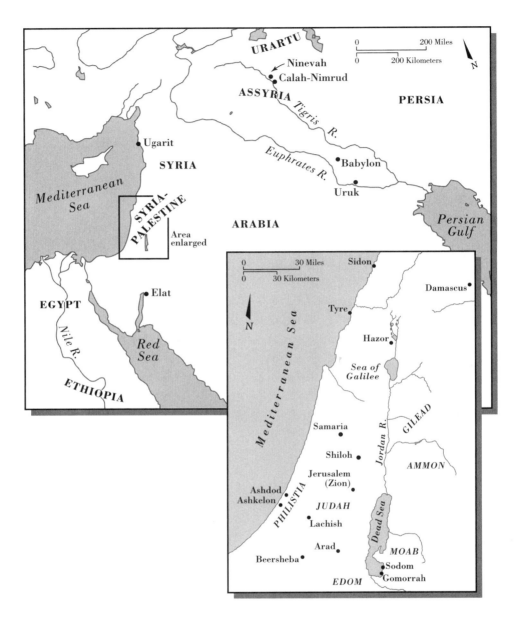

Points of Interest (Chapter 12)

12

BOOK OF ISAIAH

(ISA 1:1—66:24)

T he book of Isaiah (Hebrew: *Yesha'yahu*), the book of Jeremiah, and the book of Ezekiel preserve some of the richest and most enduring traditions in the Bible. They defined and redefined what it meant to be a Hebrew. Isaiah developed in at least three major phases (Fig. 80). The first prophetic movement was a response to several indications that, between 800 and 750 B.C.E., Judah's prosperity was coming to an end (Isa 1:1—39:8). Uzziah (783–742 B.C.E.), king of Judah, contracted leprosy, forcing him from the throne (2 Chr 26:16-20). Then, a killer earthquake struck Judah, crippling its economy (Amos 1:1; Zech 14:5). Finally, Tiglath-pileser III (744–727 B.C.E.), Assyria's great king, conducted a series of military campaigns in Syria-Palestine, threatening Judah's independence. These were signs that times were changing.

Assyrian armies first began crossing the Euphrates River shortly after 925 B.C.E. These raids and hunting expeditions were not wars of conquest. Assyria was not prepared to administer an empire. Shalmaneser III (858–824 B.C.E.) was the first great king to establish a permanent Assyrian presence west of the Euphrates. In a war memorial celebrating his fifth western campaign, this great king ratified his covenant with Jehu, the ruler of Israel. Tiglath-pileser III formally inaugurated a new age of empires. He completely reorganized Assyria's bureaucracy to gain control of the trade routes running from the Mediterranean coast inland. Any embargo in these trade lanes cut off Assyria's imports of metals, lumber, and horses.

Tiglath-pileser III proposed that Assyria ratify covenants with neighboring states either as allies, as colonies, or as provinces. Any state willing to align itself with Assyria's foreign policy and offer logistical and military assistance became an Assyrian ally or covenant partner. These covenant partners retained self-determination in their domestic policies as long as they were able to meet their tax quotas. When they did not,

1. Trial of Judah (Isa 1:1—39:8)
    a. Analysis of Judah's Domestic Policy (Isa 1:1—12:6)
    b. Analysis of Judah's Foreign Policy (Isa 13:1—27:13)
    c. Analysis of Judah's Domestic Policy (Isa 28:1—39:8)
2. Creation of Zion (Isa 40:1—55:13)
3. Isaiah's Book of Psalms (Isa 56:1—66:24)

FIGURE 80   Patterns in the Book of Isaiah (Isa 1:1—66:24)

Assyria's covenant partners lost their independence and became Assyrian colonies. In a colony, local officials retained their titles, but Assyrian personnel reviewed all domestic policies to guarantee the colony would meet the empire's budget. Their primary responsibility was to design austerity measures for local governments to implement in order to meet their debt obligations to Assyria. Refusal on the part of local officials left the colony subject to outright foreclosure by Assyria, which would deport all government personnel, redistribute the colony's population in developing regions of the empire, and assign the colony an Assyrian military governor, incorporating it completely into the empire as a province. Assyria preferred to leave local governments in place rather than to administer states directly as provinces. Local rulers did a better job of managing economies than Assyrian bureaucrats. Local soldiers provoked fewer border incidents with Egypt than Assyrian troops. Only states with healthy economies, efficient governments, and popular monarchs managed to maintain their self-determination. Assyria's budget requirements increased continually, and few local governments could meet Assyria's expectations and avoid a taxpayers' revolt. Revolutions were frequent. Israel went from the status of an Assyrian ally in 738 B.C.E., to an Assyrian colony in 732 B.C.E., and finally to an Assyrian province in 721 B.C.E.

By the time Tiglath-pileser III died, he had built Assyria into the most powerful state since the collapse of Egypt, Hatti, and Mycenae at the end of the Bronze Age. The Assyria of Tiglath-pileser III was tightly controlled. Both loyalty and rebellion were costly. Israel and Judah, like all Assyria's allies, colonies, and provinces, were deeply taxed, and any moves toward independence were penalized by stiff military reprisals. Loyalty to Assyria cost Ahaz (735–715 B.C.E.), ruler of Judah, a staggering amount to pay for Assyrian troops who defended him against Syria and Israel. In response to Israel's declaration of independence from Assyria, Sargon II (721–705 B.C.E.) completely destroyed Samaria and reduced Israel to the status of an Assyrian province with little or no self-government in 721 B.C.E. Finally, in 701 B.C.E., Judah's declaration of independence from Assyria led to invasion.

Isaiah was an important player in the politics of these times. There were at least five major campaigns in phase one of the Isaiah movement. The first campaign focused on the role of the monarch as provider for the state, and attempted to change royal domestic policy. The next four campaigns focused on the role of the monarch as the protector of the state, and attempted to change royal foreign policies.

Trials of Judah
(Isa 1:1—39:8)

Isaiah Movement, Phase One, 740–700 B.C.E.

Trial of Judah
(Isa 1:2-31)

Covenants between one state and another were under the jurisdiction of Yahweh and the divine assembly. Sometimes prophets served the divine assembly as prosecuting attorneys, sometimes as defense attorneys, and sometimes as jury foremen, who announced the decisions of the assembly to the defendants. Any state that disturbed the peace by revolution, by war, or even by negotiating for logistical supplies like food and weapons, was subject to trial before Yahweh and the divine assembly.

The book of Isaiah opens with a Trial of Judah (Isa 1:2-31) composed of an indictment (Isa 1:2-10), a sentence (Isa 1:11-17), and an appeal (Isa 1:18-31). Both the indictment and the sentence are introduced by a summons addressed to the members of the divine assembly (Fig. 81). The first summons impanels the heavens and the earth to hear the case against Judah (Isa 1:2). The second impanels the cities of Sodom and Gomorrah (Isa 1:10). The heavens (Deut 30:19; 31:28) and the earth (Deut 4:26; 30:19; 31:28) appear here because, in contrast to Israel and Judah, the heavens and the earth are faithful to their covenants with Yahweh. Similarly, Sodom and Gomorrah have suffered the tragic consequences of their own actions in violating their covenants with Yahweh. As converts, they are models of born-again faithfulness to others.

The indictment charges Judah with forgetting that Yahweh is the divine patron who provides its people with food. The ox and the ass know that whoever feeds them is their master. In contrast, the people of Judah eat the food that Yahweh provides, and think they feed themselves and have no master. They think that they have grown or negotiated for the food that they eat.

indictment (Isa 1:2-3)

> Let the heavens hear and the earth listen when Yahweh speaks:
>
> "I have been faithful to Israel and Judah,
>   But they were unfaithful to me.
>
> An ox knows its owner, and an ass knows
>   who fills its manger,
>   But my people do not."

lament (Isa 1:4-9)

> Shame! Only the unclean are unfaithful to Yahweh,
>   Only fools abrogate their covenants with the Holy One,
>   Only the shamed do such evil.
>
> Judah, your body is covered with wounds, yet you still rebel?
>   Your whole head is bleeding,
>   Your heart is scarcely beating.
>
> From head to foot, you are covered with bruises.
>   Wounds and welts . . . infected, unbandaged, untreated.
>
> Your villages are laid waste,
>   Your cities are burned to the ground.
>   Your crops feed strangers,
>
> Jerusalem looks like Sodom and Gomorrah.
>   The chosen city looks like a harvester's hut abandoned
>   in a vineyard,
>   Zion looks like a farmer's hut left in a melon patch. . . .

sentence (Isa 1:10-17)

> Let Sodom hear the word of Yahweh,
>   Let Gomorrah listen to the commandments of Yahweh. . . .
>
> "Trample my courts no more, bring no more worthless
>   offerings.
>   Your incense is loathsome to me.
>   Your new moons, Sabbaths, assemblies, octaves, and
>   festivals I detest. . . .

(continued)

You lift your hands, I close my eyes. The more you pray,
the less I listen.
Your hands are full of blood, wash yourselves clean.
Get evil out of my sight, cease doing evil.
Learn to do good, make justice your aim.
Redress the wronged.
Hear the orphan's plea.
Defend the widow."

appeal (Isa 1:18-31)

"Though your sins be scarlet, they will become white as
snow," says Yahweh.
"Though they be crimson, they will become white as
wool.

If you are faithful, you shall eat produce from the land,
If you are unfaithful, the sword shall eat you. . . ."

Therefore Yahweh Sabaoth rules: "I will take vengeance on
my foes."
The Mighty One promises: "I will fully repay my enemies.

I will be a crucible smelting out dross,
I will be a forge burning out impurities.

I will reestablish the city assembly, and appoint new elders.
You shall be called 'City of Justice' and 'Faithful City.'

Zion will be delivered from its enemies by its judgment,
The repentant will be delivered by their justice.

Rebels and sinners shall be threshed,
Deserters shall be burned.

Sacred trees will shame you, sacred groves will embarrass you.
You shall become a leafless tree, and a waterless garden.

The gardener shall turn to tinder, his garden shall burst
into flames.
Both shall burn together, no one shall quench the flames."

FIGURE 81   Trial of Judah (Isa 1:1-31)

The indictment has been elaborated with a lament like those found in the book of Psalms (Isa 1:4-9). When the mourners hear the charges brought against the rulers of Judah, they cannot believe that these monarchs do not learn from the excruciating suffering that their flawed foreign policies impose on the land and its people. Even when every covenant for food results in famine and starvation, and every covenant for arms results in war and invasion, they continue making new covenants. They never seem to learn that the people will be fed and the land will be protected only when they are fed and protected by Yahweh.

Judah's foreign policy of negotiating covenants for food from other states always results in the complete destruction of its own farms and pastures. Here the sentence is imposed in the form of a decalogue. The first four stipulations (Isa 1:12-15) describe the infertility that covenants with other states have imposed upon Judah. The last six describe how the people of Judah can renew their covenant with Yahweh (Isa 1:16-17).

The trial concludes with an appeal (Isa 1:17-31) that mourns the suffering of the people of Judah caused by the foreign policies of their monarchs, and describes the renewal of the covenant between Yahweh and Judah.

Trial of Jotham, 740–735 B.C.E.
(Isa 5:1-7)

Isaiah is not looking into the far future, but simply ahead to the near-term consequences of the actions of the monarchs Uzziah, Jotham, Ahaz, and Hezekiah. Isaiah observes the trial of these rulers before Yahweh and the divine assembly for violating the covenant between Yahweh and Judah. In the covenant, Yahweh promises to protect and provide for the land and its people. Uzziah, Jotham, and Ahaz violate Yahweh's prerogatives by negotiating covenants with other states to protect and provide for Judah. Their actions show that they do not believe that Yahweh can, or that Yahweh will, fulfill the stipulations of the covenant.

The sentence is framed by two indictments. Jotham is on trial because he negotiated a covenant between Judah and Assyria (Fig. 82). He and Ahaz, his successor, were faithful to that covenant with Assyria despite the invasion of Judah by Israel and Syria and despite strong pressure from Isaiah to remain neutral. Despite the labor and care lavished on the land by Yahweh and the farmers of Judah, its monarchs continued to use the wine of Judah to negotiate covenants with foreign states for food and protection. Covenants in the world of the Bible were like insurance policies today. Clients like Judah paid patrons like Assyria premiums to guarantee that, when Judah was in crisis, they would come to its aid. Premiums were generally paid in grain and wine and olive oil. The wine of Judah so laboriously produced by Yahweh and the farmers of Judah

Assyrian Cherubim Guard Palace of the Great King
(Nimrud 883–859 B.C.E.; alabaster 4.4 m)

was shipped out of the land to Syria, to Israel, to Philistia, and to Assyria as Judah's premium payments on its covenant insurance.

The first indictment (Isa 5:3-4) is introduced by a hymn (Isa 5:1-2). Like the women of Shiloh who played instruments, danced, and sang hymns in the vineyards to celebrate the end of the grape harvest, Isaiah leads the hymn (Judg 21:16-24). It begins with a call to worship: "Sing of a lover. Sing of his love for a vineyard" (Isa 5:1). This call is followed by a creation story, which celebrates Yahweh for founding Judah like a farmer constructing a vineyard. It describes each painstaking step.

A vineyard was labor-intensive to install and to maintain. Yahweh and the farmers of Judah had to carve vineyards into rugged hillsides. They cleared away stones, built retaining walls, and brought in new topsoil. Only then could they plow and plant.

hymn (Isa 5:1-2)

> *Sing of Yahweh as a lover!*
> > *Sing of Yahweh's love for the vineyard of Judah!*
>
> *My lover built a vineyard.*
> > *Yahweh built it on a fertile hillside.*
>
> *My lover spaded it, cleared it of stones,*
> > *Yahweh planted choice vines.*
>
> *My lover built a tower to watch over it.*
> > *Yahweh hewed a winepress out of rock.*

indictment (Isa 5:3-4)

> *When my lover looked for fine domestic grapes,*
> > *Yahweh found garbage.*
>
> *"Let Jerusalem and Judah judge between me and my vineyard.*
> > *What could I do for Judah that I had not done?*
>
> *When I looked for fine domestic grapes,*
> > *I found garbage.*

sentence (Isa 5:5-6)

> *Therefore, the hedge of the vineyard will be cut down so*
> > *goats can graze.*
> > *Strangers will breach its wall, and trample the vines.*
>
> *The vineyard shall return to chaos.*
> > *The vineyard shall not be pruned or hoed,*
> > *The vineyard shall be overgrown with thorns.*
>
> *The clouds will not open.*
> > *The clouds will not send rain upon the vineyard."*

indictment (Isa 5:7)

> *The vineyard is the land of Judah.*
> > *The land is Yahweh's chosen vine.*
>
> *Yahweh looked there for judgment (Hebrew:* mishpat*),*
> > *Yahweh found bloodshed (Hebrew:* mispah*).*
>
> *Yahweh looked there for justice (Hebrew:* tsedaqah*),*
> > *Yahweh heard the cry of the poor who farmed*
> > *(Hebrew:* tse'aqah*).*

FIGURE 82   Trial of Jotham, 740–726 B.C.E. (Isa 5:1-7)

They used hardy vines as rootstock, to which they grafted cuttings from choice vines (Ps 80:11; 1 Kgs 4:25).

To protect the vineyard, Yahweh and the farmers planted a hedge of cactus or built a wall with the rocks cleared from the hillside. Both prevented grazing animals and strangers from eating fruit that they did not work to produce (Song 2:15; Ps 80:12). The hedges and walls were complemented by a tower where children watched for birds or raiders. Before vines began to produce, they had to be hoed and pruned for as long as five years. The ground around the vines was hoed in January and February. The vines were pruned in March (Lev 25:4). Finally, a two-vat winepress was carved out of bedrock. In one vat the grapes would be crushed into a mash. In the other the juice was allowed to drain from the mash, and the sediment would be allowed to settle before the juice was transferred to large storage jars to ferment (Jer 13:12-14).

Yahweh and the farmers of Judah are not just working the land, they are making love to it. A farmer was also a lover. The story describes everything Yahweh and the farmers do for the beloved vineyard using the same erotic language that appears in the Song of Solomon (Song 2:15; 4:16; 6:1; 8:12). They farm or make love to the vineyard, and the fruit of their lovemaking is the harvest of grapes (Jer 31:39; Hab 3:17; Ezek 38:20). In Semitic languages the connotations of words for farming, sexual intercourse, war, sacrifice, eating, and learning overlap, because all six activities fully engage all five human senses (Gilg I:iv:16ff.; Song 5:1; 6:11-12; 7:11-12). Lovemaking and farming are particularly interchangeable because fertility was understood as the ability of a household to have a child, which was the work of lovemaking, and to have a harvest, which was the work of farming.

The second indictment (Isa 5:7) makes it clear that Yahweh and the farmers are not simply unrequited lovers. A play on words here defines the love with which the trial opens not simply as a matter of emotion, but as a matter of justice. Yahweh and the farmers look for judgment and justice, but find only oppression and cries for help. The words "judgment" and "oppression," as well as "justice" and "cries for help," sound alike in Hebrew. Despite all the hard work that Yahweh and the farmers do for Jotham, the people of Judah starve. Vineyards should have been prized possessions whose produce would bring prosperity to the farmers of Judah for generations (1 Kgs 21:2-3). Nonetheless, Jotham and the other monarchs of Judah collected virtually everything that the farmers produced in their vineyards as taxes (Deut 28:39; Isa 5:5-6; 1 Chr 27:27). These taxes were supposed to be used to feed and protect the people of Judah, but Jotham and the other monarchs of Judah squandered the taxes, and let the households of the farmers starve. Therefore, the predators who steal the harvest are not animals or strangers, but the monarchs who own the vineyards. These royal vineyard owners turn the hard work of the farmers into garbage. Jotham dashes the farmers' hopes and leaves them with nothing but grapes rotting on the vine.

Because Jotham allows the people of Judah to starve, Yahweh and the divine assembly sentence him to watch his vineyards and, consequently, his tax income, vanish (Isa 5:5-6). Sentences in trials announced by the prophets were always intended for monarchs. When Assyria began its conquest of Syria-Palestine, however, its diplomats often challenged a local ruler's authority by negotiating directly with the people of a place (2 Kgs 18:13-37). During the same period, prophets like Isaiah began to employ this technique by announcing directly to the people the sentences imposed by Yahweh and the divine assembly on rulers. Consequently, Isaiah promulgates this verdict of Yahweh and the divine assembly against Jotham at the temple, during the festival celebrating the end of the grape harvest. The temple was not simply where Yahweh lived, but also where Jotham and the other monarchs of Judah stored the grain, wine, and olive oil that they collected in taxes. During the festival, the farmers built the same kind of lean-to huts for their households that they threw up in the vineyards during the harvest itself (Neh 8:13-18). On the first and last day of the eight-day festival, the farmers gathered at the temple to deposit their taxes on the season's harvest.

Worked land was precious. To physically destroy the terraces, hedges, walls, towers, and vines is out of character for resource-conscious people like the Hebrews. The sentence is apocalyptic. The destruction of the vineyards will bring the old world created by the household of David to an end. Terraces will collapse and erosion will wash away the soil. Without cultivation and pruning, vineyards will fill with weeds. The land will look like it had never been worked. Ironically, the sentence uses the same words that appear in the hymn introducing the first indictment. The same words that celebrated the work of Yahweh and the farmers of Judah are used to describe the work of the Babylonians as they advance through Judah toward Jerusalem. Finally, rains would stop. The land would, once again, be without life. Only this destruction of the old world created by the household of David will allow a new world to begin.

By the time Isaiah promulgated the Trial of Jotham, the Assyrians were already crossing the Euphrates River and campaigning in Syria-Palestine (858–823 B.C.E.). The Trial of Jotham would still be vivid when the Babylonians tore down the walls of Jerusalem and destroyed the vineyards of Judah (587 B.C.E.). Jotham may have thought this sentence was intended for Israel, and not for Judah. He may have even enjoyed hearing that Judah's longtime rival to the north was to be invaded and destroyed like an unproductive vineyard. While Jotham may have misunderstood the sentence, the farmers who had come to Jerusalem to pay their taxes to Jotham did not.

Inauguration of Isaiah at Jerusalem
(ISA 6:1-13)

Despite the great respect that the prophets of ancient Israel enjoy today, in their own time they were persecuted. The call story or inauguration story is the "apology" or defense of the prophets against their critics. Apology is a literary technique that appears not only in eastern Mediterranean traditions like the Bible but in western Mediterranean traditions like the "Apology of Plato," which defends Socrates against the criticisms that the people of Athens level against him. Apologies assume, but do not repeat, the criticisms leveled at the prophets. The Inauguration of Isaiah at Jerusalem (Isa 6:1-13) assumes that the people of Judah accuse Isaiah of being ambitious, of being incompetent, of being a failure, and, therefore, of being a false prophet. Inauguration stories deny some criticisms outright, and allow some criticisms to stand, but reinterpret them.

Like most stories, inauguration stories have a crisis, a climax, and a denouement. The action in these episodes is carried out by Yahweh, the protagonist, who sets out to commission a candidate as a prophet. The candidates are antagonists, who try to prevent Yahweh from commissioning them (Fig. 83).

To counter the criticism that prophets were ambitious, the crisis episode often describes candidates as fully occupied with other tasks at the time of their inaugurations. Neither Moses, nor Isaiah, nor Jeremiah, nor Ezekiel are portrayed as looking for work as a prophet when they are called by Yahweh. At the time of his call, Isaiah is attending the funeral of Uzziah, not waiting for Yahweh to commission him as a prophet.

The people of Judah loved Uzziah as much as they had loved David. Like David, he brought years of war to an end. Amaziah (800–783 B.C.E.), Uzziah's predecessor, had unsuccessfully invaded both Edom and Israel, and then he was killed during a civil war (1 Kgs 14:1-20). Uzziah, in contrast, provided Judah with secure borders and a prosperous economy. These accomplishments were coupled with the lack of foreign intervention by Assyria, Syria, or Egypt that allowed Judah to thrive. Like David, Uzziah extended Judah's frontiers west into Philistia and east into Ammon and Edom. By 745 B.C.E., the state of Judah ruled by Uzziah was as large as it had been under David. Nonetheless, when this popular monarch contracted leprosy, change was inevitable. Leprosy vindicated Uzziah's political opponents and discouraged his supporters. His government went to caretakers and he withdrew from public life, casting a pall over Judah.

The crisis episode also describes how Yahweh lures candidates into sacred space with a theophany. The theophany attracts the attention of the candidate, who then investigates it. At the outset, the theophany is extraordinary, but not an obvious sign of the presence of Yahweh. The theophany here occurs when an earthquake rattles the temple and destroys cities and villages throughout the land. Isaiah describes the dust rising from the floor of the temple, when the earthquake shakes its foundations, as the hem of Yahweh's cloak. Isaiah sees only the hem of Yahweh's cloak, not Yahweh.

Earthquakes were frequent in the Syria-Palestine of Isaiah. They took a terrible toll in life and property. Consequently, they became signs that Yahweh and the divine assembly were dismantling the old world in preparation for creating a new world (Gen 19:24-29; Exod 19:18; Num 16:30-34; 1 Sam 14:15; 1 Kgs 19:11-12). The books of

Amos (Amos 1:1), Isaiah (Isa 6:4; 29:6), and Zechariah (Zech 14:5) also take this view of the earthquake in 750 B.C.E. that shook the temple and that also completely destroyed Uzziah's royal city at Hazor north of the Sea of Galilee.

---

crisis (Isa 6:1-2)

Lure: During King Uzziah's funeral, Yahweh, our Creator, sat enthroned high above the temple. The hem of Yahweh's cloak draped into the sanctuary. Six-winged seraphim served as honor guard. Two wings covered their faces. Two covered their sexual organs. Two kept them aloft.

Investigation: (Isa. 6:1a) I stared in amazement.

climax (Isa 6:3-5)

Greeting: "Holy, holy, holy is Yahweh Sabaoth," one seraph after the other cried out. "The land of Judah is full of Yahweh's glory."

Kenosis: The pillars of the earth trembled at the sound of their voices. The House of Yahweh filled with dust. I began to mourn. "Shame on me. I am only one human among many, yet I have seen Yahweh Sabaoth with my own eyes."

denouement episodes (Isa 6:6-13)

Stay of execution: Then a seraph flew to me, holding a red-hot piece of charcoal taken with tongs from the altar. Like a metalworker, the seraph forged my mouth with the coal. "See," the seraph said, "now all the dross has been removed, and your mouth is strong as iron." Then I heard Yahweh saying, "Whom shall I send? Who will speak for the divine assembly?"

Ready formula: "Here I am," I said, "send me."

Commission: Then Yahweh gave me this commission: "Order the people of Judah to listen carefully, but not to understand; to look intently, but recognize nothing. Harden the hearts of this people. Like an embalmer preparing the body of the dead for burial, plug their ears and shut their eyes. Otherwise, their eyes will see, their ears hear, their hearts understand, and they will repent and be healed."

Demurral: "How can this be?" I asked.

Talisman: Yahweh will remove the people from the land. The cities will have no citizens. The houses will have no households. There will be no life in the land. Yet if only a tithe of the people of Judah survives, this stump of the sacred tree, this holy oak will bloom again, unless Yahweh burns it out as well.

Compliance report: . . .

FIGURE 83   Inauguration of Isaiah at Jerusalem (Isa 6:1-13)

Isaiah also hears the seraphim snakes, who guard Yahweh. They are comparable to the uraeus snakes who guard Pharaoh. Seraphim and the cherubim are composite creatures that combine the most respected and most feared qualities of different creatures. The cherubim are part human, part ox, part lion, and part eagle. Humans were respected for their intelligence, oxen for their strength, lions for their fierceness in battle, and eagles for the ability to fly (Ezek 1:1-28). The seraphim here combine the body of a snake with the flames of a fire and the wings of an eagle. They have six wings. Two wings cover their faces so that they do not violate the prohibition against seeing Yahweh. Two wings cover their reproductive organs so that they do not violate the prohibition against appearing naked before Yahweh (Exod 20:26). Two wings allow the seraphim to hover aloft. The seraphim chant "Holy, Holy, Holy" to warn pilgrims to the temple that they are entering the divine plane, which is clearly distinct from the human plane. Humans who enter the divine plane are as radically altered as humans who are exposed to radiation today. They are physically changed, and they can change or harm other humans with whom they come into contact. Most cultures physically mark off the boundaries of the divine plane. Sometimes priests are posted at regular intervals along the path or stairway into the sanctuary. As pilgrims approach, these priests challenge them to be sure they meet the qualifications for entering sacred space (Ps 15:1-5; 24:1-10). Sometimes sanctuary land is simply fenced by a low temenos-wall to remind pilgrims to enter advisedly. Cultures not only mark off the holy, they also mark off those who enter and then leave. When Moses leaves the presence of Yahweh, he wears a mask (Exod 34:29-35), which clearly identifies him as someone who speaks for Yahweh.

In the climax episode, Yahweh greets the candidate who is investigating the theophany. The greeting makes it obvious that the extraordinary event is a sign of Yahweh's presence. Candidates respond by prostrating themselves. This prostration puts candidates in the fetal position like a child in its mother's womb or a dead body in its grave. It signifies that the candidate is dead to the old world, and in position to be raised to life in a new world. The candidate dies to the old world, and is commissioned to serve as a prophet in the new. Isaiah dies like the prosperous Judah under Uzziah, which the earthquake brings to an end, but is raised from the dead to accompany an impoverished Judah under constant financial and military pressure from Assyria.

Isaiah acknowledges the end of the old order with the words: "I am a man of unclean lips" (Isa 6:5). In the Bible, being "unclean" has little, or nothing, to do with hygiene. It is a label applied to households that are politically and economically at risk, or on probation, and are no longer eligible to participate in the daily affairs of the village. To be "unclean" or "impure" is to be "shamed" or "foolish." Isaiah affirms that, like a leper, his household has no standing in the new world that has just begun.

In the denouement, Yahweh commissions the candidate as a prophet. Isaiah is outfitted by the seraphim for his new role with lips of iron. They manufacture this unique tool using the charcoal burner in the sanctuary as a forge. Ironworking played a significant role in the development of cultures in Syria-Palestine. It became a foundational metaphor for states that are economically sound. These new iron lips will prepare Isaiah to help the monarchs of Judah make economically sound decisions in their struggle with Assyria. The household of Isaiah is no longer unclean: "guilt has departed and . . . sin is blotted out" (Isa 6:7). It has status in the new world.

The words with which Yahweh commissions Isaiah seem bizarre. They sound like the exact opposite of the words that the audience should expect. Yahweh commissions Isaiah to prevent Judah from listening to him, rather than to promote its understanding of his message.

What distorts the sound of the commission is that the world of the Bible functioned on the principle of primary causality. Western European cultures today function on secondary causality. The Hebrews considered Yahweh to be the cause of everything that happened. Yahweh is the primary cause of both good and evil. In Western European cultures, God is the cause of good alone. Secondary causes like the devil, the inhumanity of one person to another, and fate are considered to be the causes of evil.

Nonetheless, the last thing the Hebrews wanted to consider was that they were not under the primary care of Yahweh. They would shudder to think that, when they were suffering, Yahweh was not caring for them. As a matter of fact, Israel and Judah did not listen to Isaiah. Israel was invaded and destroyed by the Assyrians in 721 B.C.E. Judah was occupied by the Assyrians from the reign of Ahaz until the reign of Hezekiah, who paid a staggering ransom to Sennacherib, the great king of Assyria, for the city of Jerusalem in 701 B.C.E. Therefore, since Israel and Judah did not listen, the people of Judah considered Yahweh to have commissioned Isaiah to tell them "not to comprehend . . . not to understand" (Isa 6:9). Whatever happened, Yahweh had caused it to happen. Despite Isaiah's failure, neither Isaiah, nor Judah, was ever out of Yahweh's care and control. The inauguration does not deny that he was a failure. It simply argues that Yahweh commissioned Isaiah to fail.

Trial of Ahaz, 735–715 B.C.E.
(Isa 7:1 — 12:6)

As ruler of Judah, Ahaz pursued a strong pro-Assyrian policy (2 Kgs 16:7-16) and invited Assyrian troops to protect Judah against Israel and Syria. In a Trial of Ahaz (Isa 7:1—12:6), Isaiah uses two children, Shear-jashub and Immanuel, in pantomimes to indict Ahaz for calling on Assyria for help (Fig. 84). These pantomimes are poignantly staged in light of cultural expectations that during a military crisis monarchs like Ahaz would offer their heir as a human sacrifice (2 Kgs 16:1-20).

The war of 734–732 B.C.E. is called the "Syro-Ephraimite War," because Syria and Israel, ruled by the household of Ephraim, attacked Judah. This military crisis erupted when the foreign policies of Assyria, Syria, Israel, and Judah collided. Assyria wanted to free its trade lanes in Syria-Palestine from taxation and piracy. Syria wanted to free itself from its covenant with Assyria. Israel wanted to free Judah from the isolationist policies of the household of David. Judah wanted to free itself from its covenant with Israel, which obligated it to follow Israel's foreign-policy initiatives. By putting Judah on alert and fulfilling his covenant obligation to Assyria, Ahaz refuses to support the anti-Assyrian policies of Pekah (737–732 B.C.E.) and abrogates Judah's covenant with Israel (Isa 8:11-15). Some in Judah supported Ahaz's policy of seeking Assyrian aid to gain Judah's independence from Israel. Some supported Syria's policy of seeking Israel's and Judah's aid to gain independence from Assyria.

Assyria was not the only state bent on conquering Syria-Palestine. By 742 B.C.E., Syria was aggressively pursuing an expansionist policy of its own. With the support of Pekah, who was leading a revolt against Pekahiah, the ruler of Israel (738–737 B.C.E.), Syria occupied Israel's grain-producing region of Gilead east of the Jordan River (Amos 1:3-5). It also negotiated a covenant with Edom to seize Judah's port at Elat on the Red Sea (2 Kgs 16:6). Despite the loss of Gilead and Elat, neither Israel nor Judah was seriously interested in revolting against Assyria. Consequently, without their support, Syria delayed its plans to challenge Assyria and joined Israel and Judah during 738 B.C.E. in paying their taxes to subsidize Tiglath-pileser III's war with Urartu on Assyria's northern boundary. During his administration, Tiglath-pileser III filed annual reports on the implementation of his foreign policy on the palace walls at Calah-Nimrud. In these annals, he duly reported the taxes that Assyria's covenant partners provided for this campaign.

In 735 B.C.E., with the help of Syria, Pekah finally succeeded in assassinating Pekahiah, which gave Syria a strategic base in Israel for increasing military action against Judah. Initially, Syria also tried to assassinate Ahaz in Judah (2 Chr 28:7). The plot failed. Consequently, by 734 B.C.E. Syria and Israel were preparing to invade Judah (2 Kgs 15:29-30+37; 16:5-9; 2 Chr 28:5-21), and to turn Judah over to the household of Tabeel from Tyre, which had ruled Judah during the time of Ahab and Jezebel (873–851 B.C.E.) and their daughter Athaliah (843–837 B.C.E.).

Isaiah represents those attempting to keep Judah nonaligned, or at least only minimally compliant with its obligations to Assyria. The interventions that Isaiah makes are preserved today in more than one place in the book of Isaiah (Isaiah 7–8; 9:8-21; 17:1-6; 28:1-4). The language in these traditions reflects an education available only to the elite of Jerusalem. Although it is unlikely that Isaiah was a bureaucrat serving in the government, he certainly had access to the court (Isa 8:2; 22:15-16) and to the monarch as well (Isa 7:3). The most powerful intervention that Isaiah makes in support of nonalignment appears in this Trial of Ahaz.

indictment (Isa 7:1-2)

Whereas the heart of Ahaz, who are the elders of Jerusalem, and the heart of the people, who are the elders of Judah, cannot decide how to respond to the message that the soldiers of Syria and Israel are on the border of Judah, even though their invasion will ultimately fail to capture Jerusalem,

sentence (Isa 7:3-9)

Therefore, Yahweh and the divine assembly direct you, Isaiah, to take your son, "Surviving Remnant" (Hebrew: *Shear-jashub*), and meet with Ahaz, monarch of Judah, while he inspects the Siloam channel and its reservoir. If Ahaz remains neutral, then these fires of rebellion, kindled by Rezin in Syria and Pekah in Israel, will only smolder and their campaign to invade Judah and replace Ahaz with a monarch from the household of Tabeel in Tyre will fail.

Yahweh and the divine assembly have already found Rezin, monarch of Syria and Damascus, and Pekah, monarch of Israel and Samaria, to be guilty of breach of covenant. Syria has been sentenced to death and will be completely destroyed by Assyria. Israel has been sentenced to slavery and will be occupied by Assyria for sixty-five years.

indictment (Isa 7:10-12)

Whereas Isaiah said to Ahaz: "Ask for a sign that Yahweh will protect and provide for Judah. Let the sign be deep as the world below, or high as the world above. Do not doubt that Yahweh can and will protect this land, and do not believe that Assyria can or will protect it."

Whereas Ahaz answered: "I will not ask. I will not give Yahweh any legal cause to curse Judah for breach of the covenant between Assyria and Judah."

sentence (Isa 7:13-16)

Therefore, Yahweh and the divine assembly find Ahaz to be guilty of breach of the covenant between Yahweh and Judah, and sentence him to death. The execution of the sentence will not take place until...Yahweh gives you this sign. Behold, a virgin of Judah (Hebrew: *'almah*; Greek: *parthenos*) shall conceive and give birth to a child named "our Creator is with us" (Hebrew: *immanu el*). By the time the child can reject evil and choose good, he shall be living on yogurt and honey and the lands of those two, who threatened Judah so much, will be deserted.

commentary (Isa 7:17-25)

In other words,

On that day, Yahweh will bring Assyria's army down on Judah creating a crisis worse than when Israel seceded from Judah after the death of Solomon.

(continued)

On that day, Yahweh will whistle for every fly in the farthest streams of Egypt and for all the bees in Assyria. They shall bivouac on every ravine, cliff, thornbush, and pasture in Judah.

On that day, Yahweh will send the great king of Assyria across the Euphrates River to shave every hair off Israel's head, genitals, and beard.

On that day, every household will have only one cow and a couple of goats and need every drop of milk to make enough yogurt to feed everyone. Yogurt and date honey shall be the daily rations of those who survive.

On that day, briers and thorns will replace the thousands of grapevines, each vine once worth more than a villager earns in nine months. Briers and thornbushes will cover the countryside, making it good for nothing but hunting. They will blockade the terraces, whose soil farmers once worked with hoes and mattocks, making them fit only for cattle to graze and sheep to trample.

FIGURE 84   Trial of Ahaz (Isa 7:1-25)

The crisis that Ahaz and his advisers face is complex. On the one hand, as the ruler of an Assyrian colony, Ahaz has a legal responsibility to put down any rebellion against Assyria. On the other hand, as a covenant partner of Israel, Ahaz has a legal responsibility to support Israel's struggle for freedom. Regardless of whether Ahaz decides to support Assyria or Israel, Judah faces dire consequences. If Ahaz does not join their struggle against Assyria, Israel and Syria will invade Judah. If Ahaz does join in their struggle, Assyria will invade Judah. Ahaz and his assembly are unable to reach a decision. They shake "as the trees of the forest shake before the wind" (Isa 7:2).

Problem solving was handled by an assembly of elders and warriors (1 Sam 30:26-31). These assemblies were the "heart" of Judah and Jerusalem. In the Bible, the word "heart" refers not only to the human heart, but also to the heart of Yahweh and the heart of the sea. None of these references, however, refers to an assembly of elders and warriors. Akkadian traditions, however, do use "heart" in reference to royal officials, where the phrase "to devote the heart entirely" identifies advisers to the great king. Therefore, in this Trial of Ahaz "the heart of Ahaz" could carry the connotations not just of his own human heart, but of those officials totally dedicated to him as well. If the phrase "the heart of Ahaz" can carry the connotations of the elders of Jerusalem, then "the heart of his people" may well refer to the elders of Judah. Judah and Jerusalem regularly appear in the Bible as the two power brokers that determine royal policy.

When the assembly cannot reach a decision, Ahaz calls a recess, and leaves to inspect the defenses of Jerusalem. Regardless of which decision the assembly makes, there will be an invasion, and Jerusalem must prepare for siege. Nonetheless, the primary strategy of a recess is to offer the deadlocked elders time to negotiate with one another.

The Gihon Spring in the Kidron Valley east of the city is Jerusalem's main water source. Springs were left outside the walls of cities in order to protect them from pollution. Yet leaving springs outside the walls, which protected them during peace, put them in harm's way during war. Protecting a city's source of water during a siege was a logistical nightmare. Ahaz inspects the Siloam Canal (Isa 7:3) to assess the task. This canal drew water from the Gihon Spring and moved it south along the Kidron Valley to the Siloam Reservoir, where fullers used its water to wash the wool they manufactured into cloth. They used large quantities of water to shrink and thicken the cloth, which is why their factory was adjacent to Jerusalem's major water system.

Ahaz's inspection tour takes him outside the city and away from the assembly, which gives Isaiah the opportunity to lobby him to remain nonaligned. Isaiah bases his argument on the assumption that Jerusalem and Zion, its citadel, are impregnable because they are

Prophet-as-Actor	Prophet-as-Ascetic	Prophet-as-Docent
1 Kgs 22:11		
2 Kgs 13:14-19		
Hos 1:1—3:5		
Isa 7:1-9		
Isa 8:1-4	Isa 20:1-6	Isa 7:10-25
Jer 13:1-11		
Jer 19:1-15	Jer 16:1-4	Jer 13:12-14
Jer 17:1—28:17	Jer 16:5-7	Jer 18:1-12
Jer 32:6-44	Jer 16:8-13	Jer 35:1-19
Jer 43:8-13		
Ezek 5:1-5		
Ezek 12:1-20		
Ezek 21:23-32	Ezek 4:1-15	
Ezek 24:1-14	Ezek 24:15-23	
Ezek 37:15-28		

FIGURE 85   Categories of Prophetic Pantomimes

defended by Yahweh. Isaiah also argues that Yahweh, and Yahweh alone, can provide for and protect Judah. If Ahaz decides to put Judah on alert or if he decides to join Syria and Israel, he will be casting a vote of no confidence in Yahweh's ability or Yahweh's faithfulness. In an effort to convince Ahaz to remain nonaligned, Isaiah announces the verdict that Yahweh and the divine assembly have already issued against Israel and Syria.

Isaiah endorses his words to Ahaz with two pantomimes. Pantomime or dance is the ancient and universal art of movement. Quite distinct from story, which appeals to the sense of hearing, pantomime appeals to the sense of sight. Pantomime is not solely representational art that describes coming events, but also sympathetic ritual that brings about events.

Prophets mastered not only the sounded art of words in their trials, but the silent art of pantomime as well. They used three kinds of pantomimes. Sometimes prophets performed a single dramatic gesture. Sometimes they extended the dramatic gesture into an ascetic practice. They also simply identified the silent action or craft of another. In this third kind of pantomime, the prophet served as a docent (Fig. 85).

Both pantomimes in this Trial of Ahaz involve children. One pantomime focuses on parenting, the other on pregnancy. The nonviolent character of the pantomimes and their focus on children contrast sharply with the saber-rattling response of Ahaz and his assembly to the threat of invasion.

In the first pantomime, Isaiah performs a single dramatic gesture by bringing his son, Shear-jashub, along on Ahaz's inspection tour of Jerusalem's water system. The irony in the pantomime is biting, because, according to Annals of Ahaz (2 Kgs 16:1-20), Ahaz sacrificed his own son when messengers first brought him word that Israel and Syria were on the border of Judah (Fig. 86). By prohibiting human sacrifice (Gen 22:12; Exod 34:20; Deut 18:10), the Bible admits that human sacrifice was practiced in ancient Israel (Exod 22:29-30; Judg 11:30—31:39; 1 Kgs 16:34; 2 Kgs 16:3+21:6). For Ahaz, sacrificing his son was a gesture of piety indicating that his fate and the fate of Judah were totally in Yahweh's hands. Fathers who sacrificed their sons forfeited the protection and provision that these heirs would provide to them in their old age. Without an heir, testators died of starvation and neglect (Deut 21:19-21). By sacrificing his son, Ahaz joined the widow, the orphan, and the stranger, who depend completely upon Yahweh.

In contrast, Isaiah refuses to sacrifice Shear-jashub, who serves as a reminder that Yahweh can protect even a child from Syria and Israel. Isaiah brings Shear-jashub to Ahaz in order to challenge him to be the father of the "surviving remnant," which is the meaning of the name "Shear-jashub" in Hebrew. The first pantomime is intentionally ambivalent. The good news is that Judah will survive. The bad news is that the resulting damage will be extensive.

The rulers of cities under siege often sacrificed their children. Examples of child sacrifice appear in many traditions in the world of the Bible. In one creation story, for example, El, the divine patron of Syria-Palestine, delivers a city during a siege by sacrificing a child. The people of Ugarit had a special prayer that was to be said during the sacrifice. In 850 B.C.E., Mesha, ruler of Moab, sacrificed his son when Israel laid siege to his capital city (2 Kgs 3:26-27). In 332 B.C.E. the ruler of Tyre considered sacrificing his child when Alexander of Macedonia laid siege to the city.

Sometimes the fathers of the household of a city, not just its ruler, also sacrificed their children. War memorials of Seti I (1306–1290 B.C.E.), Merneptah (1224–1214 B.C.E.), and Ramses III (1194–1163 B.C.E.), and the Beit el-Wali memorial of Ramses II (1290–1224 B.C.E.), portray the fathers of the households of Ashkelon and other cities sacrificing their children when these pharaohs laid siege to their cities.

In the seventeenth year of Pekah, heir of Remaliah, king of Israel, Ahaz, heir of Jotham, was crowned king of Judah when he was twenty years old. He ruled sixteen years in Jerusalem, but did not do what was right in the sight of Yahweh, our Creator, as his ancestor David had done. He walked in the way of the rulers of Israel, and even sacrificed his own son, an abominable ritual practiced by the peoples whom Yahweh expelled from Syria-Palestine. Furthermore, he sacrificed and made offerings on the high places, on the hills, and under every green tree.

Then Rezin, king of Aram, and Pekah declared war on Judah. They laid siege to Jerusalem. . . . The king of Edom recaptured Elath. . . . Ahaz sent the message to Tiglath-pileser, Great King of Assyria: "I am your slave and your covenant partner. Come and rescue me from Aram and from Israel, who are preparing to attack me." Ahaz also took the silver and gold in the House of Yahweh and in the royal treasury, and sent them to the Great King. Consequently, the Great King marched against Damascus. He conquered the city, executed Rezin, and deported its people to Kir.

When Ahaz went to Damascus to meet Tiglath-pileser, he so admired the altar at Damascus that he sent the priest Uriah a model. Uriah built an altar like the one in Damascus. When Ahaz returned from Damascus, he dedicated the altar with burnt offerings and grain offerings, wine offerings, and splashed the blood of his offerings on the altar. He moved the bronze altar that was between his new altar and the House of Yahweh, and installed it on the north side of the new altar. Ahaz commanded Uriah: "Upon the great altar offer the morning burnt offering, and the evening grain offering, and the king's burnt offering, and his grain offering, with the burnt offering of all the people of the land, their grain offering, and their drink offering; then dash against it all the blood of the burnt offering, and all the blood of the sacrifice; but I will use the bronze altar for divinations." Uriah did everything that Ahaz commanded.

FIGURE 86   Annals for Ahaz of Judah (735–715 B.C.E.) (2 Kgs 16:1-20)

Isaiah's first pantomime fails to convince Ahaz. Isaiah then repeats his plea for Ahaz to keep Judah nonaligned, but this time he asks Ahaz to choose an appropriate pantomime with which to endorse the proposal.

There is a cosmic quality to the sign that Isaiah invites Ahaz to request. Earthquakes are "a sign . . . deep as Sheol." Floods are "a sign...high as heaven." They are not simply meteorological or seismic confirmation of Yahweh's presence in Judah (Isa 5:14; Num 16:31). Floods and earthquakes destroy old worlds to prepare for the creation of new worlds. Isaiah challenges Ahaz to face the end time with the confidence of Noah and Lot. Even if war comes, Isaiah argues, Yahweh will use it to destroy the old world to make way for a new world. Isaiah invites Ahaz to let go of the old world and embrace the new world that Yahweh is creating.

Requesting a sign can be either an act of piety, as it is for Gideon (Judg 6:17), or an act of presumption, as it is for Moses (Exod 17:2; Deut 6:16). By refusing to "tempt Yahweh," Ahaz refuses to give Yahweh legal cause to invoke the sanctions that enforce the covenant between Assyria and Judah. Yahweh is one of the divine witnesses to this covenant. If Judah breaks its covenant with Assyria, Yahweh must impose the curses described in the covenant on Judah. Just as Ahaz considers nonalignment presumptuous because it makes Yahweh completely responsible for Judah's defense, Isaiah considers the king's decision to fight Israel and Syria presumptuous because it makes the monarch completely responsible for Judah's defense.

The elders of Judah and Jerusalem want Judah to fulfill its legal obligations to Assyria. Eventually, Ahaz will comply with their advice (2 Kgs 16:1-20). For following their advice, instead of the advice of Isaiah, Yahweh sentences Ahaz to suffer the consequences of his own actions. He will die, and Judah will suffer the ravages of war. Assyria will invade Judah with plagues of soldiers, vicious as killer bees (Deut 1:44). Yahweh will whistle like a beekeeper (Isa 5:26), and Assyrian soldiers will swarm into the one small hive of Judah, reducing it to chaos. Judah's refugees will survive on soft cheese and wild honey (Isa 7:15). The food of paradise and the food of the poor are identical.

Nonetheless, Yahweh postpones Ahaz's execution until his son is grown. Isaiah marks the mother of the royal household as a living calendar. Her pregnancy will count off the days remaining until Ahaz's execution. In this second pantomime, Isaiah identifies the silent action of another by drawing attention to the pregnancy of Immanuel's mother and the silent growth of her child. The actor in the pantomime is not Isaiah, but the woman, who silently proceeds with her pregnancy.

The Hebrew word for "virgin" or "young woman" identified the mother of the royal household with the land of Judah (Isa 7:14). The land delivers the harvest that Yahweh promised to Abraham and Sarah, and the mother of the royal household delivers the children. The titles that the Hebrews use for the land of Judah are also the titles that they use for the mother of the royal household. They refer to the land of Judah as a "virgin," and they refer to the mother of the royal household as a "virgin."

Here the label "virgin" is a label of shame. It identifies a land and the mother of its royal household as infertile. They are shamed, unclean, or impure because they have no harvest, and because they have no children. The harvest and the children of Judah are divine gifts, not human works.

The title "Virgin of Judah" is particularly significant to describe Judah between 734 and 732 B.C.E. The harvests of Judah were seized or destroyed by the soldiers of Syria and Israel. These same soldiers disemboweled pregnant women, and smashed the heads of the newborn of Judah against the walls of their homes. Both the fields and the women of Judah were infertile. They were virgins. Likewise, the mother of the royal household is also a woman whose child has been sacrificed. Therefore, she is infertile. She is a virgin.

To conceive a child during famine and war is a sign, because the birth declares that a new world has begun, even though the agony of the old world is not yet complete. The child is at risk, but the child is also a promise that life will triumph over death.

The day of Immanuel's birth celebrates both the death of the old world and the birth of the new world. It is both a birthday and a wake. Every time Ahaz looks at his wife or his son, he will see not only the blessings of land and children but the curse of his death sentence (Hos 1:1—3:5). The announcement that this woman of Judah is expecting a baby at the same time that the land of Judah is expecting an invasion contrasts Isaiah's confidence in Yahweh's ability to deliver Judah, infants and all, from destruction with Ahaz's confidence only in his own diplomacy and Judah's military preparedness.

When Isaiah announces the verdict of Yahweh and the divine assembly against Judah (Isa 7:10-25; 8:5-8), he is not a traitor. His verdicts against Judah's enemies (Isa 8:1-4; 9:7-20; 17:1-6; 28:1-4) and announcements of the ultimate restoration of Judah under an ideal monarch from the household of David (Isa 9:1-6) demonstrate his patriotism. For Ahaz, only the strong will survive. With the help of Assyria, Judah will survive. For Isaiah, only the weak—the widow, the orphan, and the stranger—survive. With the help of Yahweh, even this newborn will survive. War destroys nothing but the armies and supplies that Judah has stockpiled in an effort to protect and feed itself. The child survives because it depends completely upon Yahweh for food and protection. Judah collapses because it does not.

Isaiah's proposal is revolutionary. The two pantomimes are powerful. The pregnant who bear children and the parents who rear them testify that only the weak survive. The silent courage of the powerless continues to challenge the powerful, who believe that war alone can feed and protect the land and its people.

Trials of Judah and Its Covenant Partners

(ISA 13:1—23:18)

In Trials of Judah and Its Covenant Partners, the sentences, or "execrations," are accompanied by pantomimes. Archaeologists have recovered two collections of execrations. One collection is inscribed on bowls preserved today in the Berlin Museum. The other appears on small statues preserved in the Cairo and Brussels museums. These sentences are imposed on rulers, cities, and peoples. When the bowls and statues on which they were written were broken and buried, the sentence was set in motion.

By smashing the bowl or statue, Egypt smashed the social organization of its enemy. Anarchy deprived a community of its life-support systems as completely as covenant created them (Hos 7:13; Isa 22:4). Crops fail and women miscarry (Leviticus 26; Num 5:21-27; Deut 28:16-68; Isa 24:6-12; Jer 23:10).

The connection between smashing the bowl or statue and anarchy may be a legal, as well as a natural, gesture of anarchy. Sellers sealed miniature figures of the grain or livestock sold in a ceramic envelope. The caravan drivers or herders delivered these bills of lading to the buyer along with the grain or livestock. Upon delivery, buyers smashed the envelope and verified the shipment, thus terminating the contract. Therefore, smashing a bowl or statue represented not only that a particular act of commerce had ended, but that all commerce between Egypt and its enemy had ended.

Prophets proclaimed to the people of Israel and Judah the indictments and the sentences of the trials that came before Yahweh and the divine assembly. Here, in Trials of Judah and Its Covenant Partners, Isaiah stands at the temple in Jerusalem. From this position at the sacred center of Judah, Isaiah announces the indictments against Judah and its covenant partners, and the sentences that Yahweh and the divine assembly have imposed on them.

Isaiah announces seven separate trials. The first six are trials of Judah's covenant partners. The seventh is a trial of Judah itself. The number "seven" stresses the thoroughness of the analysis that Yahweh and the divine assembly have made of the foreign policy of Judah.

The assemblage of ceramic bowls recovered in Egypt contains names of more than thirty rulers and of about twenty cities in Syria-Palestine. Among others are Jerusalem, Ashkelon, Beth-shean, Aphek, Acre, Mishal, Achshaph, and Tyre. Three bowls indict Egyptians. Therefore, the motif of putting yourself on trial after putting your covenant partners on trial appears on the bowls recovered in Egypt, as well as here in the book of Isaiah.

Five defendants are named on one of the Egyptian bowls. Twenty defendants are named on another. Therefore, the pattern of seven here in the book of Isaiah does not appear on these bowls from Egypt.

The second set of execration texts appears on an assemblage of small clay statues. These statues are shaped like prisoners squatting with their arms tied behind their backs.

Sixty-four cities are named on the statues. Most of cities became important during the early Iron Age (1200–1150 B.C.E.) when the first Israelite villages appear in Syria-Palestine. Among the sixty-four cities named on the statues are: Jerusalem, Ashkelon, Aphek, Acco, Achshaph, Shim'on, Pehel, Hazor, Laish, Ashtaroth, and Tyre. Five or six hundred years later these same cities are named in the Bible.

Fourteen—or two sets of seven—defendants are named on the statues. Therefore, the motif of seven that appears in the book of Isaiah appears here on the statues as well.

The ritual that accompanied these execration texts assumes that Isaiah would stand at the temple and then face each of Judah's covenant partners in turn (Fig. 87). First, Isaiah would face northeast toward Babylon (Isa 13:1—14:23) and Assyria (Isa 14:24-27). Second, like a motorist tightening the lug nuts on a tire rim, Isaiah would turn 180 degrees to face Philistia (Isa 14:28-32), southwest of Jerusalem. Isaiah would continue to use this ritual of alternating diagonals until all six judgments against Judah's covenant partners had been announced. Third, Isaiah faces Moab (Isa 15:1—16:13), southeast of Jerusalem. Fourth, Isaiah turns and faces Damascus (Isa 17:1-14), northeast of Jerusalem. Fifth, Isaiah faces Ethiopia (Isa 18:1-7) and Egypt (Isa 19:1—20:6), southwest of Jerusalem. Sixth, he turns to face Arabia (Isa 21:1-17), east of Jerusalem. Having announced the judgments against six of Judah's covenant partners, Isaiah now promulgates the judgments against Judah (Isa 22:1-14) and Israel (Isa 22:15-25). Two of the bowls recovered in Egypt contain a list of sentences that may or may not follow this diagonal pattern in execrations in the Bible.

Over time, additional trials were added to the Trials of Judah and Its Covenant Partners. The Trial of Babylon and Its Great King (Isa 13:1—14:23) was added to the Trial

1. Execration
    a. NE: Trial of Babylon and Assyria (Isa 13:1—14:27)
    b. W: Trial of Philistia (Isa 14:28-32)
    c. E: Trial of Moab (Isa 15:1—16:13)
    d. NE: Trial of Damascus (Isa 17:1-14)
    e. SW: Trial of Ethiopia and Egypt (Isa 18:1—20:6)
    f. SE: Trial of Arabia (Isa 22:1-17)
    g. Center: Trial of Judah and Israel (Isa 22:1-25)
2. Commentary: Trial of Tyre and Sidon (Isa 23:1-18)

FIGURE 87 Patterns in Trials of Judah and Its Covenant Partners
(Isa 13:1—23:18)

of Assyria (Isa 14:24-27). The Trial of Egypt (Isa 19:1—20:6) was added to the Trial of Ethiopia (Isa 18:1-7). The Trial of Arabia (Isa 21:13-17) was added to the Trial of Edom (Isa 21:11-12). The Trial of Shebna and Eliakim (Isa 22:15-25), who were royal officials in Judah, was added to the Trial of Judah (Isa 22:1-14).

The Trial of Tyre and Sidon (Isa 23:1-18) supplements the entire trial (Isa 13:1—22:25), which originally would have concluded with a Trial of Israel. The Trial of Tyre and Sidon and the Trial of Babylon (Isa 21:1-10) were added to commemorate the destruction of these cities. Tyre, which was an island citadel like Gibraltar, and the great city of Babylon were considered impregnable. Their trials were added at the point in the structure where they best conform to the diagonal pattern in the tradition. Babylon is northeast on the compass, across from Ethiopia and Egypt, which are at the southeast point on the compass. Tyre and Sidon are at the northwest point of the compass. The Trial of Judah or Israel concludes the standard judgment, so the Trial of Tyre and Sidon is added as an appendix rather than integrated into the series of six judgments whose arrangement is canonized before the destruction of these twin cities.

The Trial of Ethiopia and Egypt (Isa 18:1—20:6) contains a pantomime (Isa 20:1-6) that describes Isaiah walking naked through the streets of Jerusalem for three years. The pantomime describes what the prophet does (Isa 20:1-2), and the indictment and sentence describe what the prophet says (Isa 20:3-6). Prisoners of war were stripped of both their weapons and their clothes to immobilize them and make them easy to identify. Prisoners whose buttocks and genitals are also exposed are reduced to the status of children. Clothes are the uniform of a sexually active adult. An adult whose buttocks and genitals are exposed is impotent. In 711 B.C.E. Egypt and Ethiopia promised to help the Philistine state of Ashdod to gain its independence from Assyria. Judah watched closely the events taking place on its border. If Ashdod was successful, then Judah would make a bid for its independence as well. Isaiah walks naked to announce that not only Ashdod, but Egypt and Ethiopia as well, will be overwhelmed by the Assyrians, and led away powerless into slavery.

Creation of New Heavens and a New Earth
(Isa 24:1—27:13)

Despite Isaiah's best efforts, Hezekiah did declare Judah to be independent from Assyria when Great King Sargon died in 705 B.C.E. (2 Kings 18–20; 2 Chronicles 29–32; Isaiah 36–39; Jer 26:17-19). In preparation for an Assyrian invasion, Hezekiah closed all Judah's regional sanctuaries to Yahweh, including those at Beersheba and Arad, and moved their stores of goods and supplies to Jerusalem. The move virtually guaranteed that Assyria would have to take Jerusalem to resupply its army. Hezekiah also commissioned the digging of a 1,749 foot aqueduct from the Gihon Spring to the Siloam Reservoir to supply Jerusalem with an undisturbed water supply during a siege (2 Chr 32:4-30; 2 Kgs 20:20). He also negotiated with Babylon, Assyria's ancient enemy in southern Mesopotamia, for help. Nonetheless, by 701 B.C.E. Assyria had destroyed Lachish, Jerusalem's last defense on the road to the Coast Highway, and laid siege to Jerusalem itself. To prevent Assyria from destroying Jerusalem, Hezekiah paid a heavy ransom with all the gold, silver, weapons, and troops he could find in the city. The Ark of the Covenant, covered with gold leaf, may well have been part of the tribute paid to Sennacherib (704–681), the new Great King of Assyria.

As a world power, Assyria was not simply a threat to Judah and to the other states in Syria-Palestine. Assyria was doomsday. None were exempt from the crushing taxes imposed by Assyria, and none could defeat its army. To emphasize the seriousness of these times, the book of Isaiah concludes its analysis of the foreign policy of Judah with a Creation of New Heavens and a New Earth, also titled an Apocalypse of Isaiah (Isa 24:1—27:13; Fig. 88). The tradition is an emphatic reminder that no matter how total the destruction of the land and its people by Assyria, Yahweh always draws cosmos out of chaos. Chaos is the womb from which cosmos emerges. Chaos is the death that is the mother of new life.

A Creation of New Heavens and a New Earth is parallel to the Enuma Elish Stories, which were told at the Akitu New Year in Mesopotamia. These stories celebrate Babylon's conquest of Mesopotamia and the enthronement of Marduk as leader of the divine assembly. Isaiah's Creation of New Heavens and a New Earth tells the Enuma Elish Stories backwards to reverse the process that brought Judah's enemies to power in the first place. The Creation of New Heavens and a New Earth celebrates the defeat of the enemies of Judah and the enthronement of Yahweh as leader of the divine assembly. Reversal was a technique for abrogating a covenant and decommissioning a cosmos. A marriage covenant was contracted when a man announced to a woman: "I am your husband, you are my wife," and a woman announced to a man: "I am your wife, you are my husband." To effect a divorce, a man announced: "I am not your husband, you are not my wife" (Hos 2:2).

A Creation of New Heavens and a New Earth does not simply take delight in seeing the old world destroyed, nor does it promote the enjoyment of seeing the wicked get what is coming to them. Creation stories focus on the new world that is coming. During labor, midwives do not direct the birth mothers' attention to their pain, but rather help them focus on the impending birth. Creation stories do not focus on loss, but rather on the opportunity that loss creates for renewal. The destruction of Jerusalem offers survivors the ability to rebuild their lives, and frees them from all the limitations of the old world that has now been destroyed. The stories look forward to the building of a new world without the suffering and the injustice of the old.

The sterility affidavit that opens Isaiah's Creation of New Heavens and a New Earth is a hymn. It is followed by a cosmogony (Isa 24:21—27:11) that is a series of six hymns

I. Analysis of Judah's Domestic Policy (Isa 1:1—12:6)

II. Analysis of Judah's Foreign Policy (Isa 13:1—27:13)

   A. Analysis of Judah's Foreign Policy Proper (Isa 13:1—23:17)

   B. Creation of New Heavens and a New Earth (Isa 24:1—27:13)
     1. sterility affidavit (Isa 24:1-20)
       a. creation story (Isa 24:1-13)
       b. call to worship (Isa 24:14-20)
     2. cosmology (Isa 24:21—27:11)
       a. *On that [first] day* (Isa 24:21—25:5)
       b. *On this mountain* (Isa 25:6-8)
       c. *On that [third] day* (Isa 26:9-12)
       d. *On that [fourth] day* (Isa 26:1-21)
       e. *On that [fifth] day* (Isa 27:1)
       f. *On that [sixth] day* (Isa 27:2-11)
     3. covenant (Isa 27:12-13)
       a. creation story (Isa 27:12)
       b. call to worship (Isa 27:13)

III. Isaiah's Analysis of Judah's Domestic Policy (Isa 28:1—39:8)

FIGURE 88   Patterns in a Creation of New Heavens and a New Earth
(Isa 24:1—27:13)

punctuated with the refrain: "On that day." The covenant that concludes the Creation of New Heavens and a New Earth endows Judah with the city of Jerusalem, where "those who were lost in the land of Assyria and those who were driven out to the land of Egypt will come and worship Yahweh" (Isa 27:12-13).

The hymn describes the death of the old world in two different ways. The first is a flood story (Isa 24:1-3+17-20). "The windows of heaven are opened" (Isa 24:17) and everyone and everything in the old world is washed out of order. Chaos prevails. The old world returns to the water womb from which it came. There is no social structure (Isa 24:1-2), no childbirth (Isa 24:3-6), no wine (Isa 24:7), and no music (Isa 24:8). That is the bad news. The good news is that this same chaos creates precisely the conditions that invite Yahweh to begin work on a new world.

Creation stories often portray the old world that is about to be destroyed as a monster or dragon with a variety of names. In the Enuma Elish Stories, the monster is

Tiamat. Here the monster is called "The Insolent" (Isa 25:2), "The Fortified City" (Isa 25:2), "A Strong People" (Isa 25:3), "Fierce Nations" (Isa 25:3), and "The Wanton" (Isa 25:5). The monster is characterized as arrogant or self-sufficient, in contrast with the poor who are totally dependent upon Yahweh for survival.

The climax of the creation story is a cosmogony (Isa 24:21—27:11) that describes how Yahweh builds the new heavens and new earth. Dividing this cosmogony at the phrases "on that day" and "on the Mountain of Yahweh" (Isa 25:6) creates a series of six days of creation. The phrase "on that day" carries the connotations of a birthday. A similar use of the phrase appears in the book of Job: "Perish that day on which I was born, the night when they said, 'The child is a boy!'" (Job 3:3). The day is associated with creation, because creation is understood as the separation of light or daytime from darkness or nighttime. Before creation, the rhythm of daytime and nighttime is missing. Chaos is always dark. The pattern is also similar to that which appears in the Stories of the Heavens and the Earth, where each episode in the cosmology is punctuated with the phrase "and there was evening and there was morning, the first day" (Gen 1:5). The formula "the first day" (Gen 1:5) and "the second day" (Gen 1:8) serves as a marker dividing one episode of creation from the other. The words "that day" or the "Day of Yahweh" carry the connotations of a day of death and judgment. They focus on the destruction of the old world, which precedes the building of the new world.

Creation stories use three important metaphors to describe the creation of human beings: a womb, a tomb, and a dungeon. The womb is the primary metaphor. Both the grave or tomb and the dungeon or a pit dug into the earth are regarded as wombs from which new life emerges. All three are dark and wet, which are also the two most common ways in which the Bible describes the chaos from which Yahweh builds a new world. These metaphors characterize Yahweh as a midwife, who pulls back the placenta covering the newborn (Isa 25:7-8), the shroud covering the dead, and the blindfolds worn by prisoners (Fig. 89).

The verb "pour" is the root of another significant term in Isaiah's Creation of New Heavens and a New Earth (Isa 25:7-8), which refers to the leather bag from which the wine is poured. In the book of Proverbs (Prov 8:23-26), the wise woman describes her

> *On the Mountain, Yahweh will remove*
> *the shroud covering all peoples,*
>
> *On the Mountain, Yahweh will remove*
> *the bindings wound around all nations.*

FIGURE 89   Creation of New Heavens and a New Earth (Isa 25:7-8)

birth as if she were poured out by Yahweh. "Poured" may be the technical term for describing "breaking the water" of an expectant mother. Thus, the midwife "poured" the child like wine. The act by which she began the delivery of the child became the expression used to describe the delivery itself.

Here Isaiah casts Yahweh as a midwife who frees prisoners from a dungeon with the same skills necessary to deliver a child from its mother's womb (Isa 24:22). The prisoners are gathered together in a dungeon to prepare them for birth or liberation. The clothes of a prisoner are like the placenta or shroud that is removed and replaced with ordinary clothing when prisoners are liberated.

Only the powerless in the old world will be reborn into the new world. The poor were not allowed inside the city gates. Only those who could pass the security check had the right to spend the night in the city (Ps 24:3-6). This Creation of New Heavens and a New Earth (Isa 25:4-5) teaches that the poor will be allowed inside the city in the new world, while the rich will sleep in the fields, where they become easy victims for robbery, assault, and marauding animals.

Creation stories do not idealize poverty (Isa 25:4). In these traditions, poverty is knowing who is responsible for giving you life. Storytellers do not want to ignore the suffering and hardship and injustice connected with poverty. They simply point out that those with no material resources are more likely to acknowledge their dependence upon Yahweh.

Rebirth in the Creation of New Heavens and a New Earth takes place on "The Mountain" (Isa 25:6-7). Cultures regard certain mountains as sacred because they are shaped like the distended uterus of an expectant mother. Certain mountains mark the spot where the earth is pregnant. Through these sacred centers life flows from the God-mother into the communities that she creates. The human navel is a strong physical reminder of the dependence of one human being on another for life. A sacred center is a strong physical reminder of the dependence of a community on its creator.

Creation is celebrated at sacred centers with a sacred meal. These meals close the time of transition during which only rations are consumed. Wine and other holiday food or "rich food" is served. These meals "wipe away the tears from all faces" (Isa 25:8) as effectively as nursing a newborn stills its crying.

Curiously, the call to worship in the hymn for the fourth day does not invite the congregation to "Praise Yahweh!" Instead, it invites the community to "come . . . enter . . . shut" (Isa 26:20-21). Before the creator enters the definitive battle with chaos, the spectators are placed in a coma or some form of protective sleep. No one can witness this struggle primeval without being destroyed, just as no one can look with the naked eye at a nuclear explosion without being blinded. Therefore, the man sleeps while Yahweh creates the woman, and Jonah sleeps in the boat while the wind of Yahweh subdues the sea of chaos.

The women in the hymn are herders who follow grazing livestock to break off the dry branches for firewood (Isa 27:11). In contrast to people from every walk of life who thronged to Jerusalem during its heyday, only these poor women visit the city after it is destroyed.

Creation of Zion
(ISA 40:1—55:13)

Isaiah Movement, Phase Two, 587–537 B.C.E.

The Creation of Zion is set in the days after 587 B.C.E. when Babylon conquered Judah and destroyed Jerusalem. Assyria, which had ruled the world of the Bible from 744 to 605 B.C.E., appeared omnipotent. Nonetheless, Babylon conquered Assyria and became as fearsome to Judah alone as Assyria had been to Israel and Judah together. In its day, Assyria had invaded and plundered Judah. Babylon conquered Judah and Jerusalem. The Creation of Zion developed during the exile that followed.

The destruction of Jerusalem inaugurated a new way of life for the people of Judah. Households in Judah, which were covenant partners with the household of David in Jerusalem, were deported to Tel Aviv, the ruins of an ancient settlement outside the city of Babylon. The founders of the largest city in the state of Israel today chose the same name for their city. "Tel Aviv" means "the ruin that blooms like spring." Tel Aviv was a phoenix. Babylon then redistributed the land of Judah to households that did not have covenants with the household of David.

The households that were deported developed the Creation of Zion to direct the formation of their new life in a new land. Babylon left no monarch, no capital city, no temple in Judah. The old world had come to an end. The Creation of Zion developed to interpret that chaos, and offer the people of Judah advice on how to survive.

The Creation of Zion has also been called "Second Isaiah." These traditions contain some of the most powerful laments in the entire Bible (Isa 42:1-9; 49:1-6; 50:4-11; 52:13—53:12). Here mourners powerfully protest the loss of the land and the children of Judah to Babylon. To deal with this intense grief, they propose a new understanding of Yahweh. In the creation stories in the books of Genesis and Exodus, Yahweh frees the Hebrews from suffering. Here, in the Creation of Zion, Yahweh joins the Hebrews in their suffering. In the book of Isaiah Yahweh is not only a divine warrior, but also a suffering servant.

Like most stories, the Creation of Zion has a crisis (Isa 40:1-31), a climax (Isa 41:1—48:22), and a denouement (Isa 49:1—55:13). In the crisis, Yahweh commissions a "Suffering Servant" to announce the destruction of the old world of Babylon (Isa 40:1-11).

This old world is being reduced to chaos, so that a new world can be created. The people of Judah respond to their inauguration with a hymn celebrating Yahweh as creator and healer (Isa 40:12-31). The climax describes Yahweh decommissioning the old world where Israel and Judah are occupied by Babylon (Isa 41:1—48:22). Then, the denouement promulgates a covenant defining the conditions of life in the new world of Zion (Isa 49:1—55:13). The people also respond to the promulgation of the covenant with a hymn.

Sterility Affidavit
(Isa 40:1-31)

Inauguration of a Servant of Yahweh
(Isa 40:1-31)

The Inauguration of a Servant of Yahweh consists primarily of the commission that Yahweh and the divine assembly decree for the prophet to carry out. Except for this commission and an allusion to the lure that draws the candidate into the desert, the other elements of a standard inauguration story are missing.

The lure describes Yahweh as a powerful wind, or voice, howling, or crying out, in the desert (Isa 40:3). A similar wind appears in the Creation of the Firstborn of Israel (Exod 14:21-25). In both traditions, Yahweh creates the wind by exhaling. In the book of Exodus, Yahweh's breath cuts a highway through the Red Sea (Exod 15:8). In the book of the Isaiah, this divine wind cuts a highway through the desert. By contrast, Marduk is a powerless wind (Isa 41:29).

Yahweh addresses the servant as "you who bring good tidings" (Isa 40:9). This servant is to be a messenger announcing the good news that the highway from Babylon to Zion is open (Isa 40:3-5). "Zion" is the new name for the new Jerusalem. This highway that Yahweh constructs is patterned on the sacred road along which Marduk led the members of the divine assembly from Babylon to the sanctuary where they celebrated the Akitu New Year, and reaffirmed Marduk's authority over the heavens and the earth. The highway that Yahweh builds is a direct challenge to Marduk. The people of Judah are the people of Yahweh. They are not the prisoners of Babylon.

In response to the inauguration of the prophet, the people of Judah sing a hymn celebrating Yahweh as creator and healer (Isa 40:12-31). The hymn is almost entirely a creation story. There is only one explicit call to worship: "Lift up your eyes on high and see" (Isa 40:26). The rest are implicit calls to "Praise Yahweh." Then, the hymn catalogs all of the great works of Yahweh as a rationale for acknowledging Yahweh as their divine patron. The language of this hymn and the language of one of Yahweh's arguments in the book of Job are parallel (Job 38:1—41:5).

In the hymn, and throughout a Creation of Zion, there is a satire on the Babylonians' use of sacred sculpture. These traditions consider the statues of the divine assembly that were carried into Babylon for the Akitu New Year to be powerless (Isa 40:18-20; 46:5-7). Here the book of Isaiah considers them to be paralyzed. They cannot move by themselves. They also cannot speak, and therefore cannot bring Babylon to life in the new year. Babylon must speak to Marduk, but it is Yahweh who speaks to Israel. Only Yahweh can speak, and therefore only Yahweh can create.

By remembering the times when Yahweh spoke to Israel in the past, a Creation of Zion applies them to the events unfolding in the present. The Hebrews remembered their traditions so that every generation could participate in the experiences of every other generation. Remembering was retelling the stories of what Yahweh did and said in the past. Telling these stories defined the people as Hebrews.

Cosmogony
(Isa 41:1—48:22)

The cosmogony in the Creation of Zion follows some of the same patterns found in the cosmogony in the Death of the Firstborn of Egypt (Exod 7:14—13:10). In both stories, the world that Yahweh creates is contrasted with the worlds that Amon Ra and Marduk create. In both stories, Yahweh creates a world that is full of life, whereas the worlds created by Amon Ra for Egypt and Marduk for Babylon are plague-ridden. Yahweh is portrayed as a creator who is life-giving. Marduk creates statues that are speechless. Yahweh is the divine patron of both the powerful like Cyrus, and the powerless like the people of Judah who are slaves or a "Suffering Servant." Yet even Yahweh's suffering servant possesses more vitality than Marduk's statues of wood and metal. Nothing great or small occurs that Yahweh does not authorize and direct.

Inauguration of a Servant of Yahweh
(Isa 42:1-9)

A Creation of Zion does not announce the restoration of the household of David as rulers of Judah. Instead, it redirects the promises from the household of David to all the people of Judah taken into exile by the Babylonians. They, and not the household of David, are now "the Servant of Yahweh."

The Servant of Yahweh has been exiled from Judah to Babylon, not as a punishment, but rather as a time of preparation for a divine mission. Four hero stories describe how the Servant of Yahweh delivers the nations from their enemies (Isa 42:1-9; 49:1-6; 50:4-11; 52:13—53:12). Yahweh and the divine assembly use the formula "behold my servant, whom I uphold, my chosen in whom my soul delights" to designate the servant as their agent or vicar. A similar adoption formula appears in the hero stories in book of Judges: "the spirit of Yahweh came upon him so that he became Israel's judge" (Judg 3:10). The words are patterned on those used by a father when he adopted a newborn into the household. The titles "judge," "hero," or "chief" in the book of Judges, "Servant of Yahweh" in the book of Isaiah, and "Son of Man" (Dan 7:13) in the book of Daniel all empower the candidates who receive them to create a new world.

The last of the four hero stories, Servant of Yahweh Delivers the Nations (Isa 52:13—53:12), is the most powerful. Yahweh and the assembly authorize the Servant of Yahweh to use the divine spirit (Isa 42:1). This divine spirit is the power that Yahweh and the divine assembly use to create. It is the same spirit that hovers over the waters from which Yahweh creates the heavens and the earth (Gen 1:1). This spirit also drives back the sea when Moses raises his staff (Exod 14:21), and it comes upon Othniel and the other chiefs to allow them to create a new people from slaves (Judg 3:10). It is the breath of Yahweh.

Unlike the standard hero stories that authorize a chief to deliver only the people of Judah from their enemies, the hero stories in a Creation of Zion authorize the Servant to deliver all nations from their enemies. The "coastlines" are the islands and shores of the Mediterranean. They are the ends of the earth (Isa 42:4). These lands serve as seawalls protecting the earth from the waters above and the waters below it. Yahweh builds this seawall, part of which is Mt. Ararat, where Noah's ark runs aground at the end of the flood, and which the book of Proverbs (Prov 8:29) refers to as the "limit." Arabic-speaking cultures identify these mountains at the end of the earth as the "circle" (Job 26:10; 38:8-11). In the Eridu Stories from Mesopotamia, Marduk constructs this seawall to protect the earth.

A Creation of Zion describes, with a set of stunning metaphors, how Yahweh creates. To create is to build a seawall. To create is to pitch a tent: "who created the heavens and stretched them out" (Isa 42:5). To create is to farm: "who spread forth the earth and what comes from it" (Isa 42:5). To create is to deliver a child: "who gives breath to the people upon it and spirit to those who walk in it" (Isa 42:5). To create is to have a child: "taken you by the hand and kept you" (Isa 42:6). Like the men in a village, Yahweh built and farmed. Like the women in the village, Yahweh pitched tents, bore children, and delivered newborns.

"To open the eyes that are blind, to bring out the prisoners from the dungeon, from the prison those who sit in darkness" (Isa 42:7) also describes Yahweh creating the new world of Zion. These actions are parallel to those with which Yahweh brings the Hebrews through the Red Sea and out of slavery in Egypt. "Blind eyes" are unfinished eyes. "Prisoners from the dungeon" are like statues still locked in the stone or clay from which the sculptor will release them. Statues were dedicated by "opening their eyes." The eyes and the nose were the most important parts of a sacred statue. Unlike humans, who consumed food by putting it into their mouths, Yahweh and the members of the divine assembly consumed sacrifices by looking at them and smelling their aroma. Like a midwife, Yahweh calls out the unborn child by announcing its name, while its mother is still in labor. Obediently the child responds: "before they spring forth I tell you of them" (Isa 42:9). The Creation of the Heavens and the Earth in the book of Genesis also celebrates Yahweh's talent as a midwife who creates by announcing the names of the light, the sea, the dry land.

Injustice was not so much a breakdown in which a perfectly created cosmos deteriorated. Injustice was a cosmos in its unfinished condition. The Servant of Yahweh will "bring forth justice to the nations" and finish creating the cosmos. The creative work of the Servant of Yahweh is nonviolent, which contrasts with the way in which the book of Exodus describes the actions of Yahweh in delivering the Hebrews from slavery in Egypt, and the book of Judges describes the actions of Yahweh in delivering them from their enemies in Syria-Palestine. In the books of Exodus and Judges, the actions of Yahweh are violent, but in the book of Isaiah they are not. The Servant of Yahweh is to deliver the nations by suffering, and not by conquest.

The celebration of suffering in a Creation of Zion is a development of Israel's understanding of itself as powerless. Unlike other nations, the Hebrews did not brag that Yahweh chose them because they were powerful. Yahweh chose them because they were powerless. The Hebrews were slaves. Judah was a virgin (Isa 7:14). Jacob was a worm (Isa 41:14). The political and economic power of other nations revealed nothing about their divine patrons. Great warriors and mighty rulers built empires that were simply the results of human ability. Gilgamesh, for example, boasts that he has built the walls of Uruk from fired, not just sun-dried, bricks, and shaded its houses with orchards and parks. The success of a powerless people like the Hebrews revealed a powerful divine patron, who alone was responsible for protecting and providing for this people and its land. When slaves who were despised, rejected, stricken, smitten, and afflicted stood alongside the powerful, and divided the spoils of the strong, this was a divine and not a human work. A Creation of Zion teaches that it is Yahweh, and Yahweh alone, who protects and provides not only for Israel, but for all nations. The taxes and soldiers and cities and slaves of monarchs are ultimately powerless to protect and provide for the people and their land. A Creation of Zion celebrates a Yahweh who is the divine patron of slaves oppressed by the Egyptians and prisoners of war tortured by the Babylonians. In the worldview of a Creation of Zion, it is the last who will be first, the weak who will be strong, the exiles who will be freed, and the dead who will be raised.

Initiation of Cyrus

(ISA 44:24—45:13)

In an Initiation of Cyrus, Yahweh anoints the ruler of Persia (557–529 B.C.E.) as a messiah who will conquer Babylon and free the people of Judah from slavery. Persia was east of the Tigris River, where the state of Iran is today. Similar initiations appear in the book of Psalms (Psalms 2, 110). Nonetheless, Cyrus is the only messiah celebrated by the Bible who is not a Hebrew. He is a Persian.

Hormuzd Rassam (1826–1910) recovered a cylinder inscribed with a Decree of Cyrus from Ashurbanipal's library at Nineveh for the British Museum (Fig. 90). It provides an important parallel to this initiation by explaining why the people of Judah so honored Cyrus. This Persian conqueror had promulgated the decree shortly after his conquest of Babylon in 540 B.C.E. The inscription was in Akkadian cuneiform on a cylinder about nine inches long.

The decree indicts Nabonidus, whom Cyrus defeated, for failing to acknowledge Marduk as the divine patron of Babylon. It then orders the repatriation of the hostages whom Nebuchadnezzar and Nabonidus had deported from the lands that they had conquered, like the people of Judah deported between 597 and 587 B.C.E. (2 Kings 24-25; Jer 34:1-7). The decree also provides royal subsidies to these peoples so that they can rebuild the sanctuaries of their divine patrons (Ezra 1:1-4; 6:3-5). Parallels to the Decree of Cyrus appear both here in the book of Isaiah and also in the book of Ezra. The temple would not actually be rebuilt until after 515 B.C.E., during the reign of Darius, the successor of Cyrus. The book of Ezra (Ezra 6:1-15) describes how Darius searched the royal archives for the Decree of Cyrus before providing the people of Judah with more financial support for the project.

During the celebration of the Akitu New Year, Marduk renewed his authorization of the ruler of Babylon for another year. Both the Babylonians and their prisoners, like the people of Judah, knew the Akitu New Year ritual well. The Inauguration of Cyrus mirrors the ritual. Yahweh, however, takes the place of Marduk, and the ruler of Babylon is now a Persian. The initiation ends, as did the Akitu New Year, with the planting and watering of the first crops. The rain that Yahweh sends allows the dry earth to open and the plants to sprout. The days of starvation and war that marked the reign of Nabonidus are over; the new world, ruled by Cyrus, has begun. Yahweh has anointed Cyrus, who will see that the harvest of Babylon will come in, and the people of Judah will go free.

Nabonidus turned the worship of Marduk, ruler of the divine assembly in Babylon, into an abomination. He also enslaved the people of Babylon to work for the state year round.

Marduk heard the people of Babylon when they cried out. Therefore, he and the other members of the divine assembly left the sanctuaries that had been built for them in Babylon. Marduk searched all the lands for a righteous ruler to lead the Akitu New Year procession. He chose Cyrus, the ruler of Anshan (Arabic: *tall-i Malyan*), and anointed him as the ruler of all the earth. . . . Because Marduk was pleased with the good deeds of Cyrus and with his upright heart, Marduk commissioned him to march against Babylon. They walked together like friends. The soldiers of Cyrus strolled along without fear of attack. Marduk allowed Cyrus to enter Babylon without a battle and delivered Nabonidus, who would not lead the Akitu New Year procession for Marduk, into the hands of Cyrus.

The elders and soldiers of Babylon surrender to Cyrus and his son, Cambyses, who resume the worship of all the members of the divine assembly with sanctuaries in the city.

I entered Babylon as a friend of Marduk and took my seat in the palace. Every day I offered sacrifice to Marduk, who made the people love and obey me. Therefore, I ordered my soldiers not to loot the streets of Babylon, nor to rape the women of Sumer and Akkad. I no longer enslaved the people of Babylon to work for the state, and I helped them to rebuild their houses, which had fallen into ruin. Every ruler from the sea above the earth to the sea below it, rulers who dwell in palaces in the east and rulers who live in tents in the west, came to Babylon to bring me tribute and to kiss my feet.

I returned the statues of the divine patrons of every land—Ashur, Susa, Agade, and Eshnunna, Zamban, Me-Turnu, Der, and Gutia—to their own sanctuaries. When I found their sanctuaries in ruins, I rebuilt them. I also repatriated the people of these lands and rebuilt their houses.

Finally, with Marduk's permission, I allowed statues of the divine patrons of Sumer and Akkad, which Nabonidus had moved to Babylon, to be returned to their own sanctuaries, which I rebuilt. May all the members of the divine assembly, whose statues I have returned to their sanctuaries, ask Bel and Nebo for a long life for me every day. May they remember me to Marduk, my divine patron, with the prayer: "Remember Cyrus and his son, Cambyses. They are the rulers who worship you by bringing peace to this land. They are the rulers who have filled your land with ducks and doves. . . . They are the rulers who have rebuilt your sanctuary."

FIGURE 90　Decree of Cyrus (Matthews and Benjamin 1997: 193–95)

Isaiah's Book of Psalms

(Isa 56:1—66:24)

Isaiah Movement, Phase Three, 537–332 B.C.E.

The third phase of the Isaiah movement developed after 537 B.C.E., when Cyrus resettled some of the people of Judah in the Persian province "Beyond the River." The Babylonians deported the peoples whom they conquered to prevent them from revolting, and to educate them in the Babylonian way of life. The Persians returned these peoples to their land of origin in order to develop it. Persian foreign policy considered natives to be the more successful at exploiting the natural resources of a land than Persian governors and workers displaced from other lands. The Persians wanted economically prosperous colonies whose produce they could tax. Therefore, the Persians returned to their homelands the people of Judah and the other peoples whom the Babylonians had deported.

Isaiah's Book of Psalms reflects the struggle of the people of Judah, who had dreamed of returning to their land once flowing with milk and honey, when they return only to find the city of Jerusalem in ruins and the villagers of Judah barely surviving. The land that had fed the Hebrews as abundantly as a nursing mother was infertile. The tradition uses many of the same kind of hymns and laments found in the second phase of the Isaiah movement to create a book of psalms (Isa 56:1—66:24).

Not all the people of Judah were anxious to return to Judah. They had not become Babylonians, but they did believe, as the letter of Baruch in the Bible today reflects, that Yahweh had permanently moved them from Judah to Mesopotamia. They remained as a new people in this new land and thrived as a distinctly Jewish culture until the twentieth century.

The households who did return to Judah in the time of Cyrus found themselves to be strangers in a strange land. The households that had not been deported by the Babylonians did not welcome the return of these households of David, whose policies had led to war and to defeat at the hands of the Babylonians. These people of the land had left Jerusalem in ruins, much as their ancestors had left Jericho in ruins, in order to remind themselves that cultures that become states place themselves at the mercy of monarchs, who impose taxes that are spent on the waging of wars and the building of cities. They had no enthusiasm for the policies of these returning exiles to reestablish the old ways. These people of the land made their point with enough of the households returning from Babylon to delay the reconstruction of Jerusalem and the lands of the royal household. The traditions of this third movement in the book of Isaiah reflect the struggle between these two divergent visions in Judah after 537 B.C.E. A Hymn to Yahweh as Creator (Isa 60:1-21) and a Hymn to Yahweh as Builder of Jerusalem (Isa 65:17-25) from this tradition propose that it is not the returning exiles who will rebuild Jerusalem, but only Yahweh.

Hymn
(ISA 60:1-22)

In Isaiah's Book of Psalms, this hymn questions not so much how the people of Judah will see Yahweh, but rather how the people of Judah will reveal Yahweh. "Nations shall walk by your light" (Isa 60:3) commissions them to contribute their light to the light of the world.

Yahweh will appear in Jerusalem, but not as a divine warrior. In the book of Judges and some of the teaching traditions in the Bible, the appearance of Yahweh signals the beginning of the great war that will bring the old world to an end. Yahweh's appearance is described as a series of battle commands like "Light the signal fire." In this hymn, however, Yahweh appears as "a light of safety to the mothers and their children, to those who go down to the sea in ships, to those who come from Sheba." Not only will the exiles go home, but they will make a home for all nations.

The command: "Rise up!" brings the mourning of the exiles to a close. Ordinary life in the new world now begins. This is the word of the midwife to the newborn: "Open your eyes!" This is the light in the face of a human, and the light of a star rising. This is the same light that led the Hebrews out of Egypt, but that will now be their light to lead others to freedom. No longer will armies march against Jerusalem, but pilgrims will stream into the city. The people taken as hostages and those who fled as refugees return to Jerusalem. They will cross the desert on camels and the sea in ships.

The mother motif appears frequently in the world of the Bible. In the Enuma Elish Stories, Tiamat, as Mother Huber, conceives an army of hideous monsters. In the European children's story, Mother Hubbard has "so many children she doesn't know what to do." Pyotr Ilich Tchaikovsky (1840–93) uses the same motif in casting Mother Ginger in his ballet, *The Nutcracker*. This hymn (Isa 66:7-17) uses the mother motif to describe the Jerusalem that Yahweh will rebuild. The "breasts" (Isa 66:11), the "knees" or "arms" (Isa 66:12), of Jerusalem are the ridges of Mt. Moriah and Mt. Ophel to the east and of Mt. Zion to the west, separated by the Tyropaean Valley, across which the city climbs. Since 3000 B.C.E., these twin ridges have hung like breasts and have stretched out like arms of the hills of Judah to embrace and to nurse the people of Jerusalem.

The standard denouement in creation stories is a covenant. Here the denouement also describes Yahweh freeing prisoners, returning exiles to their countries of origin, and raising the dead from their graves. This hymn is a good example of an emancipation episode in a creation story. The emancipation reenacts the creation of humanity. Consequently, this hymn and the creation stories in the book of Genesis share many of the same motifs. In both traditions, Yahweh endows humans with Eden as their home. Here, the creator endows the exiles, who are newly created humans, with Jerusalem. The expulsion from Eden, like the expulsion from Jerusalem, is not a punishment, but a preparation for a divine mission. The people primeval leave Eden to evangelize their world, just as the exiles from Jerusalem are sent to the corners of their world to "announce my glory" (Isa 66:19).

The hymn asks the people of Judah: "Where do we wait while the old world is being destroyed?" Most human communities believe that some special place is their natural, God-given home. The painful experiences of travelers, refugees, and exiles all testify to the disorientation that develops in communities away from home.

Yahweh's coming does not bring personal salvation, but social justice. Justice is not a world without pain, but a society without prisons. The exiles are anointed to announce that all prisoners are free. Their role is not just to open the doors of prisons, but to share the life of the imprisoned. Their preaching is not door to door, but the silent campaign of living in this world with reverence and commitment. They are called to sense the gentle presence of Yahweh in all times. They are called to work for social justice in the public life, realizing that the way they will live will affect others. The exiles are called to live without mindlessly oversimplifying the challenges of living, and without mercilessly overpowering others. Yahweh comes not to wrap the exiles in the splendid isolation of a protected environment where they will see no evil, hear no evil, and speak no evil. For Isaiah, the exiles are invited to share in Yahweh's work. Salvation is not what Yahweh has done for the exiles, but their realizing how much Yahweh will expect them to do for others.

The end of the exile is a time for the silent contemplation and recognition that the people of every land are one, and of what a difference the exiles will make in the lives of other peoples. They are not called to be patronizing or arrogant, but grateful for this interdependence. The exiles are called to joyfully and confidently acknowledge how often their own pain and suffering can open their hearts and make tender their feelings toward the sufferings of others.

Hymn
(Isa 65:17-25)

One of the last hymns in Isaiah's Book of Psalms celebrates Yahweh as the builder of Jerusalem. It consists of a call to worship (Isa 65:18) and a creation story. The call to worship summons the people of Judah to "be glad and rejoice" (Isa 65:18) because Yahweh is "about to create new heavens and a new earth" (Isa 65:17).

The new Jerusalem that Yahweh is creating reverses all the suffering that plagued the old Jerusalem destroyed by Babylon. Newborns will thrive, and adults will live to be one hundred years old. Households will work their own land and enjoy the produce from their own harvests. Strangers will no longer occupy Jerusalem and take away its people and harvests as taxes. The creation story closes with the same wonderful images found in part one of the book of Isaiah: "The wolf and the lamb shall feed side by side, the lion shall graze with the ox, but the snake shall eat dust. They shall not hurt or destroy anywhere on my holy mountain" (Isa 65:25).

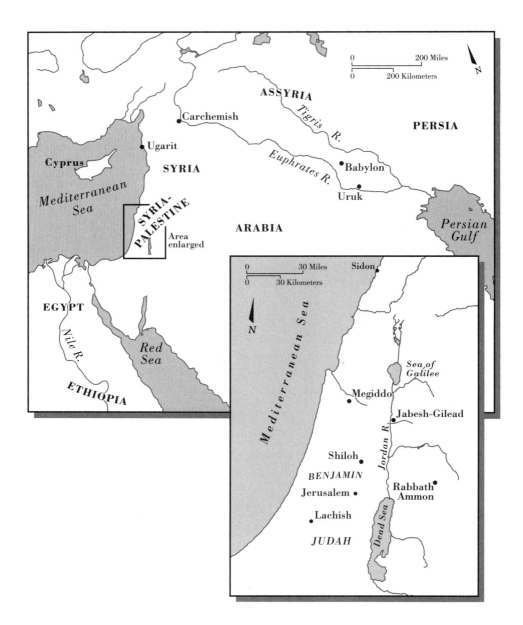

Points of Interest (Chapter 13)

13

BOOK OF JEREMIAH

(JER 1:1 — 52:34)

The book of Jeremiah (Hebrew: *Yirmeyahu*) began its development during some forty years that reflected the best of times and the worst of times for Judah. The best of times were the reform of Josiah. The worst of times were Josiah's war with Egypt and Assyria, Jehoiachim's war with Babylon, and Zedekiah's war with Babylon, which ended with the destruction of Jerusalem. Between the coronation of Josiah as the king of Judah in 640 B.C.E. and the occupation of Judah by Nebuchadnezzar of Babylon in 587 B.C.E., Jeremiah launched four major campaigns challenging royal policies for protecting and providing for Judah.

The events that launched Jeremiah's first campaign began when Ashurbanipal (668–627 B.C.E.), the Great King of Assyria, died after a forty-year reign. Taking advantage of Assyria's weakness, Babylon expelled Assyria's diplomats and merchants. Josiah followed suit. The Babylonians eventually conquered Nineveh, the capital of Assyria, in 612 B.C.E.

The book of Jeremiah was certainly sympathetic with Josiah's bid for independence. A more vivid picture of Josiah's designs for Judah and his military accomplishments, however, is preserved in the books of Deuteronomy and Joshua. Because Josiah considered himself a new Moses and a new Joshua, these books reflect the political and economic reforms carried out by Josiah.

Even though Josiah declared Judah's independence from Assyria, he was not interested in becoming a colony of Babylon. Therefore, in an act of political expediency, he led Judah into battle at Megiddo in 609 B.C.E. as an ally of Assyria. His calculated risk was a military and political disaster. Neco, pharaoh of Egypt, fought on the side of Babylon. Babylon and Egypt won the battle of Megiddo, and Neco executed Josiah for treason.

Assyria's last stand against Babylon took place at Carchemish in 605 B.C.E. Here again Babylon won a decisive victory over Assyria, and then turned on Judah as part of its effort to take possession of Syria-Palestine and the rest of Assyria's former empire (2 Kgs 23:30-34). Babylon's victory at Carchemish made it the new and uncontested superpower.

Jeremiah's second campaign ended when Egypt surrendered Judah to Babylon, which made Judah a Babylonian colony. The third campaign ended after the Babylonian army occupied Judah, and Egypt surrendered. The fourth campaign ended when Egypt granted Jeremiah political asylum. The book of Jeremiah preserves traditions from each of these four campaigns.

Inauguration of Jeremiah in His Mother's Womb
(JER 1:4-19)

An Inauguration of Jeremiah in His Mother's Womb dates his call from the first moment of his conception. There was never a moment in the life of Jeremiah when he was not a prophet. The inauguration considers the physical position of Jeremiah's fetus in his mother's womb to be his acceptance of his prophetic vocation. The fetal position is one of humility or dependence, and the relationship of a fetus and its mother models the appropriate relationship between Judah and Yahweh, a relationship that Jeremiah would work to restore.

In the inauguration, Yahweh is cast as Jeremiah's midwife. Yahweh negotiates the marriage covenant between Jeremiah's mother and father, which includes the stipulation that they would have a son. This is the connotation of the words "before I formed you in the womb, I knew you; before you were born, I set you apart" (Jer 1:5). Yahweh palpates the uterus of Jeremiah's mother to determine that she is in fact pregnant, and that her fetus is correctly positioned. Yahweh delivers Jeremiah from his mother's womb. Yahweh sings a hymn celebrating the birth of this special child, who was to be the voice of Yahweh guiding Judah during the terrible days after 614 B.C.E., while Assyria and Babylon struggled over Syria-Palestine. He would be a "Prophet to the Nations" (Jer 1:5).

Jeremiah, like other candidates commissioned for divine missions, demurs by pleading that he cannot speak for Yahweh. He does not simply mean that fetuses cannot physically speak, but that no human can responsibly speak for Yahweh. Moses pleads that: "I have never been eloquent, neither in the past nor since you have spoken to your servant; I am slow of speech and tongue" (Exod 4:10). Likewise, Isaiah demurs by saying: "I am a man of unclean lips" (Isa 6:5).

Yahweh reassures Jeremiah by touching his mouth, and customizing it for his work as a prophet. Jeremiah now has a mouth uniquely designed for speaking a divine word. Yahweh also promises Jeremiah: "I am with you" (Jer 1:8). Yahweh will not only train Jeremiah for his mission, but be right there to coach him through every confrontation with the rulers of Judah.

Amun Calls Tutakhamun from a Lotus Womb
(Valley of the Kings 1333–1323 B.C.E.; wood)

Although, in life, Jeremiah did not go immediately from his mother's womb to his divine work, in the Bible the call of Jeremiah is immediately consummated by two divinations against Judah and Jerusalem (Jer 1:11-19). Divinations are pantomimes that interpret omens or spontaneous occurrences.

Pantomimes are a form of movement-art, like dance. There are at least three kinds of pantomime in the Bible (see Fig. 85). First, prophets can mime with a single action. In the Pantomime of the Unwashed Clothes, Jeremiah buys, and wears, an item of clothing, but does not take care of it (Jer 13:1-11). These pantomimes have the same sensational effect on the audience as newspaper headlines. They are shocking, and trigger questions in their audiences. The answers develop into commentaries notarized with the formula: "says Yahweh" (Jer 16:11).

Second, prophets can mime with repeated or sustained movements. Jeremiah remains celibate (Jer 16:1-4), and does not attend funerals (Jer 16:5-7) or weddings (Jer 16:8-9). Celibacy is a form of asceticism.

Third, prophets can mime, not as actors, but as docents or guides, who interpret the actions of others such as a vintner (Jer 13:12-14) or a potter (Jer 18:1-12). They draw the attention of the audience past the surface of wine-making or pottery-making to its deep significance. Divinations belong to this third type of pantomime.

In the first divination, Jeremiah sees an almond tree bloom. Most farming cultures watch for the blooming of a particular tree to announce that the growing season is under way. The Hebrews watched for the blooming of the almond tree to define their growing season. They called it the "watching tree," whose blossoms looked like eyes. They watched for the tree, which watched for the growing season to get under way. Yahweh tells Jeremiah that the divine assembly has not only sentenced Judah and Jerusalem to death for repeatedly violating its covenant, but also that the events that will execute the sentence are already under way. When the almond tree blooms, the harvest is inevitable, and the old world of Judah and Jerusalem is about to be destroyed.

In the second divination, Jeremiah sees a cooking pot tip over on the fire. He sees the burning logs under a pot of boiling water collapse, tipping the pot and instantly scalding the land south of it in a river of steam and boiling water. Like a parent who turns to see a child pull a pan of boiling water off the stove, Jeremiah is a paralyzed witness to a disaster he can do nothing to change. He recovers consciousness slowly as the steam clears, and realizes that, in just such an instant, Babylon will sweep out of the north like a flood of boiling water and wash Judah and Jerusalem away.

Trial of Jerusalem
(JER 2:1—3:5)

The indictment in a Trial of Jerusalem charges the household of David, which rules Jerusalem, with trespassing on Judah by imposing crushing taxes on its farmers and herders. The sentence describes, at length, how the domestic policies of the household of David turned this once fertile land into a desert (Jer 2:9—3:5). Because the household of David was afraid that Yahweh could not or would not feed and protect Judah, it scrambled to negotiate covenants with Egypt and other states (Jer 2:20-28). Consequently, it needed more and more taxes to pay the premiums on these covenants.

The trial introduces Yahweh as the divine patron "who brought us up from the land of Egypt" and "who led us in the wilderness" (Jer 2:6). Yahweh's more common titles are: "Yahweh, who brought us up from the land of Egypt" and "Yahweh, who led us into the land flowing with milk and honey." Curiously, the trial parallels Yahweh's companionship to the Hebrews in the desert with Yahweh's companionship to the Hebrews crossing the Red Sea. Both are mighty or divine acts. Both should have convinced the household of David to have trust in Yahweh, but they did not.

The indictment contrasts the Hebrews in a lifeless desert who trusted in a life-giving Yahweh with the household of David in life-giving Judah that trusts in a lifeless Egypt (Jer 2:5). In a desert full of sinkholes and tar pits, the Hebrews trusted Yahweh enough to let him court her. In a desert without water during the day, and without light during the night, the Hebrews trusted Yahweh enough to become his bride. In a desert without a single village, the Hebrews trusted Yahweh enough to give birth to his children. In the desert, the Hebrews were faithful.

Neither the book of Jeremiah nor the book of Hosea idealizes the desert time as a time of naïveté or innocence. Traditional cultures like ancient Israel regard naïveté or innocence as inexperience, not as virtue. Only those who have faced challenge, not those who have avoided it, are mature.

When the Hebrews leave the desert and enter the land, Yahweh plants them in Judah, and then posts the property. Judah is holy or off-limits. The land belongs to Yahweh, not to the Hebrews. The harvests and herds of Judah are Yahweh's gifts to the Hebrews. It should have been obvious to them that, in contrast to the desert, Judah was a fertile land where they would be fed and where they would be safe. It was an Eden. Ironically, it was here in this fertile land that the household of David could not trust Yahweh enough to allow him to feed and to protect the city and its people from Assyria. Instead, they mined the land, destroying its soil. They trespassed on its harvests and herds in order to use them to negotiate covenants with Egypt and other states for food and protection.

One of the strategies that the household of David used to intensify agricultural production in Judah was to develop villages in areas of Judah without natural springs. These villages were dependent on cisterns to catch rainwater (Jer 2:13). In this trial, Jeremiah argues that if Yahweh wanted people to live in a place, it would have a spring. Both the domestic policy of developing more and more villages dependent on catch-water and the foreign policy of negotiating covenants for food and protection failed miserably. The drought came, and the Babylonians invaded.

The drought and the invasion were not simply accidents. They were a sentence for trespassing. The household of David forgot what Yahweh had done (Jer 2:13, 32), even while Yahweh continued to remember (Jer 2:2). The difference between Yahweh and the household of David is that Yahweh remembers; the household of David forgets.

As the drought begins (Jer 3:3), the household of David thinks its covenant with Egypt will feed the people (Jer 2:16). The trial argues that Egypt cannot do, and should not do, what Yahweh has promised to do. Judah is a land of natural rain; Egypt the land of unnatural irrigation. The desert is infertile land that is not sown (Jer 2:2), in contrast to Jerusalem, which is a fertile land "flowing with milk and honey."

The consequence of being a client of an infertile patron like Egypt is that Judah will become infertile. The household of David talks like a fool and negotiates with fools. Consequently, the divine assembly sentences it to death by drought. The household of David will die by the consequences of its own actions.

The sentence is demanded because no other people, as far west as Cyprus or as far east as Arabia, ever abrogated its covenant with its divine patron, even with divine patrons who failed to provide for and to protect their clients. The household of David, however, traded paradise for purgatory, so Yahweh and the divine assembly appoint the heavens to execute the sentence by withholding their rain from the land. This is the bad news. The good news is that the drought will not only turn Judah into a desert from which Yahweh can create a new cosmos (Jer 3:1-5), but also will turn the Hebrews, once again, into a devoted, loving, and merciful covenant partner.

Trial of Judah and Jerusalem
(JER 13:1-11)

Prophets connected powerful words with powerful actions. To execute the sentence of a Trial of Judah and Jerusalem, Jeremiah enacts a single, shocking pantomime.

The pantomime has two parts. There is a description of the action (Jer 13:1-7). Jeremiah buys and wears an expensive pair of underwear. Shockingly, he never washes it, and then he buries it in a riverbank, where the moisture will cause it to rot. The word for "river" (Hebrew: *perat*) also appears in the name of the Eu-*phrat*-es River, but here it simply means "river." Jeremiah does not travel all the way to the Euphrates or the Nile. Finally, Jeremiah digs up his underwear, and puts it on again.

The second part of the pantomime is a commentary on the action (Jer 13:8-11). The commentary explains that Jeremiah is Yahweh, and the underwear is Judah. The relationship of Jeremiah to his underwear is an example of the intimate relationship between Yahweh and Judah. "For as the waistcloth clings to the loins of a man, so I made the whole house of Israel and the whole house of Judah cling to me" (Jer 13:11). The covenant between Yahweh and Judah is as intimate as a man and his underwear.

The pantomime shocks its audience. Has Yahweh abandoned Judah on a riverbank? Both Babylon and Egypt were river cultures, one along the Euphrates and Tigris, the other along the Nile. Some of the people of Judah in Jeremiah's time would be buried along the Nile in Egypt, others along the Euphrates. Ostensibly, the fertility of the exiles would rot. In reality, the relationship between Yahweh and Judah was only changed, not destroyed. Yahweh would recover Judah and restore their covenant relationship.

Trial of Judah
(JER 13:12-14)

In a Trial of Judah, Jeremiah directs the attention of his audience to wine makers filling clay jugs with wine. Once the jugs are filled with wine, the wine makers label them with royal seals designating them as part of the tax payment of the village to the king of Judah.

Ideally, watching the wine-makers at work should give villagers a sense of security. The wine being jugged completes the payment of their taxes to the rulers of Judah, who in return will protect them from their enemies and maintain a stable economy in which they can profitably farm their fields and herd their livestock.

Jeremiah, however, challenges the villagers' sense of well-being. This wine will not bring them security. It is a wine that will set in motion the destruction of their world. It is not a wine that will celebrate the harvest, but a wine that will make Judah collapse like a drunk. Jeremiah shocks the audience into realizing that they are not watching the beginning of a new season of planting and grazing, but the end of the world as they know it.

Trial of Jerusalem
(JER 16:1-13)

In a Trial of Jerusalem, Jeremiah does not marry, and he does not attend weddings or funerals. He becomes a celibate and lives in solitude. These pantomimes are not a single action but a way of life.

Soldiers, in the world of the Bible, did not marry (1 Sam 21:6; 2 Sam 11:4). They were celibate. Marriage and farming, children and harvests were the blessing of peace. Recruits who had recently married, worked a field, or started a house were exempt from military service (Deut 20:5-8). The life of a soldier was a pantomime of the end time, during which the old world came to an end and a new world was being created. War was a time of transition from one world to the next. Until the new world came into existence, the young were not married, the old were not buried, and households celebrated no passages.

By remaining celibate, Jeremiah pantomimes the life of soldier who does not marry. He will remain celibate until the old world of Judah is destroyed by Babylon, and the new world is created.

Likewise, Jeremiah does not celebrate weddings or funerals. These are the rituals that unite the present generation to its ancestors in the past and its descendants in the future. Judah, however, will be destroyed. Time is suspended. There is no past and there will be no future.

Jeremiah's pantomimes are imitative rituals. They not only portray what will happen to Jerusalem in its last days, but also set those final days into motion. The war between Judah and Babylon will bring marriages, funerals, and all household celebrations to an end.

The defendants named in the indictment are the ancestors of Jerusalem (Jer 16:11). The defendants punished in the sentence, however, are their sons and daughters (Jer 16:2). During these final days, there was an intense debate about who should suffer. The covenant between Yahweh and Israel stipulates that Yahweh is "jealous, punishing children for the iniquity of parents to the third and the fourth generation of those who reject me, but showing steadfast love to the thousandth generation of those who love me and keep my commandments" (Exod 20:5-6). That tradition is reiterated here. Other traditions in the book of Jeremiah (Jer 31:29-30), as well as some in the book of Ezekiel (Ezek 18:1-32), argue that only those generations that break their covenants with Yahweh will suffer, and that future generations will be judged only on their own actions.

Trial of Jerusalem and Judah
(JER 19:1-15)

By breaking a cooking pot, Jeremiah pantomimes the sentence that Yahweh and the divine assembly have imposed on the rulers of Judah and the people of Jerusalem (Jer 19:1-15). He breaks a cooking pot or eating bowl, which sentences to death the household of David that eats from the pot, and the monarch of Judah who uses the bowl. In Egypt, archaeologists recovered a set of broken eating bowls that were inscribed with curses or execrations. These execration texts sentenced to death the lands and the peoples that they named.

A Teaching on Adultery and Jealousy in the book of Numbers (Num 5:12-31) directs that a woman charged with adultery must scatter grain from her eating bowl at a sanctuary before witnesses. An eating bowl is not only a symbol of the fertility of the land that fills it with food, but of the uteruses of its women, filled with the seed of their sexual partners. The bowl symbolizes the union between the land that feeds a household and the children that its women bear.

By breaking a cooking pot, Jeremiah sentences Judah and Jerusalem to infertility. The pantomime plays on the words for "ruin" and "pot," which sound alike in Hebrew (Jer 19:7). The Valley of Hinnom, where the people of Jerusalem dump their broken pottery and garbage, will become the "Valley of Ruin." There will be no food to fill the pot, and there will be no one to eat from it. Men will be impotent; women will be infertile. Miscarriages and crib death will multiply. Rain will not fall, crops will fail, and life in the land will come to an end.

The Valley of Hinnom is west of the Mt. Zion ridge in Jerusalem. It once marked the border between the tribe of Judah to the south and the tribe of Benjamin to the north (Josh 15:8; 18:16; Neh 11:30). There was a royal sanctuary in the valley where monarchs of Israel and Judah sacrificed their firstborn sons to prompt Yahweh to prevent an enemy from crossing the border and invading the land (2 Chr 28:3; 33:6; Jer 7:31; 32:35). Without an heir, a household was helpless, and totally dependent upon Yahweh to feed and protect it. Without a royal heir, Israel and Judah were totally dependent upon Yahweh to deliver them from their enemies.

An eternal flame burned in the sanctuary to commemorate these sacrifices. Greek speakers called the Valley of the Household of Hinnom "Ge-henna," which became a synonym for a white-hot metalworker's forge, and later for hell.

Jeremiah condemns child sacrifice, not only because of its violence and its abuse of the innocent, but also because it distorts the character of Yahweh (Jer 7:32; 19:6). Villages and states used child sacrifice to remind their divine patrons to deliver them from their enemies. For Jeremiah and other prophets, it was outrageous to think that Yahweh needed to be reminded to provide for and protect the people of Judah. The people of Judah could forget their commitments to Yahweh, but Yahweh would never forget the people of Judah. Yahweh was preeminently "The Divine Patron Who Remembers." Yahweh was a promise keeper.

Lament of Jeremiah
(JER 20:7-18)

One of the most powerful genres in the book of Jeremiah is the confession or lament. Because these laments have often been understood as insights into the agony of the prophet himself, they have inspired generations of Jews, Christians, and Muslims during their own suffering. They have been read as a reflection on the pain and frustration that fill the lives of people of faith. Like the words of Job, the laments of Jeremiah have been read as a protest against Yahweh for failing to help and support the faithful. This interpretation has helped many people of faith survive suffering. If Job and Jeremiah suffer, then suffering is not the result of failure or sin. If Job and Jeremiah cry out in protest against Yahweh, then it is not failure or sin for other people of faith to do the same.

The world of the Bible, however, did not focus either on individuals or on internal feelings. The Hebrews looked at the world from the perspective of the community. The base community was the household. The Hebrews considered external actions to be more important for understanding their world than internal feelings. Therefore, although the laments describe plots against the life of Jeremiah himself (Jer 11:18-23; 12:1-6;

15:10-21, 17:14-18; 18:18-23; 20:7-13), it is better to read them as the words of a Jeremiah who mourns not only for himself, but also for Judah and Jerusalem. Jeremiah speaks for Jerusalem and Judah. He cries out against Yahweh for failing to feed them and to protect them against Babylon. A similar lament for a city about to be destroyed appears in the books of Samuel-Kings (1 Sam 11:1-15). The messengers come to the village of Saul and, like mourners, lament the imminent destruction of Jabesh-gilead by the soldiers of Rabbath Ammon.

One lament (20:7-18) indicts Yahweh for having negotiated a covenant with Jeremiah, Judah, and Jerusalem in bad faith: "you deceived me" (Jer 20:7-8). The covenant stipulated that Yahweh would protect them from their enemies, and that Yahweh would feed them with abundant harvests. Now that the land is overrun and the people are starving, Jeremiah petitions Yahweh to turn back the calendar to the day of their birth and abort them: "Let the people of Judah perish in the dark and watery womb of slavery, rather than deliver them into the light and dry freedom and then destroy them." To have died without having known freedom, Jeremiah laments on their behalf, is not as painful as having died after having gone from slavery to freedom (Jer 20:14-18).

Nonetheless, Jeremiah praises Yahweh for protecting and providing for the people of Judah (Jer 20:13) even when their enemies make fun of them (Jer 20:9-12). Those who practice the biblical virtue of patience do not demand that the stipulations of the covenant be fulfilled in order to believe that Yahweh, in fact, will fulfill them.

Trial of Jerusalem
(Jer 34:1 — 35:19)

A Trial of Jerusalem indicts the city for slavery. At one point during the Babylonian assault on Jerusalem, the people of Judah emancipated their slaves. By freeing their slaves, they plead with Yahweh to free them from the Babylonians. This also allows the newly freed slaves to join the soldiers on the walls of Jerusalem and to fight for their lives. Regardless of whether this act of liberation was sincere or cynical, the siege was suspended and the Babylonians withdrew, at least temporarily. Jeremiah promulgated this trial "while the army of the great king of Babylon was fighting against Jerusalem and Lachish and Azekah, which were still holding out. These were the only fortified cities left in Judah" (Jer 34:7).

Azekah is eighteen miles southwest of Jerusalem, and Lachish is thirty miles southwest of Jerusalem. Between 1932 and 1938, J. L. Starkey, Henry Wellcome, and Charles Marston recovered twenty-one pieces of broken pottery with writing on them at Lachish. These letters were in the ruins of a guardroom in the western gate of the city, where they were buried after Azekah and Lachish were destroyed by Nebuchadnezzar, the great king of Babylon, in 587 B.C.E. In one letter the commander of Lachish writes: "this let-ter certifies to the commanding officer in Jerusalem that I remain on duty to carry out your orders. Judah's signal fire at Lachish still burns, even after the only other remain-ing signal fire at Azekah has gone out." It may well be that Nebuchadnezzar temporar-ily withdrew his troops from Jerusalem for the final assault on Lachish.

Almost immediately following the withdrawal of the Babylonians from Jerusalem, the people of the city reclaimed their slaves. Jeremiah is outraged. How could the people whom Yahweh freed from slavery enslave others? The whole point of the covenant between Yah-weh and Judah was to prevent slavery, not to free one people and enslave another. How could the people of Judah so clearly recognize the importance of freeing slaves by releas-ing them during the siege, and then so callously void their vows and reclaim them?

The trial contrasts the Rechabites with the people of Judah (Jer 35:1-16). The Rech-abites were metalworkers who lived in tents and did not drink wine. They crisscrossed the land in search of ore, and in search of work. They were itinerants. There was not enough work in one place, and they continually needed to replenish their supply of iron ore from distant mines. Because their work was dangerous and because it was dirty, even the vil-lages that they served did not allow them to work in the village itself, where the fires of these smiths could cause harm, and the heat and smells of the their forges could cause inconvenience. The Rechabites did not drink wine for fear that if they got drunk they would reveal just how they were able to mine and to forge iron into tools and weapons.

Although the lifestyle of the Rechabites was not unusual in early Israel, most of the people of Judah in the time of Jeremiah lived in houses, and enjoyed drinking the wine that they fermented from the harvests of grapes that the land provided. Jeremiah does not idealize the Rechabites as the only true believers who remain faithful to a nomadic way of life. They are eccentrics. They remain faithful to a way of life that no longer had any practical purpose and no covenant significance. It is this faithfulness to insignificant and meaningless customs that Jeremiah uses to contrast them with the people of Jerusalem who are unfaithful to the significant and meaningful stipulations of the covenant between Yahweh and Judah. The Rechabites remain faithful to their traditions of refusing to farm, of living in tents, and of abstaining from wine, which are eccentric and meaningless, while the people of Jerusalem abandon their tradition of freeing the slaves, which is central to the covenant and full of meaning for the descendants of the people whom Yahweh had freed from slavery. The Rechabites, as politically and eco-nomically eccentric as they are, will survive because they keep their covenants (Jer 35:18-19). The people of Judah, as politically and economically successful as they are, will not survive because they do not keep their covenants (Jer 35:17). Like most of the prophets, Jeremiah considers kept promises the only guarantee that the land and its people will be well fed and safe from their enemies. Only when the people of Judah allow Yahweh to protect the land and its people will there be peace.

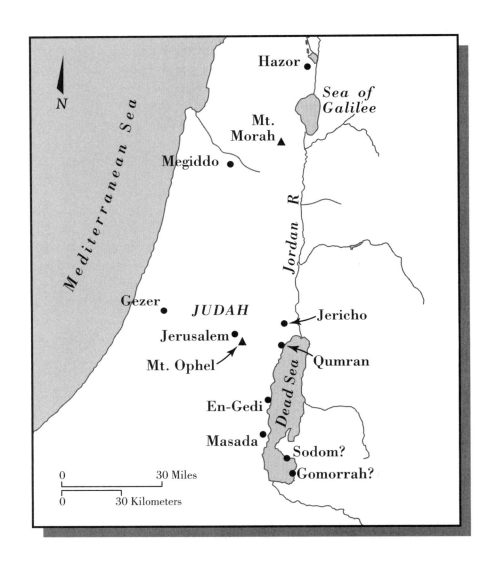

Points of Interest (Chapter 14)

14

BOOK OF EZEKIEL

(EZEK 1:1—48:35)

Babylon was a city whose name meant "The Gate of the Divine Assembly." Founded around 5000 B.C.E., Babylon became a world power twice: once during the Middle Bronze period under Hammurabi (1792–1750 B.C.E.) and once during the Iron Age under Nebuchadnezzar (604–562 B.C.E.). The shifting of power in Mesopotamia from Assyria to Babylon at the beginning of Nebuchadnezzar's reign, and the death of the grand old monarch, set dramatic political and economic changes into motion. The book of Ezekiel (Hebrew: *Yehezqe'l*) monitored the effect of these changes on Judah. The most dramatic change was the deportation of the household of David, and the subsequent destruction of the city in 587 B.C.E.

Babylon settled its exiles on abandoned sites to redevelop them, while their former rulers were carefully reeducated at the palace. Tel Aviv was the section of the city assigned to the household of David for restoration, while King Jehoiachin (598 B.C.E.) "ate at Nebuchadnezzar's table" (2 Kgs 25:27-30) in Babylon. During his forty-year reign, Nebuchadnezzar used the plunder and prisoners from his wars to rebuild and expand Babylon. To complement the city's ziggurat tower, named "The Foundation of the Heavens and the Earth," he built three palaces, The Ishtar Gate, and The Hanging Gardens. Babylon eventually covered some two thousand acres.

Theodicy is the study of incomprehensible divine actions, like how a good God can permit the innocent to suffer and the wicked to prosper. The deportation of the household of David and the destruction of Jerusalem were incomprehensible.

Yahweh had negotiated a covenant with Abraham and Sarah to feed and to protect the land and its people. The book of Ezekiel asks if the Babylonians were able to conquer the land and deport its people because Yahweh had lied to Abraham and Sarah, or if Yahweh had been killed when the Babylonians destroyed the temple. Time and again Judah was invaded, but Jerusalem survived. In 701 B.C.E., Sennacherib suddenly broke off a prolonged siege of Jerusalem and marched his soldiers back to Assyria. Hezekiah, the ruler of Judah, may have paid Sennacherib a ransom to spare the city and its temple. A plague may have broken out in the Assyrians' battle camp, or news of political unrest in Assyria may have reached Sennacherib. Nonetheless, when the siege ended, the people of Judah considered it a confirmation of their faith that Jerusalem and its temple were indestructible. Therefore, when the Babylonians broke through the walls of Jerusalem and razed its temple to the ground in 587 B.C.E., the people of Judah were devastated. The book of Ezekiel preserves some of the traditions that try to make sense of the incomprehensible act of Yahweh's allowing the Babylonians to take away the land and children promised to Abraham and Sarah.

When Babylon invaded Judah, some households were convinced that Yahweh had abrogated the covenant with Judah and was no longer their divine patron. Some of their traditions appear in the book of Ezekiel today (Ezek 8:1-18). Most households, however, were convinced that when the rulers of Judah negotiated with the rulers of neighboring states for food and for protection, they broke the covenant by transferring the responsibilities of Yahweh to these strangers. Their traditions argue that whenever the people of Judah tried to feed and to protect themselves by negotiating covenants they inevitably suffered from famine and from war. Only Yahweh could feed and protect Judah and its people. Whenever Judah broke its covenant with Yahweh, famine and war plagued the land and the people. Nonetheless, the chaos that famine and war create became the womb from which Yahweh delivered the people of Judah, ending their exile and restoring them to their land.

Creation of the City of Immanuel
(Ezek 1:1 — 48:35)

Sterility Affidavit
(Ezek 1:1 — 12:28)

The book of Ezekiel is a creation story that opens with a sterility affidavit describing the death of Judah and Jerusalem, ruled by the household of David. The Inauguration of Ezekiel, who will play an important role in the decommissioning of this old world, introduces this creation story just as the Inauguration of Moses on Mt. Horeb introduces the Death of the Firstborn of Egypt in the book of Exodus. The climax of the Creation of the City of Immanuel is a cosmogony (Ezek 13:1—32:32), and its denouement is a covenant (Ezek 33:1—48:35).

Hebrew Refugees Flee Lachish with Wagon
(Nineveh 694 B.C.E.; limestone 250 cm x 18.9 m)

Inauguration of Ezekiel in Babylon
(EZEK 1:4—3:15)

The household of David regularly indicted prophets like Ezekiel as imposters. The length of the Inauguration of Ezekiel indicates how many questions the monarchy raised about Ezekiel's legitimacy. Among the most serious indictments against him is his location in Babylon. No true prophet had ever been inaugurated by Yahweh outside the land of Israel and Judah. For the household of David, Yahweh could not leave the temple in Jerusalem. Therefore, Ezekiel could not encounter Yahweh outside Jerusalem. The Inauguration of Ezekiel in Babylon (Ezek 1:4—3:15) argues that Yahweh is not confined to the temple, but moves freely throughout the ancient Near East. The inauguration uses wings, wheels, and eyes to stress the mobility of Yahweh, who comes and goes effortlessly.

The crisis episode (Ezek 1:4-28) in the Inauguration of Ezekiel assumes that Ezekiel is sitting on the outskirts of Tel Aviv. Babylon is built on a plain that is subject to sudden and violent storms. This storm crosses the plain like an invisible hand pulling a dark curtain over a window. Ezekiel sits and watches the ominous cloud stalk the city.

Confronted with the new, the different, the unexpected, the impossible, the prophet prays: "Why are the people of Judah here, alone and without Yahweh? Is Judah an orphan who has no divine patron? Has Babylon put Yahweh to death?"

Israel prohibits images of Yahweh. There are, however, two classic exceptions. Yahweh is a pillar of fire by night and a cloud by day. The cloud was a massive thunderhead churned up like dust by the wheels of the chariot of Yahweh riding across the dome of the sky to do battle with the raging Mediterranean Sea (Deut 33:26-29). The pillar of fire was a bolt of lightning fired like an arrow from the chariot of Yahweh to drive the sea away from the land (Fig. 91).

As Ezekiel watches the storm crossing the plain, he expects to see Yahweh ride out of the cloud like a divine warrior in order to attack Babylon and free the people of Judah. Instead, he sees a refugee's wagon, glowing with the static electricity created by St. Elmo's fire, rumble out of the storm (Ezek 1:5). This is the same wagon that Ezekiel sees leaving Jerusalem when Yahweh evacuates the temple (Ezek 10:18-22). The same kind of wagon appears in the reliefs of Sennacherib's victory over Lachish. The image evokes the feelings of humility and identity with the poor evoked when the body of Martin Luther King Jr. processed in a farm wagon to his grave, or when the family in *Grapes of Wrath,* the 1939 novel by John Steinbeck (1902–68), load their truck to leave Oklahoma. Marduk rides in a war chariot; Yahweh in a refugee's wagon. Yahweh does not process triumphantly like Marduk into Babylon, but enters the city humbly among all the other prisoners of war to share the suffering of the household of David in exile.

Yahweh does not come to conquer Babylon or to set the exiles free. The wars that the rulers of Judah waged to protect the land and its people in fact destroyed the land and exiled the people. Yahweh comes, not as a covenant partner to the rulers of Judah in order to continue the war, but as a companion to those who suffer the consequences of these ill-fated war policies of the monarchy.

The wagon is loaded with the furniture that most characterized Yahweh. The cherubim (Ezek 1:5-13) are fearsome creatures who guard the Temple of Yahweh. These composite creatures combine the most respected qualities of the most respected creatures: the intelligence of humans, the strength of oxen, the courage of lions, the flight of eagles. Here, these former bodyguards are now harnessed together in two unmatched teams drawing Yahweh's wagon (Exod 37:6-9; 2 Sam 22:8-20; Ps 18:11; 79:2; 99:1).

Like the cherubim, the seraphim are also part of the household of Yahweh who evacuate Jerusalem with him. They carry the weapons of Yahweh. Ezekiel does not see "torches" (Ezek 1:13), but rather bolts of lightning flashing like fire from the chariot.

The wheels and wings are also an important component of the theophany (Ezek 1:8-20). The inauguration presents Yahweh as on the move. David and Solomon built the temple to be the House of Yahweh, but in time it became a prison that the rulers of Judah believed that Yahweh could not leave. According to Ezekiel, Yahweh can leave the temple, Jerusalem, and Judah and move in any direction across the earth. The inauguration describes Yahweh moving to Babylon. The Dedication of the City of Immanuel describes Yahweh moving back to Judah (Ezek 40:1—48:35).

call to worship

> Praise the divine patron of Israel without equal!
>   Shout as Yahweh rides across the heavens to save us!

creation story

> Yahweh subdues the ancient enemies,
>   Our divine patron shatters the forces of old;
>
> Yahweh drives out the enemy before you,
>   Our divine patron decrees: "Destroy them!"
>
> So Israel lives in safety,
>   Untroubled is Jacob's abode
>
> In a land of grain and wine,
>   Where the heavens drop down dew.
>
> Blessed are you, O Israel! Who is like you,
>   A people saved by Yahweh;
>
> Yahweh is your helpful shield,
>   Yahweh is your victorious sword.
>
> Your enemies shall surrender to you,
>   You shall put your foot on their backs.

FIGURE 91   Hymn (Deut 33:26-29)

In the Creation of the Heavens and the Earth (Gen 1:6), Yahweh designs a firmament or dome to create a habitat where creatures who breathe can survive in a liquid universe. The dome is Yahweh's patented design. This dome is also on the wagon (Ezek 1:22).

In the Flood Stories, Yahweh unstrings the divine war bow and hangs it on the wall of the heavens (Gen 9:1-17). This disarmed weapon becomes a peace symbol. Yahweh is no longer at war with the people of Noah's day. The flood is over. The rainbow is an amulet that no longer needs to be fired in anger, but simply hangs on the walls of the heavens to protect the earth.

The great storm out of which Yahweh's wagon emerges onto the plains of Babylon lures Ezekiel into the divine presence. In contrast to the elaborate theophany in the inauguration, the report of his investigation is starkly simple. "I stared at this mirage" better translates the Hebrew than "such was the appearance of the splendor all around.

This was the appearance of the likeness of the glory of Yahweh" (Ezek 1:28). Only when he investigates the mirage, as Moses investigates the burning bush, does Ezekiel become aware that it is Yahweh.

"The glory of Yahweh" is a gloss on "mirage." It is an umbrella term for the theophany that the Bible uses to indicate the presence of Yahweh. Here, the glory of Yahweh is made up of furniture like the cherubim and seraphim who serve as temple guards, the dome, the throne or Ark of the Covenant, and the war bow.

Yahweh greets Ezekiel as "Son of Man" (Ezek 1:28). In a standard inauguration, Yahweh calls the name of the candidate twice: "Moses, Moses" (Exod 3:4). "Son of Man" means "mortal," and contrasts Ezekiel with Yahweh, who is immortal. This particular title stresses that a human being has no business asking what Yahweh is doing in letting Babylon destroy Jerusalem. The book of Job provides the same answer to Job's demand for an explanation of his suffering. Human beings cannot understand what Yahweh does, so they ought to stop asking.

Ezekiel's response to Yahweh's greeting is a prostration: "I fell prostrate" (Ezek 1:28). Candidates take the fetal position with their knees and their foreheads pressed to the earth upon hearing Yahweh call their names. "As I heard a voice say to me 'Son of Man,' I fell upon my face." The greeting and the kenosis are simultaneous.

The standard stay of execution is the formula: "Fear not!" Here in the Inauguration of Ezekiel (Ezek 2:1), however, Yahweh grants Ezekiel a stay by ordering him to stand up. The gesture of raising Ezekiel to an upright and standing position simulates raising him from the dead. As a human being, Ezekiel enters the presence of Yahweh and takes the fetal position or dies. Yahweh then raises him up from the dead and he leaves the presence of Yahweh as a prophet on a divine mission.

Yahweh commissions Ezekiel not only to explain, but also to use pantomimes to set in motion the events that will bring the old world of Judah to an end (Ezek 2:2—3:11). Like all prophets, he is a master, not only wielding Yahweh's creative words, but acting to set those words into motion as well.

The book of Ezekiel considers the loss of the land of Judah to be the first phase in the termination of the covenant between Yahweh and Judah. Ezekiel declares Judah to be in a time of transition, and establishes his headquarters at Tel-Aviv or "Spring Hill," where the earth, full and round and pregnant, is preparing to give birth to a new world. The violation of the covenant between Yahweh and Judah by the household of David, and not the armies of Babylon, drove Yahweh from Jerusalem. By covenant Yahweh agreed to feed Judah and to protect Judah from its enemies. Repeatedly the household of David made covenants with Egypt and other states to feed and protect itself. These negotiations demonstrated that the household of David had no faith in Yahweh's willingness or Yahweh's ability to feed and protect Judah. Since the household of David wanted to feed and protect Judah and its people, Yahweh evacuated Jerusalem to allow the household of David to feed and protect the land and its people, which, of course, it was incapable of doing.

Trial of the Old Jerusalem
(EZEK 4:1-17)

Ezekiel consummates his inauguration by pantomiming a Trial of the Old Jerusalem. This pantomime is only the first of a number of them in the book of Ezekiel (Ezek 3:22-27; 5:1-15; 12:1-20; 21:11-12; 24:15-23; 37:15-28). Here he pantomimes the siege of Jerusalem, whose outline is cut into a brick. When cities were founded, a ground plan of its walls and major buildings was drawn on a brick, and then laid as the cornerstone of the first building.

During the siege, Ezekiel fasts as the defenders of Jerusalem fast during the siege. He rations his bread and water. As the rations run out, he begins to make bread from leftovers, mixing various kinds of grain because there is not enough of one kind to make even a single loaf of bread.

Initially, Yahweh directs Ezekiel to cook the bread on chips of dried human excrement. Ezekiel, however, negotiates to cook the bread on chips of dried cow dung. The kind of fuel indicates the length of the siege. When the siege of a city began, its citizens cooked on charcoal fires. When charcoal ran out, they cooked on dried animal dung. The same kinds of cow chips and buffalo chips were used by pioneers crossing the treeless plains into California during the nineteenth century. Eventually the citizens under siege slaughtered their animals for food, which they cooked on their own dried excrement.

Ezekiel is not shocked at the use of dung for fuel, but by the length of the siege to which Yahweh sentences Jerusalem. Consequently, Ezekiel appeals the sentence, and Yahweh agrees to shorten it. Jerusalem will fall after the charcoal is used up, but before all its animals have been slaughtered.

Cosmogony
(EZEK 13:1—32:32)

The climax episode of the Creation of the City of Immanuel is a cosmogony. The divine assembly commissions the creation of a new Judah and a new Jerusalem to be ruled by Yahweh alone. Unlike the old Judah and the old Jerusalem, which Babylon has destroyed, this new Judah and new Jerusalem will fulfill the stipulations of the covenant. Yahweh, and not the household of David, will feed its people and will protect its land. The cosmogony is composed of a variety of trials, teachings, and pantomimes.

Trial of Judah
(EZEK 14:12-23)

Prophets not only promulgated the verdicts of the divine assembly, they appealed them. When prophets felt the sentence of Yahweh would destroy Israel and Judah rather than reform them, they asked Yahweh to reconsider. The prophet as intercessor is a common motif in the book of Ezekiel (Ezek 18:1-32).

In one tradition (Ezek 14:12-23), however, Yahweh preempts an appeal by warning Ezekiel that not even the three most renowned negotiators, Noah, Daniel, and Job, could successfully appeal the decision to allow Babylon to win its war with Judah. "Son of Man, when a land sins against me by acting faithlessly, and I stretch out my hand against it, and break its staff of bread and send famine upon it, and cut off from it human beings and animals, even if Noah, Daniel, and Job, these three, were in it, they would save only their own lives by their righteousness, says Yahweh, our Creator. If I send wild animals through the land to ravage it, so that it is made desolate, and no one may pass through because of the animals; even if these three men were in it . . . they would save neither sons nor daughters; they alone would be saved, but the land would be desolate" (Ezek 14:12-16).

Trial of the Old Jerusalem
(EZEK 16:1-63)

Like most trials, a Trial of the Old Jerusalem in the book of Ezekiel is made up of an indictment and a sentence (Fig. 92). The indictment begins by describing the loving-kindness that prompts Yahweh to adopt, and then to marry, Jerusalem. Yahweh's adoption of Jerusalem preserves the most complete list in the Bible of a midwife's postpartum services. Midwives cut and tied off the umbilical cord, plunged it into a bath of seawater, rinsed the placenta off the newborn, and then wrapped it in a receiving blanket.

Because the father of the household into which Jerusalem is born does not adopt the child, it is taken from the birthing room and placed, unwashed, in an uncultivated field beyond the border of the village. This ritual places the child up for adoption. By placing the newborn outside the village in the same condition in which it left the womb, the household waives its own right to adopt the child, and declares that it is eligible for another household to claim.

Yahweh sees the newborn and calls out: "Live!" thus becoming Jerusalem's adoptive parent. Jerusalem is now a member of the household of Yahweh.

Jerusalem matures in the household of Yahweh. She becomes an adolescent whose breasts and pubic hair indicate she is capable of sexual intercourse, but whose nakedness indicates that she is still infertile. As head of the household, Yahweh not only adopts Jerusalem, but marries the city as well.

Swaddling a newborn and clothing a bride are both rituals of adoption. Clothing is a uniform that identifies humans as members of a household.

Jewelry not only identifies the household to which a woman belongs, but is an indication that she is fertile. Like clothing, jewelry is an indication of the social status of the household. Jewelry accents the erotic parts of the body. Yahweh accents the arms, the neck, the nose, the ears, and the head of Jerusalem with jewelry. Not every culture considers the same parts of the body to be erotic.

Having told the story of how loving and kind Yahweh has been to Jerusalem, the indictment then charges the city with ingratitude. Despite all the evidence that Yahweh can, and will, feed and protect the city, Jerusalem negotiated covenants with neighboring states to feed and protect itself.

For prophets like Ezekiel, the covenant between Yahweh and Judah is a "marriage," whereas the covenants that Jerusalem negotiates with other states are "adultery" (Ezek 16:15). As part of its premium payments on these covenants, the city gave away Yahweh's gifts of gold, silver, incense, bread, flour, oil, and honey (Ezek 16:15-19). Jerusalem also drafted its young men and women and sent them to serve in the armies and factories of its covenant partners (Ezek 16:20-34). The city turned these sons and daughters of Yahweh over to strangers. "As if your adultery were not enough! You slaughtered my children and delivered them up as an offering to them" (Ezek 16:20).

There was virtually no state with which Jerusalem would not negotiate a covenant for food and protection. "You built yourself a platform and made yourself a lofty place in every square; at the head of every street you built your lofty place and prostituted your beauty, offering yourself to every passerby" (Ezek 16:24-25). Jerusalem was even willing to turn the exodus around, and send its sons and daughters back into slavery in Egypt (Ezek 16:26).

Yahweh and the divine assembly convict Jerusalem of breach of covenant, but commute the city's sentence to the war and famine that it has already suffered. Despite the chronic insecurity of the rulers of Israel and Judah, and their labor-intensive efforts to negotiate food and protection for the land and its people, the results for the prophets are always the same. The Hebrews starve, and their land is invaded. Israel and Judah repeatedly suffered the consequences of the actions of their rulers.

Teaching on Responsibility
(EZEK 18:1-32)

Like the Book of Ecclesiastes, a Teaching on Responsibility in the book of Ezekiel audits sayings from the book of Proverbs. A parallel tradition is preserved in the covenant at the end of Ezekiel (Ezek 33:10-20).

The first saying from the Proverbs tradition that the book of Ezekiel audits is: "parents have eaten sour grapes, and their children's teeth are set on edge" (Ezek 18:2). The second saying is: "why should not the son suffer for the iniquity of the father?" (Ezek 18:19). The intention of the audit is not to discredit the sayings, but to point out their limitations.

The sayings stress the importance of community. An individual was not socially viable in the world of the Bible. The household was the smallest viable social unit.

inauguration of Ezekiel (Ezek 16:1-2)

"Son of Man, this is your commission:

"In the Trial of Jerusalem, Yahweh and the divine assembly find the city guilty of breach of covenant.

indictment (Ezek 16:3-34)

"Whereas, your father, an Amorite from the west, and your mother, a Canaanite from the east, abandoned you, Jerusalem, in the land of Egypt.

"Whereas you were born without a midwife to cut and tie your umbilical cord, to wash the afterbirth from your face, to rub your tender skin with oil, to plunge you into water from the sea, to wrap you in swaddling clothes.

"Whereas no household adopted you as its own or looked on you with pity or compassion.

"Whereas your father and your mother dumped you on the ground like so much human excrement, I, Yahweh, passed by and saw you gagging in your blood, and decreed: 'Live!'

"Whereas, you, Jerusalem, were only a wildflower growing in a open field.

"Whereas you were a naked animal, maturing, beginning to menstruate, developing breasts, growing pubic hair, I, Yahweh, passed by and saw you staggering blindly into adulthood. I proposed to you, swore a marriage covenant with you. I bathed your body, perfumed your hair, softened your skin with delicate oils. I dressed you in an embroidered gown, put expensive leather sandals on your feet, draped an imported linen stole from your shoulders, gave you a choice of silk gowns for the evening. I showered you with jewelry. I gave you bracelets to highlight your arms, a collar to accent your neck, a cuff for your nose, studs for your ears, a tiara for your head. You were plated with gold and silver; draped in imported linen, silk, and damask; dined on cake made from the most expensive flour, honey, and oil. Jerusalem, you were so beautiful. You were my queen. I created Jerusalem to be the most beautiful woman in the world. . . ."

[Whereas you negotiated covenants with other states for food, despite Yahweh's promise to provide for you . . .] (Ezek 16:15-19)

[Whereas you negotiated covenants with other states for troops, despite Yahweh's promise to protect you . . .] (Ezek 16:20-34)

sentence (Ezek 16:35-63)

[Therefore, Yahweh and the divine assembly convict you for breach of covenant . . . but commute your sentence to the suffering you have already endured, and assign you as a ward of this divine assembly to begin rehabilitation. . . .]

FIGURE 92   Trial of Jerusalem (Ezek 16:1-63)

The household consisted of four generations: the father of the household; his parents; his sons and their sons. This Teaching on Responsibility does not want to replace community with individuality, but to prevent the emphasis on community from becoming an excuse for avoiding the responsibility for acting decisively.

The audit indicts both the royal households remaining in Judah and the royal households that the Babylonians began deporting in 597 B.C.E. Neither were ready to accept responsibility for the loss of the land and people of Judah to Babylon. Neither were ready to take the initiative to recover them.

The royal households remaining in Judah quoted the sayings in the audit to argue that the Babylonian invasion was the consequence, not of their actions, but of the actions of their fathers. The royal households in exile argued that they were cut off from their land and their people, and so were helpless to initiate change.

Ezekiel charges both branches of the household of David with apathy, and holds them responsible for Judah's loss of Yahweh's gifts of children and land. Ezekiel seeks to empower the household of David to regain the children and the land of Judah. What the monarchy has lost by its lack of responsibility, it can regain by its conversion and repentance. The audit demonstrates how strongly Ezekiel campaigned to overcome the apathy of the royal household and those who supported it.

Ezekiel's teaching is not a call for individual moral responsibility; it is a call for the household of David to be responsible. The "man" or "son" in the teaching is not a single individual, but the royal household, which protested that it could do nothing. This teaching tries to convince the household of David that, regardless of the sins of its predecessors, it could still make a difference. It appeals to the households of David in Judah to allow Yahweh to protect and to provide for Judah instead of trying vainly to negotiate last-minute covenants with other states for food and for soldiers to protect and to provide for Judah. The teaching also appeals to the households of David in Babylon to continue to live according to the stipulations of the covenant between Yahweh and Judah, even though they have already lost their land and their children. The teaching argues that despite the fact that Judah has been destroyed, the household of David can still affect the future of the people of Yahweh by its virtue and its sins.

Ezekiel wants the household of David to forget the past. No household is responsible for its past sins, nor can any household rely on its past virtues. Conversion is complete forgiveness of past debts, and a completely new identity. It is a re-creation that the household of David can use to make "a new heart and a new spirit" (Ezek 18:31). There is no past for the newborn. The household of David will be judged by what it is doing now, not what it has done in the past.

Ezekiel Cooks a Meal
(EZEK 24:1-14)

Every meal reflected the awareness of the people of Judah that this food was a gift, not a wage. Every meal also reflected the social order in which each household knew its place and fulfilled its responsibilities to its own members and to the village.

When Ezekiel Cooks a Meal (Ezek 24:1-14), he pantomimes a Trial of Jerusalem. He invites the fathers of the royal households to a meal. He places a corroded pot on the fire and fills it with water and blood-soaked pieces of meat. As the water begins to boil, the rust and blood turn the water a deadly red. He then serves the meat randomly, making no attempt to choose pieces of meat appropriate to the status of the households. With these actions Ezekiel indicts Jerusalem for forgetting that it is Yahweh, and not the household of David, who feeds its people, and for creating such competition between the households of Judah that only the powerful survive.

The pot that Ezekiel sets on the fire represents the city of Jerusalem (Ezek 24:3). The royal households bragged that the walls of Jerusalem were as impervious to the enemies of Judah as a metal pot was to the flames licking at its sides. The discoloration of the water by the blood and rust inside the pot pantomimes that Jerusalem will be destroyed by the blood shed by the royal household inside the walls, and not by the Babylonians outside the walls.

The rust that eats away at the walls of the pot is the damage that competition of the royal households with one another has done to Jerusalem (Ezek 24:6). The covenant between Yahweh and Judah established a decentralized, subsistence village economy in which both the powerful, like the royal households, and the powerless, like the widow, the orphan, and the stranger, would be fed. The competition that the household of David set into motion by founding a centralized, surplus state economy, however, made it possible for only some households to survive. The rest rust. The innocent blood of the powerless is shed by the powerful. Ezekiel's pantomime stresses that if all the metal in the pot does not survive, then none will.

The people of Judah carefully drained all the blood from the animals that they slaughtered, not only to prevent the meat from spoiling, but also to acknowledge that these animals were gifts from Yahweh, not products of their own work. The only blood drained from the meat in the pantomime is that which splashed on the rocks while the animal was being slaughtered (Ezek 24:7-8). There was no gratitude in the butchering of these animals, only greed. Cooking meat from which the blood had not been drained was comparable today to eating without saying grace or returning thanks.

Having shocked his guests with the way in which he prepared the meal, Ezekiel further startles them by the way in which he serves it. In the world of the Bible those who ate together sat in an order that emphasized their role in the household. The best cuts and prime portions were served to those whom the household wished to honor.

Ezekiel serves his meal in total disregard for the status of his guests (Ezek 24:6). By making the first to be last and the last to be first, Ezekiel pantomimes the chaos that will follow the conquest of Jerusalem. On that day the social status of all the households of Jerusalem will be destroyed.

When the first meal is finished, Ezekiel prepares a second meal. This time, he carefully separates the bones from the meat. Then, he marinates the meat thoroughly in spices to draw the blood out of the meat and to season it. Finally, by overheating the empty pot on the fire, he scours it clean so that it will be safe and ready to use. By cleaning the pot with the intense heat of the fire, Ezekiel pantomimes the siege of Jerusalem as Yahweh's way of preparing a new Jerusalem. Once the pot is clean, the households in the marinade of the exile will be safely placed in the pot, and a new world will begin.

Covenant
(EZEK 33:1—48:35)

The Creation of the City of Immanuel closes with a covenant describing the dedication of the city. The Akitu New Year celebrated Marduk's re-creation of the city of Babylon and its people. The book of Ezekiel uses the pattern of the Akitu New Year to celebrate Yahweh's re-creation of Jerusalem and its people. A Trial of Judah (Ezek 36:16-38), the Creation of a New People from Dry Bones (Ezek 37:1-14), and the Dedication of the City of Immanuel (Ezek 40:1—48:35) are important components of this covenant.

Trial of Judah
(EZEK 36:16-38)

A Trial of Judah opens with an indictment (Ezek 36:16-21), which is typical of the genre, but it concludes with a pardon instead of a sentence (Exod 36:22-38). The trial indicts Jerusalem for adultery. "Son of Man, when Israel lived in its own land, the people shamed the land by what they said and did. They behaved like a shameful woman during menstruation" (Ezek 36:16-17).

The analogy of Jerusalem as a menstruating woman appears elsewhere in the book of Ezekiel (Ezek 7:19; 18:1-32; 22:1-31). Menstruation was treated differently in the world of the Bible than it is treated today (Gen 31:35; Lev 15:19-24; 18:19; 20:18; 2 Sam 11:4; Isa 30:22; Lam 1:17; Ezra 9:11). Because menstruation could not be controlled, because only women menstruated, and because menstruation ended a period of fertility, the Hebrews labeled menstruating women as shamed, "impure," or "unclean." The label had little or nothing to do with hygiene, but indicated that menstruating women were exempt from ordinary responsibilities, including intercourse with their husbands. They were set apart from the household. Because menstruating women were without fertility, they were without intimacy. Similarly, the trial sentences Jerusalem to be separated from Yahweh. She is quarantined like the ruins of Jericho, and becomes as infertile as Sodom and Gomorrah.

The messenger formula "Thus says Yahweh, our Creator" (Ezek 36:22, 33) introduces each companion pardon. The pardons promulgate Yahweh's decision to negotiate a new covenant and once again to bless Judah with land: "Fallow land shall be tilled . . . abandoned cities shall be rebuilt and resettled" (Ezek 36:34-36). Here, and elsewhere in creation stories, Yahweh is an urban architect who builds not only the City of Immanuel (Ezek 48:35), but also Eden, Enoch, Babel, and The Great Tent. Yahweh "will also increase its population like a flock" (Ezek 36:37) to live in and to care for the City of Immanuel.

Creation of a New People from Dry Bones
(EZEK 37:1-14)

Prophets were committed to reforming the old world; seers wanted to replace it. If they were automobile mechanics, prophets would tell you to fix your car; seers would tell you to sell it. Sometimes the book of Ezekiel portrays him as a prophet committed to reform; sometimes it portrays him as a seer committed to replacement.

The Creation of a New People from Dry Bones (Ezek 37:1-14) is time voyage, a genre in which a member of the divine assembly takes a seer like Ezekiel or Daniel from the human plane on a tour of the divine plane. These voyages are time-warp experiences in which seers pass like shamans into the divine plane. Time travel is still a popular motif in television series like *Star Trek*, *Dr. Who*, *Sliders*, and *Quantum Leap*.

The crisis episode is an epiphany of a messenger who will guide Ezekiel. Sometimes the seer is guided by Yahweh, not just a messenger of Yahweh.

The climax is a tour that contains a number of stops. At each stop, the guide instructs the seer with a catechism. The catechism consists of a question posed by the guide and an answer given by the seer, which the guide then interprets with a commentary explaining what is happening on the human plane or what is happening on the divine plane.

The denouement episode in a standard time voyage is a health report. There is no denouement in the Creation of a New People from Dry Bones.

The crisis opens when the spirit of Yahweh draws Ezekiel into a trance or sleep (Ezek 37:1). Then the "Hand of Yahweh" (Ezek 37:1), Yahweh's personal secretary, leads him into the divine plane. The first stop on the tour is "the midst of the valley," which is the center of the earth (Ezek 37:1).

At the first stop, Ezekiel observes the creation of a new people. The tradition uses elements from the Stories of Atrahasis and from the book of Genesis to describe the creation (Fig. 93). In the Stories of Atrahasis, Nintu, the divine midwife, shapes workers from clay and then moistens them with a slip of flesh and blood (Atra I:200–230). In a Story of the 'Adam as a Farmer (Gen 2:4-17), Yahweh moistens the clay with the saliva that breathing causes to condense on it. "Yahweh, our Creator, sculpted an 'adam

> Nintu said to the divine assembly:
>   "I cannot do Ea-Enki's work.
>   Only Ea-Enki has the clay to create."
>
> Ea-Enki spoke: "I will bathe to mark my time . . .
>   At the new moon, the seventh day, and the full moon, I
>   will wash.
>
> Let the divine assembly sacrifice We-ila.
>   Let them bathe in his blood.
>
> Let Nintu thin my clay with his blood.
>   Let Nintu mix clay with blood, the human
>   with the divine.
>
> Let the drum mark off the days,
>   Count down the time.
>
> Let We-ila's blood give these workers life,
>   Let the midwife call out to them: 'Live!'"
>
> The divine assembly agreed,
>   The annunaki elders consented.
>
> At the new moon, the seventh day, the full moon, Ea-Enki
>   bathed.
>   The divine assembly sacrificed We-ila the wise. . . .
>
> Nintu thinned the clay . . . with his blood.
>   The drum marked off the days . . . counted down the time.
>
> We-ila's blood gave the workers life,
>   Nintu-Mami called out to them: "Live!"

FIGURE 93   Stories of Atrahasis, I:200–230 (Matthews and Benjamin 1997: 33)

from clay, made it live by breathing moisture onto the clay" (Gen 2:7). In a Story of the *'Adam* as a Man and a Woman (Gen 2:18-24), Yahweh moistens a rib with flesh and blood (Gen 2:21). Here in the Creation of a New People from Dry Bones Yahweh moistens the unburied bones strewn across a battlefield with dew, which the gentle breeze at dawn causes to condense on them.

Today the difference between the living and the dead is a muscular heartbeat or an electrical brainwave. In the world of the Bible, the living were moist and the dead were dry. When someone stopped breathing, the household first placed the body where it could dry. This primary burial marked a time of transition. No one was truly dead or gone until the bones were completely dry, when a secondary burial took place.

Raising the dead here, and freeing the slaves in the book of Exodus, are parallel to the creation of the man and the woman in the book of Genesis. The commentary on this vision of Ezekiel (Ezek 37:11-14) emphasizes the parallel. "Behold, I will open your graves, and raise you from your graves, O my people; and I will bring you home into the land of Israel" (Ezek 37:11). Yahweh will create a new people for the new Jerusalem from the bones of the old people who died defending the old Jerusalem. Judah will once again be blessed with land and children.

Dedication of the City of Immanuel
(Ezek 40:1 — 48:35)

Today's idea that the world will come to an abrupt end, and then eternity will begin, would have been foreign to the Hebrews. They expected every old world to be replaced by a new world. Like the ruler announced by Isaiah (Isa 7:14), the city described by Ezekiel (Ezek 48:35) is named "Immanuel." The Dedication of the City of Immanuel (Ezek 40:1—48:35) surveys a new land. It designs a new temple, promulgates a new code of law, and establishes a new liturgy (Fig. 94).

The time voyage is dated to "the twenty-fifth year of our exile, at the beginning of the year, on the tenth day of the month, in the fourteenth year after the city was conquered" (Ezek 40:1) or April 19, 573 B.C.E. The significance of the date, however, is more psychological than chronological. Like the date *1984* (1949) in the novel by George Orwell (1903–50) or the date *2001—A Space Odyssey* (1968) in the film by Stanley Kubrick (1928–99), "the twenty-fifth year of our exile" offers the audience the information it needs to set its psyche, rather than its watch. Shock insulates victims from the initial pain of trauma. When the Babylonians began deporting the people of Judah in 597 B.C.E., and even when they destroyed Jerusalem in 587 B.C.E., shock allowed the people of Judah to hope that this old world would be restored. Twenty-five years after their deportation, however, the exiles were ready to come to terms with reality and to begin their rehabilitation. Nothing could be gained from denial. The Dedication of the City of Immanuel encourages the exiles to begin planning for life in a new world, a teaching that also appears in a letter of Jeremiah. In this new world there would be no monarchs. Never again would royal policies be able to bring about wars, like those between Babylon and Judah, which took away the land and children that Yahweh had bestowed upon the people of Judah.

Ezekiel is taken to the mountain on the divine plane where Yahweh, who is described as "a man, whose appearance was like bronze, with a line of flax and a measuring reed in his hand" (Ezek 40:3), is prefabricating a city. After having dispatched the armies of

A. Dedication of the City of Immanuel (Ezek 40:1—48:35)—
   a time voyage
   1. certificate for walls (Ezek 40:5)
   2. certificate for outer gates (Ezek 40:6-27)
   3. certificate for inner gates (Ezek 40:28-43)
   4. certificate for temple (Ezek 40:44—41:26)
   5. certificate for inner court (Ezek 42:1-14)
   6. certificate for outer court (Ezek 42:15-20)
   7. certificate for "glory of God" (Ezek 43:1-9)

B. New Covenant (Ezek 43:10—46:18)
   1. altar stipulation (Ezek 43:10-27)
   2. gate stipulation (Ezek 44:1-3)
   3. foreigners stipulation (Ezek 44:4-9)
   4. Levites stipulation (Ezek 44:10-14)
   5. priests stipulation (Ezek 44:15-31)
   6. land stipulation (Ezek 45:1-8)
   7. weights and measures stipulation (Ezek 45:9-17)
   8. Passover stipulation (Ezek 45:18-25)
   9. Sabbath stipulation (Ezek 46:1-15)
   10. prince stipulation (Ezek 46:16-18)

C. Endowments (Ezek 46:19—48:29)
   1. food endowment (Ezek 46:19-24)
   2. water endowment (Ezek 47:1-12)
   3. land endowment (Ezek 47:13-29)

Colophon (Ezek 48:30-35)

FIGURE 94   Patterns in Dedication of the City of Immanuel (Ezek 40:1—48:35)

Babylon to destroy the old Jerusalem, this new Jerusalem will be moved from the divine plane and installed on the human plane. The gift of Yahweh is a city.

Neither Eden nor the City of Immanuel is a wilderness. Both are urban habitats. The Story of the 'Adam as a Farmer says little about the architecture of Eden, whereas the book of Ezekiel describes the City of Immanuel in great detail. Both stories emphasize that the city is well irrigated and lavishly gardened (Gen 2:8-17; Ezek 47:1-12). Throughout, the city that Yahweh is building is contrasted with the palace and temple that the household of David built.

Ezekiel has a bird's-eye view of the city, which the guide describes in only two dimensions, length and width. The tradition is a verbal blueprint. Although the book of Ezekiel indicts the household of David, whose political policies precipitated the war between Babylon and Judah, it does admire the architectural accomplishments of the household. For example, the City of Immanuel will have gates constructed in the same pattern as those that the rulers of Israel and Judah installed at Hazor, Gezer, and Megiddo, when those cities were renovated for use as administrative centers (Ezek 40:5-16).

When the construction of the city is completed, Ezekiel and his guide watch Yahweh officially depart from Babylon and enter the City of Immanuel through its eastern gate (Ezek 43:1-12). Yahweh's entrance into the City of Immanuel parallels Yahweh's evacuation of Jerusalem in 587 B.C.E. (Ezek 10:1-22) and Yahweh's entrance into Babylon (Ezek 1:4—3:15). Ezekiel and his guide witness Yahweh officially taking possession of the City of Immanuel: "this is the place of my throne and the place for the soles of my feet, where I will reside among the people of Israel forever" (Ezek 43:7).

The commission stresses that the palace and the royal cemetery have not been constructed right next door to the temple (1 Kings 6). "The household of David shall no longer defile my sanctuary with its foreign wives and its gravestones. When the household of David placed its threshold by my threshold and its doorposts beside my doorposts, with only a wall between me and them, it shamed my holy name" (Ezek 43:7-8). The old Jerusalem was the City of David; the new Jerusalem is the City of Immanuel. The physical separation of royal space from divine space constitutes an emphatic statement that here only "Yahweh is Lord." In the old Jerusalem, the fathers of the household of David took the title "king." In the City of Immanuel they will be called "chief." There will be no kings and no queens in the City of Immanuel.

The code of honor for the household of David in the City of Immanuel identifies the fathers of the household as priests who are to serve, not kings who are to rule (Ezek 46:1-24). These fathers have only limited authority. They are to live modestly and deed their land only to children born inside the household. No member of the household can serve as a priest for more than seven years, and no other household is to be evicted from its land to support the household of David. In this new world, the household of

David is to ponder and to celebrate the great stories of how Yahweh delivered the Hebrews from slavery and endowed them with land (Deut 17:14-20). They do not live in the temple compound, but enter Yahweh's sacred space only to offer the morning sacrifice and to lead pilgrims in procession to the temple.

The morning sacrifice declared that the City of Immanuel is open for business. Then, like the vizier of Pharaoh, the fathers of the household of David unlocked the shops of each household licensed to do business in the city.

Once Yahweh officially takes possession of the city, "Hand of Yahweh" escorts Ezekiel to the dedication of the city's spectacular new water system (Ezek 47:1-12). The first stop on the tour is the Gihon Spring in the Kidron Valley. Early in the Iron Age, Jerusalem was located on a low, fifteen-acre ridge of land called Mt. Ophel, cut out of the central hills by the Kidron Valley on the east and the Central Valley on the west. Today, this spur juts out to the south of the Temple Mount constructed by Herod on Mt. Moriah, and is outside the Old City walls built by Suleiman (1494–1566). Jerusalem's principal water source is the Gihon Spring, located at the foot of the Mt. Ophel ridge in the Kidron Valley (1 Kgs 1:33). The Gihon is a siphon spring that pumps intermittently for about thirty minutes every four or five hours.

Ezekiel watches as the Gihon Spring pumps enough water to turn the Kidron Valley into a massive reservoir, which then overflows and runs down the road from Jerusalem to Jericho on the shores of the Dead Sea. Even when the freshwater from the spring reaches the saltwater in the Dead Sea, the Gihon continues to pump. In this new city the Gihon Spring pumps enough freshwater to sweeten the saltwater of the Dead Sea, from the oasis of En-gedi just north of the fortress of Masada to a spring at Qumran just south of Jericho. "When the freshwater enters the Dead Sea it becomes fresh. Wherever the river goes, every living creature that swarms will live, and there will be very many fish, once these waters reach there. It will become fresh, and everything will live where the river goes" (Ezek 47:8-10). Nonetheless, Yahweh is environmentally sensitive. Enough salt marshes will be preserved that the communities who historically have depended on the salt marshes in this forbidding terrain are protected. "Its swamps and marshes will not become fresh. They are to be left salt" (Ezek 47:11).

When Ezekiel's great time voyage ends, he has seen what Yahweh sees. The war and the exile brought the old world built by the house of David to an end, but those same events set the new world built by Yahweh into motion. The time voyage put the tragic events of his world into perspective. Despite the elaborate detail with which Ezekiel recounts his experience of the City of Immanuel, the voyage has a single and simple message for the people of Judah. Yahweh, not the household of David and not the Great King of Babylon, is the architect of all human events. It is Yahweh, and only Yahweh, who protects the land and feeds the people.

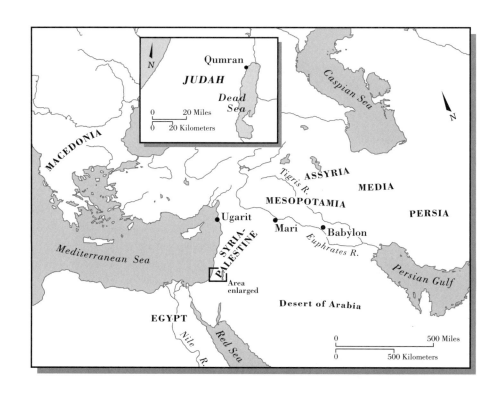

Points of Interest (Chapter 15)

15

BOOK OF DANIEL

(DAN 1:1 — 12:13)

anil" or "Daniel" (Hebrew: *Daniyye'l*) is a popular Semitic name that also appears in the books of Samuel-Kings (2 Sam 3:3), Ezekiel (Ezek 14:14-20; 28:3), Job (Job 14:14-20), Ezra (Ezra 8:2), Nehemiah (Neh 10:7), and Chronicles (1 Chr 3:1). The name develops from the call to worship: "Praise our Creator, who delivers us from our enemies."

Several cycles of Daniel stories developed in the world of the Bible, and the character of Daniel is slightly different in each. In the Stories of Aqhat from Ugarit, Daniel is a wise ruler. Daniel, Job, and Noah are great prophets in the book of Ezekiel (Fig. 95). In the teaching stories (Dan 1:1—6:29) that open the book of Daniel, Daniel is an adviser to the great kings of Mesopotamia. In the apocalypse stories (Dan 7:1—12:13), Daniel is a seer who time-travels like a shaman from the human plane to the divine plane to witness the end of the old world and the creation of the new world. In the teaching stories that close the book of Daniel in the Greek (Dan 13:1—14:42), Daniel is a wise young man who exposes the corruption of the old men in Judah.

The Greek Bible also contains a prayer of Azariah and a hymn sung by Hananiah, Mishael, and Azariah as they are being tortured by Nebuchadnezzar, the great king of Babylon (604–562 B.C.E.). Fragments of the book of Daniel were found among the Dead Sea Scrolls from three caves at Qumran. A hymn of Nabonidus (555–539 B.C.E.) and the three fragments of the book of Daniel in Aramaic, which do not appear in the Bible today, were recovered from Cave IV alone.

When the book of Daniel developed, Greeks ruled the world of the Bible. Nonetheless, the book of Daniel telescopes the Greek conquerors of Syria-Palestine with the Babylonians, the Medes, and the Persians as antagonists. In 612 B.C.E., the Medes ruled by Cyaxares and the Babylonians ruled by Nebuchadnezzar captured Nineveh and destroyed the Assyrian empire. Babylon took over the empire of Assyria and then

The once-powerful Danil is now powerless,
   He is shamed for lack of a son.

Surely he should have a son like his brothers,
   He needs an heir like his covenant partners.

He has blessed the divine assembly with food,
   He has filled their sanctuaries with drink.

Bless Danil with a son and show that you are El, the Bull.
   Build Danil a house with a child and show that you
   are my father.

Raise up a son for his household and show that you are
   father of all.
   Establish an heir in his palace.

Give Danil a son to erect a stele for the divine patrons
   of his ancestors,
   To build a shrine for the household of Danil in their
   sanctuary.

Name Danil a son to free him from death,
   To walk beside him to the grave.

Lift up Aqhat to punish those who revolt against his father,
   To drive out those who invade his land.

Make Aqhat strong enough to support Danil, when he
   drinks at the sanctuary,
   To put Danil's arm over his shoulder, when he is filled
   with spirits,

To eat his funeral meal in the sanctuary of Baal,
   To offer sacrifice in the house of El,

To patch Danil's roof after it rains,
   To clean threatening stains from his clothing.

FIGURE 95   Stories of Aqhat (Matthews and Benjamin 1997: 67)

extended it by the conquest of Judah in 587 B.C.E. In 539 B.C.E., the Persians ruled by Cyrus conquered the Medes and captured Babylon from Nabonidus and his heir, Belshazzar (539 B.C.E.). The technique of speaking about one antagonist or event while meaning another is common in the book of Daniel. Similar codes appear in political satire and editorial cartoons today.

Teaching Stories
(DAN 1:1—6:29)

The book of Daniel is composed of two kinds of stories. It begins (Dan 1:1—6:29) and ends (Dan 13:1—14:46) with teaching stories. The core of the book (Dan 7:1—12:13) is a series of apocalypse stories.

The teachers of the Daniel traditions and their audiences spoke Greek, Aramaic, and Hebrew. These Hebrew (Dan 1:1—2:4+8:1—14:46), Aramaic (Dan 2:4—7:28), and Greek (Dan 13:1—14:46) traditions testify not only to their language skills, but also to their assessment of the political climate for the people of Judah after Alexander of Macedonia (who ruled from 336 to 323 B.C.E.) conquered Syria-Palestine in 332 B.C.E. In the beginning, the relationship between the people of Judah and the Greeks was good. The people of Judah were welcome in this Hellenistic world as teachers, as advisers, and as interpreters of dreams. The teaching stories with which the book of Daniel opens view the role of the people of Judah in this new Hellenistic world positively, and therefore these stories were told in Aramaic, which was the common language used by the people of Judah and the Greeks. These stories encouraged the people of Judah to live like Daniel by making themselves useful to their foreign rulers without losing their cultural identity.

Slowly, conditions in Syria-Palestine began to change. Greeks began to discriminate against the people of Judah. A single apocalypse story told in Aramaic (Dan 7:1-28) was added to the teaching stories to encourage the people of Judah to participate in the old Hellenistic world, but to do so with caution. This Hellenistic world was about to be destroyed by the "ancient one" (Dan 7:9). Like Daniel, they must prepare to follow the Son of Man (Dan 7:13) into a new world where all the peoples of the earth would be welcome and equal. Nonetheless, the status of the people of Judah in the old world continued to deteriorate. Greeks began to consider the Semitic lifestyle of the people of Judah to be barbaric, their way of doing business to be primitive, and their worldview to be treason. Consequently, Antiochus Epiphanes IV (175–164 B.C.E.), the Greek ruler of Syria-Palestine, mounted a campaign to Hellenize the people of Judah.

Hellenism was a worldview that developed in western Mediterranean cultures like Greece and Rome, and it is the worldview of western European cultures today. It was radically different from the Semitic worldview that developed in ancient Israel and throughout the world of the Bible.

The language of Hellenism was Greek, a form of Indo-European speech like English. Greek speakers considered Semitic languages like Hebrew to be no more sophisticated than the growling of dogs.

The traditions of Hellenism were handed on in the *Iliad* and the *Odyssey* of Homer. Hellenists considered traditions like the Enuma Elish Stories and the Bible to be crude and barbaric.

The base community in Hellenism was the city, whose hundreds, and sometimes thousands, of citizens created a centralized and surplus economy with vast trade networks bringing luxury goods from the ends of the earth. The base community in ancient Israel was the household, whose thirty to fifty members created a decentralized and subsistence economy with little trade and virtually no luxury goods.

Hellenism considered the human body to be the most exquisite divine creation. Consequently, Hellenistic piety expected everyone to exercise and groom their bodies with devotion. The baths and the games were rituals in which Greeks exercised stewardship of this divine gift. Likewise, the Greeks developed a high-energy diet based on pork. The Hebrews were not prudish. They did not hate their bodies. For the Hebrews, however, Yahweh's greatest creation was not the human body, but the cosmos, of which the human body was only a part. Consequently, the Hebrews cared for their bodies just as they cared for their land and for their herds. They pruned their vines to increase their fertility, and they circumcised their sons so that they might sire more children. Circumcision outraged the Greeks. They considered it a mutilation of a divine work of art. The Hebrew diet was ascetic. Hebrews, and most other Semitic peoples, did not eat pork. Eating modestly and fasting regularly reminded the Hebrews that the physical power to bring in a harvest or to conceive a child was a gift from Yahweh, and not the result of a high-protein diet.

Some Hellenists understood and appreciated the Semitic worldview, and converted to a Semitic way of life as "God-fearers." Even more people of Judah converted to Hellenism, and embraced a lifestyle identical to their Greek and Roman conquerors. Most Hellenists, and many people of Judah, however, considered the worldview of the other to be foolish and the worst form of heresy and treason. The east was the east, and the west was the west. Conflict was inevitable.

To continue its dialogue with these changing political conditions, the book of Daniel added more apocalypse stories (Dan 1:1—2:4+8:1—12:13). These final additions were told in Hebrew, the ancient language of the people of Judah, in order to encourage them to withdraw from the Aramaic-speaking world of their Greek rulers.

Splendor of Greece—an "Abomination" in Dan 11:31
(Pergamon 200 B.C.E.; marble 39.5 cm)

The book of Daniel was complete before the death of Antiochus Epiphanes, because, although its apocalypse stories announce his imminent death, none describes the precise circumstances in which it actually occurred. Antiochus Epiphanes died in 165 B.C.E. while leading an invasion of Persia to the east. One of the apocalypse stories, for example, assumes he will be killed leading an invasion of Egypt to the south (Dan 11:45).

Daniel and Three Friends Thrive on Vegetables and Water
(DAN 1:1-21)

Daniel and Three Friends Thrive on Vegetables and Water is a teaching story that takes place at the royal court in Babylon (Dan 1:1-21). Teaching stories describe a wise protagonist surviving a crisis by applying the sayings and analogies of his teachers. Like the Teachings of Joseph (Gen 37:2—Exod 1:6), the six teaching stories with which the book of Daniel opens emphasize dream interpretation. Dream interpretation was a highly technical skill, which was respected by rulers and open to foreigners throughout the world of the Bible. Interpreters of dreams, like Joseph and Daniel, acquired wealth and power for their households. The book of Daniel casts him as both a dreamer and an interpreter of dreams.

The teaching stories in the book of Daniel are also parallel, in some ways, to the Stories of Elijah and Elisha. Like Elisha Changes Bad Vegetables into Good Vegetables (2 Kgs 4:38-41), Daniel and Three Friends Thrive on Vegetables and Water teaches its audiences how to turn bad food into good food. Like shamans, Elisha and Daniel can draw more power out of nature than ordinary human beings can. Babylonians would starve on the same diet. Teaching stories continued to be popular in later Jewish writings like the Mishnah (200 C.E.) and the Talmud (600 C.E.).

Diet was a major difference between the people of Judah and the Greeks. Pigs had been domesticated during the Neolithic period (8500–4300 B.C.E.) in this part of the world. By the Bronze Age (3300–1200 B.C.E.), however, they were herded only in villages with good rainfall, which could produce enough grain for both the pigs and the villagers. Initially, pigs were moved out of the mainstream food chain for economic reasons. They competed too strongly with humans for water and grain. Furthermore, centralized urban economies could not easily store, transport, and divide pork for redistribution. Pigs were reintroduced into Syria-Palestine by the Philistines (1200–1000 B.C.E.), and then by the Greeks (332 B.C.E.–640 C.E.).

Hebrews, however, did not shun pork for economic reasons (Leviticus 11; Deuteronomy 14; Isaiah 65–66; Tob 1:10-11; Jdt 10:5; 12:1-2; 1 Macc 1:62-63; 2 Macc 5:27; 6:8-31; 7:1). Pork was a key ingredient in the high-protein diet of the Greeks, and was an important tool in the toning and sculpting of the human body. The people of Judah considered this Greek diet to be arrogant. Building strong bodies violated their Semitic sense of humility. They considered it to be a human attempt to take over a divine work. Hebrews believed that those who arrogantly overfed themselves, in due time would starve (Deut 8:2-16; Ps 55:19). Those who fed on pork were shamed (Prov 3:34; 15:33; 18:12). Those who fasted, in due time would thrive (2 Sam 22:28; Ps 18:27). To humble oneself by fasting on a low-protein diet of water and vegetables identifies Daniel, Hananiah, Mishael, and Azariah as persons of honor who, unlike the Babylonians, depend upon Yahweh completely (Lev 26:41; 1 Kgs 21:29; 2 Kgs 22:8-20; Ps 69:10). Ironically, their diet also makes them more fit than the Babylonians themselves to serve Nebuchadnezzar, the great king.

Apocalypse Stories

(Dan 7:1 — 12:13)

Today, "apocalypse" is a threatening genre that warns the powerful of an impending end-of-the-world battle between God and Satan, after which an elite will govern a one-thousand-year empire in God's name. In the world of the Bible, "apocalypse" is a consoling genre that promises the powerless that their suffering will end soon, and that in the end good, not evil, will prevail. The apocalypse that threatens describes works like *The Late Great Planet Earth* (1979), by Hal Lindsey. The apocalypse that consoles describes works like the *Anne Frank: The Diary of a Young Girl* (1929–45), written by a Jewish teenager during the years she and her family spent in hiding from the Gestapo in Amsterdam during World War II, or the writings of Elie Wiesel (1928–), a Jewish survivor of the Nazi death camps whose works chronicle the suffering and the survival of those years.

The book of Daniel is a consoling apocalypse. It does not call upon the people of Judah to take up arms and attack their enemies, but to renew their faith in Yahweh as the divine patron who delivered them from the Babylonians, from the Medes, and from the Persians, and who, in due time, will deliver them from the Greeks as well. They are not to take up arms and wage war against the Hellenists, but to wait patiently for Yahweh to deliver them.

The apocalypse stories in the book of Daniel are the legacy of seers or "watchers," who call themselves "the holy ones of the Most High" (Dan 7:15-27). These seers have much in common with the shamans in Siberian cultures, in Native American cultures, and in the cultures along the Amazon River in South America. Their stories are not simply exotic coded messages for tracking the events leading to the destruction of the old world. Seers prepare their followers to pass safely through the crisis of dismantling the old world and entering into the new world. The most important skill that seers teach their followers is the ability to recognize authentic leaders. Apocalypse stories give their audiences a crash course in the discernment of spirits.

Seers develop their apocalypse stories by using the ritual of ecstasy, which allows them to time-travel from the human plane into the divine plane. Some meditate to induce ecstasy (1 Kgs 18:41-46). Some fast (1 Kgs 19:1-8), while others induce ecstasy with music or drumming (Exod 15:20-21; 1 Sam 10:5; 16:14-18; 19:19-24; 2 Kgs 3:15-19). Some dance, some use drugs or lapse into ecstasy following a prolonged illness. Ecstasy refocuses the senses of seeing, hearing, smelling, touching, and tasting from the human plane to the divine. Although while in ecstasy, seers appear dead because they cannot see, hear, smell, touch, or taste, they are quite alive. Their senses are simply now trained on the divine plane.

Ecstasy appeared in the prophets of Israel, Judah, Syria-Palestine, and Mari (1 Sam 19:19-24; 1 Kgs 18:1-46). The Egyptian diplomat Wen-Amon, for example, describes an encounter with a prophet while traveling in Syria-Palestine between 1100 and 1050 B.C.E.,

> One day when Prince Tjeker Baal was offering sacrifice to his gods, a spirit possessed one of his servants, who became ecstatic. . . . The servant said: "Summon this Egyptian envoy and his statue of Amon, Patron of Travelers, who dispatched him to Syria."
>
> The prophecy occurred on the same night that I had located a freighter headed for Egypt. I had loaded my possessions on board and was only waiting for it to get dark, so that I could smuggle my statue of Amon, Patron of Travelers, on board.

FIGURE 96   Stories of Wen-Amon (Matthews and Benjamin 1997: 325)

who reveals that Wen-Amon is ready to leave the state without permission of its ruler (Fig. 96). Even the hieroglyphic letters in the Egyptian word for "prophet" used in Wen-Amon's memoirs show a human figure in violent or epileptic convulsion.

Seers extend their moments of ecstasy by living ascetic lifestyles. "Shaman" is a Tungus or Siberian word borrowed from Sanskrit that means "ascetic." They limit the use of their senses on the human plane to a minimum. They keep their eyes closed or lowered, they keep silent, eat simply, and keep their hands folded. Such sensual minimalism makes it easier for seers to detach themselves from the human plane and enter the divine plane.

Ecstasy and asceticism make seers aware that the human plane is part of a much larger world. What is happening on the human plane is placed in the larger context of what is happening on the divine plane. For seers the real world is not the human world, but the divine world. Everything that happens on the human plane is a result of something that has happened on the divine plane.

The book of Daniel is told by seers who used their heightened level of awareness to take readings of the crisis of Hellenism, which threatened to destroy the land and children of Judah. Their apocalypse stories are not describing something before it happens, but indicating the significance of events that are happening. The intention of their stories is similar to weather forecasts today. Forecasters want to give their audiences information that will help them recognize atmospheric conditions that will affect them, and therefore be better prepared to enjoy them or survive them. Weather forecasts do not change conditions. They change their audiences. The same is true of apocalypse stories. The fall of old worlds and the rise of new worlds, like the weather, run in recognizable and predictable cycles. Apocalypse stories educate their audiences to recognize changes in cosmic conditions that will affect them, and to prepare to survive this breakdown of the cosmos so that, as pioneers, they are ready to enter the new world soon to be created.

There are two kinds of apocalypse stories. One is a time voyage that portrays a seer traveling from the human plane to the divine plane (Ezek 40:1—48:35). The other is a fantasy (Dan 7:1-28). In both, the protagonist is ecstatic or suspended in a trance described as "sleep." The experiences of the seer during the time voyage or fantasy are described as "dreams" or "visions." Daniel, for example, has "a dream and visions as he lay in his bed" (Dan 7:1-2).

In everyday speech, "fantasy" carries the connotation of something unreal or imaginary. Here fantasy describes a real experience of the divine like a vision, theophany, or epiphany. Fantasies, however, are more than visions. Seers experience the divine with all their senses, not just sight. They see, hear, touch, taste, or smell the presence of Yahweh. In the first fantasy in the book of Daniel, there are two epiphanies. In one, Daniel sees Yahweh and the divine assembly conducting a trial (Dan 7:9-10), and in the other he sees Yahweh as the Ancient of Days ordaining a "Son of Man" to be a messiah.

An apparition is a vision that does not involve Yahweh. The indictment session of the trial in the first fantasy contains five apparitions of various human conquerors of the world of the Bible (Dan 7:2-8).

Seers summon members of the divine assembly to be their guides. These guides often appear to them as animals. Among Daniel's guides is "One of Those Who Stood There" (Dan 7:16). Sometimes these titles are translated into names, sometimes they are not. Nonetheless, all of them are intended to characterize the guides as highly placed and reliable sources. "Gabriel" is not just an angel with a Hebrew name, but a "Bodyguard of Our Creator," who has the most intimate and continuous access to Yahweh. In time voyages, guides ask the seers questions to be sure that they do not overlook anything. In fantasies, seers ask their guides to explain the experiences. In time voyages, guides tour-guide seers, whereas in fantasies guides tutor them.

Ordination of a Son of Man
(Dan 7:1-28)

The Ordination of a Son of Man opens with Daniel entering ecstasy in order to view the actions of Yahweh and the divine assembly safely. Divine actions are too intense for any human to observe while fully conscious. Therefore, Daniel falls into ecstasy, which allows him safely to observe what Yahweh is doing in Judah.

As in many apocalypse stories, the crisis episode is coded. It telescopes time by collapsing the past, present, and future into a single fantasy. Telescoping also divides time into periods, and lays them out on a grid for comparison. In the first fantasy, the persecutions that the people of Judah suffered under Babylon, Media, Persia, and Greece are laid side by side.

A fierce storm on the coast of the Mediterranean Sea is the first apparition. The sea is attacked by four winds. The number "four" is comparable to the number "three" in English expressions like "three strikes and you're out." Four receives its ominous character from the understanding that Yahweh has surrounded the sea with winds attacking from all four points on the compass. The same divine winds subdue the waters of chaos in the Creation of the Heavens and the Earth (Gen 1:12) and the Red Sea in the Creation of the Firstborn of Israel (Exod 14:21-31).

Under attack from every direction, the sea surrenders its covenant partners. There is Babylon the Winged Lion, Media the Bear, Persia the Leopard, and the empire of Alexander, a Four-Headed Beast. The lion, the leopard, and the bear that appear in the apparition are the divine patrons of Babylon, Media, and Persia. These are the totem animals who have taught the people of these great states how to survive in a highly competitive world.

Totem animals are intimately associated with the people whom they represent. The totem animal is an ancestor. Human protégés treat their totem animal with reverence to show how strong their belief is in the relationship that exists between them. People name children for their totem animals, and eat the totem animal only at special times. The turkey was an early totem for the United States. This large and once abundant wild bird was a blessing for the first European colonists. It is still the traditional meal at the nation's observance of Thanksgiving.

Daniel sees the deadly physical characteristics of each animal, and hears the commission describing how each will attack. The schematic for the lion describes the plucking of its wings. The sea is not clipping the wings of the lion so that it cannot fly, but outfitting it for battle. Once it is ready, Daniel hears the lion commissioned to think like a human. "A human mind was given to it" should be read like the command: "arise, devour much flesh" (Dan 7:5). The lion is not simply to act on instinct, but to make decisions.

Next Daniel sees Media as a bear with fangs, "raised up on one side" (Dan 7:5). The bear is standing on its back paws and poised to attack with its front.

The apparitions of the sea, Babylon, Media, Persia, and the empire of Alexander are followed by a theophany (Dan 7:9-14) of Yahweh, who is called "The Ancient One." Yahweh is accompanied by the "thousands upon thousands" who are the stars or divine warriors. Yahweh first destroys the old world and its violent rulers, and then ordains a "Son of Man" to create a new world. Yahweh sends this human messiah to avoid overwhelming the earth and to see that everything on earth is in the proper order before Yahweh arrives.

The Son of Man "comes on the clouds of heaven," which is Yahweh's war chariot whose wheels stir up clouds of dust. "Cloud Rider" is Yahweh's title as the divine warrior (Ps 68:1-5; Fig. 97). Baal carries the same title in the traditions of Ugarit. The Son of Man is then ordained or transfigured, and commissioned with the credentials needed to act on Yahweh's behalf in creating a new world. The apocalypse story concludes with two catechisms in which the seer and the guide interpret the significance of both the apparitions and the theophany.

The name of Daniel's guide "One of Those Who Stood There," carries the same connotations as "a source close to the president." The guide acts as a guarantee that the fantasy has been given under oath or in the presence of witnesses. The seer is not simply suffering some form of delusion. Daniel's guide confirms that the empire of Alexander, which is the fourth creature, is the worst of Israel's enemies. Again, four is the ominous number. Babylon, Media, and Persia were nothing compared with the Greeks.

All ten rulers between Alexander and Antiochus Epiphanes are "horns." A horn is a phallic symbol representing a male exposing himself and blatantly abusing his power. That is the bad news. The good news is that the days of Antiochus Epiphanes are numbered. He will rule only "for a time, two times, and half a time" (Dan 7:25) or three and one-half years. The same sentence appears in the books of Maccabees (1 Macc 1:54—4:52). Actually, Antiochus Epiphanes ruled almost nine years, but his reign did come to an end, and the Greeks were ultimately driven out of Judah.

---

creation story

> *Yahweh awakes.*
>> *Yahweh scatters the enemies of Israel.*
>> *Yahweh routs those who attack Israel.*
>
> *Like smoke blown by the wind,*
>> *Our enemies are driven away.*
>
> *Like wax melted by a flame,*
>> *Those who attack Israel are routed.*

call to worship

> *Rejoice!*
>> *Exult before Yahweh!*
>> *Celebrate!*
>
> *Praise Yahweh!*
>> *Praise the name of Yahweh!*
>
> *Sing to Yahweh who rides upon the clouds!*
>> *Celebrate Yahweh, the divine patron of Israel!*
>> *Exult before Yahweh!*

FIGURE 97   Hymn to Yahweh (Ps 68:1-5)

New Heavens and a New Earth in 3½ Years
(DAN 8:1-27)

New Heavens and a New Earth in 3½ Years is an apocalypse story that, once again, describes the chaos that Antiochus Epiphanes is causing. Here, he conquers the heavens (Dan 8:10) and the earth (Dan 8:24), including the "holy ones" (Dan 8:24) who told these apocalypse stories.

The date of the story is coded to the reign of Belshazzar of Babylon, who is introduced as the "Son of Nebuchadnezzar." Actually, Belshazzar was not the immediate successor of Nebuchadnezzar, but of Nabonidus. Nabonidus was at odds with the Babylonian priests and withdrew to Teima in the Arabian desert for ten years. In his absence, Belshazzar was regent for Babylon, but he did not have the authority to take the monarch's place in the Akitu New Year, so the feast went uncelebrated.

The Ordination of a Son of Man (Dan 7:1-28) and New Heavens and a New Earth in 3½ Years (Dan 8:1-27) are two panels of a single diptych. As a result, their structures are very similar. Based on the pattern established in the Ordination of a Son of Man, there are four, not two or three, apparitions. What separates one panel from the other is not the animals, but the different configurations of horns.

The ram and the goat were the astrological signs for Persia and Syria-Palestine. Here, the ram is Persia and the goat is the Syria-Palestine ruled by Alexander. As in the Ordination of a Son of Man, these configurations of horns are coats of arms for the various states struggling to control the world of the Bible. Strangely, Daniel sees a single two-horned ram, as if the Medes and Persians ruled one great state (Dan 8:2-4). In fact, the Medes and Babylonians conquered the Assyrians and were, in turn, conquered by the Persians. The Medes and the Persians ruled much of the same land, but not at the same time. The goat with one big horn is the empire of Alexander (Dan 8:5-7). The four-horned goat represents the four regions into which Alexander's empire was divided after his death in 332 B.C.E. (Dan 8:8). The goat with one small horn is the Syria-Palestine of Antiochus Epiphanes, who ruled this region of Alexander's empire (Dan 8:9-12).

The battle report: "the great horn was broken" (Dan 8:8) precedes its schematic: "four conspicuous horns toward the four winds of heaven." In the final battle report Antiochus Epiphanes, as the little horn, is charged with having thrown down "to the earth some of the divine warriors and some of the stars, and trampled on them" (Dan 8:10). Even the "prince of the divine warriors" (Dan 8:11) is a victim of the little horn, who, like the planet Venus, appears to be pulling stars down from the heavens toward the earth.

Stories explaining why the planet Venus comes so close to the horizon of the earth in the morning and evening were popular throughout the world of the Bible. Two stories are preserved in the Bible and a third in the traditions of Ugarit. Venus is called the "Morning Star" or the "Evening Star" because it is clearly visible on the horizon just before dawn and just after sunset. This great "star" seemed out of place so close to the earth. It appeared to be a "fallen star," exiled from the heavens, where the other stars shine during the night. This fallen star could only shine during the brief periods between the end of the day and the beginning of the night, and between the end of the night and the beginning of the day, and it could shine only against the horizons that separated the heavens from the earth.

In the book of Isaiah, the fallen star is "Lucifer" or the "Day Star," who is the "Child of the Dawn," exiled for masterminding a conspiracy against the divine assembly (Isa 14:12). In the traditions of Ugarit, this star is "Athar the Awesome." Each is defeated and condemned to live between the heavens and the earth. In the book of Daniel, this star is Antiochus Epiphanes, condemned to live between the heavens and the earth for offering a sacrifice to Zeus in the temple during the dedication of Jerusalem as a Hellenistic city in December 167 B.C.E. This was the "abomination that makes desolate" or "abomination of desolation" (Dan 11:31; 12:11; 1 Macc 1:54; 2 Macc 6:1-5).

The act by which Antiochus Epiphanes had intended to inaugurate a Hellenistic state in Judah that would live forever would in fact destroy it. At the outset, Antiochus Epiphanes appears to succeed. He assimilates the House of Yahweh in Jerusalem into the chain of temples for Zeus throughout the Hellenistic world, and buries Yahweh, who is called the "Chief of the Divine Warriors" (Dan 8:11+25).

The "holy ones" who guard the tomb of Yahweh are members of the divine assembly after whom the "holy ones" who developed the apocalypse stories in the book of Daniel named themselves (Dan 8:25). The seers appropriate the title "holy ones" to identify themselves with the work of the divine assembly. Daniel hears them discussing the fate of Yahweh. At this point, Daniel seems only to hear the voices of the holy ones, but not to see them.

The climax episodes are two fantasies in which Daniel both hears and sees his guide, Gabriel, explain the apparitions. One is a short interpretation (Dan 8:15-17) and one is a long interpretation (Dan 8:18-26). In each, Daniel begins his question with a prostration: "I was frightened and fell on my face" (Dan 8:17) and "I fell into a deep sleep with my face to the ground" (Dan 8:18). The short interpretation simply confirms that Antiochus Epiphanes has inaugurated the endtime by granting Jerusalem the status of a polis city and celebrating the event by erecting a statue of Zeus in the House of Yahweh. Consequently, he will fall and destroy himself and Jerusalem in the process. In due time, Yahweh will create new heavens and a new earth.

The old world of Antiochus Epiphanes will come to an end in "two thousand three hundred evenings and mornings" (Dan 8:14) or eleven hundred fifty days. Eleven hundred fifty days is almost the three and one-half years that appears as the length of his reign in the Ordination of a Son of Man (Dan 7:25) and in a Resurrection of the Dead (Dan 12:7). The book of Daniel is emphatic. The end of the reign of Antiochus

Epiphanes has already been determined by the divine assembly. The people of Judah have only to be patient.

A New Heavens and a New Earth in 3½ Years is critical, not only of Antiochus Epiphanes, but also of any human solution to the crisis created by Antiochus Epiphanes. From its perspective, the matter will be settled on the divine plane, not on the human plane. The book of Daniel does not support revolutionaries; it refers to them as a "human hand" (Dan 8:25) or "little help" (Dan 11:34). The book of Daniel encourages the people of Judah to see the immediate crisis surrounding the administration of Syria-Palestine by Antiochus Epiphanes on the larger scale. By putting it in perspective, they may better survive the persecution. The apocalypse wants them to let Antiochus self-destruct rather than taking any direct action against his policies. His overvaulting ambition will destroy him. Resistance will only postpone his government's inevitable collapse.

The denouement certifies that Daniel was in ecstasy for days before he was able to return to his work at the palace. Curiously, despite the help of his guide, Daniel "did not understand" (Dan 8:27) this fantasy. Daniel has four experiences that are virtually identical (Dan 7:1-28; 8:1-27; 9:1-27; 10:1—12:13), but he still "could not understand" (Dan 12:8). Actually, it is not so much a question of understanding the experiences as it is of the willingness of Daniel and the people of Judah to act on them. In fact, the people of Judah did not patiently wait for Yahweh and the divine assembly to bring the old world of Antiochus Epiphanes to an end, and to create new heavens and a new earth. They fought for their own independence from the Greeks, and created their own Hasmonean state. Daniel and the people of Judah knew what their guides were saying. They just did not want to believe it, and they did not. The books of Maccabees tell the stories of this war of independence.

New Heavens and a New Earth in 7x70 Years
(DAN 9:1-27)

A New Heavens and a New Earth in 7x70 Years is an apocalypse story that consists simply of a climax and a denouement. There is no crisis. The story does not describe the fantasy of Daniel; it simply provides an interpretation. The interpretation assumes that he has an experience of the divine that is similar to those in the Ordination of a Son of Man and in New Heavens and a New Earth in 3½ Years (Fig. 98).

The catechism in the climax of New Heavens and a New Earth in 7x70 years explains that the sentence of seventy years that the book of Jeremiah imposes on Jerusalem is actually seventy sabbatical years or 490 years. A similar reading appears in the book of Leviticus (Lev 26:18) and the books of Chronicles (2 Chr 36:21).

crisis (missing)
climax (Dan 9:1-27)

question (Dan 9:1-19)

citation (Dan 9:1-3): I, Daniel, read in the scroll of Jeremiah (Jer 25:11-12; 29:10) that Jerusalem will lie in ruins for seventy years. So I turned to Yahweh, our Creator, for an interpretation of this passage.

lament (Dan 9:4-19)
answers (Dan 9:20-27)

While I was praying, Gabriel . . . came to me in swift flight at the time of the evening sacrifice. He came and said to me, "Daniel, I have come to give you wisdom and understanding. . . .

"There will be 490 years (*70 jubilee years* or 70 times 7 calendar years representing 373 calendar years) between 537 B.C.E., when Cyrus, the great king of Persia, liberated the people of Judah in Babylon and sent them home to rebuild the holy city of Jerusalem, and the death of Antiochus Epiphanes, the ruler of Syria-Palestine who persecuted the people of Judah from 175 B.C.E. until his death. Nonetheless, Yahweh, our Creator, will put an end to the persecutions of Antiochus Epiphanes . . . and rededicate the Temple.

"There were 49 years (*seven jubilee years* or 7 times 7 years representing 48 calendar years) between the decree of Cyrus in 537 B.C.E. to . . . rebuild Jerusalem until Zerubbabel was anointed Prince of Judah and rebuilt the Temple during hard times in 489 B.C.E.

"There were 434 years (*62 jubilee years* or 62 times 7 years representing 317 calendar years) between the decree of Cyrus in 537 B.C.E. and the assassination of Onias III, the high priest in Jerusalem, by Antiochus Epiphanes and the occupation of Jerusalem and its temple by his soldiers. Nonetheless, Yahweh, our Creator, will drive Antiochus Epiphanes and his soldiers out of Jerusalem and its temple.

"Antiochus Epiphanes will rule Judah for only 7 years (*1 jubilee year* or 7 times one years representing 8 calendar years). For 3½ years (*half of the week*) Antiochus Epiphanes will forbid the priests to offer sacrifice to Yahweh, our Creator, in the temple, and he will offer an abominable sacrifice (*abomination that desolates* or *abomination of desolation*) until Yahweh, our Creator, sentences this executioner (*desolator*) to death."

denouement (missing)

FIGURE 98   New Heavens and a New Earth in 7x70 Years (Dan 9:1-27)

Cyrus repatriates the people of Judah, 537 B.C.E.	373 calendar years
seventy weeks of years (490 years)	
Zerubbabel rebuilds the temple, 489 B.C.E.	48 calendar years
seven weeks of years (49 years)	
Reign of Antiochus Epiphanes, 175–164 B.C.E.	9 calendar years
one week of years (7 years)	
a time, two times, and half a time (3½ years)	
2,300 evenings and mornings (3½ years)	
1,290 days (3½ years)	
1,335 days (3½ years)	
Onias is assassinated, 172 B.C.E.	317 calendar years
sixty-two weeks of years (434 years)	

FIGURE 99   Calendar in the Book of Daniel

Nonetheless, the reign of Antiochus Epiphanes is taking place during the last seven years or "last week of years" of the sentence. The calendar that the seers are using begins with the decree of Cyrus of Persia to rebuild Jerusalem in 537 B.C.E. The actual work on the temple was delayed for forty-nine years or "seven weeks of years" until 489 B.C.E. when Zerubbabel, the "Anointed Prince" (Ezra 2:2; 3:2; Hag 1:1-14; Zech 6:9-14), served as governor of Judah under Darius I (522–486 B.C.E.), and Joshua was high priest (Fig. 99).

Between 489 B.C.E. and 172 B.C.E., when the people of Judah who supported Antiochus Epiphanes, the "Prince Who Is to Come," murdered the high priest, Onias III, the "Anointed One," for opposing Antiochus Epiphanes, the story counts 434 years or "sixty-two weeks of years." Mathematically, there are only 317 years between the two dates, so the number must have some other significance for the seers.

The year 172 B.C.E. marked the beginning of the last seven years of the sentence. In a Resurrection of the Dead (Dan 10:1—12:13) that follows a Creation of New Heavens and a New Earth in 7x70 Years and in an Ordination of a Son of Man, which precedes it, this seven-year sentence is further reduced to three and one-half years or "a time, two times, and half a time" (Dan 12:7).

Resurrection of the Dead
(Dan 10:1 — 12:13)

A Resurrection of the Dead, like a New Heavens and a New Earth in 7x70 Years (Dan 9:1-27), is an apocalypse story without a crisis and without a denouement. There is only a climax in which "a man clothed in linen with a belt of gold from Uphaz around his waist" (Dan 10:5; Ezek 1: 27; 9:1-2) offers three interpretations of Daniel's fantasy. The story assumes Daniel's fantasy to be similar to those that are described fully in an Ordination of a Son of Man and New Heavens and a New Earth in 3½ Years.

Although the guide tells Daniel that his "words have been heard, and I have come because of your words" (Dan 10:12), the story itself describes only Daniel's actions.

Daniel asks his question by fasting. He eats only simple meals, and does not bathe (Fig. 100).

---

catechism (Dan 10:1-14)

question (Dan 10:2-3): In 536 B.C.E., the third year of Cyrus of Persia (559–530 B.C.E.), I, Daniel, had been mourning for three weeks. I had not eaten rich food, meat, or wine, and I had not bathed.

answer (Dan 10:4-14): On the twenty-fourth day of the first month, as I was standing on the bank of the Great River, Tigris, I looked up and saw a man clothed in linen, with a belt of gold from Uphaz around his waist. His body was like beryl, his face like lightning, his eyes like flaming torches, his arms and legs like the gleam of burnished bronze, and the sound of his voice like the battle cry of a great army. I, Daniel, alone saw the vision. The people who were with me did not. When they began to tremble with fear, they fled and hid. So I was left alone to see this great vision. My body was weak, and my complexion grew deathly pale. I was exhausted. When I heard his voice, I fell into a trance, face to the ground.

His hand touched me and lifted me to my hands and knees. "Daniel, greatly beloved, listen carefully. Stand up." So while he was speaking, I stood up trembling. "Do not be afraid, Daniel, for from the first day that you set your mind to gain understanding and to humble yourself before our Creator, your prayers have been heard, and I have come to answer your prayers. The guardian angel of Persia prevented me from coming for twenty-one days. So Michael, one of the archangels, came to help me, and I left him there with the guardian angel of Persia, and have come to help you understand what is to happen to the people of Judah in the endtime."

FIGURE 100   Catechism (Dan 10:1-14)

catechism (Dan 10:15—12:4)

question (Dan 10:15-17): While the guide was speaking, I turned my face toward the ground and was speechless. Then he touched my lips, and I said, "My lord, the vision of you causes me such pain that I am too weak to talk. I am trembling, powerless and breathless."

answer (Dan 10:18—12:4): My guide touched me again and said, "Do not be afraid, greatly beloved, you are safe. Be strong and courageous!" When he spoke, my strength returned and I said, "Speak, my lord." Then he said, "Do you know why I have come to you? Shortly, I must return to fight against the guardian angel of Persia, and when I am through with him, with the guardian angel of Greece. Before I go, I will tell you what is written in the Book of Truth. "I was appointed guardian angel to Persia in the first year of **Darius the Mede (521–486 B.C.E.).** Three more kings, Ahasuerus, whose throne name will be **Xerxes I (485–465 B.C.E.), Artaxerxes I (464–425 B.C.E.), and Darius II (423–405 B.C.E.),** ruled Persia. Darius II was the richest, and declared war on Greece. **Alexander the Great (356–323 B.C.E.)** ruled a great empire. After Alexander's death on June 10, 323 B.C.E., at the age of thirty-three, his empire survived even though it was divided into four: Macedonia under Cassander; Thrace and Asia Minor under Lysimachus; Syria, Mesopotamia, and Persia under Seleucus; and Egypt under Ptolemy. Not one of these generals was a natural son of Alexander, nor native-born in the land that he ruled. "**Antiochus IV Epiphanes (175–164 B.C.E.)** is an illegitimate ruler, who usurped the throne of Syria-Palestine. He slaughtered the soldiers of Judah and assassinated Onias III, their high priest, in 172 B.C.E. Although Antiochus negotiated a covenant of peace with Judah, he cannot be trusted. His small party of supporters in Judah will plunder the richest parts of the land like none of his predecessors have done. He has plans to take over every city in Judah. None of this will last. He plans to invade Egypt, but Egypt shall defeat him, and those who eat at his table shall betray him and his soldiers. Many shall die and many shall be sold as slaves. Ptolemy and Antiochus will negotiate a covenant of peace in bad faith. They shall sit at the same table and lie to one another. The peace shall not last, because their world will come to an end at the appointed time. Antiochus IV shall return to Damascus rich with plunder, and his heart still set on taking Judah away from Egypt. Therefore Antiochus shall invade Egypt again, but Roman ships shall threaten his army. He shall lose heart and withdraw. He shall take revenge against Judah with the help of traitors whose loyalty he will buy. Antiochus shall send soldiers to occupy and profane the temple and its fortress of Akra. They shall abolish the regular sacrifices to our Creator, and erect a statue of Zeus, 'the abomination that makes desolate.' Despite the traitors who support Antiochus, those loyal to our Creator shall stand firm. These wise shall inspire many. For a time the wise shall be beheaded, burned at the stake, thrown into prison, and have all their property confiscated. A few will share their suffering, but most will feign faithfulness to the covenant between our Creator and Judah. The wise must be martyred, so that they

(continued)

may be refined, purified, and cleansed during the days before the end time. During the days before the end time, Antiochus IV shall do as he pleases. He shall declare himself to be divine, and shall speak blasphemously against our Creator. He shall, however, prosper only until these days of suffering are complete. What our Creator has decreed shall be done. Antiochus shall pay no respect to the divine patrons of his ancestors, nor to Tammuz, the divine gardener loved by women. He shall consider himself to be greater than them all. Antiochus shall only honor Zeus, Baal Shamem, the divine patron of imperial cities (Greek: *polis*) all over the world. Zeus is a divine patron whom his ancestors did not know, yet Antiochus shall honor Zeus with gold and silver, precious stones, and costly gifts. He shall dedicate all the major cities in his kingdom to this divine patron of strangers. Antiochus shall enrich those who acknowledge Zeus with wealth and land. In the end-time Egypt shall attack him, but Antiochus IV shall counterattack like a whirlwind with chariots, cavalry, and ships. Antiochus shall invade lands like a flood. He shall invade Judah, the beautiful land, and slaughter tens of thousands. Edom, Moab, and most of Ammon, however, shall escape from his power. He shall declare war against many states, and even Egypt shall not escape. He shall become ruler of the treasures of gold and of silver, and all the riches of Egypt. The people of Libya and Ethiopia shall be part of his empire. He shall march his army out of Egypt to answer alarming reports from the east and the north by destroying everything in his path. He shall pitch his royal tents between the sea and Mt. Zion, the beautiful mountain. Yet he shall come to his end. No one will help him. Go your way, Daniel, for the words are to remain secret and sealed until the end time. There shall be three and one-half years from the time that the regular burnt offering to our Creator is taken away from the temple and 'the abomination that desolates' to Zeus is erected there. Blessed are those who persevere for three and one-half years. Go. Rest. You shall rise for your reward in the end time."

FIGURE 101 Catechism (Dan 10:15—12:4)

At the end of three weeks, an epiphany takes place. A member of the divine assembly arrives to be Daniel's guide. His face was "like lightning, his eyes like flaming torches" (Dan 10:6). Lightning is often described as "fire" (Dan 10:1-6). In Elijah Divines Rain on the Carmel Mountains, lightning strikes the altar and drives back the water that had flooded it. The winter storms along the Mediterranean coast were understood as a struggle between the Creator and chaos. The waves are the weapon of chaos, and lightning is the weapon that the Creator hurls into the waves to subdue them. Although lightning was frightening, it was regarded as the weapon that the Creator was using to protect the human community from chaos. Daniel's guide is a divine warrior, a member of the Sabaoth commanded by Yahweh.

The guide first explains that the day on which Daniel began to fast was the day on which the old world of Persia began to come to an end. During the three weeks of Daniel's fast (Dan 10:2, 13), his guide and Michael had been at war with the divine patron or "Prince" (Dan 10:13) of Persia on the divine plane in order to set the people of Judah free.

Daniel then asks his guide a second question (Dan 10:15-17). The guide responds by explaining that, before the people of Judah can be set free, there will be four Persian rulers and five Greek rulers of Syria-Palestine (Fig. 101).

Although historically there were eleven Persian rulers, only four are named in the Bible: Cyrus (550–530 B.C.E.), Ahasuerus or Xerxes I (486–465 B.C.E.), Artaxerxes I (465–424 B.C.E.), and Darius II (423–404 B.C.E.).

The five Greek rulers described here are Alexander, Ptolemy I, Ptolemy III, Antiochus III, and Antiochus IV Epiphanes. Alexander (336–323 B.C.E.) is the "Warrior King" (Dan 10:19—11:4). Ptolemy I (323–285 B.C.E.) is the "King of the South" (Dan 11:5-6) in Egypt. Ptolemy III (246–203 B.C.E.) invades "the fortress of the King of the North" (Dan 11:6-11) in Syria-Palestine. Antiochus III (223–187 B.C.E.) launches an unsuccessful invasion of Egypt (Dan 11:10-19). Antiochus IV Epiphanes (175–164 B.C.E.) is "a contemptible person" (Dan 11:20-45) who launches an invasion of Egypt, but is driven off by a Roman fleet, described as "the ships of Kittim" (Dan 11:29).

In support of his claim to all of Syria-Palestine, described by the guide as the "Beautiful Land" (Dan 11:41), and to appeal to the people of Judah to support him against the Greek rulers of Egypt, Antiochus Epiphanes raises Jerusalem to the status of a *polis* city, and makes it his capital in the region. The guide describes this tour de force with contempt. "Forces sent by Antiochus Epiphanes shall occupy and profane the temple and its fortress. They shall abolish the regular burnt offering and set up the abomination that makes desolate" (Dan 11:31).

As long and involved as the guide's explanation to Daniel may be, it makes a single point. None of this jockeying for power by the Greek rulers of Syria-Palestine will last. "It will not succeed, for there remains an end at the time appointed" (Dan 11:27). Yahweh, and Yahweh alone, protects and provides for the people of Judah. Even those who die as victims in these endless wars will be raised from the dead (Dan 12:1-4).

The book of Daniel is the only tradition in the Hebrew Bible that refers explicitly to the resurrection of the dead. Other traditions understand death as the end of the covenant between Yahweh and Israel. The dead no longer acknowledge Yahweh as their divine patron (Ps 115:17). Like the book of Daniel, however, the books of Maccabees (2 Macc 7:1-42) and the Wisdom of Solomon (Wis 2:1—3:19) in the Greek Bible understand the resurrection of the dead as the fulfillment of Yahweh's promise to provide for and to protect the people of Judah from their enemies.

The books of Daniel, Maccabees, and the Wisdom of Solomon develop their explicit faith in the resurrection of the dead from traditions about the fate of the dead in the books of Isaiah and Ezekiel. For Isaiah, the dead will cover the ground like dew only until morning, when they will rise into the sunlight (Isa 26:19). For Ezekiel, even the dead who remain unburied for so long that every trace of flesh and blood has disappeared will be moistened again with a breath of wind from Yahweh (Ezek 37:1-14). They will be re-created like the *'adam* in the book of Genesis (Gen 2:7).

In the world of the Bible, the difference between life and death was not breath, but moisture. Bodies that were still damp, whose bones were still moist with flesh and blood, were technically not yet dead. The dead were pronounced dead only once their bones were dry. Yahweh brings the *'adam* to life by moistening the clay with the condensation produced by breathing on it (Gen 2:4-17). Yahweh uses the same technique to raise the dry bones to life in the book of Ezekiel (Ezek 37:1-14). It is the moisture that the breeze deposits on the bones that brings them to life. Therefore, the guide promises Daniel that the rain will fall again in Judah, and that divine moisture will lift the crops from the dust and the dead from their graves.

Despite the detail in the second catechism, and the guide's remarkable affirmation that even the victims of Antiochus Epiphanes will be raised from the dead, Daniel repeats his question for a third time (Dan 12:5-6). He wants to know how much longer the people of Judah will have to suffer under Antiochus Epiphanes.

The guide gives Daniel three answers. The suffering of the people of Judah will end in "a time, two times, and half a time" (Dan 12:7), or "one thousand two hundred ninety days" (Dan 12:11), or "one thousand three hundred thirty-five days" (Dan 12:12). Each figure is approximately three and one-half years. What is important is not the number itself, but that the date has been set, and that the people of Judah should wait patiently for their suffering to abate. The last words of the guide to Daniel are the repeated message of each of the apocalypse stories. "Go your way, and rest. You shall rise for your reward at the end of the days" (Dan 12:13).

Teaching Stories
(Dan 13:1 — 14:46)

The teaching stories with which the book of Daniel in the Hebrew Bible begins encourage the people of Judah to survive by making themselves useful to their Greek rulers. The teaching stories with which the book of Daniel in the Greek Bible ends warn the people of Judah against collaborating with their Greek rulers. In the first cycle of stories, the Greeks respect and protect the people of Judah because of their learning. In the second cycle of stories, the Greeks despise the people of Judah even though they embrace their Hellenistic way of life.

A Beautiful Woman Remains Faithful
(DAN 13:1-64)

A Beautiful Woman Remains Faithful, in the Greek Bible, is a teaching story. The story was a popular masterpiece retold again and again. Stories of a bathing woman who becomes a swan, of a chaste wife, and of a clever judge and his unique decision, appear in both eastern and western Mediterranean cultures. There are parallels in the books of Tobit (Tob 6:12) and Judith (Jdt 8:7-8) in the Greek Bible, as well as in a story of Ali Chadsa in *A Thousand and One Nights*, which developed after 800 C.E.

The protagonist is Susanna, a beautiful and faithful woman, who is wise. The antagonists are two elders, who are fools. In the crisis, they attempt to rape Susanna, and then charge her with adultery. The books of Leviticus (Lev 24:14) and Deuteronomy (Deut 13:9-10; 17:5-7) describe the ritual of placing their hands on their heads, which the elders use to charge Susanna with a capital crime (Dan 13:34).

The climax episode combines more than one telling of the story, one told in Greek, the other in Aramaic. In the Aramaic version, the elders are asked "Where?" but not "Under what tree?" Susanna meets her lover (Dan 13:52-59). In Greek, the elders' answers are puns; in Aramaic, they are not. When one elder says the couple makes love under a weeping willow or cut tree, Daniel sentences him to be cut in two. When the other elder says the couple makes love under a live or sawed oak, Daniel sentences him to be sawed in two. He uses the principle of reciprocity (Deut 19:8-19), which punishes witnesses guilty of perjury with the same sentence their false testimony seeks to inflict on the defendant (Dan 13:60).

Like the other traditions in the book of Daniel, the story of A Beautiful Woman Remains Faithful developed as a response to the introduction of Hellenism into Syria-Palestine following its conquest by Alexander in 332 B.C.E. The two elders are converts to Hellenism, who try to convert Susanna, who represents the people of Judah. "It is better for me to fall into your power without guilt than to sin before Yahweh" (Dan 13:23) is the creed of all the martyrs who refused to embrace the Hellenistic way of life. The story teaches the people of Judah that they, like Susanna, can resist the rape of assimilation and survive.

The book of Daniel was only one of several traditions that developed to help the people of Judah cope with the challenge of Hellenism. The traditions in the book of Maccabees challenge the people of Judah to join an armed revolt against Antiochus Epiphanes (1 Macc 1:29-38). The book of Enoch, which is not included in the Bible, wants them to negotiate a treaty with the Greek rulers of Egypt to be their allies in a revolt against Antiochus Epiphanes. In contrast to these calls to arms, the book of Daniel is nonviolent. Its apocalypse stories promise the people of Judah that Yahweh alone will deliver them. It also warns them against the dangers of trying to deliver themselves. For the book of Daniel, the virtue of those who survive is patience, which is the ability to wait for Yahweh to complete the work begun.

In the end, however, it was the books of Maccabees and Enoch that reached the hearts of the people. By 142 B.C.E. a war of independence led by the household of Hashmon had liberated Judah from the Greek rulers of both Syria and Egypt. For the first time since 587 B.C.E., the people of Judah lived in an independent state. The Hasmoneans ruled this Judah until 63 B.C.E., when it was conquered by the Romans, and the people of Judah were once again confronted with the challenge of surviving in yet another Hellenistic world.

Points of Interest (Chapter 16)

16

BOOK OF HOSEA

(Hos 1:1 — 14:9)

Hosea (Hebrew: *Hoshe'a*) or Hoshea (2 Kgs 17:1), like Joshua (Num 13:8; Deut 32:44), Josiah, and Jesus, is a name that means "Yahweh is my Savior." Archaeologists have recovered several seals and seal impressions belonging to Semitic men named "Hosea." An important theme in the book of Hosea is that Yahweh—not the monarchs, not the prophets, not the priests, not the soldiers—is the savior of Israel.

The book of Hosea, like the books of Joel, Micah, Zephaniah, and Zechariah, is introduced by a series of formulas. These formulas create a title page. The title page of the book of Hosea labels it as the "Word of Yahweh."

"Hosea, son of Beeri" is the patron to whom the tradition is dedicated. It celebrates the household of Hosea for its courage in confronting the monarchs of Israel. Some title pages list the trade in which the household of its patron worked, and the village that was its domicile.

When title pages date a tradition, they calendar the time in the book politically or meteorologically. The date for the Book of Hosea is political: "during the reigns of Uzziah [783–742 B.C.E.], Jotham [750–735 B.C.E.], Ahaz [735–715 B.C.E.], and Hezekiah [715–687 B.C.E.], who ruled Judah, and the reigns of Jehoash [801–786 B.C.E.] and Jeroboam [786–746 B.C.E.], who ruled Israel." The time in the book of Hosea is 750–725 B.C.E., but the time when this particular way of talking about the events developed is after 721 B.C.E., after the Assyrians had conquered Israel.

Jeroboam, ruler of Israel, was an accomplished politician whose military covenants and trade agreements gave Israel a thriving surplus economy. During his reign the people of Israel enjoyed a very high standard of living. Jeroboam's covenants with states having common borders with Israel were intended to feed Israel during famine and protect Israel during war.

429

When Tiglath-pileser III (744–727 B.C.E.) became the great king of Assyria, however, he inaugurated a new age of empires by completely reorganizing Assyria's bureaucracy to gain political and economic control of the trade routes running from the Mediterranean coast inland. At least two of these major routes ran through Israel. During the days of Hosea, Assyria downgraded the status of Israel from an independent ally of Assyria in 738 B.C.E., to a closely supervised colony in 732 B.C.E., and finally to a province conquered in war in 721 B.C.E.

Marriage, adultery, and divorce are significant metaphors in the book of Hosea. The Trial of Israel, with which the book of Hosea opens, reflects on the failed marriage between Hosea and Gomer to better understand the failed covenant between Yahweh and Israel. The painful reason for the failure of both relationships is not so much sexual promiscuity, but human insecurity. Hosea and Gomer, like the rulers of Israel, did too much to care for themselves and too little to trust in Yahweh to care for them.

In the world of the Bible, there were certainly sexual relationships that reflected deep personal and emotional love of one person for another. There was romance in ancient Israel, just as there is romance in every culture. The Bible describes romance between unmarried men and women (Song 8:1-4; 5:10-16), between the fathers and mothers of households (Gen 24:67; 29:16-20; Judg 14:3; 1 Sam 1:5; 18:20; 25:44; 2 Sam 3:15; 11:27; 13:12), and between the fathers of households and their secondary wives (Exod 21:7-11; Judges 19).

Nevertheless, sexual language in the Bible does not simply describe romance. For example, the "wife of your youth" (Prov 5:18-20) and the "good wife" (Prov 31:10-31) in the book of Proverbs refer to the wise woman who teaches students to be disciplined, not to a woman with whom the learner is in love. The "loose woman" (Prov 5:2-5) is a fool who teaches the student that success can be achieved without discipline, not a woman with whom the learner is having an affair.

Even marriage had more to do with economics and politics than with romance. Marriage was a delicately negotiated covenant to bring together two households, who were willing to exchange substantial goods and services with each other over a significant period of time (Gen 34:21; 24:3-4; Exod 2:21; 1 Sam 18:17-28; 25:43). Marriage was more a matter of business than of pleasure.

Couples themselves rarely chose their own sexual partners. Fathers of households were responsible for safeguarding the status of the men and women in their households. They also applied the legal codes to determine who was eligible to marry and who was not. Eligibility to marry in these codes was determined differently for men than for women.

"Virgin" is the technical term for a woman who is legally eligible to marry. Fathers were responsible for the virginity, or legal eligibility for marriage, of the women in the household. Fathers of households were also responsible for the chastity, or legal

Noble Woman like Gomer Gazes from Her Window
(Nimrud 800–750 B.C.E.; ivory 10.7 cm)

compliance, of these women with the terms of their marriage covenants (Deut 22:13-21). Fathers who negotiated marriages for women in their households who were not virgins, that is, who were legally ineligible to marry, forfeited their land and children. Likewise, fathers who failed to see that women in their households remained chaste or fulfilled the terms of their marriage covenants also lost the patrimony that these marriages were intended to increase and multiply.

The legal codes in some households were exogamous and required fathers to choose marriage partners from different clans. Exogamous marriages were typical of economically aggressive and expanding households. Such marriages expanded the property rights and holdings of households as well as their political power. They were financially high-risk, high-return investments. If an exogamous marriage succeeded, both households enjoyed significant economic returns. If it failed, the financial loss was substantial.

The legal codes of other households were endogamous and required fathers to choose marriage partners from the same clan. Marriage partners also had to come from households that had an existing economic relationship with one another. Endogamous marriages were financially conservative. They strengthened an already existing and proven relationship between two households. The financial risks were small and, in general, so were the financial rewards. Endogamous marriages were designed to keep property within the village.

The most common endogamous marriage in the Bible combines the households of two brothers. Therefore, the bride and the groom were cousins, not necessarily blood relatives, but at least legal relatives. The words "uncle" or "father's brother" often refer to a covenant partner, not necessarily a sibling. The relationship between a man and his uncle was as important as the relationship between a man and his father. The uncle's son had a legal right to marry his parallel cousin. Very often when the Bible describes marriage (Genesis 24; 27:46—28:2), it describes cross-cousin marriage. Nahor marries his cousin to establish a covenant with his uncle (Gen 11:29).

The legal codes also eliminated some marriage partners altogether. The book of Leviticus (Lev 18:6-18), for example, directs fathers not to arrange a marriage between a man and his widowed mother, his father's wife, his sister or half-sister, his grand-daughter, his paternal or maternal aunt, his daughter-in-law, or his sister-in-law. These women were taboo as marriage partners. These taboos involved a variety of factors, but generally prohibited marriage between two households whose existing covenants would be threatened or duplicated by a new covenant. One woman, for example, could not fulfill the responsibilities of both the wife of a father and the wife of his son.

Most households in the world of the Bible were patrilocal. After they married, the couple generally lived with the household of the groom until the father of the household chose an heir. Rebekah joins the household of Abraham and Sarah after her marriage with Isaac (Gen 24:58-67), and the sons of Micah live within his house-hold (Judg 17:5).

Some few cultures in the Mediterranean world were matrilocal, and expected men to live with the households of their wives. Jacob leaves the household of Isaac and Rebekah and lives with Leah and Rachel in the household of Laban, their father (Genesis 29–30).

Marriage was not a single event, but a process of negotiations. Each negotiation furthered the covenant between the two households and spelled out their obligations to one another in more exact terms. To tender a proposal of marriage (Mal 2:14), the father of the groom's household sent a gift to the father of the household of the bride (Gen 34:12; Exod 22:16; Deut 22:29; 1 Sam 18:25). The father of the bride accepted the proposal by allowing the groom to take the bride to his household (Deut 20:7; 28:30; Exod 21:10). The marriage covenant was ratified when the groom "went into" the tent of the bride. Once he spread his cloak or "wings" over the bride (Ruth 3:9), their mar-riage was consummated.

Men conferred one of two titles on the women they married. One woman in the household held the status of "primary wife" or "mother of the household." Her title is generally translated "wife" or "mother." Other women held the status of "secondary wife." Their title is generally translated "concubine." Each title is not so much an indication of the sexual behavior of a particular woman, but rather of the economic status of the relationship between her household and the household of her husband (Fig. 102).

Marriage vows were simple. The wife said: "You are my husband. I am your wife." The husband said: "You are my wife. I am your husband." The words of divorce were equally brief: "You are not my wife. I am not your husband." The same kinds of words were used to seal the covenant between Yahweh and Israel: "You are my people. I am your divine patron" (Hos 1:9).

When the marriage was ratified, an exchange of property took place. An elaborate framework developed to administer the property that was exchanged. The honeymoon lasted for one year, during which the couple were freed from their obligations to the village. "When a man is newly married, he shall not go out with the army or be charged with any related duty. He shall be free at home one year, to be happy with the wife whom he has married" (Deut 24:5).

Inheritance was an integral part of marriage. The father of the household had to appoint an heir and a legal guardian. Inheritance in ancient Israel was patrilineal. Possessions were handed on by the father of the household to his son. Fathers often handed over their household to natural sons, but they could also appoint their daughters as heirs (Num 36:2-12; Josh 17:3-6), or someone to whom they were not related by blood kinship (Gen 15:2).

> Solomon sealed his many covenants with marriage. He married a daughter of Pharaoh, daughters of Moab, daughters of Ammon, daughters of Edom, daughters of Sidon, and daughters of Hattusas . . . seven hundred primary wives and three hundred secondary wives in all.

FIGURE 102 Annals of Solomon
(1 Kgs 11:1-3)

Trial of Israel
(Hos 1:2-3)

In the Trial of Israel (Hos 1:2-3), which opens the book of Hosea, the marriage of Hosea and Gomer is a pantomime. Like Jeremiah, who does not marry or attend any household celebrations, and like Isaiah, who goes naked for three years (Isa 18:1—20:6), Hosea extends the single dramatic gesture of his marriage to Gomer into a lifestyle.

"So he went and took Gomer the daughter of Diblaim" is the official document that records the marriage covenant between Hosea and Gomer. Gomer is the "Daughter of Diblaim," which is the title of a woman of honor. She is not a prostitute.

Hosea cites their marriage certificate, and then reflects on its significance. It is a human accomplishment, not a divine gift. It is adultery, not marriage. Legally, Hosea and Gomer marry, but morally, they are guilty of adultery. Similarly, the rulers of Israel legally negotiate covenants with neighboring states for food in times of famine and troops in times of war. Morally, they are guilty of a breach of the covenant between Yahweh and Israel, which stipulates that Yahweh alone will feed and protect Israel.

For Hosea and the prophets, only when the rulers of Israel allow Yahweh to feed and protect the land and its people is there a "marriage." When the rulers of Israel try to feed and protect the land and its children by negotiating covenants with neighboring states, that is "adultery." "Adultery" is doing for themselves what Yahweh has promised to do for them.

Many English translations use "prostitution," "harlotry," and "whoredom" here instead of "adultery." The connotations of these words are of paying someone for sexual intercourse. The connotations of "adultery" imply any relationship—sexual, economic, or political—that establishes independence or self-sufficiency.

Hosea and Gomer prepared for their marriage by carefully following the rituals used in the world of the Bible to guarantee that, once a couple was married, they could have children. Similarly, the monarchs of Israel and Judah carefully followed diplomatic rituals of covenant making to guarantee that the state would be protected and economically sound. Nonetheless, the covenant between Yahweh and Israel stipulates that the fertility of a household—and the fertility of the state—is a divine gift. Couples and monarchs do not protect and provide for their households and their states; Yahweh does. Couples, like Hosea and Gomer, and monarchs, like Jeroboam II, who usurp these divine responsibilities to protect and provide for the land and its people are indicted for adultery by prophets like Hosea, because they are trying to do what Yahweh has already promised to do. By doing for themselves what Yahweh has promised to do for them, they are saying either that Yahweh cannot, or that Yahweh will not, fulfill the promises of the covenant. They are saying that Yahweh is a liar, or that Yahweh is powerless. Therefore, in all of the prophetic traditions in the Bible, the covenant between Yahweh and Israel is a "marriage," and the covenants that the monarchs of Israel and Judah negotiate with neighboring states are "adultery." Likewise, couples who trust in Yahweh to bless their households with land and children are "married." Couples who trust in fertility rituals to bring their households harvests and children are guilty of "adultery."

Hosea uses his marriage to Gomer, and the births of their children, to assess Jeroboam's administration from two points of view. First, the traditions of Hosea are committed to the development of a subsistence economy in Israel, and are radically opposed to the surplus economy of the monarchs of Israel. Jeroboam II, in contrast, is committed to strengthening Israel's economy through competition. There needs to be a surplus in order to provide goods to trade, and luxuries for the people at home. For Hosea, a surplus economy, and the covenants that make it possible, are too independent of

Yahweh. Only a subsistence economy allows the Hebrews to profess their faith that it is Yahweh who feeds them and protects them, that Yahweh is their divine patron.

Trial of Israel
(Hos 1:3-5)

The indictment of another Trial of Israel cites the birth certificate of Hosea and Gomer's first child: "Gomer conceived and bore him a son." The name "Jezreel" is hideous because it is a battle cry. Naming one's child "Jezreel" is similar to naming one's child "Remember Pearl Harbor."

In the course of its history, Israel had several capital cities. One was Jezreel; another was Samaria. Israel also had two state sanctuaries dedicated to Yahweh. The one in the north was Dan; the one in the south was Bethel.

Both Egypt and Babylon have periods in which political and religious power in the state is centered in more than one place. The Babylonian ruler Nabonidus (555–539 B.C.E.) relocates the capital from Babylon to Tema. Pharaoh Amenophis IV changes his name to Akhenaten (1369–1353 B.C.E.) and relocates the Egyptian capital from Thebes to Akhetaten. David relocates the capital from Hebron to Jerusalem. Transitions in government are often connected with the foundation of a new capital.

Samaria was the city of Israel's monarchs. Jezreel was the village of Israel's chiefs. Samaria was like Washington, D.C.; Jezreel like Camp David. Rulers exercised a different style of leadership in each place.

Hosea looks at the birth certificate of his son, and remembers the day when Jehu rushed past the king's bodyguards and murdered King Jehoram, who was recovering from battle wounds at Jezreel. Hosea considers Jehu to be the epitome of human arrogance. Just as Jehu is arrogant enough to kill Jehoram, his king, Hosea and Gomer are arrogant enough to think they can conceive and bear a child on their own.

Trial of Israel
(Hos 2:2 — 3:5)

In yet another Trial of Israel, Hosea, the prosecuting attorney, speaks as if he is Yahweh. As father of the household, Hosea pleads with the rulers of Israel. He begs them to intercede with Israel, their mother country, and convince her to stop negotiating covenants for food with other states. Yahweh wants Israel to fulfill the stipulations of their covenant. Israel's covenants with other states are without any validity. They are infertile. They are adultery.

The mother of the royal household enjoyed such a distinct status that she became a symbol of Israel itself. West Semitic peoples referred to their prominent cities as "mothers," and the villages within a city's sphere of influence as her "daughters" (Josh 15:45-47; Judg 1:17). Not only Israel, but also Babylon and Ugarit, referred to their cities as mothers. Phoenician coins depict cities that have the same names as their divine husbands, like some cities in the Bible, as women with the title "Lady" or "Godmother" (Josh 9:10; 15:9).

Consequently, when the book of Deuteronomy and other legal codes in the Bible refer to women and deal with women's issues, they are seldom interested simply in regulating physical relationships between men and women. The vocabulary dealing with women, and with sexuality, is concerned far more with property than with gender and genital contact. These law codes are concerned with more sweeping issues of social justice, and the equitable distribution of goods and services by maintaining a subsistence economy. For traditional societies, social justice, and not sexual conduct, is the basis of morality. Consequently, teachings dealing with virginity, marriage, divorce, infidelity, adultery, promiscuity, and rape are not only concerned with the sexual relationships, but with the social and economic relationships between the households in the village as a whole.

When Hosea pleads with Israel to "put away adultery" (Hos 2:2), he is asking for a fundamental realignment of royal foreign policy. Israel in the days of Hosea was committed to building its international network of alliances. Hosea considers it a flawed policy that will strip the country of its resources, not protect it from famine and invasion.

By stripping a woman convicted of adultery naked, a household excommunicated her (Hos 2:3). Clothes were not worn for modesty, but for identification. Clothing was not simply an accessory reflecting individual style or personal preference. Its style, weave, and color functioned as a uniform.

Changing clothes did not simply reflect a practice of good hygiene, but a change of status. Those who changed clothes were preparing to play new roles. Ruth does not bathe, comb her hair, and put on her best clothes simply to appear more physically attractive to Boaz, but to signal to him that she is an official representative of the household of Elimelech and Naomi (Ruth 3:3).

In Mesopotamia, the word "to clothe" also meant "to exercise power." Therefore, when monarchs put on their cloaks, they were taking up the power of their office. David has the opportunity to kill Saul, who unknowingly comes into a cave near the oasis of En-gedi where David and his warriors are hiding. David's warriors see it as an opportunity to kill him (1 Sam 24:4). David, however, simply cuts a tassel off Saul's cloak. David is neither teasing Saul nor frustrating his warriors' desire for victory. The tassel represents Saul's authority as ruler. David takes Saul's honor, and leaves him with shame.

The "children" in this Trial of Israel are its rulers. They are the "children of adultery" (Hos 2:4) because they rely on the support of the rulers of other states for their authority to rule Israel. Legitimate monarchs in Israel rely only on Yahweh, and not on their covenants with foreign monarchs to feed and protect Israel.

The "lovers" whom Israel pursues are the states that are its neighbors (Hos 2:5). The monarchs of Israel pay the premiums on their covenants with neighboring states with the grain, wool, flax, olive oil, and wine that the land of Israel produces.

Grain, wine, and olive oil are the primary trading goods in the world of the Bible. They are portable. They can be moved from villages to sanctuaries, and from sanctuaries to the soldiers and bureaucrats who will use them. They are storable. Grain, wine, and oil can be kept for extended periods of time without spoiling. They are divisible. Grain, wine, and oil can be stored in large quantities and then broken down into smaller amounts in order to be distributed.

Hosea does not indict the rulers of Israel for becoming clients of divine patrons other than Yahweh. They are not worshiping strange gods, but worshiping Yahweh strangely. Elijah makes the same indictment against Ahab and Jezebel. The rulers of Israel worship Yahweh triumphally as the Great King of a state with a surplus economy. For Elijah and Hosea, the Hebrews should worship Yahweh as the Good Shepherd of a state with a subsistence economy. "Baal" and "Yahweh" were comparable divine titles in the villages of early Israel. After the formation of the state of Israel, the prophets used "Baal" as a label of shame for the way monarchs worshiped Yahweh in royal sanctuaries.

Yahweh and the divine assembly impose a two-part sentence upon Israel. The first sentence is siege (Hos 2:6-8). The land will be invaded by an enemy who will completely seal off the city of Samaria with a "hedge of thorns." They will blockade the city with a rampart.

Once the siege is set, Samaria is completely cut off. Its messengers are unable to work their way through the enemy lines to call on Israel's covenant partners for help. Israel "shall seek them, but shall not find them" (Hos 2:7). Unable to leave the land and seek help from other states, Israel will then remember Yahweh, her "first husband." Only when these other states cannot protect Israel does Israel ask Yahweh for protection. The siege teaches Israel that it cannot protect itself.

The second sentence is drought and famine, which teach Israel that whenever it does not remember that it is Yahweh who sends the grain, the olive oil, and the wine, Yahweh takes them away (Hos 2:9-13). There will be no grain and wine and oil; therefore there will be no harvest festivals. There will be no flax to weave into linen, and therefore Israel will be naked. There will not even be enough linen to make underwear, and so even Israel's vagina or "shame" will be exposed (Hos 2:10). The land will be so poverty-stricken that no other state will want to be its covenant partner. Israel will be a wasteland, where only wild animals are at home (Hos 2:12).

The sentence is extreme, but it is also therapeutic. Without the soldiers of other states to protect its land during war, and relief aid to feed its people during famine, Israel is ripe for courting. The bad news is that Israel is in dire straits. The good news is that Israel is now willing to listen. Therefore, in her suffering, Yahweh "speaks tenderly to her" (Hos 2:15). The covenant between Yahweh and Israel is renewed, and the land and its people bloom once again.

The first appeal (Hos 2:14-23) is mirrored in a second appeal (Hos 3:1-5). Israel is guilty of adultery because only its covenant with Yahweh is a marriage. Its covenants with all the other states are infertile. No matter how many "raisin cakes" and other aphrodisiacs are eaten at the wedding banquet ratifying these covenants, Israel will lose its land and children.

Raisin cakes are patties of sun-dried grapes (Song 2:5; 1 Sam 25:18-31; 2 Sam 16:1-4; 1 Chr 12:40; Isa 16:7; Jer 7:18). Grapes, and by association wine and raisins, are considered to promote fertility because their shape was similar to the shape of testicles.

Orgies of eating, drinking, and sexual intercourse are not just human communities out of control. They are rituals that are designed to remind nature to reproduce. Throughout Syria-Palestine, these fertility rituals were a catalyst to fertility. The Hebrews did not object to fertility rituals because they were puritanical about physical pleasures. They objected to the idea that Yahweh had to be reminded to send the harvest and the child. Yahweh was faithful without prodding.

The bride-price that Yahweh pays for Israel is a bargain. The once-great land is auctioned for salvage. Unlike the elaborate exchanges of goods with which the monarchs of Israel celebrated the ratification of their covenants with neighboring states, Yahweh offers only simple gifts.

Likewise, there is no orgy at the ratification of the new covenant between Yahweh and Israel. What sets the cycle of fertility in motion is not abundance, but need. Yahweh responds to infertility, not excess. Therefore, Hosea takes Israel through a prolonged period of drying out. Everything that suggests that Israel feeds and protects itself must disappear. All of Israel's covenants will be allowed to expire. "You will not play the whore." No children will be born. "You shall not have intercourse with a man, nor I with you." There will be no harvest for the monarch to tax, or sacrifice under the pillar or sacred tree. These great oak trees or terebinths marked sacred centers throughout the land. The shape of their crown of leaves and branches reminded the people of the uterus of their Godmother, and its trunk was the birth canal through which they were delivered onto the human plane. Just as there was no harvest of grain, there was also no roundup of livestock to be sheared and slaughtered. Therefore, there were no priests dressed in ephod aprons processing the meat. Finally, since there was no land worth buying or selling, households had no teraphim statues, which were deeds or titles to the land. Only when the land and people of Israel are virtually dead can it be absolutely clear that its fertility is the work of Yahweh, and not the work of their own hands, and the hands of their covenant partners in other states.

The traditions of Hosea do not rant and rave against unfaithful women, but against the kind of human arrogance that leads to self-sufficiency, and ultimately self-destruction. These traditions indict Israel for forgetting that it is Yahweh who protects and defends. The price of forgetting is to do without until the memory of how Yahweh fed and protected them in the desert between Egypt and the land begins to return.

Trial of Israel
(Hos 11:1-11)

In the Trial of Israel that opens part one of the book of Hosea, Yahweh is a marriage partner. In another Trial of Israel (Hos 11:1-11) in part two of the book of Hosea (Hos 4:1—14:9), Yahweh is a parent (Fig. 103).

Yahweh indicts Israel because it "refused to come back to me" (Hos 11:1-5). Although Yahweh, like a human mother, taught Israel to walk, it walked away from her rather than back to her. Israel did not recognize that the source of its strength was the outstretched arms of its Godmother. By teaching a child to walk, a parent lays down its life for its child. The parent must give its child everything and expect nothing in return. Parents teach their children to walk, and their children often walk away from them.

As an infant, Israel took its first step from slavery to freedom toward the hands that Yahweh held out to it. These outstretched hands are the hands of a mother teaching a child to walk, and are implicitly contrasted with the raised hand and mighty arm (Jer 21:5) of a divine warrior about to kill his enemies. Hosea prods the audience to consider which hands are more powerful: those of a mother or those of a warrior.

Egyptian traditions regularly portray pharaohs with their hands and arms raised, holding a war club and preparing to destroy their enemies. The Semites were only one of Egypt's nine ancient enemies. Likewise, the book of Exodus portrays Yahweh with an arm raised to deliver the Hebrews (Exod 6:6; 15:16), dueling with a pharaoh whose arm is raised to destroy them. This trial indicts Israel for having walked away from the outstretched hands of peace in search of an arm raised in war. The Hebrews misunderstood the gentleness of Yahweh's outstretched hands for weakness, and so they have sought to protect themselves with the raised arms of the soldiers of Egypt and Assyria.

Yahweh loved and called Israel. "Loved" and "called" are not only terms of emotional endearment, but also terms of covenant obligation. Yahweh loves Israel, because

indictment (Hos 11:1-4)

> When Israel was a child, I loved him,
>> Out of Egypt I called my son.
>
> The more I called Israel,
>> The more they went from me.
>
> They kept sacrificing to me as Baal,
>> They kept offering incense to statues.
>
> I taught the household of Ephraim to walk,
>> I took them up in my arms;
>> They did not know that I healed them.
>
> I led them with cords of human kindness,
>> I led them with bands of love.
>
> Like a parent I lifted them to my cheek,
>> I cradled them in my arms and nursed them.

sentence (Hos 11:5-7)

> They shall return to slavery in Egypt,
>> Assyria shall conquer them.
>> Because they refuse to come back to me,
>
> The sword will destroy their cities,
>> The sword will kill their priests. . . .
>
> Because my people turn from me. . . .
>> When they call on the Most High, I will ignore them.

appeal (Hos 11:8-11)

> How can I give you up to your enemies, Israel?
>> How can I hand you over as prisoners, Israel?
>
> How can I destroy you like Admah?
>> How can I punish you like Zeboiim?
>
> My heart recoils within me.
>> My compassion grows warm and tender.

(continued)

> *I will not act in anger.*
> > *I will not destroy Israel again.*
>
> *For I am divine, not human,*
> > *The Holy One cannot come in anger.*
>
> *The Hebrews return to Yahweh roaring like a lion,*
> > *Yahweh roars and cubs come obediently from the west.*
>
> *They come obediently as geese from Egypt,*
> > *They come obediently as swallows from Assyria.*
> > *I will take them back, says Yahweh.*

FIGURE 103   Trial of Israel (Hos 11:1-4)

Yahweh fulfills the stipulations of the covenant between them. Yahweh calls Israel "Son," because Yahweh and Israel are covenant partners. The trial indicts the monarchs of Israel for continuing to negotiate covenants with other states to feed Israel in the event of a famine, and to protect Israel in the event of war, despite Yahweh's faithfulness in feeding the people and protecting the land.

Yahweh did not just feed Israel like cattle, but nursed Israel like a mother. As slaves in Egypt and exiles in the empire of Assyria, Israel was like a hungry child crying out to be fed. Yahweh lifted Israel to the breast, and leaned gently over it so that Israel could nurse (Hos 11:4). Israel was as secure and as well fed in the land into which Yahweh had lifted it as a nursing child in its mother's arms. Nevertheless, Israel climbed down and walked away to look for security and food elsewhere. Next time Yahweh will ignore Israel's cry for food, and allow Egypt and Assyria to feed and protect it (Hos 11:7).

Hosea, on behalf of Yahweh, appeals Israel's sentence of death by starvation (Hos 11:8-10). "My heart recoils within me. Although I am furious, I will not execute my fierce anger. I will not again destroy Ephraim. . . . my compassion grows warm and tender" (Hos 11:8). The English word "compassion" here translates a Hebrew word that means "womb." The womb of Yahweh that carried Israel remembers the child, even when the child forgets its Godmother. Yahweh cannot forget Israel, even when Israel forgets Yahweh. Yahweh will roar, like a female lion who has made a kill, and Israel will come running like cubs, and swoop down on the carcass like birds of prey (Hos 11:10). For Hosea, the bond between husband and wife, and between mother and child, is ultimately indestructible.

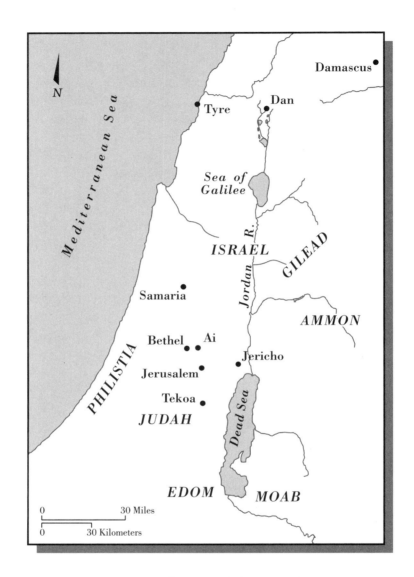

Points of Interest (Chapter 17)

17

BOOK OF AMOS

(Amos 1:1—9:15)

Amos (Hebrew: 'Amos) is introduced without a patron or "father," but he is not introduced as a poor man. Amos was a wealthy rancher or a grower. When Amaziah charges him with being a "professional prophet" paid by the ruler of Judah to destabilize Israel, Amos argues that he makes his living as a herder and farmer (Amos 7:10-17). He has the mobility to leave Judah, where Tekoa is located, and travel to Bethel in Israel. His style of speaking and his familiarity with the traditions of ancient Israel identify Amos as well educated.

Amos is the loyal opposition to Jeroboam II (786–746 B.C.E.), who ruled Israel in its prime. Jehoash (801–786 B.C.E.) is Jeroboam's patron. He appointed Jeroboam his heir. The book of Amos is a careful analysis of the consequences for the people of Israel of the covenants that Jeroboam negotiated with surrounding states.

Tekoa is ten miles south of Jerusalem just at the edge of the well-watered farmlands to the west, and the dry hills overlooking the Dead Sea to the east. Amos travels from Judah in the south to Israel in the north. Bethel marks the intersection of two great ancient highways fifteen miles north of Jerusalem. The sanctuary was founded after 2000 B.C.E., when it was called "Luz."

Bethel, like its sister city, Dan, is a border city that tradition celebrated as both a holy city and a sacrilegious city. Some of the Bible's most-told traditions developed here. Hebrews laid claim to Bethel in the book of Genesis, in Abraham and Sarah Negotiate with Yahweh (Gen 11:27—12:8) and the Inauguration of Jacob at Bethel (Gen 28:10-22). These ancestors celebrated their commitment to Yahweh by erecting a great stone at Bethel.

In the story of his inauguration at Bethel, Jacob does not actually see a ladder, but Esagila, a ziggurat or great stepped platform that the members of the divine assembly used to enter and leave Babylon. The Flood Stories (Gen 11:1-9) satirize the same ziggurat as the "Tower of Babel." The Inauguration of Jacob at Bethel confers the status of the Gate of the Divine Assembly in Mesopotamia on the House of Our Creator (Hebrew: *Beth El*) in Syria-Palestine. Nearby Bethel are Jericho and Ai, where villagers celebrated Yahweh's gift of new land to them by telling Stories of Rahab and Stories of Joshua. Bethel was also part of the territory where the Ark of the Covenant Stories and the Stories of Samuel were told.

Around 925 B.C.E., Israel declared its independence from Judah. Jeroboam I (925–905 B.C.E.), Israel's first ruler, designated Bethel as the place where this revolution would be commemorated as a new exodus from slavery. A gold bull was installed as a pedestal on which Yahweh could stand victorious (1 Kgs 12:1-32). Prophets like Elijah and Elisha also sanctioned Bethel's new status (2 Kgs 2:1-25).

Understandably, Judah's monarchs (Josh 7:2) and prophets (Hos 4:15) did not consider Bethel to be an authentic sanctuary or the House of Our Creator, but caricatured it as a House of Sacrilege. These two titles for the sanctuary at Bethel sound alike in Hebrew. The monarchs and prophets of Judah did their best to destroy or discredit Bethel. Twice, Judah's armies overran Bethel (2 Chr 13:1-23; 1 Kgs 12:33—13:34; 2 Kgs 22:1—23:30). The Stories of a Golden Calf (Exod 32:1—34:35), which compare Israel's secession from Judah with Aaron's rebellion against Moses, and the Trial of a Priest of Bethel (Amos 7:10-17) preserve the kind of satire that Judah used to discredit the venerable sanctuary. Nonetheless, its reputation remained intact. Even the Assyrians who conquered Israel in 721 B.C.E. publicly acknowledged Yahweh's sanctuary there (2 Kgs 17:1-41).

Trials of Israel and Its Covenant Partners
(AMOS 1:3—2:16)

The Trials of Israel and Its Covenant Partners (Amos 1:3—2:16), with which the book of Amos opens, is actually a series of seven trials or execrations. Just as in the Trial of Judah and Its Covenant Partners in the book of Isaiah (Isa 13:1—23:18), it is a compass that provides the logic for arranging the series. Israel is the centerpoint of the compass, and the place where Amos stands. He rotates to face each defendant while announcing the verdict that Yahweh and the divine assembly have imposed. He alternates diagonally from one compass point to the other.

Divine Gardener like Amos Dresses Tree (Amos 7:14)
(Nimrud 875–860 B.C.E.; alabaster 141 x 95 cm)

Damascus, which is northeast of Israel, is sentenced first (Amos 1:3-5). Philistia, which is southwest of Israel, is sentenced second (Amos 1:6-8). Amos then announces the sentence of Tyre, which is northwest of Israel (Amos 1:9-10). Then Edom, which is southeast of Israel, is sentenced (Amos 1:11-12). Ammon, which is east of Israel, is sentenced (Amos 1:13-15); then Moab in southern Jordan, which is south-southeast (Amos 2:1-3). Finally, Amos announces the sentence against Judah and Israel (Amos 2:14-16). The diagonal pattern ties down the sentence of the final defendant, and builds suspense like a knife thrower in a carnival sideshow.

Each trial is introduced with the formula "Thus says Yahweh." The prophet, as foreperson of the jury, announces the verdict of Yahweh and the divine assembly with the formula "Thus says Yahweh" (Amos 1:3). In courts today, the judge asks: "Has the jury reached a verdict?" To which the foreperson replies: "We have, your honor." The language is stylized, so that audiences will realize that a public event is being conducted by duly authorized officials, not simply an informal exchange between two individuals.

Each trial also uses a counting motif. By using two successive numbers in increments of one: "for three transgressions . . . and for four" (Amos 1:6), the trial builds suspense in the audience. The same technique is used in numerical proverbs (Prov 30:18-19). Today, parents often count to three or ten to motivate a youngster to start or finish a chore: "I am going to count to three, and you'd better be upstairs and putting on your pajamas." Although here the numbers total seven, the emphasis is on the counting, not on the total. Likewise, in courts of laws today, defendants are charged with a certain number of "counts" of a crime, indicating that they are repeat offenders, which is precisely what Amos stresses. Israel and its covenant partners are criminals of excess. Their violence is as excessive as their luxurious lifestyle. For the book of Amos excessive luxury and excessive violence go hand in hand.

The trials give examples of the excessive violence of the defendants. Damascus, for example, is indicted for "threshing" Gilead (Amos 1:3). Threshing is a process by which the husks of wheat and barley are removed. The stalks are dried on flat, paved surfaces or threshing floors (1 Chr 21:20-23). Then the kernels are separated from the husks by beating the stalks with long, flexible wooden poles called "flails," crushed by the hooves of animals driven over the stalks, or by a "sledge" or a wooden sled with stone-studded or metal-covered runners dragged across the threshing floor by an ox or a donkey (Deut 25:4).

Different cultures dispatch the wounded left on the battlefield in different ways. On the one hand, the soldiers of Damascus may have put the wounded to death by dragging a sledge back and forth across the battlefield, leaving no survivors. On the other hand, the soldiers of Damascus may have so excessively plundered the crops of Gilead that none of the people of the land could survive until the next harvest. Regardless, the book of Amos considers their battle tactics to be excessive and barbaric. They take more than victory from their enemies.

War and slavery were standard institutions in the world of the Bible. They were violent, but they were not lawless. Likewise, the Philistines are indicted for excessively harvesting prisoners of war from their enemies. The protocol of war expects that the victors will deport the ruling household of their enemies, but not "entire communities" (Amos 1:6).

People of the land could be enslaved for failing to repay debts, but they could not be sold to outsiders. Only prisoners of war could be sold to strangers. The people of Tyre, however, were excessive in their practice of slavery. They "did not remember the covenant of kinship" (Amos 1:9), but sold the people of Damascus, who were their covenant partners, into slavery.

The Hebrews considered the Edomites to be the people of Esau, who hunted his brother Jacob. They made enemies of their own households. War was a strategy for dealing with outsiders, but Edom "pursued his brother with the sword" (Amos 1:11). Edom was the land of civil war, which for the book of Amos was war to excess.

Ammon was a state to the south of Gilead. Damascus was a state to the north. The people of Ammon are as excessive in their practice of war as the people of Tyre are in their practice of slavery. They not only attacked the soldiers of Gilead who came out to meet them on the field of battle; they "ripped open pregnant women" (Amos 1:13) and waged war on the unborn.

Similarly, the soldiers of Moab not only made war on the living, but "burned to lime the bones of the king of Edom" (Amos 2:1). Once they had defeated the soldiers of Edom, they attacked the dead of Edom in their graves. Moab is not indicted for waging war, but for waging total war against its enemies.

Judah and Israel, like their covenant partners, are indicted for excessive injustice. For the book of Amos, the teaching of Yahweh established moderation (Amos 2:4). Its statutes were intended to create a society in which the poor could survive. In contrast, the economies of Judah and Israel were excessively competitive. "They sell the righteous for silver, and the needy for a pair of sandals" (Amos 2:6).

Sandals were the uniform that distinguished landowners, who walked off the land in sandals to mark its boundaries. Sandals were title to land. When landowners mortgaged their property, they surrendered their sandals to creditors as collateral. If they defaulted on their debt, creditors sold the land for which the sandals were the title to recover their investment. Here in the book of Amos creditors in Israel are ruthless. Instead of extending landowners time to pay, they promptly foreclosed on their land. The creditors auction the land or "sandals," which their debtors have offered as collateral, in order to recover the value of their loan, which is far less than the land itself is worth.

The households of Israel not only compete excessively with the poor; the fathers of households compete against their own heirs. "Father and son have intercourse with the same woman" (Amos 2:7). The indictment does not simply charge the men with sexual promiscuity, but with excessive economic competition.

The sentence imposed upon Israel and each of its covenant partners is that Yahweh will no longer feed their peoples and protect their lands. They must feed and protect themselves, which ultimately none of the states indicted will be able to do. "The strong shall not retain their strength, nor shall the mighty save their lives; those who handle the bow shall not stand, and those who are swift of foot shall not save themselves, nor shall those who ride horses save their lives; and those who are stout of heart among the mighty shall flee away naked in that day" (Amos 2:13-16).

From the perspective of Amos and the other prophets, the covenants that the monarchs of Israel and Judah negotiate with their neighbors for food and military assistance are useless. Yahweh, and only Yahweh, can feed the people and protect the land. The sentence to which Yahweh and the divine assembly condemn Israel and its covenant partners is that they must depend on themselves to survive. Ultimately, human efforts lead only to war and starvation, not peace and plenty. For the prophets, Yahweh does not inflict pain. Yahweh simply allows Israel and Judah to suffer the consequences of their actions.

Trial of Israel
(AMOS 7:1—9:15)

One Trial of Israel (Amos 7:1-9) portrays Amos as the defense attorney who negotiates a mitigation of the sentence imposed upon Israel by Yahweh and the divine assembly. The first sentence imposed on Israel is a plague of locusts. "Yahweh, our Creator, was about to hatch a plague of locusts just as the second harvest began to sprout" (Amos 7:1).

There were two harvests in Syria-Palestine. The entire first harvest was collected by the monarchs as taxes. The second harvest was all the households had to eat. Yahweh had sentenced Israel to lose its entire second harvest to locusts (Joel 1:1-12). Amos objects. The goal of a sentence is to rehabilitate Israel, not to destroy it. Destroy the second harvest, Amos argues, and you destroy Israel. "Yahweh relented. 'It shall not be,' said Yahweh" (Amos 7:3).

The second sentence imposed on Israel is a drought so severe that even the Mediterranean Sea would evaporate. "Yahweh, our Creator, was about to dispatch a drought to devour the Great Sea and to eat the farmland" (Amos 7:4). Again Amos objects. Israel is too small a state to survive such a catastrophe. Again Yahweh mitigates the sentence.

The third sentence imposed on Israel is invasion. Amos sees Yahweh as a military engineer drawing up a plan of attack against Israel's capital city of Samaria. "Yahweh was standing beside the wall of the city with a plumb line in hand. Yahweh asked me: 'Amos, what do you see?' I said: 'I see a plumb line.' Then Yahweh said: 'I am using this plumb line to cut Israel in two. I will abandon both the sanctuary that the household of Isaac built for me in Jerusalem and the sanctuary that the household of Jacob built for me in Samaria. I will lead the attack against the household of Jeroboam'" (Amos 7:8-9).

As in the book of Daniel, here Yahweh is a divine architect who knows every weak point and every blind spot in the walls of Samaria. There is no appeal of the third sentence. Israel and Judah will both be invaded and their capital cities will be destroyed. Those magnificent architectural monuments that were the showplaces of the rulers of Israel and Judah are powerless to defend the land and to defend themselves. For Amos, Yahweh was the only wall that could withstand the enemies of Israel and Judah. When the rulers of Israel and Judah built their own walls, Yahweh departed, and Yahweh's departure was a death sentence for Jerusalem and Samaria.

After the cities built by the household of David and the household of Jeroboam have been destroyed, however, Yahweh will build new cities. "On that day I will replace the hut that David built. I will rebuild on its ruins" (Amos 9:11). Only the cities that Yahweh builds last. Only the walls that Yahweh constructs are strong enough to protect the people from their enemies.

Likewise, only the fields that Yahweh plants thrive. "The time is surely coming, says Yahweh, when the farmer who plants will overtake the farmer who harvests. The wine maker who presses the grapes will overtake the farmers who harvest them" (Amos 9:13). One harvest will follow the other so quickly that workers will hardly have time to harvest a field before they have to sow it. Farmers will not have enough time to process the wine before they have to return to the vineyards and bring in the grapes. Covenants that rulers negotiate for food with neighboring states cannot compete with the abundance Yahweh provides. "The mountains shall drip fine wine, and all the hills shall flow with it" (Amos 9:13).

The message of Amos is: "Let Yahweh do it." It is self-destructive arrogance for the monarchs of Israel and Judah to do what Yahweh has promised to do. They cannot feed the people and protect the land no matter how many covenants they negotiate, and how many cities they build. For Amos, Yahweh is the only faithful covenant partner for Israel and Judah. Every other covenant is a heresy that sentences the people and their land to death. Israel and Judah will survive only when they are able to let Yahweh "plant them upon their land and they shall never again be plucked up out of the land that I have given them" (Amos 9:15).

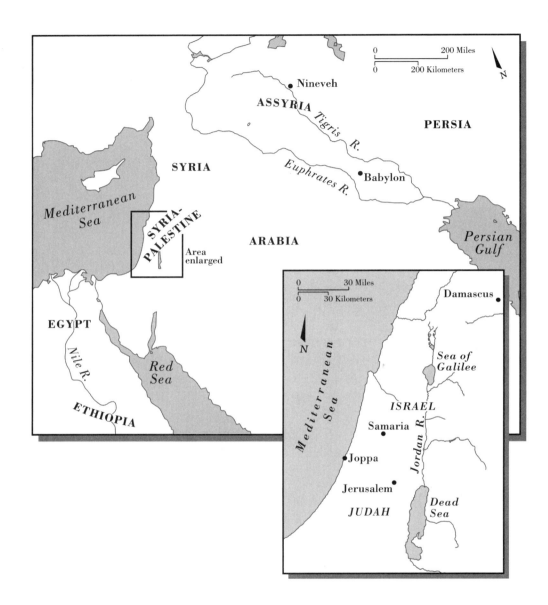

Points of Interest (Chapter 18)

18

BOOK OF JONAH

(JONAH 1:1—4:11)

The book of Job asks: Why do good people suffer? The book of Jonah (Hebrew: *Yonah*) asks: Why do bad people go unpunished? These were burning questions among the people of Judah living in the Diaspora, the non-Jewish worlds of their enemies. These are also the burning questions in the classics of every culture, like *Moby Dick* by Herman Melville (1819–91). The book of Jonah is one of the shortest, and one of the most powerful, of these classic struggles.

Again and again, the Hebrews became strangers in strange lands: when the Assyrians destroyed Samaria in 721 B.C.E., when the Babylonians destroyed Jerusalem in 587 B.C.E., and when the Greeks conquered Syria-Palestine in 332 B.C.E. They were outraged that Yahweh had not protected them from their enemies. Jonah is their voice.

Crisis Episode
(JONAH 1:1—3:9)

A theodicy is a tradition that struggles to reconcile faith in a divine patron, who is good, with a world in which there is evil. Both the book of Job and the book of Jonah are theodicies. They impeach Yahweh for breach of covenant for allowing good people to suffer and bad people to go unpunished. The genre of the book of Job, however, is a trial. The genre of the book of Jonah, like the book of Ruth, is a parable.

One difference between trials and parables is that trials are conducted in the first person, whereas parables are told in the third person. In the Trial of Israel and Its Covenant Partners (Amos 1:1—2:16), for example, Amos announces: "Thus says Yahweh: 'For three counts of breach of covenant, and for four, I will indict Damascus'" (Amos

451

1:3). In the book of Jonah, however: "Yahweh sent a Great Fish to swallow Jonah. For three days and three nights, Jonah was down in the belly of the Fish, which turned him back toward Yahweh" (Jonah 1:17).

Another difference between trials and parables is that the characters in trials are all human. In a Trial of Israel (Hos 11:1-11), Yahweh and the rulers of Israel plead their cases before the divine assembly: "When Israel was a child, I loved him, and out of Egypt I called my son." Parables, however, use fable. The fable technique casts non-human characters like plants and animals as if they were human characters. The Great Wind (Jonah 1:4), the Great Fish (Jonah 2:1), the Plant (Jonah 4:6), the Worm (Jonah 4:7), and the East Wind (Jonah 4:8) all have human attributes in the book of Jonah.

The book of Jonah begins, as all stories begin, when a crisis disturbs the peace. The life of the Faithful Prophet is turned upside down when the Creator of the Heavens, the Sea, and the Land commissions him to preach against the Great City.

Some language in the opening episode imitates the inaugurations of prophets, for example, "Now the word of Yahweh came." (Jonah 1:1). Most language in the opening episode is from parables, for example, "Jonah, son of Amittai," which was originally heard generically as "the Faithful Prophet." The other characters in the book of Jonah, like the characters in most parables, are also generic. The protagonist is the "Creator of the Heavens, the Sea, and the Land." Only Jonah addresses this Creator as "Yahweh."

Jonah's name is ironic, which is a common literary technique in parables. Irony uses incongruity or anomaly. The audience is aware of the contradiction between the words and actions of a character even though the character is not. Irony often causes such outrage in the audience that it wants to interrupt the action of the story in order to object. Thus, irony gets the audience to take an active part in the story by actually playing a role. In Hebrew the word "Jonah" means a "dove," a gentle, obedient, and faithful bird. Likewise, the Hebrew words "son of Amittai" also mean "faithful." The words do not identify Jonah's father, but Jonah's character. The audience is aware that Jonah is anything but obedient and faithful.

Jonah's commission is also a mix of inauguration language and parable language. "Go. . . . Cry out!" is language common in the inauguration of a prophet. "Against Nineveh, the Great City," however, is generic parable language. The "Great City" represents, not just the city of Nineveh in Assyria, but also all the enemies from whom Yahweh did not protect Judah.

Seven episodes make up the crisis portion of the book of Jonah (Jonah 1:1—3:9; Fig. 104). Each episode has a report of an action by the Creator of the Heavens, the Sea, and the Land, and a report of a reaction by the Faithful Prophet. The Creator "sends" for the Faithful Prophet; Jonah "goes down" to get away from his divine patron. The Creator's relentless pursuit of the Faithful Prophet and Jonah's repeated reluctance is one of the defining motifs of the parable.

Jonah 3:6-9 Reverses Humiliation of Jehu before Shalmaneser
(Nimrud 858–824 B.C.E.; alabaster 2 x 0.6 m)

First, the Creator acts by "sending" a word to the Faithful Prophet. Jonah reacts by "going down" from Jerusalem to Joppa, and "going down" from the dock onto the deck of the Sea Dragon.

The Creator of the Heavens, the Sea, and the Land acts because: "wickedness has come up before me" (Jonah 1:2). Just as in a Story of Noah and the Rainbow (Gen 8:21), where the aroma of Noah's sacrifice reaches the heavens, so the aroma of Nineveh's sacrifices also reaches the heavens. The aroma of Noah's sacrifice is enticing. The aroma of Nineveh's sacrifice is repulsive. The eyes and nose are the primary senses through which divine patrons communicated with their human protégés. Members of the divine assembly consumed food offerings by gazing at them, or inhaling their aroma, not by putting them in their mouths.

Second, the Creator acts by "sending" a Great Wind to attack the Sea Dragon. The sailors react by praying to their own divine patrons. Jonah reacts by "going down" from the deck into the hold of the ship to sleep. That the sailors are devout, while the prophet is a renegade, is ironic.

Third, the Creator acts by "sending" the captain of the Sea Dragon to wake up the Faithful Prophet. The sailors react by asking the Faithful Prophet: "What's your story? Because of your crime we are being punished. For whom are you working? From whom are you running? What is your land? Who are your people?" (Jonah 1:8).

Jonah's answer is ironic. Jonah says: "I am a Hebrew. . . . I worship Yahweh, the Creator of the Heavens, the Sea, and the Land" (Jonah 1:9). He ought to say, "I used to be a Hebrew." It is obvious to the audience that Jonah is not following Yahweh, but running away from Yahweh. When Jonah proclaims that it is Yahweh who is the Creator of the Heavens, the Sea, and the Land, the sailors react by praying to Yahweh, and then throwing Jonah "down" from the deck of the Sea Dragon into the sea (Jonah 1:14).

crisis (Jonah 1:1—3:9)

Once the Creator of the Heavens, the Sea, and the Land *sent* the word to Jonah the faithful prophet: "Get up. Go to the Great City of Nineveh. Cry out against its crime reeking to the heavens." Jonah, however, got up and set out for a godforsaken land at the end of the earth. He went *down* to Joppa, where he found the Sea Dragon bound for the end of the earth. He paid the fare and went *down* on deck with the others for the godforsaken land at the end of the earth.

Then Yahweh *sent* the Great Wind onto the sea. The Great Wind churned up waves, which began to break the Sea Dragon apart. . . . Each cried out to his own divine patron, while together they jettisoned the cargo on board the Sea Dragon to lighten its load. Jonah, however, went *down* below deck into the belly of the ship. He lay down and fell into a deep sleep.

Then Yahweh *sent* the captain to Jonah. "What are you doing sound asleep? Get up. Cry out to your divine patron." Jonah reluctantly replied: "Will not Yahweh remember us and keep us from drowning?"

Then Yahweh *sent* the Great Wind even more forcefully against the sea. The sailors made a pact with one another. "Throw the dice. Find out for whose crime we are being punished." They threw the dice and Jonah lost. "What's your story," they demanded. "Because of your crime we are being punished." "For whom are you working?" "From whom are you running?" "Where is your land?" "Who are your people?" So Jonah grudgingly confessed. "I am a Hebrew. I follow Yahweh, the Creator of the Heavens, the Sea, and the Land." The sailors were overwhelmed with zeal for Yahweh. "How could you commit such a crime?" they asked as they learned by listening to his story that he was running from Yahweh. "How must we punish you so that this raging sea will settle down around us?" Jonah insisted: "Offer me up. Throw me overboard into the sea and it will settle down. It is punishing you for my crime." Instead, the sailors rowed, but were not able to return to shore because the sea continued to rage against them. They cried out to Yahweh. "Do not punish us for taking this man's life. Do not indict us for shedding innocent blood. We are only doing what you, Yahweh, commanded us to do." Finally, they offered up Jonah and threw him *down* into the raging sea. Zeal for Yahweh overwhelmed the sailors as they began to offer sacrifices and make vows to their new divine patron.

Then Yahweh *sent* the Great Fish to swallow Jonah. For three days and three nights, Jonah was *down* in the belly of the Great Fish, which turned him back toward Yahweh.

Then Yahweh *sent* word to the Great Fish, and it delivered Jonah to the shore. Once again Yahweh *sent* word to Jonah. "Get up. Go to the Great City of Nineveh. Cry out against it as I told you." This time, Jonah got up and went to Nineveh as Yahweh ordered. For three days Jonah wandered the Great City of Nineveh. It was

(continued)

awesome. On the first day Jonah went into the Great City he cried out: "Nineveh must be turned around in forty days." Immediately, every citizen of Nineveh put faith in Yahweh and cried out: "Repent." Powerful and powerless alike wore nothing but burlap. When word reached the great king of Nineveh, he got up, took off his robe, put on burlap and sat down among the beggars in the city's garbage. He also issued a proclamation for Nineveh: "By order of the great king and the city assembly no human or animal, large or small, will eat or drink anything. Every human and animal will wear nothing but burlap. They will cry out as loud as they can to the Creator of the Heavens, the Sea, and the Land. All the citizens of Nineveh will turn their feet from evil, their hands from violence. Who knows when the Creator of the Heavens, the Sea, and the Land will turn back, change heart, recall this burning anger so that we will not be annihilated?"

FIGURE 104 Crisis Episodes (Jonah 1:1—3:9)

Fourth, the Creator acts by "sending" the Great Fish to swallow the Faithful Prophet. The Great Fish reacts by taking Jonah "down" into its belly. It is ironic that the non-human creatures in the story such as the Great Wind, the Great Fish, the Plant, and the Worm are obedient to their Creator, while Jonah, the Faithful Prophet, is not.

Fifth, the Creator acts by "sending" the words of a lament to the Faithful Prophet. The Great Fish reacts by taking Jonah "down" into the heart of the sea. For three days, the Great Fish physically forces Jonah to prostrate himself before Yahweh.

Jonah is not only physically forced into the position to pray, but he is also given the words of the prayer as well. The audience, like the daughters of Jerusalem in the Song of Solomon, or like Eliphaz, Bildad, and Zophar in the book of Job, pleads with Jonah to join in the words of its lament (Jonah 2:3-9; Fig. 105). While he is in the belly of the Great Fish, Jonah can hear the words of this lament, composed of excerpts from the book of Psalms, with which the audience is coaxing him to turn back to Yahweh (Ps 30:1-12; 32:1-11).

Jonah's descent brings him at last to the fetal position in the belly of the Great Fish at the womb of the earth. "You cast me into the deep. You cast me into the sea. Judge River engulfed me. Breakers and billows washed over my head. Abyss smothered me. 'Sea of No Return' was tattooed on my forehead. I went down at the base of the mountains, the earth disappeared behind me forever." What is on Jonah's forehead is his destination. The lament does not refer to seaweed wrapping itself around the head of Jonah as he drowns, but rather that Jonah has been marked for delivery to the Sea of No Return, as far away as possible from where Yahweh lives.

Lament for Jonah (Jonah 2:3-9)

In agony, I cried out to Yahweh.   CONFESSION OF FAITH
    Yahweh answered me.

From the pit of Sheol, I begged for help;
    Yahweh heard my voice.

You cast me into the deep,   COMPLAINT
    You threw me into the sea.

Judge River engulfed me,
    Breakers and billows washed over my head.

I cried out, "I can no longer see your face.   PETITION
    Give me one last look at your holy temple."

Water choked me,   COMPLAINT
    The abyss smothered me.

"Sea of No Return" was tattooed on my forehead.
    I went down at the base of the mountains.
    The earth disappeared behind me forever.

You delivered my life from   CONFESSION OF FAITH
    the pit of Sheol.
    Yahweh, you are my divine patron . . .

With my last breath,
    I remembered Yahweh.

I turned back to you,
    I looked toward your holy temple.

Those who follow worthless patrons   VOW
    desert a merciful one.
    I will gratefully offer sacrifice to you.

What I have vowed, I will fulfill.
    "Yahweh is my deliverer."

FIGURE 105   A Lament for Jonah (Jonah 2:3-9)

Sixth, the Creator acts by "sending" a word to the Great Fish. The Great Fish reacts by dropping Jonah "down" on the beach of Assyria. The Great Fish is not vomiting, but giving birth. The Creator is giving Jonah a second chance. He is reborn.

Seventh, the Creator acts by "sending" a word to the Faithful Prophet. Finally, Jonah reluctantly accepts his commission, and walks through Nineveh for three days preaching: "Nineveh must be turned around in forty days."

Hyperbole is the technique of making an extravagant exaggeration, which is also characteristic of parables. Although Nineveh, at its peak, covered some two thousand acres, it is an exaggeration or hyperbole to say it would take a three-day journey to cross it (Jonah 3:3; Esth 1:1-8; Jdt 1:1-6; Song 6:8-9).

Climax Episode
(JONAH 3:10—4:8)

The climax of a story presents the most intense point of conflict. Here Yahweh spares the Great City and the Faithful Prophet revolts (Jonah 3:10—4:3). The climax invokes the principle of reciprocity. The people of Nineveh turn away from the evil destroying their lives, and Yahweh turns away from the evil destroying their city (Jonah 3:10).

The Assyrians at Nineveh, whose reputation for arrogance was legendary, repent in sackcloth and ashes, while the Faithful Prophet is incorrigible. Each acts in exactly the opposite way that the audience expects. The actions of both are ironic.

People wore sackcloth and ashes in times of crisis to plead no contest to the charges that Yahweh brought against them and to offer to plea-bargain. Sackcloth is woven from goat or camel hair. Sackcloth and ashes were the uniform of those who were shamed (Gen 37:34; 2 Sam 3:31; 2 Kgs 6:30; Esth 4:1).

Jonah converts the most evil nation in the world of the Bible with a sermon only five words long in Hebrew, that he preached during only three days. In contrast, the Bible preserves sixty-six chapters of Isaiah's preaching. Not one prophet, including Isaiah, Jeremiah, and Ezekiel, was able to convert the people of Yahweh in spite of a lifetime of lengthy sermons. The audience expects Jonah to fail. Nonetheless, he succeeds, which is ironic.

Hyperbole appears in the climax, where not only the people of Nineveh repent, but their rulers and their livestock as well. Such repentance was unheard of in any other prophetic tradition.

Although the fire that burned in Yahweh is out, the fire of anger in Jonah is lit. Here the parable is using a play on words. Elijah is called a "person on fire," because of his ability to become ecstatic and leave the human plane for the divine plane. Jonah, however, is not ecstatic; he is angry. The spirit that takes possession of Jonah is an evil, not a good, spirit. Jonah turns on Yahweh in anger, not back to Yahweh in repentance.

Denouement Episode
(JONAH 4:9-11)

In most stories, the denouement repairs the damage caused by the crisis and climax episodes. Because parables are consciously thought-provoking, however, they do not resolve a crisis. The situation remains open-ended, and parables simply end with a question.

The parable's question has no satisfactory answer. It is a paradox, a statement that although seemingly a contradiction, is actually true. The intention of the parable is to give the audience an appreciation of a mystery, not the answer to a problem.

Faced with significant or unexpected developments in their lives, prophets often withdraw to pray. After the people of Judah have been deported to Babylon, for example, Ezekiel goes the edge of the village to pray: Has Yahweh betrayed us? Jonah's withdrawal, however, is ironic. Jonah prays for death, not in submission to the will of Yahweh, as Ezekiel does, or Elijah does (1 Kgs 19:1-8), but in rebellion against it.

When the Creator questions the Faithful Prophet, Jonah asks why allowing bad people to go unpunished should not make him angry. In the book of Exodus, Yahweh is both "a divine patron merciful and gracious, slow to anger, and abounding in steadfast love and faithfulness, keeping steadfast love for thousands, forgiving iniquity and transgression and sin" (Exod 34:6), and a divine patron who visits "the iniquity of the fathers upon the children and the children's children, to the third and the fourth generation" (Exod 34:7). Unlike the book of Exodus, a tradition in the book of Jeremiah links the behavior of Yahweh to human behavior. "If that nation, concerning which I have spoken, turns from its evil, I will repent of the evil that I intended to do to it. And if at any time I declare concerning a nation or a kingdom that I will build and plant it, and if it does evil in my sight, not listening to my voice, then I will repent of the good which I had intended to do to it" (Jer 18:7-10). It makes Jonah angry that his divine patron forgives bad people instead of punishing them.

The denouement in the book of Jonah (Jonah 4:3-5) is followed by an anticlimax (Jonah 4:6-8) with its own denouement (Jonah 4:9-11; Fig. 106). These denouements ask: "Is it good for you to be angry over the City?" (Jonah 4:4). "Is it good for you to be angry over the Plant?" (Jonah 4:9). "Should I, Yahweh, not have sympathy for Nineveh with its huge population of 120,000 humans, who are like children, and all its cattle?" (Jonah 4:11).

Jonah does not react. He remains silent. The reaction must come from the audience, whose role Jonah has been playing throughout. The parable is a living theater in which the audience participates as a full character. Generally, the audience observes and can only participate by identifying with a character, that nonetheless still has all the lines. In parables, the audience must write the reaction to Yahweh's final challenge. The question leaves the audience to resolve the crisis. The technique is a wonderful teaching tool. Long after the parable has ended and long after the teller has gone, the audience is still pondering the question. The teaching life of a parable is greater than any other form of story.

denouement (Jonah 4:9-11)

Yahweh said: "Is it good for you to be angry over the Plant?" Jonah answered: "My anger is good enough to kill me." Then Yahweh said: "You have so much sympathy for this Plant, which you did not sow, nor tend; which sprang up overnight and withered overnight. Should I not have sympathy for the Great City of Nineveh with its population of 120,000 humans, who are only children, and all its cattle?"

FIGURE 106   Denouement Episodes (Jonah 4:9-11)

The book of Jonah asks its audience: Should the Creator show less concern for the City than the Faithful Prophet shows for the Plant? Should Yahweh show less concern for the enemies of Judah than Yahweh shows for Judah? Why should the Creator, who forgives the Faithful Prophet, not forgive the City? Jonah wants to die rather than to let Yahweh forgive Nineveh. The question remains: Will the audiences who hear this parable choose to do the same?

Anonymous, 20th century. Untitled.
1920–1930. Ricco/Maresca Gallery (New York, NY, U.S.A.).

19

LIVING THE BIBLE

Living the Bible is the reason most people study the Bible. The ways in which people refer to the traditions of ancient Israel reveal much about how those traditions help them live the Bible.

Many scholars refer to the traditions of ancient Israel as the "Hebrew Bible" or the "Hebrew Scriptures." These labels emphasize that most of the traditions of ancient Israel were composed in Semitic languages like Hebrew and Aramaic, and that these traditions are sacred to Jews or Hebrews.

Jewish people refer to the traditions of ancient Israel as "Tanak." Tanak is an acronym that makes a word from the first letter of *torah*, *nebiim*, and *ketubim*. *Torah* is the Hebrew word for "teaching." *Nebiim* is the Hebrew word for "prophets." *Ketubim* is the Hebrew word for "writings" (Fig. 107).

Many Christians use "Bible," "Scripture," or "Word of God" exclusively for the traditions of ancient Israel and early Christianity. Technically, however, these are generic terms that can identify the core traditions of any religion or culture. Consequently, the Qur'an of Islam; the Tao te Ching of Taoism; the Vinaya of Buddhism; the Vedas, Upanishads, and Bhagavad Gita of Hinduism; and the Book of Mormon of the Latter-Day Saints are all "Bibles," "Scriptures," or "Words of God" in their own traditions.

What Does the Bible Teach?

The Bible arranges stories and laws in a dramatic sequence to express Israel's common faith. The arrangement is not historical or chronological, but educational. The Bible arranges its laws and stories artfully like photographs in a scrapbook or patches in a

The Torah
Genesis
Exodus
Leviticus
Numbers
Deuteronomy

The Prophets
Joshua
Judges
1–2 Samuel
1–2 Kings
Isaiah
Jeremiah
Ezekiel
The Book of the Twelve: Hosea, Joel, Amos, Obadiah, Jonah, Micah, Nahum, Habakkuk, Zephaniah, Haggai, Zechariah, Malachi

The Writings
Psalms
Job
Proverbsa
Ruth
Song of Solomon
Ecclesiastes
Lamentations
Esther
Daniel
Ezra-Nehemiah
1-2 Chronicles

FIGURE 107   The Books of the Bible

quilt, and not randomly like buttons dumped in a box. The Bible carefully chooses and arranges to tell Israel's story and to explain its unique way of looking at human life.

For those who live the Bible, the traditions of ancient Israel are a "canon." In Egypt, the canon was a length of measurement like a meterstick or a yardstick (1 Kgs 14:15; Ezek 40:5). As a canon, the Bible is the core curriculum that hands on the basic culture of ancient Israel. The way of life that developed in ancient Israel is the basis on which those who live the Bible develop their own ways of life. Therefore, the Bible is the foundation of the Talmud for Jews, the foundation of the New Testament for Christians, and the foundation of the Qur'an for Muslims. The Bible is "The Book" on which their books stand.

The relationship between Jews, Christians, and Muslims—the "peoples of the Book," as the Qur'an calls them—and the Bible has not always been constructive. For some, "living the Bible" has meant not only destroying the traditions of ancient Israel, but also killing Jews. For example, in 641 C.E., some Christians in Egypt burned twenty thousand books from the great library in Alexandria because they considered the writings of past, pre-Christian cultures, including the Bible, to be worthless.

Between 139 and 144 C.E., a charismatic Christian teacher named Marcion argued that the only thing Christians can learn from the Bible of ancient Israel is what not to do. For Marcion, only parts of the New Testament had any value. Similar tendencies appear among Muslims, who consider the Bible, and the New Testament, to be only examples of how Jews and Christians misunderstood God.

The nineteenth-century German philosopher Friedrich Nietzsche (1844–1900) studied similarly negative views about the past. There are still those who consider the past in general, and the Bible in particular, as having little or nothing to offer today. But the Greek philosopher Socrates (ca. 470–399 B.C.E.), in Plato's *Apology,* taught that the unexamined life is not worth living, and the American philosopher George Santayana (1863–1952) emphasized that those ignorant of history will repeat its mistakes. Without a sense of the past, it is virtually impossible for those who want to live the Bible to acquire a sense of their place in the human community.

To call the traditions of ancient Israel the "Bible," "Scripture," or "Word of God" is to make the commitment that yesterday is important for understanding today. It is impossible to understand the Talmud, the New Testament, or the Qur'an without understanding the Bible. The Bible is a mirror for understanding what it means to be a Jew, or a Christian, or a Muslim. This revelation is never static; it is always revolutionary because Jews and Christians and Muslims never look into the mirror from the same place in their lives, and the image changes each time they do. Today's question is different from yesterday's question or the question of the day before yesterday. Therefore, what the peoples of the Book learn today is different from what they learned yesterday or the day before yesterday.

By studying the Bible, Jews and Christians and Muslims discover that where they are is not yet where they want to be. Looking back is not an exercise in nostalgia. Studying the Bible is an opportunity for those who live the Bible to see themselves as part of a long and wonderful struggle of humanity in its most inspiring and most frightening moments. For those who make the time to learn from it, the Bible is an introduction to the story of their own lives.

The Bible also has a more modest sense of human accomplishment than most Jews and Christians and Muslims do today. The Hebrews realized how little each generation accomplishes to put its visions into practice. For the Bible, human history is long, but human achievement is not. The result is not despair, but rather a sense of satisfaction with small achievements and modest gains. The Bible reminds Jews and Christians and Muslims that there were visionaries in the past, whose own time was as crucial as the present time. Consequently, when people who want to live the Bible are tired of struggling, unsure of success, exhausted from generosity, they can learn from the past that there have been others like them who have struggled, who have suffered, who have survived, and who have shared. The Bible teaches Jews and Christians and Muslims today that they are not alone, and that, in itself, should give them confidence.

Studying the past is also an antidote for omnipotence. It tempers judgments. Without a knowledge of the past, those who want to live the Bible can be fooled into thinking that they make no mistakes, that they have no faults, and that there are no limits. The candor of the Hebrews' reflections is certainly one of the most refreshing qualities of the Bible. The Hebrews not only admitted their sins, but were courageous enough to offer others the opportunity to learn from them, and perhaps to realize that humans are best understood in terms of their limits.

Admittedly, the Hebrews looked at their world then differently than Jews and Christians and Muslims look at their worlds now. The Hebrews were as comfortable talking with Yahweh as they were talking with one another. Today such events would be extraordinary, but in the world of the Bible they were ordinary.

Likewise, both ancient Israel and the United States celebrate their ancestors. The Hebrews honored Abraham and Sarah just as Americans honor George Washington and Martin Luther King Jr. Biblical people, however, were much more modest in their expectations of ancestors. They evaluated their ancestors from only one perspective. Abraham and Sarah Negotiate with Pharaoh (Gen 12:9—13:1) celebrates them as ancestors who used fast talk and good looks to trick their enemy into giving them land and children. Abraham is shrewd. Sarah is attractive. The story never considers whether Abraham is also a liar, and Sarah the victim of a chauvinist husband. The Bible celebrates ancestors for a single virtue and takes for granted that even the virtuous are not perfect. Today leaders are evaluated from every possible perspective. Public scrutiny of leaders today demands virtual perfection.

The Bible also has a very different sense of nature. Nature is not a machine to be predicted, but a creature to be understood. The Hebrews respected nature. They did not seek to control it. It would be wrong to consider them pantheistic. They were not. The Bible, however, reflects a wonderful ecology where humans are only part of the world, and it offers some wonderful opportunities to think about living within nature, rather than living to conquer it.